Regional Identities in Southeast Asia:
Contemporary Challenges, Historical Fractures

REGIONAL IDENTITIES IN SOUTHEAST ASIA

Contemporary Challenges, Historical Fractures

Edited by

JAYEEL CORNELIO

and

VOLKER GRABOWSKY

SEATIDE-CRISEA-Silkworm Books series

Series editors: Yves Goudineau, Andrew Hardy, Jacques Leider, Chayan Vaddhanaphuti

This study was written for the École française d'Extrême-Orient (EFEO) in the framework of the project "Competing Regional Integrations in Southeast Asia" (CRISEA, 2017–2021) funded by the European Commission. CRISEA was a successor project to the project "Integration in Southeast Asia: Trajectories of Inclusion, Dynamics of Exclusion" (SEATIDE, 2012–2016), also funded by the European Commission.

The research leading to these results as well as their publication have received funding from the European Commission's Horizon 2020 Framework Programme under Grant Agreement N°770562.

CRISEA partners
École française d'Extrême-Orient (France)
University of Hamburg (Germany)
University of Naples L'Orientale (Italy)
University of Oslo (Norway)
University of Lodz (Poland)
University of Social and Political Sciences (Portugal)
University of Cambridge (United Kingdom)
Centre for Strategic and International Studies (Indonesia)
University of Malaya (Malaysia)
University of Mandalay (Myanmar)
Ateneo de Manila University (Philippines)
University of Chiang Mai (Thailand)
Vietnam Academy of Social Sciences (Vietnam)

ISBN 978-616-215-190-3

© 2023 by École française d'Extrême-Orient (EFEO)

All rights reserved

No part of this publication may be reproduced, stored in a retrieval system, or transmitted, in any form or by any means, electronic, mechanical, photocopying, recording or otherwise, without the prior permission in writing of the publisher.

First edition published in 2023 by
Silkworm Books
430/58 M. 7, T. Mae Hia, Chiang Mai 50100, Thailand
info@silkwormbooks.com
www.silkwormbooks.com

Typeset in Minion Pro 10.5 pt. by Silk Type
Printed and bound in the United States by Lightning Source

Contents

Foreword	vii
Acknowledgements	xi
Introduction	1
Volker Grabowsky and Jayeel Cornelio	

Generations

1. Generational Support for ASEAN Integration and Identity: An Indonesian Perspective   33
   Medelina K. Hendytio
2. Hakka Dialect Identity and Chinese Identity in Malaysia   55
   Danny Wong Tze Ken
3. Kola Identity at the Pailin Frontier Gem Mines: Generations of Autonomy, Integration, and Upheaval   75
   Natasha Pairaudeau
4. Tin Mining in Laos: Contested Resources, Labor Mobility, and Precarious Livelihoods   105
   Oliver Tappe

Transnationalism

5. Transnational Indigenism in Southeast Asia   125
   Prasit Leepreecha
6. Transnational Malay Identity: Stage Performances and the Revival of Royal Patrons in the Riau Islands   151
   Alan Darmawan and Jan van der Putten
7. Skilled Migration in Post-2011 Singapore: Filipino Professionals in the Talent Capital of Southeast Asia   181
   Filomeno Aguilar Jr.
8. The Religious Imaginary: Filipino Missionaries in Thailand   205
   Jayeel Cornelio and Erron C. Medina

CONTENTS

9 Christian Missions and the Reconstruction of Identities: 225
The Talaku Karen on the Thailand-Myanmar Borderland
Kwanchewan Buadaeng

10 Buddhist Pilgrimages and Architectural Restoration in 247
the Upper Mekong Basin: Revival of Tai (Transnational) Identities
Sirui Dao and Volker Grabowsky

11 Death of the Last King: Contemporary Ethnic Identity 271
and Belonging among the Tai Lü of Sipsòng Panna
Roger Casas

Violence

12 Anticriminality and Democracy in Southeast Asia 293
Erron C. Medina and Bianca Ysabelle Franco

13 Papuan Youth Identity: Violence, Oppression, 317
and Marginalization in the Context of ASEAN Integration
Vidhyandika Djati Perkasa

14 Violence and Belonging: Conflict, War, and Insecurity 347
in Arakan, 1942–1952
Jacques P. Leider

15 Democratic Kampuchea's Revolutionary Terror in the 1970s: 373
The Role of Cambodian Youth in Mass Violence
Volker Grabowsky

16 Mass Violence, Ethnic Conflict, and the Expanding State 407
in the Vietnamese Highlands: The Sơn Hà Revolt as
Event and Memory
Đào Thế Đức and Andrew Hardy

17 Youth, Violence, and Identities of Insecurity in Timor-Leste 439
Janina Pawelz

Contributors 457
Index 461

vi

Foreword

Diverse forces drive regional integration in Southeast Asia and these forces compete for power, resources and legitimacy. This premise is central to the research conducted under the project "Competing Regional Integrations in Southeast Asia" (CRISEA). Funded by the European Commission's Horizon 2020 program, the project is part of Europe's investment in the social sciences and humanities that aims to provide knowledge of the world and help the EU and its member states make coherent and culturally relevant foreign policies.

The CRISEA project ran from 2017 to 2021 and was conducted with a strong awareness that the issue of integration is important for Europeans and Southeast Asians, who – precisely because of their different approaches to the subject – have much to learn from each other. The first "learners" in this respect were the members of the research teams, as CRISEA brought together scholars from six universities and institutes in Southeast Asia and seven in Europe. Their institutional diversity was matched by a multiplicity of disciplinary background, as economists and political scientists worked together, both in the field and at regular meetings, with anthropologists, historians and sociologists. The interplay of micro and macro perspectives was entirely appropriate to a project whose prime assumptions were the plurality of integration processes and the competitive nature of regional integration.

The project investigated the competing forces of regional integration in several arenas, including the economy, the state, the environment and the Region. Its research into these arenas and the progress of its dissemination activities may be followed on its website (https://crisea.hypotheses.org) and its results – published in working papers, articles, policy briefs and documentary films – can be consulted in its web archive (https://hal.archives-ouvertes.fr/CRISEA/). CRISEA built on the insights achieved by an earlier European project, "Integration in Southeast Asia: Trajectories of Inclusion, Dynamics of Exclusion" (SEATIDE, 2012–2016), which examined some of the assumed benefits of integration, focusing on the tensions and contradictions within and between communities that inhere to processes of integration. Readers may access this project's findings on its website (https://seatide.hypotheses.org) and web archive (https://hal.archives-ouvertes.fr/SEATIDE/).

One arena of competition identified by CRISEA is the issue of identity. Led by Volker Grabowsky of the University of Hamburg and Jayeel Cornelio of Ateneo de Manila University, this research set out from the observation that migration, travel, communication technologies and other forms of globalised modernity have brought new voices to clamour for the attention, allegiance and identity of Southeast Asia's population. One of these voices is ASEAN, which was in many ways at the origin of Southeast Asia's sense of region and is now embarked on its own socio-cultural project in the context of the ASEAN Community. But many other home-grown and external forces shape the identities of Southeast Asia's people and compete to foster a sense of belonging among them. What those forces are, how they interact and what effects they have on the ground is the subject of the research presented in this volume.

$$* * * *$$

Southeast Asia is home to many ethnic and religious identities, which – through historical processes dating to colonial and pre-colonial times – have shaped the nationalism of modern nation-states. Local loyalties were formed by inclusion in broader ideological frameworks, both national and transnational, including systems like Buddhism, Christianity, Communism, Confucianism, Hinduism and Islam. In the post-independence period, they have been further impacted by choices and conflicts associated with decolonisation, nation-building, the Cold War, the processes and technologies of globalisation, the rising influence of China. Internal and external forces have appealed and continue to appeal to the allegiances of Southeast Asian people in different ways with different results.

These identities underpin Southeast Asian citizens' sense of their membership of the ASEAN Community. In recent years, ASEAN has paid attention to the emergence of new forms of collective imaginations about the region's future, committing it to directions that reach beyond the politico-economic realm. These initiatives remain shallow, however, and the current global context places pressure on the values of multilateralism and the possibility of plural and transversal identities, and poses a threat to ASEAN's framework-building efforts in the socio-cultural sphere. There is a risk that more exclusive visions, whether national, religious, ethnic or other, will hold sway.

CRISEA builds on research conducted by SEATIDE into the ethnic and religious dimensions of Southeast Asia's identities (published as *Ethnic and Religious Identities and Integration in Southeast Asia*, edited by Ooi Keat Gin and Volker Grabowsky, Silkworm Books, 2017). It examines three factors – generations, transnationalism and violence – that CRISEA's research team saw as key to the emerging identities of the region. These are discussed in detail by Jayeel Cornelio and Volker Grabowsky in their introduction.

Here it suffices to note that, taken together, this volume's seventeen case studies eloquently portray the contested nature of belonging in Southeast Asia. Each of them focuses on one of the above-mentioned factors: generations, transnationalism and violence. Yet each in its own specific context also demonstrates the relevance of all three factors for our understanding of regional identities in Southeast Asia. The pace of generational change is high in Southeast Asia, in line with the region's high rate of economic growth. Modernisation is driven by transnational mobilities of people, ideas and technologies and the emergence of cross-border connectivities nurtured by globalisation and regional integration that were unimaginable a few decades ago. And the peace enjoyed by the current generation has allowed most of the population – though regrettably not all, as the violence in Myanmar continues – to move on from the region's many twentieth-century episodes of violence, whether experienced by nations or small groups, whether inflicted by outsiders or neighbours.

These case studies recognise the importance for regional solidarity not only of the reality of peace but also of a sense of security. The issue of past violence raises a question about the way people move on: how is the event remembered, forgotten and unforgotten by later generations? The question of violence thus has a historical dimension of acute contemporary relevance. For collective futures to nurture future communities and generate loyalty to shared values, collective pasts must be settled and ways found for people to come to terms with memories of violence and other forms of alterity. And this, in turn, means that people have to settle the present. To this extent, the contemporary challenge turns on how people feel. Reaching across boundaries of nation, ethnicity and religion, a sense of regional community, security and belonging needs to be fostered and enhanced in each generation. Historical fractures can be resilient and extremism competes to be seen as a legitimate influence on identity construction.

Andrew Hardy
École française d'Extrême-Orient
CRISEA Coordinator

Acknowledgements

THIS collection is a milestone for the project "Competing Regional Integrations in Southeast Asia" (CRISEA). As Andrew Hardy puts it in his foreword to this volume, the members of this project came together "with a strong awareness that the issue of integration is important for Europeans and Southeast Asians, who—precisely because of their different approaches to the subject—have much to learn from each other." That our team of researchers—what we refer to as our Work Package on "Identity"—has been able to reach this far is an important achievement in itself. Coming from different disciplines and academic institutions, we have on many occasions presented our findings, exchanged notes, and identified common themes that are now articulated throughout this collection. Every member of our team deserves recognition and appreciation for having joined to produce an important volume like this, composed of 17 chapters written by 20 authors. We are particularly thankful for their collegiality and willingness to participate in every event we organized in Manila, Hanoi, Chiang Mai, and Procida/Naples.

Beyond our team, we also wish to extend our gratitude to other people who have supported our project in every way. The European Union, through its Horizon 2020 Programme, must be recognized for enabling us to pursue our research and engagements in different parts of Southeast Asia. Apart from this book, our work package has also produced several technical reports and policy briefs that were presented to various EU dignitaries in the region and in Brussels. We are grateful too to the École française d'Extrême-Orient (EFEO) for having supported us in many ways. A substantial grant came from EFEO so that this book could be eventually made open access. Four colleagues from EFEO are worth mentioning for their administrative support: Andrew Hardy (CRISEA Coordinator), Jacques Leider (Scientific Coordinator), Elisabeth Lacroix (Project Manager), and Yves Goudineau (Special Advisor). Hardy and Leider have also been part of our work package and are contributors to this volume.

We would also like to thank colleagues who have contributed to this collection's production at various stages. Kornkanok Khetnongbua prepared the maps that appear in several chapters. At an early stage of the book project,

Natthaly Natschke provided editorial assistance. Karandeep Sing prepared the index. To our reliable publisher at Silkworm Books, Trasvin Jittidecharak, and our copy-editor, Noor Azlina Yunus, we express our deep gratitude, thanking them for their trust and patience.

Finally, we wish to say that this volume is the product of our long-standing collective work in and on Southeast Asia. Over time we have established deep bonds with communities whose histories and narratives are recounted here. It is to them that we dedicate this collection.

Jayeel Cornelio and Volker Grabowsky

Introduction

VOLKER GRABOWSKY AND JAYEEL CORNELIO

ASEAN as a regional entity shapes collective imaginings about the future of the region. These visions rest on the three pillars that support a community ideal: economy, security, and culture. As the violent polarizations of the Cold War give way to post-conflict mobilities of people and information, Southeast Asia's population is becoming culturally aware of its own creative diversity and its place in Asia and the world. Local and global forces clamor for its attention and loyalty, forging new multiple identities of a wider regional belonging. But as these are undermined by the crisis of globalization, the embrace and celebration of difference—at the heart of regional integration—risk being subsumed in nationally and culturally conferred forms of legitimacy.

The struggle for legitimacy of non-state actors is relevant in two ways. At one level, it shows that within traditional markers such as ethnicity, religion, generation, and movements, non-state actors are looking for legitimate ways of self-definition. At another level, it demonstrates how such markers bring together actors around Southeast Asia (Hau and Kasian 2011). In so doing, they contribute to a reimagining of the region's future. This is a search for legitimacy that responds to issues that confront the region as a whole.

ASEAN as a region also relies on networks built by its citizens based on ethnic, religious, and generational affinities. Our research reflects this reality, and seeks to investigate ethnic, religious, and generational responses across the region. For this reason, the areas we examine include violence and trauma (Timor-Leste, Myanmar, Thailand, Cambodia, Vietnam), climate change (Malaysia), exclusion (Vietnam, Myanmar), and mobility (the Philippines). In our view, these are issues that, ostensibly at least, would compel the peoples of Southeast Asia to respond in a collective fashion. Taken together, the individual chapters in this volume all question to what extent non-state actors are taking part in shaping, or contesting, regional integration. At the same time, their initiatives demonstrate both the potential and limits of regional integration.

In this volume we examine three areas that are shaping competing identities in Southeast Asia: generations, transnationalism, and violence. *Generational configurations* are the focus of studies on the national, ethnic, religious, and regional identities of Southeast Asian youth and the motivation of young women and men to seek a role shaping the future idea of ASEAN (Thompson and Chulanee 1996). *Transnational ethnoreligious groups*, possessing a capacity both to imagine solidarity and to exacerbate tensions, are studied for their potential to support or contest regional integration (Hirsch 1996). Finally, for collective futures to nurture loyalty, collective pasts must be settled and ways found for people to come to terms with memories of intercommunal *violence*. This has a contemporary dimension; violent extremism still competes to assert itself as a legitimate influence on identity construction.

Generational Configurations

Generational identity, the theme of Part I, is defined as an individual's awareness of his or her membership in a generational group and the significance of this group to the individual himself (Joshi et al. 2010). This is in line with Mannheim's (1952) definition that generational affinities are about sharing a common outlook on the basis of its members' common experiences. In that sense, the use of the term "generation" is meant to characterize the people living in a particular historical period. To put it differently, generations are not so much defined by their age brackets as they are by shared experiences.

Thus, the concept of generations is not an abstract idea but one based on shared economic, historical, social, political, and cultural experiences. Identity formation is consequently rooted in such defining moments. In other words, specific events shape the identity of specific generations. Researchers thus take note of shifts in society in the form of demographic transitions, democratization, social conflicts, or violence. These factors can foster new social conditions in which specific generations are growing up. Different formative experiences when they interact with lifecycle and aging processes could shape people's views of the world (Wyn and Cahill 2015).

Why do these moments matter? Mannheim (1952) claims that political and economic struggle have the potential to affect an individual's consciousness leading to the search for a new identity. For example, a generation that experienced violence tends to shape its identity in a particular way, such as by contesting a more collective national identity and forming a more secluded or primordial identity. In this regard, violence or trauma is a potent generational marker. Several studies argue this point. For example, the conflict in the Maluku Islands in Indonesia gives a clear picture of how generations, identity, nationalism, and violence relate to one other. Bjorkhagen's (2013) research on the conflict in the Moluccas in the early 2000s suggest this very point. For youth, many of whom were under eighteen then, the conflict in the Moluccas was the result of resentment among the Muslims toward a legacy of Dutch colonial rule that favored only Christians. Thus, when conflict erupted in 1999, violence led to segregation along religious lines. In this context, identity formation is unavoidably linked to religion.

The nationwide popular uprising against military dictatorship in Myanmar (Burma), with key events occurring on August 8, 1988, gave rise to a generation of students, young monks, civil servants, and workers whose political worldview was very much shaped by decades of fighting for democracy and the restoration of civilian rule. This was the moment at which the Burmese "8888 generation," now in their late forties and early fifties, came into being (Maung Maung 1999). Further to the east, in Thailand, the collective experiences of persons born in the 1950s were very much shaped by the struggle of the 1970s for democracy and against military domination culminating in the uprising of October 14, 1973 and facing a traumatic setback with the massacres at Thammasat University on October 6, 1976. Members of that "October Generation" (who adopted the collective identity of "Octobrists") joined hands in the pro-democracy movement of 1992 and also led the street protests of 2006–14, both on the sides of the "yellow shirts" (conservative monarchists) and the "red shirts" (pro-Thaksin populist) movements (Kanokrat 2012; see also Thongchai 2020).

Transnationalism, such as that engendered by migration, contributes as well to the formation of identity among generations. This can be seen in the Papuan case where indigenous Papuans who have been living in Indonesia for many years have suffered economic, political, and cultural discrimination exacerbated by human rights violations. Due to such treatment, they only reluctantly identify themselves as "Indonesian" and have sought independence from the Indonesian nation-state. Yet, since the early 1960s they have been struggling to establish an exclusive Papuan nationalism.

Toblize (2008) has observed that a generation's value system or characteristics could be generated through interaction among its members. Members of a generation share common experiences that influence their thoughts, values, behavior, and reactions. Over time, these experiences would foster the specific characteristics of a unique generational group. For Toblize, individuals bring with them "personalities, influences, and particular backgrounds from their race, class, gender, region, family, religion and more, but some broad generalizations are possible among those who are born in approximately the same years. Values tend to be similar among members within each generation" (2008, 1).

The fact that social factors shape identity indicates that it is fluid, and can be changed, in so far as it involves people's adaptation to different social contexts (Dimock 2018). Cornelio (2015) and Anagnost et al. (2013) argue that political participation, social engagement, and religiosity are also elements that form new identities. By taking the case of Salafi followers in Indonesia, Cornelio has shown that religiosity can shape young people's new identity formation. He quotes Hasan's study on *The Drama of Jihad: The Emergence of Salafi Youth in Indonesia* (2010) that Salafism is an alternative channel for youth to find their identity and establish their place in an Indonesian society whose modernization has left them alienated, an alienation exacerbated by poverty and unemployment. By wearing the prescribed dress (*jalabiya* and turban), growing a beard, and praying and reciting the Quran with the right accent, youth can internalize a "total Muslim" identity. These phenomena suggest that, according to Dimock (2018), identity formation within a specific generation is also transboundary. This means that, regardless of their country or community of birth, when faced with similar issues across national borders, people affected by the same events and sharing similar experiences are likely to have similar underlying value systems. These "value systems" have an impact on behavior and attitudes.

Yet, it could be asked what accounts for different value systems among different generations. The work of Howe and Strauss (2007) on generational theory postulates that different generations develop different value systems. A similar view can be found in the study of Paul Taylor (2010), who argues that each generation has aspirations which are necessarily different from those of other generations. A crucial factor, amongst others, that influences value systems is the personal experience shared with numerous other members of the same generation. Mannheim's work (quoted in Kertzer 1983) shows that the different value systems of each generation could be driven by their unique experiences.

A similar observation was made by Crodington (2008), who found that historical context also plays an important role in shaping a generation's value system. This can be seen from the fact that individuals could form a generational consciousness. As Taylor (2010) observes, life experiences, such as war or economic crisis, have an impact on how a generation defines itself. The experiences of the generations of the Great Depression, World War II, and the Cold War period reflect the link between specific situations in the past with certain characteristics attached to generational identity later. Most Southeast Asian countries went through such generational experiences in the last sixty years, for example, the wars in Vietnam and Laos in the 1960s and early 1970s or the 1965 massacres in

Indonesia. Such traumatic experiences of a generation could even impact on the psychological makeup of their children's generation (Herman 1992).

Based on the discussion above, scholars, commentators, and journalists have developed the following generational labels: Generation Z (born 1996 and later); Millennials (or Generation Y, born 1977 to 1995); Generation X (born 1965 to 1976); Baby Boomers (born 1946 to 1964); and the Traditionalists or Silent Generation (born 1945 and earlier). Now, however, the years vary from one source to another. But what needs to be emphasized here is that while these labels are widely used around the world, scholars from Southeast Asia have also cautioned on their relevance in local contexts. The work of Cornelio (2020), for example, calls into question the usefulness of these generational labels in countries like the Philippines. That young people remain fragmented when it comes to access to education and technology and that they are also exposed to conflict and other forms of vulnerabilities means that using these Western generational labels is inappropriate. These labels, he argues, carry normative expectations of mobility and cosmopolitanism that are simply irrelevant to the experience of Filipino youths.

Transnational Ethnoreligious Groups

Non-state actors are also involved in shaping Southeast Asian identities. In our volume we pay attention to transnational non-state actors who draw on religion, gender, ethnicity, and other social markers that bring together different people. Advocacy is also crucial in this regard. The chapters under the theme of transnationalism investigate to what extent ordinary citizens and their respective organizations offer alternative pathways to articulating identity in the region. In doing so, we seek to adopt what the literature describes as the transnational optic to examine "the boundaries and borders that emerge at particular historical moments" and explore "their relationship to unbounded arenas and processes" (Khagram and Levitt 2008, 5).

Privileging Non-state Actors

The literature on transnationalism privileges non-state actors to show that ties are forged not only by governments in national frameworks, but by other social forces. These non-state actors range from migrant workers and missionaries to multinational corporations and the media. Collectively, they make transnationalism possible. By transnationalism we mean the "multiple ties and interactions linking people or institutions across the borders of nation-states" (Vertovec 1999, 447). This broad approach to transnationalism embraces different kinds of collaboration that have to do with advocacy groups, movements, mobility, and political action. They have potential contributions to institutionalizing legal norms and diffusing cultural values in the wider public (Kearney 1995). A narrower approach to transnationalism, by contrast, focuses only on identifiable and purposeful "coalitions and actors" who attempt to "achieve specific political goals in the 'target' state of their activities" (Risse-Kappen 2008, 461). As opposed to the broad approach, the analytical advantage of this restrictive definition lies in clearly identifying the policy impact of transnational activities.

Regardless of the approach, transnational studies show that identity is often an organic basis of these ties and coalitions. Transnational interactions revolve around identity, either by drawing from existing ones or creating new expressions. For example, identity is very much reflected in the religious, linguistic, and ethnic affinities of diasporic people. Such affinities are shared by these individuals even if they may be globally dispersed. In this sense, the transnational identity is not only a social formation but also a type of consciousness. This consciousness, however, is not only oriented in one direction. Migrants may have emotional connections to both their home country and the place where they currently reside. Cultural practices may also reflect a transnational identity in terms of people's everyday choices over fashion, music, and language. These cultural influences are made readily available by transnational platforms such as migration and the media. Identity is clearly a major area in transnational studies.

Why is the transnational angle important in studying regional integration? In our view, this angle is a conceptual and empirical corrective to nuance appreciations of regional integration as a state-led process. Often the process is driven by concerns for security and prosperity. In the first place, the region's modern configuration is a result of strategic thinking after World War II (Osborne 2016). In the late 1990s, the Association of Southeast Asian Nations (ASEAN) also articulated its vision of regional integration and prosperity based on a "common regional identity." What that identity constitutes, however, remains contested (Jones 2004). What is clear though is that ASEAN, which presents itself as the official representation of the region, is typically seen as a regional bloc for trade and security. As the succeeding sections show, this narrative has generally gained traction among the peoples of Southeast Asia. At the same time, other regional identities are being articulated which owe much to the ethnic, linguistic, and religious diversity of the region. In some ways, the pervasiveness of this diversity precedes and, in the contemporary period, challenges existing state boundaries (Ooi and Grabowsky 2017). The challenge lies in the fact that, on the one hand, these identities rely on transnational networks and, on the other, they are shored up to respond to risks and other social problems in the region.

To put it differently, these identities become the bases of "transnational 'community ties'" (Beck 2008, 227). Sometimes they rely on organic "family resemblances" among beliefs and practices (Antweiler 2017, 74). But at other times they are deployed for strategic purposes. The point is that privileging non-state actors in these transnational connections sheds light on alternative regionalisms at work (Rother and Piper 2015). A quick caveat: The writings cited in this introduction cover recent developments. But transnational linkages in the region are much older, as in the case of the spread of nationalism in the wake of anticolonial movements and the different waves of student activism in Southeast Asia (Hau and Tejapira 2011; Weiss et al. 2012).

Southeast Asian/ASEAN Identity

There is no denying that the strength of ASEAN as a regional configuration has been to foster peace and prosperity among its member states. This is in spite of its weak responses to some current regional issues, such as maritime disputes in the South China Sea and the Rohingya crisis. However, ASEAN is perceived as an elite gathering of decision-makers in the government and the business sector. Journalists have thus observed that "there appears to be limited public awareness of why ASEAN matters" (Hussain 2017). At the same time, a sense of regional citizenship among its people is lacking which is why the "one identity" and "one community" ambition it aspires to remains elusive. If ever such a community exists, it does so only among the region's policy elites who gather on a regular basis, as Murti (2016) critically argues. It is the policy elites who are aware of the norms that govern intraregional relations, such as non-use of force in settling disputes, non-interference in members' internal matters, and decision-making by consensus.

The last point is important even if a conceptual distinction were made between ASEAN identity and Southeast Asian identity. The scientific literature makes the case that the two are very much conflated as far as both the organization and the public are concerned. Acharya (2017, 29) notes that "the very idea of Southeast Asia as a region in itself, distinct from China and India, has much to do with the role of ASEAN." This is in spite of the fact that Southeast Asian identities have their own histories, which proceed based on ethnic, linguistic, and religious affinities (Osborne 2016). It is crucial to recognize this tension, particularly because these affinities predate the formation of territorially bounded nation-states. For example, Kwanchewan Buadaeng's (2013) work on the Talaku movement on the Thai-Burma borderland demonstrates the tensions generated by the state's interventions to form its modern citizens.

How did this conflation between the geographical category and the formal region occur? One factor is grounded in the very history of ASEAN itself. The regional organization was founded in the spirit of securing peace and prosperity for its member states that had emerged in the postcolonial period with strong nationalist and developmentalist aspirations. For ASEAN's founders, the regional identity that was framed was not so much cultural as it was economic, thus developmentally oriented while not impinging on nationalist sentiments. It was only much later that the idea of ASEAN as also a cultural community came to be articulated by the organization (ASEAN 2016). According to the ASEAN Charter ratified in 2008, "One Southeast Asia" is a community with a diversity of cultures and heritages. The Association seeks to foster greater awareness of this diversity (Acharya 2017).

Fostering this awareness, nevertheless, remains a challenge. A recent study shows that citizens in different sectors of the population are more familiar with the ASEAN's economic pillar than they are with its other pillars related to security and culture (Intal and Ruddy 2017). That it remains an economic institution in the public's mind feeds back into the perception that ASEAN is elitist. In this light, expert recommendations on forging a regional identity have been generally targeted promoting ASEAN as its embodiment. It has been advised that there should be "dialogue by engaging the diverse communities … by establishing their rights and responsibilities, giving voice to their concerns, activating their potential, and affirming the opportunity to be engaged as citizens of a dynamic region" (Jones 2004, 149).

The perception that ASEAN integration is elitist is the background to our interest in the role of transnational non-state actors in fostering alternative regional identities. More specifically, the contemporary interest in alternative regionalism in which "non-state actors such as domestic firms, transnational corporations, NGOs, and other types of social networks and social movements" (Igarashi 2011, 4) are involved, provides a springboard for our research. This is the kind of regional integration that takes place from below. The succeeding sections spell out how this point has been argued in the literature by examining three themes: active transnational engagements for raising ASEAN awareness; transnational constructions based on shared identities; and critical approaches.

INTRODUCTION

Active Transnational Engagements for Regional Awareness

The first theme concerns transnational initiatives that foster regional awareness in Southeast Asia. One important sector in this regard is education. In the past decades, a number of initiatives have been undertaken in order to create opportunities for students from different countries to interact with one another. Established in 1995, the ASEAN University Network (AUN) is an example. Although spearheaded by ASEAN, it relies on collaboration among its member universities from around the region. Apart from working to enhance quality among its member universities, AUN is also driving student mobility. This attempt is crucial so that students in the region are exposed to different cultures and academic environments. Other initiatives have also been introduced, such as innovative classes that promote ASEAN awareness. One program is the link created between two universities in Indonesia and Malaysia so their respective students could interact online (Azmawati and Quayle 2017). In spite of technological difficulties, their Skype sessions proved successful in encouraging dialog among their students. This is a very good example of transnational learning.

How successful has the education sector been in raising regional awareness? A practical caveat clearly exists in that the quality and viability of the education system is very uneven across Southeast Asia (Chao 2016). This unevenness poses a challenge to regional initiatives to integrate universities, to develop human capacity, and to foster intercultural interactions among their students. It is not surprising, therefore, that the intervention described above is not commonplace. In fact, other studies show that the scale of other initiatives in the wider region is still low (Hou et al. 2017).

Nevertheless, some studies suggest that regional awareness does exist. One example is the landmark study on young people's familiarity with ASEAN (Thompson et al. 2016). When university students in the region's ten countries were asked to describe ASEAN, they used words that related to both regionalism and culture. For the students, the region was about cooperation, development, and poverty reduction. But it was also about transcending cultural diversity: 82 percent of the respondents felt that they are citizens of ASEAN. Yet, the important point about this study is that the awareness of the region is tied to perceiving ASEAN as an economic community. Even recommendations to heighten awareness are still framed in terms of what the Association does to address development challenges in the region. Thus, they are aimed at correcting the elitist impression the public has of ASEAN.

Transnational Coalitions Based on Shared Identities

The second strand in the literature on transnationalism and identity has to do with the transnational networks of civil society actors. These actors, who are brought together by their shared identities and advocacies, are involved in what the literature calls an alternative form of regionalism, or integration that takes place from below. Although they are not the main policymakers, their presence has been notable. In fact, one author has argued that regionalization is "progressing rapidly on the basis of actions undertaken by those involved in the civil society" (Igarashi 2011, 8). Other scholars have observed this reality in Southeast Asia by examining its particular characteristics. In the region, many civil society organizations have active partnerships with ASEAN itself. Some notable civil society organizations are the ASEAN Chamber of Commerce and Industry (ASEAN-CCI) and the ASEAN Institute of Strategic and International Studies (ASEAN-ISIS). To these can be added the ASEAN People's Forum and the ASEAN Youth Forum. These are civil society organizations affiliated with ASEAN. Such partnerships exemplify a model adopted in Southeast Asia that is aimed at transforming perceptions of ASEAN as limited to an elite group of policymakers. At the same time, these partnerships are strategic for transnational civil society in making their voices heard at the level of the region, which is otherwise neglected at the level of some member states. These alternative spaces are valuable for members of the political opposition or marginalized groups.

However, according to Rother (2015), the caveat is that they have to strike a careful balance between their roles as partners of government and as advocacy groups. On the one hand, they may be seen as being merely co-opted entities. On the other, they have demands as outsiders that could make them lose their access to ASEAN or government agencies. At the same time, there are some concerns about the power of ASEAN to vet accredited civil society organizations. It is instructive to refer to the list of accredited organizations, which includes the ASEAN Federation of Accountants, the Federation of ASEAN Shipowners' Association, and even the ASEAN Kite Council. None, however, is related to human rights concerns, which are sensitive issues for the different state actors in the region (ASEAN 2015).

It is for this reason that there is a need for other studies that focus on non-affiliated civil society organizations. Many of these organizations and networks are transnational in character, based on shared identities or advocacies about specific problems like human rights violations. Student activism based on a common educational experience is one area where a shared identity is at play. Although the extent of transnational linkages has varied over the years, there have been several waves of student activism contesting authoritarian and corrupt regimes in Southeast Asia over the years (Weiss et al. 2012). Other types of advocacies have also been consolidated based on other shared identities, such as those pertaining to religion, ethnicity, and citizenship. The fact that they are not accredited at the formal ASEAN level makes their advocacy work at times difficult. But this non-recognition also provides an opportunity for them to exercise their agency in different ways. Indeed, agency is critical to respond creatively to various issues.

Migrant workers, for example, in spite of their being drawn from different nationalities, have ongoing interactions in the region to organize themselves. Two influential networks are the Migrant Forum in Asia (MFA) and Coordination of Action Research on AIDS and Mobility (CARAM Asia) (Rother and Piper 2015). Another transnational case is explored in Leider's (2017) work on the Rohingya movement. The study identifies several transnational coalitions monitoring human rights issues in Myanmar. One coalition is the Alternative ASEAN Network on Burma (ALTSEAN), which documents human rights abuses against Muslims in Rakhine State. Another recent study demonstrating agency is that by Baird on the multiple transnational affiliations of indigenous groups in Laos. In fact, instead of transnational networks, he uses "translocal assemblages" to refer to the different regional affiliations that are helping ethnic groups in Laos to internalize their indigenous identity (Baird 2015, 56). In contrast to other countries in Southeast Asia, Laos has not adopted the term "indigenous people" as a legal category. This has had some consequences on the weak social protection of marginalized communities in Laos itself. But, by being connected to advocacy groups such as the Indigenous Knowledge and Peoples Network (based in Chiang Mai), the Co-Management Learning Network (based in Phnom Penh), and the Asian Indigenous Peoples' Pact (also based in Chiang Mai), local ethnic groups and their representatives have participated in activities around the region. In such interactions they learn about minority rights and environmental management.

Critical Approaches to Transnationalism and Identity

The third approach to transnationalism and identity in Southeast Asia is critical. Studies using this approach are important insofar as they call into question the coherent and cohesive narrative of ASEAN. In the previous section, the transnational coalitions discussed (whether ASEAN-affiliated or not) in one way or another provide support to the Association. In this section, by contrast, the social configurations discussed challenge the narrative of ASEAN as a formal regional bloc. These social configurations may either be formal (institutional) or informal (cultural). Whether the way they challenge ASEAN is explicit or otherwise, the point is that these cases illustrate ways in which identity and integration are critically engendered from below.

One strand of the scholarship on these social configurations is derived from anthropology and the humanities. These studies exemplify the broad approach to transnationalism that examines the diffusion of cultural values, practices, and norms. Unlike the examples highlighted above, they show that regional identity is not so much reliant on organized entities as it is on less formal arrangements brought about by migration and the media. In so doing, the regional identity engendered this way is more fluid both in terms of its character, and also its social boundedness. The argument is that cultural experiences are alternative ways of thinking about regional identity by critiquing the state of affairs in the region. Cinema, which has a long history in Southeast Asia, is instructive in this regard (Ainslie 2016).

Other studies in the region show that the transnational encounter is a nexus of social, political, and economic power. This means that people and institutions, depending on their physical and social locations, will have different experiences of the transnational. In some cases, it affords them greater choices while in others it limits their possibilities. This is why Hannerz (2008, 248) notes that in the transnational realm there are different kinds of "kinship, friendship, collegiality, business, pursuits of pleasure, or struggles for security" that may either take a "peripheral or a central part." For instance, the variegated experiences of transnational migrants are endowed with both possibilities and limitations. For example, migrants in diasporic networks have been described as reclaiming their ethnic identities. Ethnic communities like the Tai Lü, who were dispersed in the wake of World War II and the Cultural Revolution, are rediscovering not just their religious heritage but also economic benefits through cross-border movements in the Upper Mekong valley. As a result, even its ancient manuscript culture that uses the Tai Lü script to document historical and Buddhist narratives seems to be making a comeback. These movements "allow the Tai Lü diaspora in Laos, Burma and elsewhere to associate themselves with their ancient homeland in Sipsong Panna" (Grabowsky and Techasiriwan 2013, 8).

Yet, other scholars such as Benton and Gomez (2014) are cautious about romanticizing diasporic ethnic identities. They note, for example, that Chinese identities among migrants are adopted to the extent that they generate profitable opportunities, especially for entrepreneurial migrants such as the Chinese diaspora in Southeast Asia. At the same time, vis-à-vis state authorities, transnationalism cannot be taken to justify unrestricted freedom of movement for all kinds of migrants. Borders are tighter for specific types of migrant workers than they are for highly skilled professionals. This is certainly the case for many transnational migrant women in Southeast Asia who are beholden to contractual arrangements to undertake domestic work in the region. Their contractual work and inability to secure citizenship in their respective countries of employment limits not just their career choices but also their modes of intimacy with their left-behind children who cannot join them in the future (Hoang et al. 2015).

The concept of alternative regionalism in Southeast Asia is instructive to tease out the different ways in which alternative regionalism has been deployed. Chandra's (2009) work on ASEAN suggests that transnational civil society actors may be categorized as either mainstream or progressive regionalists. The former tend to be supportive of neoliberal policies while the latter push for more socialistic ideals. The progressive regionalists contest the neoliberal agenda of ASEAN. Their activities are underpinned by a different vision for a region, which scholars of alternative regionalism see as a "social construct that is built actively by various agencies rather than being a passive object" (Igarashi 2011, 4). One example is the Solidarity for Asian People's Advocacy (SAPA), an international non-governmental organization. In the statement that it submitted to ASEAN as its Charter was being deliberated more than a decade ago, the network articulated its commitment to labor standards, trade unions, and a debt-free region (SAPA 2006). Another example is the networks of non-government organizations and international development agencies working for sustainability and environmental preservation in the region. These advocacies are targeted at unhampered tourism that destroys the region's ecology. NGOs in mainland Southeast Asia, for example, have worked with local partners for community-based ecotourism. But as Parnwell argues, much work needs to be done "in convincing tourists to act as ethical consumers who can potentially wield immense power over the future direction of sustainable tourism development in Southeast Asia" (Parnwell 2008, 253).

Alternative regionalism, however, is not always a successful endeavor. Networks can become dormant, as in the case of the People's Agenda for Alternative Regionalisms (PAAR). This is indicative of the institutional weaknesses of such transnational coalitions. While studies have welcomed their critical contributions in forging regional identities, they also problematize their narratives. Rother (2015), for example, questions their legitimacy because some of these transnational coalitions are also elite-driven. It thus casts doubt not only on their potential in terms of activism but, more fundamentally, on their status as the "true voice of the people" (Rother 2015, 104).

Violence

A crucial but widely overlooked area that is shaping competing identities in Southeast Asia is violence. Violence is understood as "the intentional use of physical force or power, threatened or actual, against oneself, another person, or against a group or community, that either results in or has a high likelihood of resulting in injury, death, psychological harm, maldevelopment or deprivation" (WHO 2002, 4). In this volume, we exclude both self-directed violence (including suicide) and violence committed by an individual or a small group of individuals against other individuals (including homicide). Our focus is on all acts of collective violence committed by large groups of people, such as state security forces, organized political groups, militia, and terrorist organizations. Collective violence is often tied to warfare in which both military and civilian actors are involved. In our understanding of collective violence by large groups, the victims are often civilians. It is the impact of violence on civilians that we are most interested in.

Collective violence or mass violence "is a collective tactic pursued because it promises to serve a collective purpose" (Boudreau 2010, 141). It occurs at different levels: at a local or regional level in the form of subnational conflicts (e.g. separatist movements); at the level mainly of the nation-state (e.g. civil wars and anticolonial struggles); and at the transnational level in the form of interstate and international conflicts (e.g. wars between nation-states). The impact of group violence on identity will be discussed at all three levels against the background of the Southeast Asian experience of the last century. Moreover, specific cultural, social, demographic, and psychological conditions—either favoring or impairing the outbreak of mass violence—need to be addressed. Finally, the question of how violence has shaped social, political, and other forms of identities in Southeast Asia will be taken into consideration.

Subnational Violent Conflicts and Identity

The vast majority of violent conflicts in Southeast Asia since World War II have been fought at a subnational level. In many cases, these conflicts revolve around demands of ethnolinguistic and religious groups for political autonomy and self-determination within a nation-state. Very often these groups articulate historical claims to justify their cause. In spite of underlying political and economic factors, ethnoreligious conflicts occur in cultural contexts deeply embedded in identity issues. Croissant and Trinn (2009) argue that such culturally grounded political conflicts "do not primarily hinge on a clearly definable, interest-based (and thus essentially negotiable) object" (2009, 6), which makes them more explosive than other kinds of conflicts. There are, thus, good reasons for assuming a connection between identity and violence. Smelser (2007) argues that groups based on particularistic identities—ethnic, religious, and racial—may be particularly prone to violence since identity groups tend to have primordial ideological foundations containing a powerful exclusionary distinction between themselves and the "others."

One prominent form of subnational violence are secessionist armed conflicts over control of a subnational territory within a sovereign state. Such conflicts have affected half of the current eleven nation-states of Southeast Asia over the last thirty years. Among the countries in the region, Myanmar (Burma) is probably the one most seriously affected by secessionist movements, which have been challenging the territorial integrity of the state since its independence from Britain in January 1948. Myanmar is the only Southeast Asian country divided into "ethnic states," some of which were given a special status as "protected territories" by the British colonial administration. Political conflicts centered on issues of ethnolinguistic, religious, and historical animosities between the Bamar (the country's ethnic majority) and the minorities have become increasingly violent, especially after the military coup d'état of 1962 (Smith 1999, 2007; South 2008). A separate issue is the subnational violence in Rakhine State where an ethnoreligious conflict bordering the Chittagong Hill Tracts of Bangladesh continues to simmer. Despite the intervention of Burmese military forces and the demands of Rohingya extremists for an autonomous state in Sittwe in northern Rakhine, the main protagonists of the violent conflict seem to be, on the one side, the Rohingya Muslims claiming Rakhine (or a part of the territory) as their ancestral homeland and calling for Burmese citizenship through a claim for ethnic recognition. On the other side can be found the Buddhist (Rakhine-) Burmese who argue that the Rohingya are illegal settlers, the majority of whom migrated from Bangladesh in recent times (Leider 2013). In contrast to the Malay Muslims in southern Thailand and the Moros of Mindanao, who both have strong cases as primordial ethnoreligious groups, the claims of the Rohingya to primordial locality in Rakhine appear rather weak (Kosuta 2017, 29). In any case, the Rakhine conflict clearly demonstrates how mutually exclusive historical and cultural claims of identity groups engender violence.

While the Cambodian and Lao nation-states did not experience subnational conflicts that involved ethnoreligious groups calling for autonomy or secession—with the Hmong army in Laos during the Second Indochina War being only partially an exception (Lee 1982)— Vietnam faced secessionist conflicts until the 1970s. The Front Unifié de Lutte des Races Opprimées (FULRO), founded in 1964, was an organization of ethnic minorities in the Vietnamese central highlands fighting all kinds of Vietnamese hegemony, both that of the pro-American Republic of Vietnam in Saigon and, after 1975, their Communist adversaries, the Socialist Republic of Vietnam. Though the FULRO insurgency finally subsided at the end of the 1980s, its impact on the politics of ethnic relations was profound and indeed survived the insurgency's demise: into the twenty-first century, state policies and officials' decisions on ethnic minorities were shaped by fears of a recrudescence of ethnonationalist violence. The Khmer minority in the Mekong delta is another group which instigated an insurgency, though at a rather low level, against the Vietnamese state in the decades following the collapse of French rule in 1945 (Forest 1980). The communal violence between Khmer Krom villagers and pro-Communist Vietnamese forces reached its peak between 1945 and 1947 when the French colonial authorities were very weak, both politically and militarily. In his study of the role of ethnicity and violence in Khmer-Vietnamese relations, Shawn McHale observes that the high degree of indiscriminate violence by indigenous inhabitants and civilians in Cochinchina coincided with the breakdown of rural order, thus "[a] wide variety of groups, from brigands to armed political bands, took advantage of the opportunity" (McHale 2013, 380).

Thailand, or Siam as the country was known until 1939, is proud of being the only country in Southeast Asia that escaped colonialism by European powers. However, the country's present-day borders are the outcome of unequal treaties which the Siamese kingdom was forced to conclude with France and Britain. As a result, large territories inhabited by non-Siamese ethnic groups fell under French (Laos) and British (the Malay sultanates of Kelantan, Terengganu, and Kedah) rule, while significant areas inhabited by the same peoples became part of the modern Thai nation-state, such as the predominantly Lao-inhabited Northeast (Isan) and the former Malay sultanate of Patani (now the three southern border provinces of Pattani, Yala, and Narathiwat). Whereas political regionalism in Isan during the 1940s and 1950s did not develop with armed movements calling for autonomy or even secession from the Thai state (Keyes 1967), the Malay Muslim minority in the deep south, which make up a large majority in the region itself, remained resilient. Its resurgence since the beginning of the twenty-first century, following two decades of relative peace, gave intercommunal relations in southern Thailand a stronger religious thrust. During the last two or three decades, it has led to a radicalization of the Thai-Buddhist minority, increasingly fearful of being marginalized and even threatened in its very identity, as explored by McCargo (2012). There is a growing militarization of the Buddhist Sangha and laity in Thailand's deep south. A study by Jerryson (2011) reveals the hidden existence of armed Buddhist monks in a highly volatile and contested border region.

Violent Conflicts at the National Level and Their Relation to Identity Politics

The characteristics of individual states and the international context have been crucial in the shaping of mass violence in Southeast Asia. Robinson (2010, 70) points out that all states in the region have influenced or even conditioned mass violence in one way or the other, either as perpetrators, facilitators, or models of violence. Though the examples highlighted by Robinson exclusively pertain to the modern nation-state, his conceptual framework also seems valid for the colonial or, perhaps, even the precolonial state as well. The role of the state as the principal perpetrator of violence is obvious in the mass killings in Indonesia in 1965–66, in Cambodia during the Khmer Rouge regime (1975–78), and in East Timor during the time of Indonesian occupation (1975–99). These three cases of mass killings perpetrated by the state against its own people or certain segments of the population (defined by ethnicity, class, political affiliation, or other criteria) have alone caused the death of several million people and have thus been qualified as "genocide" by many scholars. We also need to refer to the persecution of political opponents in Myanmar by the military following the crackdown of the people's uprising in August 1988, the nationwide hunting down of leftist students before and after the military coup d'état of October 6, 1976 in Thailand (see Thongchai 2002; Beemer n.d.), and the repression of "landlords and reactionaries" during the North Vietnamese land reform (1954–56). Although causing the death of "only" hundreds or thousands of people, these examples also indicate that such mass violence at a national level does not necessarily resurface in the absence of a strong state but, on the contrary, is more "often the result of strategic calculation by political and military leaders" (Robinson 2010, 76).

Even in cases where the states in Southeast Asia have not been the main perpetrators of mass violence, they have often played a decisive role in instigating, provoking, or facilitating it. In many cases, they did so through the vector of identity policies based on a xenophobic mobilization of the population. States have produced and disseminated inflammatory propaganda which was, for example, the root cause of the anti-Vietnamese riots that broke out in Cambodia in the weeks after Lon Nol's coup d'état of March 1970, with thousands of ethnic Vietnamese murdered during communal riots and more than 200,000 fleeing to South Vietnam (Kiernan 2008). Or they have mobilized civilian paramilitary groups, as which was what happened in Thailand during the short-lived democratic period from 1973 to 1976 when various right-wing militia like the Nawaphon (New Force) and Krathing Daeng (Red Gaurs) committed acts of violence against members of leftist organizations threatening conservative notions of Thai identity and who were, thus, accused of being "anti-Thai traitors" (Bowie 1997). In a similar vein, when the armed conflict between Vietnam and Democratic Kampuchea escalated in 1977–78, the Pol Pot leadership accused its opponents of having "Khmer bodies with Vietnamese minds" (Kiernan 1996; Morris 1999).

Moreover, state authorities have facilitated and provoked violence through their engagement with non-state actors committing acts of violence in the face of extreme and unlawful violence of their own security forces. Through such behavior, states have contributed to the spread of violence as a preferred political strategy among non-state groups. The mass killings of members and supporters of the Communist Party of Indonesia in 1965–66, with radical Muslim militias being encouraged by the military, are probably the most striking example of this phenomenon. Most of the violence carried out by military and paramilitary forces of the state in battling Communist insurgents fits also into this pattern. Half of the countries in Southeast Asia have faced Communist uprisings in the post-World War II period. While some were relatively short-lived and at a rather low level, like in Thailand (1965–early 1980s), others inflicted damage over longer periods, such as the Communist insurgencies in Malaysia (before independence), in Myanmar, and in the Philippines. In some countries, Communist insurgencies succeeded in seizing state power as in the case of South Vietnam, Laos, and Cambodia in 1975.

Though less obvious, states in Southeast Asia have also played central roles in the formation and spread of a sociopolitical culture where political disagreements and conflicts tend to be resolved through violent means. However, Hardy and Duc present in their study of the Sơn Hà revolt in the Vietnamese highlands a case whereby the violence was perpetrated by a non-state society which rejected the expansion of the state though that state did spread the sociopolitical culture of violence (see chapter 16 in this volume). Through the unparalleled institutional reach of state power, "distinctive forms, repertoires and discourses of violence have been normalized, and have been employed by non-state actors in their own conflicts even where the state has not played a central role" (Robinson 2010, 77). The dramatic spread of violence perpetrated by local militia groups during the late years of the "New Order"

(1966–98) in Indonesia clearly illustrates this pattern: these groups consciously emulated the style and organization of the Indonesian military and adopted the latter's violent institutional culture.

Wars between States and Foreign Interventions

Since their independence in the post-World War II years, the nation-states of Southeast Asia have experienced numerous border disputes, many of which resulted from the legacy of the colonial period. Nevertheless, armed conflicts, not to speak of outright wars, between Southeast Asian states remained exceptional. The most serious border conflict was Indonesia's *konfrontasi* policy toward Malaysia during the late Suharto period (1963–66). Claiming the whole of northern Kalimantan—the sultanates of Sarawak and Sabah as well as Brunei—as Indonesian territory, the Republic of Indonesia questioned the very existence of its northern neighbour. A total of 740 people were killed on both sides and hundreds more wounded in the military clashes ending with a final peace agreement in August 1966. The short Thai-Lao border war (December 1987–February 1988) over the suzerainty of the village of Ban Romklao and three smaller settlements in the Lao province of Sainyabuli (Xayabouri) claimed by Thailand, caused over 1,000 casualties. It ended with the complete withdrawal of Thai forces from the contested area. In more recent times, the frozen conflict between Thailand and Cambodia over the suzerainty of the Preah Vihear temple complex escalated after the main temple was registered as a Cambodian World Heritage site by UNESCO in July 2008. Between October 2008 and May 2011, skirmishes between Thai and Cambodian border troops flared up from time to time in a disputed area surrounding the temple, resulting in dozens of dead and wounded soldiers on both sides and the flight of civilians from the area. Since then, the situation has de-escalated, partly owing to mediation efforts by ASEAN, thus averting a full-scale war between Thailand and Cambodia (see Grabowsky 2017; Strate 2015).

Since 1945, there have been only two cases of full-scale wars between Southeast Asian states. One of these, the war between Indonesia and East Timor (Timor-Leste) broke out in the aftermath of East Timorese independence, which was unilaterally declared on November 28, 1975 by the Revolutionary Front for an Independent East Timor (Fretelin), one of several contending parties in a civil war that had broken out shortly after the sudden withdrawal of the Portuguese in late 1974, though it could be argued that East Timor at the time was not a sovereign nation-state. Because the opponents of the Marxist-oriented Fretelin called for

Indonesian military intervention and supported the subsequent integration of East Timor into the Indonesian state, the violent conflict in East Timor might not necessarily be interpreted as a war of aggression by Indonesia against a neighboring state (Taylor 1995; Kammen 2015). The conflict could alternatively be interpreted as either the continuation of an ongoing civil war or as a subnational war of secession from Indonesia led by a pro-Communist insurgency.

The second case, the Vietnamese invasion of Cambodia, which started on December, 25 1978, was without doubt a full-scale war between two sovereign states in Southeast Asia. Following a year and a half of border skirmishes, with Khmer Rouge troops making incursions deep into Vietnamese territory in the strategically important Parrot's Peak area, thirteen Vietnamese divisions, estimated at 150,000 soldiers, well-supported by heavy artillery and air power, occupied the heartland of Cambodia, including the emptied capital of Phnom Penh, within two weeks. This first "Red Brotherhood at War" (Evans and Rowley 1984) entailed the bloody Chinese "punishing campaign" against Vietnam in February and March 1979, leading to an estimated 30,000 casualties on each side. The Cambodian conflict, also called the "Third Indochina War," claimed the lives of more than 15,000 Vietnamese soldiers and of more than 100,000 Cambodian soldiers and civilians.

Mass Violence and Identity

How is mass violence related to the feeling of belonging on the part of perpetrators, victims, and third parties? Southeast Asian evidence suggests that this sense of belonging is shaped by the experience of mass violence. The shared memories of past violence shape ethnic, religious, social, and political identities. Bonds of loyalty are created and deepened through such memories, providing the justification and the models for future mass violence. Those who have experienced violence directly are invariably transformed by it, regardless of whether they are perpetrators, victims, or merely witnesses. This is especially true for the personal experience of extreme violence, such as beheadings, rape, and torture. It is more this shared experience and collective memory of violence, rather than economic or political grievances, that inspire loyalty and create group identity. Members of minority groups—Karen, Shan, Kachin, etc.—fighting the Burmese army, Malay Muslims in Thailand's Deep South, and members and supporters of the New People's Army in the Philippines, all provide evidence of the relationship between mass violence and group identity. In his insightful study of mass violence in East Timor, Douglas Kammen observes that in East Timor and elsewhere the recurrence of violence is of central importance to the narrative of indigenous resistance against colonial oppression, providing the oppressed with a sense of a common destiny, that is, a sense of belonging, even though the "Timorese peoples were not inherently or culturally predisposed to violence" (Kammen 2015, 168). The role of remembering (and forgetting) of past traumatic violence in the shaping of collective identities has been discussed with regard to the concept of collective memory as outlined by Halbwachs (1992) and Nora (1996). "Mourning, reparation, and the working-through of violent histories require a relational politics, including a politics of emotion that crosses the divide between victims and perpetrators" (Schwab 2010, 104). Thongchai (2020) has further pushed the boundaries of analysis of Southeast Asian violence and belonging in his discussion of the Bangkok massacre of October 6, 1976 and the "unforgetting"—or memory impasse—that developed in its aftermath, whereby the event was neither publicly remembered nor forgotten.

The power of violence to shape identities and to motivate further violence does not function automatically. Local communities, like nations as a whole, may have histories of mass violence or cultural patterns of violent behavior but then afterwards enjoy longer periods of peace and stability, which one day might be ended by renewed waves of collective violence, as the history of the Balkans in the nineteenth and twentieth centuries has demonstrated. Robinson (2010) highlights the importance of "violence specialists," like the notorious *preman* (thugs for hire) in Indonesia and semi-official militia groups, who consciously encourage acts of mass violence through the evocation, manipulation, and even distortion of experiences and memories of past violence. Boudreau (2010) observes that the degree of segregation between populations that movements (political, class, ethnic, religious, generational) attack, and the populations from which they recruit, determines the pressure they face to moderate attacks and make them more discriminate. Some theorists have suggested that youth cohorts may develop a generational consciousness, especially out of an awareness of belonging to a generation that possesses an extraordinary size and strength, thus enabling their members to act as a collective. Urdal (2004, 2) notes, however, that although collective violent action can only be carried out by identity groups, "it is not necessary that identity groups are generation-based for youth bulges to increase the likelihood of armed conflict."

Violence should not be understood simply by reference to exogenous causes (economic problems, social injustice, foreign intervention, etc.), but rather as a critical element in the process of shaping the identities, motivations, and methods of future violence. Social and political dynamics at a local, national, or regional level do not operate independently in the creation of violence, they become pertinent only under certain historical conditions. Smelser (2007, 35–36) identifies four sets of variables explaining the occurrence of violence exercised by identity groups or identity movements (either holding or opposing state power). These variables are a facilitating ideology; opportunities for the use of violence; access to the means of violence; and the actual unavailability of alternative political means to achieve specific ends. It is therefore debatable whether a democratic political environment gives identity groups more voice for a non-violent articulation than authoritarian regimes (Gurr and Harff 1994). An effective state is often more important in avoiding or regulating ethnic violence than the form of government, as Umar (2007) has suggested in discussing the Nigerian case.

Structure of the Volume

This volume is interested in the different ways in which non-state actors in Southeast Asia have responded to the formation of regional identity over time. As we have indicated at the outset, this has been a project of ASEAN as a community of states. But as the chapters in this volume demonstrate, the formation of regional identities among Southeast Asians has a much longer history, which continues to this day. In their own ways, these chapters spell out how non-state actors have either shaped or contested these regional identities. The chapters have been categorized according to the three themes of generations, transnationalism, and violence.

Part I contains four chapters based on the theme of generations as a social configuration around which identities within ASEAN member countries are forged. Most ASEAN members are developing countries and, as a result, have young populations. In economic terms, the youthful population is framed as a potent resource for regional integration and development, especially through the participation in the workforce of those who are highly educated, mobile, and skilled. In Chapter 1, Medelina K. Hendytio analyzes the Millennial generation's attitudes toward ASEAN in various Southeast Asian countries, in particular Indonesia. She seeks to do so from a comparative perspective in order to appreciate the organization's relevance for the emergence of an ASEAN regional identity. In Chapter 2, Danny Wong Tze Ken investigates the evolution of Chinese identity in Malaysia and its neighbors Indonesia and Singapore by focusing on dialects. Dialects, which were regarded as the primary basis of Chinese identity in Southeast Asia, have undergone generational change, especially when the larger ethnic Chinese identity takes precedence over dialect identity in the face of meeting greater challenges confronting the community at national level. In Chapter 3, Natasha Pairaudeau explores the past and present experiences of ethnic Shan migrants called Kula who were long-standing caravan traders in the Thai-Lao border area before taking up work in the gem mines in the border area of Pailin in northwestern Cambodia. Her research looks at the impact of decolonization and nation-building on their identity and examines the violence that accompanied these processes. In Chapter 4, Oliver Tappe pays attention to labor as well, this time on the generations of Vietnamese tin miners who migrated to neighboring Laos over a century. He recounts their common experiences of precarity, mobility, hope, and resilience.

The chapters of Part II discuss how alternative regional identities are engendered on the ground across transnational coalitions. These formal and informal networks are crucial in actively defining different visions, or imaginings, about Southeast Asia's future in relation to the economy, mobility, and labor. Special attention is paid to non-state actors who may not necessarily be organized as transnational coalitions. For example, in Chapter 5 Prasit Leepreecha analyzes the transnational coalition of indigenous peoples in ASEAN. He shows how international laws and organic collaborations among indigenous groups have made this transnational coalition possible. Migration is crucial in forging transnational solidarities. Malays migrating from the peninsula to Indonesia, as Jan van der Putten and Alan Darmawan discuss in Chapter 6, reimagine their ethnic identity to cover a much wider geography. Both authors investigate the process of identity formation in the contemporary context, focusing on how the Malay communities in Southeast Asia attempt to link with each other. In Chapter 7, Filomeno Aguilar Jr. investigates the circumstances and consequences of the decision of many Filipinos to acquire Singaporean citizenship. His chapter probes its implications for nationhood and for people's sense of belonging in Southeast Asia. While migration is often an economic decision, as might be the case for these Filipinos in Singapore, it could be religiously motivated as well. In Chapter 8, Jayeel Cornelio and Erron C. Medina make this case as they trace the work of Filipino missionaries in Bangkok and the transnational communities that they create. For them, Thailand is a harvest field to which they have been called as missionaries in Southeast Asia.

Two chapters in Part II pay attention to identities formed around borderlands. The work of Kwanchewan Buadaeng among the Karen is an example. In Chapter 9, she explores the ways in which the Talaku Karen ethnoreligious people reconstruct their identities in the context of political and economic transformations in the borderlands. The Talaku Karen are integrated under the Thai and Burmese state and under the global network of Christian organizations. The Talaku's ways of constructing and reconstructing their identities involves the process of working and connecting with specific types of networks and movements. Chapter 10 by Sirui Dao and Volker Grabowsky focuses on transborder pilgrimage as a practice to preserve ethnoreligious identity. The chapter draws on extensive ethnography among a sizeable Tai Lü refugee community living along the Myanmar-Thailand border, a group barely studied by scholars in the field. For the communities living in eastern Myanmar and northern Thailand, the reconstruction of a holy stupa in the Sipsòng Panna homeland is considered a meritorious deed, not only aimed at karmic benefits for the individual donor but also at overcoming traumatic experiences caused by past violence. The Tai Lü as a transnational community are linked by an identification with their homeland of Sipsòng Panna or Moeng Lü, embodied by its traditional ruler, the *chao fa* ("Lord of Heaven"). Roger Casas explores in Chapter 11 the reactions to the death of the last ruler (*chao fa*) in October 2017, deposed by the Chinese communists in 1950, and how he acted as a symbol of a traditional, transnational Tai Lü identity that spills over the borders of the Chinese polity.

The chapters in Part III turn to violence and how it intersects with identity. These chapters are useful in making sense of violence and trauma around Southeast Asia. Violence, for example, is discursively tied to national identities. State-sponsored violence in the form of anticrime campaigns could be a political project set as a precondition for social order and economic growth. This seems to be a pattern for many politicians across Southeast Asia, as Erron C. Medina and Bianca Ysabelle Franco discuss in Chapter 12. This discourse makes anticrime campaigns popular among the people while still being dangerous for democratic change and good governance.

In other cases, experiences of violence foster a strong sense of collective identity. This is true in two local studies presented here. In Chapter 13, Vidhyandika Djati Perkasa examines Papuan youth identity as the result of violence, oppression, and marginalization. In the Papuan case, as the chapter shows, national identity is undermined by a more exclusive form of local identity. A violent conflict at a local level, but with transnational implications is dealt with in Chapter 14. Jacques P. Leider pays attention to ethnoreligious entanglements in the Bengal-Myanmar borderlands. From a historical perspective, his chapter looks at the impact of communal and state violence on the political conscience and identity of people in the Rakhine heartlands.

Other chapters affirm the same point by focusing on national experiences of violence. In Chapter 15, Volker Grabowsky examines mass violence at the national level. His work investigates the role of Cambodian youth in the revolutionary terror of the Khmer Rouge regime in the second half of the 1970s. He analyzes how the leadership of the Communist Party of Kampuchea exploited the idealism of Cambodian youth for their political ends. Special emphasis is given to the mechanisms of recruitment of young cadres into the military and political apparatus of the Khmer Rouge. Another case study, this time by Đào Thế Đức and Andrew Hardy, points to the impact of violence on collective memory and identities at the level of a single district. Chapter 16 narrates the historical context that led to the killings of ethnic Viet inhabitants by their Hrê neighbors in the early 1950s. The chapter discusses the impact of this experience on present-day ethnic relations and political culture. Turning to Timor-Leste, Janina Pawelz in Chapter 17 narrates the experience of martial arts groups that gained notoriety as instigators of violence and insecurity in the country. She employs social identity theory to make sense of youth identities in a conflict setting.

Conclusion

This volume has been a long time in the making, a major output of the Work Package on Identity under the project Competing Regional Integrations in Southeast Asia (CRISEA). All the contributors to this volume are grateful to the European Commission for a generous grant under the Horizon 2020 Programme. CRISEA has enabled us to form an interdisciplinary community of scholars working on collective identities in Southeast Asia. In keeping with the thrust of our work package, this volume's main contribution is in bringing to the surface the extensive work of non-state actors in shaping alternative regional identities. In that sense, the volume showcases the struggle for legitimacy among non-state actors in forming transnational solidarities. At the same time, the volume shows how regional identities are contested, especially with respect to ASEAN as an entity and identity.

Finally, the other contribution of the volume lies in the themes that transverse its different chapters. Throughout we pay attention to several transversal themes. The first is mobilities. The experience of mobile populations, such as labor migrants, pilgrims, tourists, and refugees, help us recognize whether their movements compete with or legitimize forms of Southeast Asian identity. Another transversal theme is the importance of security for regional solidarity, conceived in several different respects, including human security from violence and social exclusion. As we explore identity construction, gender is another traversal theme that informs our analyses. Religious resurgence has taken various forms among Muslim men and women, ranging from pious feminism to radical patriarchy, while similar contestations engage Buddhist monks and nuns and Buddhist societies and moralities at large.

References

Acharya, Amitav. 2017. "The Evolution and Limitations of ASEAN Identity." In *Building the ASEAN Community: Political-Security and Socio-Cultural Reflections*, eds. Aileen Baviera and L. Maramis, 25–38. Jakarta: Economic Research Institute for ASEAN and East Asia.

Ainslie, Mary J. 2016. "Towards a Southeast Asian Model of Horror: Thai Horror Cinema in Malaysia, Urbanization, and Cultural Proximity." In *Transnational Horror Cinema: Bodies of Excess and the Global Grotesque*, eds. Sharon Siddique and R. Raphael, 179–204. Basingstoke, UK: Palgrave Macmillan.

Anagnost, Ann, Andrea Arai, and Hai Ren, eds. 2013. *Global Futures in East Asia: Youth, Nation, and the New Economy in Uncertain Times*. Stanford, CA: Stanford University Press.

Antweiler, Christoph. 2017. "Area Studies @ Southeast Asia: Alternative Areas Versus Alternatives to Areas." In *Area Studies at the Crossroads: Knowledge Production after the Mobility Turn*, eds. Katja Mielke and Anna-Katharina Hornidge, 65–82. New York: Palgrave Macmillan.

ASEAN. 2015. Register of Accredited Civil Society Organizations. http://www.asean.org/wp-content/uploads/images/2015/May/list_of_Entities_Associated_with_ASEAN/Accredited%20Civil%20Society%20Organisations%20%20as%20of%2011%20May%202015.pdf.

————————. 2016. *ASEAN Socio-Cultural Community Blueprint 2025*. Jakarta: ASEAN Secretariat.

Azmawati, D., and L. Quayle. 2017 "Promoting ASEAN Awareness at the Higher Education Chalkface." *Contemporary Southeast Asia: A Journal of International and Strategic Affairs* 39: 127–48.

Baird, Ian. 2015. "Translocal Assemblages and the Circulation of the Concept of 'Indigenous "Peoples' in Laos." *Political Geography* 46: 54–64.

Beck, Ulrich. 2008. "The Cosmopolitan Perspective: Sociology of the Second Age of Modernity." In *The Transnational Studies Reader: Intersections and Innovations*, eds. S. Khagram and P. Levitt, 222–30. London: Routledge.

Beemer, Bryce. "Bangkok Postcard: Forgetting and Remembering 'Hok Tulaa', the October 6 Massacre." http://www.2.hawaii.edu/~seassa/explorations/v1n1/ art6/ v1n1-frame6.html.

Benton, G., and E. T. Gomez. 2014 "Belonging to the Nation: Generational Change, Identity and the Chinese Diaspora." *Ethnic and Racial Studies* 37: 1157–71.

Bjorkhagen, Martin. 2013. *The Conflict in the Moluccas: Local Youths' Perceptions Contrasted to Previous Research*. Malmo: Faculty of Culture and Society, Department of Global Political Studies, Malmo University.

Boudreau, Vincent. 2010. "Recruitment and Attack in Southeast Asian Collective Violence." In *Political Violence in South and Southeast Asia: Critical Perspectives*, eds. Itty Abraham et al., 141–67. Tokyo: United Nations University Press.

Bowie, Katherine. 1997. *Rituals of National Loyalty: The Village Scout Movement in Thailand*. New York: Columbia University Press.

Chandra, Alexander C. 2009. *Civil Society in Search of an Alternative Regionalism in ASEAN*. Winnipeg: International Institute for Sustainable Development.

Chao, Roger. 2016. "Changing Higher Education Discourse in the Making of the ASEAN Region." In *Global Regionalisms and Higher Education: Projects, Processes, Politics*, eds. S. Robertson et al., 124–42. Cheltenham, UK: Edward Elgard Publishing.

Cornelio, Jayeel. 2015. "Youth and Religion in East and Southeast Asia." In *Handbook of Children and Youth Studies*, eds. J. Wyn and H. Cahill, 903–16. Singapore: Springer.

————————. 2020. "The State of Filipino Millennials: An Alternative View." In *Rethinking Filipino Millennials: Alternative Perspectives on a Misunderstood Generation*, ed. J. Cornelio, 2–28. Manila: UST Publishing House.

Crodington, Graeme. 2008. "Detailed Introduction to Generational Theory." http://ngkok.co.za/sinode2016/intro-generations.pdf.

Croissant, Aurel, and Christoph Trinn. 2009. *Culture, Identity and Conflict in Asia and Southeast Asia*. Gütersloh: Bertelsmann Stiftung.

Dimock, Michael. 2018. *Millennials End and Post-Millennials Begin*. Washington, DC: Pew Research Center.

Evans, Grant, and Kelvin Rowley. 1984. *Red Brotherhood at War: Indochina Since the Fall of Saigon*. London: Verso.

Forest, Alain. 1980. *Le Cambodge et la colonisation française: histoire d'une colonisation sans heurts (1897-1920)*. Paris: L'Harmattan.

Grabowsky, Volker. 2017. "Heritage and Nationalism in the Preah Vihear Dispute." In *Ethnic and Religious Identities and Integration in Southeast Asia*, eds. Ooi Keat Gin and Volker Grabowsky, 405–48. Chiang Mai: Silkworm Books.

Grabowsky, Volker, and Apiradee Techasiriwan. 2013. "Tai Lü Identities in the Upper Mekong Region: Glimpses from Mulberry Paper Manuscripts." *Aséanie* 31: 11–34.

Gurr, Ted R., and Barbara Harff. 1994. *Ethnic Conflict in World Politics*. Boulder, CO: Westview Press.

Halbwachs, Maurice. 1992. *On Collective Memory*. Chicago, IL: University of Chicago Press.

Hannerz, Ulf. 2008. "Nigerian Kung Fu, Manhattan Fatwa and the Local and the Global: Continuity and Change." In *The Transnational Studies Reader: Intersections and Innovations*, eds. S. Khagram and P. Levitt, 235–50. London: Routledge.

Hasan, Noorhaidi. 2010. *The Drama of Jihad: The Emergence of Salafi Youth in Indonesia*. Oxford: Oxford University Press.

Hau, Caroline, and Kasian Tejapira. 2011. *Traveling Nation-Makers: Transnational Flows and Movements in the Making of Modern Southeast Asia*. Singapore: NUS Press/Kyoto: Kyoto University Press.

Herman, Judith. 1992. *Trauma and Recovery: The Aftermath of Violence: From Domestic Abuse to Political Terror*. New York: Basic Books.

Hirsch, Philip, ed. 1996. *Seeing Forests for Trees: Environment and Environmentalism in Thailand*. Chiang Mai: Silkworm Books.

Hoang, L. A., T. Lam, and B. Yeoh. 2015. "Transnational Migration, Changing Care Arrangements and Left-behind Children's Responses in South-east Asia." *Children's Geographies* 13: 263–77.

Howe, Neil, and William Strauss. 2007. "The Next 20 Years: How Customer and Workforce Attitudes Will Evolve." *Harvard Business Review* 85(7–8): 41–57.

Hou, AYC., C. Hill, KH-J Chen et al. 2017. "A Comparative Study of Student Mobility Programs in SEAMEO-RIHED, UMAP, and Campus Asia: Regulation, Challenges, and Impacts on Higher Education Regionalization." *Higher Education Evaluation and Development* 11: 12–24.

Hussain, Z. 2017. "Time to Have a Deeper ASEAN Identity." http://www.straitstimes.com/asia/se-asia/time-to-have-deeper-asean-identity.

Igarashi, Seiichi. 2011. "The New Regional Order and Transnational Civil Society in Southeast Asia: Focusing on Alternative Regionalism from Below in the Process of Building the ASEAN Community." *World Political Science Review* 7: 1–31.

Intal, Ponciano, and Lydia Ruddy. 2017. *Voices of ASEAN: What Does ASEAN Mean to ASEAN Peoples?* Jakarta: Economic Research Institute for ASEAN and East Asia.

Jerryson, Michael K. 2011. *Buddhist Fury: Religion and Violence in Southern Thailand*. New York: Oxford University Press.

Jones, Michael. 2004. "Forging an ASEAN Identity: The Challenge to Construct a Shared Destiny." *Contemporary Southeast Asia* 26: 140–54.

Joshi, Aparna, John C. Dencker, Gentz Franz, and Joseph J. Martocchio. 2010. "Unpacking Generational Identities in Organizations." *Academy of Management Review* 35: 392–414.

Kammen, Douglas. 2015. *Three Centuries of Conflict in East Timor*. New Brunswick, NJ: Rutgers University Press.

Kanokrat Lertchoosakul. 2012. "The Rise of the Octobrists: Power and Conflict among Former Left Wing Student Activists in Contemporary Thai Politics." PhD dissertation, London School of Economics and Political Science.

Kearney, M. 1995. "The Local and the Global: The Anthropology of Globalization and Transnationalism." *Annual Review of Anthropology* 24: 547–65.

Kertzer, David. 1983. "Generation as a Sociological Problem." *Annual Review of Sociology* 9: 125–49.

Keyes, Charles F. 1967. *Isan: Regionalism in Northeastern Thailand*. Ithaca, NY: Southeast Asia Program, Cornell University.

Khagram, S., and P. Levitt. 2008. "Constructing Transnational Studies." In *The Transnational Studies Reader: Intersections and Innovations*, eds. S. Khagram and P. Levitt, 1–18. London: Routledge.

Kiernan, Ben. 1996. *The Pol Pot Regime: Race, Power, and Genocide in Cambodia under the Khmer Rouge, 1975–79*. New Haven, CT: Yale University Press.

———. 2008. *Genocide and Resistance in Southeast Asia: Documentation, Denial & Justice in Cambodia & East Timor*. London: Transaction Publishers.

Kosuta, Matthew. 2017. "Postcolonial Religious Conflict in Southeast Asia." *Contemporary Postcolonial Asia* 22(1): 24–30.

Kwanchewan Buadaeng. 2013. "Talaku Movement among the Karen in Thai-Burma Borderland: Territorialization and Deterritorialization Processes." In *Mobility and Heritage in Northern Thailand and Laos: Past and Present*, eds. Olivier Evrard, D. Guillaud, and Chayan Vaddhanaphuti, 167–84. Chiang Mai: Good Print.

Lee, Gary Yia. 1982. "Minority Policies and the Hmong in Laos." In *Contemporary Laos. Studies in the Politics and Society of the Lao People's Democratic Republic*, ed. Martin Stuart-Fox, 199–219. St. Lucia: University of Queensland Press.

Leider, Jacques. 2013. "Des musulmans d'Arakan aux Rohingyas de Birmanie: origines historiques et mouvement politique." *Diplomatie, Affaires stratégiques et relations internationales*, January–February, 70–71.

——————. 2017. "Transmutations of the Rohingya Movement in the Post-2012 Rakhine State Crisis." In *Ethnic and Religious Identities and Integration in Southeast Asia*, eds. Ooi Keat Gin and Volker Grabowsky, 191–239. Chiang Mai: Silkworm Books.

Malarney, Shaun Kingsley. 2001. "The Fatherland Remembers Your Sacrifice: Commemorating War Dead in North Vietnam." In *The Country of Memory: Remaking the Past in Late Socialist Vietnam*, ed. Hue Tam Ho Tai, 46–76. Berkeley, CA: University of California Press.

Mannheim, Karl. 1952. "The Problem of Generations." In *Essays on the Sociology of Knowledge*, ed. Paul Kecskemeti. London: Routledge and Kegan Paul.

Maung Maung. 1999. *The 1988 Uprising in Burma*. New Haven, CT: Yale University Southeast Asia Studies Program.

McCargo, Duncan. 2012. *Mapping National Anxieties: Thailand's Southern Conflict*. Copenhagen: Nordic Institute of Asian Studies Press.

McHale, Shawn. 2013. "Ethnicity, Violence, and Khmer-Vietnamese Relations: The Significance of the Lower Mekong Delta, 1757–1954." *Journal of Asian Studies* 72(2): 367–90.

Morris, Stephen J. 1999. *Why Vietnam Invaded Cambodia: Political Culture and Causes of War*. Stanford, CA: Stanford University Press.

Murti, G. L. 2016. "ASEAN's 'One Identity and One Community': A Slogan or a Reality?" *Yale Journal of International Affairs* 1: 87–96.

Nora, Pierre. 1996. *Realms of Memory*. New York: Columbia University Press.

Ooi Keat Gin and Volker Grabowsky. 2017. "Introduction." In *Ethnic and Religious Identities and Integration in Southeast Asia*. eds. Ooi Keat Gin and Volker Grabowsky, 1–27. Chiang Mai: Silkworm Books.

Osborne, Milton. 2016. *Southeast Asia: An Introductory History*, rev. edn. Sydney: Allen & Unwin.

Parnwell, M. 2008. "A Political Ecology of Sustainable Tourism in Southeast Asia." In *Tourism in Southeast Asia: Challenges and New Directions*, eds. M. Hitchcock, V. King, and M. Parnwell, 236–53. Honolulu, HI: University of Hawaii Press.

Risse-Kappen, Thomas. 2008. "Bringing Transnational Relations Back." In *The Transnational Studies Reader: Intersections and Innovations*, eds. S. Khagram and P. Levitt, 459–73. London: Routledge.

Robinson, Geoffrey. 2010. "Mass Violence in Southeast Asia." In *Political Violence in South and Southeast Asia: Critical Perspectives*, eds. Itty Abraham et al., 69–90. Tokyo: United Nations University Press.

Rother, Stefan. 2015. "Democratizing ASEAN Through 'Alternative Regionalism'? The ASEAN Civil Society Conference and the ASEAN Youth Forum." *ASIEN The German Journal on Contemporary Asia* 136: 98–119.

Rother, Stefan, and Nicola Piper. 2015. "Alternative Regionalism from Below: Democratizing ASEAN's Migration Governance." *International Migration* 53: 36–49.

SAPA. 2006. Submission on the Economic Pillar for the Eminent Persons Group on the ASEAN Chart. http://www.alternative-regionalisms.org/wp-content/uploads/2009/07/ sapasubmissionasean charterecon.pdf.

Schwab, Gabriele. 2010. *Haunting Legacies: Violent Histories and Transgenerational Trauma*. New York: Columbia University Press.

Smelser, Neil J. 2007. "Uncertain Connections: Globalization, Localization, Identities, and Violence." In *Identity Conflicts: Can Violence Be Regulated?*, eds. J. Craig Jenkins and Esther E. Gottlieb, 23–39. London: Transaction Publishers.

Smith, Martin. 1999. *Burma: Insurgency and the Politics of Ethnicity*. Bangkok: White Lotus/London: Zed Books.

——————. 2007. *State of Strife: The Dynamics of Ethnic Conflict in Burma*. Washington, DC: East-West Center, Policy Studies Series no. 36.

South, Ashley. 2008. *Ethnic Politics in Burma: States of Conflict*. London: Routledge.

Strate, Shane. 2015. *The Lost Territories: Thailand's History of National Humiliation*. Honolulu, HI: University of Hawai'i Press.

Taylor, John G. 1995. "The Emergence of a Nationalist Movement in East Timor." In *East Timor at the Crossroads: The Forging of a Nation*, eds. Peter Carey and G. Carter Bentley, 21–41. London/New York: Cassell/Social Science Research Council.

Taylor, Paul. 2010. *Confident. Connected. Open to Change*. Washington, DC: Pew Research Center.

Thompson, Eric C., and Chulanee Thianthai. 1996. "Attitudes and Awareness Toward ASEAN: Findings of a Ten Nation Survey." http://www.aseanfoundation.org/ documents/ Attitudes%20and%20 Awareness%20 Toward%20ASEAN.pdf.

Thompson, Eric C., Chulanee Thianthai, and Moe Thuzar. 2016. *Do Young People Know ASEAN? Update of a Ten-Nation Survey*. Singapore: Institute of Southeast Asian Studies.

Thongchai Winichakul. 2002. "Remembering/ Silencing the Traumatic Past: The Ambivalent Memories of the October 1976 Massacre in Bangkok." In *Cultural Crisis and Social Memory: Modernity and Identity in Thailand and Laos*, eds. Charles F. Keyes and Shigeharu Tanabe, 243–83. London: Routledge/Curzon.

——————. 2020. *Moments of Silence: The Unforgetting of the October 6, 1976, Massacre in Bangkok*. Honolulu, HI: University of Hawai'i Press.

Tolbize, Anick. 2008. "Generational Differences in the Workplace." Minneapolis: Research and Training Center on Community Living, University of Minnesota.

Umar, Muhammad Sani. 2007. "Weak States and Democratization: Ethnic and Religious Conflicts in Nigeria." In *Identity Conflicts: Can Violence Be Regulated?*, eds. J. Craig Jenkins and Esther E. Gottlieb, 259–79. New Brunswick, NJ: Transaction Publishers.

Urdal, Henrik. 2004. "The Devil in the Demographics: The Effect of Youth Bulges on Domestic Armed Conflict, 1950–2000." Working Paper No. 14. Washington, DC: Social Development Department, The World Bank.

Vertovec, Steven. 1999. "Conceiving and Researching Transnationalism." *Ethnic and Racial Studies* 22: 447–62.

Weiss, Meredith, Edward Aspinall, and Mark Thompson. 2012. "Introduction: Understanding Student Activism in Asia." In *Student Activism in Asia: Between Protest and Powerlessness*, eds. Meredith Weiss and Edward Aspinall, 1–32. Minneapolis, MN: University of Minnesota Press.

World Health Organization/WHO. 2002. *World Report on Health and Violence: Summary*. Geneva: World Health Organization.

Wyn, Johanna, and Helen Cahill, eds. 2015. *Handbook of Children and Youth Studies*. Singapore: Springer Science and Business Media.

GENERATIONS

Generational Support for ASEAN Integration and Identity: An Indonesian Perspective

MEDELINA K. HENDYTIO

Since 1967, Southeast Asia has seen the most ambitious regional integration project outside of Europe, pursued through the Association of Southeast Asian Nations (ASEAN). On August 8, 2020, ASEAN turned fifty-three years old. On the positive side, there has been a high level of regional stability for the last fifty years, even though it has not been without internal and external generated conflicts on the political-security front.

Since its inception, ASEAN has made extraordinary progress in promoting economic cooperation and integration as well as social development. Mobility within ASEAN countries has significantly increased, which has facilitated closer people-to-people collaboration and connectivity among the member countries of ASEAN. Intraregional trade and connectivity have also made visible achievements in ASEAN trade, setting almost zero tariffs and visa-free travel for ASEAN nationals. Meanwhile, the ASEAN Socio-Cultural Community (ASCC) has shown considerable social progress in reducing the number of people living in poverty, i.e. on less than US$1.25 a day, from one in every two people to one in every eight within two decades, as well as minimizing infant and maternal mortality in the region. Furthermore, the average life expectancy in ASEAN member countries has risen from 55.6 years in 1969 to 70.9 years in 2016 (Pakpahan 2019).

Despite its remarkable achievements, ASEAN still faces many challenges. Against a reduction in absolute poverty, several member countries are challenged by the fact that many of their people still live below the poverty line. Significant income and wealth inequity is an additional challenge. In the economic sector, economic integration benefits have not been distributed evenly between member countries and, more importantly, within the populations of those countries. ASEAN members and their external partners face disruptive migration flows, inter-ethnic conflicts, and territorial disputes. As a result, the domestic discourse of ASEAN members has contested border openness challenges in recent years.

Territorial disputes have led to the rise of nationalism and sovereignty issues and caused tensions among different ASEAN countries in the effort to settle these disputes. These problems could potentially erode "Southeast Asian Integration," which is the framework enabling members to opt for cooperation when it is useful while also ensuring the ability to retain national sovereignty. Mohammad Fajar Ikhsan et al. (2016) have argued that in practice regional integration is a cooperative model created among the states involved in making positive possibilities and opportunities to fulfill their national agenda. In short, integration is not an end but a process to support economic growth strategies, greater social equality, and democratization (Haokip, 2012). This approach is reflected in the ASEAN Charter and the ASEAN Community Vision 2025, which state that the deepening integration process is designed as an action plan for human development and civic empowerment (ASEAN 2015, 13).

Southeast Asia integration cannot be separated from the pursuit of a common identity, and since its institutional inception, ASEAN has called on its member nations to share a regional identity. This vision and subsequent initiatives for Southeast Asian integration appear to depend on citizens' acceptance of regional identity, or at least an awareness that beyond the nation-state to which they belong is a collective body that offers security and protection. The strong co-dependency between regional integration and regional identity becomes imperative when ASEAN member countries need to mobilize their respective nations for a common goal that unites the region. The integration will bear responsibility for each member's government to ratify and respect regional visions, commitments, and rules. The document *ASEAN Vision* 2020 set a goal for ASEAN integration so that by 2020 the ASEAN community would be conscious of its historical ties, aware of its cultural heritage, and bound by a common regional identity (ASEAN 1997).

The fact that social factors shape identity indicates that identity is fluid and liable to change (Dimock 2018). Accordingly, we cannot take the integration of ASEAN through "identity" as fixed. It is socially constructed and thus a continuous process. Identity in the Southeast Asian context must be treated like an ongoing project that can guarantee cohesion among ASEAN member states, a project that can "glue" the region together. This is where the concept of ASEAN identity becomes relevant. Acharya (2017, 27) has made a distinction between ASEAN identity and Southeast Asian identity: "ASEAN identity reflects Southeast Asian identity but is not identical to it. Southeast Asia's regional identity anchors ASEAN's institutional identity. ASEAN is not a region;

Southeast Asia is. ASEAN identity is more recent, artificial, and dependent on political and strategic forces than Southeast Asia's. Southeast Asia's regional identity is more enduring than ASEAN's, although the loss or weakening of ASEAN will adversely impact Southeast Asian identity. But the critical point here is that one cannot understand the nature of and prospects for ASEAN identity without considering the wider context of Southeast Asian identity within which it is nested."

The question arises as to whether a sense of common ASEAN identity can be developed sustainably to form the fundamental element for ASEAN integration in the future. To pursue this objective, there needs to be a "leading actor" in society that will underpin this development and play a key role in determining ASEAN's future. Among the many generation categories, Millennials will play a significant leadership role in ASEAN's future. In accordance with this, we have sought answers to two questions. How do the younger generations or millennials perceive regional integration and ASEAN identity? What are their aspirations for ASEAN's role and function?

On ASEAN Millennials

The main objective of this study was to understand the younger generation's perceptions and expectations in ASEAN countries, particularly among millennials. The focus on millennials is based on the observation that they are an essential cohort in ASEAN countries because not only do they make up a high percentage of young people but also a third of the total population in the ASEAN region. Although there is no agreement on definitive thresholds by which millennial generational boundaries are defined (Dimock 2018), Smola and Sutton (2002) define Millennials as those born between 1979 and 1994, Generation X between 1965 and 1978, and Baby Boomers between 1946 and 1964. Another categorization was made by Policy Solutions and FEPS (2016): Gen Z, iGen, or Centennials were born in 1996 or later, Millennials or Gen Y in the period 1977–95, Generation X in 1965–76, Baby Boomers in 1946–64, and Traditionalists or Silent Generation in 1945 and earlier. (See also the classification by Grabowsky and Cornelio in the Introduction to this volume.) This study defines Millennials as aged 23–38. It is crucial to understand how this cohort perceives regional integration and ASEAN identity because their perspective on ASEAN will determine whether they will support and defend this regional organization and ensure its sustainability in the future.

At the same time, it is also essential to understand whether younger generations seek a role in shaping ASEAN's future and, if so, how they can help forge a harmonious identity for ASEAN now and in the future. We must assume, however, that younger generations have different expectations of ASEAN compared to their predecessors. Taylor (2010) states that a generation has identity and aspiration, which are necessarily different from other generations. A factor that influences value systems, among others, is personal experience. In Mannheim's view (cited in Kertzer 1983), the different values of each generation are driven by experience, how they adapt to their surroundings, and the value systems they have inculcated against the realities of life. The Deloitte Millennial Survey (August 2017) captured some characteristics of the millennial generation, noting that they are optimistic but are concerned about issues that directly impact the individual and threats and uncertainties such as conflict, climate change, and scarcity.

While high-level officials may best handle security issues at the regional level, broad commitments on social welfare should involve citizens in the decision-making process to a certain extent. Most citizens currently have little say in ASEAN's decision-making process even though issues such as health, migration, and the environment all directly impact them (UNCTAD 2017, 7). From this perspective, ASEAN should consider the role of millennials and acknowledge their existence in the ASEAN agenda to support an integrated society.

Observing how millennials are shaping collective political imagination about ASEAN identity is critical as many scholars argue that ASEAN identity is essentially elitist. From the point of view of Anderson (1991), regional configurations like ASEAN are imagined communities in many ways; its regional identity-building experience can be likened to a quest for identity. Although it involves history and culture, a sense of identity cannot be separated from media and elite socialization in creating a sense of community. This process could lead to an "artificial" sense of identity, especially if the creation of "ASEAN identity" is more of an institutional, political, and strategic endeavor. This poses the question of whether, or not, a sense of ASEAN identity exists among millennials, as ASEAN identity is also a result of generational differences.

One distinctive characteristic of millennials may influence their perception and expectation of ASEAN identity compared to their predecessors. As a generation born after the establishment of ASEAN, the millennial generation may not consider the historical factors that the ASEAN leaders used as a vehicle for developing a sense of Southeast Asian identity and building regional awareness. As quoted by Acharya (2017, 27), S. Rajaratnam, Singapore's Minister for Foreign Affairs at the time and one of ASEAN's founders, stated:

"The actions of ASEAN's founders were purposive and rational. But they were also underpinned by a sense of history and identity. Its founders were 'imagining' themselves to be part of a collective entity, or a region, by drawing upon a shared historical heritage as well as identifying common goals in a contemporary setting."

Research Questions and Methodology

Having different characteristics and views from their predecessors, millennials have a different interpretation and perspective on how regional identity should be built, understood, and manifested. In exploring millennial aspirations on integration and identity, this study posed three questions. First, how do millennials perceive ASEAN? We wanted to pay particular attention to their level of awareness and knowledge. The discourse at this stage centered around the notion that the Information Age has shaped a well-informed millennial generation. ASEAN's awareness and perception are essential in developing a collective entity as a part of the region, eventually forming a sense of belonging. Creating a "we feeling" requires millennials to have a conscious desire and make a deliberate effort to engage in various ASEAN areas such as the arts, education, and tourism that promote mutual understanding amongst societies. This process could not happen without millennials' awareness and understanding of ASEAN.

Secondly, what do millennials perceive as their contribution to strengthening ASEAN integration and identity? Information and data on this issue informed us about millennials' fundamental views on achieving regional integration and fostering a shared identity. An enquiry followed this question into millennials' perception of the benefit and significance of ASEAN. Perceptions of ASEAN's significance and benefits indicated what millennials expect from and gauge their understanding of ASEAN's function in society. It also showed what millennials understood about ASEAN's role in bringing progress and development to the region. This analysis contends that the regional integration of political and economic systems will only be successful when citizens perceive that it can accommodate their diverse interests. They would strive to become part of and prosper within.

Thirdly, what do millennials perceive as factors that could weaken ASEAN integration and ASEAN identity. The information gathered around this issue is vital if the younger generation is expected to have a sense of ASEAN integration and identity. How can there be regional integration when problems challenge its unity? The final question is related to millennials' perceptions of regional identity. This part was aimed at gathering information on the notion of the "so-called" ASEAN identity. Does it exist? If so, how do the respondents perceive ASEAN identity?

There have been several studies focusing on millennial perceptions of ASEAN (Dimock 2018; Filatrovi 2021; Deloite Millennial Survey 2017). Our work does not replicate those studies but instead is aimed at complementing them. Our research's strength lies in observing the transformation of ASEAN's perceptions and expectations by comparing millennials and previous generations in our sample cohort and the factors that have influenced such transformations or changes.

Methodologically, we used a combination of quantitative and qualitative methods. In the quantitative method, we surveyed 1,960 Indonesians from different generations. We consolidated our understanding of the survey results with qualitative research through in-depth interviews and Focus Group Discussions (FGDs). The national survey was conducted in thirty-four provinces in Indonesia using multistage random sampling. Apart from considering gender and urban and rural balance, the 1960 respondents were selected according to five age cohorts: Generation Z (under 22), Generation Y (Millennials) (23–38), Generation X (39–54), Generation Baby Boomers (55–73), and Generation Silent (74–91). The survey aimed at obtaining a preliminary understanding of how Indonesian millennials (23–38) perceived ASEAN. To complement the survey, in-depth interviews were conducted with Indonesians and Filipinos, which focused on capturing their understanding and expectations of ASEAN and what they perceive as their contribution in constructing an ASEAN identity. We chose to conduct interviews with Filipinos as a point of comparison to Indonesian millennials because of the similarity in the democratic trajectory. Both groups had faced authoritarian regimes in the past and had played a crucial role in challenging government suppression, and both groups came from countries with separatism problems. The data and information were enriched by two Focus Group Discussions (FGD) conducted with millennials from the Philippines and Malaysia.

Data analysis was conducted by comparing the generational perceptions of ASEAN. This comparison is a way of looking at variations in ASEAN's perceptions and expectations between generations. Although data collected from various ASEAN countries' millennials could not represent the overall opinion of ASEAN millennials, it reflects the diversity of opinions. Of the respondents involved in the survey (fig. 1), 39.9 percent were classified as Generation X (39.9 percent), Generation Y Millennials (31.7 percent), and Baby Boomers (19.6 percent). Although our respondents covered all five age cohorts, we focused our analysis on one age cohort, Generation Y Millennials aged 23–38.

Fig. 1. Demographic Age of Generations

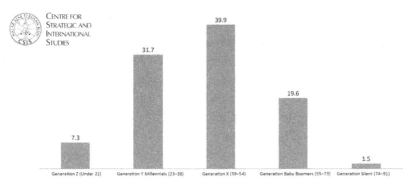

Source: CSIS National Public Opinion Survey, March 15–22, 2019.

Results from the Survey

Awareness of ASEAN

In his research, Severino (2006) underlined the importance of awareness and understanding of ASEAN. He argued that identity, awareness, and knowledge would contribute significantly and were essential to building a security community in Southeast Asia. They would be necessary for regional norms to be adopted and common values to be shared. They would make regional cooperation easier on a broad range of security concerns. The following table shows the awareness of millennials and other age cohorts about ASEAN.

Table 1. Awareness of ASEAN, by Age

 Q: Have you ever heard of ASEAN?

Category	Baseline of Sample	Yes	No	Total
Generation Z (Under 22)	7.3	68.5%	31.5%	100.0%
Generation Y Millennials (23-38)	31.7	55.9%	44.1%	100.0%
Generation X (39-54)	39.9	43.8%	56.2%	100.0%
Generation Baby Boomers (55-73)	19.6	27.9%	72.1%	100.0%
Generation Silent (74-91)	1.5	31.0%	69.0%	100.0%
Total	100.0	46.1%	53.9%	100.0%

Source: CSIS National Public Opinion Survey, March 15–22, 2019.

Interestingly, when analyzed by age, awareness of ASEAN was high among Millennials compared to Generation X or Baby Boomers. In theory, Generation X and Baby Boomers should have a high recognition of ASEAN since it was established in 1967 during their lifetime. Yet, from table 1 we can see that 55.9 percent of millennial respondents had heard of ASEAN compared to only 27.9 percent of Baby Boomers. This indicates that millennials have received more exposure to ASEAN than the previous generations. It is important to note that a sense of history and identity mostly underpin ASEAN's awareness for the Baby Boomer generation, especially those who witnessed the inception of ASEAN. For the millennials, ASEAN awareness is mostly gained by knowledge transfer.

It is also interesting to understand where millennials have acquired their knowledge of ASEAN. From the survey, we noted that schools, television, and the Internet helped with the "socialization" of ASEAN among the younger generation (fig. 2).

Fig. 2. Source of Information about ASEAN

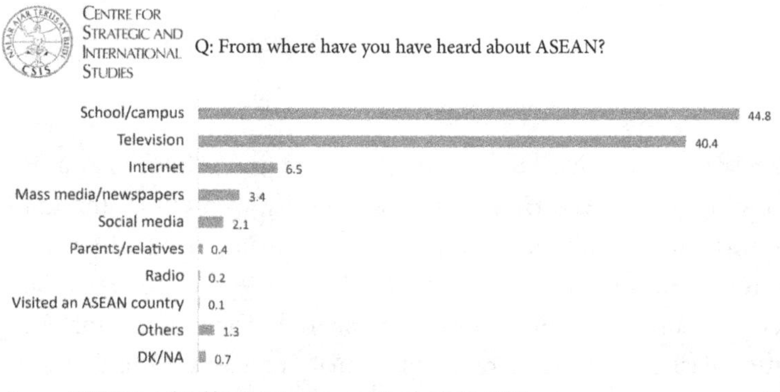

CENTRE FOR STRATEGIC AND INTERNATIONAL STUDIES

Q: From where have you have heard about ASEAN?

Source	Percent
School/campus	44.8
Television	40.4
Internet	6.5
Mass media/newspapers	3.4
Social media	2.1
Parents/relatives	0.4
Radio	0.2
Visited an ASEAN country	0.1
Others	1.3
DK/NA	0.7

Source: CSIS National Public Opinion Survey, March 15–22, 2019.

If we break down the category, however, we can see in table 2 that schools play a more significant role in exposing ASEAN to Millennials (46.7 percent) compared to television, which is more influential among Generation X (60.4 percent) and Baby Boomers (52.3 percent). Only 3.4 percent and 2.1 percent, respectively, of these respondents had heard about ASEAN through the mass media and social media. The survey findings were confirmed by interviews and FGD, where both Malaysian and Filipino millennials indicated they had gained awareness and knowledge of ASEAN mostly from schools or universities. However, school information was usually very basic, such as the history of the establishment of the organization, member states, aims and purposes, and structure. Those who have a particular interest in ASEAN seek further information from social media or mass media where ASEAN's development and activities are readily available.

Table 2. Source of Information about ASEAN, by Age

Q: From where have you have heard about ASEAN?

Category	Baseline of Sample	Internet	Mass media/ newspapers	Parents/ relatives	Visited an ASEAN country	Radio	School/ campus	Social media	Television	Others	DK/NA	Total
Generation Z (Under 22)	7.3	2.0%	1.0%	2.0%	0%	0%	76.5%	6.1%	12.2%	0%	0%	100.0%
Generation Y Millennials (23-38)	31.7	11.0%	3.2%	0.3%	0%	0.3%	46.7%	2.6%	34.0%	1.7%	0.3%	100.0%
Generation X (39-54)	39.9	4.1%	3.5%	0.3%	0.3%	0.3%	37.6%	1.2%	50.4%	1.5%	0.9%	100.0%
Generation Baby Boomers (55-73)	19.6	4.7%	5.6%	0%	0%	0%	34.6%	0%	52.3%	0.9%	1.9%	100.0%
Generation Silent (74-91)	1.5	0%	11.1%	0%	0%	0%	22.2%	0%	66.7%	0%	0%	100.0%
Total	100.0	6.5%	3.4%	0.4%	0.1%	.2%	44.8%	2.1%	40.4%	1.3%	0.7%	100.0%

Source: CSIS National Public Opinion Survey, March 15–22, 2019.

Table 3. Awareness of ASEAN by Education

Q: Have you ever heard of ASEAN?

Category	Baseline of Sample	Internet	Mass media/ newspapers	Parents/ relatives	Visited an ASEAN country	Radio	School/ campus	Social media	Television	Others	DK/NA	Total
Primary and Middle School	57.9	2.8%	1.9%	0.6%	0.3%	0.3%	35.1%	0.9%	55.7%	1.6%	0.6%	100.0%
High School	32.0	7.7%	3.7%	0.5%	0%	0%	50.6%	2.3%	33.8%	0.7%	0.7%	100.0%
College and University	9.8	10.3%	5.8%	0%	0%	.6%	49.4%	3.8%	26.9%	2.6%	0.6%	100.0%
NA	0.3	33.3%	0%	0%	0%	0%	0%	0%	66.7%	0%	0%	100.0%
Total	100.0	6.5%	3.4%	0.4%	0.1%	0.2%	44.8%	2.1%	40.4%	1.3%	0.7%	100.0%

Source: CSIS National Public Opinion Survey, March 15–22, 2019.

We can see that ASEAN has a better outreach among the younger generation compared to older age groups (table 3). In the three age cohorts, better quality of education may also expose ASEAN to the younger or older generations who have received a good education. From table 3 we can see that awareness of ASEAN correlates positively with High School (68.4 percent) and College and University Graduates (80.8 percent). The millennials' positive attitude toward ASEAN is in line with the findings of Thompson and Thianthai's Survey (2008, xii), which states that students across the region have a relatively good knowledge of ASEAN. Further, "they consider themselves ASEAN 'citizens' and demonstrate generally positive attitudes towards the Association."

ASEAN Relevance and Benefits

As mentioned previously, one crucial question that we wished to explore in this study was millennials' perception of ASEAN's relevance and significance. According to table 4 below, we can see that in all age cohorts, the respondents stated that ASEAN is still essential, relevant, and should be maintained: Millennials (90.5 percent), Generation X (92.7 percent), and Baby Boomers (90.7 percent). That ASEAN is not relevant is a minority sentiment among Millennials (4.6 percent), followed by Generation Baby Boomers (3.7 percent) and Generation X (3.5 percent). In our qualitative research, most respondents also forwarded a counterargument that underlined ASEAN's irrelevance: this was related to the perception of ASEAN's incapacity to solve regional issues such as the Rohingya case.

Table 4. Relevance of ASEAN, by Age

CENTRE FOR STRATEGIC AND INTERNATIONAL STUDIES — Q: According to you, is the presence of ASEAN still relevant/important to be maintained?

Category	Baseline of Sample	Yes, it is still important and relevant	No, it is not important or relevant (ASEAN should be disbanded as it does not bring any advantage)	DK/NA	Total
Generation Z (Under 22)	7.3	88.8%	9.2%	2.0%	100.0%
Generation Y Millennials (23-38)	31.7	90.5%	4.6%	4.9%	100.0%
Generation X (39-54)	39.9	92.7%	3.5%	3.8%	100.0%
Generation Baby Boomers (55-73)	19.6	90.7%	3.7%	5.6%	100.0%
Generation Silent (74-91)	1.5	100.0%	0%	0%	100.0%
Total	**100.0**	**91.3%**	**4.5%**	**4.2%**	**100.0%**

Source: CSIS National Public Opinion Survey, March 15–22, 2019.

The argument above on ASEAN's irrelevance is corroborated by our data suggesting a limited understanding among respondents about ASEAN. From table 5, ASEAN was understood purely in "economic terms" or economic benefits. Millennial respondents perceived that ASEAN brings economic benefits through job creation.

When asked what kind of cooperation millennials would benefit from by becoming an ASEAN member, 64.8 percent answered from economic cooperation, 6.6 percent from sociocultural cooperation, 7.5 percent from information and technology cooperation, 5.2 percent from defense cooperation, and 4.9 percent from educational cooperation. These results are consistent with in-depth interviews where both Indonesian and Filipino millennials admitted that the ASEAN Economic Community (AEC) had opened opportunities to access jobs in other ASEAN countries. Despite such opportunities, however, unemployment or difficulties in getting a job had become a big concern for millennials. In 2011, the World Bank published data stating that, globally, a young person's risk of being unemployed was three times higher than that of an adult. Furthermore, the World Bank Group Entrepreneurship snapshot (UNFPA 2016, 2) predicted meager job creation growth, specifically in Indonesia's entrepreneurship sector, with less than 2 percent. This is low compared with the entrepreneurship sector in Thailand (4.1 percent) and Singapore (7.2 percent). The importance of economic cooperation among ASEAN countries, especially in the area of poverty reduction and development, was expressed by young, educated ASEAN nationals in Thompson and Thianthai's survey (2008, 8).

Table 5. Benefits of ASEAN Cooperation, by Age

CENTRE FOR STRATEGIC AND INTERNATIONAL STUDIES Q: According to you, is the presence of ASEAN still relevant/important to be maintained?

Category	Baseline of Sample	Economic cooperation	Health cooperation	Environment cooperation	Defense/ security cooperation	Politics cooperation	Sociocultural cooperation	Educational cooperation	Information technology cooperation	Others	DK/NA	Total
Generation Z (Under 22)	7.3	55.1%	3.1%	2.0%	5.1%	7.1%	7.1%	8.2%	8.2%	1.0%	3.1%	100.0%
Generation Y Millennials (23-38)	31.7	64.8%	1.4%	1.7%	5.2%	1.7%	6.6%	4.9%	7.5%	0.9%	5.2%	100.0%
Generation X (39-54)	39.9	66.5%	1.5%	1.2%	6.4%	2.0%	7.3%	3.2%	6.1%	1.5%	4.4%	100.0%
Generation Baby Boomers (55-73)	19.6	67.3%	1.9%	0%	7.5%	0.9%	2.8%	4.7%	5.6%	1.9%	7.5%	100.0%
Generation Silent (74-91)	1.5	66.7%	0%	0%	11.1%	0%	11.1%	0%	11.1%	0%	0%	100.0%
Total	100.0	64.7%	1.7%	1.3%	6.0%	2.3%	6.5%	4.5%	6.9%	1.2%	4.9%	100.0%

Source: CSIS National Public Opinion Survey, March 15–22, 2019.

Despite their concerns, millennial respondents argued that each country should not solve its problems alone if it was a part of ASEAN. For example, the high unemployment rate would not be solved by individual countries but could be solved at a regional level. A millennial from the Philippines further explained that one benefit from the Philippines joining ASEAN is that she could get cheaper products imported from ASEAN countries compared to the price of local products. However, during in-depth interviews, another millennial warned that employment in other ASEAN countries is only accessible to those with skills and IT capacity who are technology-savvy, mobile, and more highly educated. It could mean leaving behind many other millennials lacking such skills and who not ready to embrace the competition in other ASEAN countries.

ASEAN also aims to be beneficial in other sectors beyond economics, such as health, environment, politics, education, and the socio-cultural arena, which requires multilateral networking and solutions. However, the respondents perceived some challenges from ASEAN in tackling these problems. As indicated in fig. 3, in general one-third of all generations surveyed stated that they never felt they received any benefit from ASEAN. Discussions with Filipino and Malaysian millennials revealed that ASEAN was beneficial for its member countries, for example, through economic cooperation in trade, tariff barriers, and infrastructure. However, they do not recognize ASEAN's benefit as individuals, except for some millennials who had obtained ASEAN scholarships or were involved in some ASEAN youth programs.

Fig. 3. Personal Benefits from the Presence of ASEAN

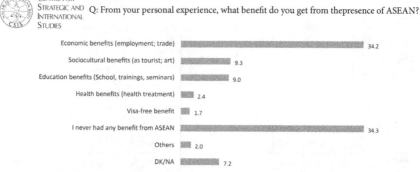

Source: CSIS National Public Opinion Survey, March 15–22, 2019.

Factors Weakening and Strengthening ASEAN Integration

Table 6. Issues that Could Weaken ASEAN Solidarity, by Age

Q: Generally, which of the issues below that could deteriorate the relation between ASEAN member states?

Category	Baseline of Sample	Human rights violations issues	Labor issues	Economic inequality	Environ-mental degradation	Money laundering	Cultural theft	Natural resource theft	The discrepancy of relation's orientation with superpower states such as, China, United States of America and Japan	Human trafficking and refugee	DK/NA	Total
Generation Z (Under 22)	7.3	22.4%	14.3%	12.2%	1.0%	4.1%	13.3%	10.2%	14.3%	5.1%	3.1%	100.0%
Generation Y Millennials (23-38)	31.7	22.8%	20.7%	17.6%	2.9%	1.2%	7.2%	11.2%	4.6%	4.6%	7.2%	100.0%
Generation X (39-54)	39.9	25.1%	19.2%	16.3%	3.2%	2.6%	4.1%	11.1%	4.7%	4.7%	9.0%	100.0%
Generation Baby Boomers (55-73)	19.6	29.0%	22.4%	9.3%	4.7%	2.8%	9.3%	13.1%	0.9%	.9%	7.5%	100.0%
Generation Silent (74-91)	1.5	66.7%	11.1%	11.1%	0%	0%	11.1%	0%	0%	0%	0%	100.0%
Total	100.0	24.8%	19.6%	15.5%	3.0%	2.2%	7.0%	11.2%	5.2%	4.2%	7.4%	100.0%

Source: CSIS National Public Opinion Survey, March 15–22, 2019.

In this rapidly changing world, ASEAN's cohesiveness as a regional organization is threatened by various issues. The three main age cohorts (table 6) all agreed that issues such as human rights, labor mobility, cultural theft, and economic inequality could weaken ASEAN relations and thus integration. For the millennials, 22.8 percent answered regarding human rights violation issues, which could be an alarming issue for ASEAN cohesiveness. Cross-border human rights issues, such as illegal fishing, migrant workers, and the Rohingya case, could potentially disrupt ASEAN cohesiveness if not appropriately handled. This information is critical for decision-makers to understand how to integrate citizens into the broader regional identity or regional citizenship (Jones 2004). According to Filipino and Malaysian millennials, ASEAN integration is weakened when ASEAN cannot take collective action to address its common problems rather than relying on individual countries to solve the problems based on each country's interest. In the South China Sea disputes, no single ASEAN country supported the Philippines in its conflict with China based on the principle of non-interference.

Despite issues that could erode ASEAN cohesiveness, the study also identified issues that could strengthen ASEAN cohesiveness (table 7). The three age cohorts all agreed that terrorism and radicalism, poverty and injustice, and natural disasters needed collaborative work in a multilateral framework due to their cross-border implications.

Table 7. Issues that Strengthen the Relation of ASEAN Member States, by Age

Q: Generally, which of the following issues below that could strengthened the relation between ASEAN member states?

Category	Baseline of Sample	Threats coming from foreign countries, such as China or North Korea	Poverty, inequality and injustice	Drugs	Human trafficking and refugee protection issues	Climate change	Terrorism and radicalism	Natural disaster	Others	DK/NA	Total
Generation Z (Under 22)	7.3	18.4%	18.4%	8.2%	6.1%	3.1%	19.4%	21.4%	1.0%	4.1%	100.0%
Generation Y Millennials (23-38)	31.7	15.9%	18.7%	7.8%	6.6%	0.9%	22.8%	15.6%	2.0%	9.8%	100.0%
Generation X (39-54)	39.9	12.8%	19.2%	9.0%	5.5%	1.7%	22.4%	18.4%	2.0%	8.7%	100.0%
Generation Baby Boomers (55-73)	19.6	12.1%	14.0%	12.1%	1.9%	0.9%	26.2%	15.9%	5.6%	11.2%	100.0%
Generation Silent (74-91)	1.5	22.2%	11.1%	11.1%	0%	0%	11.1%	22.2%	22.2%	0%	100.0%
Total	100.0	14.6%	18.3%	8.8%	5.5%	1.4%	22.6%	17.4%	2.5%	8.8%	100.0%

Source: CSIS National Public Opinion Survey, March 15–22, 2019.

Almost all generations supported cooperation among ASEAN member countries on matters of counterterrorism and radicalism, natural disasters and poverty alleviation in order to strengthen ASEAN relations. The three issues were seen as the most pressing problems in ASEAN countries. Radicalism and terrorism have become a serious threat in the region, especially in Indonesia and the Philippines. They are manifested through direct attacks or by inspiring action by homegrown extremists. Many young people, both male and female, who are recruited into terrorist groups play essential roles, such as suicide bombers, or under-recognized roles in advancing their group's mission. It is also not surprising that ASEAN cooperation on natural disasters is listed because Southeast Asia is known as one of the most disaster-prone regions in the world and most vulnerable to climate change's adverse effects. Indonesian millennials are also concerned about foreign threats, which suggests the importance of cooperation within ASEAN in tackling such issues. Regardless of their country, people are likely to feel closer to one another when facing similar issues across national borders, impacted by the same events and sharing similar experiences.

Millennial Contribution

Finally, when the millennial respondents were asked how they might contribute to sustaining an ASEAN sense of belonging or identity, 31.4 percent said they wanted to contribute to the economic sector, 11.8 percent to the sociocultural sector, 6.6 percent to diplomacy, 5.8 percent to the environment, and 4.3 percent to technology (table 8).

Table 8. Public Contributions to the Development of ASEAN Cooperation, by Age

Q: In what field, will you be interested in contributing to the development of ASEAN cooperation?

Category	Baseline of Sample	Diplomacy	Economy	Environment	Politics	Sociocultural	Technology	Not interested	DK/NA	Total
Generation Z (Under 22)	7.3	8.2%	18.4%	11.2%	4.1%	17.3%	7.1%	28.6%	5.1%	100.0%
Generation Y Millennials (23-38)	31.7	6.6%	31.4%	5.8%	1.2%	11.8%	4.3%	32.3%	6.6%	100.0%
Generation X (39-54)	39.9	5.8%	33.2%	4.4%	3.2%	9.0%	5.5%	33.8%	5.0%	100.0%
Generation Baby Boomers (55-73)	19.6	9.3%	24.3%	6.5%	1.9%	13.1%	5.6%	29.9%	9.3%	100.0%
Generation Silent (74-91)	1.5	22.2%	22.2%	11.1%	0%	22.2%	0%	22.2%	0%	100.0%
Total	100.0	7.0%	29.8%	6.0%	2.3%	11.6%	5.2%	32.1%	6.1%	100.0%

Source: CSIS National Public Opinion Survey, March 15-22, 2019.

More than half of the surveyed millennials felt confident about their influence, especially in contributing to the economy. During interviews, millennials frequently mentioned IT and connectivity as their primary focus. Mobile Internet, in particular, is regarded as a useful tool for overcoming Southeast Asia's geographical barriers and widening access to information, products, and services.

It is important to note that this survey, as indicated in table 8, found that 32.3 percent of Indonesian millennials were not interested in contributing to ASEAN cooperation. From the interviews, we found several reasons for this. First, they do not know how to engage with ASEAN and contribute to the organization. Secondly, many Indonesian youths are not catching up with the development of organizations like the ASEAN Economic Community and their benefits to Indonesia.

One of the highlights for young Indonesians is that with ASEAN integration, Indonesia's millennials will face tougher competition with "foreigners" from other ASEAN countries hoping to work in Indonesia. Finally, the fact that inequality between and within ASEAN persists prompted a significant number of respondents to say that they never perceived any benefit from ASEAN.

ASEAN Identity

A critical piece of information that we wanted to gather from this study concerned the notion of ASEAN identity. From the survey result, as indicated in table 9, most of the respondents, including millennials, viewed ASEAN as related to "the spatial proximity of one ASEAN country to the other." To them, ASEAN identity is about "territorial closeness," which has contributed to the "shared feeling" of being part of ASEAN. The other factor supporting ASEAN identity is cultural similarities, such as food, values, norms, and *serumpun* (meaning "of the same root" in Malay and Indonesian).

Table 9. Understanding of ASEAN Identity, by Age

Q: According to you, what do you understand about ASEAN identity?

Category	Baseline of Sample	Historical similarity (for instance, having experienced as former colonized countries)	Cultural similarity (for instance, "as group" (serumpun), art, food, values and norms)	The spatial proximity of one ASEAN country to another	The similar "fate" as developing countries and potentially having threats coming from countries outside the ASEAN region	The physical similarity (skin color, hair)	There is no such thing as ASEAN identity	Others	DK/NA	Total
Generation Z (Under 22)	7.3	14.3%	22.4%	43.9%	10.2%	1.0%	4.1%	1.0%	3.1%	100.0%
Generation Y Millennials (23–38)	31.7	13.5%	20.7%	42.1%	11.8%	0.6%	0.9%	0.9%	9.5%	100.0%
Generation X (39–54)	39.9	13.7%	23.6%	34.7%	12.0%	2.0%	2.3%	.6%	11.1%	100.0%
Generation Baby Boomers (55–73)	19.6	12.1%	18.7%	38.3%	13.1%	0.9%	1.9%	3.7%	11.2%	100.0%
Generation Silent (74–91)	1.5	22.2%	33.3%	11.1%	11.1%	0%	11.1%	11.1%	0%	100.0%
Total	100.0	13.6%	21.9%	38.7%	11.8%	1.2%	2.0%	1.2%	9.5%	100.0%

Source: CSIS National Public Opinion Survey, March 15–22, 2019.

However, millennials' perception of the critical role of cultural similarity and the geographical proximity needed in building a common identity is challenged by multicultural nations and the multiethnicity of ASEAN member countries. Previous works (Acharya, 2017) have shown that it is difficult for the region to create a common identity with multiple competing cultural identities. Understanding difficulties in forming this shared identity, Severino (cited in Jones 2004) did not powerfully articulate the regional identity vision. Instead, he sees ASEAN as a "cohesive mass that can come only from geographical propinquity" that requires member nations' commitment to maintaining ASEAN's cohesion and strengthening its solidarity. From Severino's statement, we can argue that having a shared culture among ASEAN member countries does not guarantee movement toward integration.

Empirical evidence of this is observable in the experiences of Indonesia and Malaysia: they share historical and cultural similarities, but those similarities have also become a source of conflict and confusion. In recent years, disputes have arisen between these countries concerning cultural heritage. Indonesia accused Malaysia of stealing Indonesian cultural practices such as the Pendet dance from Bali, batik from Java, and the "Rasa Sayange" folk song from the Maluku Islands. In 2010, tensions climaxed when Malaysians claimed the Indonesian bamboo musical instrument or *angklung* as part of their national heritage. Later, the Indonesian government registered the instrument, and in 2010 UNESCO listed *angklung* as an Indonesian intangible cultural heritage (Suharjono 2012).

Anti-Malaysian sentiment has declined, but the residual antagonism remains to this day and is easily provoked if sensitive issues like labor or border issues arise. Poor relations between Indonesia and Malaysia are evident from the fact that some Indonesians are reluctant to buy Malaysian products, such as petroleum and the Malaysian-made car, the Proton Saga. Although such negative sentiments have not destroyed the relationship and cooperation between the two countries, they can teach lessons. Cultural similarity does not automatically foster unity or construct a shared identity but can, instead, trigger conflict.

The above conclusion echoes the findings from a discussion with a Malaysian millennial, who argued that ASEAN identity does not exist. Even the "ASEAN Way" that has been viewed as an essential source of regional collective identity is not enough to identify a shared heritage. The essential ingredient for collective identity is the shared value systems generated through a collaboration with each other when facing similar issues, impacted by the same events, and sharing similar experiences. The shared value systems will eventually become the guiding principles of collective thought and behavior and thus be respected and accepted by the community. Shared value systems are therefore the drivers of behaviors and attitudes and are good predictors of behavior and expectations.

The regional identity of ASEAN is "imagined" in the context of relations with the outside world. However, the fact that ASEAN people live in proximity to each other and have similar physical and cultural characteristics contributes to people feeling a part of a distinct region. In that respect, the feeling of "we" and "them" emerges. Similar findings were found in public opinion surveys commissioned by the Jakarta-based ASEAN Secretariat (2015) and the ASEAN Foundation (Ng 2015). These surveys showed that most respondents were aware of ASEAN's existence but were not aware of what the regional organization did and how it affected their lives (ibid.). Therefore, the tough task of ASEAN member countries is to provide their people with diverse culture to form an ASEAN identity or develop civic-minded people with a sense of belonging, or at least create people's awareness beyond the nation-state.

Conclusion

The future of ASEAN lies in the millennial generation that has the task of sustaining, strengthening, and manifesting ASEAN identity to support Southeast Asian integration. Millennials' active involvement in the construction of an ASEAN identity could address the regional organization's elitist and top-down conception.

This study reveals that between millennials and the previous generations there are different values and priorities about how ASEAN could benefit its community. Their perceptions of ASEAN are based on their practical needs and whether ASEAN has been beneficial not only at the state level but also for the individual. Without undermining ASEAN achievement, millennials believe that the extent to which ASEAN member states individually put regional interests before their national ones could weaken ASEAN integration. National interests that have differentiated each member are facing "foreign threats," including China's political and economic influence which has impacted and jeopardized the sense of togetherness. This problem needs to be resolved, otherwise, it will undermine other efforts to maintain cohesion and solidarity.

From the survey result of Indonesian millennials and interviews with other millennials, we can argue that most respondents are well aware of ASEAN. Education and social media have contributed significantly to raising awareness about ASEAN. However, ASEAN's function is viewed primarily as economic cooperation and hence "undervalues" or understates other critical missions, such as socio-cultural, education, political, and environmental spheres. This understanding of ASEAN exclusively in economic terms may be derived from various factors, ranging from sharp economic inequality among ASEAN member countries to a perception that economic cooperation is the greatest benefit of ASEAN.

The fact that all generations stated that ASEAN is still relevant poses good momentum to strengthen this regional organization. This survey has also shown how education and social media have played an essential role in ASEAN. Thus, it needs to be further utilized to maximize its potential in advancing knowledge of ASEAN. With the fact that ASEAN identity is only understood or even felt because of "geographic proximity" means that more work and exploration need to be conducted so that an ASEAN identity can be established in each citizen of ASEAN.

Conscious desire and effort to engage millennials in various areas are needed to develop the sense of belonging of becoming part of ASEAN and creating a "we identity." The key attributes of a sense of ASEAN identity for millennials are real life experiences, real benefits, greater interaction, as well as togetherness in overcoming common problems. The efforts of current leaders to spark millennials' interest in ASEAN are also needed, since a significant number of millennials are not interested in contributing to ASEAN development because they feel they have never benefited from ASEAN. ASEAN should make millennials more aware of what has been done by these regional cooperation initiatives. It needs to employ more creative strategies and information dissemination, including social media, that show the concrete actions and benefits of what ASEAN has been doing for the people. The approach should be less elitist and more accessible to the average person and more aligned with the concerns and interests of ASEAN millennials.

From the millennial perspective, ASEAN's concerted efforts in their region to handle terrorism and radicalization, natural disasters, and foreign threats will help to deepen the sense of ASEAN belonging and community. Millennials also view tackling human rights violations, labor violations, and the destruction of natural resources as significant hurdles for regional integration. Diverse cultures, competing for national interests and varying political structures in ASEAN, have made efforts to address issues in these three sectors difficult. To be more specific, there are also "forces" that have recurrently jeopardized bilateral relationships, such as the "cultural theft issue" between Malaysia and Indonesia, and even issues that could have regional implications, such as haze and pollution and other hazards like terrorism and illegal fishing. These problems need to be permanently solved with the involvement of millennials in identifying the problems and finding solutions.

The way forward in addressing these vital concerns at the regional level is to strengthen regional cooperation in human rights, labor, and natural resources theft while balancing competing national interests. The concerning issues which millennials have identified should also involve them in seeking policy prescriptions. This endeavor is one way to create a sense of belonging and ownership among millennials that their contribution significantly determines ASEAN's future.

Most millennials who participated in the survey, in-depth interviews, and group discussions stated that ASEAN identity is artificial and is based more on geographical proximity and physical and cultural similarities than on shared values. This study also shows that after more than fifty years, ASEAN is still facing the same challenges in its effort to establish some kind of regional identity, especially among millennials who individually feel they do not get any benefit from ASEAN. According to millennials, two critical components that form a sense of identity—mutual responsiveness and shared values—are missing. Many Millennials who have participated in ASEAN youth programs or have had the chance to interact with millennials from different countries have a more positive view on regional identity.

To conclude, many things still need to be done to maintain ASEAN integration and to foster the so-called ASEAN identity. Millennials are already sitting in the "driving seat." The question is, will there be a more serious effort, political will, and trust given to millennials to steer the future of ASEAN? The answer is yet to be known.

References

Acharya, Amitav. 2017. "The Evolution and Limitations of ASEAN Identity." In *Building ASEAN Community: Political-Security and Socio-cultural Reflections*, vol. 4, eds. Aileen Baviera and Larry Maramis, 25–38. Jakarta: Economic Research Institute for ASEAN and East Asia.

Anderson, Benedict R. 1991. *Imagined Communities: Reflections on the Origin and Spread of Nationalism*. London: Verso.

ASEAN. 1997. "Forging an ASEAN Identity: The Challenge to Construct a Shared Destiny Introduction: An Evolving Regional Identity." *Policy Report from the 1997 ASEAN Summit Meeting*, 15 December, last accessed 30 August 2022.

————. 2015. "Forging Ahead Together." Jakarta: ASEAN Secretariat, December.

Deloitte Millennial Survey. 2017. https://www2.deloitte.com/global/en/pages/about- Deloitte/articles/millennial-survey-making-impact-through-employers.html#empowerment, August.

Dimock, Michael. 2018. *Millennials End and Post-millennials Begin*. Washington, DC: Pew Research Center.

Filatrovi, E. Willy. 2021. "The Understanding of Millennials Generation Behavior in Asean." *International Journal of Business and Accounting* 5(3): 865–73.

Foundation for European Progressive Studies. 2017. "Study on Millennials Perception Towards Europe."

Haokip, T. 2012. "Recent Trends in Regional Integration and the Indian Experience." *International Area Studies Review* 15(4): 377–92.

Jones, M. Ernest. 2004. "Forging an ASEAN Identity: The Challenge to Construct a Shared Destiny." *Contemporary Southeast Asia* 26(1): 140–54.

Kertzer, David I. 1983. "Generation as a Sociological Problem." *Annual Review of Sociology* 9: 125–49.

Mohammad Fajar Ikshan, Ahmad Bashawir Abdul Ghani, and Muhammad Subhan. 2016. "Re-thinking of ASEAN Regional Integration: People-Oriented Towards Communitarian Approaches." *Proceedings of the 6th International Conference on International Studies*, Universiti Utara Malaysia, Kuala Lumpur, August 20–22.

Ng, Candida. 2015. "ASEAN Community: What's That Again." Singapore: ASEAN Investment Report. https://www.reportingasean.net/asean-community-whats-that-again/, last accessed 30 August 2022

Pakpahan, Beginda. 2019. "ASEAN At 52: Achievements and Challenges Ahead." *Global Asia* 14(3). https://www.globalasia.org/v14no3/feature/asean-at-52-achievements-and-challenges-ahead_beginda-pakpahan, last accessed 30 August 2022.

Severino, Rodolfo C. 2006. *Southeast Asia in Search of an ASEAN Community: Insights from the Former ASEAN Secretary-General*. Singapore: Institute of Southeast Asian Studies.

Smola, K. W., and C. D. Sutton. 2002. "Generational Differences: Revisiting Generational Work Values for the New Millennium." *Journal of Organizational Behavior* 23: 363–82.

Suharjono, Lilik, A. 2012. "Battling for Shared Culture Between Indonesia and Malaysia in the Social Media Era." *Humaniora* 3(1): 58–69.

Taylor, Paul. 2010. "Confident. Connected. Open to Change." Washington, DC: Pew Research Center.

Thomson, Eric C., and Chulanee Thianthai. 2008. *Attitudes and Awareness Towards ASEAN: Finding of a Ten-Nation Survey*, Report No. 2, ASEAN Studies Centre. Singapore: Institute of Southeast Asian Studies.

UNCTAD. 2017. "ASEAN at 50: Achievements and Challenges in Regional Integration." Geneva: UNCTAD.

UNFPA. 2016. *Youth Advisory Panel (YAP). Issue Brief The Power of the Millennials: Boosting Economic Development through Creative Economy and Innovation*. Jakarta: UNFPA Indonesia.

Hakka Dialect Identity and Chinese Identity in Malaysia

DANNY WONG TZE KEN

Ethnic identification is very important in the lives of Malaysians. Who you are in terms of ethnicity has a bearing on many things that affect daily life, including access to higher education, positions in the public service, and certain economic advantages. The introduction of the New Economic Policy (NEP), a social engineering or affirmative action policy, in 1971, has contributed to this situation. For the Chinese community, this ethnic differentiation has contributed significantly to transforming the manner the Chinese in Malaysia identify themselves—from dialect-based to a collective unified Chinese identity. Yet, while dialect-oriented identity, including the use of dialect as spoken language, has declined, it has not been entirely eliminated. Instead, there seems to be a revival of the importance of dialect identity, especially amongst the Hakka dialect group.

This chapter endeavors to investigate the way the Hakka dialect identity has developed since the Hakka established themselves in the country, and how this distinctive dialect group became part of the effort to foster dialect identity by both the dialect group and the state. The former jealously guarded their dialect identity, while the latter exploited this identity as a way of identifying the Chinese community as a whole. In so doing, the state or government, initially represented by the British colonial administration and later by the Malayan and Malaysian government, created a framework of identity for the Chinese based on dialect identity, including the endorsement of dialect-based Chinese organizations, cemeteries, schools, and most important of all, a population census that categorized the Chinese by dialect groups. The chapter will also trace the changes in different eras, including the rise of Chinese nationalism, Japanese military occupation, postwar Emergency, and post-Independent Malaysia, how this dialect identity coped with the changes and demands of each of these eras, and how the Hakka dialect survived. Finally, the chapter will also examine the impact of the state's policy toward this dialect identity and how the dialect organizations, including the Hakka, responded.

Migration and Colonial Legacies

Like some countries outside China with a sizable Chinese community, such as Thailand, Indonesia, and Singapore, the Chinese community in Malaysia is organized based on dialect groups. This is a legacy of both the Chinese migration process and colonial policies; both factors strengthened the importance of dialect identity in the country.

The Hakka were part of the Chinese migration to the region known today as Malaysia in the late nineteenth century and first half of the twentieth century. The Hakka are considered as latecomers compared to several other dialect groups like the Hokkien and Teochiu, who arrived earlier, followed by the Cantonese speakers. Upon their arrival, the Hakka organized themselves based on dialect identity as well as subdialect identity. The Hakka who came to Malaysia are not a homogeneous community. There are subdialect groups organized based on the county of origin. They are broadly organized into two large categories based on the manner the counties were organized in Guangdong, China, during the late nineteenth century and the turn of the twentieth century. The first centers on Huizhou Prefecture, which covers counties such as Bao An, Zijin, and Bo Luo; and the second centers on Jia Yin Zhou Prefecture, which covers the so-called Hakka heartland of Meizhou (Meixian), Wuhua (Zhangle), and Laolung (Longchuan).

The early Hakka organizations were not known as Hakka associations. Instead, they were organized as groups representing the respective counties or prefectures, such as the Jiaying Zhou Association, the Huizhou Association, the Zeng Cheng Association, and the Chayang Association (Dapu). It was at a much later period that names like Hakka Association emerged; even then, it was originally known as Hakka Affiliated Association (Keshu Gonghui), acting in both name and actuality as an umbrella over various Hakka community subgroups. Apart from not being homogeneous in their organization, the Hakka also fought each other in the Perak civil wars of the 1860s–1870s (Khoo 1978), as well as in other parts of the Malay Peninsula, including Negeri Sembilan and Selangor. The Hakka dialect identity formation was similar to that of other dialect groups which also set up their own subdialect organizations as a way of mutual support. The Chinese way of dialect identification had much to do with the manner they had emigrated and settled in the country. In most cases, settlers would encourage their relations to join them. The miners in Perak and Selangor, many of whom were from Huizhou, would return to their home counties to ask their relatives to join them. In the same way, recruiting agents for the various mines and estates would turn to familiar places to recruit labor. Upon arrival, these new recruits would be joining a workforce which had similar origins and background. Thus, concentration of the Hakka of respective related counties resulted in the gradual establishment of Hakka settlements in different parts of the country.

Closely related to the Hakka associations were temples, churches, cemeteries, and schools. As dialect organizations were being established throughout the country, they also took on the task of organizing the community's welfare. Primary to this were the religious organizations and places of worship established by the various dialect organizations. In Malaysia, two types of Chinese religious entities (and respective deities) were closely tied to the Hakka community: Dabo Gong (Tai Pak Kung) and Tan Gong (Tham Kung). Both deities were related to the Hakka just as Mazu was linked to the Fujian community. There are many Tai Pak Kung temples in Malaysia, including the famous one in Penang which dates to the late eighteenth century. There are also at least seven Tan Gong temples in Malaysia, including a famous one in Sandakan which is considered a heritage site. All these temples served as reminders to the Hakka of their dialect cohesion and solidarity. Many of the Hakka who migrated to Sabah had ties to the Christian churches. The Basel Church, which was established by the Swiss-based Basel Missionary Society and originally operated in Guangdong and Hong Kong, helped many Hakka Christians to migrate to Sabah (and Sarawak), and the community established their own churches in Sabah. The Basel Church became one of the most important Christian churches in the country, and the only one which is Hakka-based. This church remained the main social organization for Hakka Christians who were brought into the state via special arrangements between the Basel Mission and the state government (Wong 1999, 131–58). There was no Hakka organization on the west coast of Sabah until 1940. Even then, the first chairman and the executive committee of the West Coast Hakka Association were the pastor and members of the Basel Church.

The Chinese cemeteries in Malaysia were also established partly in relation to the dialect organizations. While the Chinese Chamber of Commerce was normally the main body in many towns that ran Chinese cemeteries, known as the Zhonghua Yishan, the various dialect groups also established cemeteries. In this case, the Hakka were subsumed under the Guangdong Yishan, though in many of these there were also those based on counties. Apart from being organized in this manner, the Hakka would be reminded of their country of origin through tombstones or headstones; on these, in addition to the names of the deceased and their immediate descendants, the name of the province and county of origin would be inscribed. All these served as constant reminders of their Hakka-ness.

Schools also helped in the reinforcement of Hakka identity in Malaysia, at least in the late nineteenth and early twentieth centuries; the Chinese in Malaysia established schools to cater for the future of their offspring. Most of the schools were, again, organized by dialect-based associations. The Hakka also took the initiative to establish their own schools. These included, in Kuala Lumpur, Shun Ren; in Ipoh, Pei Feng; in Kuching, Chung Hwa; in Kota Kinabalu, Tshung Tsin; in Penang, Penang Chinese Girls School and Sin Min (Liew 1999). Initially these schools used the Hakka dialect as the medium of instruction. However, with the introduction of the national school system following the establishment of the new Chinese Republic in 1912 and later, following the May Fourth Movement of 1919, the curriculum and medium of instruction were changed to Mandarin. Nonetheless, the Hakka associations held on to their schools and organized boards of directors which remained the link between the organizations and the schools they had established. One of the last schools to be started by a Hakka association was the Tshing Tsin Secondary School in Kota Kinabalu. Founded in 1965 as a Chinese independent school (Du Zhong), it is one of the largest schools in the state. But apart from the annual board of directors' meetings and the speech day or annual dinners when the Hakka Association board of directors would attend, there is very little Hakka identity remaining in these schools.

The Hakka associations only became Hakka associations after the 1920s, especially following Hu Wenfu's efforts to organize the Federation of Nanyang Hakka Associations. His efforts, which were supported by the academic framework on Hakka identity and Hakka studies by Luo Xianglin, formed the basis for the other Hakka organizations to come together to form larger Hakka associations. But for many years the actual nomenclature was not Hakka associations; rather, it was Hakka-affiliated organizations, or *ke shu*, and the continuation of the various county-based subdialect associations.

As part of the larger community, however, Chinese organizations, including the Hakka associations, were part of the larger branches of the Chinese Chamber of Commerce established at the national (that is, the whole of Malaya), state, and even district levels. Representations to the Chamber were normally made through the respective dialect organizations. For instance, the Sandakan Chinese Chamber of Commerce in East Malaysia that was started in 1908 had representatives from the various dialect groups—three representatives each from the Cantonese, Hokkien, Hakka, and Teochiu groups, and two from the

Hainanese, a smaller group (Wong 1998, 67). The Selangor Chinese Chamber of Commerce founded in 1904 had a similar arrangement (Low 1985).

The Hakka method of dialect-based identification was further reinforced by the British administration's way of identifying the different groups within the Chinese community, through dialect identity. Thus, from the first detailed census in 1891, the Chinese in Malaya, Sarawak, and North Borneo were all classified based on dialect group. Hence, in the population census, the Chinese were subdivided into Cantonese (Guangfu), Hokkien (Fujian), Hakka (Kejia), Teochiu (Chaozhou), Hainanese (Hainan), Kwangsi (Guangxi), and Henghua (Xinhua). Henghua is part of Fujian Province, so their existence as a category in the national census as a sub-Chinese group is an anomaly but is, at the same time, a historical legacy since the British had earlier recognized them as a separate group. Such identification continues. However, since the 2000 population census, the subgroup categorization of the Chinese is no longer given in the main census report. One needs to apply and pay for the detailed breakdown.

The British administration's method of intraethnic identification was, however, not confined to the population census. It extended to the administration's method of inviting Chinese representation to the various local committees or councils. From the lowest level of representation in the sanitary boards in the various townships to the state legislative councils, or appointment to the Federal Council, the basic principle was to obtain representation from the various dialect groups. Again, this applied to the entire country, including North Borneo (present-day Sabah) and Sarawak, which were not part of Malaysia until September 1963; at that time, they were British protectorates.

In this way, the importance of dialect identification was reinforced. With China out of sight and out of mind, the lack of a national (nation-state) identity, and the land of their residence still under British colonial rule, Chinese and dialect identity was then confined to being Chinese, or being a Hakka, or a Cantonese, depending on one's dialect group. This reinforcement ensured that dialect identity remained strong. There were, of course, challenges, which are the focus of the next section.

Chinese Identity and Hakka Identity

The pioneer immigrant dialect-based affinity began to face challenges during the 1920s with the rise of a more assertive Republican China, especially the Nanjing government, since 1927. Many Chinese migrated abroad to escape the harsh economic life in China, but many also left because of disillusionment with the political situation in China. The Hakka were no different. The post-Taiping Rebellion failures had triggered a mass exodus of Hakka abroad, adding to the already large Hakka contingents of earlier migrants. Many of the Chinese overseas continued their political links with China through their participation in the anti-Manchu activities, including supporting Dr. Sun Yat-Sen's campaign to overthrow the Manchu rule. When the Manchu fell in 1912, the mood began to change among the Chinese migrants abroad, hopeful for a new China under the Republic. But when Yuan Shih Khai usurped the revolution and, upon his death in 1916, China was thrown into a state of warlordism, the Hakka and other migrants turned their support to the Kuomintang, founded by Dr. Sun Yat-Sen and later led by Chiang Kai Shek, to unite China. This rise of Chinese nationalism and the institutional changes that accompanied it, including cultural unity and education reform, also had a lasting impact on the way the Chinese living abroad began to look at themselves. In North Borneo and Sarawak, they began to identify themselves more as Chinese than by their dialect identity.

The changes that took place in China began to invoke a stronger response from the Hakka and other Chinese and reshaped the way they looked at China. Thus far, most of the Hakka had looked at China, ruled by the Manchu, as a hostile regime. Those who were involved with the Taiping Rebellion, for instance, could not imagine returning to the country. Others found China increasingly distant from their memories and daily lives. But the events of 1912 and 1916 began to change them. For the first time, many began to see the problems in China from the perspective of nationalism, the need to rescue a nation that was increasingly being usurped by warlords. As details of the 1919 Versailles Accord vis-à-vis the Japanese position in Liaodong became public, resulting in the May Fourth Movement that denounced the national government in Peiping (Beijing) and demanded a renewal of China, the Hakka and other Chinese in Malaya were also caught up in this national fervor. This started a change in the orientation of the Hakka; instead of placing emphasis on their Hakka-ness, the Hakka began to speak as Chinese versus others. They began to participate in the various activities that had national fervor, which emphasized a national identity, including providing support to anti-Japanese demonstrations, the boycott of Japanese goods, anti-Western imperialism activities, and support for the Kuomintang. All these events reignited a fire that had deserted many of the Hakka and other Chinese migrants, but it was culture and education which started a process that would have a lasting effect on the Hakka identity of those in Malaysia.

The May Fourth Movement that aimed at the renewal of China began to see Hakka and other Chinese in Malaya introducing various initiatives aimed at reigniting and promoting Chinese-ness rather than dialect (in this case, Hakka-ness). The introduction of a national education syllabus was in store, with Mandarin as the medium of instruction. The focus of the day would be national revival and national unity. The school syllabus would place great emphasis on these issues. The most fundamental was the change in the medium of instruction. The "Speak Mandarin" campaign, made popular with Hu Shih's introduction of Baihua, or plain language Mandarin (in contrast to classical Mandarin) as the medium of instruction, made an impact on the Chinese school system in Malaysia. The emphasis on Mandarin saw the use of dialect as the medium of instruction quickly being phased out. New teachers, often graduates of reputable national universities, were recruited. This change impacted the nature of the Chinese school to its core. The new school leavers were now conversant in the national language and could thus identify with the national aspirations of the new Republic. With greater emphasis on Mandarin, the place of Hakka as a medium of instruction became a thing of the past. The various campaigns aimed at promoting Mandarin in the schools and the banning of dialect use began to erode the use of Hakka and other dialects among the students.

Changes began to take on greater urgency with the establishment of the Kuomintang National Government in Nanjing in 1929. With relative peace at hand, the Nanjing government was able to focus on fulfilling the Three National Principles propounded by Dr. Sun Yat-Sen, and education in China received a massive boost.

In Malaya, the changes in China and the reestablishment of a viable national government further invoked the sense of a national Chinese identity. By 1933, all Chinese schools had adopted the national education syllabus similar to that used in China. The fervent nationalist tone in the syllabus and the teaching materials also attracted the attention of the British colonial administration, which began to feel uneasy over the hostile phrases on anti-Western imperialism found in the textbooks. The British administration took measures to vet the imported textbooks, and many of them were banned and refused entry into Malaya. To the Hakka, these were very exciting events which also saw them embracing this new national fervor.

Another medium of communication undergoing change was the Chinese newspapers. While very few Chinese newspapers were associated with a particular dialect group, but were the main medium through which Chinese organizations, including the dialect associations, had news of their activities publicized. With so many happenings taking place in China following the setting up of the nationalist government, the newspapers also began to provide greater coverage on the events. Together with the news came the ideas of national unity and national rejuvenation. Space given to this coverage also meant that local news, especially news pertaining to dialect associations, was considered as news of lesser importance. While the local press never abandoned local events, they began to play second fiddle to "national news" in China, thus rekindling the reorientation of the Chinese, including the Hakka, to China.

When the Japanese Army began to attack Shenyang (Mukden) in September 1931, Chinese all over the world condemned the move. In Malaya, various demonstrations were held to protest the Japanese Army's aggression in Manchuria. A boycott of Japanese goods was also initiated. When the Japanese Navy attacked Shanghai the following year, similar protests were organized. The newspapers also had a field day lambasting the Japanese and, at the same time, heightening the feeling of nationalism and the need for national salvation. When total war finally broke out between China and Japan following the Lukuo Qiao (Marco Polo Bridge) Incident of July 7, 1937, the Chinese in British Malaya and British Borneo fully embraced the mission of national salvation and anti-Japanese activities began to dominate public life. The various organizations and movements that emerged from this anti-Japanese sentiment were all organized in the regional and national sense. The main body of the China Relief Fund, for instance, was organized by the Chinese Chamber of Commerce in various towns and states. The newspapers also played their part by publishing subscription lists of people who donated to these funds.

With all these events taking on a national posture and fostering a strong sense of national identity, it is a wonder that dialect identity, including Hakka identity, was able to endure. There was an event which, amidst the rise of Chinese nationalism and the forging of a national Chinese identity, gave the Hakka identity a certain boost, hence providing a slightly different response to the question of identity. In 1929, Aw Boon Haw founded the Federation of Nanyang Hakka Associations. Born in Rangoon (Yangon), Aw Boon Haw and his brother Aw Boon Par made their fortune by manufacturing and selling an ointment known as Tiger Balm. A Hakka of Yongding origins, Aw Boon Haw's initial idea was to bring the various Hakka organizations together.[1] But in 1939, when evaluating the effect of ten years of its existence, Aw Boon Haw realized that the federation had achieved very little. In fact, it was almost becoming an embarrassment.[2] This is clearly an indication that events in China had absorbed the attention of the Hakka more than their concerns for Hakka identity or Hakka solidarity.

Even though Aw Boon Haw tried to inject some initiatives towards the solidarity of the Hakka in Southeast Asia, very little was achieved, save for a few places which responded to his calls. For instance, the Hakka on the west coast of

Sabah decided to formally set up a new Hakka Association in Jesselton (present-day Kota Kinabalu) in 1940; it was led mainly by members of the Basel Church on the west coast (Wong 2013, 254–55). In the same way, Hakka Associations in Johor in the southern Malay Peninsula, Sarawak, and Myanmar were established or reorganized following Aw Boon Haw's call for Hakka unity. This was a reverse trend in the plight of dialect organizations in Southeast Asia and Malaya, where Hakka dialect organizations were once again attracting attention and diverting the Hakka interest to the national agenda and concerns of China as a whole. Even then, Aw Boon Haw and his Hakka ventures went big in so far as they were able to steer within the confines of the campaigns for national salvation. The activities at the tenth anniversary celebration of the Federation of Nanyang Hakka Associations in Singapore in August 1939 were closely tied to the various campaigns to raise funds for the war victims fund in China as well as a declaration for the starting of such a fund. Thus, in this manner, the dialect focus of the celebration was still subsumed under this greater weight of a national agenda.

But to be fair to Aw Boon Haw, he did something more than merely call for Hakka solidarity. With the establishment of the Federation of Nanyang Hakka Associations, he provided a certain way of thinking about Hakka-ness and Hakka studies. He encouraged and promoted Luo Xianglin's concept of Hakka-ness and Hakka identity.[3] Luo Xianglin, who taught at Hong Kong University, published a seminal work on the question of Hakka-ness, in which he defined Hakka identity and gave it a conceptual framework hinged on the idea that the Hakka originated from the Zhong Yuan, or heartland of China, in the Yellow River basin, but had been displaced and emigrated to the south. This idea was an important departure from all previous attempts to unify the Hakka people. Since its publication there have been different views about the concept of a northern origin of the Hakka and their migration to the south (*Nanyang Daily*, December 23, 2005).

Through Luo Xianglin's work, Hakka existence was given a new breath of life. Hakka-ness was now gaining recognition and those associated with the community were now proud to learn that their dialect group, which had thus far been associated with a rural existence, was given a different interpretation in which a dialect group was deemed to be sophisticated. These efforts to promote the virtues of Hakka-ness helped to provide a certain sense of pride and unity among those who professed to be Hakka. This would lay the basis for the establishment of Hakka organizations at a global level. That would come only later. But in 1933 and 1939, Aw Boon Haw's promotion of the idea of Hakka-ness and Hakka identity went as far as the physical establishment of more Hakka associations. However, it was still not embraced by all Hakkas.

Another group of Hakka leaders who shared Aw Boon Haw's concerns for Hakka unity and the future of the Hakka identity were the leaders of the Tshung Tsin Association in Hong Kong. The organization went on to organize academic discussions on the origins and migration of the Hakka people, and their works were very academic in nature. The focus was, of course, on the Hakka community in China, their origins and their southward migration. But ultimately the challenge was to transfer the idea of Hakka identity and Hakka-ness to the ordinary Hakka so that he or she would be able to identify with this collective identity. For the ordinary Hakka, this Hakka identity came not from the in-depth studies of scholars but from the more down-to-earth dissemination of ideas and concepts in newspapers. For this, Aw Boon Haw had the answers in the numerous newspapers that he owned or could influence. These included the *Yangon Ribao*, *Myanmar Morning News Sin Chew Daily*, *Sin Bin Ribao*, and *Sinsiam Ribao*. Chief of these was the *Sin Chew Daily*, the flagship newspaper under Aw's newsgroup. It was through these newspapers that the idea of being a Hakka was being expounded by the various scholars. Even Aw Boon Haw contributed articles on the Hakka to the paper. In 1938, he published an article on "Spirit of Hakka."[4] He also distributed Luo Xianglin's seminal work on the Hakka in mass numbers. Some of the ideas in the book were also serialized in the newspapers.

The various efforts to promote Hakka identity, including those by Aw Boon Haw and others, were admirable, but came at a time when the Chinese, the Hakka included, were confronted by bigger issues of national survival. Thus, it is not surprising that, despite all the efforts, the notion of Hakka identity could only have an effect on those involved in Hakka organizations or those who were genuinely interested in the plight of the Hakka.

Local Hakka Identity?

When the Japanese Army attacked Malaya in December 1941, all concerns were on Malaya's war efforts, including putting up defence. The Chinese also began to join anti-Japanese activities, including serving in the volunteer forces of the Straits Settlements or the Malay States. But in all these activities, the notion of Hakka-ness was not apparent nor was there any effort to further promote the idea of Hakka identity in times of emergency. This situation persisted during the Japanese occupation when anti-Japanese activities were organized not based on dialect group but on the notion of being Chinese.

In the immediate postwar years, when reconstruction was actively pursued, the Hakka associations throughout the country went through a period of reregistration and updating of membership and office bearers, and their premises became social meeting places. The winds of change that were blowing included the political radicalization of a sizable section of the Chinese community. Leading the field was the Malayan Communist Party (MCP), which had led a rather successful anti-Japanese military force (the Malayan People's Anti-Japanese Army) during the occupation. Interestingly, many of the MCP members were Hakka, probably because many who lived in the fringe of the jungles or were displaced persons were Hakka.

When Emergency was declared in June 1948, once again the concerns of the Hakka centered less on their dialect identity than on the larger question of being Chinese. The MCP were predominantly Chinese, and most of the security forces were Malays, while the rest were troops from Commonwealth countries. The MCP, through their civilian support organization, the Min Yuen, infiltrated the general Chinese population to elicit support and supplies. The Min Yuen's prime targets were the Chinese living on the fringes of rural and jungle areas. Many of these Chinese were former miners, most of them Hakka, who had been laid off during the Great Depression years and settled in these marginalized fringe areas. This posed a security problem to the authorities who aimed at eliminating support for the MCP. This was also a problem for the Chinese as they were constantly suspected of aiding the MCP. Many Chinese were unable to identify with the MCP's struggle and were content to be left alone to seek a decent living, but the situation was being forced upon them.

The resettlement scheme introduced in 1951, known as the Briggs Plan, was a massive operation that aimed at resettling more than 500,000 Chinese (and a few non-Chinese) who were living on the fringes of the jungle, mainly on state-owned land, and thus were susceptible to the influence of the MCP and Min Yuen. The plans called for the construction of more than 400 settlements, known as New Villages, into which the 500,000 Chinese would be forced to move. This massive operation was assisted by Chinese organizations, including the Malayan Chinese Association (MCA), which was established in 1949 as an alternative to the MCP. In the resettlement process, the Chinese were identified solely as Chinese and not by dialect group even though the majority were Hakka. The New Villages were massive camps with fences and security. Social and basic amenities were established, mainly in the form of health clinics, village administration, libraries, and schools. The new schools were run as Chinese schools, not dialect schools. While the medium of many of these New Villages remained dialect-based, whether Cantonese, Hokkien, or Hakka, the place of dialect within these villages also gradually eroded, giving way to the idea of being Chinese. This situation was to last even up to the point of independence in 1957.

While the situation in the Malay Peninsula presented one of the most successful resettlement schemes in combatting communism, the case in Sarawak was quite different. During the time of negotiation for independence and the formation of Malaysia, some Chinese were averse to the idea of joining the new federation. They were convinced that Malaysia was not for them. In their struggle against the British and, later, Malaysian government, they formed a guerrilla force known as the Tentera Nasional Kalimantan Utara (North Kalimantan National Army) which had ties to the Indonesians. These people crossed over to Kalimantan and established the Sarawak Clandestine Organisation (SCO), which began to recruit young Chinese into its ranks and put them through military training. The SCO worked in tandem with the North Kalimantan National Army, which was established under President Soekarno in his bid to derail the establishment of the new Federation of Malaysia. Most of the Chinese involved in the movement were Hakka. In a memorial to more than 700 SCO members who were killed by security forces, at least 70 percent of them were of Hakka origin.[5] This should not come as a surprise as, similar to their counterparts in the Malay Peninsula during the Emergency era, most of the Hakka in Sarawak also lived in rural areas, and thus were also considered vulnerable to influence by the SCO, or were perceived by the security authorities to be lending support to the SCO, which later also took on a communist slant in their struggle. Thus, the security forces introduced plans similar to those in the Briggs Plan and set up camps that would group the Hakka villages together.

One of the more recent developments in this regard was the continued marginalization of the Hakka in rural Sarawak. Many of them were bitter about the entire experience. Many of those who came out of the jungle following the peace accord at Seri Aman in 1971 were detained over long periods and, upon release, found themselves marginalized and remained poor. Feelings of loss and exasperation characterized these people. A recent work on the Hakka of Sarawak focuses on these disfranchised Hakka (Kee 2013). Yet, despite their plight, the group's Hakka identity was retained, if not sustained, by the actions of the state and perhaps even as a result of the isolation imposed by other Chinese, who were often seen through the prism of dialect groups.

The two cases of resettlement in new villages had different outcomes for the preservation of Hakka identity. In the peninsula, the large number of Hakka-majority new villages resulted in the emergence of some Hakka areas, including Menglembu near Ipoh, Tanah Merah in Perak, and Serdang and Chempaka in Selangor. But sustaining their ethnic identity was problematic as their resettlement had nothing to do with dialect grouping or origins. In the case of Sarawak, the feeling was different as the Hakka believed that they were targeted by the authorities and, hence, victimized. They have a stronger sense of being Hakka than their brethren in the Malay Peninsula.

In the Peninsular New Villages, two important factors mitigated against the fostering of a stronger Hakka identity. The first was the role played by the MCA, a Chinese-based political party which had championed the interests and rights of the Chinese community since 1949. The party was also part of the independence movement and part of the government since 1955. As a national party, the MCA sought to promote the existence of a single Chinese identity instead of dialect identity. Therefore, despite many New Villages being populated by a certain dialect majority, MCA's socio-economic programs did not have any dialect inclination. The emphasis was on Mandarin as the official language, used in official functions in the New Villages, and all programs emphasized Chinese unity to fight communism and, later, as Chinese in a larger sense of the nation, and also vis-à-vis other ethnic groups. The second factor was the effect of the exodus of young people from the New Villages. After the dismantling of the security fences, the New Villagers were no longer confined to life in a closed compound. Many of them later sought employment elsewhere, especially in the larger cities. Younger people also moved out for better education. The effect of this change was significant in eroding the Hakka identity in the New Villages. As younger people were leaving for the cities, they left behind the older generations, with no one else sustaining or continuing the Hakka dialect or even tradition. In the larger cities, where the use of the Hakka dialect, which is not a commercial language, was at best negligible, Hakka speakers would have very few occasions to use their original dialect (Tan 2000. Instead, many adopted the main dialect used in their new location, usually either Cantonese or Hokkien. Only in places such as Sabah, where the Hakka comprise around 60 percent of the Chinese population, is Hakka the main lingua franca. The migration history of the state and its ties to the Hakka-speaking Basel Christian Church ensured that Hakka became the main Chinese dialect.

The next section will examine the manner Hakka identity fared in the setting of the new nation-state of Malaysia.

Chinese Identity Formation in Malaysia

When Malaya achieved independence, the new state inherited the census categories of ethnic groups and subethnic groups as established by the British at the turn of the twentieth century. Therefore, in every census the Chinese were asked for their dialect origin. This continued until the end of the twentieth century but was less emphasized in the post-2000 census. Yet, the country's ethnic composition is still based on the main ethnic configuration of Malays, Chinese, Indians, and others. This was underscored all along and was evident in at least three moments in the country's history. The first moment was the British government's stress in its response to Malaya's demand for independence. When Tunku Abdul Rahman and his Alliance Party, which originally consisted of the United Malays National Organisation (UMNO) and the MCA, demanded independence from the British, the latter's reply was that the Malayans need to ensure that they had all the major ethnic groups with them. Hence, the Tunku and his allies invited the Malayan Indian Congress (MIC) to join them in the pursuit of independence. Later negotiation delegations always contained representatives of all three major races, and the interests of the various ethnic groups were also negotiated, especially in the manner they were represented. This set the tone for the ethnic bargaining that became a permanent feature of Malaysian politics and life, so the Chinese needed to put up a united front, via the MCA, in order to champion the welfare of the larger Chinese community.

The second moment was the racial riot of May 13, 1969, which saw racial clashes taking place in the new nation's capital, Kuala Lumpur, following the announcement of the May 1969 General Election results. The opposition parties had made significant gains, and squabbling between supporters of different political parties soon took on a racial line. The ensuing clashes resulted in many deaths. The event reinforced the importance of ethnic identity. In the case of the Chinese, it was Chinese vis-à-vis the rest, especially the Malays. In this regard, dialect identification was seen as a mark of division which, if it needed to be emphasized, should concentrate on culture and tradition, not as a form of identification vis-à-vis other ethnic groups.

The third defining moment was the introduction of the New Economic Policy (NEP) in 1971 in the aftermath of the racial riot. As parliament had been suspended, the National Operations Council proposed that one of the root causes of the racial riot was the economic imbalance in the country. The NEP aimed at addressing this imbalance and eradicating poverty, but it also proposed affirmative action measures aimed at improving the equity holdings of the Bumiputera community to 30 percent. The policy was to last for twenty years. But in 1991, the evaluation showed that the policy was still short of the target. It was hence replaced by the New Development Policy and, later, the New Vision Policy. All these policies, noble as they set out to be, were a major challenge to the Chinese community. Their implementation inevitably placed the Chinese in a disadvantaged position, not only in the public service but also in terms of economic opportunities. In trying to mitigate against the impact of these policies, political parties like the MCA (and Chinese-based opposition parties) had to work hard to create more opportunities and space for the Chinese community to operate. However, again, it was the Chinese identity that was underlined and not dialect identity. In this way, even though the state did not have direct impact on dialect identity, the introduction of state policies brought about the need for a unified response, one that could only derive from a united Chinese position.

Where, then, was Hakka identity in the midst of all this? Throughout the challenging years of building a new nation-state and the many issues that demanded a unified Chinese response, the role and place of Hakka and other dialect identities also declined significantly. This, however, did not mean that Hakka associations were closed and abandoned. That was hardly the case. Most Hakka associations continued with their mission of promoting Hakka culture and serving as a bonding mechanism to preserve Hakka tradition and identity, with a strong sense of purpose. There was, of course, a decline in interest among younger people, but most Hakka associations continued with their activities of holding regular worship rites for their deities as well as supporting the schools started by their forebears in the previous century. While the Hakka associations survived, they paid a heavy price. To many, they are the domains of the senior group of Chinese who were brought up speaking the dialect. The Hakka associations have very little appeal to younger groups of Hakka who are inclined to speak Mandarin and who view dialect associations as archaic and not very progressive. Others join simply to look for gains, for example, benefits such as scholarships, or to use the association for social mobility. Therefore, there is little genuine effort to identify themselves with Hakka dialect organizations.

Even as the Chinese community weathers the challenges of being a unified community vis-à-vis other ethnic groups and, at the same time, negotiating through government policies that place the Chinese in a disadvantaged position, the existence of Hakka (and other dialect) associations remind the Chinese that in the back of their minds something called dialect identity exists.

The last section will examine the way in which the Hakka identity experienced some revival, with impetus from within and outside of the country.

The Revival of Hakka Identity

In recent years, at least two events provided some impetus for a revival of interest in Hakka associations and Hakka-ness. The first was the World Hakka Conference. The original conference, held in Hong Kong in 1971, was organized by the Tshung Tsin Association, to which Luo Xianglin belonged. The meeting was meant to be a serious affair with a strong slant toward academic pursuit. Subsequent years saw the meeting take on a wider role, also becoming a forum for Hakka leaders, especially Hakka businessmen, to gather to exchange views and, most important of all, to reinforce their common dialect identity as Hakka. Originally a biannual event, the World Hakka Conference has, since 2010, been organized annually.

The economic and business consideration of organizing the conference received a great incentive with the rise of China as an economic power. It is no wonder that attendance at these conferences has increased. From the humble beginnings of a few hundred delegates, the number of attendees rose to one thousand in the 1980s and 1990s, and to two thousand for the first time in 1996 in Singapore. The 24th meeting in 2011 in Guangxi had six thousand delegates, and two years later in Jakarta, the figure went up to eight thousand. Since its inception, nine of the meetings have been held in China.

Malaysian delegates have been attending the conference since its inception. More importantly, Malaysia has twice played host to the conference. The first was in 1990, in Kota Kinabalu, Sabah, one of the Hakka heartlands in Malaysia (Sabah State Museum 1990). The second was in Kuala Lumpur in 1999. On both occasions, the federal and state governments provided a great deal of support toward the successful organizing of the conferences. With the organization of the two conferences, the Hakka in Malaysia received a wonderful boost in terms of both morale and pride. It was nice to be known as Hakka again.

A second impetus came from Taiwan. With the establishment of the Hakka Commission at the State Council level in 2001,[6] Taiwan experienced a revival of interest in Hakka studies. A number of universities, including the National Chiao Tung and the National Central University, began to offer Hakka studies as a study program, while others set up research institutes, including the Kaoshiung Normal University and Taiwan Normal University. Annual conferences were held, and scholars were invited to present papers and join research projects initiated by Hakka studies scholars in Taiwan. This, in some way, inspired the introduction of research on the Hakka in Malaysian universities. The University of Malaya Malaysian Chinese Research Centre, for instance, has initiated at least two research programs on the study of the Hakka in Malaysia and Southeast Asia, conducted in collaboration with colleagues from Taiwan and China. In the same way, Tunku Abdul Rahman University also has research projects focused on various aspects of Hakka studies in Malaysia.

There is also a Hakka TV station in Taiwan that delivers its programs in two Hakka tones. This provides enormous encouragement and inspires pride in

Hakka visitors to Taiwan. In Malaysia, the Hakka dialect is only found in the Hakka News Bulletin, which is a broadcast of only fifteen minutes.

Within the Hakka associations there is also a sense of revival and renewal, partly through realizations when interacting with Hakka from other places, especially Taiwan and China. The fact that after so long (since 1948), the Hakka in Malaysia are able to visit their ancestral home has rekindled that strong sense of identity and solidarity toward their home.

As a result of such contacts, interest was rekindled, and some of the Hakka associations began to launch major projects aimed at promoting Hakka identity in their respective locality. The Hakka Association of Penang proposed the construction of a *tulou* structure that would serve as the center for Hakka identity. The building is to take the shape of a rounded fortress and will house a museum and shopping complex (*Sin Chew Daily*, June 15, 2008; *The Star*, June 12, 2010). In Kota Kinabalu, the Hakka Association opened a Sabah Hakka Complex in 2015 which staged some very important exhibits (*Daily Express*, March 9, 2015).

In 1979, in the face of new challenges to sustain Hakka identity, the Malaysian Federation of Hakka Associations was established. This was an important development which reflected the need to unite as well to respond to the erosion and decline of Hakka identity. The Federation hoped to engage in ongoing socioeconomic developments and also have their voice heard in political spheres. This was a noble effort, but thus far it has not made significant difference. However, that has not prevented it from becoming one of the largest Chinese federations in Malaysia (Hsiao and Lim 2007, 429–30).

The recent revival of Hakka identity was nothing compared to the original Hakka identity of the late nineteenth and early twentieth centuries when dialect consciousness was everything. The late twentieth century revival concentrated more on culture and heritage. This is inevitable as the question of being a Hakka in the economic or political sense means little in facing the challenges of being a Chinese in present-day Malaysia. Therefore, this revival was limited in nature but given the state of affairs of the Hakka dialect identity which had suffered a gradual decline over the years, it was indeed a sort of reversal in fortune. In actual fact, the trend was irreversible.

Conclusion

When the Hakka arrived in the territories that eventually formed the new federation of Malaysia, their Hakka identity played a very important role in defining who they were and how they should live their lives in the new land. The Hakka in Malaysia, like their counterparts from other dialect groups, have seen their dialect identity undergoing transformation from being the most defining identification in the late nineteenth and early twentieth centuries to experiencing a gradual decline and erosion on all fronts. This erosion, however, was not a direct result of the British administration in Malaya. In fact, the British, to some extent, helped to reinforce and sustain this Hakka identity by incorporating dialect as a way of categorizing the Chinese. They also used dialect categories to select representation to government-related institutions.

For a Hakka, dialect identity was an important way of defining who he was. His life, the settlement of his home, and his social institutions evolved around dialect organizations. In some cases, even the school that their children attended was started by the Hakka association. This began to change in the 1920s, but the drive to change was not the local British government but, rather, events in China that had a stronger bearing on the future of dialect identity in Malaysia.

The establishment of the new Chinese Republic and the reorganization of the education system to favor Mandarin education had no place for dialect identification. The new ideal of Chinese identity prevailed. For the Chinese in Malaysia, the changes were profound and perhaps even swift in the way that the Hakka dialect identity gave way to a unified Chinese identity. Events of the 1930s, especially reaction toward Japanese military aggression in China, invoked a stronger embracing of this Chinese identity and, with it, Chinese nationalism. This was to be sustained through World War II and even in the immediate postwar years. Compared to other dialect groups, the Hakka dialect had some theoretical framework as established by Luo Xianglin. This set them apart when discussing dialect identity.

Events in post-1945 Malaysia saw the Chinese identity being forged as a way of responding to the challenges of the MCP and, later, for independence. Even though there were elements of the Hakka dialect in the New Villages, they, too, were subsumed under the overall Chinese identity vis-à-vis other ethnic groups.

Post-independent Malaysia was no different. Hakka identity eroded further with the challenges of ethnic politics, where the Chinese had to stand united against certain government policies. The introduction of the NEP following the May 1969 racial riots further weakened the Hakka identity.

The position of dialect identity seems to be experiencing a revival, but with encouragement from abroad. First was the World Hakka Conference, and second, the promotion of Hakka studies in Taiwan. However, dialect identification and Hakka-ness are now more of a cultural and traditional concern.

Endnote: Hakka Dialect Identity and Chinese Identity in Malaysia

1. For a study of Aw Boon Haw (1984), see 康吉父,《胡文虎傳》, Hong Kong: 龍門文化.康吉父, 1984.
2. 黄力堅, 南洋客總與抗戰前期的中國—以《新加坡南洋客屬總會十十週年紀念特刊》為研究中心, 臺北: 行政院客家委員會獎助客家學術研究計畫, 黃力堅, 2010, 439.
3. 羅香林《客家研究導論》, 台北: 南天, 1992. Originally published in Guangdong in 1933 by 興寧希山書藏社初版發行.
4. I am indebted to Dr Chang Jung-Chia for her paper on Aw Boon Haw, where she tried to develop the notion of Aw Boon Haw promoting Hakka identity through various means. Her paper, "The Shaoing of the Hakka Community: Aw Boon Haw and His Hakka Group," was presented at the 3rd Taiwan International Hakka Studies Conference, National Chiao Tung University, Hsinchu, November 8–9, 2014.
5. See 《浩气长存》 2013, Kuching: Ex-Comrade Association.
6. Retrieved from http://www.hakka.gov.tw/mp1.html., last accessed on 30 August 2022.

References

Chang Jung-Chia. 2014. "The Shaoing of the Hakka Community: Aw Boon Haw and His Hakka Group." Paper presented at the 3rd Taiwan International Hakka Studies Conference, National Chiao Tung University, Hsinchu, November, 8–9.

Hsiao, Michael, and Lim Khai Tiong. 2007. "The Formation and Limitation of Hakka Identity in Southeast Asia." In *Hakka Ethnic and Local Society: The Experiences of Taiwan and Global*, eds. Chiu Chang Tye and Michael Hsiao, 429–30. Taipei: National Central University Press. http://www.hakka.gov.tw/mp1.html., last accessed on 30 August 2022.

Hsiao Hsin-Huang, ed. 2011. *Changing Faces of Hakka in Southeast: Singapore and Malaysia*. Taipei: Center for Asia-Pacific Area Studies, RCHSS, Academia Sinica.

Kee Howe Yong. 2013. *The Hakka of Sarawak: Sacrificial Gifts in Cold War Era Malaysia*. Toronto: University of Toronto Press.

Khoo Kay Kim. 1978. *The Western Malay States*. Kuala Lumpur: Oxford University Press.

Liew Kam Ba. 1999. "Hakka and Chinese Education." *Nanyang Daily*, October 17. See also *Oriental Press*, February 24, 2009.

Low, Y. K. 1985. *Sejarah Perkembangan Dewan Perniagaan Cina Selangor* [History of the Selangor Chinese Chamber of Commerce]. Bangi: Universiti Kebangsaan Malaysia.

Sabah State Museum. 1990. *The World Hakka Conference 1990*. Kota Kinabalu: Sabah State Museum.

Tan Chee Beng. 2000. "Socio-Cultural Diversities and Identities." In *The Chinese in Malaysia*, eds. Lee Kam Hing and Tan Chee Beng. Shah Alam: Oxford University Press.

Wang Gungwu. 2001. "The Hakka in Migration History." In *Don't Leave Home: Migration and the Chinese* by Wang Gungwu, 217–38. Singapore: Times Academic Press. Originally published in *Proceedings, International Conference on Hakkalogy*, 1995. Hong Kong: The Chinese University of Hong Kong Centre for Asia-Pacific Studies.

Wong Tze Ken, Danny. 1998. *The Transformation of an Immigrant Society: A History of the Chinese of Sabah*. London: ASEAN Academic Press.

——————. 1999. "Chinese Migration to Sabah Before the Second World War." *Archipel* 58(3): 131–58.

——————. 2013. "The Hakka in Sabah before World War Two: Their Adaptation to New Environment, Challenges and the Forging of New Identity." In 張维安,《東南亞客家及其周邊》, Taipei: 中央大學出版中心 & 遠流, 254–55.

《浩气长存》 2013, Kuching: Ex-Comrade Association.

康吉父,《胡文虎傳》, Hong Kong: 龍門文化. 1984. [Kang Jifu. 1984. *A Biography of Aw Boon Haw*, Hong Kong: Longman Wenhua].

羅香林《客家研究導論》, 台北: 南天, 1992; first published in Guangdong in 1933 by 興寧希山書藏社初版發行.

黄力堅, 南洋客總與抗戰前期的中國—以《新加坡南洋客屬總會十十週年紀念特刊》為研究中心, 臺北: 行政院客家委員會獎助客家學術研究計畫, 2010. [Huang Lijian, The Pre-War Nanyang Hakka Federation and China in "The Singapore Nanyang Hakka Federation Ten Anniversary Magazine as Research Focus." Taipei: Hakka Commission Research Project Proposal, 2010].

Kola Identity at the Pailin Frontier Gem Mines: Generations of Autonomy, Integration, and Upheaval

NATASHA PAIRAUDEAU

In 1884 the French explorer Auguste Pavie traveled from Chanthaburi to Pailin, which was then under Siamese administration. The well-established route was dotted with *sala* or open-sided rest stops, built by wealthy gem merchants to make merit and publicly demonstrate their success. As if the Siamese needed reminding, this infrastructure underlined effective control of the area by a group of people who called themselves Kola (Lunet 1910, 417).[1] Pavie's encounter with one of the migrant miners was another reminder of who was in control. In his journal Pavie recorded how, much to his irritation, an aggressive fellow shoved his face up close, stuck his hand in the Frenchman's plate of stew, and declared, "I am Koula" (Pavie 1884, 60–61).

Pailin is a plateau abutting the northeastern slopes of the Cardamom Mountains (Khe Kravanh in Khmer; Bao Patat in Thai), where this range marks the border between modern-day Thailand and Cambodia. Mining settlements sprung up at Pailin from the early 1870s after Shan prospectors discovered sapphires and rubies in the riverbeds and surrounding hills. These prospectors came from a relatively long distance to reach Pailin; the Shan are ethnic Tai from the hill tracts northeast of Burma who traditionally paid tribute to the Burmese kingdom. They continued nevertheless to make up the vast majority of the miners drawn to these gem tracts and formed an elite who controlled the mining economy as it developed. They were joined in smaller numbers by other peoples from Burma and its tributary states.

European observers often referred to this migrant mining population as "Burmese," a convenient if imprecise blanket term for a more complex set of social and legal identities. The Siamese and Khmer, though, who occupied the lowlands surrounding the frontier ruby and sapphire mines, used Kola, a derivation of the Burmese word for "foreigner," to identify the miners who had appeared in the hills. The Burmese transcription for Kola is ကုလား. In Thai it is rendered กุลา, and in Khmer កុឡា.[2]

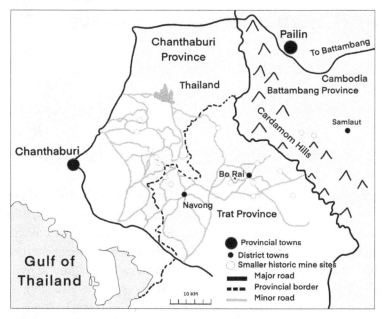

Map 1. The Chanthaburi-Pailin gem districts (adapted from Smyth 1898).

Long before the term Kola became attached to the migrant gem miners, the term was already used in Siam for a different group of people. Itinerant traders from Burma and its tributaries who plied caravan routes across north and northeastern Siam were also known to the Siamese as Kola (กุลา) (Koizumi 1990; Chonpairot et al., 2009).[3] This linguistic connection reinforces the suggestion that Kola traders were the first to be attracted to rumors of gems in the hills beyond the Siamese port of Chanthaburi (Filleau 1920, 424). The Shan miners also willingly accepted the term Kola to identify themselves. They did not like it, the visiting British geologist Herbert Warington Smyth noted in 1895, when Europeans called them "Burmese": "*Gula* is the term most commonly used for them both by themselves and by Siamese" (Smyth, 1898, 181).

In a relatively short span of time, Kola became not just a functional category, but a term attached to a meaningful identity. This identity changed over time in the Pailin region as circumstances changed, from the latter half of the nineteenth century when the migrant miners settled on the plateau, to the recent past and its unsettling events which have displaced and nearly eliminated the Kola population.

Pailin's Kola history, and with it the construction of Kola identity, has three broad phases. A first phase witnessed Pailin's mining heyday, beginning with the initial Shan discovery of gems at Pailin in the early 1870s. At that time the plateau was under Siamese administration. Later, from 1907, it was subject to French rule within the protectorate of the Kingdom of Cambodia. Despite these extensions of sovereignty (and despite British consular oversight of the miners, the majority of whom were British subjects), the Kola retained a remarkable level of autonomy over their mining region. Despite, too, their apparently isolated position in the hills, they were connected to commercial flows and attuned to the modernizing impulses of the outside world.

French authorities sought to remove the special administrative powers the Kola enjoyed. They were troubled by the threat posed by the many heavily armed Kola at the mines, frustrated at having to stand by as the Kola headman retained large sums in tax from an agreement out of their control, and humiliated by the "state within a state" within an area supposedly under French protection. Although France managed to diminish the powers of the Kola headman in 1915, the Kola continued their economic hold over the district and its gem mining.

Kola control over the gem-mining district did not disappear with Cambodian independence from French rule in 1953. Kola history entered gradually into a second phase from the late 1950s as conditions in the newly independent country began to affect the mining region. By the late 1960s, outplayed by Chinese and Khmer entrepreneurs, the Kola had definitively ceded their monopoly over gem mining. They were outnumbered, too, by incomers in search of a livelihood and refuge from conflict elsewhere in the country. Pailin's integration into the new nation-state was characterized by this loss of Kola power, and their gradual departure or assimilation into the local population.

Before this second phase had fully played itself out, however, events took a different turn. Both the Kola and the incomers who were in the process of displacing them in the 1960s and early 1970s were scattered, killed, or exiled by the radical program of social reconstruction under the Khmer Rouge. When the Khmer Rouge were ousted from central power in 1979, Pailin became a hold-out for its prominent leaders. Effectively, Pailin became once again a semiautonomous zone, a status officially recognized by the central government in Phnom Penh in the late 1990s when Pailin's Khmer Rouge fugitives struck a deal in "surrender" to these powers. To this day, Pailin remains in the hands of the supporters and relatives of these former Khmer Rouge leaders. The vast majority of Pailin's inhabitants, Khmer Rouge fighters who settled in Pailin in peacetime, are not familiar with the term Kola. Those who are, or were, Kola have all but disappeared, while a new identity, which obscures their recent past and ignores the complexities of their longer history, is being created for them as one of the nation's minority ethnic groups.

Pailin, I argue here, witnessed two initial phases of its history which each produced a distinctive Kola identity. These identities formed in tandem with the dynamics of local autonomy and forces of regional and national integration. Latterly, in a third phase, people identifying as Kola are all but gone from Pailin, while Kola identity has been reconstructed by the region's newer inhabitants and power brokers.

This account is pieced together from historical archives as well as contemporary press sources and documents. Most of these sources are in English or French but the archives include petitions and testimonies translated from originals in Thai, Khmer, Burmese, and Shan. Where sources use terms drawn from other languages, as they often do for Pailin, I have retained the transcription used in that source, while providing where possible the correct modern spelling in the original language and script. This account also relies on interviews conducted during a visit to Pailin and the region in September 2019. There I worked, where necessary, through local interpreters.

Becoming Kola

The mines and population settlements at Pailin grew rapidly following the initial discovery of gems there. By the 1880s Pailin's population stood at 4,000, with another 3,000 at Navong, a related site on the southwesterly slopes of the Cardamom Hills some 80 kilometers to the south (Smyth 1898, 181; Brien 1885, 352). Such was the draw of Pailin's gem rush, coupled with political disruptions in Upper Burma and the Shan States, that one source put Pailin's population by the late 1880s as high as 10,000 (*Echo Annamite* 1939).

The latter figure may have been exaggerated, yet there is no doubt that at the end of the nineteenth century a vibrant mining culture and a rich ethnic mix existed at Pailin. Different peoples assumed distinctive roles at the mining sites, but the Shan were the undoubted masters. It was also the Shan, initially at least, who were referred to locally as Kola, and readily, even proudly, accepted the name.

It was Shan, venturing north from the earlier discovered site at Navong, who first appreciated the potential for ruby and sapphire mining at Pailin in the 1870s. As prospectors and mine owners, they continued to seek out promising sites on the Pailin plateau and in the surrounding hills. Over the years they secured rights over much of the best gem-yielding land. They built a network of canals which greatly extended the number of viable mining sites and which, crucially, gave them control over access points to water (Black 1895).

The gem mines themselves remained no more than small open pits. The miners dug until they reached a gem-bearing gravel layer, which was removed and washed with water to search out the precious stones (Black 1895). Mines dotted the valley and hills but could equally be found in the streets of the mining settlements. By 1895 Smyth noted that the successful Kola were overseeing, rather than directly engaged, in this hard work. Lao laborers, "the short strong-limbed Lao," were hired by wealthier Shan miners to carry out heavy labor "where the sinking of pits exceeds a few feet" and where canals needed digging. The "gay Gulas in their gaudy *passohs*," as Smyth observed them, looked on, "squatting and smoking over their pits" (Smyth 1898, 205).[4]

Another early observer at Pailin was the British consular officer, Stewart Black. In 1895, the same year as Smyth's visit, Black conducted the first "consular tour" to the gem-mining region; the tour became thereafter an annual occurrence (Black 1895). Its purpose was to register miners as British subjects with the consulate at Bangkok, to carry out "all the year's litigation," and to investigate any difficulties British subjects encountered under the Siamese administration (Wood 1965, 35–36). Under the Bowring Treaty (1855), Siam recognized extraterritorial protection for British subjects, which extended to protection for those subjects of Britain's colonial empire. Britain had an interest in ensuring Siam respected its treaty rights, and British imperial subjects were keen to avail themselves of the advantages this protection gave them (Hong 2003).

On his initial visit, Black registered three-quarters of the mining population as British subjects (2,500 people of a total population of 3,500 at Pailin). Of these newly registered British subjects he stated: "They are natives of Upper Burmah, from the districts of Mone, Mokmai, and Mandalay, and there are also a good many *Tongsoos* [Karen] from Lower Burma. A few hail from Chieng Tung and even from Bhamo" (Black 1895).

Those referred to as Lao workers, meanwhile, were itinerant wage laborers from "Bassac" (Champasak) or Ubon, who established their own encampments adjacent to the mining settlements (Black 1895; Lunet 1910, 417). Despite their position at the lower end of Pailin's social structure, the smooth running of the mines depended upon them. Outbreaks of malaria were common in the early years before forest was cleared around the mining settlements. Lao wage laborers, with less to lose than mine owners, were the first to flee, and over several years mining operations were seriously disrupted by the population flight. In 1899 a smallpox epidemic again emptied villages of laborers, crippling mining operations and raising the price of labor (Carlisle 1899).

The ethnic Burmese, for their part, worked as gem dealers or were stationed at Pailin as intermediaries to buyers in Chanthaburi, Bangkok, and to gem markets farther afield in Burma and Bangkok. In addition, a small number of Chinese, Siamese, and Vietnamese merchants had shops along the main street of Pailin town, where they sold goods brought up from the port at Chanthaburi (Filleau 1920, 427). The neighboring Khmer people in the plains to the east tended to stay away from the mining sites at Pailin as they were unwilling to risk their health in the face of the prevailing fevers and diseases (Brien 1886, 11). Their reluctance to travel to Pailin contributed to the mining plateau's reputation as an isolated place.

By contrast, the "natural immunity" of the Shan, which allowed them to remain in the hills while others kept away, was much remarked upon (Stringer 1898; Smyth 1898, 180, 202).[5] In truth, the Shan were not completely invulnerable. When the mines were first discovered, they too "died in the jungle or succumbed to lingering fever" and were forced to abandon some badly affected sites (Black 1895).

The Europeans who described Pailin in the late nineteenth century were men versed in the ethnographic understandings of their own time. They tended to attribute the ethnic division of labor to the innate capacities of different distinctive "races."[6] Thus, Smyth declared that the Shan, in addition to their natural resistance to malaria, possessed an innate capacity for finding gems.[7] Their ability to detect the color and quality of precious stones was pronounced, they had a "roving spirit," and were irresistibly attracted to the "charm" of gems and the thrill of their pursuit.

The bodily relationship between the Shan and their gems made their gem-seeking abilities appear even more primordial. Like many Shan from their homelands, Kola men covered their chests and legs in blue and red tattoos in the belief this protected them from maleficence and made them invulnerable (Smyth 1898, 173, 180). In addition to these markings, men were known to insert gems under their skin. These were intended either as internal talismans to increase the potency of their tattoos or as a very sure method to guard their wealth from theft. Possibly they were both (Badens 1886; Brien 1886, 19; Smyth 1898, 217; Wood 1965, 89).

In Smyth's view, the Burman could almost equal the Shan in virtues and strengths, but "does not have the same energy or constitution.": It followed that he acted at the mines as a middleman (Smyth 1898, 180).

Early assertions that Pailin society was shaped by ethnically (or racially) determined characteristics belied a less than tidy situation on the ground. The Shan were mainly prospectors, but this did not preclude their involvement in gem dealing. People of Burma's other ethnic groups are mentioned at Pailin, albeit in much smaller numbers, but it is difficult from the sources to pin down the roles they assumed. Indians, Chinese, Vietnamese, and Siamese traded in basic goods, but they too became increasingly involved in negotiating gems. And while mining laborers were described as "Lao" by reputation, Khmer labor was not unknown at the mines and increased over time (Black 1895).

Observers' assertions about the gender makeup at the mines did not appear either to fully capture a more complicated picture on the ground. Some travelers of the 1880s insisted the migrant miners were typically single men, while others asserted that they often formed relationships, and families, with local women (Brien 1885, 349; Boulangier 1887, 305). By the 1890s there were signs of established families in the mining villages. Smyth speaks of women and children who would search the shallow gravel once it had been "nearly worked out" for any gem fragments that might remain (Smyth 1898, 204–5). These laboring women may have been the partners of laboring Lao men, but Smyth also romanticized the "pretty Shan maidens" who wore "roses in their hair" as they strolled the "palm-fringed street" at Pailin (Smyth 1898, 202). Accounts from the 1910s describe "elegant women" in Pailin's main town, seemingly of higher status, dressed in styles which can be understood as Shan and Burmese (Smyth 1898, 202; Lunet 1910, 417; Filleau 1920, 428).

The Shan migrants and the Siamese shared linguistic ties which added another layer of complexity to their existence as distinct peoples at Pailin and the surrounding region. The Shan are Tai in linguistic terms, a trait which connects them to other speakers of Tai languages spread from Northeast India across the Southeast Asian massif.[8] "Shan" was a Burmese term used to identify Tai speakers within British Burma and the Yunnan-Burma frontier area and was adopted in the same sense in British colonial circles. Yet, to the west and southwest of Burma, as anthropologist Edmund Leach wrote in the 1950s, the term Shan "creates some ambiguity since the Burmese distinguish Shans from Siamese, although both groups call themselves Tai" (Leach 1972, 29).

When migration brought these two Tai-speaking groups into contact at Pailin, their affinities as well as their differences were thrown into relief. Smyth claimed in the 1890s that the whole Shan mining population "spoke Siamese, even among themselves. Their own language is so similar ... that they end up speaking it" (Smyth 1898, 181). He took this as proof of "a great affinity of race and language between the *Koulas* and the Siamese," but language use at Pailin was far from stable, and the urge to mark distinctions appears to have outweighed the desire to demonstrate affinities (Smyth 1898, 181). Some twenty years later, contrary to Smyth's observations, the French delegate at Pailin,

Gilbert Filleau de Saint Hilaire, insisted that the "Koula" readily used both Siamese and English in their business dealings, but "spoke among themselves in the Burmese language" (Filleau 1920, 431). This discrepancy may have been produced by the observers' own strengths and limitations, but it also suggests that the Kola's use of language was contextual.[9] Speaking Burmese between themselves might have been a convenient way of keeping their conversations from (Tai-speaking) outsiders. What is clear is that the Shan of Pailin remained "foreign" (quite literally Kola) to their Siamese neighbors. Becoming Kola, it could even be said, was a way for the Shan to preserve their distinction from the Siamese despite their Tai language affinity.

Tai-speaking peoples not only shared a common linguistic heritage but in locations spread across the upper valleys of the Southeast Asian massif they displayed a remarkable uniformity in their social and political structures. They cultivated wet rice in mid-level valleys, they were organized into minor polities or *müang*, and they shared the practice of Theravada Buddhism (Leach 1972, 37).

Shan practice at Pailin continued to resemble that of the Tai *müang* in one respect, in that Theravada Buddhism remained a central force in their lives. From the tall stupa on a hill which overlooked the main town, to "the many-roofed *Pungyi Kyoung*" [Buddhist monastery] at its base, to local pagodas in the villages, a profusion of Buddhist monuments punctuated the landscape (Smyth 1898, 202). These were financed (like the *sala* enroute to Chanthaburi) as acts of devotion. Miners accumulated merit—and further good fortune in mining—by such acts, and by their contributions to a busy calendar of religious festivals (Brunet 1914, 7; Filleau 1920, 427).

Whether Pailin's distinct form of enlightened autocracy—of which more later—approximated the political structure of the Tai *müang* is debatable. Regarding agricultural practice, the Shan/Kola were far from existing on the wet rice cultivation of their forebears. They grew no rice at all, living instead in a cash economy where fresh produce was brought into the district by Khmer traders from the east, and imported items came up through Chanthaburi to the west. Beef, milk and bread—all European influences—were part of the miners' diet and readily available locally (Smyth 1898, 210). Imported luxuries remained popular as long as there was the chance of a good day's gem mining: "Sardines and tinned salmon seem rather favourites of the Shan miners when they can afford them" (Carlisle 1899). Their Siamese neighbors, including the Chanthaburi traders who carried whisky and English biscuits as well as the sardines up from the port town, were just as distant as the Pailin miners from the classic Tai upland polity.

The Shan miners appeared to have come a long way from their places of origin. To understand how the so-called Kola may have emerged at Pailin, it helps to look at ways in which anthropologists in the mid-twentieth century were rethinking how ethnic identities were produced. They turned on its head the formulation that people possessed distinctive traits because of their ethnic identity. Rather, it was the geographical, social, and political context that produced ethnicity. This was supported in Burma by evidence that "Shan" were not just those people who were born "Shan." People from surrounding hill tribes, if they came down and lived among the Shan, became "Shan" as they were accepted into these valley cultures (Scott 2009, 243).

A similar, if somewhat complicated, process of ethnicity production was at work in Pailin. Both Smyth in 1895 and Filleau twenty-five years later, insisted the Shan migrants and Shan culture were dominant at Pailin and that the Shan readily embraced the name Kola. The Shan did not like to be mistaken for the Burmese, Smyth noted. Filleau remarked that the Burmese seemed "to have little desire to be mistaken for Shan" (Smyth 1898, 181; Filleau 1920, 430). Yet, despite the importance for these two peoples to preserve some distinction between them, the neighboring peoples were liable to call all migrant miners Kola as long as they were in gem mining and had come from somewhere beyond to the east. And further to Filleau's declaration that "from the moment the Shan arrived in this region they were known as *Koula* (foreigners)," he went on at length to argue that becoming "Koula" was not just a local change in name but a deep-rooted transformation of identity: "At Pailin they had "lost from day to day the dominant traits of the primitive [Shan] race to become a special type in the region: the *Koula*" (Filleau 1920, 430–31).

Kola Modernity

The distinguishing trait of this "special type" was a remarkable sense of progress, modernity, and self-confidence. It was this modernity, and Pailin's particular political and socioeconomic conditions, which was producing Kola and not the other way around.

Pailin's vibrancy belied its isolated geography: "It is a surprise for all who visit Pailin," wrote Filleau, "to find themselves in a center they never imagined could be so bustling and lively, and larger in size than most agglomerations in Cambodia" (Filleau 1920, 427). It also ran counter to another important sociopolitical dynamic between the lowlands of mainland Southeast Asia and the peoples of the upland frontiers. Populations in the plains had long considered borderlands to be inhabited by less civilized peoples who had yet to be absorbed into the lowland state. This was an understanding readily assumed by European colonial administrators, reinforced in turn by the developing nineteenth-century anthropology of primitive peoples (see Keyes 2002).

Filleau was not the first to observe that these supposedly "primitive" *birmans de la montagne* (Burmese mountain people) were remarkably progressive. Accounts of Pailin from the 1890s already spoke of "order and neatness," "comfort and a certain luxury," which set it apart from "the squalor of southeast Indochina." The district boasted "a good road, equipped with bridges and comfortable *salas*," which connected Pailin's headquarters at Boyakar and the settlement of Bodineo five miles south (Black 1895; Smyth 1898, 201). Compared with the debauchery associated with mining encampments in the "civilized" world, the Shan gem-digging villages demonstrated an uncommon "mutual confidence and respect for order" (Smyth 1898, 201).

Fig. 1. Pailin Street Scene ca. 1900 (postcard).

By the 1910s the settlement at Bodineo had expanded and merged with smaller outlying villages to become Pailin town, an urban agglomeration divided into neat quarters (Filleau 1920, 437). Pailin's main street was lined with shops selling imported goods brought in from Siam. These included "many tins of an English firm's biscuits ... hats, shoes, umbrellas, cloths ... bottled beer and cheap brands of whisky and brandy" (Brunet 1914). In Bo Pohir, a quarter to the north, lapidaries sorted and polished stones. Beyond lay a village of Laotian diggers (ibid., 427).

More than any other, the quarter of Bo Laphok gave proof of the civility which characterized Pailin. In this residential neighborhood, gem dealers made their homes in wooden houses decorated with delicate carved lattices and surrounded by abundant rose gardens. Gem brokers were in the habit of rising late, but by mid-morning would be gathering over teacups in these gardens, negotiating purchases and discussing the value of one gem or another. Young women passed, selling flowers in the streets or carrying trays of offerings in procession to the pagodas (Lunet 1910, 417; Filleau 1920, 428).

Kola identity was by no means forged at the expense of long-standing cultural traditions. Pailin maintained and adapted a busy schedule of religious festivals. Its many pagodas were illuminated by petrol lamps for festivities that featured music, games, processions of offerings, and operas that went on long into the night. Siamese troupes were brought in from Chanthaburi or Bangkok to perform. Audiences gathered in the open air, talking over the actors at tables laid with "bad coffee with condensed milk, and Huntley & Palmers biscuits." Malabar merchants made a tidy profit selling stronger drinks, and gambling was a popular pastime at these events (Brunet 1914; Filleau 1920, 429).

Most astonishing of all, in Filleau's view, were the civilized manners of the Kola: "In everyday life, the Koula seeks to distinguish himself by the civility of his manners and his attitude.... His warm hospitality, the cleanliness of his abode, and above all his rapid grasp of things, his desire to enlighten and teach himself, render him an agreeable person" (Filleau 1920, 431).

These outward-looking attitudes, Filleau reckoned, were the result of continuous Kola contact with the outside world, of the journeys of its "tireless travelers, merchants and lapidaries." who "in the course of their stay in big cities such as Bangkok, Rangoon, Calcutta," had "come to govern and civilise themselves" (Filleau 1920, 431).

Kola advancement showed in the modern decoration of wealthy houses: "Burmese engravings compete with photographs of European and Asian sovereigns. Tables, chairs, and armchairs from Hong Kong make up the practical furnishings. Nothing is lacking for receiving the European." Even in the most modest houses, the highly literate Kola kept "bibles, copies of the laws of Manou, books edited in Burmese." Newspapers received from Rangoon, Mandalay, and Bangkok kept them up with current affairs (ibid.).

The desire to learn was also being bred into a new generation of Kola. Boys were sent to the pagoda as novices, where along with religious instruction they were taught the Burmese script. By 1915 there were three secular primary schools in Pailin, with provision for boys and girls. A few young Kola went on to further their studies in Bangkok or were sent away to schools in British Burma or India. Thus was Pailin producing further generations of "individuals accustomed to ideas of civilization and well-being in life" (ibid., 432).

Kola Autonomy

There is a sharp contrast between the admiration expressed by outside observers of Kola openness to the world and their often-scathing assessment of Pailin's local leaders. The privilege of the truly civilized, for those who mused on the virtues of civilization in the late nineteenth century, was the right to govern themselves. For the likes of Smyth (whose visit in the service of the Siamese Department of Mines was intended to resolve conflicts arising with the granting of rights to European concessionaires) and later Filleau (posted to the district to strengthen French military and administrative control over the area)—their praise of Pailin ended when it came to the mining districts' powerful leaders. This was so even though the order and civility they observed can only have been connected with the leaders who ran Pailin as a "state within a state." Pailin's population was not only organized, confident, and self-possessed, it was also heavily armed. Miners openly carried long sabers and rifles to protect themselves and protect their wealth.[10] This, and the amount of effective control that became concentrated in the hands of the Kola leaders, made them less a subject of ethnographic interest and more one of deep political concern.

The first of these Kola autocrats was a wealthy miner named Maung Keng. The foundation was laid for Kola autonomy, and for Maung Keng's rise to power, when the Siamese administration first extended the tax farms it had established in Battambang Province to Pailin in 1877, in line with Siam's arms-length governance of the culturally Khmer province under its occupation (Boulangier 1887, 255). In that year, tax collection for the mining region's several vices—gambling, alcohol, and opium consumption—were contracted out to a local Kola miner.[11] Shortly afterwards, the Siamese government sought to impose a more direct tax on mining, but this did not go well. The Kola objected to the presence of the Siamese official sent to reside at Pailin for this purpose; officials were just as resistant to living in a region they perceived as wild and unhealthy. When the last such cadre succumbed to fever in 1881, the prominent prospector Maung Keng was charged with collecting this mining tax (Smyth 1898, 206).[12]

When Maung Keng became collector for the mines, or Nai Phasi, he was already serving as headman for the British Consul in Bangkok.[13] In the latter role he liaised with the Consul to serve the interests of the many British subjects at the mines, to maintain records of this registered population, manage deceased estates, and settle minor disputes (ibid.). In 1884 Maung Keng gained control of the trio of tax farms at Pailin (gambling, alcohol, opium), and with this the most important local positions at Pailin were united in his hands (Filleau 1920, 436).

His reach did not stop there. Siam's granting, in 1889, of the first gemmining lease to a European investor looked to herald the end of Kola power. The mismanagement of this concession, though, produced the opposite effect. The concession was granted not at Pailin but at Navong, the earlier established and smaller Kola-run gem tract to the south. The Anglo-Italian company that secured the lease, Sapphires and Rubies Limited, came in heavy-handed. Its investors in distant London insisted all stones were "to be sold to the Company, whose expert would fix a value" (Black 1895). It then tried to enforce bodily searches on the miners. These measures deeply offended the fiercely independent Kola, the pioneers who, it should be stressed, had discovered the sources of precious stones in the first place. The result, as Black noted in 1895, was "unexpected and disastrous" (ibid.). A mass exodus ensued from Navong, and its population plummeted from 2,800 miners in 1889 to a few hundred in 1895 (Smyth 1898, 181).[14]

The Kola were not easily replaced. Few, if any local people had the desire, expertise, or constitution to work the gem mines. Sapphires and Rubies Limited was forced to give up its claim to preemptive purchase and its bodily searches. It reverted to a simple license fee per head, but the change came too late and the company collapsed in 1894 (Black 1895). In the same year, Siam leased rights over mining at Pailin to another British syndicate, Siam Exploring Company Limited. This company acted quickly to buy out the failed concession at Navong, thus securing rights over the Kola gem tracts on both sides of the Cardamom range.

It was at this juncture that Maung Keng further consolidated his power at Pailin. The Siam Exploring Company hoped to gain from the bitter experience of its predecessor and sought to manage the mines through a local sublessee. Maung Keng was the obvious choice. Predictably, perhaps, the arrangement was not without conflict. The company transferred Maung Keng's lease to a rival faction when he declared the raise in rent was impossible to pay, but he returned to successfully outbid this group at Navong and Pailin. His sway over the region and its "excitable parties of men all fully armed" was a deciding factor (Smyth 1898, 206–7, 212; Stringer 1898, 48).

Smyth met Maung Keng in 1895, by which time the "small, short man with the wrinkled face," as he described him, had earned a solid reputation as "an autocrat, who was practically *Sawbaw* of this far-away little Shan state" (Smyth 1898, 206).[15] The Siamese administration and the mining company between them had many complaints against him. The Siamese suspected him of routinely underreporting the number of registered miners at Pailin to reduce his burden of head tax, and of extorting far more from his tax farms than he was contracted to pay (Brien 1886, 40–41). He applied his own laws to administer justice, using his powers to enrich himself and his faction. Once he became the sublessee of the Siam Exploring Company, the Nai Phasi repeatedly demanded reductions in his rent, or refused outright to submit the full contracted sum. His leverage was the warning that the miners would desert if too heavily taxed, or the threat, more carefully veiled, that they might use their stock of arms to rebel (Moor 1900).

British consular officials were more willing than other observers to excuse Maung Keng's shortcomings and to credit him with the efficiency and order so evident at the mines. The consular headman's complaints of arbitrary Siamese taxes or illegal corvée were valuable opportunities to defend British treaty rights. Maung Keng, in turn, was a gracious host on their annual tours (Black 1895; Moor 1900; 1901). The British concessionaires' similar expectation of support from their Consul, however, had consular authorities treading carefully between conflicting interests.

Maung Keng was eventually unseated, not by his Siamese or European detractors but by the uncertainties of the gem trade and his internal rivals. Ruby prices were volatile as Pailin entered the twentieth century. They shot up briefly as India's princes prepared themselves for the Delhi Durbar of 1900, only to drop sharply with the advent of artificial gems shortly afterwards (Government of Indochina 1914, 138; Lunet 1910, 417). A 1901 poll tax created a labor shortage, as it prompted the Lao diggers to leave. The tax applied to Lao and Khmer but not—after intervention from their consul—to the Kola British subjects. Maung Keng was bankrupt by October of that year, and was forced to resign. The prime motive of the British consulate and the mining company, when they sought to reappoint a leader or leaders to the now vacant positions, was the maintenance of public order and local cooperation (Carlisle 1902).

In the event, and after some short-term shuffling, another strongman stepped forward, prominent Kola mine owner and prospector Maung Say. Initially, he captured the mining lease and tax farms (Carlisle 1909). He held on to his newfound positions when Battambang Province was returned to Cambodia under the 1907 Franco-Siamese Treaty, and the border was redrawn to include Pailin in the Cambodian kingdom under French protection. The European companies had done little more than to act as rent-seeking middlemen at the gem mines, all the while accusing Pailin's autocrats of the very same thing. French authorities nonetheless honored the Siamese government's contract with the Siam Exploring Company, and Maung Say's role as sublesee, for the few years remaining until the expiration of that contract (ibid.).

In January 1908 Maung Say completed his power play by securing the role of British consular headman. This came about following petitions to the British consulate from miners at Pailin denouncing the standing headman Muang

Chong Soo, whom vice-consul Tom Carlisle initially appointed to replace Maung Keng (ibid.). The appointment was now subject to French approval. Carlisle presented Maung Say as the preferred British choice in the interest of keeping the peace. The French delegate grumbled at what he saw as a "crafty" move to maintain British leverage in the newly French territory. It was just as characteristic, though, of how factions within Pailin made use of outside authorities to gain power over one another (Filleau 1914).

French delegates got off on a poor footing with Maung Say when, following a 1908 anti-French attack in Battambang, they accused the headman of harboring dacoits, and confiscated Kola guns and sabers (Carlisle 1909). Yet, with no better option, when the mining company's lease came to an end in 1910, they negotiated a direct contract with Maung Say, granting him the mining lease and the three tax farms until March 1915 (Resident Supérieur du Cambodge 1914).

French confidence that they would be able to treat Maung Say "like the head of a foreign congregation, as a simple intermediary between the Burmese [*sic*] of Pailin and the administration of the French Protectorate" was short-lived (Filleau 1914). Maung Say was no less trouble for the French than Maung Keng had been for the Siamese. He was soon "the absolute master of Pailin district." The delegate Filleau de Saint Hilaire would later ruminate more calmly on Kola civility, but in 1914 he was livid. Maung Say was "vain and self-important." He was slavishly obeyed "by the retinue of well-armed cavaliers that he treats, depending on the occasion, as a guard of honour or a police force." He was a small king, a *roitelet* of "the minor realm of Pailin, exerting his absolute authority in many ways, and receiving in return the veneration of all those under his protection." He had the respect and devotion of people who were "under his thumb or directly dependent upon him," who could "almost be considered his direct subjects." "He holds court in the sumptuous houses which he owns in Pailin; he hosts public festivities day and night to which he makes it a point of pride to invite everybody" (Filleau 1914).

Filleau continued: Maung Say ruled on legal affairs over which he had no jurisdiction, yet it was impossible for French law to reach anyone under his protection. He profited from tax extracted indiscriminately from Pailin's inhabitants while his close friends and family were never taxed. Neither were many of the Chinese traders doing business at Pailin, who bought Maung Say's protection and escaped their *patente* or trading tax (ibid.).

Like Mang Keng before him, Maung Say made repeated demands, difficult to ignore, for reductions in his rent. The French Resident's weary response expressed official French feelings: "Maung Say has given us nothing but grief since we appointed him the head of Pailin district" (Resident Supérieur 1911).

By 1911 French officials were looking for a way to replace the "special regime." Like the Siamese before them, they were chastened by the power Maung Say wielded and the armaments his miners possessed (200 rapid-fire pistols, they reckoned in 1911, in addition to hunting rifles and sabers) (Breucq 1911). They were maddened that they were being taken for fools, and even more maddened when they estimated Maung Say's actual earnings. Their contracts with him were pitched too low and the sums he earned far too high. Filleau asked baldly, "Why would we not put our hands on these [sums]?" (Filleau 1914).

The French Resident at Phnom Penh had suggested pitting Maung Say's rivals against him (Breucq 1911). When Maung Say was ousted—his contract was not renewed when it came due in 1915—his local rivals did indeed come to the fore. Yet, it is doubtful this was due to a successful French intervention in local politics. They seemed, as did the Siamese and the British, too out of their depth at Pailin for such a fine strategy. The French delegate declared nonetheless that Pailin would no longer remain "a Burmese [sic] enclave hostile to France." The conditions that enabled the autocrat's removal were worse now than in Maung Keng's time. The outbreak of World War I, which caused European demand for luxuries to plummet, generated a severe and long-lasting crisis that not only allowed Maung Say's ouster but signaled the end of the Kola heyday at Pailin.

Filleau's glowing 1920 article concluded with a statement that was manifestly false: "The *Koulas* ... have become loyal subjects of France, hoping with an active and sincere ardour for Her and her noble Allies the triumph of Law, Justice, Liberty and the annihilation of Modern Barbarians" (Filleau 1920, 419). The modern outlook of the Kola, as his article itself demonstrated, did not come to them as a virtue of French occupation. It existed long before that. There was little to show by 1920 that the Kola had suddenly become loyal subjects of France. Even the "Barbarian" leadership, Filleau's statement admitted, was modern in its own way. They were condemned ultimately not for their corruption or paternalism, but for holding on so resolutely to the principle of self-government.

In 1939 the Vietnamese nationalist newspaper *L'Echo Annamite* described Pailin as a region whose best days were behind it. The district population was down to 2,500 persons. A slight recovery in gem prices in the interwar years had not bolstered the region, nor had the 1931 tarmacking of the road to Battambang. Good stones were now rare. Some miners had gone back to Burma while others headed to northeastern Cambodia in search of zircons. Those who remained were returning to old pits in search of inferior stones, or digging where they had previously passed over, in private gardens or coconut plantations. Many mining families had begun for the first time to cultivate fruit trees to supplement their income. New restrictions on movement following

World War I strained their connections with Burma, including the Shan States, and they became a more closed community. What was left of Pailin's diminished mining economy, however, remained in Kola hands (*Echo Annamite* 1939; Blanadet 1970, 349).

National Integration

In November 1953, when Cambodia declared its independence from French rule, Pailin went from an embarrassment for French colonialists to a distant outpost of the nascent Cambodian nation. In the first decade of independence, other parts of the country were in a state of disruption, wracked by revolts of the Khmer Issarak and the Viet Minh. Pailin retained its reputation as a place whose fiercely independent and heavily armed inhabitants were a law unto themselves. Yet, relatively speaking, it was peaceful, and the mines experienced a revival as migrants sought refuge from the turbulence outside. The first migrants from the new Cambodia came spontaneously. The new Cambodian state, meanwhile, was occupied by more pressing matters and initially took little notice of Pailin, neglecting even to tax gem extraction in the first decade of Cambodia's independence (Blanadet 1970, 359).

Modern Cambodia came to know Pailin through one of the first novels published in the Khmer language. Thaëm Gnok's 1943 *The Rose of Pailin* presented the mining district to the new Cambodia as a romantic trope rather than a political problem. Armed bandits lay in wait on the road from Battambang, and anyone who reached the remote and dangerous place, unlike the hardy "Burmese," was liable to succumb to its legendary fevers. Yet, within the rose-filled gardens of the mining town, romance could bloom. The two main characters are both clearly Khmer, telling of the physical and sociocultural distance that still divided the Kola of the mining district from the Khmer of the plains (Thaëm 1943).

Many Khmer once knew long passages of *The Rose of Pailin* by heart, and it was a staple of the school curriculum right up until 1975. By then, however, Pailin had been integrated into the national whole in ways decidedly more real than romantic, and at the expense of long-standing Kola autonomy in the gem fields.

The Cambodian state mounted a half-hearted initiative in the 1960s to open the region to agricultural development. The real catalyst for Pailin's integration came not from Phnom Penh though, but from Rangoon. Burmese prime minister Ne Win's 1963 nationalization of the Mogok ruby mines in the northeastern Shan hills, sharply cut the supply of rubies on the world market.

The Pailin ruby tracts suddenly gained in importance as the price of these gems rose on the world market. This revived Kola fortunes, but also spurred increased interest in the region. Ethnic Cambodians (Khmer Krom) who had fled from southern Vietnam arrived, as did greater numbers of Khmer and Chinese entrepreneurs from other parts of Cambodia. Pailin's population nearly doubled, from barely 6,000 in 1964 to over 11,000 in 1967 (Blanadet 1970, 359). Its ethnic composition changed too; 60 percent of the population was now Khmer, and Chinese entrepreneurs were much more prominent in the urban center, which now boasted its own Chinatown (ibid.).

A practice dating back to the earliest gem rush allowed the first claimant on any mining tract to claim land and water rights over it. This custom was enshrined in French agreements with the miners when they took control of the region in 1907 (Filleau 1920, 435). It was viewed by prospectors as fair practice, even if occasional disputes arose. Long-established Kola had resolved problems of irregular rainfall by creating water courses to help with the washing of alluvial soils, and the ownership of water courses became a sound indicator of elite status (Blanadet 1970, 357).

French geographer Roger Blanadet studied Pailin's resources in 1966 and found the Shan/Kola owned only 10 percent of the land in Pailin but, unsurprisingly perhaps, up to half of all gem-yielding land. More importantly, Kola miners controlled virtually all access to the water vital for washing the gem-bearing gravel (ibid.). To newcomers this was perceived as foreign control of national land and water resources, and thus grossly unfair. Despite these disadvantages, Chinese entrepreneurs managed by the late 1960s to break the Kola monopoly. They did so by astutely balancing fruit cultivation, a new industry, with leasing of water rights. They also gained a foothold in the middleman trade with new Khmer miners who were hesitant to deal with the Kola. Finally, water rights lost their relevance as Kola elders succumbed to the pressure of the new situation and ceased to collect them. At the end of the 1960s, Blanadet concluded, the "old and opulent Burmese [sic] bourgeoisie has stepped back and is in the process of ceding to these young rival forces" (ibid., 359).

Pailin's Kola population in the late 1960s was far less mobile than it had been in the past. Habitual movements from Pailin across Siam to the Shan States and Burma prior to the outbreak of World War I came to a standstill. It is unclear whether this was a consequence of new routes for the marketing of gems, the end of Kola political interest in their place of origin, more regulated movement with the post-World War I introduction of the passport, or a combination of all these things. By 1966 Pailin's Kola were characterized as a community "definitively cut" from its place of origin, who were accepting their gradual assimilation into the national majority: "All have long since adopted Cambodian nationality; they speak Shan [among themselves] but all speak some Khmer and their children learn at the national schools they attend. They no longer practice endogamy and while fusion has only just begun it has definitely begun" (ibid.).

While the Kola slowly ceded power in Pailin, Lon Nol's government drafted a new mining law intended to capture more mining revenues for the state. The 1968 mining law was never to come into force, however, as the deep divisions becoming evident in Khmer society would come to change the course of the country's history (ibid., 366). Norodom Sihanouk (formerly king, and then prime minister) promoted education in the first years of Cambodia's independence, but it produced a growing number of qualified young people "who could not find jobs they considered to be good enough for them" (Kiernan 1972, 2–3; Osborne 1971, 40).[16] Visiting Pailin in late 1966, historian Milton Osborne found graduate "coolies" among those flocking to the mines in search of work: "As I passed one of the holes I found myself addressed in excellent French. The young man who spoke to me had received five years of secondary education ... there were others, he assured me who ... like him found the prospects for work elsewhere so limited that they had come to Pailin, where the work was hard but there was always the chance that a rich find of stones could bring temporary relief from poverty and hard physical labour. He was clearly a person who resented his low position and who found the domination of the Shans in Pailin ... particularly galling. It would have been bad enough if he were working for a Cambodian in these conditions but to suffer as a coolie for a foreigner, that was the final indignity" (Osborne 1979, 41).

Fig. 2. A new gem rush, 1974.

When thousands of frustrated villagers from Battambang Province revolted against government mistreatment and fled in late 1967 to the *maquis* of anti-government leftist revolutionaries, this educated but dissatisfied sector of the population was among them. Their discontent gave rise to the Samlaut Uprising of April 1967, a serious outbreak of violence which spread across the country and which for some historians marks the beginning of Cambodia's long civil war (Kiernan 1972, ii). The uprising did not reach Pailin, although it originated just 80 kilometers south of the mining settlements, in the same forested hill range. It was an early indicator of just how valuable this region and its resources would become in Cambodian politics in the next few decades.

The photographs of Colin Grafton, a Phnom Penh-based British teacher who visited Pailin in 1974, offer a compelling last glimpse of the fading Kola mining settlement before the country as a whole came under a drastic program of social reorganization. The Kola presence is visible in the distinctive delicate wooden architecture, which appears to have still been well-maintained. The new rush for gems, though, had grown to a torrent, as shown by the throngs of people panning for stones in the riverbed, overseen from the bank by forbidding characters sporting dark glasses and Hawaiian shirts. As Grafton writes, half of Pailin was now made up of shacks which housed "cafes and restaurants, bars and brothels.... People walked around with shirt breast pockets stuffed with banknotes. It was an expensive place. The prices were almost double those of Phnom Penh. There was a nightlife. Filipino bands played in the bars."[17]

The Kola and the Rule of Angkar

In 1974 the only safe means of reaching Pailin was by military helicopter as Communist Party supporters occupied the stretch of road to Battambang.[18] The Khmer Rouge or "Red Khmer," as they were dubbed by the outside world, had steadily gained hold of the countryside and would take Phnom Penh in April of the following year. Calling itself Angkar ("The Organisation") once it took power, the Khmer Rouge promptly began a mass evacuation from urban areas in a radical program aimed at transforming Cambodia into a classless agriculturalist society. In pursuit of this goal, up to two million people lost their lives, dying in the evacuation itself, through hardships endured by the collapse of the most basic structures of social and economic life, or at the hands of executioners as unwanted intellectuals, city residents, minority peoples, or traitors to the party (Khamboly 2007, 1–3).

Like so much of Cambodian history in this period, the story of what happened to the Kola is fragmented. One group of Kola fled to Thailand before the Khmer Rouge advance on Pailin. A resident monk claims they left at the urging of the head monk at Wat Phnom Yat (the main hill temple), who was prompted by a premonition: "If you go east, he said, you will be killed" (discussion at Wat Khaong Kang, September 2019). How many were in this group and where they ended up is not known.

Reports in the Thai press in 1975 claimed that Pailin's Khmer, Chinese, and Vietnamese populations were forcibly evacuated from the town on April 26, 1975. The Kola were also made to leave, but not until a week later (Kiernan 2002, 301). Within a few days of the Khmer Rouge arrival in Pailin, according to another account, the Kola people were relocated to different places in Battambang Province. Many of them were sent to the Bovel district north of Pailin, where they were expected to clear and farm new land. Some escaped to Thailand, but many would have been killed by the Khmer Rouge, or died due to starvation and overwork (email communication with Lor Then, December 2020).

A rare Kola testimony corroborates reports of forced Kola evacuation from Pailin to land-clearing sites north of Pailin. Me Khin Me, daughter of a Kola gem dealer and a Khmer mother, relates in first-hand testimony to the Documentation Centre of Cambodia that in early May 1975 the Khmer Rouge removed everyone from the mining villages. Her mother's (Khmer) relatives escaped to Battambang town. Her husband, another Kola gem dealer, stood his ground, believing the Khmer Rouge might let them stay. Threats at gunpoint soon convinced him otherwise, and Me Khin Me's family joined the exodus. Their belongings were confiscated and at several sites further north they were forced to clear land and cultivate rice. In the course of these stays, "Hundreds of families died. There I lost my three children, father, and husband. It was absolutely miserable. A lot of Kola died…. Aside from illness, many Kolas lost their lives to landmines or were gunned down by the Khmer Rouge while trying to escape to Thailand" (Sophal 2005, 19).

Me Khin Me's account raises questions about the extent to which her Kola identity contributed to the hardship she experienced. She maintains the Khmer Rouge "did not mistreat the Kola" because they "trusted the Kola's integrity." Yet, when they were kept together with other Kolas, she observes, life was more difficult. It became more bearable only when she was moved to a place whose residents were "all Khmer." Once warned that "speaking the Kola language" could have her killed, she switched to Khmer with her surviving children (ibid.).

Remarkably, Me Khin Me's is the only recorded testimony of Kola experience under the Khmer Rouge. There are still no statistics on how many Kola perished, nor are there numbers on the few known to have escaped to Thailand, some of whom went on to third countries (Kiernan 2002, 300–1; email with Sovicheth Meta, December 2020).

Khmer Rouge Refuge

In January 1979 Vietnamese troops and a united front of dissident Cambodians captured Phnom Penh and drove out the Khmer Rouge. When the capital fell, the core of Khmer Rouge leadership and thousands of Khmer Rouge fighters fled to the western border with Thailand. This area, including the Pailin plateau, became the site of drawn-out conflict between the forces of the newly installed government (and their Vietnamese backers) and the remaining Khmer Rouge. In its frontier refuge, the ousted regime continued to equip its fighters with support from Thai generals and a trade in gemstones and hardwood timber (Kiernan 2002, 442).

By October 1989, with the Vietnamese withdrawal from Cambodia, four of the highest-ranking Khmer Rouge leaders had established themselves at Pailin. They included Khieu Samphan, official head of state from 1976 to 1979 and the group's nominal leader in the 1980s; Nuon Chea, second-in-command to Pol Pot and the architect of much of the extremist ideology; Ieng Sary, Foreign Minister and "Brother Number Three"; and Ieng Thirith, Pol Pot's Social Affairs Minister, his sister-in-law, and Ieng Sary's wife (Gluck 1998; Kitigawa 2002, 110; BBC 2007; Fogarty 2008).[19]

As the guerrilla war ceased in the area, Ieng Sary became the new autocrat of Pailin. Over the next two years he leased gem-mining rights to multiple Thai companies. Their work was extraction in its most basic form. Miners hauled out the raw gravel, which was shipped away in heavy trucks. Only when it reached Thailand was it washed and sifted (Palm 2016).

Me Khin Me had no desire, nor any reason to return to Pailin once the conflict was over. "It would remind me of the tragic past." Her house and land were occupied by others (Sophal 2005, 20). Other Kola, however, remained in the Pailin area or returned there after 1979. One man of Kola origin, who still resides at Pailin, described working alongside other Kola in the early 1990s as hired labor for the Thai mining companies. Once the wholesale mining operations stripped out the gemstones from the area, around 1995, and after the defeat and final surrender of the Khmer Rouge in 1996, most of these remaining Kola miners left the country. He claimed they had returned to Burma, but he had not maintained contact with any of those who left (N., Pailin, September 2019).

The near cessation of gem mining at Pailin through the Angkar years, and the continued limit on the export of rubies from Ne Win's Burma, spurred an exponential increase in the value of rubies on the world market. By 1979 they were worth far more than diamonds (Kurtis 1981). Ieng Sary, along with his cohorts and lessees, amply profited from this rise. The ruby and sapphire tracts across the Thai side of the Cardamom Mountains, which had once been considered inferior to those at Pailin, also benefitted. The district of Bo Rai, in Trat Province, was gripped by a new gem fever which lasted from the 1960s through the 1990s. This was enhanced by its role as a gateway for smuggled Khmer Rouge gems (Keller 1982; Panu and Prapan 2017). A morning gem market at Bo Phloy, the district township, easily turned over 100 million baht in daily trade in the 1980s, and every trader carried a gun (S., attendant at Bo Rai gems museum, September 2019).[20] The economic depression that hit Bo Rai in the late 1990s was due not only to the exhaustion of the gem supply in the immediate vicinity, but from the surrender of the Khmer Rouge when the cross-border trafficking of supplies and gems came to an end (Panu and Prapan 2017).

Ieng Sary defected to Hun Sen's government in August 1996, along with thousands of former Khmer Rouge fighters. He was pardoned by the newly returned king and continued to live freely in Pailin, which became a special administrative zone, carved off from Battambang Province, under the authority of the former Khmer Rouge forces (Saing, 2014; Palm 2016). When the two other key leaders, Nuon Chea and Khieu Samphan, in turn defected to the Cambodian government in late 1998, they too returned to live freely in Pailin for the next decade (Gluck 1999).

It looked, then, like the former Khmer Rouge leaders had become the new generation of autocrats, ably capitalizing on Pailin's isolated position and valuable resources. In 2007, however, all four Pailin-based former Khmer Rouge leaders were arrested. In 2011 the three men were put on trial on multiple charges by a joint Cambodian-United Nations tribunal (Ieng Thirith was judged mentally unfit to stand trial). Ieng Sary died in 2013 with his trial ongoing; Ieng Thirith died in 2015 (Chandler 2013). Nuon Chea and Khieu Sampan were both convicted and imprisoned. Nuon Chea died in 2019, but Khieu Samphan remains in prison where it is expected he will live out his sentence (Chandler 2019).

Nowadays, the first sight on entering Pailin on the road from Battambang is the pagoda-topped hill, familiar from visitors' descriptions of over a century ago. At its base sits a massive concrete statue of a gray-haired woman wrapped in glittering cloth, with offerings at her feet. A leaflet provided by the nearby tourist bureau describes her as Yeay Yat, or Grandmother Yat, a legendary figure beloved of "villagers of the Cola tribe" who "lived in the Pailin area". This promotional literature claims, somewhat optimistically, that Pailin "has become a thriving tourist resort" (Cambodian Ministry of Tourism, 2019).

According to a plaque to one side of this giant figure, the statue was dedicated in 2011 by Y Chhien, Governor of Pailin Province and formerly Pol Pot's chief bodyguard (Saing 2014). The chief Khmer Rouge are now dead or behind bars but succeeding them is a power bloc of relatives and supporters in prominent provincial, and now central, positions. Ieng Vuth, son of Ieng Sary and Ieng Thirith, has long held the position of deputy governor of Pailin. Y Chhien governed Pailin for nearly two decades after Ieng Sary's 1998 defection (Chandler 2013). His wife Ban Sreymo assumed the post in December 2020; Y Chhien has since been made secretary of state at the Ministry of Defence (Sen 2020).

As for the Kola, in the wake of the Khmer Rouge upheaval very few now live there. We do not know how many were killed or survived and left permanently to other countries. The Kola overseas make their mark in the new Pailin, albeit in a way that goes virtually unnoticed to the present population. At Wat Khaong Kang, the monastery at the foot of the pagoda-topped hill, a covered corridor is painted with the names of Kola living in France, the US, Australia, and Canada, who return occasionally and make donations to the temples in the name of relatives who once lived there (discussion with head monks, Wat Pa Hy and Wat Khaong Kang, Pailin, September 2019). Whether they still consider themselves to be Kola is a hanging question.

Fig. 3. Pailin's "pagoda-topped hill" in 2019.

Those Kola who survived but remained in Cambodia express hesitation, as Me Khin Me has done, to return to a place which carries painful memories of the past and that no longer belongs to them (Sophal 2005; Lewis and Phorn 2015).

How many Kola remain in the country is no more than a wild guess; there are no more than five or six families with Kola forebears remaining in Pailin (Lewis and Phorn 2015; discussions in Pailin, September 2019). Whether these people continue to call themselves Kola is another hanging question. Living separated in different locations very likely strains the shared culture, values, relationships, occupations, and experiences that once shaped their group identity.

The implications of this sharp reduction in the Kola population within Cambodia, and their separation from one another, were evident in the ways in which the one Kola we met perceived of his identity. To him, the Kola were people who originated from Burma, from different peoples of Burma, but his ancestors came a long time ago and he did not know what group they belonged to. In his childhood he always spoke "Kola" because there were many Kola around; now he only very occasionally uses it when he meets one of the few remaining Kola. He felt proud of his Kola heritage he said, but then showed us his Cambodian identity card and emphasized that he is a Khmer national and a member of Khmer society. His name did not identify him as distinctly Kola. His children study in Khmer at school, and he sees little reason to speak to them in Kola. He was at pains to explain what "Kola language" was. Was it Burmese? Shan? Thai? An amalgam of all of these? He introduced his wife as "Khmer Rouge," adding a laugh which suggested there is much more to untangle (N., Pailin, September 2019).

Conclusion

The migrant miners at Pailin shaped a distinctive social, political, and occupational identity through succeeding generations, as outside authority shifted around the place in which they had settled. They carved out a solid place for themselves in the upland frontier gem tracts, so solid that the label "foreigner," or Kola, was a well-established identity by the 1920s. While Siamese, French, and British actors all vied to control them, they retained a remarkably high degree of autonomy.

Kola autonomy weakened in the newly independent Cambodia. Gradual assimilation with the incoming populations accompanied a loss of economic control over the mines. Then, in 1975, the Khmer Rouge stopped this process in its tracks. They displaced the Kola from Pailin and eliminated an unknown number of them. Khmer Rouge leaders went on to capitalize upon the very resources and geographical features that the Kola had used earlier to secure their own autonomy. Under the Khmer Rouge the Kola disappeared entirely as a distinct community. They are being curiously revived in the present day as an ethnic group, albeit in the absence of any sizeable or coherent grouping of Kola within the country.

It could be thought a welcome move that the Pailin tourist board acknowledges the "Cola tribe" as a people who used to inhabit the area and that Pailin's new leaders have taken the trouble to resurrect Grandmother Yat and her legend. Perhaps it is a way of laying aside the violence of the past and moving on. The current popularity of the "Pailin Peacock Dance" in the rest of the country might be understood in the same way. This dance, attributed to "the Kola ethnic group," is performed regularly by the Royal Khmer Ballet. It is included in the UNESCO inventory of intangible cultural heritage (UNESCO 2004).[21] At the Cambodian Cultural Village, a theme park at Siem Reap catering to tourists flocking to the nearby Angkor temple complex, an artificial "Kola village" headlines the same dance.[22] Yet, in contrast to the absences and ambiguities in Pailin itself, this kind of "moving on" looks like ethnicity used to smooth over and forget an uncomfortable history.

The Kola did not fit within the ethnographic assumptions that prevailed during their heyday at the gem tracts. They had come from Burma's borderlands and installed themselves at another hill frontier, but they were not an unchanging upland people. Instead, they kept abreast of the times and were determined, and sometimes difficult interlocutors in the region's politics and economy. The Kola case shows the value of studying the people of Southeast Asia's borderlands in political and historical terms, not just ethnographic ones. This chapter reveals but a small part of the Kola's rich history. It merely scratches the surface of Pailin's complex politics. As rich as some of the early outsider descriptions of the gem mines may be, they barely begin to gain a grasp of direct Kola experience. When the political projects and aspirations of Kola gem miners and their cohorts are examined and taken seriously, this plateau tucked into the Cardamom hills becomes much less marginal to the politics and economics of the region long before the Khmer Rouge made of it a last stronghold.

Endnote: Kola Identity at the Pailin Frontier Gem Mines

1. *Sala* were open platforms used to provide accommodation to passing travelers.

2. Various spellings are used in French and English language texts, including Gula, Cola, Coulah, and Koulah. I have used Kola in this text as it is the most commonly recognized spelling in the present day but have retained the original spelling when quoting sources.

3. The word Kola is also used in Vietnamese, but its meaning changed from the 1950s when *cù là* came to denote "medicated balm." This was due to an enterprising Kola migrant who established a medicinal balm empire in Cambodia and Vietnam in the 1950s and 1960s. See https://vi.wikipedia.org/wiki/Dầu_cù_là [accessed October 2022].

4. *Passoh* indicates a sarong or hip wrapper.

5. One curious feature of Pailin in the present day, still not fully understood, is that strains of malaria resistant to drugs have always appeared first in this region (Panu and Prapan 2017; McKie 2018).

6. See Keyes 2002 for a succinct overview of the historical development of European ethnology in mainland Southeast Asia. See also the Chapter "Ethnogenesis" in Scott 2009.

7. Their resistance to malaria was undoubtedly built up during their long stay in the malarial highlands. This would explain why they fell sick on first arrival and succumbed less frequently later on.

8. The Burmese "Shan" relates linguistically to "Sam," the term used in the Jinghpaw language of the Kachin to refer to the same people. It is also tied to Siam, the Siamese and the Tai-speaking Ahom or Assam on India's northeastern border with Burma. Other close cousins draw their names from the Tai of their language group: the Dai in China's Yunnan Province, the Tày and Thái of Vietnam, and the Thai of modern Thailand (Leach 1972, 29; Chit 2007, xxxix; Jumsai 1992, v).

9. It is difficult to gauge who was the better observer. Smyth spoke Siamese, likely to a high level, but was in Pailin for a few days only in 1895; Filleau had no Siamese but was posted for several years at Battambang (ca. 1911–19) and visited Pailin frequently.

10. See, for example, Boulangier 1887, 233–34. It is not clear whether the right to bear arms came as part of their recognition in Siam as British subjects.

11. Tax farmers were given the right to collect taxes from the public revenue in return for a fixed sum to government coffers. Southeast Asian states frequently used them as a means to extend their fiscal reach, but by the turn of the twentieth century they were being replaced by state bureaucracies which they had helped to finance. See Butcher and Dick 1993, 3.

12. This tax amounted to three *ticals* for an individual, and five for a head of household. Every person present in the district was subject to the tax regardless of whether they were involved in mining or other activities (Filleau 1920, 435–36).

13. Nai Phasi: its literal meaning (in Thai) is "tax collector." At Pailin it was understood to refer to the head of the mines in all his powers, and was later printed as a title on the leader's letterhead.

14. Nearby Bo Yaw, under the same lease, stood at a mere 54 in 1895, from 1,200–1,500 men when the company assumed management.

15. Sawbaw: the royal title for Tai/Shan rulers (lit. "lord of the sky"). Sawbaw was the accepted transcription in British Burma. It is now more frequently rendered as *saopha* with reference to Shan rulers. The Thai cognate is เจ้าฟ้า (*chao fa*).

16. Sihanouk took over the throne from his grandfather Monivong in 1941. He led Cambodia to independence in 1953, abdicating in favor of his father Suramarit in order to participate in politics. His party, Sangkhum, elected him prime minister following its 1955 election win. On Sihanouk's life, see Osborne 1994.

17. See https://colingrafton.wixsite.com/phnompenh1973/pailin-1974-2017 [accessed October 2022].

18. Yet, as in the days of Siamese and French control, Pailin continued to be better connected westwards. Grafton observed Thai traders and Thai baht moving freely into Pailin from Chanthaburi.

19. Ieng Thirith's sister was Khieu Ponnary, Pol Pot's first wife (*Cambodia News Daily*, 2019).

20. See also Bo Rai Gems Museum https://www.museumthailand.com/en/781/storytelling/Gem-Rush/ [accessed October 2020].

21. See https://intocambodia.org/content/robam-kngork-pailin-pailin-peacock-dance [accessed October 2022].

22. See https://en.wikipedia.org/wiki/Cambodian_Cultural_Village [accessed October 2022].

References

ANOM Archives Nationales Outre Mer, Aix en Provence, France
CNA Cambodian National Archives, Phnom Penh
IOR India Office Records, British Library London

Badens, Cdt. 1886. "Letter from Commandant Badens, Provisional Resident General of Cambodia, General Begin, Interim Governor of Indochina, 17 January". File Indo (Amiraux) GGI 12663 A.s. Des birmans enrôlés parmi les rebelles au Cambodge, ANOM.

BBC. 2007. "Senior Khmer Rouge Leader Charged." BBC News online, September 19.

Black, J. S. 1895. "Report on the Sapphire and Ruby Mines of Siam, 27 February 1895." File 491, L/PS/3/345, IOR.

Blanadet, Roger. 1970. "Pailin une region du Cambodge en voie de mutation." *Les Cahiers d'outre mer* 24: 353–78.

Boulangier, Edgar. 1887. *Un hiver au Cambodge: chasses au tigre, à l'éléphant et au buffle sauvage, souvenirs d'une mission officielle remplie en 1880-1881*. Tours: Alfred Mame et fils.

Brien, M. 1885. "Aperçu sur le Province de Battambang." *Excursions et Reconnaissances* 1(10): 341–56.

———. 1886. "Aperçu sur le Province de Battambang." *Excursions et Reconnaissances*, 2(11): 5–44.

Breucq, M. 1911. Civil Services Administrator Battambang to French Resident for Cambodia, 31 October. File GGI 2923 Concession anglaise de Pailin (Mines), ANOM.

Brunet, Lt. 1914. "Rapport sur la région de Pailin par le Lieutenant BRUNET, Commandant le poste de Thvéa-Amphil." File no. 5898, CNA.

Butcher, John, and Howard Dick, eds. 1993. *The Rise and Fall of Revenue Farming*. Houndsmills, Basingstoke: Macmillan.

Cambodia News Daily. 2019. "Khieu Ponnary, Wife of Pol Pot." May 3.

Cambodian Ministry of Tourism. 2019. "Pailin, Ruby City." Phnom Penh: Government Publishing.

Carlisle, T. 1899. "Mr. Carlisle to Mr. Greville." File no. 2057, L/PS/3/370, IOR.

———. 1902. "Report by Mr. Assistant Carlisle upon journey to Pailin District, 22 February." File IOR/L/PS/20/FO81/1, June 1903, IOR.

———. 1909. "Report on Affairs at the Pailin Mines, by Consul Carlisle." 28 April 1909. File no. 3398, L/PS/3/449, IOR.

Chandler, David P. 2013. "Ieng Sary Obituary." *Guardian*, March 14.

———. 2019. "Nuon Chea Obituary: Cambodian politician and member of the Khmer Rouge who was found guilty of genocide and crimes against humanity." *Guardian*, August 4.

Chit Hlaing, F. K. L. 2007. "Introduction: Notes on Edmund Leach's Analysis of Kachin Society and Its Further Applications." In *Social Dynamics in the Highlands of Southeast Asia, Reconsidering Political Systems of Highlands Burma by E.R. Leach*, eds. François Robinne and Mandy Sadan. Leiden: Brill.

Chonpairot, MingKwan, Souneth Phothisane, and Phra Sutdhisansophon. 2009. "Guideline for Conservation, Revitalization and Development of the Identity and Customs of the Kola Ethnic Group in Northeast Thailand." *The Social Sciences* 4(2): 167–73.

Echo Annamite. 1939. "Les resources Minières du Cambodge: le District de Pailin," May 23.

Filleau de Saint Hilaire, Gilbert. 1914. "Letter to Resident Supérieur de Cambodge," April 14, 1914. File no. 5896, "Dossier de l'affaire de Mang Sai de Pailin – contrat passé avec Mang Sai pour les divers fermages de Pailin," CNA.

———. 1920. "Le District Minier de Phailin." *Revue Indochinoise Illustré* vol. 56 (January): 417–48; vol. 7–8 (July): 28–55.

Fogarty, Philippa. 2008. "Tribunal Views from Khmer Rouge Town." BBC News online, June 9.

Gluck, Caroline, 1998/1999. "Row Over Khmer Rouge Defectors." BBC News online, December 27, 1998 and January 3, 1999.

Government of Indochina. 1914. "Orfèvrerie et Bijouterie – Joaillerie." *Bulletin Economique de l'Indochine* 107: 138.

Grafton, Colin, "Pailin 1974" and "Pailin 2017" [text and photographs]. https://colingrafton.wixsite.com/phnompenh1973/pailin-1974-2017 [accessed October 2022].

Hong Lysa. 2003. "Extraterritoriality in Bangkok in the Reign of King Chulalongkorn, 1868-1910: The Cacophonies of Semi-Colonial Cosmopolitanism." *Itinerario: European Journal of Overseas History* 27(2): 25–46.

Jumsai, Manich. 1992. "Foreword." In *The Dai or the Tai and their Architecture and Customs in South China* by Zhu Liangwen. Bangkok: DD Books.

Khamboly Dy. 2007. *A History of Democratic Kampuchea (1975–1979)*. Phnom Penh: Documentation Centre of Cambodia.

Keller, Peter C. 1982. "The Chanthaburi-Trat Gem Field, Thailand." *Gems and Gemmology* (Winter): 186–96.

Keyes, Charles F. 2002. "Presidential Address: 'The Peoples of Asia' – Science and Politics in the Classification of Ethnic Groups in Thailand, China, and Vietnam." *The Journal of Asian Studies* 61(4): 1163–1203.

Kiernan, Benedict. 1972. "The Samlaut Rebellion and Its Aftermath, 1967–1970: The Origins of Cambodia's Liberation Movement. Part I." Melbourne: Monash Centre of Southeast Asian Studies.

—————. 2002. *The Pol Pot Regime: Race, Power and Genocide in Cambodia under the Khmer Rouge, 1975–1979*. New Haven, CT: Yale University Press.

Kitigawa, Takako. 2009. "The Emergence of Pailin: The Land of Sapphires." *The Memoirs of the Toyo Bunko* 67: 109–27.

Koizumi, Junko. 1990. "Why the Kola Wept: A Report of the Trade Activities of the Kola in Isan at the end of the 19th Century." *Southeast Asian Studies*, Tokyo, 28: 2.

Kurtis, Bill. 1981. "A Worldwide Scramble for the Rarest Rubies." *New York Times*, November 8.

Leach, E. R. 1972 [1954]. *Political Systems of Highland Burma: A Study of Kachin Social Structure*. Boston: Beacon Press.

Lewis, Simon, and Phorn Bopha. 2015. "The Kola of Cambodia." *Irrawaddy Magazine*, January 9.

Lunet de La Jonquière, E. 1910. "De Saigon à Singapour, par Angkor, Autour du Golfe de Siam." *Le Tour du monde: nouveau journal des voyages* XVI(35): 409–20.

McKie, Robin. 2018. "The town that breeds resistance to malaria drugs." *The Observer*, April 8.

Moor, G. H. R. 1900. "Report by Mr. G. H. R. Moor." Enclosure 1 in No. 50, L/PS/20/FO80, IOR.

—————. 1901. "Report on the Annual District Court, held in the provinces of Chantaboon and Phailin." Enclosure in No. 45, L/PS/20/FO80, IOR.

Osborne, Milton. 1979. *Before Kampuchea: Preludes to Tragedy*. London: George Allen and Unwin.

—————. 1994. *Sihanouk Prince of Light, Prince of Darkness*. Honolulu: University of Hawai'i Press.

Palm, Anya. 2016. "The Khmer Rouge's Last Stronghold in Cambodia." *The Diplomat*, May 5.

Panu Wongcha-um and Prapan Chankaew. 2017. "Thailand battles drug-resistant malaria strains that imperil global campaign." Reuters online, December 15.

Pavie, Auguste. "Journal de Marche, 1883–84." Item 1, file 1, Pavie Papers 46 APC/1, ANOM.

Resident Supérieur du Cambodge. 1911. Telegram from French resident Cambodia to French delegate Battambang, 8 December. File no. 22, Concession minière de Pailin accordée au chef birman Mangsai 1911, CNA.

—————. 1914. Letter from French Resident in Cambodia to Governor General of Indochina, dated 23 November. File GGI 2923 Concession anglaise de Pailin (Mines), ANOM.

Saing Soenthrith. 2014. "Y Chhien to Be Replaced as Pailin Governor." *Cambodia Daily*, May 30.

Scott, James C. 2009. *The Art of Not Being Governed: An Anarchist History of Upland Southeast Asia*. New Haven, CT: Yale University Press.

Sen, David. 2020. "Ban Sreymom appointed as Pailin Province governor." *Khmer Times*, December 20.

Smyth, Herbert Warington. 1898. *Five Years in Siam from 1891 to 1896, Vol. II*. London: John Murray.

Sophal Ly. 2005. "Ma Khin Me: What is Angkar?" *Searching for the Truth (Special English Edition)*. Documentation Centre of Cambodia (DC-Cam), Third Quarter, 18–20.

Stringer, C. E. W. 1898. "Mr Stringer's Report on the Mines at Chantabun and Pailin." File 2096, L/PS/3/366 2096, IOR.

Thaëm Gnok 1995 [1943]. *La Rose de Pailin*, trans. Gerard Groussin. Paris: L'Harmattan.

UNESCO. 2004. *Inventory of Intangible Cultural Heritage of Cambodia: A Joint Publication of the Ministry of Culture and Fine Arts and UNESCO*. Cambodia: JSRC Printing House.

Wood, W. A. R. 2003 [1965]. *Consul in Paradise: Sixty-Eight Years in Siam*. Chiang Mai: Silkworm Books.

Tin Mining in Laos: Contested Resources, Labor Mobility, and Precarious Livelihoods

OLIVER TAPPE

In 1901, on his tour across Laos, the French explorer and prolific travel writer Alfred Raquez visited the tin mines in the valley of the river Nam Phathaen (Khammouane Province, central Laos). He noted the peculiar landscape surrounded by steep limestone outcrops, perforated by countless holes and tunnels. Those were the result of extensive mining activities by local Lao miners. Raquez provided detailed descriptions of artisanal mining practices along the Nam Phathaen and discussed the potential for industrial resource extraction with a French engineer who was struggling to establish modern mining facilities, given supply problems and labor shortage (Raquez 1902, 499–503).

More than a hundred years later, I traveled to the old tin-mining area where today more than 90 percent of the local villagers still engage in artisanal mining—next to large-scale mining operations (LSM) that are mainly run by Vietnamese and Chinese investors (Lahiri-Dutt et al. 2014; Earth Systems and BGR 2019). The parallels with Raquez's account were striking. The miners still use basic tools to dig out holes and shafts and produce ore while their wives and daughters wash the latter with simple pumps. This genuine family business of Lao artisanal and small-scale miners (ASM) often takes place in the direct vicinity of the roaring excavators of the big mining operations.

Tin mining in the Nam Phathaen valley of Khammouane Province is characterized by a precarious coexistence of ASM and LSM. It is the product of a long history of local peasant-miner livelihoods, the emergence of industrial mining under French colonial rule, and the more recent foreign investments in resource-rich Lao PDR by countries like China, Vietnam, and Thailand. Investigating local labor relations and livelihoods in this specific context of tin mining requires the combination of local perspectives with perspectives at the

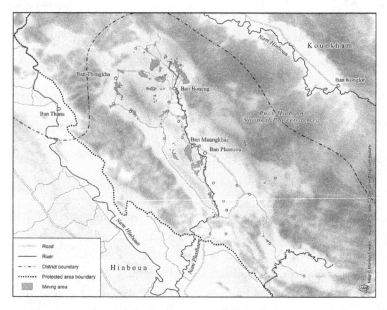

Map 1. Khammouane Province, Lao PDR.
Drawn by the cartographer Monika Feinen.

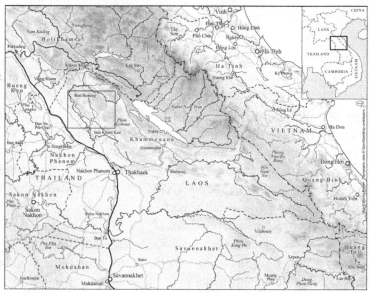

Map 2. Nam Phathaen Valley in Khammouane Province.
Drawn by the cartographer Monika Feinen.

macro level, such as the nation-state, regional and global economic dynamics, as well as historical depth.[1]

Lao Tin Mining in Regional Perspective

By taking global capitalism as a vantage point, and by mirroring present tendencies (for example, the Belt-and-Road-Initiative) with colonial economic dynamics, this study aims to reveal historical parallels with regard to contested natural resources and transregional dynamics of labor and migration. In the case of the tin mines of central Laos, French commercial interests certainly fostered rapid economic development and, in consequence, transformations of local lifeworlds through new socioeconomic configurations and labor mobilities.

This chapter also addresses questions of local identity within the broader context of regional economic integration exemplified, for instance, by generations of Vietnamese work migrants to Laos. A historical, transgenerational approach to the study of a small mining area in Laos contributes to understanding local agency and aspirations vis-à-vis contesting regional forces. Siam and French Indochina in the past, Thailand, Vietnam and China today—the frictions of such geopolitical macro contexts—arguably shape local livelihood strategies and identification processes over generations.

In the Nam Phathaen valley, located 60 kilometers from the provincial capital of Thakhaek, the proximity to the Thai border and a history of Vietnamese migration are two factors that affect local ASM settings. This chapter investigates tin mining from two perspectives: (1) a diachronic approach focusing on historical labor relations, including the significant Vietnamese worker migration which has shaped the labor-intensive sectors of the Lao economy until the present day; and (2) a synchronic approach which explores the current coexistence of ASM and LSM and the related tensions and contradictions at different scales (local, national, global). Shifting between multiple micro-macro perspectives is essential for this research.

This chapter combines historical and anthropological research methods in a *longue durée* perspective on labor relations and livelihoods over several generations. While research in the French colonial archives sheds light on the emergence of industrial labor and corresponding migration dynamics, anthropological field research in the mining communities addresses the question of how the precarious relationship between ASM and LSM shapes the everyday life of the local population. In both components of the project,

Vietnamese labor mobility is important with regard to geopolitical aspects, regional economic integration, demography, and local identity. One goal is to understand local and migrant workers' everyday experiences and their embeddedness in regional sociopolitical contexts, dependencies, and identification processes.

In the following, I trace the history of tin mining in Khammouane and investigate local lifeworlds in the past and present. In the first sections, I explore the history of the colonial *mise en valeur* of the Lao tin-mining area in the Nam Phathaen valley, with a particular focus on changing patterns of Vietnamese labor mobility. After that I discuss present tendencies and legal issues of ASM and LSM in the Nam Phathaen valley. Finally, I investigate the challenges of local ASM families, especially with regard to adjacent industrial mining activities and related environmental degradation.

Mining in Laos: An Overview

Mining is a key economic sector for GDP growth in Lao PDR, which is essentially resource-driven (Menon and Warr 2013; Mottet 2013). Gold reserves, for instance, attracted the attention of generations of entrepreneurs and venturers since colonial times. In the 1990s, the World Bank identified mining as fundamental for socioeconomic development and revenue generation. Until today, the mining sector generates important state revenues and attracts a large share of Foreign Direct Investment (FDI), especially from the economic regional powerhouses China, Thailand, and Vietnam.

The Lao Ministry of Energy and Mines estimates that there are more than 150 mineral deposits in the country, including gold, copper, tin, iron, bauxite, lignite, and potash. Besides the two big industrial copper and gold-mining areas in Sepon (Savannakhet Province) and Xaysomboun Province, a great number of smaller mining areas such as the Nam Phathaen valley punctuate the Lao uplands. In addition, an estimated 15 percent of the villages in Laos consider artisanal and small-scale mining as a component of their subsistence strategies (see Barney 2018; Keovilignavong 2019; Tappe 2021; 2022).

Tin Mining in Colonial Laos

Towards the end of the nineteenth century, French administrators noted the mining activities of Lao peasants in Khammouane and started exploring the alluvial tin reserves of the Nam Phathaen valley (for the case of the much larger tin reserves on the Malay Peninsula, see Ross 2014). In precolonial Laos, tin was an important tributary gift and tax, sent by local Lao rulers to the court of Bangkok (Grossin 1933, 64). It was used for the production of bronze statues and weights for fishing nets (Deloncle 1930, 113).

Lao villagers of the Nam Phathaen valley practiced artisanal tin mining for only two months during the dry season. Alfred Raquez (1902, 499–503) provided detailed descriptions. The villagers dug narrow vertical shafts in the ground, between 10 and 20 meters deep with a diameter of 80 to 150 centimeters. Then they dug out tunnels, extracted the ore, crushed it with stones, and washed it in wide bowls or coconut shells (techniques still used today, see below). Finally, the miners melted the mineral in small earthen ovens and made small nuggets out of them to sell in the Mekong towns or to give them to Chinese merchants in exchange for textiles, salt, dried fish, and sometimes rice in cases of local famine.

Raquez also noted a recent phenomenon, namely Vietnamese peddlers buying or trading tin and other local products—the vanguard of the numerous Vietnamese migrants who later dominated the economic sector in the Lao Mekong towns and became the main workforce. At the turn of the twentieth century, however, it was still difficult for the French engineers who explored the tin reserves to recruit sufficient labor in order to exploit the mines in a profitable way. After all, eight villages were involved in mining, with the men doing the digging and the females the washing of the minerals, a division of labor that we still find today. Yet, rice cultivation remained the main subsistence activity, and only land-poor villages demonstrated mentionable mineral extraction.[2]

In most upland regions of Laos, such as Attapeu or the surroundings of Luang Prabang, non-Lao ethnic groups whom the French called "Kha," practiced artisanal gold mining and traded the precious metal with lowland groups for salt, cloth, and other commodities (see, for example, Coussot 1898; Bernard 1990). In contrast, the peasant-miner communities in the Nam Phathaen valley were predominantly Lao. We can only speculate how they developed these specific livelihoods that contradict the stereotype of the Lao as pure wet rice farmer. One possibility is that local elite's demand for tin drove people to the valley. Arguably, Lao peasants were coerced to mine for a specific amount to pay tributes to local notables who, in turn, were vassals of Siamese rulers.

However, it was not an easy task for the French colonial administration to transform this kind of corvée labor into modern contract labor. What is more, the villages, if at all, did the mining only for two months, in November and December after the harvest season, which makes practical sense. Moreover, the fear of malevolent spirits in the rivers prevented mining during the rainy season (Raquez 1902, 503).[3] This is considered dangerous until the present day and the reason for diverse ritual activity (see below). However, colonial sources indicate that by the start of the boom years in the 1920s, local tin mining seemed to have proceeded as well—a "small indigenous industry," according to French observers.[4]

Indeed, labor scarcity was one of the biggest challenges for industrial mining in Laos. Lao peasants were reluctant to work for the French mines as wage labor throughout the year would collide with the necessities of agricultural production. Thus, French capitalists resorted to Vietnamese migrant labor, as will be discussed in more detail below. However, Lao were gradually employed by the French as well, not least because the expansion of the extractive industry in the fertile river basin increasingly affected local agricultural livelihoods.[5]

Industrialization in Europe and the United States, notably the automobile and railroad industries, created a high demand for tin. Tin was used for white alloy, solder, babbit, and bronze.[6] The 1920s witnessed a veritable tin boom and the emergence of a number of French enterprises in Khammouane. Inspired by the tin-mining industry in British Malaya, ambitious French entrepreneurs and metropolitan capital founded the Société des Études et Éxplorations des Mines de l'Indochine, the Société des Étains du Cammon, and the Société des Étains de l'Indochine, the latter two forming the Compagnie Fermière des Étains d'Extrême-Orient, in cooperation with the Société des Étains et Wolframs du Tonkin which had already successfully exploited the tin reserves in northern Tonkin. (For an insightful study of the French mining enterprises in Laos, see Mouscadet 2013.)

The colonial administration was busy with building infrastructures to assist the interests of the metropolitan capital (see Goscha 2012; Brocheux and Hémery 2009). Those conditions attracted a number of venturers, fueling rush and speculation and sparking the hopes of a "Klondike Indochinois and New Bolivia" in Laos (Deloncle 1930, 116; Gunn 1988). The global economic crisis resulted in the bubble's burst. The drop in prices was caused by the downturn of white alloy and the automobile industry in the US. Only larger companies like the Société des Études et Éxplorations des Mines de l'Indochine (SEEMI) continued operations.

The Nam Phathaen valley remained a key site of industrialization and an important source of revenue for the fledgling Lao nation-state after independence in 1953. French engineers remained in charge before Russians took over after the communist revolution of 1975 (Mouscadet 2013; Lahiri-Dutt et al. 2014). For many years, a Lao-North Korean joint venture continued to operate the old SEEMI mine of Phontiou before it was taken over by a Chinese mining enterprise (ibid.). Today, the ruins of an old Catholic church oversee some scattered old machines and wreckage.

Historical Patterns of Labor and Migration

The French mining enterprises employed thousands of Vietnamese workers, the so-called "coolies," from impoverished regions of coastal Vietnam. While labor demand on the rubber plantations in Cochinchina was met by thousands of contract workers from Tonkin (see Aso 2018), the Lao tin mines experienced a mix of local seasonal labor recruitment and a combination of state-organized and spontaneous labor migration from northern Annam. The local Lao peasantry preferred seasonal artisanal mining and by and large resisted all-year labor recruitment as already indicated above. However, the French managed to tap this limited workforce via the system of compulsory corvée labor as part of the colonial system of taxation (Gunn 1990, 47–52).

Vietnamese migration was not restricted to labor-intensive industry and construction, though. In the Mekong towns of Vientiane, Thakhaek, Savannakhet, and Pakse, the French employed Vietnamese for local administration and public works, followed by numerous Vietnamese (and Chinese) traders. As one report noted in 1928, 2,000 "coolies" crossed the mountains from Vinh to Khammouane, flanked by caravans of Vietnamese traders "squeezed like canned herring" (Monet 1930, 85–86) with their various goods. Missionary sources explicitly mentioned the two large "Annamite" communities in the tin mines of Phontiou and Bonaeng, and the Missions Étrangères took precautions to send Vietnamese-speaking priests to the Lao tin-mining area.[7]

Vietnamese migration resulted in massive demographic changes in the Mekong River towns like Thakhaek, where the Vietnamese constituted 85 percent of the urban population, the highest percentage of Vietnamese among all Lao towns (Pietrantoni 1957, 230; Goscha 2012). This was an effect desired by many French administrators who considered the allegedly more "industrious" Vietnamese "race" as key to the development of sparsely populated Laos (ibid.). An *arrêté* of 1935 even formalized the creation of Vietnamese villages in Laos (Gunn 1990, 49).

While the Vietnamese in the Lao towns created a small administrative and commercial elite, the Vietnamese "coolies" in the mines suffered from hard work and harsh living conditions (as their fellows did in the southern rubber plantations; Tappe 2016).[8] After the economic crisis, salary cuts aggravated their plight (Gunn 1988, 75). As many workers hailed from the Nghe Tinh region, early communist strongholds in Vietnam, the mines on the Nam Phathaen witnessed the first communist cells and organized labor movements in Laos (Gunn 1988, 36).

Thus, Vietnamese migration had been a key factor for social and political developments in central Laos. For the year 1932, Gunn (1990, 48) counted a workforce of 1,157 (down from 6,000 in 1929), 921 of them Vietnamese, 156 Lao. This ratio indicates Vietnamese dominance in the labor sector, but also the fact that at least seasonal work in the colonial mines had become a part of local Lao livelihoods, perhaps parallel to agriculture and fishing.

The economic crisis after 1929 (and later the refugee waves in 1946 and after 1975) led to a reduction of the Vietnamese element in Khammouane's society. The close connections to the Vietnamese coast and to the large Vietnamese community on the Thai Mekong bank remained a key factor for the sociopolitical and cultural dynamics in the region, though. Current tendencies for a new generation of Vietnamese workers to move into labor-intensive sectors of the Lao economy, and the complex cross-border trade networks between Vietnam, Laos, and Thailand, echo the economic entanglements of colonial Indochina. Today, numerous families in Thakhaek and the surrounding areas, including the Nam Phathaen valley, refer to a mixed Lao-Vietnamese origin. It is no coincidence that the Ho Chi Minh Memorial in Savannakhet further down the Mekong, opened in 2013, was constructed with financial support from the local Lao-Vietnamese community.

Tin Mining and Labor Relations Today

What historian Geoffrey Gunn (1990, 35) has identified as a "localized agromineral sphere" in colonial Laos can still be observed today. The historical vicissitudes of colonialism, socialism, and globalization in Laos notwithstanding, the Nam Phathaen valley (population approx. 12,000) displays a strong local peasant-miner identity (see Lahiri-Dutt 2014; Lahiri-Dutt et al. 2014). ASM in the Nam Phathaen valley includes mining with simple tools in abandoned mines or running concessions, as well as panning in the rivers. About 95 percent of the working-age population practice ASM, which accounts for an estimated 70 percent of household income. Local livelihoods are vulnerable to a vicious cycle of land degradation and other negative impacts of mining and also to an increased dependence on mining activities.

As already indicated, a large part of the Vietnamese community in Laos moved to Thailand after the communist revolution of 1975. Yet, the Vietnamese remain a prominent part of the population of Khammouane, especially in the urban center of Thakhaek. Today, they face new challenges. Still taking advantage of economic opportunities and long-standing ethnic networks that link the Vietnamese coast with the Lao and Thai cities along the Mekong River, they often live and work under precarious conditions. Lacking legal security in Laos, they depend on the goodwill of their employers and local authorities (Baird et al. 2019; Tappe 2019, 13–15). Working illegally on a 30-day tourist visa, they are used to crossing the bridge between Thakhaek (Laos) and Nakhon Phanom (Thailand) for monthly "visa runs," a practice now obstructed by Thai authorities. Thus, cases of visa overstay and corresponding insecurity are increasing among the Vietnamese migrant community.

In the mines, Vietnamese laborers earn less than the official minimum wage in Laos (1,200,000 Kip; 128 US$). Given the extreme poverty in some regions of Vietnam and the favorable exchange rate of the Vietnam Dong to the Lao Kip, working in Laos remains an attractive opportunity for impoverished and mobile parts of the Vietnamese population. Due to better roads and efficient communication networks cultivated by Lao-Vietnamese middlemen, seasonal work migration to Laos is convenient for both employers and employees. Therefore, a transregional perspective is key to understanding labor relations in mining and other labor-intensive economic sectors of past and present Laos.

While Vietnamese (and Chinese) companies apparently find it more efficient to recruit migrant labor, local Lao seem to prefer freelance artisanal mining to employment under a fixed contract. Low salaries and difficult working conditions make formal jobs in the mining sector less attractive, anyway. Since the job skills of the Lao miner-peasants are considered insufficient for better-paid jobs, such as engineer, the Lao rarely obtain regular work contracts. Accordingly, ASM miners lack even the little work security that Vietnamese formal workers have.

Unskilled workers earn hardly more than the minimum wage of 1.2 million Kip in the mines while skilled workers, such as excavator operators and mechanics, can earn up to 3 million Kip (320 US$). Regrettably, hardly any local Lao can get one of these well-paid jobs due to lack of skills and the preference of Chinese and Vietnamese companies for their countrymen. Unskilled labor is also often done by migrants because Lao artisanal miners can earn more than the minimum wage in ASM and dislike direct employment with long hours of hard work in the mines. Young Lao prefer to accept precarious working conditions in neighboring Thailand (as local people in Ban Muangkhai emphasized during my interviews in 2019).

More than 90 percent of the working population in the Nam Phathaen valley is active in freelance artisanal and small-scale mining, either in closed mines or operating concessions. Artisanal mining may generate more than 200 US$ per month depending on the amount of ore and its tin concentration. On bad days, it may be half of that and without the small benefits such as insurance which direct employment provides. Artisanal miners enter the pits without protective gear and other means of work security. Accidents occur very often but health risks are exempt from the equation when people talk about income opportunities (Interviews, February 2019; see also Earth Systems and BGR 2019). Another negative factor is the general legal insecurity as discussed in the next section.

Problems of Lao Mining Legislation

Tin mining in the Nam Phathaen valley is regulated by the Ministry of Energy and Mines, primarily through the Law on Minerals (2017). The Ministry is responsible for approvals and oversight of prospecting, exploration, mining, and closure. The Ministry of Natural Resources and Environment is responsible for approving Environmental and Social Impact Assessments, providing Environmental Compliance Certificates, and routine monitoring for compliance according to the Law on Environmental Protection throughout construction, operations, and closure (Earth Systems and BGR 2019).

The Ministry of Planning and Investment is arguably one of the most influential ministries in Lao PDR and enjoys considerable decision-making power with regard to foreign investment and the distribution of concessions. Poor communication is a major problem in Laos, as well as competition between ministries and different administrative levels of the respective ministries (national, provincial, district). What might appear neat and clear at the national level looks completely different at the district or village level (cf. Lu and Schönweger 2019; Keovilignavong 2019). This hints at a general problem in Lao PDR—a disjuncture between national and local planning processes as in the case of land governance and land use across scales (Suhardiman et al. 2019).

Amendments to the Law on Investment Promotion may even contradict regulations for environmental compliance and mining management. A recent advisory report (Earth Systems and BGR 2019) notes a lack of commitment to the enforcement of core legislation throughout the approval process, exploration, and mining from the responsible ministries and their provincial and district counterparts. Moreover, district and provincial authorities are highly dependent on financing from mine operations to conduct monitoring. Not surprisingly, only limited funding is provided. Obviously, local ASM communities are caught in the crossfire of competing and contradicting legal regulations on different and arguably disparate scales.

What exactly counts as ASM remains an ongoing debate. The Law on Minerals (2017) clearly distinguishes between artisanal mining and small-scale mining. While artisanal mining mainly means panning for alluvial gold and tin, a lowly mechanized and communal operation, small-scale mining includes digging and blasting mineral on an area below 10 hectares. Lao village communities or single households are entitled to obtain official permissions and legal rights to do small-scale mining. And yet, larger mining concessions granted to foreign companies are often superimposed on such communal rights (see Barney 2018; Keovilignavong 2019; Tappe 2021, 4–6; 2022).

The specificities of ASM in the Law on Minerals make it also difficult to legally reckon recent trends of mechanization and intensification in ASM and the rise of domestic and foreign small-to-medium-scale mining activities that escape such categorizations. Many mining operations in Laos outside the relatively well-monitored LSM, thus navigate in legally ambiguous waters. Increased mechanization, migration, and other unintended effects of mining development entail a variegated pattern of ASM, which poses considerable challenges for effective legislation and governance (Barney 2018, 354–55).

Many LSM concessions in the valley were granted before most of the aforementioned regulations were introduced. As a consequence, there is now a number of community - or family - run ASM operations on concession grounds of Chinese or Vietnamese mining enterprises. Although artisanal mining within a concession is de facto illegal, exploiting a concession without proper land titles is legally ambiguous as well. What looks orderly at the macro level of ministerial planning is more complex on the ground, the whole process yielding unexpected, contingent results depending on mining sites.

The interaction of artisanal miners and mining companies is certainly complex; it can be conflictual or mutually beneficial. While many mining enterprises tolerate ASM activities on concession grounds to take advantage of local informal labor or in recognition of local customary rights, others try to remove ASM from their concessions, largely unsuccessfully due to the many access points and after-hours mining (Earth Systems and BGR 2019). However, such concessions were sometimes granted without the required consultations at district or village level. According to the Law on Minerals, concessions granted without considering village boundaries or existing land titles are illegal. Thus, the companies also find themselves in a legal gray zone and are reluctant to provoke local resentment and unnecessary attention on higher levels.

Zooming between the macro level of contradictory national legislations and international investment politics and the implementation at the micro level thus reveals considerable tensions. According to local informants, one Chinese company was frustrated when it learned after the concession was granted that it overlapped with village land on which the local community held official legal mining rights (based on the Law on Minerals). After some negotiations with village and district authorities, they came to the agreement that villagers were allowed to practice ASM on concession grounds as long as they sell the ore at a fixed price to the company itself. They were also allowed to use the company's processing facilities.

Precarious Livelihoods of ASM Communities

For the villagers the situation is ambivalent because although they sometimes have some wiggle room to negotiate traditional mining rights, they still bear all the risks. In Ban Bonaeng, a tin-mining area since colonial times, a group of villagers, including women and children, used an old shaker table owned by a Chinese company to process ore. Protective gears (hard hats, ear protection, and security boots) were largely absent. For this informal workforce, the foreign mining companies deny any responsibility and thus operate outside Lao labor legislation.

Lao mining legislation largely ignores these aspects and offers only little protection. Companies can deny any responsibility for accidents that occur on their mining sites (for example, landslides). They are also not held accountable for pollution even if the law calls for sustainability and post-closure rehabilitation. These are so far hardly ever enforced. Increased LSM activities result in vast stretches of degraded land and reduced agricultural options. Therefore, villagers carry the risks of mining opportunities. They are often ignorant of laws that can protect them. Local communities suffer a lot from land degradation, pollution, noise, and other side effects of mining (Earth Systems and BGR 2019, 10–16).

Negative impacts on the environment and local land use include the destruction or pollution of arable land and water reserves. The absence of proper planning, controls, and rehabilitation in ASM and LSM tin-mining practices certainly contributes to local precariousness. Moreover, the fact that the local villagers have to buy fish, rice, and drinking water (unlike the average Lao village community) eats into their income. Finally, the uncontrolled use of chemicals in both ASM and LSM produces health risks (Barney 2018; Keovilignavong 2019; Tappe 2022).

People and landscape both bear the marks of a century of intensive mining in the Nam Phathaen valley that has had a profound impact on local livelihoods. The population of the valley demonstrates a specific miner-peasant identity that Kuntala Lahiri-Dutt aptly describes as "mining by peasants" even though some households in the valley do not cultivate the land at all—while still insisting on living from the resources of the valley's earth (Lahiri-Dutt 2014, 3). In this regard, it does not matter if the respective families are of Lao, Vietnamese, or mixed origin. They share the identity with the valley, their particular ASM livelihoods, and corresponding opportunity and precarity.

This local identity is marked by ritual practices that recall Raquez's descriptions of the rituals and taboos of artisanal miners. For example, village elders from Ban Muangkhai told me about the annual ritual offerings to the two spiritual sisters Nang Bo Kut and Nang Bo Dat who dwell in the river. These dangerous female *nang* (spirits), associated with the water, carry the word *bo* ("mine") in their names. Their agency is associated with water-induced hazards during the rainy season, such as flooding and landslides that can be fatal for miners. My interview partners in 2019 made it clear that ritual ignorance would result in more mining-related accidents. These aspects certainly deserve more thorough ethnographic research that would connect with seminal case studies in the anthropology of mining, such as June Nash's (1979) work on the Bolivian tin mines and related sociocosmological relations.

The spiritual domain adds to the complex mining assemblages that shape the Nam Phathaen valley, including diverse international and domestic political and entrepreneurial actors. Always integrated into larger political and economic contexts, from Siamese tributary systems and French colonial *mise en valeur* to socialist development aid by the Soviet Union, North Korea, China, and Vietnam, and not least the recent Belt-and-Road Initiative. Even if these macro tendencies shaped the landscape and its people (and spirits), local identification processes with the land and the specific peasant-miner livelihoods have shown a strong resilience over many generations.

Conclusion

The case of the Lao tin mines has demonstrated how local processes of socioeconomic change are embedded in regional dynamics of capitalist expansion and corresponding mobilities. From colonial times to the present, local communities as well as Vietnamese migrants experience changing regimes of resource exploitation and demonstrate adaptive strategies. Legal ambiguities and environmental degradation contribute to a general sense of precariousness, implying uncertainty and anxiety but also flexibility and adventurousness. Local identity is thus characterized by an ambivalent sense of place, both sustained and disrupted by mining activities. The preceding discussion has demonstrated how different macro levels, such as national legislation, transnational migration, and investment politics, and global economic dynamics affect generations of local artisanal and small-scale miners as well as work migrants in different ways.

By linking micro-macro and transgenerational perspectives of a century of industrial resource extraction on the mining communities in the Nam Phathaen valley (their labor relations, resource governance, and local livelihoods), their impact becomes clear. From colonial economic policies to present FDI flows, local communities in Laos have long witnessed the impact of global capitalism. The macro-perspective of a Lao "resource frontier" which is open to accumulation processes and exploitation, must be complemented with micro-studies that reveal the variegated outcomes of and obstacles to capitalist enclosure (see Barney 2009). While the French struggled with the difficult terrain and the shortage of labor, today Chinese investors complain about ambiguous legal frameworks and costly negotiations at district and village level.

Shifting between different analytic scales conveys an understanding of capitalist relations and market integration and resulting local economic and sociocultural transformations in past and present Laos. What happens at the national or global level has effects on the ground, while arguably local economic and political dynamics can also yield effects on larger scales. That said, this should not be understood as an argument for an academic division of labor between, for example, anthropological micro and the macro perspectives of political scientists. Rather, interdisciplinary exchange and collaboration is essential to bringing the research framework to fruition—together zooming in and out, aiming to understand local life worlds in the context of larger regional and global economic and political dynamics.

Endnotes: Tin Mining in Laos

1. This chapter is a revised version of my CRISEA WP5 Working Paper on Macro-Micro Dialogue Studies; http://crisea.eu/wp-content/uploads/2020/12/Del-5.3-Working-Paper-Macro-Micro-Dialogue-Studies.pdf (see as well Tappe 2022).
Research in Laos and in the French archives has been enabled through the generous support of CRISEA and the Small Grants Program of the German Association of Asian Studies.

2. Letter, 25 April 1898, Commissaire du Gouvernement (Cammon/Khammouane) à Monsieur l'Administrateur du Syndicat des Mines du Laos; Archives nationales d'outre-mer (Aix-en-Provence), ANOM RSL/E8.

3. This reminded me of a similar case from Houaphan Province in the far northeast of Laos. The Phong, an upland group from the Austroasiatic language family, also practiced iron mining for a very short time off-season, in fact only for nine consecutive days and with specific rituals to appease the spirits. During those days, the village was declared khalam, which means taboo, off-limits to strangers (Lagrèze 1925). Such ethnohistorical material offers interesting perspectives to investigate the link between mining and sociocosmological relations, also in diachronical comparative perspective (see Badenoch and Tappe 2021 for an ethnolinguistic and ethnohistorical study of the Phong of Houaphan).

4. Copie de l'Option sur les Mines d'étain de Pak-Hin-Boun (mars 1926); Archives nationales du monde du travail (Roubaix), Fonds Belugou 176 AQ 23.

5. "L'industrie minière en Indochine en 1927." Bulletin Économique de l'Indochine. 1928, 878.

6. Ibid., 869.

7. See, for example, Bulletin de la Société des Missions Étrangères de Paris, 1933, 311; 1935, 527.

8. As Robequain (1944, 260) observes in the 1940s: "Work is done by gangs and goes on continuously since the machines can only be stopped at great expense, at night this isolated basin surrounded by rugged mountains and dotted with electric lights which furnish illumination for the coolies as they work to the accompaniment of the mill's unrelenting rhythm, is a striking picture."

References

Aso, Michitake. 2018. *Rubber and the Making of Vietnam: An Ecological History, 1897–1975*. Chapel Hill: University of North Carolina Press.

Badenoch, Nathan, and Oliver Tappe. 2021. "Neither Kha, Tai, Nor Lao: Language, Myth, Histories, and the Position of the Phong in Houaphan." *Japan-ASEAN Transdisciplinary Studies Working Paper Series*, vol. 12. Center for Southeast Asian Studies (CSEAS), Kyoto University. https://doi.org/10.14989/TDWPS_12.

Baird, Ian G., William Noseworthy, Nghiem Phuong Tuyen, Le Thu Ha, and Jefferson Fox. 2019. "Land Grabs and Labor: Vietnamese Workers on Rubber Plantations in Southern Laos." *Singapore Journal of Tropical Geography* 40: 50–70.

Barney, Keith. 2009. "Laos and the Making of a 'Relational' Resource Frontier." *Geographical Journal* 175(2): 146–59.

——————. 2018. "Reassembling Informal Gold-mining for Development and Sustainability? Opportunities and Limits to Formalisation in India, Indonesia and Laos." In *Between the Plough and the Pick: Informal, Artisanal and Small-scale Mining in the Contemporary World*, ed. Kuntala Lahiri-Dutt, 335–70. Canberra: ANU Press.

Bernard, Auguste. 1990. Les gisements miniers du Laos. *Péninsule* 20: 1–98.

Brocheux, Pierre, and Daniel Hémery. 2009. *Indochina: An Ambiguous Colonization, 1858–1954*. Berkeley, CA: University of California Press.

Coussot, Alfred. 1898. *Douze mois chez les sauvages du Laos*. Paris: Challamel.

Delamarre, Émile. 1931. *L'émigration et l'immigration ouvrière en Indochine*. Hanoï: Imprimerie d'Extrême-Orient.

Deloncle, Pierre. [1930] 2011. "The Development of Laos." In *Laos in the 1920s: The Gods, Monks and Mountains of Laos* by J. Renaud, 103–21. Bangkok: White Lotus.

Earth Systems and BGR 2019. *Impacts of Tin Mining in the Hinboun District, Lao PDR*. Vientiane: Ministry of Energy and Mines.

Goscha, Christopher E. 2012. *Going Indochinese: Contesting Concepts of Space and Place in French Indochina*. Copenhagen: NIAS Press.

Grossin, Pierre. 1933. *Notes sur l'histoire de la Province de Cammon.* Hanoï: Imprimerie d'Extrême-Orient.

Gunn, Geoffrey C. 1988. *Political Struggles in Laos (1930–1954): Vietnamese Communist Power and the Lao Struggle for National Independence.* Bangkok: Editions Duang Kamol.

——————. 1990. *Rebellion in Laos: Peasant and Politics in a Colonial Backwater.* Bangkok: White Lotus.

Keovilignavong, Oulavanh. 2019. "Mining Governance Dilemma and Impacts: A Case of Gold Mining in Phu-Hae, Lao PDR." *Resources Policy* 61: 141–50.

Lagrèze, Antoine. 1925. *Dictionnaire Kha Pong.* Files of the Résidence Supérieur du Laos, Archives nationales d'outre-mer, Aix-en-Provence; ANOM RSL/Z.

Lahiri-Dutt, Kuntala. 2014. "Extracting Peasants from the Fields: Rushing for a Livelihood?" *ARI Working Paper Series* no. 216. Asia Research Institute, National University of Singapore.

Lahiri-Dutt, K., Kim Alexander, and Chansouk Insouvanh. 2014. "Informal Mining in Livelihood Diversification: Mineral Dependence and Rural Communities in Lao PDR." *South East Asia Research* 22(1): 103–22.

Lu, Juliet, and Oliver Schönweger. 2019. "Great Expectations: Chinese Investment in Laos and the Myth of Empty Land." *Territory, Politics, Governance* 7(1): 61–78.

Menon, Jayant, and Peter Warr. 2013. *The Lao Economy: Capitalizing on Natural Resource Exports.* ADB Economics Working Paper Series No. 330. https://www.adb.org/sites/default/files/publication/30138/economics-wp330-lao-economy.pdf.

Monet, Paul. 1930. *Les Jauniers.* Paris: Gallimard.

Mottet, Éric. 2013. Au Laos, la nouvelle aventure minière pourra-t-elle se dérouler sans conflits? *Les Cahiers d'Outre-Mer* 262: 217–46.

Mouscadet, Marc. 2013. L'exploitation des resources du sous-sol au Laos à l'époque coloniale de 1893 à 1940. Mémoire, Paris: Inalco.

Nash, June 1979. *We Eat the Mines and the Mines Eat Us: Dependency and Exploitation in Bolivian Tin Mines.* New York: Columbia University Press.

Pietrantoni, Eric. 1957. "La population du Laos en 1943 dans son milieu géographique." *Bulletin de la Société des Etudes Indochinoises* 32: 223–43.

Raquez, Alfred. 1902. *Pages laotiennes.* Hanoi: F.H. Schneider.

Robequain, Charles. 1944. *The Economic Development of French Indo-China.* London: Oxford University Press.

Ross, Corey. 2014. "The Tin Frontier: Mining, Empire, and Environment in Southeast Asia, 1870s–1930s." *Environmental History* 19: 454–79.

Suhardiman, Diana, Oulavanh Keovilignavong, and Miles Kenney-Lazar. 2019. "The Territorial Politics of Land Use Planning in Laos." *Land Use Policy* 83: 346–56.

Tappe, Oliver. 2016. "Variants of Bonded Labour in Precolonial and Colonial Southeast Asia." In *Bonded Labour: Global and Comparative Perspectives (18th–21st Century)*, eds. Sabine Damir-Geilsdorf, Ulrike Lindner, Gesine Müller, Oliver Tappe, and Michael Zeuske, 103–31. Bielefeld: transcript.

——————. 2019. "Patterns of Precarity: Historical Trajectories of Vietnamese Labour Mobility." *TRaNS: Trans-Regional and -National Studies of Southeast Asia* 7(1): 19–42.

——————. 2021. "Artisanal, Small-scale and Large-scale Mining in Lao PDR." *ISEAS Perspective*, 2021/44. https://www.iseas.edu.sg/articles-commentaries/iseas-perspective/2021-44-artisanal-small-scale-and-large-scale-mining-in-lao-pdr-by-oliver-tappe/.

——————. 2022. "Frontier Capitalism in Colonial and Contemporary Laos: The Case of Tin Mining." In *Extracting Development: Contested Resource Frontiers in Mainland Southeast Asia* by Oliver Tappe and Simon Rowedder, 172–96. Singapore: ISEAS Publishing.

TRANSNATIONALISM

Transnational Indigenism in Southeast Asia

PRASIT LEEPREECHA

The movement of indigenous peoples in Asia especially in South, East, and Southeast Asia, has become a prominent and powerful phenomenon over the past few decades. On a global level, indigeneity—the fact of originating or living in a particular place—has been used by marginalized peoples as justification for claiming and accessing basic rights. The origin of indigeneity may be found in colonized countries where European settlers permanently settled and gradually dominated indigenous or native peoples, particularly on the North American, Latin American, and Australian continents. Unlike many settler colonies in the West, native peoples in many former colonized countries and non-colonized countries are no longer dominated by recent settlers but are still being internally colonized by the present national governments (see Abeysekara 2011; Enloe 1977; Evans 1992; Prasit and Mukdawan 2021; Tan 2020; and Thongchai 2000). This has resulted in various native and ethnic groups identifying themselves as indigenous peoples and joining the international movement of indigeneity. In recent years, indigenism has become not only a common ideological consciousness but also a transnational movement in Southeast Asia, operating at different levels of networking. Considering this, my basic questions concern why indigenism is popular among various ethnic groups in Southeast Asia, what it stems from, and how it is being used to connect with indigenous peoples' movements in other parts of the world. It is my belief that self-identifying as indigenous peoples, among marginalized ethnic groups in Southeast Asia, enhances the opportunity for power negotiation with national government and relevant agencies, and for international cooperation with concerning human rights claims. To understand these issues, we need to trace the historical development of indigeneity in former settler colonies and the influence of its achievements on the indigenous movements in Southeast Asia. Particular attention needs to be paid to the limited scope for participation of ethnic minority and marginalized groups in both the national and ASEAN arenas. Within the framework of the Southeast Asian region, the concept of transnationalism will be employed in my analytical framework.

The creation of modern nation-states in Southeast Asia emerged at the beginning of colonialism in the region, from the 1780s to the 1890s. Prior to this, the political and government systems in the region were known as tributary states, mandala systems, galactic polities, or candle states. There were also no clear geographical boundaries between states or kingdoms. Instead, there were overlapping power boundaries and multiple sovereignties of premodern states in Southeast Asia. The creation of the "geo-body," to use Thongchai Winichakul's term (1994, 129), of each modern state was based on modern cartography brought to the region by European experts. Borderline demarcation and agreement signing established clear boundaries with neighboring states. Thus, people living near a state's borders, regardless of their ethnic backgrounds, became subjects of the state. The central government was entirely controlled by either the colonial ruler or the leader who mainly represented the mainstream group in the state, while other minority and marginalized groups became ethnic groups in the modern state. In the case of former non-settler colonies in Southeast Asia, government leaders in the postcolonial period, after World War II, also came from major groups.

Throughout the region, nation-building mainly favors the identities of the mainstream group rather than equal participation and representation of diverse ethnic groups. Whether states adopt segregation or assimilation policies, ethnic peoples have been marginalized as a result, their basic rights treated differently. Even in countries that have adopted assimilative ideologies like Thailand, the successful assimilation of ethnic peoples into mainstream society has resulted in the loss of their ethnic identity. For instance, the longer ethnic students are enrolled in compulsory school, the less they are able and willing to speak their own ethnic or local languages. For states that have adopted multicultural policies like Singapore, unequal treatment may still be found but to a lesser degree. Indeed, development projects of states toward ethnic peoples often contain a hidden agenda of domestication and assimilation. Subsequently, struggles of ethnic groups for more equal rights occur on various occasions and in various forms. Some groups may use soft approaches to negotiate with state governments, while others may take up arms to fight against state forces. Previously, each group or community would normally react to state forces alone. But in the post-Cold War era and the age of globalization since the 1990s, interethnic and transnational cooperation has taken place among marginalized ethnic groups in Southeast Asian countries. Links have also been made between international movements and the achievements of indigenous peoples in Western colonized countries. Such common indigeneity movements and ideologies have been termed "indigenism" (Niezen 2003).

Unlike ethnonationalism, indigenism, as stated by Ronald Niezen (ibid., 9), "is not a particularized identity but a global one that acts almost the same way as ethnic particularism." Ethnonationalism is an ideology that centers on a single ethnic group, with distinction from others, while indigenism "identifies a boundary of membership and experience that can be crossed only by birth or hard-won international recognition. It links local, primordial sentiments to universal category." Essentially, he points out that "the indigenous peoples' movement has arisen out of the shared experiences of marginalized groups facing the negative impacts of resource extraction and economic modernization and the social convergence and homogenization that these ambitions tend to bring about." Indigenism exists on both practical and ideological levels. For the latter, according to Niezen, "With little public awareness, and with the obvious terminology ("indigenism") little used up to this point, an international movement has led to the creation of an important new "ism" (ibid.). One of the distinguishing marks of this movement is the extent to which, unlike ethnonationalism, it is grounded in international networks. To reiterate, indigenism is a transnational ideology shared by groups of people of different backgrounds who intend to claim indigeneity worldwide, although they exist in distinct contexts.

The concept of transnationalism describes a situation in which nations and communications are connected, regardless of the geographical distances that separate people, typically by new communication technologies that facilitate flows and networks of people, goods, and services (Turner 2008, 433). According to Steven Vertovec (2009, 3), transnationalism refers to "sustained linkages and ongoing exchanges among non-state actors based across national borders—business, non-government organizations, and individuals sharing the same interests." The collective attributes of such connections, their processes of formation and maintenance, and their wider implications are referred to broadly as transnationalism.

Occasionally, transnationalism is associated with the notions of "network society" (Castells 2000) and international mobility (Urry 2000). One such process is "the emergence of cross-national political and institutional networks that deploy the discourses of decolonization, human rights, and other universalistic tropes to advance the interests of heretofore marginalized groups" (Smith 2003, 19). In the case of indigenous peoples in Southeast Asia, they have adopted the transnational ideology of indigenism in their responses to modern nation-state domination.

Worldwide Emergence of Indigeneity

The movement of indigenous peoples emerged following the recognition of universal human rights and the foundation of international institutions. Initially, the rise of indigeneity derived from the relations between indigenous peoples and colonial powers in the colonized continents on which European settlers have permanently settled and later exerted dominant power over the native peoples. In the non-colonized context and postcolonial era, it can be argued that the indigeneity movement has arisen because of the internal colonialism of the modern nation-state that marginalizes minority groups. In the case of Southeast Asian, indigenous identification and movements have been influenced by such movements in Western colonized countries that have been recognized by international institutions and laws in the context of globalization.

Initiatives of indigenous movements that attracted international attention began in Canada following the end of World War I. Various groups of native peoples had inhabited Canada for more than 12,000 years before European settlers immigrated into the area in the early fifteenth century. These settlers, mainly British and French, gradually occupied the territories and lands of native peoples and dominated them economically, politically, culturally, and socially. Although grievances against colonial and state domination had been growing among native peoples in Canada for a long time, their petition reached international institutions only with the foundation of the League of Nations after World War I, based on "President Wilson's promise of self-determination for nations and the rights of minorities to protection" (Niezen 2003, 31). This is also why native peoples in Canada identify themselves as "first nations," "native," or "indigenous" peoples. Among the Six Nations of the Grand River Land near Brandford, Ontario, Levi General Deskaheh, chief of the Younger Bear Clan of the Cayuga Nation, became the representative for lobbying at the League of Nations in Geneva in 1923–24. Unfortunately, he passed away in the United States several months after leaving Geneva. Although the dispute with Canada over indigenous rights had not been resolved, Deskaheh's effort was heard by the international organization (Niezen 2003, 36). However, the League of Nations did not act on indigenous issues up until the late 1930s and the start of World War II.

A new wave of indigenous movements caught the attention of international organizations after the founding of the United Nations in 1945 and its agencies within the framework of human rights. Racism, discrimination, and fascism during World War II were major concerns for the United Nations, led by the United States. Besides the dismantling of European colonies in other parts of the world, the domination by colonial and postcolonial governments over native peoples was also determined to be a human rights violation based on the Universal Declaration of Human Rights adopted in 1948. Two additional instruments of human rights, the International Covenant on Economic, Social and Cultural Rights and the International Covenant on Civil and Political Rights, were adopted by the United Nations in 1966. These instruments formed the basis for self-determination on the rights of indigenous peoples in those postcolonial countries where they were still dominated and assimilated by mainstream European settlers and new state governments. According to Niezen (2003, 42), among the civil rights movements in the United States in the 1960s were "pan-Indian" or "pan-indigenous" groups. In 1974 and 1975, the first international indigenous organizations—the International Indian Treaty Council and the World Council of Indigenous Peoples (WCIP)—were founded in the US and Canada. The latter was the initiative of George Manuel of the National Indian Brotherhood of Canada in response to the Trudeau government's promulgation of a White Paper proposing the elimination of Indian status and repeal of the Indian Act (first passed in 1876 and later amended) (Perry 1996, 150).

In addition to those in Canada and North America, indigenous peoples in Australia and Latin America played crucial roles in transnational indigeneity. The situation in Australia was quite similar to that in North America, where European settlers had settled permanently, occupied the land, and gradually dominated indigenous peoples in various ways. In the 1780s, the first British settlement was established in Sydney by Captain Arthur Phillip. Later, Australia became a British penal colony mostly inhabited by prisoners. Eventually, however, settlers included not only convicts but also people who sought new economic opportunities, especially during the gold rush. Before the settlement of Europeans, the native peoples or Aborigines had been living in different localities for tens of thousands of years. The invasion of European settlers not only led to widespread violence and land-grabbing but also the unintentional spread of new diseases among the Aborigines. Like the experience of Canada and the United States, European settlers in Australia also carried out cultural genocide against Aborigines in the form of acts aimed at assimilation. Boarding schools and missionary work were the prominent mechanisms for weakening Aboriginal cultures.

Civil movements among Aborigines in response to colonization occurred in different forms. As reviewed by Francesca Merlan (2005), from pre-World War II to the 1960s, protests existed in the form of ritual action, such as messianic cults, rather than practical action targeted at the invaders. However, progressive indigenous activism had been operating since the turn of the twentieth century. The Native Union in Western Australia and the Australian Aborigines' League (AAL) were founded in 1926 and 1932, respectively (Clark 1965, 91; Haebich 1992, 269). In 1958, the Federal Council of the Advancement of Aborigines together with the Aboriginal Advancement Leagues of Victoria, South Australia, and Western Australia were formed with the basic task of promoting equal citizenship for Aborigines. In this way, the federal government set up a clear mandate on Aboriginal affairs and the self-determination of Aborigines in the late 1960s to early 1970s. Yet, land rights issues were raised by Aborigines against mining and land-grabbing in the same period. In response, both local and national governments initiated the Aboriginal Land Rights Act in the 1960s to 1980s.

In Latin America, indigenous peoples were exploited in both colonial and postcolonial times despite every country gaining independence after World War II. However, indigenous peoples continue to face troubles concerning environmental degradation and the intrusion of the national government in terms of economic, political, and social domination. According to Guillermo de la Pena (2005), prominent indigenous peoples' movements in Latin America have existed since the 1970s. The term "indigenismo" or indigenous people was adopted to refer to people who lived outside the "civilized" nation, in the old communities and in the wild frontier, to replace words like "Indians" and "tribes" (Pena 2005, 721). The movement for self-identification and determination, according to Pena, was also influenced by the globalization of neoliberal indigenism, a movement through which indigenous people are "not claiming political independence or artificial isolation but are demanding an inclusive definition of the nation where the right to cultural diversity is an essential aspect of citizenship" (ibid., 732–33).

The Asia Indigenous Peoples Pact (AIPP) (2014) stated that "two-thirds of the approximate 370 million self-identified indigenous peoples are in Asia, enriching the region's enormous cultural and linguistic diversity." AIPP also pointed out that governments refer to indigenous peoples collectively as ethnic minorities, hill tribes, tribal people, and highland people. Those terms have negative connotations of primitiveness or backwardness and inferiority (ibid., 1). Both colonial and postcolonial governments played crucial roles in the creation of "otherness" and marginalization towards them (Thongchai 2000). Their land and other natural resources have been strictly controlled and occupied by state governments and outsiders. They have less access to basic services and are subject to assimilation to the national culture by long-term government development projects. Similar impacts to those experienced on the abovementioned continents cause marginalized peoples in Asia to define themselves as "indigenous peoples" and join the international movement of indigeneity.

Civil movements for indigeneity in Asia, mainly in East Asia, South Asia, and Southeast Asia, have been present for decades. Previous studies on indigeneity in Asia focused primarily on case-by-case issues, country by country (Baird 2016; Dunford 2019; Prasit 2019, Morton and Baird 2019; and Theriault 2019), compared with this study that looks at the Southeast Asia regional movement of indigenous peoples. I would argue that the transnational movement of indigenous peoples in Southeast Asia empowers the marginalized native peoples at national, regional, and global levels.

Transnational Indigenism in Southeast Asia

The existence of transnational indigenism in Southeast Asia only began in the early 1990s, in contrast to indigenism in Western countries that gained momentum after World War I and went on to attract international attention after World War II. Given this slow start, I set out to discover why ethnic groups in Southeast Asia identified themselves as indigenous peoples so late, especially considering they were no longer subject to colonial occupation in the region. I was also interested in exploring how indigenous peoples, networks, and institutions mobilized the indigenism movement on different levels.

Becoming Indigenous Peoples in Southeast Asia

"For 50 years, genuine people's participation in the ASEAN has been severely limited. Despite the civic organizations' efforts to initiate engagements for constructive dialogues alongside Asean's claims of having more inclusive and meaningful spaces, Asean remains largely inaccessible to people." This statement was made by Jelen Paclarin, chair of the steering committee of the ASEAN Civil Society Conference/ASEAN People's Forum (ACSC/APF), in Quezon City, the Philippines, on November 15, 2017 (Agoncillo 2017). Parallel to the annual ASEAN Summit rotationally hosted by member countries and attended by leaders, officers of the ASEAN Civil Society Conference/ASEAN People's Forum have also organized people's organizations and social movements. Ideally, meetings are planned annually by the ASEAN People's Forum in the country that hosts the ASEAN Summit. However, it is difficult and, in some cases, impossible to hold the ASEAN People's Forum in certain countries, such as Laos, Vietnam, Burma, and Cambodia. This explains why one of the forums was held in the Philippines in mid-November 2017. Civil society leaders who gathered at that conference represented marginalized populations, including farmers, low-skilled workers, women, indigenous peoples, and members of the lesbian, gay, bisexual, and transgender communities. What they wanted was genuine inclusion in ASEAN meetings for leaders to hear people's concerns from the ground. Based on my observation, transnational indigenism in Southeast Asia is a response to ASEAN leaders' lack of attention to marginalized peoples. The movement also stems from international indigeneity in Western colonized countries in the context of globalization.

In responding to ASEAN, which primarily emphasizes regional cooperation of state leaders and the business sector, the Asia Indigenous Peoples Pact (AIPP), an international organization that represents indigenous peoples in Asia, points out the lack of participation of indigenous peoples. ASEAN has three pillars: the ASEAN Political-Security Community (APSC), the ASEAN Economic Community (AEC), and the ASEAN Socio-Cultural Community (ASCC). According to AIPP, each of these pillars has its own blueprint regarding policies, technical arrangements, action plans, and review mechanisms. The blueprints also establish clear targets and timelines for implementation and have pre-agreed flexibilities to accommodate the interests of all ASEAN member countries. However, in the implementation of each pillar, indigenous peoples are not included, even though they are affected in various ways by regional cooperation.

The first pillar, the ASEAN Political-Security Community (APSC), covers political development, the shaping and sharing of norms, conflict prevention, conflict resolution, postconflict peacebuilding, and combating terrorism. ASEAN maintains the principles of noninterference, consensus decision-making, national and regional resilience, and respect for sovereignty. It also affirms the principle of nondiscrimination when it comes to gender, race, religion, language, and social and cultural background in participating in, and benefitting from, the process of ASEAN integration and community-building. Importantly, its aspirational goals cover tolerance, respect for diversity, equality, and mutual understanding. To deal with these issues, the ASEAN Intergovernmental Commission on Human Rights (AICHR) was established.

However, according to AIPP and related networks, "its present mandate is too weak in terms of human rights protection. It does not have the mandate yet to look into cases of human rights violations and enforce adherence to human rights standards among member states, especially the protection of the collective rights of Indigenous Peoples" (AIPP, IWGIA and Forum-Asia 2010, 17). For example, customary laws of indigenous peoples across ASEAN are not even acknowledged or recognized. Their self-identification as indigenous people has not even been officially recognized by most of the member countries of ASEAN. Furthermore, indigenous leaders who play vital roles in protecting their basic rights have been killed, or have disappeared, or have been suppressed by state authorities.

The second pillar, the ASEAN Economic Community (AEC), aims to transform ASEAN into a stable, prosperous, and highly competitive region with equitable economic development and reduced poverty and socioeconomic disparities. Four main aspects under this pillar include: (1) a single market and production base; (2) a highly competitive economic region; (3) a region of equitable economic development, and (4) a region fully integrated into the global economy. Despite this, the more cooperation the AEC has developed, the more indigenous peoples have become disadvantaged or even victimized since those who benefit comprise the business sectors. As pointed out by AIPP and other organizations, "the market driven economy being promoted by the AEC endangers indigenous communities as our lands and territories will be used and exploited in the name of development that is not benefiting us" (AIPP, IWGIA and Forum-Asia 2010, 17). Their diverse ways of life to achieve self-sufficiency, based on land and resources, were completely ignored. Free Prior and Informed Consent (FPIC) for indigenous communities on development projects was not fairly conducted.

The last pillar is the ASEAN Socio-Cultural Community (ASCC). It seeks to forge a caring and sharing society that is inclusive and where the well-being, livelihood, and welfare of the people are enhanced. ASCC aims for the following: (1) human development; (2) social welfare and protection; (3) social justice and rights; (4) ensuring environmental sustainability; (5) building the ASEAN identity, and (6) narrowing the development gap. However, according to AIPP and other organizations, it "fails to acknowledge sustainable livelihoods of Indigenous Peoples. Further, the reference to regional food security ignores the production aspect, i.e. the threats of trade liberalization to small farmers and traditional livelihoods, and thus food security of Indigenous Peoples" (AIPP, IWGIA and Forum-Asia 2010, 18). It appears that only mainstream education has been promoted, while state governments ignore promoting diversity in languages, such as the provision of mother tongue education.

AIPP and related institutions of indigenous peoples in Southeast Asia were thus set up to play crucial roles in promoting the fundamental rights of indigenous peoples in the region and to aim for the recognition of collective rights and identity by the ASEAN community. These grassroots networks and organizations have gradually imposed international indigenism concerning ethnic and marginalized peoples in the Southeast Asian region. A good example of the long-term influences of indigenism in Southeast Asia is the common term for referring to those existing names and meanings mainly coined and defined by outsiders. According to AIPP and other organizations:

> Some governments in Southeast Asia use names to refer to us collectively—like "ethnic minorities," "hill tribes," "native people." There are also the names given by outsiders, some of which are not appreciated by many of us, since they often imply notions of cultural inferiority, being "primitive" or "backward." Examples are *chuncheat* (meaning "ethnicity," or literally "national people" in Cambodia) or *sakai* (literally meaning "slave") used in Thailand for some hunter-gatherer groups. We ourselves though prefer to use the names which our ancestors have given us.
>
> We are using the term "Indigenous Peoples" with a meaning that is different from that given in many dictionaries, or how it is understood by many governments. Over the past decades, the concept of Indigenous Peoples has evolved beyond the original meaning found in dictionaries, and it is now well established in international law. That is why we are writing it with capital initial letters. It is a foreign term for most of us, and it is often difficult to translate into our own languages (AIPP, IWGIA, and Forum-Asia 2010, 2).

Indigenism in Southeast Asia has gradually been influenced by indigenous movements in Western countries which have endorsed various international legal instruments, starting with the ILO Convention 169, which refers to both Indigenous Peoples and Tribal Peoples. Others are the International Covenant on Civil and Political Rights, the International Covenant on Economic, Social and Cultural Rights, and the International Convention on the Elimination of All Forms of Racial Discrimination. The most direct and recent mechanism is the United Nations Declaration on the Rights of Indigenous Peoples (UNDRIP), adopted by the General Assembly on September 13, 2007. Among the above instruments, the ILO Convention 169 and UNDRIP apply most to indigenous peoples in Southeast Asia since they explicitly refer to collective rights (AIPP and Ikap 2009, 3).

According to AIPP, there are common issues shared by indigenous peoples in Southeast Asia regarding transnational movements in the region (Maranan and Tessier 2015, 44–55). The first concerns the legal recognition of state governments in the region. Among the ten member countries of ASEAN, only the Philippines, Malaysia, and Cambodia recognize indigenous peoples at the constitutional level. In other countries, they are invisible in the fundamental law of the land and others, to the extent that the term "indigenous peoples" even remains contentious (ibid., 44).

Although some countries acknowledge the existence of indigenous peoples, the idea that they are distinct people who have been discriminated against and marginalized by state policies and the domination of mainstream groups has been ignored. Such denial, therefore, does not meet the international definition of being indigenous peoples and the principle of social justice regarding discrimination against them as affirmed by the UNDRIP. For those countries that do not recognize the existence of indigenous peoples, state governments claim that either there are no indigenous peoples or that every group is indigenous since both marginalized and mainstream groups have lived side-by-side for a long time. Taking Thailand as an example, the minister of Natural Resources and Environment, Mr. Warawut Silapa-Archa, insisted that there are no indigenous people but only ethnic groups in Thailand (Nicha 2021). Similarly, the director-general of the Department of Social Development and Human Security gave an opening speech on the celebration of World Indigenous Peoples' Day in 2011 in which he stated that the Thai are also an indigenous ethnic group since Thai people have inhabited Thailand for a very long time. Whether or not they are recognized as such, indigenous peoples are still being discriminated against or assimilated by the national governments' policies and domination of mainstream groups.

The second common issue is the violation of indigenous peoples' right to land, territories, and resources. According to legal thought and general understanding, land and resources belong to the king or state but can be granted to individuals and legitimate organizations to own and utilize, such as in the case of Thailand (Sophon 1978, 45). Therefore, it is the right of the state to revoke private ownership of land and resources. Indigenous peoples mainly reside in areas that are rich in natural resources. Their perception is that land and natural resources belong to sacred spirits. Humans only occupy and utilize them temporarily. In terms of ownership, a small piece of land may belong to a family but the vast area is owned by the community. It is a matter of collective rights. Violation of indigenous peoples' rights to land, territories, and resources occurs because of state governments' development projects and privatization. Hydropower construction, road construction, forest conservation declarations, land and resource concessions, and issuing of land titles to outside private owners are major examples of violations of indigenous peoples' rights to land, territories, and resources.

The third issue concerns violations of the rights of indigenous women and children. In dealing with both the state and their own communities, women and children are the most vulnerable groups. Their rights need to be protected and fulfilled. Indigenous women are traditionally dominated by men in various ways. They are the first group to face hardships in finding food if laws on natural resource conservation are imposed by state officers. Lack of formal education and language barriers are further obstacles to women's access to basic services, such as healthcare provided by state officials. Indigenous children normally have less opportunity for formal education because of their location in remote communities and their poverty. Those who have enrolled in school often face discrimination because of their distinct culture and stereotypical views of them. State-sponsored schools are mainly dominated by government curricula aimed at nation-building. The longer indigenous children stay in school, the more they lose their indigenous knowledge and identity.

The final common obstacle common among indigenous peoples in Southeast Asia is the lack of access to social services. Since they reside in remote communities, they are often denied state government development projects and basic services, including education and healthcare. Living in the forest area makes it difficult for state agencies to bring development projects and social services to them. In the case of Thailand, large numbers of indigenous people still lack Thai citizenship, which means they cannot get access to basic services provided by the state. For those who can access social services, the ways in which they are treated are unequal because they are perceived as lower status groups. Therefore, lack of access to social services and unequal treatment are common problems of discrimination faced by indigenous peoples in Southeast Asia.

In the face of such common problems, indigenous peoples in the region have no choice but to struggle for more equal treatment, especially from their respective government agencies. Forming their own networks and organizations is an essential strategy to empower themselves and contest state power, especially as governments in Southeast Asia have to follow international laws pertaining to indigenous peoples (see more details in Feiring et al. 2014; Prasit 2019; and Maranan and Tessier 2015).

Famark Hlawnching, the secretary-general of the Chin Human Rights Organization (CHRO), has said that one initiative of the movement was "to lobby the international community to support, as possible as it is, to those Chins who are fighting for our human rights. From the standpoints of the international human rights law, we have found out that we belong to the ethnic indigenous group" (interview Chiang Mai, November 20, 2019). According to him, the definition of indigenous people includes those who are in the current place with their history and before the invasions, those who are now dominated by mainstream society, and those who have their unique identity based on their cultural civilization and vowed to maintain that identity handed down to the next generations. Importantly, to him the term "indigenous people" refers to people in a society that is subject to domination, either by a European colony or the current nation-state. As he explains: "People usually think that colonizers come from across the sea. But, in the case of current colonization in Myanmar, there is no need to cross the sea. Burmese colonization is without crossing the sea. We also see the colonization of the neighboring countries without crossing the sea. Nowadays, colonization is easily seen through the policy and institutionalization. Burmanization is a form of colonization."

In the case of Thailand, the only country in Southeast Asia that has not been colonized by a European country, indigenism has been adopted and widely expanded for several decades. According to Sakda Saenmi, director of the IMPECT Association and secretary of the Network of Indigenous Peoples in Thailand (NIPT), the definition of indigenous people in the Thailand context is based on several components. The first is a cultural identity that has been inherited over a long history. According to him, "we are indigenous peoples because we want to preserve our identities such as culture, language, ritual, ceremony, customary law, and lifestyle. These are the issues that indigenous peoples would like to maintain and take forward from their history to the future." The second component, as addressed in UNDRIP, is that "we are not the major dominant group but we are small groups. We are people who are being disadvantaged through government policies. Unlike other colonized countries, we are dominated by government policies which impact our identity and ways of life." The last one is self-identification. According to Sakda Saenmi, "We should have a sense and rights to identify ourselves who we are." He emphasizes that "we have a common aspect of being part of the movement of indigenous peoples in Thailand. Movements of the indigenous assembly of Thailand help to concrete action on the advocacy of indigenous' self-determination." To him, people who have been involved with the indigenous movement may not have any questions about the concept of indigenous people, while those who have never participated in the movement may need to ask themselves who they are and what they would like to be—indigenous people or hill tribes (interview with Sakda Saenmi, Chiang Mai, November 21, 2019).

Overall, the birth of indigeneity in Southeast Asia at the national level has been caused by the marginalization of indigenous peoples and the violation of their rights as a result of development and nation-building. This contrasts with the indigeneity movement in Western colonized countries, which was a reaction to the European settlers who took power and dominated native peoples. At the regional level, the movement of indigenous peoples is a response to the lack of knowledge of the ASEAN community regarding their common problems. Moreover, at the international level, the emergence of indigenism in Southeast Asia was influenced by the progress and achievement of indigenous movements in Western colonized countries in the context of globalization. During the late 1980s and early 1990s, young leaders of ethnic groups in South and Southeast Asia established linkages with counterparts in Western colonized countries and learned about the international laws governing indigenous peoples. Among various indigenous networks and organizations in Southeast Asia, the Asia Indigenous Peoples Pact (AIPP) has played an essential role in mobilizing transnational indigenism in the region.

The Transnational Indigenism Movement in Southeast Asia

Although various international organizations are involved in the transnational movement of indigenism in Southeast Asia, the Asia Indigenous Peoples Pact (AIPP) has played the greatest role in propelling the movement. I have been indirectly involved with AIPP since the early 1990s, observing its development, but only recently have begun to carefully examine it closely. In this section, I want to show how indigenous peoples, networks, and institutions mobilize the movement on different levels in the region. Based on my longtime experience and recent fieldwork, I conclude that AIPP as a regional organization and other national and ethnic organizations are essential mechanisms that drive the indigenous movement in various activities and occasions. Throughout the past decades, peoples who have joined pertinent activities have gradually adopted indigenism. The movement has also been gradually introduced to the public and acknowledged by some state agencies in the region.

At the regional level, the foundation and roles of AIPP have led to the current transnational indigenism movement in Southeast Asia. AIPP was founded in Bangkok in 1992. During the 1970s and 1980s, prior to AIPP, Christian and international nongovernmental organizations bridged indigenous peoples in the South Asian and Southeast Asian regions. According to Morton and Baird (2019) and Dunford (2019), Luingam Luithui, an ethnic Naga leader from India, was one of the key founders of AIPP. After attending a few forums on ethnic minorities in the Philippines, Thailand, and elsewhere, Luithui understood the problems faced by ethnic minorities, who later defined themselves as "indigenous peoples" in South and Southeast Asia. The starting point of transnational indigenism was the Indigenous Peoples' Forum in Chiang Mai, organized by the Christian Conference of Asia (CCA), an NGO, in August 1988. Luithui became the first chair of the forum. Initially, he and other AIPP founders intended to set up their head office in Bombay, India. However, he later decided to base AIPP in Bangkok since the relationship between state and ethnic minorities was better than in other countries (Morton and Baird 2019, 17). Scholars and leaders of NGOs in civil movements also supported the establishment of AIPP. Luithui began to contact young leaders of indigenous peoples who actively ran local and national NGOs in South and Southeast Asia. He then decided to move the secretariat of AIPP to Chiang Mai in 1993 because NGOs on ethnic issues were mainly based in northern Thailand (ibid.), as well as IWGIA, an international indigenous NGO from Denmark. There were thus several networks that fitted well in supporting the future movements of AIPP.

In Chiang Mai, both religious and non-religious NGOs on highland ethnic minorities or hill tribes had existed since the 1980s. Prasert Trakarnsupakorn, the former director of Inter-Mountain Peoples' Education and Culture in Thailand (IMPECT, was one of those pioneers who had good connections with foreign activists and agencies. He had opportunities to present ethnic minority issues, especially the declaration of national parks on highland areas inhabited by ethnic groups, at the Asia Dialogue in Japan and the Philippines (interview, Chiang Mai, June 15th, 2018). According to Prasert, AIPP's forum was organized in Penang in 1992. By that time, he was the director of the Inter-Mountain Peoples' Education and Culture in Thailand (IMPECT) and joined the forum, also attended by Tuanjai Deetes, the founder of the Hill Area and Community Development Foundation which was based in Chiang Rai (interview with Tuanjai Deetes, Chiang Mai, November 21, 2019). Through that connection, Luithui found new alliances which worked with ethnic minority peoples in northern Thailand, which led to his decision to base the secretariat of AIPP in Chiang Mai.

It should be noted that the forums and civil movements for human rights and indigenous issues of the early 1990s were opportunities for ethnic leaders who were NGO workers in northern Thailand and other countries in Southeast Asia and South Asia, including other continents, to be united. In 1992, representatives of ethnic networks organized forums on both ethnic group and interethnic group levels in northern Thailand, brainstorming problems faced by their people, then brought the results and recommendations for joining the People's Plan for the 21st Century to Bangkok in December of that year. The following year, Prasert Trakarnsupakorn was the only representative from Thailand to attend and speak at the forum on the International Year of the World's Indigenous People in New York (interview, Chiang Mai, June 15th, 2018). In the meantime, Kittisak Rattanakrachangsri, director of the Indigenous Peoples' Foundation for Education and Environment (IPF), also joined the International Alliance of Indigenous and Tribal People in the Tropical Forests (IAITPTF), whose secretariat rotates among different continents and is currently based in Nairobi, Kenya (interview, June 18th, 2018). Subsequently, the first secretariat office of this alliance was set up in Chiang Mai in the mid-1990s. Later, before the office moved out of Asia, he and other colleagues, including myself, set up the Indigenous Peoples' Foundation for Education and Environment (IPF). In addition, Chiang Mai was also the base of the regional office of International Work Group for Indigenous Affairs (IWGIA) since early the 1990s.

After AIPP had permanently established itself in Chiang Mai, young indigenous leaders from Malaysia, the Philippines, Nepal, India, and other countries were brought in to staff this regional organization. Jennie Lasimbang, an indigenous leader from the Sabah state of Malaysia, served as the secretary-general of AIPP for two terms, four years each term. According to Prasert and Kittisak, Jennie Lasimbang played a crucial role in setting up the structure of AIPP, networking with regional indigenous organizations and networks, and raising funds for the organization. Environmental issues were highlighted under her administration. The second secretary-general of AIPP was Joan Carling from the Philippines. She also served for two terms, focusing on international linkage and human rights issues. It was through her hard work that AIPP became known to international indigenous-related organizations, especially at the UN level. The present secretary-general of AIPP is Gam Shimray from Nepal. At present, AIPP has forty-seven members from fourteen countries in Asia with eighteen indigenous peoples' national alliances/networks (national formations), and thirty local and subnational organizations. Of this number, sixteen are ethnic-based organizations, six indigenous women-based, four indigenous youth organizations, and one organization of indigenous persons with disabilities (https://aippnet.org/about-us/, 2021).

Those fourteen countries are organized into four subregions: South Asia (Bangladesh, India, northeast India, and Nepal), Mekong (Myanmar, Thailand, Laos, Cambodia, and Vietnam), East Asia (Japan and Taiwan/China), and Southeast Asia (Malaysia, Indonesia, Timor-Leste, and the Philippines). Although many new organizations and networks/alliances have applied to be members of AIPP, no policy for this has been presented to the General Assembly for approval as it would be difficult for AIPP to take care of a larger number of members. Over thirty years, AIPP has undoubtedly grown exponentially and played an essential role in driving transnational indigenism in Southeast Asia as well as South and East Asia. Its programs include communication, environment, human rights campaign and advocacy, indigenous women, organizational strengthening and movement building, and regional capacity building (https:// aippnet.org/about-us/, 2021). To promote indigenism, AIPP disseminates information via various means, including websites, pamphlets, and books.

At the national level, Malaysia, Indonesia, the Philippines, and Thailand are the only countries in Southeast Asia that have a local organization for uniting various indigenous organizations and networks. The AIPP, the regional movement of indigenism, played a crucial role in the emergence of those national organizations. In Malaysia, the Indigenous Peoples Network of Malaysia or Jaringan Orang Asal Se Malaysia (JOAS) is the umbrella network for twenty-one community-based nongovernmental organizations that have indigenous peoples' issues as the focus. As the focal point for indigenous rights and advocacy in Malaysia, JOAS provides the indigenous communities with representation not just nationally but regionally and internationally.

In Indonesia, the Alliance of Indigenous Peoples of the Archipelago (AMAN) is an independent community organization with a vision to create a just and prosperous life for all Indigenous Peoples in the country. This alliance represents 2,332 indigenous communities throughout Indonesia, amounting to about seventeen million members. The organization represents and advocates for Indigenous Peoples' issues at local, national, and international levels.

In the Philippines, there are many indigenous organizations because of its scattered islands. However, the two best-known ones at the national level are Cordillera Peoples Alliance (CPA) and TEBTEBBA. CPA is based in the Cordillera Administrative Region in the northern Philippines. As stated on its website, "CPA was founded in June 1984 in Bontoc, Mountain Province, by 150 delegates from 27 organizations attending the Cordillera People's Congress. The founders of CPA were mainly indigenous leaders and activists who spearheaded the widespread and successful opposition to the World Bank-funded Chico dams project and the commercial logging operations of the Cellophil Resources Corporation." CPA works on a variety of issues pertaining to indigenous peoples' rights, especially the defense of ancestor domain and for self-determination" (https://www.cpaphils.org/about1.html, 2021).

TEBTEBBA was established in 1996 to promote and disseminate indigenous peoples' worldviews and their perspectives on key issues such as individual and collective human rights, sustainable development, climate change, biodiversity, traditional knowledge, customary laws and governance, conflict transformation, and gender. According to Victoria Tauli-Corpuz, AIPP is the network of indigenous peoples in Asia while TEBTEBBA, of which she was the founder (and a former United Nations special rapporteur for the rights of indigenous peoples), is a global indigenous network. "Although TEBTEBBA is not a member of AIPP, we help each other on advocacy regarding the right of indigenous peoples on the global level, to ensure indigenous representatives' participation in global events, especially the UN" (interview, Chiang Mai, November 20, 2019).

In Thailand, where AIPP is based, the birth of the Network of Indigenous Peoples of Thailand (NIPT) and the Assembly of Indigenous Peoples in Thailand (AIPT) were influenced by AIPP. Although AIPP has been based in Chiang Mai since the early 1990s, few individuals and local indigenous organizations have worked closely with it. It was not until 2008 that NIPT was established. Previously, on August 21, 2007, I attended and observed a national workshop on "The Situation and Impacts of the International Decade of Indigenous Peoples on Thailand," held at the Chiang Mai University campus. There were around thirty participants, mostly NGO workers and local community leaders with highland ethnic backgrounds. NGO leaders who had joined the indigenous movements, both in Thailand and on the international level, presented the historical background and the importance of indigenism to the audience. A few staff members of AIPP also introduced the role of AIPP in bridging indigenous movements in the region and at the international level. It was agreed at the end of the workshop that an annual event be held on International Day of the World's Indigenous Peoples and to launch the Network of Indigenous Peoples in Thailand (NIPT). Since 2008, members of NIPT have gathered on August 9 each year to celebrate the International Day of the World's Indigenous Peoples. During the three-day event, there is a session in which a key person of AIPP makes a speech, addressing the importance of indigenism and the main theme set by indigenous organizations on the UN level.

Fig. 1. Attendees from forty indigenous groups in Thailand during the 2018 annual International Day of the World's Indigenous Peoples held at Rajaphat Chiang Rai University.

Fig. 2. A representative of AIPP reads a statement during the 2018 annual International Day of the World's Indigenous Peoples held at Rajaphat Chiang Rai University.

The NIPT is mainly responsible for organizing the annual celebration of the International Day of the World's Indigenous Peoples. In 2015, the network became an assembly (see Prasit 2019 and Morton and Baird 2019). Despite attempts to draft its act for presentation at the national congress, there has been no progress concerning the creation of a law. Recently, three versions of bills concerning indigenous peoples and ethnic groups have been drafted for presentation at the national congress of Thailand. According to Sakda Saenmi, a key person in the Assembly of Indigenous Peoples of Thailand (AIPT), "presently, there are 42 indigenous groups that have become members of the assembly. Each group may have different types of organization, such as a club, network, association, and organization which registered with the Assembly of Indigenous Peoples in Thailand" (interview, November 20, 2019). There are six strategies for the network and assembly: building capacity for indigenous peoples and organizations, enhancing the capacity of indigenous peoples at the household and community levels, promoting and protecting the rights of indigenous peoples, promoting peace and collaboration within and outside indigenous networks, disseminating information to the public and state government, and fundraising.

On the indigenous group level, as stated by AIPP, among the fortyoseven members of AIPP, sixteen are ethnic-based organizations, some founded before the creation of AIPP, others recently set up. Joining the movement of indigenous networks or organizations on the national, regional, and global levels can empower indigenous organizations. One example of an indigenous organization in Myanmar is the Chin Human Rights Organization (CHRO), founded in 1995 and legally registered in Canada and the United States. CHRO works to protect and promote human rights through monitoring, research, documentation, education, and advocacy on behalf of indigenous Chin people and other oppressed and marginalized communities in Myanmar (https://www.chinhumanrights.org/alliance-membership/, 2021). The works of CHRO cover local, national, regional, and international groups on a range of issues. At the Chin state level, CHRO works with a variety of local partners and has built strong relationships with academic institutions, the media, civil society, religious, and community-based organizations from across the nine townships in the state, as well as outside Chin state. In addition to being a member of the Myanmar Indigenous Peoples/Ethnic Nationalities Network, CHRO became a member of AIPP in 1996. According to Famark Hlawnching, the secretary-general of CHRO, this indigenous organization became a member of AIPP in 1996. Becoming affiliated with national, regional, and international levels of indigenous movements could increase the power and acknowledge the roles of this indigenous organization. To Hlawnching, "while the government is working on the drafts of policy, law, and practice, they are beginning to invite us to work together" (interview, Chiang Mai, November 20, 2019).

Other indigenous organizations in Southeast Asia that are members of AIPP include the Organization to Promote Kui Culture (Cambodia), the Hmong Association for Development in Thailand, and the Karen Network for Culture and Environment (Thailand). In theory, these organizations are the intermediate agencies linking indigenous peoples with national, regional, and international organizations regarding the rights of indigenous peoples. In reality, from what I have observed over the past decade, most indigenous members who attend the annual celebration of World Indigenous Peoples' Day and other related activities are the same every year, while new youths appear only every few years. There appears to be no workshop or clear activity for campaigning about the meaning and essence of indigenous peoples on the ground. This may explain why the majority of members of ethnic groups who have been discriminated against and marginalized are seldom aware of the movement and the concept of indigenism (Baird, Prasit, and Urai 2016). Many challenges remain for indigenous organizations or networks at ethnic group, national, and regional levels in Southeast Asia to advocate for indigenism in communities.

In summary, indigenism in Southeast Asian countries has been influenced by Western indigenous movements in the context of globalization. Transnational indigenism in the region is a response to the state-led ASEAN community, which has left marginalized ethnic groups behind. In the past decades, transnational indigenism in Southeast Asia has developed and presently occurs in groups at the regional, national, and ethnic levels. Although the original context of indigenism in Western countries is different from that of Southeast Asian countries, nowadays they share a common ideology and movement. Transnational indigenism in Southeast Asia has gained much more trust on the international level. In addition to the annual United Nations Permanent Forum on Indigenous Issues held in New York, where representatives of different levels in Southeast Asia attend and present their problems, indigenous movements in the region also gain confidence from the forum. In November 2019, the International Expert Group Meeting, under the Secretariat of the Permanent Forum on Indigenous Issues, was held on the Chiang Mai University campus. The agenda was peace, justice, and strong institutions: the role of indigenous peoples in implementing Sustainable Development Goal 16. One of its main purposes was to propose recommendations and next steps to ensure the recognition of indigenous peoples' rights and institutions. In addition to leaders of indigenous organizations in Southeast Asia, representatives of independent and state agencies also attended. The event was a strategic mechanism for fostering transnational indigenism in Southeast Asia.

Conclusion

During the ASEAN summit in Jakarta in 2016, the ASEAN Secretariat, in cooperation with the Mission of the People's Republic of China to ASEAN and the United Nations Development Program, hosted a symposium on the 2030 Agenda for Sustainable Development titled "Leave No One Behind" (https://

asean.org/asean-to-leave-no-one-behind/, 2021). At the regional level, the ASEAN Peoples' Forum, the parallel summit of civil society, attracts more and more attendees each year, comprising discriminated and excluded groups, among them ethnic or indigenous peoples. In some years, however, the host country of the ASEAN summit is not open to holding the peoples' forum, and civil activists are unable to get together. Alternatively, they have to organize the event outside the host country. At the ground level, ethnic peoples are still being marginalized. Lacking access to basic government services, ethnic groups also become victims since their rights to fruitful natural resources have been taken by the state government and outside capitalists. They face difficulties or even are displaced because of hydropower construction, land and natural concessions, national park establishment, tourism investment, etc. From time to time, local ethnic activists have been killed or have gone missing, as annually reported by IWGIA in *The Indigenous World* (Mamo 2020). Hence, identifying themselves as "indigenous people" and uniting with peoples who face the same obstacles and indigenous organizations or networks at different levels gives them hope in strengthening the power of powerless indigeneity.

Indigenism, as pointed out by Ronald Niezen (2003, 9), is a common ideology and movement of marginalized ethnic groups who face the negative impacts of resource extraction, economic modernization, and social convergence and homogenization. In addition, I would affirm that although indigenous peoples in Western colonized countries originally faced problems of domination by European settlers in the colonial era, in postcolonial times, whether in Western colonized countries or non-colonized countries, they face the same problems of state domination and capitalistic exploitation. By identifying themselves as indigenous peoples they are linked across ethnic boundaries and indigenous movements on various levels. Since it is grounded in international networks, indigenism becomes a transnational consciousness and social mobilization. At the regional level in Southeast Asia, it is my finding that indigeneity has only been adopted by native ethnic peoples in the past few decades. Scholars and activists on indigeneity in Southeast Asia clearly state that the indigeneity movement in this region stems from the influence of long-term movements in Western colonized countries. Turning points have been the Special Rapport on the United Nation's Sub-Commission on Prevention of Discrimination and Protection of Minorities by José R. Martínez-Cobo in 1981, the ILO Convention 169 in 1989, and the United Nations Declaration on the Rights of Indigenous Peoples (UNDRIP) in 2007 (Baird 2020, 2021; Erni 2008, Gray 1995; Kingsbury 1995; and Tauli-Corpuz 2008).

Transnational indigenism in Southeast Asia is a civil movement of excluded and marginalized ethnic peoples in ASEAN countries. Internally, transnational indigenism in Southeast Asia mobilizes disadvantaged peoples beyond a state's sovereignty. In reality, the freedom of movement of marginalized peoples differs among ASEAN members. As pointed out by Ian Baird, only the "governments of the Philippines and Cambodia now define particular ethnic groups of people as Indigenous, and are providing these groups with particular rights" (2019, 2). Some countries are quite receptive to indigenous peoples' movements, even though they still may not formally recognize those peoples' existence and basic rights. Meanwhile, some countries still strictly control the movement of ethnic or indigenous peoples. In such cases, any human rights movements of ethnic or indigenous peoples can be viewed as threats to national security and thus are suppressed by state governments. Internally, indigenous movements operate based on issues, especially environmental protection, educational promotion, cultural preservation, and general development. Externally, at the transnational Southeast Asian level, they share a common indigenism movement. Transnational indigenism in this region is also linked to the global level. Issues of marginalized and disadvantaged indigenous peoples in Southeast Asian countries are publicized via various mechanisms and opportunities. The problems faced by indigenous peoples in Southeast Asia are also human rights issues. The more indigenous peoples in Southeast Asia are disadvantaged and ignored by state governments and the ASEAN community, the more pressure will be imposed through the transnational indigenism movements by international indigenous and human rights-related institutions and laws.

References

Abeysekara, Ananda. 2011. "Buddhism, Power, Modernity. Gathering Leaves and Lifting Words: Histories of Buddhist Monastic Education in Laos and Thailand." *Culture and Religion* 12(4): 489–97.

Agoncillo, Jodee A. 2017. "Civil Society Leaders Push for People's Participation in Development Talks." Inquirer.net. accessed January 15, 2021. https://globalnation.inquirer.net/162513/civil-society-leaders-push-peoples-participation-development-talks.

Asia Indigenous Peoples Pact (AIPP), the International Work Group for Indigenous Affairs (IWGIA), and Asian Forum for Human Rights and Development (FORUM-ASIA). 2010. *ASEAN's Indigenous Peoples*. Chiang Mai: AIPP, IWGIA, and Forum-Asia.

Asia Indigenous Peoples Pact Foundation (AIPP) and Indigenous Knowledge and Peoples Network (Ikap). 2009. *Who We Are: Indigenous Peoples in Asia*. Chiang Mai: AIPP and Ikap.

Asia Indigenous Peoples Pact. 2014. *Overview of the State of Indigenous Peoples in Asia*. Chiang Mai: AIPP.

Baird, Ian G. 2016. "Should Ethnic Lao People Be Considered Indigenous to Cambodia? Ethnicity, Classification and the Politics of Indigeneity." *Asian Ethnicity* 17(4): 506–26.

——————. "Introduction: Indigeneity in 'Southeast Asia': Challenging Identities and Geographies." *Journal of Southeast Asian Studies* 50(1): 2–6.

——————. 2020. "Thinking about Indigeneity with Respect to Time and Space: Reflections from Southeast Asia." *Espace Populations Societies*, 1–17. Accessed January 10, 2021. https://journals.openedition.org/eps/9628.

——————. 2021. "The Complex Relationship between Indigeneity and Class in South East Asia." *South East Asia Research*, 1–19. Accessed January 12, 2021. https://doi.org/10.1080/096782 8X.2020.1859932.

Baird, Ian G., Prasit Leepreecha, and Urai Yangcheepsujarit. 2016. "Who Should be Considered 'Indigenous'? A Survey of Ethnic Groups in Northern Thailand." *Asian Ethnicity* 18(4): 543–62.

Castells, Manuel. 2000. *The Rise of the Network Society*, 2nd edn. Oxford, UK: Blackwell.

Clark, Mavis T. 1965. *Pastor Doug: The Story of an Aboriginal Leader*. Melbourne: Lansdowne.

Dunford, Michael R. 2019. "Indigeneity, Ethnopolitics, and Taingyinthar: Myanmar and the Global Indigenous Peoples' Movement." *Journal of Southeast Asian Studies* 50(1): 51–67.

Enloe, Cynthia H. 1977. "Internal Colonialism, Federalism and Alternative State Development Strategies." *Publius* 7(4): 145–60.

Erni, Christian, ed. 2008. *The Concept of Indigenous Peoples in Asia: A Resource Book*. Copenhagen and Chiang Mai: International Work Group for Indigenous Affairs (IWGIA) and Asia Indigenous Peoples Pact Foundation (AIPP).

Evans, Grant. 1992. "Internal Colonialism in the Central Highlands of Vietnam." *SOJOURN: Journal of Social Issues in Southeast Asia* 7(2): 274–304

Feiring, Birgitte et al. 2014. *United Nations and Indigenous Peoples in Developing Countries: An Evolving Partnership*. Baguio City, Philippines: Tebtebba Foundation.

Gray, Andrew. 1995. "The Indigenous Movement in Asia." In *Indigenous Peoples of Asia*, eds. R. H. Barnes, Andrew Gray, and Benedict Kingsbury, 35–38. Ann Arbor, MI: Association for Asian Studies.

Haebich, Anna. 1992. *For Their Own Good: Aborigines and Government in the South West of Western Australia 1900-1940*. Nedlands: University of Western Australia Press.

Kingsbury, Benedict. 1995. "'Indigenous Peoples' as an International Legal Concept." In *Indigenous Peoples of Asia*, eds. R. H. Barnes, Andrew Gray, and Benedict Kingsbury, 35–38. Ann Arbor, MI: Association for Asian Studies.

Mamo, Dwayne, ed. 2020. *The Indigenous World 2020*. Copenhagen, Denmark: Eks-Skolen Trykkeri.

Maranan, Luchie, and Jade Tessier. 2015. *Indigenous Peoples and ASEAN Integration*. Chiang Mai: Asia Indigenous Peoples Pact (AIPP) Foundation.

Merlan, Francesca. 2005. "Indigenous Movements in Australia." *Annual Review of Anthropology* 34: 473–94.

Morton, Micah, and Ian Baird. 2019. "From Hill Tribes to Indigenous Peoples: The Localisation of a Global Movement in Thailand." *Journal of Southeast Asian Studies* 50(1): 7–31.

Nicha Wechpanich. 2021. Samphat phiset 'Warawut Silapa-Archa' lang mati kaengkrachan pen moradokloke (Special interview 'Warawut Silapa-Arch' after Kaengkrachan becomes world heritage). Accessed July 28, 2021. https://greennews.agency/?p=24676&fbclid=IwAR2VeQF3TxFQ-nopmgohCQWI9J2NBoP8-pA9VG96YrJBMqWnBQUnfvp1xZc.

Niezen, Roland. 2003. *The Origins of Indigenism: Human Rights and the Politics of Identity*. Berkeley, CA: University of California Press.

Pena, Gullermo de la. 2005. "Social and Cultural Policies Toward Indigenous Peoples: Perspectives from Latin America." *Annual Review of Anthropology* 34: 717–39.

Perry, Richard J. 1996. *From Time Immemorial: Indigenous Peoples and State Systems*. Austin: University of Texas Press.

Prasit Leepreecha. 2019. "Becoming Indigenous Peoples in Thailand." *Journal of Southeast Asian Studies* 50(1): 32–50.

Prasit Leepreecha and Mukdawan Sakboon. 2021. "Education for Being Thai-ness among Indigenous Peoples in the North." *Thammasat Journal* 40(2): 68–97 (in Thai).

Smith, Michael Peter. 2003. "Transnationalism and Citizenship." In *Approaching Transnationalisms: Studies on Transnational Societies, Multicultural Contacts, and Imaginings of Home*, eds. Brenda S. A. Yeoh, Michael W. Charney, and Tong Chee Kiong, 2–38. Boston, NY: Kluwer Academic Publishers.

Sophon Ratanakhon. 1978. "Legal Aspects of Land Occupation and Development." In *Farmers in the Forest: Economic Development and Marginal Agriculture in Northern Thailand*, eds. Peter Kunstadter et al., 45–53. Honolulu, HI: University Press of Hawai'i.

Tan, Rhe-Anne. 2020. "We Are Not Red and White, We are Morning Star: Internal Colonization, Indigenous Identity, and the Idea of Indonesia." *Journal of International Affairs* 73(2): 271–84.

Tauli-Corpuz, Victoria. 2008. "The Concept of Indigenous Peoples at the International Level: Origins, Development and Challenges." In *The Concept of Indigenous Peoples in Asia: A Resource Book*, ed. Christian Erni, 77–99. Copenhagen and Chiang Mai: International Working Group for Indigenous Affairs (IWGIA) and Asia Indigenous Peoples Pact (AIPP).

Theriault, Noha. 2019. "Unravelling the Strings Attached: Philippine Indigeneity in Law and Practice." *Journal of Southeast Asian Studies* 50(1): 107–28.

Thongchai Winichakul. 1994. *Siam Mapped: A History of the Geo-body of a Nation*. Chiang Mai: Silkworm Books.

—————. 2000. "The Others Within: Travel and Ethno-Spatial Differentiation of Siamese Subjects 1885–1910." In *Civility and Savagely: Social Identity in Tai States*, ed. Andrew Turton, 38–62. London: Curzon Press.

Turner, Bryan S. 2008. "Transnationalism." In *International Encyclopedia of Social Sciences*, vol. 3., 2nd edn, ed. William A. Darity, 433–34. Detroit: Course Technology Cengage Learning.

Urry, John. 2000. "Mobile Sociology." *British Journal of Sociology* 51(1): 185–203.

Vertovec, Steven. 2009. *Transnationalism*. London and New York: Routledge.

Transnational Malay Identity: Stage Performances and the Revival of Royal Patrons in the Riau Islands[1]

ALAN DARMAWAN AND JAN VAN DER PUTTEN

Studying Malay identity through a transnational lens seems logical but is, at the same time, problematic. The conceptual framework of transnationalism is most often used in the field of migration studies in which the concepts of homeland and diaspora are fundamental to understand the feelings, movements, and sociopolitical behaviors of migrants to maintain connections with the people "back home." The modes and realization of such contacts are based on historical contingencies and will change over time in intensity and content (Vertovec 2009, 13). Groups of people who identify themselves as Malay are dispersed around insular and mainland Southeast Asia, an area that may be referred to as the Malay World, which straddles the nation-states of Indonesia, Malaysia, Singapore, and other Southeast Asian states. They also include groups that have settled beyond the boundaries of this region. From this perspective, of course, Malays are transnational, as the areas where they have settled belong to different nation-states.

Recent studies about Malay identity have made it clear that the terminology "Malay" was used with different definitions in the course of history and in political discourses and agendas (cf. Barnard and Maier 2004; Kahn 2006; Milner 2010; Maznah Mohamad and Syed Muhd Khairudin Aljuneid 2011; and Long 2013). The studies expound and contextualize the point that in general "Malay" has been and, in some cases, is still being used to refer to the people of insular and peninsular Southeast Asia as a whole, or as a generic term for the speakers of variants of the Malay language. In other contexts, "Malay" may refer to an ethnic community whose members traditionally live in the coastal areas of Sumatra, Borneo, and the Malay Peninsula, or Muslim citizens of the nation-states Malaysia, Singapore, Brunei, and Thailand. Even some groups in Vietnam, Cambodia, and as far away as Sri Lanka and South Africa may identify themselves as Malay. To add to this blurred definition of the term "Malay,"

Malaysian and Singapore citizens quite commonly add other ethnic epithets to that of "Malay," such as Bugis, Boyan, or Jawa, to distinguish themselves from other members within the Malay community. At the same time, they indicate a certain affectionate relationship with the homeland or home community in Indonesia (the Bugis in Sulawesi and the islands of Bawean or Java). As might be expected, boundaries between the definitions are blurred and the ongoing processes of globalization have invigorated the formation of localized forms of a shared cultural Malay identity.

In this chapter, we reflect on Appadurai's notion (1996) about how imagination fuels the activities of culturalist movements which self-consciously produce "locality" in the context of a globalized world. Therefore, we look at how the imagination of "homeland" has been localized in the Riau Islands and, at the same time, maintains relationships with other communities in the Malay World. It is our contention that ever since the elevation of the Riau Islands to the administrative level of province in 2004, officials, cultural activists, and other local agents have been actively promoting this Negeri Segantang Lada ("A Spattering of Peppercorns")—referring to the multitude of islands strewn around the South China Sea—as Bunda Tanah Melayu ("Motherland of the Malays"), another name for the province that is being popularized in the local discourse.

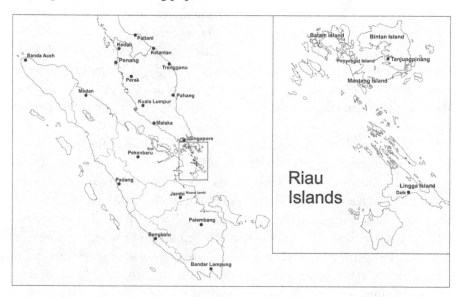

Map of Sumatra, the Malay Peninsula, and the Riau Islands. Edited by Alan Darmawan. *Source*: National Atlas of Indonesia (Atlas Nasional Indonesia) published by the Geospatial Information Agency, Indonesia, 2015. See the online atlas through this link: <https://atlas.big.go.id/eatlas1/Atlas/Tampil/25#modalNarasi> last accessed 24 September 2021.

One might say that these agents are constructing and forging the region as a Malay *kampung* or neighborhood as a situated community where revived traditions invite the inhabitants, both of local and outside origins, to become culturally Malay (cf. Appadurai 1996, 178–79). They are also packaging it as a model to be reproduced in other regions where people subscribe to the cultural values they see as significant for Malay identity. As a contribution to this volume, what concerns us most in this chapter is how certain agents in the Indonesian province of the Riau Islands (Kepulauan Riau, henceforth abbreviated as Kepri) redefine Malay identity and reconfigure its cultural significance by revitalizing or resuscitating erstwhile artistic expressions and customs and commodifying these to be performed in cyclical arts festivals which travel to other regions and nations. In this chapter we will discuss how dance and other cultural performances are being circulated throughout the Malay World and beyond, mostly originating from Kepri and Riau Province on the island of Sumatra,[2] which strive to enhance their role as innovative art centers.

The second clear Malay identity marker that we will discuss is the institution of kingship in the modern garb of a sultan who pushes for economic development in accordance with the rules of Islamic law. In this respect, a form of Islam is propagated by a newly instated sultan of Bintan in Kepri who claims part of his legitimation from the Murabitun movement, a global Sufi network that strives after the reintroduction of the gold dinar and silver dirham coins for economic exchange in agreement with Islamic law. Backed by this movement and using his personal network, this sultan of Bintan has rekindled connections with Malaysian sultanates and uses his interpretation of Islam to fortify ties with other Indonesian sultans and rulers. However, the Murabitun connection and the existence of other and possibly older contenders for a position in the new aristocracy with cultural and political ramifications, may eventually undermine the role of the new sultan to transnationalize a Kepri-based standard of Malay cultural identity.

Identity and "Homeland" in Traditional Historiography

The traditional historiography of the Malay ethnic community harks back to the legendary tale of how descendants of Alexander the Great descended from the sky to establish a new kingdom by forging bonds with the local community near Palembang, South Sumatra. For reasons left unmentioned in the tale, after some time the king went to seek a new area in which to settle. After temporary stints in the islands of Bintan and Singapore, the group of Malay royalty descended upon a small place on the west coast of the Malay Peninsula that later would become famous under the name of Melaka. This is the version that has come down to modern times through the traditional narrative *Sulalatu 'l-Salatin*, better known under the title *Sejarah Melayu*, preserved in manuscript copies from the nineteenth century. This narrative was probably compiled and copied in Johor after the Malay royal house was ousted from Melaka by the Portuguese in 1511. Being commissioned by certain factions in the Malay court, it was designed to legitimate the authority of the ruling faction and boost the reputation of the court, its history, and traditions. The latter motivation of its initial compilation was highly successful as it provided the Johor court with a predecessor of high renown and became an important source for the configuration of Malay culture. This was, at least, the case from the start of the nineteenth century onward, when the first translation in English was published by Raffles in England in 1821 and the first edition of the Malay text was printed by Abdullah Munshi at the Mission Press in Singapore in 1841. This tale is used throughout the Malay World to indicate the historicity of claims of certain parties or even regions in their efforts to revitalize the institution of the sultanate or principality as we will see below in the case of Bintan.

In Malaysia, nationalist agents used the tale's reputation to forge a Malay identity that was based on traditional pillars enhanced by the studies and measures of colonial officials and scholars. These pillars are Malay customs and good manners (*adat*), which are bound in and part of the concept of *bahasa* (language) (Maier 1993; Heryanto 1990), and Islam that was connected to the traditional leadership the sultans executed in the nine states that were part of the Federated States of Malaysia. The government of Indonesia initially withdrew all administrative and political power from the local rulers, and revolutionary militias killed several of the sultans with their families at the beginning of independence. However, with the main aim of keeping the nation together after the dismissal of President Suharto, the central government implemented far-reaching decentralization policies that encouraged a number of local polities to reinstate sultans and give them a renewed symbolic cultural position. Notions of Malay culture that are used to reconfigure the cultural identity are embedded in the culture that was established in the traditional sultanate courts that were dispersed within the Malay World and that took their model in the imagined grandeur of the Melakan court. This made Melaka the center of the Malay cultural world for a long time, but Kepri's recent activities have been vying with Melaka's focal point for the ongoing reconfigurations of Malay cultural identity. Kepri's authorities have been sponsoring festivals, art centers, and many other initiatives in a claim of becoming the rightful heir of the Malay royal traditions.

Nonetheless, the concept of "homeland" among these transnational communities that form the Malay ethnoscape has been grounded in Palembang and Jambi (Indonesia) and Melaka (Malaysia). As we argue here, however, there are signs that Kepri certainly is gaining ground in this cultural competition of claiming to be the proverbial "homeland of Malay culture." The notion of transnationalism becomes further complicated when we look into the different pillars that support the configuration of this cultural identity in the different local contexts in the Malay World.

Malay Communities, Identity, and the Initial Efforts of a Transnational Connection

Transnational activities in reconfiguring a Malay cultural identity in different localities may be a relatively recent phenomenon. In its initial stage, it nostalgically aims to reconnect groups of people who base their self-identification as Malay on their ethnic background and live as separate communities across national borders in Southeast Asia. The premise of the formation of such an identity is the imagination of a Malay cultural realm or ecumene, Alam Melayu or Malay World, which implies a narrative of united communities in a cultural space along the Strait of Melaka sharing a number of cultural elements. The 1824 London Treaty is regarded to have initiated the division of the Malay realm into a British and a Dutch sphere of influence. This division was continued by the postcolonial nation-states, which play an important role in reconfiguring the image of the Malay self and its communities on both sides of the Strait. Different formative processes leading to alternative configurations of Malay identity in Malaysia, Indonesia, and some other countries, were broadly caused by differences in political regimes and types of nation-building of these modern independent states.

Certain groups during the Indonesian revolution for independence (1945–49) pushed for the eradication of traditional rule, which triggered violent conflicts in East Sumatra. These conflicts led to the killings and persecution of Malay royal family members and the burning of their palaces (Reid 1979). Malay people who could claim communal ownership of the land lost their customary rights. The sultans had rented most of their customary lands to European and American companies since 1862, which the Indonesian state nationalized in 1958. The eviction from their lands became a structural problem that marginalized the Malay population and converted them into second-rate citizens. Moreover, a high influx of labor migrants from China, India, and

Java to the east coast of Sumatra, and groups voluntarily descending from the highlands of West and North Sumatran to take their chances in the new urban area of Medan and the plantation belt that evolved, turned the local Malays into a minority group.

Living in destitute circumstances and unable to afford proper education, Malays could not compete with migrants who strived hard to obtain land and make a living. Within the framework of national development that took place between the 1970 and 1990s, the configuration of national culture and identity was based on the creation of regional identity in the provinces (Rodgers 1993). In North Sumatra, the home of multiethnic groups, the Malay community was left out of the formation of its regional identity. In Riau Province, encompassing the islands and a vast area on the east coast of Sumatra, Malayness was made into a regional identity based on simplified and essentialized forms of cultural practices. If the awareness of being Malay in North Sumatra was related to the traumatic experiences during the process of state formation and marginalization, being Malay in Riau was associated with similar experiences caused by industrialization, exploitation of natural resources, and transmigration of laborers from other Indonesian regions, evicting local Malays from their traditional lands. Therefore, in the 1980s to 1990s, foregrounding Malay identity became an act of resistance to the Indonesian state, and the feeling of being Malay became more associated with the Malay World at large.

In Malaysia, Malays form the dominant racial group ruling over the others, comprising indigenous groups and people of Chinese and Indian origins. Since national independence in 1957, political leaders in Malaysia have always made it an important part of their agenda to promote the Malay language and culture as the basis for Malaysian national identity. The state of Malaysia developed a "Malay nation" based on racial division while putting Malayness at the center of its nation-building project. The affirmative actions contained in the New Economic Policy, which the Malaysian government adopted in 1971 to improve the socioeconomic position of the Malay people, inculcated among them a consciousness of being a modern Malay nation, of being a "new Malay" (Melayu Baru) (Rustam A. Sani 1993). Cultural aspects such as the Malay language, literature, and the arts continued to play a prominent role in Malaysia's national development. When Prime Minister Mahathir Mohamad enthusiastically launched "Vision 2020" in 1991 to develop Malaysia into one of Asia's economic tigers, it not only included the expansion of economic cooperation with its neighboring countries, but it also aimed at strengthening cultural and religious connections that were considered a good basis for economic programs and enhancing the Malaysian nation as one single and powerful people.

In this context, Malayness was deployed to connect and promote Malaysia among other Malay peoples with their organizations in the Southeast Asian region and beyond. Malaysian state authorities supported such an enhancement of transnational connections in which a few individuals and organizations played a major role in propagating transnationalism "from below." Regional dialogues and cultural festivals formed the core of these efforts to develop partnerships between Malay organizations in the neighboring countries and Malaysia. These initial efforts created the basis for further development of transnational activities in the region. The main aim of these activities was the reconstruction of the Malay cultural realm to be implanted in multiple localities across national borders to form a genuine Tanah Melayu or Malay land. These activities emphasized emotional ties with the land and the sense of belonging to a shared Malay culture and heritage in the form of language and traditional art forms. Malaysian organizations initiated these activities that were received well in other parts of the region as they boosted local pride and supported local political agendas.

The initial efforts go back to October 1970 when thirteen associations of Malay writers gathered to form the Federation of National Writers Association of Malaysia (Gabungan Persatuan Penulis Nasional/GAPENA) (Zakry Abadi 1989, 15–22). The highly respected Malay intellectual Ismail Hussein, who led GAPENA from 1971 to 2013, developed it into one of the most active organizations promoting Malay literature and culture on a national and transnational level. GAPENA strengthened networks in the Malay World by organizing a series of gatherings they named Northern Dialogue or Dialog Utara since the first gathering in Penang in 1982. In the framework of this Dialog Utara, events were organized in Medan, Aceh, Terengganu, Perak, and Patani to enhance cultural and economic ties between the northern states in the Malay Peninsula and the northern provinces of Sumatra and southern Thailand.[3] The Malaysian government supported this initiative as it wanted to use cultural efforts to boost economic cooperation in an Indonesia-Malaysia-Thailand Growth Triangle (IMT-GT). Moreover, the Northern Dialogue stimulated other dialogue series, one of which was a similar series of events in the south, Dialog Selatan, involving Singapore, Johor, and Riau (SiJoRi-growth triangle) to forge a regional network in the south of the Malay Peninsula.[4] Initiated in 1992, this Southern Dialogue also envisioned enhancing economic growth in an Indonesia-Malaysia-Singapore Growth Triangle (IMS-GT) development scheme.

In its effort to become the leader of a Malay World network in the closing decade of the twentieth century, Malaysia staged a number of big events.

Following the Malay World Conference in 1982, further initiatives were taken in 1996 to set up the Secretariat of the Malay World network in Kuala Lumpur.[5] In addition to these efforts by the central government, the regional organization Dunia Melayu Dunia Islam (DMDI, Malay World Islamic World) was founded in Melaka to position Malaysia (i.e. Melaka) at the center of the Malaysian transnational movement. In a convention held in Melaka in 2000, DMDI envisioned distributing Malay values and concepts from Melaka to the entire world (Sakai 2009, 65).[6] In all these events, dialogue series, conventions, and conferences, stage performances such as music, dance, and theater were given a central role to display the aesthetic forms of Malayness. These art performances stimulated a Malay activists forum, which further articulated Malay identity, and connected the dispersed Malay groups by propagating the narrative of a shared heritage.

As a response to initiatives by DMDI and GAPENA in developing the transnational network, Malay activists in the neighboring island tried to configure Sumatran Malayness to unite Malay communities.[7] In this respect, the concept of an integrated Malay cultural space, Alam Melayu, has been used to produce and make a sense of place. Hence, it comes as no surprise that the definition of the place of origin where the Malay kingdom of Srivijaya was situated, gains in prominence. Up until then, the dominant discourse of the Malay place of origin came from Malaysia, hailing Melaka as the very center of Malay civilization. Around the turn of the twenty-first century, Sumatra's claim as the place of origin became stronger, concomitant with the formation of Sumatran Malayness. Several political and economic factors explain this decline in Malaysia's dominance, while Indonesian provinces in Sumatra invigorated their efforts to develop a Malay transnational network.

The decentralization of the Indonesian political system is the main factor behind the reconfiguration of Malay culture and identity and the emergence of a joint Sumatran Malayness. This policy provided more authority and autonomy to the regional levels of the state's administrative system (regency and province) to stimulate economic, educational, and cultural developments. The tourist economy became an important tool for economic development, promoting commodified forms of heritage in specific regions and cities. Even though they are characterized by ethnic diversity, many regions in Sumatra stressed Malayness as their main identity. This reformation of Malay identity in Sumatra was particularly focused on traditional centers of power, such as Palembang, Jambi, Pagarruyung, Siak, and the island of Bintan. Fostering the ambition to become the heartland of the Malay World, the island of Sumatra tried to change the configuration of the previous cultural map drawn from a Malaysian perspective.

From this macro view of the Malay transnational network, we focus the discussion on the sociocultural processes taking place on a micro level in Kepri. The initiatives developed by agents in Kepri are rooted in the cultural movement active since the 1980s in Riau Province. Initially, it was a resistance movement in the 1990s against the central government in Jakarta. Riau declared its own "Visi 2020," which included turning Riau Province into the Malay economic and cultural center of Southeast Asia. Toward the end of the 1990s, political activists took the opportunity to lead a Riau independence movement against Jakarta-led exploitation of the region's natural resources and the suppression of civil rights of its population (cf. Colombijn 2003). This independence movement lost its momentum when countered with the regional autonomy regulations of the early 2000s, but it did trigger a commotion in the Riau Islands where political elites called for the establishment of an independent province separate from Riau, which was realized in 2004. The separation between the two provinces entailed the issue of how to distinguish from one the other and, at the same time, consider them as one single Malay people. This issue of cultural competition inspired cultural activists and art performers of both provinces to strive after the same goal of promoting their provinces as the "motherland of Malay culture" in a friendly but sometimes stiff bureaucratic competitiveness. In this competition, cultural festivals and heritage performances play a major role in the "Malayization" of the people in both Riaus and producing locality, while configuring a vibrant and highly dynamic Malay ethnoscape in its wake.

Malaysian efforts have declined significantly since the economic crisis of the late 1990s, which has had consequences on the force and intensity of Malaysia's cultural influence on the formation of transnational Malayness. By contrast, art festivals, predominantly engaging itinerary troupes from the Riau Islands, seem to play an increasingly important role in the formation of identity in Sumatra and other regions. This line of argument would confirm a shift of the center of cultural formations from Malaysia to both mainland Riau and Kepri, meaning that the activities that started in the 1990s in Pekanbaru and slightly later in Tanjungpinang seem to be paying off.

Transnational identity work at a local level is the main concern of this chapter where we pay particular attention to the role of cultural festivals in recreating the concept of Tanah Melayu (Malay Land), thereby reconfiguring and inculcating emotional attachment to the image of the Malay self, which contains both local dimensions and transnational entanglements. Malay identity is presented and promoted in an aesthetic form through the imagery of theater and dance performances. The concept of Malay kingship, which forms the central theme in the performances, symbolizes Malay sovereignty, territoriality, and dignity as a manifestation of Malayness that through these performances is being restored and propagated. Before discussing the circumstance surrounding the restoration of the sultanate of Bintan Darul Masyhur in Kepri, we will explore how arts festivals help to produce place and invite the multiethnic population of the region to become local subjects through a series of performed rituals (cf. Apadurai 1996, 185).

Cultural Festivals, Malay Homeland, and Transnational Entanglements

Transnationalist relations between migrants and the people in the home countries include affective ties that the people at both ends feel and cherish while often nostalgically imagining an idealized home that is no longer there. Malay transnationalism has much to do with such emotional feelings, nostalgia, and imagination of a cultural realm, a homeland, which harks back to the era before colonialism and the postcolonial nation-states. However, unlike the transnationalism of a diasporic community whose homeland is situated far away, the Malay homeland is produced "here" in the place where many Malays have lived for a long time. Since the nostalgic reproduction of a homeland is often historically configured or imagined as a genealogy based on royal lineages, former kingdoms such as Melaka and Riau-Lingga compete to be designated as such. This homeland is considered as tainted by modernization and the presence of substantial numbers of newcomers practicing their way of life in the *kampung* or Tanah Melayu. Therefore, acts of reclaiming places and the recreation of the homeland are thought to be necessary and important. Cultural activists and performers use cultural festivals to reverberate the story about ancestral origins and their subsequent migrations, and to create cultural heritage comprising paramount achievements of Malay civilization in order to reclaim the Malay land and remake the "space" into their "place."

The content and discourse surrounding cultural festivals held in Sumatra and the Malay Peninsula indicate the Malays' concern about place, cultural realm, and landscape. Such cultural events serve as a tool to reconnect people with their places and evoke a sense of belonging. It is interesting to observe the ways Malays support their claim of certain places or sites as part of their heritage. In more general terms, and with regard to the interconnectedness of the Austronesians with their places, Thomas Reuter (2006, 11) argues that

The Austronesian-speaking people articulate their sense of belonging to particular places and lay their claim to land or other territorial rights by invoking local histories of ancestral origins and migration. These accounts of human movement and emplacement might be written down but more often they are conveyed as oral histories. Origin histories are also inscribed on the physical landscape in the form of sacred sites, and on the minds of local participants through their shared experience of ritual performances held at these sites. Together these commemorative social practices generate a powerful sense of belonging and emplacement.

Reuter's contention above refers to the work of ritual performance and ritualized practices and the impact these generate. It is in such events that stories are created and retold, reanimated in bodily performances, and reinstated through traditional practices such as rituals and art performances to (re)make places. For the people and the participants, particular cultural events at heritage sites provide the opportunity to socially reconstruct and personally experience places and sites.

A memorable occasion in the Riau Islands that can exemplify the construction of a place through a cultural event is the gathering of Malay authors from across Southeast Asia (Perkampungan Penulis Melayu se-Asia Tenggara) held in Daik on the island of Lingga in 1997. Yusmar Yusuf, then head of the Center for Malay Studies at the University of Riau, gave the opening speech and commented upon historical sites and traditions that people have practiced up to modern times in Daik as their heritage from the Riau-Johor Malay dynasty, the successor of the Melaka kingdom. In this speech, he coined the name Bunda Tanah Melayu (Motherland of the Malays) for Daik, which inscribed the title to the place and, more importantly, into the participants' minds. The participants who stayed (*berkampung*) there with the local Malays for some time while experiencing the local way of life, landscape,[8] language register, and special flavors of nostalgic *kampung* cooking, wrote down and published their experiences in the form of poems, pantuns, and prose stories. The Malaysian co-organizing GAPENA published their impressions under the title *Daik Bonda Tanah Melayu* (Daik the Motherland of the Malays) (Rejab F. I. 2000). This outside recognition was a great boost for the confidence of the Riau Islands in general and the island of Lingga in particular, as it has a history of being rather marginalized within Kepri, where the focus is more on the northern islands of Batam and Bintan. The local authorities of Lingga district formalized the sobriquet to become an official epithet of the district's territory,[9] which was then followed by a Kepri governor who broadened its scale to the provincial level in 2010.

Place names, landscape names, renaming, and making sense of place all construct a narrative framework that draws a connection between the present generation and the ancestors. Place and landscape are material aspects of myths of origin, which are embedded in local knowledge and relate to the recitation of an ordered sequence of place names, or "topogeny," which "represents a projected externalization of memories that can be lived in as well as thought about" (Fox 1997, 8). The story of the origin of the Malay dynasty as contained in the *Sulalatu 'l-Salatin* recounts successive migrations from Mount Seguntang in South Sumatra to the Riau Islands, Singapore, Melaka, and back to the Riau Islands, which correspond with historical sites local Malay groups celebrate because of their cultural significance. However, the topogeny in the geographic context of the Malay World consists of several localities with their respective local configurations dispersed around the national territories of Indonesia, Singapore, and Malaysia. As a matter of course, the ensuing quest for the center of Malay civilization and its original place of birth is contested in historical studies, which interpret the remains found in such places as Kedah's Bujang Valley, Palembang, Jambi, and some other places like Kepri. These contestations over the place of origin attract attention from Malay groups across national borders, which show the transnational nature of Malay identity. Besides local configurations of identity grounded in the respective sites, there are attempts to articulate a shared imagination of the Malay land, Tanah Melayu.

A song composed in 2005, "Hymne Tanah Melayu" (Hymn of the Malay Land), illustrates these efforts of making sense of place, of inculcating a sense of devotion to the Malay land. It serves as a text that helps Malays (re)embed emotional attachment to the Malay land. Tengku Ryo Riezqan from Medan, who composed the song, stated that he wrote the lyrics as a synthesis of his observations of the Malay communities in Sumatra and Borneo. He inferred that the lives of the Malays had been seriously affected since the inception of the Republic of Indonesia that destroyed the traditional rule in several Malay kingdoms. His experience as a member of the paramilitary forces assisting Indonesian soldiers "defending" Timor Leste against a "separatist" movement, made him concerned about the fate of the former Malay territory on the east coast of Sumatra. Tengku Ryo is a member of the former ruling house of Serdang, but only in the late 1990s heard the story about the killings of family members during the so-called "social revolution" in East Sumatra in 1946. He stated that his hike to the top of the legendary Mount Ledang near Melaka inspired him even more in composing the lyrics of the hymn. He believes that the traditional ruling elites have lost control over their lands, which would have been used to develop their culture and civilization and bring prosperity to the people.[10] Based on the general feeling that Malays have been pushed aside and alienated from their lands, the hymn expresses a call to the Malay land, to make sense of it, restore peoples' attachment to it, and reclaim it firmly into their possession.

The lyrics of "Hymne Tanah Melayu," which is regularly performed in the opening ceremony of festivals, emphasize the connection with the land by repeating the phrase *Wahai Tanahku, Tanahku Melayu* ("O land of mine, my Malay land"), which is further underscored with phrases about its nostalgic beauty, such as *sungguhlah permai sedari dulu* ("truly beautiful in the past and present") and *damai berpuak menjadi satu* ("all groups are in peace to become one community"). It is full of praise for the Malay land that will affect the subject *Aku* ("I") because *Engkau* ("you") refers to the land that gave birth to *Aku* (*engkaulah satu tempat ku ber-Ibu*). In addition, the melody of the song invokes *Aku*, whom the audience and performers will identify with, to sing it solemnly and internalize its lyrics. Ever since the song was released in an album entitled *Kecik* ("Small") and uploaded to a website in 2009, Tengku Ryo has received fan mail from people who share with him that the song evokes melancholic feelings. Tengku Ryo dedicated the song to the Malays around the world, and the responses indicate a reception in the Malay world at large. Currently, it is sung by both audiences and performers at the opening of Malay cultural festivals in Medan, Riau, Lampung, and Kepri.

In Kepri, Malay activists, artists, and local government promote the region as the motherland of Malays through cultural festivals. By cultural festivals, we mean occasional events in which cultural productions, such as performing arts, spectacles, and rituals are performed. With reference to Ling and Lew (2012), festivals can be categorized based on their historical and geographic context. Most festivals in Kepri are contemporary in origin and promote local identity if the historical context is used, while they can be classified as place-specific and place-nonspecific festivals if the geographic context is used as the criterion. Place-specific festivals are rooted in a certain locality that reflects a community's sense of place (ibid., 17), which in the context of the recreation of the Malay homeland construct a narrative about associations of the landscape and/or place with three iconic symbols: historical sites, heroes, and traditions.

The narrative that associates the Malay land with historical sites emphasizes objects, physical remains, and sites as evidence of the former Malay kingdom. The Carang River Festival (Festival Sungai Carang) held annually in Tanjungpinang presents the story of early eighteenth-century Riau with its harbor and royal palace that the Johor Malay dynasty built in the upstream region of the Carang River. The Tanjungpinang municipal government supports the preservation of the palace site and the tombs of its royal occupants and celebrates these with a cultural festival. During the Festival Sungai Carang, the local government employs a number of boats decorated and named after Malay heroes whose tombs are found along the Carang River. In 2017 about fifty boats paraded from upstream of the river into Bintan Bay, watched by an audience congregated on the Tanjungpinang shoreline. A master of ceremonies briefly told the stories about the Malay nobles whose names were attached to the boats. This is an act of deploying selected historical narratives to accentuate the era regarded as the golden era of the local Malay kingdom and consecrate its former territory as the Malay land, that is, present-day Kepri with its capital Tanjungpinang.

The glorification of the former power center is a strategy to legitimate the act of invoking historical narratives to recreate a Malay cultural space. The Festival of Penyengat Island (Festival Pulau Penyengat) stages stories about the historical sites on the island as the former political and literary center of the Riau-Lingga dynasty of the nineteenth century. At the Festival Pulau Penyengat in 2018, Raja Malik Hafrizal, one of the members of the main aristocratic family and co-organizer of the festival, enumerated buildings and places on the small island to illustrate the glorious history of Penyengat Island and emphasize the achievements of his renowned ancestors, scholars of language and literature. Already imagined as one of the main pillars of Malay identity, the language as marker gains in significance to be highlighted in the case of Penyengat. As one of the region's three contributions to the pantheon of national heroes, Raja Ali Haji, a member of the viceregal family, was added because of his merits in the development of the Indonesian language. Nineteenth-century language authorities designated Malay as used in the islands to be the main source for its standardization in the nineteenth century, which later was used as an important basis for standard Indonesian.

In addition to local interests to promote Kepri's reputation as cultural and literary center in the Malay World (and attract tourists from other parts of the Malay world),[11] the Malay homeland with its landscape used in the story as backdrop implies a transnational space. This is used by Malaysian and Singaporean Malays to trace and ground part of their shared history. Moreover, both Festival Sungai Carang and Festival Pulau Penyengat amplify the significance of the Malay territory that they want to recreate.

Fig. 1. A float with a marriage ceremony conducted by a group of school children in a parade during the Festival Tamadun Melayu in 2017 in Daik, Lingga Island.

We find a similar case in Lingga with the Malay Civilization Festival (Festival Tamadun Melayu) in 2017, which nostalgically reminisced about the rule of Sultan Mahmud Riayat Syah over the Riau-Lingga kingdom and parts of the Malay Peninsula (Johor and Pahang; r. 1761–1812). Even though the festival aimed to celebrate the bestowal of the title of Indonesian national hero on the sultan, the main focus of the narrative was the *territory* under Sultan Mahmud's rule with Daik as its center. Therefore, the organizers gave a prominent role to a rebuilt royal complex to serve as a backdrop for staging heroic stories about the sultan who commanded a "marine guerrilla" strategy against the Dutch based in Tanjungpinang. He is reported to have used nearby islands and Mount Daik as natural fortresses and a sago forest as food supply for the people. This narrative frames the festival as a place-making event by connecting the hero to the Malay land of Daik which he defended against the Dutch. Delegations from Terengganu and Johor took part in the celebration and consecration of this transnational space which, at the same time, represented the local ambitions of Lingga to recreate itself as the center by celebrating the hero status of one of its sultans.

Such entanglements of local and transnational interests are also reflected in the International Literary Festival of Mount Bintan (Festival Sastra Internasional Gunung Bintan/FSIGB). In 2018 the event promoted the Malay legendary hero Hang Tuah and, as the organizers implied, Sungai Duyung, a place near Mount

Bintan, as his place of birth. FSIGB is the manifestation of the local interests in promoting the former Malay kingdom called Bentan and its heritage site around a hill located in the area of Bintan Bay named Gunung Bintan (Mount Bintan). Yet, the interests in boosting the reputation of Bintan are intertwined with the transnational dimension of Malayness, in which the territory and the kingdom called Bentan were among the places where the Malay progenitor first settled in his migration from Palembang.[12] The organizers of the FSIGB also promoted an alternative story of Hang Tuah's place of birth that is imagined to be located on Bintan. In this festival, poets from across the Malay World gathered to discuss and publicize their creative work. Many of the performed poems reinterpreted the legendary figure of Hang Tuah and glorified him with the aim of keeping the figure alive as a role model for future generations. Festival Sastra International Gunung Bintan 2020 was held online at the end of September and comprised performances of poetry readings and an online seminar in zoom which was uploaded on YouTube. This format continued in the 2021 event and is being planned as live performances in 2022.

Fig. 2. The performance of mak yong by a troupe from Mantang Island at the Festival Mak Yong 2019 in Tanjungpinang. In the foreground we see a cross-dressed female actor as the king in a dance with the clown figure, Awang Pengasuh. *Source*: Institute for Preservation of Cultural Values (Balai Pelestarian Nilai Budaya/BPNB) Kepri, 2019.

Apart from associating place with sites and heroes, the festivals also connect place with traditions. These place-specific festivals enhance the relationship between places and traditions as we encounter in the Festival Sungai Enam, celebrating a subdistrict on the south coast of Bintan. In November 2017 the festival promoted and celebrated the local Malay traditions of a theater performance called Mak Yong and a social dance named Joget Dangkong,[13] as well as the local dish *otak-otak* (fish cakes), a snack known throughout the Malay World. The event clearly aimed to make the dish into an icon of the *kampung* and enhance its place identity. Such an iconic tradition related to a certain *kampung* is also what the Festival Mak Yong Mantang presents. By making a place identity for the island of Mantang, situated just off Bintan's south coast, the festival brings to the fore a narrative that connects the Mak Yong theater to Mantang Island and strengthens its reputation as the place where the theater form was initially developed in the Riau Islands. This does not mean that the people of Mantang do not realize that the tradition is a part of heritage shared with other Malay communities in East Sumatra and the Malay Peninsula. The narrative, in this respect, shapes the identity of place and links it to the rest of the Malay World.

The consciousness of sharing a rich heritage with other Malay communities while localizing and connecting them with particular *kampung* in Kepri piecing together a Malay homeland, is prevalent in and organized through cultural festivals. Within the above frames, the festivals exhibit traditionalized cultural practices, some of which are revived, such as performing arts, ritual practices, genuine *kampung* food, literary works, textiles, and martial arts. These commodified traditions are made and remade into a shared Malay heritage in the entire Malay World. The theatrical performances of Mak Yong and Bangsawan that center on the royal court life take a prominent position among the promoted art forms. They distribute and animate images of feudal power, loyalty, kingship, and territoriality, and in addition propose court etiquettes as cultured values of Malay propriety which the people may want to follow if they see themselves as "cultured Malays."

Mak Yong and particularly Bangsawan are widely distributed in the Malay World. These art forms are considered to epitomize the Malay language, music, costume, moral values, and most intriguingly, the Malay way of life. The repertoire is predominantly fictional although Bangsawan, especially, is known for the historical sources the stage plays are based on or refer to. An example of this is the play "Sultan Mahmud Riayat Syah," which narrates the move of the sultan from Riau to Lingga and his resistance against Dutch colonial rule.[14] If Mak Yong tends to contain slapstick humor and features a clown figure who, to a certain extent, may subvert the king's authority, in contrast Bangsawan contains dialogues in a refined style of the language, gestures, and manners of the royal family and its retinue at court. If Mak Yong manifests the image that emphasizes an intimate relationship with royalty, Bangsawan performs an image of the

Malay aristocratic family in its sublime majesty. Interestingly, in the current context of their revival, both amplify a sense of loyalty and submission to the king and his power. As the reconstruction of the Malay cultural realm requires justification of certain territory as Malay homeland, Mak Yong and Bangsawan become a vehicle to instantiate the stories and imagination of Malay kingship, kingdom, and territory. These forms preserve the basic idea of the social and political structure of Malay society of the past, which the present generation may want to revive.

The (Re)appearance of Royalty and a Global Sufi Movement

In this section we will discuss one of the other pillars that is pivotal in the configuration of Malay identity and the production of a territory that might be considered as the Bunda Tanah Melayu. The different strands of its imagery are localized but also have strong transnational connections which are instrumental to explaining the inauguration of a sultan without any royal credentials, thereby outweighing local aristocratic families who may have more authoritative claims to reinstate a sultanate in Kepri. In the discussion about this recent development in local cultural politics, we refer to Arjun Appadurai's work on transnationalism and his proposition about the importance of imagination and its distinction with sheer fantasy:

> The idea of fantasy carries with it the inescapable connotation of thought divorced from projects and actions, and it also has a private, even individualistic sound about it. The imagination, on the other hand, has a projective sense about it, the sense of being a prelude to some sort of expression, whether aesthetic or otherwise. Fantasy can dissipate (because its logic is so often autotelic), but the imagination, especially when collective, can become the fuel for action. It is the imagination, in its collective forms, that creates ideas of neighborhood and nationhood, of moral economies and unjust rule, of higher wages and foreign labor prospects. The imagination is today a staging ground for action, and not only for escape (Appadurai 1996, 7).

The imagination of royalty as presented in Mak Yong and Bangsawan (re)familiarizes Malays with the notion of kingship, and therefore enhances its position as part of their cultural identity. Therefore, these theatrical forms would also be helpful in generating acceptance or other positive responses from the surrounding society about the revival of kingship in the twenty-first century. Here, too, the transnational premise of Malay culture comes to the fore in support of a general appraisal of the revival of the institution of the sultanate in Kepri. In the federated state of Malaysia, nine sultans have continued to be invested with a certain authority and governing capacity by the central government, particularly in the spheres of customs and religion. Even in Singapore, the defunct Malay royal institution was resuscitated to a certain extent by one of the members of the family of the Malay sultan installed by the British in the early nineteenth century. The descendant of the sultan's family, Tengku Mohammad Shawal Ibni Tengku Abdul Aziz, apparently does not carry the title sultan, but rather occupies the politically less sensitive function of custodian (*pemangku adat*) of Malay customs in a rather imaginary "Singapore, Riau-Lingga Sultanate." In this function he does, at least occasionally, bestow honorary titles on individuals, such as an Indonesian member of parliament, Arsul Sani, on his visit to Singapore in September 2019.[15]

This is similar, in fact, to what has been taking place in Indonesia on a much more regular basis since the turn of the new millennium, when President Suharto was forced to step down and consecutive new governments promulgated laws for administrative and political decentralization. One of the ramifications of this "communitarian turn in Indonesian politics" is that the "return of the sultan" has become such a common characteristic that Gerry van Klinken (2007, 149) suggests that "sultanship has become perhaps the symbol par excellence of local identity in Indonesia's autonomy era." According to his research, seventy of the more than three hundred principalities that existed in Indonesia at the beginning of the twentieth century had an incumbent in the early 2000s. Most of these were the result of recent revival activities of the following three types: an existing institution that raised its profile, a kingdom dismantled or destroyed in the first decades of Indonesia's independence that was resurrected or a principality that had disappeared in the more distant past and was now being reinvented (ibid.). The inauguration of a leader in the previously unknown sultanate of Bintan in Kepri is a clear example of the third type as there are only scanty indications that the island once was the seat of a Malay kingdom.

Based on her research into the change of power in Indonesia at the turn of the past millennium, Vivienne Wee (2002, 502) argues that atavistic tendencies of Malay elites in the islands have fueled efforts to recreate the idea of the Riau-Lingga sultanate as a cultural reality in contemporary times, which have also legitimated everyday practices of several customs and rituals derived from a feudal past. The Malay ruling house of Riau is considered the most senior and legitimate cultural heir of the Melaka throne, as it was in Riau that the family eventually settled after its forced departure and peregrination when the Portuguese vanquished Malay forces and occupied the town of Melaka. The other Malay royal houses still in existence in Malaysia and Indonesia came later, while the royal pedigree may not always be generally acknowledged.

Therefore, the claim of the elite that Riau-Lingga is Melaka's rightful heir is not without reason, nor is it new, but what is emphasized in this latest atavistic revival of Malay royalty is that the family returned to the *root* kingdom where the family once started and changed the area into a thriving polity. As mentioned in the introduction of this chapter, the foundational text *Sulalatu 'l-Salatin* relates how a legendary descendant of Alexander the Great settled first in Bintan before founding the settlements of Singapore and Melaka, from which they were ousted by foreign forces after they had changed them into international entrepots. By contrast, in Bintan the Palembang prince Sri Tri Buana (also known as Sang Nila Utama) was welcomed by an already established royal house, with whom he entered a family relationship by marrying the daughter of Queen Wan Seri Beni—probably the most common line of argument found in traditional historiography.[16]

Archaeological explorations in the area indicate early settlements from the fourteenth century on the coast of Bintan Bay, where pot sherds, glass, and bronze items were found that suggest international trade between the islands and China (Miksic 2013, 377–78). Combined with the legendary tales of the *Sulalatu 'l-Salatin*, this information is normally interpreted as an indication of early cooperation between roaming Malay royalty with sea nomads for whom the Riau Islands was one of the places used as a temporary base. Local historians, however, go much further in their interpretation and apply their imagination to concoct stories to fill in blanks in the history which may also be used as "fuel for action" (cf. the above quotation by Appadurai). For instance, in one of the local histories we find Bintan mentioned as the direct heir of Srivijaya because the Palembang prince replaced the local queen and mother-in-law Wan Sri Beni in 1158, after which he moved the kingdom to Singapore (Abdul Malik, et. al. 2012, 3).

The historiography follows the peregrination of Malay royalty along the mentioned paths to eventually return to firmer ground on the banks of the Carang River or Hulu Riau, near present-day Tanjungpinang, where the Malay royal family settled and thrived in the early eighteenth century. This place became their power base from where they warded off attacks by Siak forces led by Raja Kecik with the assistance of Bugis mercenary forces whom the Malay aristocrats had engaged for this purpose. This cooperation and intermarriage between Malays and Bugis had a long-lived impact on the configuration of the power relations in the Riau-Lingga sultanate lasting until 1911, when the last (Malay/Bugis) sultan, Abdul Rahman, was deposed by the Dutch colonial government. The sultan took refuge in Singapore while other members of the family went to Johor, Terengganu, or stayed in the island of Penyengat. In subsequent periods, certain factions within the sultan's family made efforts to reinstate the sultanate, but to no avail. However, in 2007, two families on Bintan who claim to be direct descendants of Tun Telanai—the caretaker of the former kingdom of Bentan after Sri Tri Buana had left on future missions—inaugurated a person without any royal credentials as custodian of Malay traditions (*pemangku adat*). Five years later, on December 12, 2012, at 12 o'clock midnight, this custodian of Malay traditions, Huzrin Hood, was installed as the first sultan of Bintan Darul Masyhur—the revived and renamed kingdom of Bentan. The surprising part here is that for some reason it was not the most eligible member of the official Malay sultan's family lineage, Tengku Husin, who was chosen to become the new head of a revived Riau sultanate. Instead, a local political figure who had led the local elite's struggle to elevate the administrative status of the region from regency (*kabupaten*) to that of province in 2004, was granted a position into the local aristocracy.

With an educational background as religious teacher and law student, Huzrin Hood went into politics in the mid-1970s and steadily made his way up the ladder in the governmental party ranks of Golkar to become the *bupati* (head of the regency) of the Kepulauan Riau by 2000. However, his term in office was cut short because of a two-year jail sentence for misappropriating funds from the regional budget after a legal process that, according to his own assessment, was fraught with political issues (*sebuah kasus hukum yang sarat muatan politis*) (Huzrin Hood et. al. 2015, 76). As champion of the struggle for the regency's elevated status, he was slated to become the first governor of the new province, but he was instead sent to Bandung to serve his sentence. The short stint he spent there obviously did not break his spirit to develop the region of his birth, and he returned with great fervor to continue where he had left off. He strengthened his network in the region designated as the growth triangle SiJoRi (Singapore, Johor, and Riau), taking the initiative to establish a youth organization, a business association, and become the founding father of the prestigious regional championship in martial arts (*pencak silat*), which is considered as a specific Malay identity marker. Huzrin Hood is also listed as director and commissioner of several companies and a number of social organizations, such as chair of the Kepri's regional branch of the Friendship Forum of Indonesian Archipelago Palaces (Forum Silaturahmi Keraton Se-Nusantara) and chair of the Indonesian Mosque Council (Dewan Masjid Indonesia).

Huzrin Hood and his assistants compiled a book about the resurrection of the Bentan kingdom and its historical background with the contemporary objectives of grounding an economy based on sharia laws. In this work, with the ominous title *Sesat di Ujung Jalan, Balek ke Pangkal Jalan* ("Lost at the End of the Road, Return to the Beginning of the Road"), Huzrin Hood stated that he wanted to revitalize trading activities as part of everyday life in accordance with Islamic law and elevate the dignity (*marwah*) of Malay customs and culture (Hurzin Hood et. al. 2015, 79).[17] In a section of the book that was summarized from an article by one of the main leaders in the global Murabitun sufi protest movement, Syeikh Umar Ibrahim Vadillo, it is explained that the Prophet Muhammad upon his arrival in Medina created two institutions: the mosque as a place of worship and a market (*souq muamalah*) as a place where people could exchange goods without paying rent for the stalls or taxes to any authority (ibid., 39–40). Fanned by the devastating financial crisis that severely affected Malaysia in 1997, the Malaysian prime minister Tun Mahathir Mohamad ogled the Islamic gold dinar as currency to fortify the nation against attacks from Western speculators, fight the near-monopolistic position of the American dollar in international trade, and unite Malaysia with its Muslim brother states in the early 2000s (cf. Abu Bakar bin Mohd Yusuf et al, 2002). In December 2019 Dr Mahathir reiterated his intention to introduce this setup, which, in his view, was an effective cure against Western economic dominance. At the end of the summit of the Organisation of Islamic Cooperation (OIC), he revealed that Iran, Malaysia, Turkey, and Qatar were seriously considering trading among themselves using the gold standard and a barter system to guard against economic sanctions (Lee 2019).

Ironic in the context is that the return of the Islamic gold dinar from before the early Muslim caliphates originates in, and was promoted globally by, a relatively small movement that predominantly consists of European converts to Islam. The Scottish convert and charismatic Syaikh Abdalqadir as-Sufi (1930–2021) established this Murabitun movement in the United Kingdom in 1969 and ever since has functioned as its spiritual leader. The Murabitun movement is a mystical order branched off from the Darqawi order in Morocco and particularly targets minorities in regions outside the core area of Islam, such as South Africa, Mexico, and the United States, to cater to "protest converts" and to prepare for a global Islamic revolution (Bubandt 2009, 108–9). The more worldly and political program of the movement is designed and led by the abovementioned Syaikh Vadillo, a Spanish convert who has settled in Kuala Lumpur. He is the chairman of the World Islamic Mint, the organization responsible for the issuing and the standards of gold and silver coins and was the founding president of the World Islamic Trading Organization. He has authored many books and travels around to promote the cause. The overall goal of the movement is to cancel the use of paper money as it leads to usury and inflation and break the control of the banking system on the exchange of goods. After this is achieved, they would be able to recreate a society that is supposed to resemble the one at the time of the Prophet Muhammad. Clearly the gold dinar and silver dirham that were introduced to pay *zakat* and other obligatory expenses related to Islam, eventually would replace the local currency. Unsurprisingly, this causes big problems for the introduction of the sharia exchange system even in majority Muslim nations, such as Malaysia and Indonesia. In a recent move by the Indonesian government, the main Indonesian representative of the movement, Ir. Zaim Saidi, who wrote the foreword in Huzrin Hood's book (2015, iv–v), was arrested and the *muamalah* market in Depok disbanded because all financial transactions should make use of the official currency, the Indonesian rupiah, as Vice-President Ma'ruf Amin explained to news agencies and on his official website.[18]

Fig. 3. Silver coin (Dirham) with a weight of 2.975 gram valued as 1 dirham, which was minted by Sultan Huzrin Hood of Bintan Darul Masyhur in 2013 (1435 A.H.). The standard of this coin (purity of its silver and weight) is authorized by the World Islamic Mint led by Syaikh Umar Ibrahim Vadillo.

The Murabitun sufi movement has been quite successful in propagating the use of the gold dinar and silver dirham among sultanates in the Malay World, such as Ternate, Cirebon, and Bintan in Indonesia, Sulu in the Philippines, and Kelantan, Kedah, and Perak in the Malay Peninsula. These kingdoms have all minted coins in the name of their sultans which are used for the payment of *zakat*, alms, dowry, and in *muamalah* markets. Shortly after he was inaugurated as the first sultan of Bintan, Huzrin Hood opened a *muamalah* market near his house with rules as stipulated by Shaikh Vadillo on the principle of creating public marketplaces as opposed to private institutions, such as supermarkets. At his Sultan's Market, nobody paid any rent for the stalls and people would trade by using the gold and silver coins that were minted with silver and gold obtained from the state-related mining company PT Antam and donations from abroad, as Huzrin proudly acknowledged in an interview in 2019.[19] He also set up a scholarship program for young people (Pendidikan Perwira Bintan) to get an education in accordance with the basic rules of the Murabitun movement so that the common people would be enabled to retrieve the power hijacked by the banks and big companies (cf. Vadillo 2002 as quoted in Bubandt 2009, 112). Another project that he has planned and is building is an integrated center referred to as Imaret, where a mosque and Islamic boarding school will be joined by small business enterprises to enhance the wellbeing of the people (Huzrin Hood et. al. 2005, 61–64). At the time of editing this volume, the Imaret was still under construction.

It is debatable how far the influence of the new sultan reaches and to what extent he will change or fortify the cultural identity of the local and translocal Malays, but many networks come together in this figure who is widely connected with other revived sultanates and principalities in Indonesia (that partly also follow the Murabitun guidelines). He is clearly a figurehead whom the local government respects and supports by financing the building of his palace and other facilities. For some unknown reason, Huzrin Hood dropped out of the 2020 provincial elections. However, it seems only a matter of time before he will combine his Sri Tri Buana's crown as sultan of Bintan Darul Masyhur with the Malay headdress, *kopiah* or *tanjak*, of the Kepri governor.

Conclusion

In this chapter we have tried to capture and explore the dynamics of Malay identity works in the relatively recently established administrative area of the province of Riau Islands (Kepri). The configurations are a good example of how local, transregional, transnational, and global forces come together in one Indonesian region, which itself borders on two other nation-states. Since the elevation of its status to an autonomous province in 2004, the local authorities have been active in reconfiguring the image of the region and its population from a backwater collection of islands strewn in the sea (Segantang Lada) at the edge of the nation populated by marginalized and destitute Malays into an island province imagined to be the center of the transnational Malay world, where the many immigrant groups will learn what it is to be a Malay by learning its literary and cultural productions. We highlighted two indicators used by the authorities, as well as by grassroot cultural activists, to manifest and propagate this new status of Malay identity, namely art festivals that help to produce place of certain sites. Performances commemorating certain historical events that took place at the site, such as the Festival Sungai Carang, augment the significance of these sites. This festival memorializes the return of the Malay sultan's family to the region by settling at the Carang River in the beginning of the eighteenth century. Such commodification of cultural expressions not only present this heightened meaning to groups of naïve tourists, but also try to persuade the multiethnic population of the region to become local subjects through a series of performed rituals (cf. Appadurai 1996, 185). Approached from a transregional and transnational perspective, people living outside Kepri who self-identify as Malay will recognize the style and may feel at home with these commodified cultural productions.

These performances are not only staged by professional cultural activists but are taught as part of the curriculum of local schools and have experienced an increasing popularity among the younger sections of the population, many of whom will not have ethnic Malay roots in the province. There seems to have been a change in the appreciation of the local culture among the local youth, who in the early 2000s were reported to opt for Indonesianess over the local Malay forms (Faucher 2006). In Kepri there are many arts training centers (*sanggar*) that specialize in Javanese, Sundanese, Balinese, and other regional cultures in Indonesia, but the Malay culture is considered as a relevant part of living in the Riau Islands.

Another significant marker of local identity is having a sultan who symbolically rules over his people, bestows the occasional title, and is a special public figure in the sociopolitical configuration of society. Since 2012 Riau officially has a new sultan after 101 years of absence and many efforts have been made to revitalize the institution during this century of absence. The fact that the incumbent has no royal credentials and that his ancestors are Javanese rather than ethnic Malay does not seem to be big issue for this public figure who is widely connected to sociopolitical organizations and private companies. He focuses his efforts on purifying the Islamic economic exchanges and returning the people's faith and dignity in their local traditions and culture. His efforts are parallel to those of the local authorities who albeit fear his power and influence, also appreciate his endeavors. With him as the sultan, they have a figurehead who can enlarge the chances of the province becoming the imaginary Bunda Tanah Melayu.

Endnotes: Transnational Malay Identity

1. The research for this chapter, comprising fieldwork in Tanjungpinang and other parts of the Riau Islands, was carried out in the framework of the EU-funded Competing Regional Integrations in Southeast Asia (CRISEA). We are grateful for being granted the opportunity to conduct the research and want to thank the members of the Research Programme for their constructive comments, particularly Volker Grabowsky and Jayeel Cornelio, whose feedback has been instrumental in improving this chapter. Any mistakes and errors are, of course, our responsibility.

2. In this chapter we use Kepri (Kepulauan Riau) to refer to the province of Riau Islands formed in 2004 and Riau Province for the province on the mainland of Sumatra with Pekanbaru as its provincial capital.

3. This information is based on the documentation of the regional dialog forums "Dialog Utara" in the form of programs and proceedings. See Dialog Utara IV 1989, Dialog Utara VII 1997, and Dialog Utara VIII 1999.

4. Zaini-Lajoubert (1992) reported on the first Dialog Selatan held in Johor. See also Dialog Selatan II 1995.

5. See the following sources: Simposium Jaringan Melayu Antarbangsa 1996, Malay World Conference 2001.

6. DMDI's vision was also reiterated in the following conventions. See Konvensyen Dunia Melayu Dunia Islam IV 2003 and Konvensyen Dunia Melayu Dunia Islam V 2004.

7. Riau Province took the first initiative to develop Sumatran Malay networks in 2006 (see Musyawarah Lembaga Adat Melayu Se-Sumatra 2006. In addition to this, see https://www.riauterkini. com/hukum.php?arr=9257). The last gathering of Sumatran Malay networks so far documented was the third conference which was held in Jambi in 2014. See https://acehprov.go.id/berita/kategori/umum/ rumpun-melayu-se-sumatera-persiapkan-musyawarah-paripurna-iii.

8. In Malay *pantun* and other genres, Mount Daik (Gunung Daik) features prominently for its peculiar three summits which are ascribed legendary, magical powers and are imagined to be the abode of invisible creatures (*orang bunian*). That the belief in such forces is still alive emerged in an interview Alan Darmawan had with a Mak Yong actor who, after having staged a Mak Yong performance in Daik, was driven to the verge of suicide. He could not cope with tensions caused by *orang bunian* who had watched the play and were enraged with him because he had failed to pay proper respect to them (interview, September 6, 2018).

9. This sobriquet of Lingga, Bunda Tanah Melayu, was officially made and included in the official logo of Lingga district following the local bylaw No. 20 of 2012 (Peraturan Daerah Kabupaten Lingga No. 20 Tahun 2012 tentang Perubahan Atas Peraturan Daerah Kabupaten Lingga No. 3 tahun 2005 tentang Lambang Daerah, Motto dan Slogan Kabupaten Lingga).

10. Summarized from the interview Alan Darmawan had with Tengku Ryo on September 27, 2020.

11. Local authorities sponsor these festivals as they are expected to have a positive impact on foreign tourist visits to Kepri who predominantly hail from Singapore (48.5 percent) and Malaysia (10.5 percent), making a total of 1.3 million visitors in 2019 (Wilda Fajriah 2020).

12. See below for a more elaborate discussion about this. As for the spelling of the name of the island and the kingdom once located on it, Bentan is used to refer to the old kingdom while Bintan is used as the present-day name of the island. The revived Kesultanan Bintan Darul Masyhur seems to make use of both interchangebly.

13. Mak Yong is a theater form that combines dance, music, slapstik comedy, acting, and storytelling. It exists currently in the Indonesian provinces of Riau Islands and North Sumatra, the northern states of the Malay Peninsula, and the southern provinces of Thailand. Joget Dangkong is a dance performed by a group of females, who in some part of their performance, invite male members of the audience to join the dance.

14. A Bangsawan theater group in Lingga, Sri Mahkota Lingga, performed this play in November 2017 at the Festival Tamadun Melayu held in conjuction with the celebration surrounding the inclusion of Sultan Mahmud into the pantheon of national heroes of Indonesia. Alan Darmawan made a copy of this play script and recorded the stage performance of the troupe at the festival. Another play about Sultan Mahmud was composed and performed by a troupe from Dabo-Singkep, Lingga, at Festival Tamadun Melayu in 2013 in Tanjungpinang (Kornhauser 2019).

15. Around 1819 a conflict about the successor of the Malay sultan in Riau-Lingga resulted in one of the contenders being inaugurated as sultan of Singapore, but there was never a sultanate under the name of Singapore, Riau-Lingga. Another contender to the throne was installed in Lingga as Sultan Abdul Rahman, who continued the family's reign as might be expected, under the watchful eyes of colonial officials. Tengku Shawal bestowed the title as part of the festivities to commemmorate the 200th anniversary of the establishment of modern Singapore, which was also the start of the Malay sultanate of Singapura (see Agus Setiawan 2019, "Sekjen PPP dapat gelar datuk di Singapura").

16. Unsurprisingly, the local and traditional stories differ in some details: in certain versions it was the daughter, in others it was the queen herself who married the prince from Palembang. The continuation of the local historiographic tradition also makes use of different versions, frequently without any attempt to verify the information that is provided.

17. In the book and other Malay sources that refer to the global dinar movement, the term *muamala* is used, often spelled with a final -h or -t. This Arabic word *mu'amala* refers to social life and intercourse as well as business transaction (Wehr 1976, 646). It may be that the Murabitun movement coined the special meaning, and in the Malay World it is used with the religious connotations, also for Islamic banking which is one of the institutions the Murabitun movement vehemently opposes (Bubandt 2009,112).

18. See website Cabinet Secretariat of the Republic of Indonesia, February 4, 2021.

19. Part of the interview can be viewed in the CRISEA documentary Malay Identity on Stage (CRISEA Website).

References

Abdul Malik, Abdul Kadir Ibrahim et al. 2012. *Sejarah Kejuangan dan Kepahlawanan Sultan Mahmud Ri'ayat Syah Yang Dipertuan Besar Kerajaan Riau-Lingga-Johor-Pahang (1761–1812)* [History of the Struggle and Heroism of Sultan Mahmud Ri'ayat Syah, the Overlord of the Malay Sultanate of Riau-Lingga-Johor-Pahang (1761–1812)]. NP: Pemerintah Kabupaten Lingga, Pemerintah Provinsi Kepulauan Riau.

Abu Bakar bin Mohd Yusuf, Nuradli Ridzwan Shah bin Mohd Dali, and Norhayati Mat Husin. 2002. "Implementation of the Gold Dinar: Is it the End of Speculative Measures?" *Journal of Economic Cooperation* 23(3): 71–84.

Agus Setiawan. 2019. "Sekjen PPP dapat gelar datuk di Singapura" [The General Secretary of the United Development Party was conferred the noble title of 'Datuk' in Singapore]. Antara News. jabar. antaranews.com/nasional/berita/1074652/sekjen-ppp-dapat-gelar-datuk-di-singapura. Last accessed March 23, 2021.

Appadurai, Arjun. 1996. *Modernity at Large: Cultural Dimensions of Globalization*. Minneapolis: University of Minnesota Press.

Barnard, Timothy P., and H. M. J. Maier, eds. 2004. *Contesting Malayness: Malay Identities Across Boundaries*. Singapore: NUS Press.

Bubandt, Nils. 2009. "Gold for a Golden Age: Sacred Money and Islamic Freedom in a Global Sufi Order." *Social Analysis: The International Journal of Anthropology* 53(1): 103–22.

Colombijn, Freek. 2003. "When there is nothing to imagine. Nationalism in Riau." In *Framing Indonesian Realities: Essays in Symbolic Anthropology in Honour of Reimar Schefold*, eds. Peter J. M. Nas, Gerard A. Persoon, and Jifke Jaffe, 333–70. Leiden: KITLV Press.

Dialog Selatan II, December 11–13, 1995. Pekanbaru: Dewan Kesenian Riau. Perpustakaan Tengku Luckman Sinar [No. 02001836].

Dialog Utara IV (Temu Sastrawan Sumatra Utara–Malaysia Utara), June 9–11, 1989. Medan: Dewan Kesenian Sumatera Utara. Perpustakaan Tengku Luckman Sinar [No. 02002260].

Dialog Utara VII, November 25–28, 1997. Ipoh-Perak, Malaysia: GAPENA. Perpustakaan Tengku Luckman Sinar [No. 02001734].

Dialog Utara VIII, December 1–4, 1999. Patani: University of Prince Songkhla, GAPENA, dan Dewan Bahasa dan Pustaka Malaysia. Perpustakan Tengku Luckman Sinar [No. 02001722].

Faucher, Carole. 2006. "Popular Discourse on Identity Politics and Decentralisation in Tanjung Pinang Public Schools." *Asia Pacific Viewpoint* 47(2): 273–85.

Fox, James J. 2006. "Place and Landscape in Comparative Austronesian Perspective." In *The Poetic Power of Place: Comparatives on Austronesian Ideas of Locality*, ed. J. J. Fox, 1–22. Canberra: ANU Press.

Heryanto, Ariel, 1990. "The Making of Language: Developmentalism in Indonesia." *Prisma* 50: 40–53.

Huzrin Hood, Amri Husin et. al. 2015. *Sesat di Ujung Jalan Balek ke Pangkal Jalan*. NP [Tanjungpinang]: Badan Perpustakaan dan Arsip Daerah Provinsi Kepulauan Riau.

Kahn, Joel S. 2006. *Other Malays: Nationalism and Cosmopolitanism in the Modern Malay World*. Singapore: NUS Press.

Klinken, Gerry van. 2007. "Return of the Sultans: The Communitarian Turn in Local Politics." In *The Revival of Tradition in Indonesian Politics: The Deployment of Adat from Colonialism to Indigenism*, eds. Jamie Davidson and David Henley, 149–69. London: Routledge.

Konvensyen Dunia Melayu Dunia Islam IV, October 6–7, 2003. Melaka: Dunia Melayu Dunia Islam. Perpustakaan Tengku Luckman Sinar [No. 02004879].

Konvensyen Dunia Melayu Dunia Islam V, October 6–8, 2004. Melaka: Dunia Melayu Dunia Islam. Perpustakaan Luckman Sinar Library [no number].

Kornhauser, Bronia. 2019. "Bangsawan in Lingga: The Vanished Era of the Lingga-Riau Sultanate." In *Performing the Arts of Indonesia: Malay Identity and Politics in the Music, Dance and Theatre of the Riau Islands*, ed. Margaret Kartomi, 127–51. Copenhagen: NIAS Press.

Lee, Liz. 2019. "Muslim nations consider Gold, barter trade to beat sanctions." Found at Thomson and Reuters, Emerging Markets. https://www.reuters.com/article/us-malaysia-muslimalliance-idUSKBN1YP04C. Last accessed March 22, 2021.

Ling Ma and Alan A. Lew. 2012. "Historical and Geographical Context in Festival Tourism Development." *Journal of Heritage Tourism* 7(1): 13–31.

Long, Nicholas. 2013. *Being Malay in Indonesia: Histories, Hopes and Citizenship in the Riau Archipelago*. Singapore: NUS Press.

Maier, H. M. J., 1993. "From Heteroglossia to Polyglossia: The Creation of Malay and Dutch in the Indies." *Indonesia* 56: 37–65.

Malay World Conference, October 12–14, 2001. Kuala Lumpur: GAPENA. Perpustakaan Tengku Luckman Sinar [No. 02001844].

Maznah Mohamad and Syed Muhd Khairudin Aljunied, eds. 2011. *Melayu: The Politics, Poetics and Paradoxes of Malayness*. Singapore: NUS Press.

Micksic, John N. 2013. *Singapore and the Silk Road of the Sea 1300–1800*. Singapore: NUS Press.

Milner, Anthony. 2010. *The Malays*. Oxford: Wiley-Blackwell.

Musyawarah Lembaga Adat Melayu Se-Sumatra, April 15–17, 2006. Pekanbaru: Lembaga Adat Melayu (LAM) Riau. Perpustakaan Tengku Luckman Sinar [no number].

Reid, Anthony. 1979. *The Blood of the People: Revolution and the End of Traditional Rule in Northern Sumatra*. Kuala Lumpur: Oxford University Press.

Rejab F. I. 2000. *Daik Bonda Tanah Melayu* [Daik: The Motherland of the Malays]. Kuala Lumpur: Malaysian Encyclopedia Research Centre.

Reuter, Thomas. 2006. "Land and Territory in the Austronesian World." In *Sharing the Earth, Dividing the Land: Land and Territory in the Autronesian World*, ed. Thomas Reuter, 11–38. Canberra: ANU E Press.

Rodgers, Susan. 1993. "Batak Heritage in the Indonesian State: Print Literacy and the Construction of Ethnic Cultures in Indonesia." In *Ethnicity and the State*, ed. Judith D. Toland, 147–76. New Brunswick and London: Transaction Publishers.

Rustam A. Sani 1993. *Melayu Baru dan Bangsa Malaysia: Tradisi Cendikia dan Krisis Budaya*. Kuala Lumpur: Utusan Publications and Distributors.

Sakai, Minako. 2009. "Creating a New Center in the Periphery of Indonesia: Sumatran Malay Identity Politics." In *The Politics of the Periphery in Indonesia: Social and Geographical Perspectives*, ed. M. Sakai, G. Banks, and J. H. Walker, 62–83. Singapore: NUS Press.

Simposium Jaringan Melayu Antarbangsa, April 19–21, 1996. Shah Alam, Malaysia: GAPENA. Perpustakaan Tengku Luckman Sinar [no number].

Vertovec, Steven. 2009. *Transnationalism*. London: Routledge.

Website Cabinet Secretariat of the Republic of Indonesia, February 4, 2021: "Vice President: Transactions in Indonesia Must Use Legal Currency." https://setkab.go.id/en/vice-president-transactions-in-indonesia-must-use-legal-currency/. Last accessed March 23, 2021.

Wee, Vivienne. 2002. "Ethno-nationalism in Process: Ethnicity, Atavism and Indigenism in Riau, Indonesia." *The Pacific Review* 15(4): 497–516.

Wehr, Hans. 1976. *A Dictionary of Modern Written Arabic*, ed. J. Milton Cowan, 3rd edn. Ithaca, New York: Spoke Language Services.

Wilda Fajriah. 2020. *Singapura dan Malaysia Bakal Semarakkan Festival Pulau Penyengat 2020* [Singaporeans and Malaysians will liven up the Penyengat Cultural Festival in 2020], OK-Zone, 18.02.2020. Last accessed January 1, 2021.

Zaini-Lajoubert, Monique. 1992. "Dialog Selatan I (Johor Bahru 24–26 Janvier 1992)." *Archipel* 44: 19–20.

Zakry Abadi. 1989. *GAPENA: Antara Politik dan Sastera* [GAPENA: Between Political and Literary Activities]. Kuala Lumpur: Penerbitan Keramat.

Skilled Migration in Post-2011 Singapore: Filipino Professionals in the Talent Capital of Southeast Asia

FILOMENO AGUILAR JR.[*]

The ASEAN Economic Community Blueprint that was signed in Singapore on November 20, 2007, specifically focused on the goal "to transform ASEAN into a region with free movement of goods, services, investment, skilled labor, and freer flow of capital" (ASEAN 2008, 5). Although the migration of unskilled labor has long been a phenomenon within the region, ASEAN does not include it as an element in regional integration—an exclusion that emanates from the evident threat that would confront domestic labor given the huge number of unauthorized migrants in the region (cf. Battistella and Asis 2003). ASEAN's focus is thus on a small proportion of the actual flows of labor within the region.

To stimulate intraregional skilled labor mobility, since 2005 ASEAN has introduced several Mutual Recognition Agreements (MRAs) that recognize an individual's training and skills in certain employment sectors and allow employment in another Southeast Asian country.[1] In practice, however, it is difficult to employ the services of a professional even for the handful of occupations covered by the MRAs, given the restrictive labor practices found in ASEAN countries. These stem from a combination of nationalist sentiment and paranoia over competition from skilled labor. In this context, the immigration rules even for those who are to be employed under MRAs can be restrictive. Thus, "professional recognition provided by MRAs can only play a secondary role and does not provide automatic market access" (Chia 2011, 244).

Regardless of ASEAN's half-hearted promotion of skilled migration, professionals have moved to other countries in Southeast Asia even before the conceptualization of the ASEAN blueprint (Iredale 2000, 895–99), and they continue to do so (Kikkawa and Suan 2019, 9–12; Corong and Aguiar 2019).

---

[*] I am very grateful to Lou Antolihao for his generous and wonderful help prior to and during my research trip to Singapore and for sending me valuable materials even after my visit to Singapore. Many thanks are also due to Argie Chua, Jayeel Cornelio, and Pastor Joey Geronimo for kind introductions to contacts in Singapore.

Evidence shows that skilled migration covered by the MRAs represents only a small subset of the overall flow of skilled migration within the region (cf. Kikkawa and Suan 2019, 12–14). In the overall context of intraregional skilled migration, the Philippines "stands out as the main supplier of skilled (also unskilled) labor to ASEAN countries" (Chia 2011, 230).[2] For its part, Singapore stands out as the host country that registers the highest number of skilled migrants coming from within as well as from outside the region (Corong and Aguiar 2019, 70).

The presence of skilled Philippine migrants in Singapore has grown considerably since the 1990s, to an estimated 200,000 at present, as discussed below, and raises several interesting issues. In the 1990s, when domestic workers from the Philippines were more numerous than professionals, Singapore's execution of domestic worker Flor Contemplacion highlighted the precarious place of Filipino skilled migrants in the city-state. Given their class sensibilities, Filipino professionals did not want to be associated with low-status migrant domestic workers who, at that time, served as the public face of Philippine migration (Aguilar 1996; cf. Aguilar 2014, 83–126). Today, despite the absence of reliable data, the consensus is that Filipino professionals outnumber domestic workers by three to two. How do these white-collar workers from the Philippines fit into Singapore society? How do they regard their residence in Singapore and the prospect of acquiring Singaporean citizenship? In what ways is their presence in Singapore a step toward building an ASEAN community? To answer these questions, this study relies on interviews conducted in April 2019 with skilled Filipino migrants as well as a Philippine embassy official in Singapore.[3] It also utilizes official documents issued by government agencies, the findings of previous studies, and a range of data that can be obtained online, including news items and blog sites that deal with the Filipino presence in Singapore.

This chapter starts by discussing the overall scenario of skilled migration to Singapore, which resulted in an unprecedented growth in the nonresident population in the first decade of the twenty-first century and in the crystallization of local-born Singaporeans' resentment toward migrant professionals in the wake of the financial crisis of 2008–2009, resulting in a political debacle in the May 2011 general election. In response to this shocking outcome (outlined below), the Singapore government introduced policy changes that seriously affected the immigration status of skilled migrants. It is against this broader backdrop that Filipino skilled migration in Singapore is discussed.

Singapore's Drive for Foreign Talent

The separation of Singapore from Malaysia in 1965 reduced the nonresident population in the city-state to a mere 2.9 percent of the total population (Yeoh and Lin 2012, 1). However, in the 1980s Singapore decided that simply upgrading its manufacturing sector was not enough to sustain itself. Its vision was to become a regional headquarters for multinational corporations as part of a strategic shift to a service-led economy (Kwon 2019, 423). Migration was thus back on the agenda, with immigration policies "becoming increasingly instrumental and market-driven" (ibid., 436). To meet the challenge of competing in the global economy, in the 1990s Singapore focused on becoming "the 'talent capital' of the global economy" (Yeoh and Lin 2012, 6).

Subsequently, Singapore liberalized its immigration policies for skilled migrants, who found it easy to gain permanent residency and citizenship. At its height, foreign skilled workers with employment passes could apply to become permanent residents (PR) after six months of living in Singapore, and the residency requirement for citizenship was reduced from ten to six years (Ortiga 2018, 958–59). Permanent residents were "entitled to most of the rights provided to citizens, except for the right to vote in general elections" (Kwon 2019, 428). Their children could study in local schools, and they were entitled to subsidized medical expenses. They could also purchase second-hand government-subsidized housing—the ubiquitous flats built by the Housing Development Board (HDB).[4] Young PR males, however, were and still are subject to a two-year mandatory military service known as National Service (NS). In 1990 permanent residents (PR) represented only 3.6 percent of the total population, but this proportion rose to 7.1 percent by 2000 and to 10.7 percent by 2010 (Yeoh and Lin 2012, 2 table 1). Within a span of two decades, the permanent resident population quintupled from 109,872 in 1990 to 541,00 in 2010 (ibid.).

The "hung[er] for foreign talent" persisted into the first decade of the twenty-first century (Wee and Yeoh 2020, 6) even as the "nonresident population increased at an unprecedented pace" (Yeoh and Lin 2012, 1). Due to the heavy influx of migrants, Singapore's population grew from 3,016,379 in 1990 to 4,027,887 in 2000 and further to 5,076,732 in 2010 (ibid., 2 table 1). Singapore has had to rely on immigration to augment its population in view of the drastic decline in total fertility rate from a low 1.60 children per woman in 2000 to an even lower 1.15 in 2010 (ibid., 9). With the growth in the migrant population, the proportion of citizens declined from 86 percent in 1990 to 74.1 percent in 2000 and to 63.6 percent in 2010. The "resident" population—

despite the addition of naturalized citizens and permanent residents to the number of native-born Singaporeans—declined from 89.7 percent of the total population in 1990 to 81.3 percent in 2000 and to 74.3 percent in 2010 (ibid.). In contrast, the "nonresident" population, deemed as temporary migrants, which represented 10.3 percent of the total population in 1990, swelled to 25.7 percent by 2010 (ibid.).

"The most rapid (absolute) increase in the foreign-born proportion of the labor force occurred in the 2000s when, following decades of healthy growth, Singapore's nonresident workforce increased 76.8 percent from 615,700 in 2000 to nearly 1.09 million in 2010" (ibid., 3). The number of "skilled and generally better-educated S-pass or employment pass holders, along with a small number of entrepreneurs" also "increased rapidly due to intensive recruitment and liberalized immigration eligibility criteria." Skilled workers and professionals represented 22 percent, or more than one-fifth of the nonresident labor force (ibid., 3, 6). As part of maintaining the racial balance of Singapore society, "the majority of skilled workers (apart from Malaysians)" that were recruited came from China and India (ibid., 6).[5]

Did the Philippine population in Singapore increase during this period of rapid growth in the foreign-born labor force? A definitive answer cannot be made given the difficulty of ascertaining the number of Filipinos in Singapore. Information from the Commission on Filipinos Overseas (CFO) is of questionable accuracy, but it can be used for now in the absence of other reliable data. The CFO (1997, 2007) data indicate that the number of Filipinos in Singapore increased by 30 percent from 120,152 in 1997 to 156,466 in 2007. The growth in the Filipino population does not, however, appear to be as rapid as the rise in the overall migrant workforce in Singapore. What is interesting about the CFO data is the huge leap in the permanent resident population from a mere 152 Filipinos in 1997 to 29,850 Filipinos in 2007, a trend consistent with Singapore's liberalized policy during this ten-year period.

The CFO data also indicate a burgeoning skilled migrant pool from the Philippines. The latest available CFO (2013) data show that by 2013 the total number of Filipinos in Singapore had risen to 203,243, of which 44,102 were permanent rather than temporary migrants. The continual rise in the number of permanent migrants is indicative of the growth of the Filipino professional class in Singapore in both absolute and relative terms. By 2014 it could be said that "[t]hese days a Singaporean professional is likely to have Filipino colleagues" (Wong 2014). Clearly this represents a dramatic change in the composition of the Philippine population in the city-state. Whereas in the mid-1990s domestic workers constituted around 60 percent of the total Philippine population, with skilled migrants accounting for the remainder, a reversal occurred so that by the mid-2010s white-collar workers made up 60 percent of the total, as estimated by First Secretary and Consul J. Anthony A. Reyes during an interview conducted on April 10, 2019 at the Philippine Embassy. Singapore's "hunger for foreign talent" has altered Philippine demographics in Singapore.

Anti-immigrant Resentment and the 2011 General Election

Singapore's relentless drive for foreign talent ignited growing hostility among the local population toward skilled foreign workers, particularly fellow Asians.[6] While unskilled migrants took up low-status jobs shunned by Singaporeans and thus were not seen as competitors, foreign skilled workers competed with native-born Singaporeans for jobs on an even plane, a competition the government reckoned "to have positive effects on the economy to offset the effect of job protectionism" (Kwon 2019, 426). In this situation, employers used "skill shortage" to justify their preference "to use temporary skilled foreigners to reduce costs and avoid risks" (ibid.).

In the early 2000s, the backlash against immigration began to heighten in public discourse, with professional migrants from China and India—despite their racial affinity with most Singaporeans—seen as "insular, racist, and unable to interact [with] other ethnic groups" and lacking "tolerance and understanding of Singapore's diversity" (Ortiga 2018, 955, 956). Although Singaporean Chinese consider themselves to be a part of the overseas Chinese diaspora, they view themselves as different from mainland Chinese. Singaporean Chinese deem themselves as not "insular" and not "racist" because of their interactions with Indians, Malays, and other "races" and "cultures," even if these interactions are with their fellow Singaporeans. Mainland Chinese, in contrast, are perceived to be without such interactions and are thus regarded as "insular" and "racist" and devoid of appreciation for Singapore's diversity, supposedly unable to tolerate Singaporean Malay and Indian practices. In this milieu, the government was blamed for its inability "to change migrants' 'racist' attitudes," which were deemed as undermining social cohesion (ibid., 955). The government was also criticized for its "global city" ambition, which had brought in "an influx of migrants who are only interested in milking the country's resources" (ibid., 958). These foreign professionals were said to not really care about Singapore.

The competition for jobs intensified with the financial crisis of 2008–2009, which "debunked the national stereotype of perpetual prosperity and transformed it into a narrative of insecurity, previously unknown in Singapore"

(Dirksmeier 2020, 2). In the struggle for jobs, the more expensive skilled Singaporean workers lost out to skilled foreigners who allegedly were (and are) willing to work for wages lower than what the former would accept. The rising unemployment among educated Singaporeans fostered the view that skilled foreigners were competitors for jobs, housing, and other scarce resources in Singapore, and the government was perceived as extending "preferential treatment" to foreigners over Singaporeans (Kwon 2019, 428). The educated Singaporeans' grievance centered on "the state's unfairness towards its own citizens" (Dirksmeier 2020, 2). Their battle cry was "Singapore for Singaporeans" (Yeoh and Lam 2016, 638).

The public's discontent with the government came to a head in the May 7, 2011 general election, when 82 of 87 seats (or 94.3 percent) were contested, the highest percentage of seats ever contested since independence. For only the second time, the ruling People's Action Party (PAP) did not officially return to power on nomination day. The PAP received 60.14 percent of the popular vote, the lowest percentage since Singapore's autonomous existence began in 1965 (Chong 2012, 283). Opposition parties won six parliamentary seats. Singaporeans' dissatisfaction with government policy on "foreign talent" and other issues, plus the rise of social media which the government could not control and for which the PAP was ill-prepared, overturned the dominance of the ruling party.

Notwithstanding policy changes and government endeavors to favor its citizens over immigrants discussed in the next section, resentment against skilled foreigners persisted after 2011. Based on 2010–14 data drawn from a representative sample of the adult Singaporean residential population, 35.7 percent—way over one-third—do not accept immigrants as neighbors (Dirksmeier 2020, 4). Ethnic Chinese, who comprise the majority, trust strangers significantly less than other ethnic groups (ibid.). In a move that turns Singapore's multiculturalism on its head (Ortiga 2018), describing oneself as "cosmopolitan" and supposedly willing to interact with other cultures as defined by the Singapore state's CMIO ("Chinese," "Malay," "Indian," and "Others") racial division of society,[7] does not reduce the risk of showing anti-immigrant attitudes (Dirksmeier 2020, 5). As Yasmin Ortiga (2018, 960) argues, Singaporeans "have countered state discourse by constructing their own discourse of multiculturalism," which like the state discourse relies on categories of race but ultimately is ultranationalist. Immigrants may be of the same "race" as Singaporeans, but these foreigners are said to be "too prejudiced or bigoted to adapt to Singapore's multiracial society," a belief that makes Singaporeans eschew skilled immigrants (ibid., 947). Thus, a Chinese Singaporean would much prefer to have a Singaporean Malay as a neighbor than a Chinese immigrant from the mainland.

In 2014 Filipinos bore the brunt of "racism and xenophobia, pure and simple" (Han 2014) when a group that called itself the Pilipino Independence Day Council (PIDC) decided to celebrate Philippine Independence Day at the Ngee Ann City Civic Plaza along Orchard Road, the city-state's central shopping district. A group on social media, "Say 'No' to an overpopulated Singapore" (SNOS), vehemently attacked the planned event based on the PIDC's promotional materials. The SNOS objected to the event's logo using an image of Singapore's skyline as well as the words "interdependence" and "two nations." Moreover, celebration was to be staged in a public space rather than in the privacy of the Philippine Embassy grounds tucked away in a quiet corner on Nassim Road (onlinecitizen 2014). Acting as if Singapore was facing a siege, the initial post that incited SNOS followers to protest the event declared, "Make your voice heard, and remind them that this is OUR LAND!" (ibid.).[8] The PIDC canceled the event over "public order and safety issues" (Suarez 2014). Prime Minister Lee Hsien Loong was "appalled" by the "thuggish behavior" of Singaporean "trolls," whom he called a "disgrace to Singapore" (ibid.; Wong 2014). Even after the event had been canceled, "anti-Filipino sentiment continued to swirl online, culminating in a blog titled "Blood Stained Singapore suggesting ways to abuse Filipinos," calling them 'an infestation'" (Wong 2014; cf. *Coconuts Singapore* 2014). This incident was a public display of the pervasive anti-immigration sentiment, this time pitting Singaporeans against another Southeast Asian nationality as well as their own government.

The Immigration Regime Post–2011 General Election

In response to the shocking outcome of the 2011 General Election, between July 2011 and January 2012 the government introduced changes that would "substantially change Singapore's policy on skilled labor" (Yeoh and Lam 2016, 643–44). Although the employment visa categories remain unchanged, the conditions are no longer those that prevailed at the height of the liberal immigration policy. For instance, to be eligible for an employment pass, the minimum monthly salary was raised from S$2,500 to S$3,300 (ibid., 644). In other words, "skilled foreigners must command 11–20 percent higher salaries before being granted the right to work in Singapore" (Yeoh and Lin 2012, 7). Foreign students who graduated from a Singapore educational institution would only have three months in which to find a job or return to their country of origin, whereas the previous allowable time was one year (ibid.). To ensure that citizens and permanent residents are given priority in employment, employers are "scrutinized or penalized if its workforce consists of an unusually high proportion of foreign workers, particularly when an employer is found to choose foreign workers over local workers" (Zhan and Zhou 2020, 1661).

The conditions governing applications for permanent residency and Singaporean citizenship have also become more stringent. As a result, "The number of new permanent residents dropped nearly two-thirds, from 79,167 in 2008 to 29,265 in 2010, and remained roughly at that level thereafter" (ibid., 1659). The implication is that "most of the highly skilled immigrants would have to work in Singapore on a temporary basis, despite their intention to settle down" (ibid.).

At the same time, Singapore officials admitted the "fear that skilled labor may be in Singapore to better their chances of facilitating migration to greener pastures … in countries like the United States, Australia, and the United Kingdom" (Mathews and Soon 2016, 39). To deal with the presumed "exploitation" of Singapore by skilled migrants in their stepwise mobility, the government officially encourages naturalization. The state prods "permanent residents who have been in Singapore for some time to more fully commit to Singapore in renouncing their citizenship status from their countries of origin and become Singapore citizens" (ibid., 41). The threat has been aired that if permanent residents do not apply for citizenship, their PR status might not be renewed (ibid., 40). The government has also sought to appease its citizenry by reducing the social benefits in education, housing, and healthcare to which noncitizens are entitled, thus substantially and materially altering the situation of so-called temporary skilled migrants in Singapore while "creating a more exclusive form of citizenship" (ibid.).[9] This approach to citizenship is meant to reassure local-born citizens who feel they "bear a disproportionate amount of the obligations of citizenship whilst receiving nearly the same amount of benefits as permanent residents" (ibid.).

Nevertheless, the government also insists that "the influx of new immigrants into the city-state must continue, albeit in a more controlled manner" (Yeoh and Lam 2016, 644). Thus, the proportion of the total population accounted for by nonresidents grew from 25.7 percent in 2010 to 29.2 percent by 2014 (ibid., 642), remaining steady at 29.4 percent by 2017 (Zhan and Zhou 2020, 1659). The proportion of nonresidents remains at the same ratio of the total population even while migrants arrive on the island and leave, a circulation of incoming and outgoing talent that Singapore attracts, resulting in a "high turnover rate of the workforce, including both highly skilled and low-skilled immigrant workers" (ibid., 1662).

In the post-2011 immigration regime, countless highly skilled migrants are left in the noncitizen category. In 2017, highly skilled migrants made up 48 percent of noncitizens (ibid.). As Shaohua Zhan and Min Zhou have argued, much like unskilled migrant workers, "many highly skilled immigrants are also subjected to employment insecurity and settlement uncertainties associated with unstable jobs, temporary residence, and risks of downward mobility" (ibid., 1655). Most skilled migrants in Singapore work on a temporary basis. In effect, skilled labor has become expendable,[10] and, much like low-skilled labor, skilled migrants find themselves in a precarious situation. The instability in employment is exacerbated by the uncertainty in immigration status, as it has become common for foreign professionals to receive multiple rejections in their application for permanent residency (ibid., 1659, 1662, 1663, 1966). As Filipino informants indicate, no explanation is ever given as to why an application for permanent residency is turned down, shrouding the entire process in mystery and uncertainty, especially when they find out that someone they know has received approval whereas they did not. Applying for permanent residency is akin to rolling a dice.

This situation highlights the contradictory role of the Singaporean nation-state. It attracts skilled migrants in order to gain the foreign talent it needs, thereby boosting the economy, but at the same time restricts their incorporation into Singapore society and the body politic as a way of managing internal political dissent. Immigration status is the valve that the state manipulates to balance the structural need to import foreign skilled labor and appease its national constituency. Thus, although skilled migrants are economically functional, they are confined to an unseen social enclave. In effect, the only sphere to which they are welcome and where they belong in Singapore is the marketplace.

Filipino Professionals: Modes of Being in Singapore

Because there is no reliable information on the number of Filipinos in Singapore, we can only use outdated CFO data, which indicate, as shown earlier, a 30 percent increase in the number of Filipinos from 156,466 in 2007 to 203,243 in 2013, despite the policy changes inaugurated in 2011. The Philippine Embassy in Singapore still uses the estimate of "200,000" Filipinos in Singapore, perhaps suggesting that the total number has not drastically changed since 2013.[11]

In addition, even if Consul Reyes says that permanent residency has become difficult to acquire and is now subject to quota, CFO data for 2007 and 2013 register an increase of nearly 48 percent of Filipino permanent residents from 29,850 in 2007 to 44,102 in 2013. Inexplicably, this rate of increase is higher than the growth in the total number of Filipinos in Singapore. However, there is no firm basis for inferring from such limited data that Filipino migration to Singapore has bucked the trend that Singapore meticulously manages.

Given the way Singapore manages the circulation and high turnover of skilled labor, the total number of Filipinos may have been maintained or even risen, but it has been on the back of innumerable skilled Filipino migrants who moved to Singapore but had to leave after they lost their employment or their immigration status, whichever came first, their place taken up by the next stream of migrants.[12] This circulatory flow notwithstanding, what is indisputable is that the class expansion of Filipino professionals in Singapore observed in the early 2010s continued in the early 2020s. These skilled migrants from the Philippines are employed in sectors such as information technology, banking, health care, and education.

A study by Karen Anne Liao suggests that these skilled Filipinos appreciate the "economic opportunities, advanced technology, efficiency and convenience of lifestyle" that Singapore offers, including the island-state's proximity to the Philippines (2019, 218). They tend to cultivate a cosmopolitan sensibility, with "interest and appreciation for the diverse multi-cultural environment in Singapore, their international and local travels, and previous migration experiences. Cosmopolitanism is also expressed through language skills, dress codes and workplace interactions, as in the case of professionals in Singapore's financial sector" (ibid.).[13]

Given this cosmopolitan outlook alongside Singapore's tighter immigration regime after 2011, how do these skilled migrants regard their stay in Singapore? In the discussion that follows, I explain four types of orientation discernible among Filipino professionals toward Singapore.

The Extended Layover

This approach to life regards Singapore as a stopover en route to somewhere else, but the layover has no definite timeframe. Depending on circumstances, the layover may be brief or protracted. The idea is not to settle down—and certainly not to retire—in Singapore. However, for as long as circumstances allow, they will remain in Singapore as *visitors*, which obviates the need to belong locally. They are permanently transient, which is the mode of being in Singapore they prefer, especially given the post–2011 immigration regime.

Filipino professionals in this group include those who have never applied for permanent residency after working in Singapore for many years because they do not want their sons to render the compulsory two-year National Service. The objection is not so much to the military training that would interfere with their children's education and career trajectories as to the idea that their sons would be serving a country other than the Philippines. For such skilled migrants, attachment to their nation of birth, a sentiment passed on to their children, is a weighty reason for not applying to become permanent residents or Singapore citizens.[14] Thus, for as long as they can find secure employment and remain in Singapore, they prefer to be in the nonresident category.

This political stance is not understood by some Singaporeans who believe that nonresidents and noncitizens remain in the city-state simply to exploit it. It is the same political affection for the nation of one's birth that in 2014 resulted in a group of Filipinos wanting to celebrate Philippine Independence Day publicly, which upset some Singaporeans.

With the withdrawal of educational, housing,[15] and medical care benefits from permanent residents after 2011, permanent residency has become an even more undesirable option for these skilled migrants who consider their stay in Singapore as an extended layover.

Becoming permanently transient in Singapore has become the default mode for many skilled migrants who believe that moving to another country other than their homeland should take place by a certain age, beyond which they feel that they would rather not undergo the rigors of adjustment to another country. If skilled migrants are already in their late thirties, there is the concern that there will not be enough time for their career to take off if they were to move to another country. As Zhan and Zhou (2020, 1662) also point out, for "those who are in their late 30s and 40s, frequent migration may not be a privilege but a burden because a job change and relocation would disrupt family life and children's education."

The sense of transience and of not belonging to Singapore is further compounded by instances of exclusion that these skilled migrants have experienced from Singaporeans. A 42-year-old male informant explains why he has not applied for permanent residency: "I still like to be Filipino, and I can't imagine myself being Singaporean." Although renunciation of Philippine citizenship is not required for permanent residency, he regards permanent residency as "a step forward toward that" eventuality, especially since he has a friend who was told that someone who is a permanent resident but does not apply for citizenship will have their permanency status revoked. This informant describes the situation as one of "forced citizenship." Asked why he cannot imagine himself as a Singaporean, his reply: "Cultural and experiential exclusion." Apart from everyday indignities—commonly experienced from taxi drivers[16]—exclusion is reinforced by the lack of meaningful social relationships with local Singaporeans, which is the situation of most Filipino migrants in Singapore. Apart from the workplace, "[m]ore profound interactions remain lacking in other social domains," as Kwon (2019, 428) has observed among skilled Asian immigrants in general. Considering themselves as mere visitors or sojourners enables Filipino professionals to cope with and even dismiss exclusion by the host society.

The Stepping Stone

This approach, which treats Singapore as a stepping stone to a future destination elsewhere, probably appeals to most skilled Filipino migrants. As Liao (2019, 220) reports in her study: "Filipino highly skilled and professional migrants shared their future plans, which gravitate towards three pathways— few of them plan to stay in Singapore permanently or to stay for a longer period of time, while most plan to either re-migrate to another country, or to return to the Philippines." They go to Singapore "to earn money and boost savings, to start a family, to gain career growth—but not for permanent settlement and retirement, because of the high cost of living" (ibid.). Their stay in Singapore is perceived as an asset, their experiences engendering confidence in their ability to negotiate the international workplace and abetting their global mobility. As one professional put it, his experiences in Singapore have "made it 'easy to relocate' (*Madaling mag-relocate*), and has trained him in cross-cultural interaction, which helps in his consultancy work" (ibid., 219).

Migration to Singapore is thus considered a strategic move over a certain period of time, which increases their chances of migrating to a country that is definitely preferred over the city-state. The stepping stone approach is like the extended layover in that no permanence and no sense of belonging in Singapore are envisioned. However, the layover approach is usually indefinite unlike the calculated approach of the stepping stone.

This category includes those who are seeking to remigrate to another, usually Western, country despite their permanent residency status or even Singaporean citizenship. Informants mentioned people they know who have moved to Australia, New Zealand, Canada, and the United States even if they already had Singaporean citizenship. In one case, a Filipino IT teacher in an international school, who migrated to Singapore in the 1990s when he was in his late thirties, was deliberately strategic. His wife and three children became Singaporean citizens, but he remained a permanent resident because he was planning to move to the US. In this man's account, it was possible to stay longer in the US with a Philippine passport than with a Singaporean one, the extended stay allowing him the time and opportunity to look for employment. When people asked him why he had not become a naturalized Singaporean, he would say that he was still looking for a stable job considering that his contract as an IT teacher lasted only for two years and required constant renewal. In 2015 he and his family left for the US. This man's tactical use of citizenship matches the state's own utilization of immigration and citizenship laws for its strategic purposes (cf. Aguilar 1999, 2018).

Kellynn Wee and Brenda Yeoh (2020) label this type of migrant as a serial migrant. "The serial migrant is necessarily a self-making subject, deliberately choosing to uproot and resettle themselves repeatedly in pursuit of a complex set of desires and dreams," which includes citizenship choices (ibid., 5). Globalization has made serial global mobility a real option for "an increasingly well-educated middle class" (ibid., 4).

It is possible, however, that someone who intends to use Singapore as a stepping stone ends up staying much longer than originally intended. For example, a 37-year-old single male computer scientist who migrated to Singapore in 2007 was planning to stay there for only two to three years. After twelve years, he is still thinking of moving on to another country but admits that he is not acting on the idea. He enjoys his work, especially as in 2016 he became assistant vice president in a global bank. He is also part of a Philippine-Singapore civil society entity, which gives him meaningful activities outside the sphere of work. He is on the verge of joining the "second home" category, discussed below.

Conversely, a migrant with no intention of serial migration could be pushed to turn Singapore into a stepping stone. One 47-year-old informant who started graduate studies in Singapore in 1999, worked formally from 2002, and had become a permanent resident six years later, intimated during an interview in April 2019 that he had received a job offer in a European country. Despite his age and after living in Singapore for two decades, he was resolute about leaving Singapore. He explained that when he was still a graduate student, during the heyday of Singapore's drive for foreign talent, he had received an invitation to acquire Singapore citizenship. He declined the invitation because there was "no incentive except the right to vote." At that time, the benefits of permanent residency were "enough to enjoy Singapore." But in 2019, the withdrawal of education and housing benefits following the 2011 general elections clinched his decision to leave Singapore for Europe. He felt particularly aggrieved that he could no longer send his three children to local schools because the government had removed the children of permanent residents from the priority list of admission to local schools, and the alternative of sending them to an international school was a steep price to pay for remaining in Singapore. Before 2019 was over, he and his family had migrated to Europe. This case reveals that the immigration regime after 2011 has not only bred a high turnover rate in skilled labor but has also precipitated the departure of otherwise settled migrants.

Skilled migrants who regard Singapore as a stepping stone are, in some respects, like Singaporeans who emigrate and leave Singapore for good. By the 2000s, "the trend for Singaporeans to emigrate permanently without necessarily contributing or returning to Singapore emerged" (Yeoh and Lin 2012, 8).[17] The numbers are not insignificant. By the early 2010s, "an average of about 1,200 highly educated Singaporeans" and an additional "300 naturalized citizens" were renouncing their Singaporean citizenship every year (ibid.). Reportedly also, in 2010 "about 1,000 Singaporeans a month were applying for a 'Certificate of No Criminal Conviction'—a prerequisite to getting permanent residence overseas. In some social surveys among Singaporean youth, more than half of those surveyed would leave the country to build their careers if given the chance" (ibid.). If a sizeable number of native-born Singaporeans see no future for themselves in the city-state, why would not those who migrated to Singapore feel the same?

The rising cost of living for all residents, the withdrawal of benefits from permanent residents, the small size of Singapore that suggests finite options, and the very structure of the global economy all encourage out-migration. Nevertheless, the same global economy brings a fresh batch of skilled migrants into Singapore, which blends with Singapore's own strategy of stimulating, through the levers of immigration, the circulation of skilled labor.

The Second Home

This approach to being in Singapore is taken up by skilled Filipino migrants who stay there for as long as possible and generally do not desire to migrate to a third country because they are content with their life in the city-state. They have lived in Singapore for many years, even decades—many settling there during the heyday of the liberal immigration policy before 2011—and have learned to call it their "second home."[18] They have secure jobs; they like their occupation and are satisfied with their salary. They are impressed by the fact that Singapore is clean, safe, efficient, and technologically advanced. They say they have no language problems because English is widely spoken. They appreciate Singapore's proximity to the Philippines, which they can visit at least twice or thrice a year. According to a 46-year-old female library specialist, Singapore is "still close enough. If I need to go home, I can go home quickly." They feel comfortable in Singapore because of the large number of skilled Filipinos with whom they can interact and pursue a social life. They may even have a sibling who also lives and works in Singapore.[19]

The personal circumstances of these migrants who regard Singapore as a second home, such as being single or, if married, having no children with them in Singapore, insulates them from the effects of the withdrawal of educational benefits from permanent residents after 2011. They already have assets in Singapore, such as ownership of an HDB flat. Many are of an age that makes them no longer keen on being serial migrants.

These skilled migrants may or may not have been granted permanent residency or even citizenship. After the tightening of rules in 2011, some migrants who had been working in Singapore for twenty or more years regretted that they did not apply for permanent residency. Thus, they have had to make adjustments, such as sending their children back to the Philippines. The nonresidents and noncitizens ultimately do not know for how long they will be in Singapore. Certainly, some of those who had treated Singapore as a second home have already been compelled to leave, as informants attest. However, unlike those in the extended layover mode, they do not feel excluded. The 46-year-old female informant mentioned above, who has lived in Singapore since 2006, applied for permanent residency three years after arrival but was unsuccessful, yet was informed that she could reapply six months later. She refiled her application in 2011, but it was again denied, and this time she was told not to reapply. Although she has a permanent job—the only Filipino in the entire organization—she must renew her immigration pass biennially, unlike every five years previously, which lends a degree of uncertainty to her tenure in Singapore. She just braces herself every two years. She feels that she blends in locally, saying, "I think I've been here long enough *hindi na nga halata na Kapampangan ako; mas ano na yong Singlish ko*" [my hailing from Pampanga is no longer apparent; my Singlish carries the day].

A 32-year-old single male engineer, who migrated to Singapore in 2007, received his permanent residency the following year. His desire to acquire Singaporean citizenship in order to purchase an HDB flat exemplifies migrants' strategic citizenship that seeks to "maximize utility" (Harpaz and Mateos 2019, 2). To pursue his Singapore dream, he does not mind losing his Philippine citizenship. Although dual nationality is allowed by Philippine law, he is not sure if he would like to reacquire his natal citizenship after his intended naturalization in Singapore becomes a reality: "I will not give a closing statement on it, but as of today I will say 'no.' I will not go back to Filipino citizenship after my acquisition of Singapore citizenship." Yet, if Singapore would someday allow dual citizenship, he would welcome it so that "I can still have my property under my name in the Philippines as well as here." Another reason for desiring naturalization is to ensure that someday his children—and he does not mind his son doing National Service—will be admitted to a local school.

Notwithstanding his utilitarian approach to citizenship, he would still want to marry a Filipina over a Singaporean woman. He even specifies that the Filipina need not have permanent residency, cognizant that this status is not required for him to be eligible to purchase an HDB flat. Explaining his choice of a partner, he says, "The culture does not change; it's just the citizenship; it's just the passport. But how you were raised is still the same, the values as a Filipino are still there." He elaborates, "At the end of the day, it does not mean that you change your passport, you change your citizenship, that you become fully Singaporean." He is aware of discrimination against foreigners, but asserts, "I'm not a person that's easy to bring down when it comes to racism and stuff like that."

Ultimately, skilled Filipino migrants who regard Singapore as their second home are not truly integrated into Singapore society. They may enjoy a degree of meaningful interaction with locals, but they still perceive themselves as a culture apart in their second home.

The Uncongenial Neighborhood

Skilled Philippine migrants who have married Singaporeans may be deemed as among those who have "made Singapore home" (Yeoh 2020), a real home, not just a second home. They form a separate category, approaching Singapore as the uncongenial neighborhood. Although some migrants have married locals whom they met in Singapore, such as Mario Lajarca Jr., who moved to Singapore in 1997 and married "a Singaporean Chinese colleague who was one of his first local friends" (ibid.), there are also those who as students or professionals met their Singaporean spouses in a third country. The latter tend to be female, whose migratory journeys dovetail with those of their Singaporean husbands. At some point, they and any children they may have move to Singapore, settling there permanently. Many of these wives relaunch their careers in Singapore and work as professionals, although some have remained housewives.

Among the different types of skilled migrants from the Philippines, the individuals who are married to Singaporeans have made the greatest adjustment to life in Singapore. For instance, they have learned to prepare meals according to the preferences of their Singaporean spouse. They have also acquired the cultural tools for negotiating harmonious relationships with their husband's relatives. They appreciate Singapore for the same reasons that some skilled migrants elect to make the city-state their second home.

Nevertheless, they are subject to social exclusion from the larger society in a way that second-home migrants are not. Because they hail from the Philippines, they are made to feel undeserving of their status in life in Singapore. Lajarca, for example, feels that some taxi drivers condescendingly tell him that he is "'lucky' when they [find] out that his wife is Singaporean Chinese" (ibid.). Filipinas married to Singaporeans are vocal about the discrimination they have experienced. A grandmother informant, who met her husband in the Middle East in the 1980s, acquired the status of a permanent resident in Singapore while overseas "because they considered the three children." After a time in the Philippines, the family finally settled down in Singapore in 2000. She exclaimed, "*Kasi hindi ko alam ang* Singapore, discriminatory *dito. May* racial *pala dito. May* religious discrimination. *May* language discrimination. *May* accent discrimination. *Pati* dress code" [I did not know that Singapore is discriminatory. But I found out there is racial discrimination. Religious discrimination. Language discrimination. Accent discrimination. Even dress code discrimination].[20]

A classic experience of exclusion is at the hands of an immigration officer at the point of entry to or exit from Singapore. Because they are female and carry a Philippine passport, they fall into the stereotype of the migrant domestic worker. Their being married to a Singaporean, even when their husband is with them, does not prevent them from being held up, scrutinized, and treated in what they feel is an undignified manner. The grandmother mentioned above recounted an incident at the airport that led her to demand to speak to the immigration officer's supervisor, even though the officer had already apologized. She berated him, "No, I don't accept your sorry. *Kasi* [Because] you're offending me. You humiliate me." She added, "*Kung sumagot ang mga* Singaporean very arrogant *sila*" [When Singaporeans reply, they're very arrogant]. Another informant in her sixties narrated that at one time, when she and her family were returning to Singapore, she was asked by an immigration officer to produce a return ticket, insisting on this requirement for entry even after the Singaporean husband said, "She's my wife." The husband was so upset that he demanded to talk to the supervisor, who, in turn, apologized, explaining that these immigration officers "are programmed that way."

After a while, these Filipinas get used to this kind of treatment and no longer feel as offended as when it first happened. But the delays and inconveniences at the airport, such as the time spent in the queue for noncitizens and the extra scrutiny of their passport, are usually the trigger for them to consider acquiring Singaporean citizenship. For one Filipina in her sixties, the 2004 Indian Ocean tsunami marked a turning point. She saw how the Japanese and Singaporean governments made every effort to account for their citizens who perished in Phuket (where her friend died together with her family). This Filipina thought that if something happened to her family, the Singapore government would do its best to locate her husband and child, but she doubted if the Philippine government would search for her or would have the capacity to find her. She pondered, "Why am I holding on to my Philippine citizenship?" That very day she decided to apply for Singapore citizenship. When the Singaporeans she knew eventually found out that she had acquired citizenship, they asked, "Since when?" She replied, "Since I decided that Singapore is worth my citizenship." She recounted that they were stunned into silence; her naturalization did not mean she groveled for political or economic advantage.

Because of their nationalist sentiment, many skilled migrants who are married to Singaporeans resist naturalization for as long as possible. "I love my country," as the grandmother declared. Her being a Filipino is indelible in her birth certificate, she said. Because Singapore requires formal exclusive allegiance, these Filipinas lament that they cannot opt for dual citizenship, which Philippine law allows. Yet, for practical reasons they eventually renounce their Philippine citizenship, but very reluctantly. Renunciation of Philippine citizenship is a highly emotional issue for them.

These migrants epitomize the tenacity of Filipino identity despite becoming, for all intents and purposes, locals. They have acquired Singaporean citizenship and have raised children who are Singaporean. But they remain inherently Filipino. In fact, the grandmother is married to a third-generation Filipino Singaporean, whose choice of a spouse from the Philippines has ensured that Filipinoness will be passed on to the next legally Singaporean generation.

Conclusion

After the 2011 general election, the immigration rules underpinning skilled migration to Singapore changed drastically. Singapore went into a delicately contradictory strategy of attracting foreign talent while restricting their incorporation into Singapore society, resulting in a rapid inflow and outflow of skilled labor that has been reduced to precarity. In 2011, antagonism against skilled foreigners was exposed, with the Singapore government perceived as favoring foreigners over locals. Singaporeans stood the state's

CMIO multiculturalism on its head to reject skilled Asians. To mollify their local constituency, the government swung to the other side. The conditions governing the acquisition of permanent residency and citizenship have become more stringent. The benefits previously given to permanent residents have been removed. Thus, both the state and society structurally exclude foreigners from Singapore society and the body politic, while desiring them as foreign talent.

In this context, skilled migrants from the Philippines can be said to pursue four modes of being in Singapore. They may be living and working with an orientation that regards the island-state as (1) an extended layover, (2) a stepping stone, (3) a second home, or (4) an uncongenial neighborhood. Depending on their orientation and indeed their strategic goals, with civil status as a crucial factor, their feeling of inclusion and exclusion varies along with the desire for permanent residency and citizenship. Yet, across all four ideal types, the sense of Filipino national identity remains strong, a sentiment that many Singaporeans do not understand because they cannot imagine themselves in the reverse position of skilled migrants whom they see as coming from poor countries that are economically far behind Singapore. Because of a paucity of meaningful social relationships with native-born Singaporeans, Filipino professionals operate in a cultural enclave, whether they are permanent residents or have Singaporean citizenship. Because they are positioned in Singapore primarily as Filipinos, either by citizenship or by ethnicity, and because that is how the Singapore state and society relate to them, their national identity is reinforced wittingly and unwittingly.

In this context, the forging of a Southeast Asian community is pushed farther away. Regional integration may be occurring in economic terms through the presence of skilled Filipino migrants in Singapore who send remittances to the Philippines, but beyond the economic sphere there has been little integration. Singapore is far from being a microcosm of a Southeast Asian regional community. ASEAN's goal of promoting regional integration through transnational skilled migration within the region remains to be accomplished, especially given the factors that have bred resentment against skilled foreigners.

Singapore remains a "plural society," a phrase that John Furnivall (1956) famously coined to refer to colonial societies where interethnic interaction was limited to the marketplace. Different ethnicities, Furnivall said, lived side by side yet without mingling. However, Singaporeans readily embraced the old ethnicities represented by "Chinese," "Malay," "Indian," and "Others" (CMIO) when they were confronted by new arrivals that they could not fit into the boxes of Singapore's official multiculturalism. In the twenty-first century, Singapore is a new kind of plural society: the "multicultural" natives live side by side with immigrants with whom they do not mingle, with immigrants they consider as interlopers. *Their* national identity, fashioned out of the CMIO divisions, remains predominate over racial affinity or regional identity.

Endnotes: Skilled Migration in Post-2011 Singapore

1. ASEAN has signed Mutual Recognition Agreements with respect to seven occupations only—engineering services (2005), nursing (2006), architectural services (2007), medical practitioners (2009), dental practitioners (2009), tourism professionals (2012), and accounting services (2014)—and one "framework arrangement for mutual recognition" for surveying (2007) (ASEAN 2019).

2. In terms of occupations covered by the MRAs, Malaysia appears to be the biggest supplier of skilled labor within ASEAN (Corong and Aguiar 2019, 61, 70).

3. In discussing informants' personal characteristics such as age and the number of years of living in Singapore, I use the ethnographic present; in other words, the reference point is 2019.

4. During the heyday of liberal immigration, only citizens could acquire brand-new HDB flats.

5. See note 7 on Singapore's policy on multiculturalism.

6. Westerners are thought to work mainly for multinational corporations rather than for Singaporean companies and hence are not perceived as competing with locals for jobs.

7. Through its policy of "multiculturalism," the Singapore state preserves "racial identities" and maintains the "racial division of society" through language policies and quotas in public housing allocation and in political representation. This policy centers on the four categories of "Chinese," "Malay," "Indian," and "Others"—the well-known racial labels of CMIO. These categories are not only to be maintained, but the balance of their numbers must hew closely to an idealized proportional distribution that is said to ensure "social harmony": with a 75 percent Chinese majority, followed by 13 percent Malay, 9 percent Indian, and a 3 percent catch-all Others, a category that encompasses a motley crowd but most notably Eurasians. Singapore's policy of multiculturalism has not only been used as a broadly conceived "instrument of social control" (Chua 2003), but it also has had specific ramifications for skilled migration. Thus, "there are quotas in place (although not made official) for the number of new immigrants who are granted permanent residency in the country" (Mathew and Soon 2016, 37–38).

8. Kirsten Han (2014) trenchantly pointed out, "We also just had a huge, expensive blow-out of a Singapore Day in London—in which we *also* used the London skyline as part of our promotional material."

9. In 2011 the state established the Singapore Citizenship Journey as a requirement for naturalization. This citizenship ritual is intended to take an immigrant deeper into things Singaporean, its "national symbols, values and institutions" and "the history, norms and values of the country" (Mathew and Soon 2016, 41). It has four key components: "an online component, a tour of historical landmarks and national institutions, a community engagement session, and … a [culminating] citizenship ceremony" (ibid., 42). In other words, this requisite "journey" weeds out the supposedly insincere even as it seeks to engender affective citizenship or "political love" (cf. Aguilar 2018) for Singapore.

10. This word was used by one of my informants, who said, "Expendable: that term hovers over me," explaining that "[i]n our workplace everybody is expendable."

11. News media put the Philippine population in Singapore in 2015 at 298,000 (Liao 2019, 2), but this figure is a guesstimate.

12. A research project that would trace skilled migrants who once worked in Singapore but have repatriated back to the Philippines would be interesting but highly challenging.

13. These skilled Filipino migrants' conception of "cosmopolitanism" is evidently different from the "cosmopolitanism" of Singaporeans who are anti-immigration.

14. Other Southeast Asians feel that letting go of their natal citizenship is difficult. For example, an Indonesian man "who was not certain if he wanted to renounce his Indonesian citizenship" could not see himself retiring in Singapore (Wee and Yeoh 2020, 11).

15. At present, to purchase a resale HDB flat requires Singaporean citizenship (https://www.hdb.gov. sg/residential/buying-a-flat/resale/eligibility), whereas during the period of liberal immigration permanent residency was sufficient.

16. It is not unusual for taxi drivers in Singapore to express sentiments that do not go down well with Filipino professionals when these drivers find out that their Filipino passengers live in private condominiums. Filipinos who experience random checks by auxiliary police in the MRT and are asked about their country of origin and to show the content of any bags they may be carrying feel that they are targeted simply because they "look different." One Filipino academic was asked, "How come they're getting Filipinos as lecturers?" See Yeoh 2020 for examples of other everyday irritants.

17. When I lived in Singapore from 1993 to 1996, I would hear Singaporeans refer to their country as "just a hotel room," which obviously is not meant to be stayed in permanently.

18. As a 47-year-old male IT informant who migrated to Singapore in 1999 puts it, "*Para na rin second home ko na ito*" [This place is already like my second home]. Another male informant, 41 years of age, says, "It's like home to me. Like my comfort zone."

19. Tessa Wong (2014) narrates that one of Singapore's most popular comic characters is a Filipino domestic worker called Leticia Bongnino, a fictional television character, who, in one sketch, announced, "Now there are a lot of Filipinos in Singapore…. Leticia is very happy as almost all my relatives are here."

20. These marriage migrants recognize that after 2011 the immigration regime has made Singapore unwelcoming to skilled foreigners, but they are also cognizant of the political reasons for the change in policies. A 62-year-old economist married to a Singaporean asked rhetorically, if she were in the shoes of other Filipino migrants, "The question now is what would make me become PR here?"

References

Aguilar, Filomeno V. 1996. "The Dialectics of Transnational Shame and National Identity." *Philippine Sociological Review* 44: 101–36.

—————. 1999. "The Triumph of Instrumental Citizenship? Migrations, Identities, and the Nation-State in Southeast Asia." *Asian Studies Review* 23(3): 307–36.

—————. 2014. *Migration Revolution: Philippine Nationhood and Class Relations in a Globalized Age.* Singapore: NUS Press; Kyoto: Kyoto University Press; Quezon City: Ateneo de Manila University Press.

—————. 2018. "Political Love: Affect, Instrumentalism and Dual Citizenship Legislation in the Philippines." *Citizenship Studies* 22(8): 829–54.

Association of Southeast Asian Nations (ASEAN). 2008. *ASEAN Economic Community Blueprint.* Jakarta: ASEAN Secretariat. https://asean.org/wp-content/uploads/archive/5187-10.pdf.

—————. 2019. "ASEAN Mutual Recognition Agreements." *Invest in ASEAN.* http://investasean. asean.org/index.php/page/view/asean-free-trade-area-agreements/view/757/newsid/868/mutual-recognition-arrangements.html.

Battistella, Graziano, and Maruja M. B. Asis, eds. 2003. *Unauthorized Migration in Southeast Asia.* Quezon City: Scalabrini Migration Center.

Chia Siow Yue. 2011. "Free Flow of Skilled Labor in the AEC." In *Toward a Competitive ASEAN Single Market: Sectoral Analysis*, eds. S. Urata and M. Okabe, 205–79. ERIA Research Project Report 2010-03. Jakarta: Economic Research Institute for ASEAN and East Asia (ERIA). http://www.eria.org/uploads/media/Research-Project-Report/RPR_FY2010_3_Chapter_4.pdf.

Chong, Terrence. 2012. "A Return to Normal Politics: Singapore General Elections 2011." *Southeast Asian Affairs* 12: 283–98.

Chua Beng Huat. 2003. "Multiculturalism in Singapore: An Instrument of Social Control." *Race & Class* 44(3): 58–77.

Commission of Filipinos Overseas (CFO). 1997. "Stock Estimate of Overseas Filipinos as of December 1997." https://cfo.gov.ph/yearly-stock-estimation-of-overseas-filipinos/.

—————. 2007. "Stock Estimate of Overseas Filipinos as of December 2007." https://cfo.gov.ph/yearly-stock-estimation-of-overseas-filipinos/.

—————. 2013. "Stock Estimate of Overseas Filipinos as of December 2013." https://cfo.gov.ph/yearly-stock-estimation-of-overseas-filipinos/.

Coconuts Singapore. 2014. "Viral Now: Bloody Blog Teaches You How to Mistreat Filipinos in Singapore 'Legally,'" 13 June. https://coconuts.co/singapore/news/viral-now-bloody-blog-teaches-you-how-mistreat-filipinos-singapore-legally/.

Corong, Erwin, and Angel Aguiar. 2019. "Economic Impacts of Skilled Labor Mobility Within the ASEAN Economic Community." In *Skilled Labor Mobility and Migration: Challenges and Opportunities for the ASEAN Economic Community*, ed. Elisabetta Gentile, 57–88. Cheltenham, UK: Edward Elgar; and Mandaluyong City: Asian Development Bank. https://www.adb.org/publications/skilled-labor-mobility-migration-asean.

Dirksmeier, Peter. 2020. "Resentments in the Cosmopolis: Anti-immigrant Attitudes in Postcolonial Singapore." *Cities* 98, art. 102584. https://doi.org/10.1016/j.cities.2019.102584.

Furnivall, John. 1956. *Colonial Policy and Practice: A Comparative Study of Burma and Netherlands India.* New York: New York University Press.

Han, Kirsten. 2014. "COMMENT: Xenophobia Rears its Ugly Head in Singapore Once More." *Yahoo!news*, 19 Apr. https://sg.news.yahoo.com/blogs/singaporescene/racism-xenophobia-rears-ugly-head-singapore-once-more-004751861.html.

Harpaz, Yossi, and Pablo Mateos. 2019. "Strategic Citizenship: Negotiating Membership in the Age of Dual Nationality." *Journal of Ethnic and Migration Studies* 45(6): 843–57.

Iredale, Robyn. 2000. "Migration Policies for the Highly Skilled in the Asia-Pacific Region." *International Migration Review* 34(3): 882–906.

Kikkawa, Aiko, and Eric B. Suan. 2019. "Trends and Patterns in Intra-ASEAN Migration." In *Skilled Labor Mobility and Migration: Challenges and Opportunities for the ASEAN Economic Community*, ed. Elisabetta Gentile, 1–24. Cheltenham, UK: Edward Elgar; and Mandaluyong City: Asian Development Bank. https://www.adb.org/publications/skilled-labor-mobility-migration-asean.

Kwon, Oh-Jung. 2019. "The Diverging Paths of Skilled Immigration in Singapore, Japan and Korea: Policy Priorities and External Labor Market for Skilled Foreign Workers." *Asia Pacific Journal of Human Resources* 57: 418–44.

Liao, Karen Anne. 2019. "Mobile Practices and the Production of Professionals on the Move: Filipino Highly Skilled Migrants in Singapore." *Geoforum* 106: 214–22.

Mathew, Mathews, and Debbie Soon. 2016. "Case Study. Transiting into the Singaporean Identity: Immigration and Naturalisation Policy." *Migration Letters* 13(1): 33–48.

onlinecitizen. 2014. "Revisiting the Protest on the Philippine Independence Day Event." *TOC*, 22 Apr. https://www.theonlinecitizen.com/2014/04/22/revisiting-the-protest-on-the-philippine-independence-day-event/.

Ortiga, Yasmin. 2018. "Multiculturalism on its Head: Unexpected Social Boundaries and New Migration in Singapore." *Journal of International Migration and Integration* 16(4): 947–63.

Suarez, K. D. 2014. "Pinoy Group in Singapore Drops Independence Day Event Plan." *Rappler*, May 26. https://www.rappler.com/world/asia-pacific/ph-independence-day-plan-singapore-dropped.

Yeoh, Brenda, and Theodora Lam. 2016. "Immigration and Its (Dis)Contents: The Challenges of Highly Skilled Migration in Globalizing Singapore." *American Behavioral Scientist* 60(5–6): 637–58.

Yeoh, Brenda, and Weiqiang Lin. 2012. "Rapid Growth in Singapore's Immigrant Population Brings Policy Challenges." *Migration Information Source*, April 3. https://www.migrationpolicy.org/article/rapid-growth-singapores-immigrant-population-brings-policy-challenges.

Yeoh, Grace. 2020. "The Many Colourful and Varied Lives of Filipinos in Singapore." *RICE*. https://www.ricemedia.co/culture-people-many-colourful-varied-lives-filipinos-singapore/.

Wee, Kellynn, and Brenda Yeoh. 2020. "Serial Migration, Multiple Belongings and Orientations toward the Future: The Perspective of Middle-Class Migrants in Singapore." Theme Issue, "Post-national Formations and Cosmopolitanism." *Journal of Sociology*. https://doi.org/10.1177/1440783320960521.

Wong, Tessa. 2014. "Unease in Singapore over Filipino workers." *BBC News*, December 29. https://www.bbc.com/news/world-asia-28953147.

Zhan Shaohua, and Min Zhou. 2020. "Precarious Talent: Highly Skilled Chinese and Indian Immigrants in Singapore." *Ethnic and Racial Studies* 43(9): 1654–72.

The Religious Imaginary:
Filipino Missionaries in Thailand

JAYEEL CORNELIO AND ERRON C. MEDINA

Thailand is an unusual destination for potential Overseas Filipino Workers (OFWs). According to the latest data, the most preferred destination of OFWs regardless of their religious affiliation is Saudi Arabia, followed by the United Arab Emirates, then Hong Kong (Philippine Statistics Authority 2020). Since 2000, however, Thailand has been attracting Filipinos to teach in basic education or to work in households or the hotel industry. In fact, Filipinos in the country are known as English teachers. Although they are often hired on a "no work, no pay" basis, Filipinos consider teaching in Thailand a lucrative career because it pays better than in the Philippines (Mala 2020). Another compelling motivation is that they have a chance to work with colleagues from a different cultural background (Ulla 2019). According to the Philippine Embassy in Bangkok, there were around 18,000 Filipinos in Thailand in 2019–20 (Novio 2020).

Riding the wave of Filipino labor migration to Thailand is the entry of Filipino missionaries. They might enter the country as tourists, but they may also be sponsored by missionary organizations, Christian schools, or churches that are already based in Thailand (Novio 2018). They play an important role in providing pastoral care for the rising number of Filipinos in the country. Currently, there are no official statistics about the number of Filipino ministers in Thailand. But very telling is the presence of many Filipino-led congregations that were established there as outreaches of Christian churches or denominations based in the Philippines or other parts of Southeast Asia. During our fieldwork, we also encountered small, independent congregations set up by Filipinos who moved to Thailand as missionaries.

These developments, in a way, are not unusual. Filipinos are present in many parts of Southeast Asia where they work in different industries. Wherever they are, they find immediate solidarity with one another in such religious spaces as a Catholic parish in Kuala Lumpur or an evangelical congregation in Singapore

(Tondo 2014; Cornelio 2008). Particularly in the twentieth century, mainland Southeast Asia has become a deliberate target of Christian missionary work. Often it is the case that the Philippines is the launching pad for these missions (Cornelio 2020a). For example, religious shortwave broadcasting set up by Americans was based in Manila and was instrumental in the conversion of indigenous communities in the region after World War II (Ngo 2009). Radio Veritas, run by the Catholic Church, was established in the 1950s and has now turned to digital broadcasting to target different audiences around Southeast Asia (Skelchy 2020). To this day, missiologists continue to develop innovative models to equip OFWs to become effective missionaries in the region and other parts of Asia (Pantoja et al. 2004; Ruger 2020). A model that might resonate with Filipinos in Thailand and other parts of Southeast Asia treats migrant workers as intentional missionaries in "creative access nations," places that are generally restrictive towards missionaries (Manzano 2015).

This chapter presents the stories of Filipino missionaries in Bangkok. It is a preliminary attempt to account for their growing presence in a predominantly Buddhist society. Specifically, we analyze their motivations in relation to how they understand Thailand as a place to carry out missionary work. The argument we make is that for Filipino Christians in Bangkok, Thailand is a "harvest field" tied to their own personal narratives. The dynamic relationship between Thailand as a harvest field and their own narratives of migration constitutes their religious imaginary. Specifically, this religious imaginary is derived from divine revelations about Thailand as a country and about themselves as Filipinos called to be missionaries in Southeast Asia. Most likely a former OFW, the missionary's story is one of a divine interruption that reimagines Thailand as a "dark spot" that needs the light of the Gospel, which Filipinos have the divine calling to bring to them. The religious imaginary has three themes: (1) the religious imaginary as an interruption, (2) the sacralization of interruption, and (3) the special calling of Filipinos as missionaries to the region.

In effect, their religious imaginary is redefining their roles as fellow citizens of the region, a point that contributes to the overall thrust of this volume on identities in Southeast Asia. But it is one that clearly challenges the long-standing Buddhist identity of Thailand and mainland Southeast Asia as a whole, at the expense of minorities (Ooi and Grabowsky 2017). In this sense, our work builds on recent scholarship on divine revelations as religious imaginaries that widen one's "horizons of expectations." Specifically, "by opening a channel between ordinary daily life and the numinous, visions draw new imaginative horizons and work as a perceptual hope" (Beneduce 2021, 19).

Method

This chapter draws on key informant interviews and participant observations to substantiate our argument. In total, we interviewed seventeen Filipinos involved in Christian missionary work in Thailand. Most of them are pastors, while some of them are part-time teachers, professionals, or full-time workers in their own churches. Some of our respondents have had previous experience in doing missionary work in other countries in the region, such as Laos, Malaysia, Cambodia, Singapore, and Taiwan. These interviews took place in Bangkok in 2019. But in preparation for our fieldwork, we also managed to interview a couple of Filipino pastors in Manila who were once based in other Southeast Asian countries. Our questions revolved around several themes. We let the participants describe their church organization and narrate a short history of their missionary work. We also asked them about their roles in the particular church or congregation and the reasons for getting appointed to these posts. But more important questions focused on their Filipino identity in church mission. We also conducted participant observations in key church-related events in Manila and Bangkok, including anniversaries and thanksgiving services.

By combining interviews with participant observations, we discovered how personal narratives about missionary work in Thailand are made legible in their congregational activities. For example, while Filipinos constitute the majority in some congregations, others, especially the smaller congregations, tend to be multinational. One even welcomes asylum-seekers who are waiting for a decision on their applications from the UNHCR office in Thailand. While some congregations are independent, others are satellite churches with active relationships with their headquarters in the Philippines or the denomination's regional network in Southeast Asia. Through these interviews and participant observations, we also discovered stories about their divine encounters and revelations from Scripture that led to their commitment to missionary work in Thailand.

Christianity and the Filipino Migrant

Our work is a contribution to the growing scholarship on the religious lives of Filipinos around the world. Theologians and missiologists have long reflected on Filipino global migration, often relating it to the experience of Jews and early Christians (Pantoja et al. 2004). These reflections suggest that although precipitated by economic needs and suffering, Filipino migration has also been providential in so far as the Gospel gets to reach restrictive places. But other religious scholars are cautious. While "God has a plan for scattering Filipinos around the world," argues Athena Gorospe (2015, 145), "there is a tendency to gloss over the negative effects of migration, extolling this model's virtues without properly addressing its problems." Specifically, her theological reading of the migration phenomenon is that it creates victims not just out of OFWs but also their families.

In the social sciences, many scholars argue that in the process of global migration of Filipinos, they carry with them Christian beliefs and practices that are unmistakably inflected with strong Filipino identity (Fresnoza-Flot 2010).[1] Functionalist in orientation, some of these writings emphasize the solidarity that Filipinos encounter when they come together in local religious spaces. Instructive in this regard, for example, is the work of anthropologist Jo Tondo (2014) carried out among domestic workers in Kuala Lumpur. Every Sunday, the domestic workers would linger at church after Mass where they could spend time with each other. Apart from deepening their relationships with one another and their devotion to Mary, these gatherings were also spaces of comfort to mitigate the impact of everyday discrimination. Camaraderie, Marian devotion, and shared experiences of discrimination galvanized Filipino identity for these domestic workers. The experience of Filipina Catholics in France reveals the same dynamics. Despite their college degrees, they are domestic workers in the country but appreciate having a "Filipino Catholic Church" with a liturgy delivered in Filipino. In a society with a strong secular tradition and rigid immigration policies, the Filipino parish serves irregular Filipina migrants as an "extension of their [Filipinos] country of origin ... that allows them to affirm their religious and linguistic identities ... a space of refuge and protection from police arrest" (Fresnoza-Flot 2010, 352). In this situation, the Catholic community has been granted a very important role in providing a safe haven for migrants, as well as material and humanitarian help in times of personal and financial crises.

Apart from building solidarity, Filipino Christianity in other countries is also an act of resistance. One interesting case of Filipino Catholic practice abroad is the celebration and performance of the Santacruzan pageant in Italy. This Filipino Catholic tradition provides migrants an "indirect way to cope with everyday life migrant status" (Saint-Blancat and Cancellieri 2014, 658). However, carried out in a visible urbanized space, this religious ritual challenges how public spaces are viewed in Padua, Italy. Belongingness to the city has been one of the primary motivations for this practice. In effect, Filipino Santacruzan[2] in Italy redefines Filipino religiosity, as it becomes a public display of piety and

Filipinoness in a foreign land. This performance of tradition has been one of the important topics addressed in religion and transnationalism. Filipino Catholics in Italy indirectly negotiate their presence, which can also challenge how Italians understand and accept them in their locality. Indeed, there is a complex dynamic between locals and migrants with respect to religious rituals in urban space. In this case, the need to affirm religious identities in another society is central to transnationalizing religion.

A similar case can be made about the Sinulog Festival in Hong Kong. Domestic helpers organize the feast in honor of Santo Niño (Child Jesus), a spectacular practice that is derived from the annual event that takes place in Cebu, a province in Central Philippines. In Hong Kong, the practice, which began in 2008, replicates the street performance, dancing, and merrymaking associated with the Sinulog Festival (Oracion 2012). Their celebrations even include a beauty pageant. To the Filipino domestic workers, organizing the event is not only a form of worship but also an assertion of legitimacy and quest for recognition by the Catholic Church in Hong Kong, the Philippine Consulate General, and even Hong Kong society at large.

These cases point to how religion and transnational life are studied among overseas Filipinos (Yap 2015; Liebelt 2010). The functionalist account usually tackles how the Catholic Church as an institution provides help and space for migrants. In fact, Catholicism affords even second-generation Filipino migrants the resources to construct their identities (Caneva 2016). These studies present an instrumental view of Christianity and religious practices. At the same time, anthropologists have also revealed how religious and spiritual belongingness is achieved, which can be very difficult in the case of migrants. Aside from the spiritual dimension, Christianity has also enabled Filipinos to assert their presence and visibility in the foreign land. By exercising and celebrating religious activities, they contend meanings and spaces in their host countries, which challenge the dynamics of sacred and secular and migrant and local.

The Religious Imaginary

In the sections that follow we go beyond solidarity and resistance, themes that are well rehearsed in the scholarship on Filipino Christianity among migrant workers. While these ideas are discernible in our interviews with Filipino missionaries, a more recurring theme concerns their religious subjectivity and their religious views about Thailand and their calling in the country. We approach these religious views about the self and the country to which they believe they have been called to work as missionaries as the religious imaginary.[3]

In the literature, the religious imaginary, broadly speaking, is a religiously inspired "view of how the world is and works" (Beneduce 2021, 3). Individuals develop these views as a result of divine encounters, usually in the form of visions, dreams, and voices. They can also be derived from existing religious cosmologies based on tradition (Gravers 2015). These encounters provide the religious language or lexicon to account for personal experiences and imbue them with meaning for individuals. In Taiwan, for example, the New Testament Church's (NTC) claim on Mount Zion in Kaohsiung City is directly inspired by a dream. One night, at the foot of the mountain, Elijah Hong, NTC's leader, had a dream that paralleled Jacob's in Genesis 28. Based on that dream, the church believes that Mount Zion "has moved from Israel to Taiwan" and that "it has been chosen by God as His and that it is the site for the impending Tribulation" (Farrelly 2012, 183). Similarly, Beneduce's (2021) ethnographic work in southern Italy demonstrates the power of visions in helping subaltern mystics recognize the religious meanings behind their sufferings. He writes about the mystic Tony, who receives messages directly from God in the local vernacular, which his followers receive as specific messages for them.

But these visions are not only about the individual. Often, they are commentaries about the status quo that enables individuals to envision future events. For being divine, religious imaginaries, therefore, are powerful narratives that locate individuals in history, from which they are summoned to do more. "By opening a channel between ordinary life and the numinous, visions draw new imaginative horizons and work as perceptual hope" (Beneduce 2021, 19). In the case of the mystic Tony's followers, the horizon of hope that opens is about forming communities of acceptance and healing. The experience of poor Karen migrants around the border of Thailand and Burma validates this point (Gravers 2015). Inspired by the work of charismatic Buddhist monks, their religious imaginary underpins their vision of a new moral order that maintains peace with Christians and fellow Buddhists in an otherwise violent area. They have sought refuge in monasteries catering for Karen migrants where they encounter ascetic practices and humanitarian work for internally displaced people. In effect, they become part of lay Buddhist communities that apply a "Buddhist cosmological imaginary" to build monasteries, schools, and other infrastructure in a manner that brings together spirituality with development aspirations (ibid., 68).

Although these illustrations demonstrate the power of the religious imaginary to build solidarities, other scholars note its divisive consequences. Religious imaginaries, for being "cosmological and ontological notions" specific to a culture, can create divisions and even be violent at the expense of those who do not belong to the community, or worse, those who threaten its integrity (Taylor 2013, 269). Taylor's incisive commentary on the Rwandan genocide brings in the religious imaginary that underpinned the hostilities against the Tutsi. He proposes that the Hutu extremists believed that President Habyarimana was no longer able to fulfill his responsibility as a conduit for celestial order—a precolonial view of sacred kings. They held the Tutsi, a minority ethnic group, responsible. In their view, the Tutsi blocked the celestial order, and were thus a threat to the progress of Rwanda. The Tutsi "had become the 'blocking beings', and they were everywhere—neighbors, colleagues, sometimes even wives and mistresses. No pity could be shown" (ibid., 278).

The lesson from Taylor's provocative analysis is that the religious imaginary is also divisive. The task of the scholar is thus to identify the boundaries that are being drawn in the name of the religious imaginary. Religious beliefs, in other words, can define the enemies of society and deepen the public's moral panic. In the course of the twentieth century, the Philippine Catholic hierarchy produced official documents that echoed the state's rhetoric against illegal drugs, for example (Cornelio and Lasco 2020). In the contemporary period, emerging Christian groups in the Philippines are, in their own ways, making discursive claims about the Christian identity—the religious imaginary—of the country by drawing on Scriptures, visions, and other divine encounters (Cornelio 2020a). Claiming the nation for Christianity erases the presence of other religious minorities, including the Moro.

Filipino Christianity in Thailand

In what follows, we adopt the religious imaginary as a useful heuristic tool in accounting for the decision of Filipino missionaries, many of whom gave up lucrative professional careers, to commit their lives to evangelistic work in Thailand. As we have pointed out above, three themes are salient from our interviews: the religious imaginary as an interruption, the sacralization of interruption, and the special calling of Filipinos as missionaries to the region. Like the scholars we mentioned above, we propose that the religious imaginary provides a far richer explanatory power, than, say economic factors. We note, for example, the observation that the "evangelistic zeal of religious laity combined with the economic opportunities to migrate and carry out their mission to spread the gospel" creates unique self-understandings which "do not always 'make sense' when evaluated from a purely economic perspective" (Cruz 2013, 48). In effect, through the religious imaginary "religions are taking part in a network society that cuts across borders" (Michel et al., 2017, 1). Bold predictions from the past about the inevitable weakening of religion as societies modernize are belied by the observations made by many scholars who pay attention to the power of the religious imaginary to move people around.

Religious Imaginary as Interruption

We begin with the recurring narrative among our informants that their decision to be missionaries was not necessarily intentional. It is often couched as an interruption brought about by a divine encounter. Consistent with the general motivation of other OFWs, many of them left the country as economic migrants. Low-cost international travel, lack of opportunities at home, and the promise of better economic payoffs have enabled Filipinos to go abroad (Aguilar 2014; San Juan Jr. 2009). State policies have also been instrumental in pursuing opportunities abroad. The establishment of the Overseas Workers Welfare Administration in 1977 and the Philippine Overseas Employment Administration in 1982 have created a separate process for would-be OFWs to ensure that their transactions and plans are assisted by the government. Since then, all Filipinos deployed in legal overseas jobs are supervised by these state agencies. Interestingly, the Philippine House of Representatives approved a bill in 2020 that instituted a "Department of Filipinos Overseas and Foreign Deployment" aimed at protecting OFWs from illegal recruitment and helping Filipinos in distress abroad (CNN Philippines 2020).

While some of our interlocutors are currently employed as English teachers, others were once sales personnel, factory workers, or industrial engineers. On average, our informants have been in Thailand for more than ten years. Some of them have been pastors not only in Thailand but also in neighboring Asian countries like Laos, Cambodia, Indonesia, and Taiwan. But before becoming pastors and missionaries, most of them were not interested in leaving the Philippines. In fact, some of them were already part of churches in the country

During our fieldwork, we noticed that many of our informants left the Philippines not as missionaries but as migrant workers. Over time, an interruption took place in their lives—often explained as a divine encounter— that convinced them to leave their careers. Max, 53 years old, an assistant pastor for the International Christian Assembly in Bangkok, shares his experience: "Actually, I never thought that I would work abroad because this was not my desire really.... My desire was to stay in the Philippines. But later on I had to leave and work as a factory manager and a production manager in Indonesia. So, just before my contract ended, somehow the Lord impressed upon me that I needed to go full time in the ministry in Bali. There was one preacher that came during our service. He prayed for me that the Lord would use me in a different way. That convinced me to leave my career and go full time in the ministry."

This experience is an example of an interruption to the "normal life story" of our interlocutors as economic migrants before anything else. While they were busy at work, circumstances took place that prompted them to consider Christian ministry. Pastor Rudy of the Jesus is Lord (JIL) Church Bangkok shares with us the same narrative. His church is a worldwide network of evangelical congregations that originated in the Philippines (Cornelio 2018, 128–29). After getting his college degree, he went to Taiwan for work. He aspired then to be the best in his field—fine arts—but it seemed that God had a different plan for him. In Taiwan, he committed his days off for church ministry, distributing tracts for evangelism. As the Filipino Christian community grew, JIL decided to form their own congregation in Taiwan. Pastor Rudy was appointed to lead a service. For Pastor Rudy, "I really wanted to be a professional in the field that I chose. But you cannot escape God. You cannot run away from him. Even Jonah didn't escape." In 2003, he finally obtained his missionary visa for Taiwan and has been a church pastor in other countries in the region. He has currently been pastoring JIL in Bangkok for more than two years.

For others, the interruption took place as a disappointing turn of events in their lives. In the case of Pastor Lando, 53 years old, the missionary was running a business in Manila. Before that, he also worked in Thailand as a restaurant manager. However, his business "went south" in the Philippines "in spite of being a Christian already." He describes himself then as "mere Christian, but not a serving Christian." As he struggled with his finances and other problems in the family, he realized that "God was calling him through brokenness also." As nothing aligned with his plan, he realized that "there's no way [for me] to go except to follow God." This led him to do volunteer work, first for the International Christian Assembly. The volunteer work then led him to another church that would be his spiritual home for the years to come, the Lord's Blessing International Church Bangkok.

Another example is Pastor Allen, a native of Bukidnon Province in southern Philippines. When he was young, he was already spending time on church ministry. He was even successful in setting up churches and linking local congregations with international networks such as the Assemblies of God in the same province. After realizing that he was done with the groundwork for his local congregation, he expressed his desire to his church leaders "to go outside." This desire was accompanied by an invitation from his sister to go to Bangkok for a vacation. While enjoying his vacation in the city, he was invited to a Christian service, which turned out to be a pivotal moment. The simple invitation led him to "sense Thailand" as a "strange land." After discovering the minority status of Christians in Thailand, he felt that the Lord had "birthed a mission" for him. This led him to interpret the simple vacation he was supposed to be on as a divine inspiration to set up a new congregation, Jesus for All Nations.

These stories confirm the potent pull of religious matters and spirituality for migrants (Sheringham 2010, 1688). While other studies show that religious institutions in host societies provide spiritual shelter for immigrants, the case of Filipino missionaries in Bangkok adds a different layer to this narrative. Here, our respondents felt an interruption in their work and life-changing experiences to be "called" for missionary service in Thailand, a foreign land that, in their view, needs Christianity. In this sense, the acquisition of a religious imaginary was an interruption in an otherwise mundane life guided by economic needs and career ambitions.

Sacralization of Interruption

While we have already identified the divine encounters that interrupted the lives of Filipinos as migrant workers, here we turn to the power of visions and revelations in validating their decision to become missionaries. As we have also noted above, the religious imaginary, as a religiously inspired view of the world, finds its potency in divine encounters usually in the form of visions and revelations from Scripture (Beneduce 2021; Gravers 2015). These encounters provide a transcendental basis for viewing Thailand as a country that needs the message of Christianity. Predictably, the Bible has been a recurring basis for the religious imaginary. Almost all our respondents refer to Jesus's commandment in Matthew 28: 19–20 to "go and make disciples of all nations." For them, this has taken on a more urgent meaning as they navigate their space in Thai society.

In addition to this commandment from Jesus, some of them received spiritual messages and signs that validate their missionary work in Bangkok. This point became clear to us toward the end of our interview with Pastor Rudy. Pastor Rudy, 45 years old, a father of three children who commands authority with his height, echoes exactly this point about his divine calling for Thailand. Speaking in a soft voice, he recounted to us a vision he saw as he was praying while walking along the Mekong River near the boundary between Laos and Thailand. This took place a year before his Bangkok appointment: "Then suddenly I saw two rainbows. I don't know, it's supernatural. It's not so easy for others to interpret this vision. I was standing near the boundary of Laos and Thailand. I saw two rainbows. The ends of the two rainbows were in two different countries. I was praying to God, 'Lord, what is the meaning of this? What is your message?' And then I realized that the Lord has prepared something to do for me for these two countries."

The vision became fact during his life. Pastor Rudy became the pastor of JIL in Laos before being appointed to lead his congregation in Bangkok, where he is a respected pastor. As a factory worker in Taiwan in 1997, he did not anticipate that his time there would be his first involvement in JIL, which set him on a path of missionary work for the rest of his life. Even though it has been difficult for him to be away from his family, he is grateful that church-sponsored travel for his family allows them to visit him once a year in Bangkok.

Our other interlocutors have also had dreams which they believe were from God. Pastor Allen, a youthful and energetic pastor in his late thirties, preaches and plays the guitar for his church. He shares with us what happened to him: "But I woke up one day and then I saw Thailand, Thai people. They were spiritually dead. Do you know the Valley of the Dry Bones? It was like that. They were lifeless." Pastor Allen interprets Ezekiel 37 to refer to a foreign land that needs spiritual rejuvenation. For him, Thailand is that empty place that is also the center of his ministry. Brother Roger, who has been a lay worker for Seventh-day Adventists in Thailand since 2001, agrees with this observation. Brother Roger is also the principal of an Adventist school in Bangkok. Its logo bears the image of Thailand but shaded in black. When we ask him why this is so, he does not hold back: "We know that this is a Buddhist country.… Thailand in the school logo is in black. We are in a dark country because we are in a non-Christian country."

It is not surprising, then, that Bangkok represents for our informants a "mission or harvest field." This harvest field can include various groups of people: Filipino migrants who have turned away from their faith, Thai citizens who are not yet Christians, and other immigrants who need immediate help. For Pastor Max, 54 years old, an engineer with a small build, the geographical importance of Thailand for doing missions is undeniable. Fluent in English, Pastor Max is the head of an outreach ministry and connects various groups to his church in Bangkok. According to him, "Thailand is a hub. It's the heart of Southeast Asia. So, this will be a great ground, if we can develop this ground for Christianity, to move around towards all parts of Southeast Asia."

Even though they acknowledge that explicit proselytizing may be "too aggressive" for Thais, their perseverance and patience do not falter. For Pastor

Bob and Sister Linda of Bangjak Filipino Ministry, a married couple who have been involved in Thai mission for more than three years, the preexisting beliefs of Thais make them a harvest field. According to them, the strong Buddhist orientation of Thais made it difficult for previous American missionaries to introduce Christianity. Since Filipinos are "skilled, trustworthy, and teachable," they believe that Filipino Christians can do far more significant work. For Pastor Bob, "We teach Filipinos and these Filipinos will also reach out to Thais. If we wanted to evangelize Filipinos, then we should have just stayed in Manila, not Thailand."

They are also aware of the differing circumstances between the two countries. Since their children are already professionals, they admit that living in the Philippines would be very comfortable. However, they believe that "their conviction is in Thailand... The challenge that no one dared to take up, we will take up." Pastor Bob believes that Bangkok is a large spiritual opportunity: "When people do not belong to the Lord, they will face punishment. And when you're a child of God, you know that they have souls, they still have hope. You can reach out to them. If no one will do that, who else?" When we ask him about his future prospects, he tells us that he wants "to serve God and die in Thailand."

The challenge to serve Thais was accepted by Sister Joy, a lay missionary worker from the Pentecostal Missionary Church of Christ (4th Watch). Sister Joy always has a positive view in life, evident in her round, smiling face. She finished her Bible training in Manila before leaving for Bangkok. For her, to be a deliverer of God's word is "the highest profession." She invests her youthful life in doing mission even if that has meant giving up university education and her relationship with her longtime boyfriend in the Philippines. Life outside missions, for Joy, is unimaginable. When she experiences homesickness in Bangkok, she consoles herself by reminding herself of God's promise that her ministry and family will be blessed if she is faithful to God. She even cites for us Luke 9:62 to assert that anyone "who puts his hand to the plow and looks back" is disqualified from the kingdom of God. When we ask her whether God has a plan for Southeast Asia, she answers in the affirmative: "In my view, the Lord has a great plan for Southeast Asia. But before it can be fulfilled, we really need to undergo hard tests to see how determined we are to fulfill the plan."

In another interview, Pastor Lando, a 55-year-old former businessman, could not help but echo the importance of steadfastness in the mission field. For him, "Thailand is special because God loves its people too and that the souls of Thais, Cambodians, and others are precious because they are not many. The Philippines has so many Christians already. Here, they are few.... So, one soul saved here in Thailand is like equivalent to so many souls in the Philippines."

Pastor Lando has been doing church ministry in Thailand for nine years. Unlike the other pastors that we interviewed, he lives with his family in Bangkok where his children are also studying.

The Special Calling of Filipinos

During our interviews, we also noticed that many of our informants are convinced that Filipinos have a special calling in Thailand and the wider region. This is discernible in the visions and narratives we presented above, in which Thailand is imagined as the heart of Christian missions in mainland Southeast Asia. Indeed, being in Bangkok has developed a deeper sense of Christian mission for our informants. For them, Filipino Christians have a "special calling" to fulfill the divine destiny of Thailand.

Brother Leo and Sister Linda attest to this. They are a married couple who have been in Thailand for more than four decades. They belong to the first generation of Filipino migrants who came to Thailand as English teachers in the late 1950s. They were hosted in Bangkok under the auspices of the Seventh-day Adventist Church. At that time, they were affiliated with Mountain View College, a Seventh-day Adventist educational institution in Bukidnon Province. For them, that Filipinos are "the only English-speaking, Christian country" in Southeast Asia plays a big role in the Christian work in Bangkok. Based on experience, they believe that because of their English-speaking skills, Filipinos in Thailand are able to gain the respect of locals. Over time, this impression has given them the professional credibility to share God's message with their students, both Thais and non-Thais. According to the couple, Filipino Christians are also suitable to do evangelistic work because of their human values. For example, they say that "Filipinos are hospitable ... and Thais know that we are peace-loving as well." For them, it is an advantage that Filipinos can get along with both Buddhists and Muslims. Being a Filipino Christian also gives them a special edge in missionary work: "We are able to identify ourselves with their needs because they are also Asian. And we also look like them. Indeed, we are no different in appearance unless we open our mouth. But when we speak, ... they say, 'Oh you are so good because even if you are Filipino, you've tried to know our language.'"

This flexibility is important as well for Pastor Victor, 59 years old. As a minister, he commits his time and energy to JIL Bangkok. He began missionary work in other provinces in southern Philippines, including Zamboanga and Tawi-Tawi. These are now successful congregations. Because of his humble and multifaceted preaching style, JIL appointed him to conduct various missionary work in Hong Kong, Singapore, Canada, and then California. His most memorable experience was in Hong Kong. While serving the congregation there, Pastor Victor coordinated legal assistance for Filipina domestic workers who were abused by their employers or laid off from their jobs. Brother Roger, a former computer teacher and lay worker for Seventh-day Adventists, shares the same story. He has witnessed many financial struggles for their faith-based school, but he attributes the resilience of the school to the involvement of Filipinos. He even compares the missionary work done by Filipinos to other nationalities. For Brother Roger, "the Philippines is one of the Christian countries in East Asia, although Korea is also a Christian country. The rest are all non-Christian countries. But, unlike Filipinos, Koreans won't go out of their country just to work except to be a missionary."

Here, Brother Roger interprets the poor economic conditions that force Filipinos to go abroad as a springboard for another, even greater, calling. This calling allows them to "earn a living while being a missionary." For Brother Roger and other missiologists, being a missionary is not a monopoly of people who exclusively dedicate their life to sharing the faith. Rather, anyone can be a missionary as long as they carry their faith to influence non-believers in different capacities, especially in what scholars refer to as "creative access nations," places that restrict missionary work and thus call for unique ways of entering them (Manzano 2015).

Pastor Gino, a pastor in his mid-40s who speaks with a commanding voice, echoed this point in another interview. He has led an underground evangelical church in Kuala Lumpur for Filipinos based in the city. Pastor Gino, however, provides a different reading of the economic and social struggles of Filipinos. He proposes that "we are molded by God! It's no surprise that the Philippines is a third world country because only those who know suffering and poverty can withstand the challenges in the mission fields." Pastor Gino also argues that "the Philippines will be a missionary-sending country." He even suggests that "for now, the gospel movement is not concentrated in Jerusalem. But time will come, it will return to Jerusalem and before that happens, there will be a revival in countries in Southeast Asia." Pastor EJ, the Regional Pastor of JIL in Southeast Asia, reinforces this point. Describing his church, it is important that JIL is "a Filipino church, born in the heart of God, started in the Philippines ... that will give Filipinos and all nationalities of the world the opportunity to hear the word of God." Based on our interviews, we know that this viewpoint is not unique to JIL pastors. It is common among the missionaries we have come across. Pastor Gino is now assigned to JIL Hongkong and continues to maintain a low profile.

Additionally, Pastor Lando sees a greater purpose for OFWs: "God has a purpose through ... economic (hardships), for us to be dispersed, to be OFWs. But I see it with a missionary eye that OFWs are not just Overseas Filipino Workers, but they are Overseas Filipino Witnesses." This statement articulates a "theology of migration" which stresses that Filipinos can play a big role "in order to help men and women, lost in their earthly sojourn, find their way back home to God" (Groody 2009, 649).

Above, we have presented how this reading of the plight of Filipino migrant workers informs the diaspora theology among local missiologists as well (Pantoja et al., 2004; Gorospe 2015). These thoughts from our respondents afford special roles or calling to the Filipinos in the evangelization of Southeast Asia. All the struggles and challenges, big or small, seem to make sense as they hear and heed their calling. That they see themselves as a people with a special calling from God fits their religious imaginary of Thailand as a "mission field" for Christianity.

When we attended some of the church activities in Bangkok, we immediately noticed how their prayers, preachings, and proclamations echoed exactly this point. When we attended a regular Sunday service of the Bangjak Filipino Ministry, we observed that although the congregation was small, it was diverse. Its Sunday School teacher was an American while attendees were Thais, Filipinos, and even asylum-seekers from South Asia. The same was evident in the International Christian Assembly, a large and affluent congregation, which had its own property in a central part of Bangkok. Surrounding the hall were flags that represented the different nationalities present in the congregation. Pastor Max, a Filipino, serves as its assistant pastor. Even congregations that mainly catered for Filipinos, like the Pentecostal Missionary Church of Christ (4th Watch), embodied elements that signified their calling in Thailand and Southeast Asia. During their anniversary celebration, the guest speaker was their pastor assigned in Singapore who rehearsed for them Thailand's need to encounter Christ.

Conclusion

Our study advances the scholarly work on the state of Filipino Christianity around the world. In an earlier section, we noted how most studies highlight the significant role of Christianity for migrants, most of them focused on Filipino women who are employed as domestic or care workers abroad. Apart from those that have been offered by missiologists, deliberate focus on Filipinos doing missionary work has not been carried out extensively. In addition, Catholicism dominates the discussion, overlooking other Christian denominations. Filipino Catholics have been the primary subject of studies about Filipino Christianity and transnationalism. This chapter has diversified by examining other Christian denominations. In this light, we are advancing recent developments in the study of religious diversity in the Philippines, which is only beginning to recognize the influence and even global presence of other Christian denominations (Cornelio 2020b; Cornelio 2017; Cornelio and Aldama 2020; Baring 2011; and Sapitula 2013).

This chapter has been concerned with the experience of Filipino missionaries in Bangkok. While Thailand is not a conventional destination for Filipino migrant workers, the country has, in recent years, seen an influx of Filipino teachers, engineers, and other professionals. Young scholars who are drawn to this phenomenon, echo the economic promise that these migrant workers find in Thailand (Novio 2018). Aligned with the thrust of this volume, our work also examines how religion underpins the movement of Filipinos in Southeast Asia. While we have focused only on those who are in Bangkok, the narratives of our informants show that before becoming missionaries many of them were based elsewhere in the region as migrant workers. The religious imaginary—articulated as an interruption in their lives, a sacralization of this interruption, and as a special calling—are compelling explanations for their commitment to missionary work.

However, it needs to be made clear that the religious imaginary, while articulated from the point of view of individuals, is at the same time about Thailand (and arguably even Southeast Asia at large). Thailand is a mission field, a religious imaginary drawn from visions, dreams, and Scriptural references (Beneduce 2021; Farrelly 2012). In other words, there is a dynamic relationship between the idea that Thailand is a harvest field and their own narratives of migration. Therefore, the religious imaginary that they carry with them reframes their personal identity as Filipino missionaries as much as it does the identity of Thailand from a Buddhist society into a harvest field. But the religious imaginary also means that it has a confrontational tone to it, evident even in some of our interviews that depict Thai society as a "dark spot." Given this orientation, Filipinos might be carrying an attitude towards non-Christians that may result in unintentional disregard for religious and cultural diversity. The religious imaginary among Filipino missionaries makes them new agents of evangelization, which replaces the role of American and European Christians in Southeast Asia.

Indeed, the literature on religious imaginary is cautious about its divisive character, which, in some cases, has underpinned violence against those who do not belong to the community (Taylor 2013). In the context of our research, this note raises questions about the conflicts the religious imaginary engenders in the everyday lives of these Filipino missionaries. Building on our exploratory work, succeeding research must explore the contested relationship between their religious imaginary and their religious citizenship as Christian migrants in a Buddhist society (Lau 2020). Future studies may also explore the religious imaginary of other global Filipino churches. Iglesia Ni Criso and the Kingdom of Jesus Christ, which both claim millions of members around the world, may be good starting points. For embracing a non-Trinitarian theology, they are considered sectarian by mainstream churches in the Philippines.

Endnotes: The Religious Imaginary

1. For more on Filipino Catholicism, see the special issue of *Philippine Studies: Historical and Ethnographic Viewpoints* dedicated to this topic (Cornelio 2014).

2. Santacruzan is an annual pageant conducted in many villages and towns in the Philippines. Featuring women who represent different religious entities, including Queen Helena of Constantinople, the pageant commemorates the historical search for the True Cross.

3. In this way, our work aligns with recent ethnographic accounts about religion and citizenship, specifically among expatriates in mainland China. Lau's (2020) incisive observations reveal how these Christians, who originate from other countries, bring with them a particular religious subjectivity. Even though they are foreigners, they would like to be exemplary residents to represent Christianity in a society where proselytization is under surveillance.

References

Aguilar, Filomeno Jr. 2014. *Migration Revolution: Philippine Nationhood and Class Relations in a Globalized Age*. Quezon City, Philippines: Ateneo de Manila University Press.

Baring, Rito V. 2011. "Plurality in Unity: Challenges toward Religious Education in the Philippines." *Religious Education* 106 (5): 459–75. doi: 10.1080/00344087.2011.613342.

Beneduce, Roberto. 2021. "Vision, Subalternity, and Religious Imaginary in Southern Italy." *Social Compass* 68(1): 3–24.

Caneva, Elena. 2016. "The Role of Catholicism in the Identity Construction Processes of Filipino Second Generations Living in Italy." In *Migration, Transnationalism and Catholicism*, eds. Dominic Pasura and Erdal Marta Bivand, 235–56. London: Palgrave Macmillan.

CNN Philippines. 2020. "House Approves OFW Department Bill." News. CNN Philippines. March 11, 2020. https://www.cnnphilippines.com/news/2020/3/11/House-approves-OFW-department-bill.html.

Cornelio, Jayeel. 2008. "New Paradigm Christianity and Commitment-formation: The Case of Hope Filipino (Singapore)." In *Religion and the Individual: Belief, Practice, Identity*, ed. Abby Day, 65–77. Aldershot, UK: Ashgate.

—————. 2014. "Guest Editor's Introduction." *Philippine Studies: Historical & Ethnographic Viewpoints* 62(3–4): 309–12.

—————. 2017. "Religion and Civic Engagement: The Case of Iglesia ni Cristo in the Philippines." *Religion, State and Society* 45(1): 23–38.

—————. 2018. "Jesus is Lord: The Indigenization of Megachurch Christianity in the Philippines." In *Pentecostal Megachurches in Southeast Asia: Negotiating Class, Consumption and the Nation*, ed. Terence Chong, 127–55. Singapore: Institute of Southeast Asian Studies.

—————. 2020a. "Claiming the Nation: Theological Nationalism in the Philippines." In *What Does Theology Do, Actually? Observing Theology and the Transcultural*, eds. Matthew Robinson and Inja Inders, 149–65. Leipzig: EVA.

—————. 2020b. "The Philippines." In *Edinburgh Companions to Global Christianity: Christianity in East and South-East Asia*, eds. Kenneth Ross, Todd Johnson, and Francis Alvarez, 242–53. Edinburgh: Edinburgh University Press.

Cornelio, Jayeel, and Gideon Lasco. 2020. "Morality Politics: Drug Use and the Catholic Church in the Philippines." *Open Theology* 6.

Cornelio, Jayeel, and Prince Kennex Aldama. 2020. "Religious Diversity and Covenantal Pluralism in the Philippines." *Review of Faith & International Affairs* 18(4): 74–85.

Cruz, Joseph Nathan. 2013. "Faith in Exile: Evangelical Communities and Filipino Migrant Workers." MA thesis, Department of Sociology, National University of Singapore.

Farrelly, Paul. 2012. "The New Testament Church and Mount Zion in Taiwan." In *Flows of Faith: Religious Reach and Community in Asia and the Pacific*, eds. Lenore Manderson, Wendy Smith, and Matt Tomlinson, 183–200. Dordrecht and Heidelberg: Springer.

Fresnoza-Flot, Asuncion. 2010. "The Catholic Church in the Lives of Irregular Migrant Filipinas in France: Identity Formation, Empowerment and Social Control." *Asia Pacific Journal of Anthropology* 11(3–4): 345–61.

Gorospe, Athena. 2015. "What Does the Bible Say about Migration? Three Approaches to the Biblical Text." In *God at the Borders: Globalization, Migration and Diaspora*, eds. Charles Ringma, Karen Hollenbeck-Wuest, and Athena Gorospe, 125–59. Mandaluyong City: OMF Lit.

Gravers, Mikael. 2015. "Religious Imaginary as an Alternative Social and Moral Order: Karen Buddhism across the Thai-Burma Border." In *Building Noah's Ark for Migrants, Refugees, and Religious Communities*, eds. Alexander Horstmann and Jin-Heong Jung, 45–76. New York: Palgrave Macmillan.

Groody, Daniel G. 2009. "Crossing the Divide: Foundations of a Theology of Migration and Refugees." *Theological Studies* 70: 638–67.

Lau Sin Wen. 2020. *Overseas Chinese Christians in Contemporary China: Religion, Mobility, and Belonging*. Leiden: Brill.

Liebelt, Claudia. 2010. "Becoming Pilgrims in the Holy Land: On Filipina Domestic Workers' Struggles and Pilgrimages for a Cause in Israel." *Asia Pacific Journal of Anthropology* 11(3–4): 245–67.

Mala, Dumrongkiat. 2020. "Filipino Teachers Feel the Pinch." https://www.bangkokpost.com/thailand/general/1919728/filipino-teachers-feel-the-pinch. Accessed February 10, 2020.

Manzano, Jojo. 2015. "Preparing Overseas Filipino Workers." In *God at the Borders: Globalization, Migration and Diaspora*, eds. Charles Ringma, Karen Hollenbeck-Wuest, and Athena Gorospe, 204–7. Mandaluyong City: OMF Lit.

Michel, Patrick, Adam Possamai, and Bryan Turner, eds. 2017. *Religions, Nations, and Transnationalism in Multiple Modernities*. London: Palgrave Macmillan.

Ngo, Thi Thanh Tam. 2009. "The 'Short-waved' Faith: Christian Broadcastings and the Protestant Conversion of the Hmong in Vietnam." In *Mediating Piety: Technology and Religion in Contemporary Asia*, ed. Francis Khek Gee Lim, 139–58. Leiden: Brill.

Novio, Eunice Barbara. 2018. "Tourist to Ajarn: The Filipino Teachers in Thailand." การประชุมวิชาการเสนอ ผลงานวิจัย ระดับชาติและนานาชาติ 1(9).

————. 2020. "Undocumented Filipinos in Thailand Face a Long Wait for Repatriation amid the Coronavirus Outbreak." *Thai Enquirer*. https://www.thaienquirer.com/10469/undocumented-filipinos-in-thailand-face-a-long-wait-for-repatriation-amid-the-coronavirus-outbreak/

Ooi Keat Gin and Volker Grabowsky. 2017. "Introduction." In *Ethnic and Religious Identities and Integration in Southeast Asia*, eds. Ooi Keat Gin and Volker Grabowsky, 1–27. Chiang Mai: Silkworm Books.

Oracion, Enrique. 2012. "The Sinulog Festival of Overseas Filipino Workers in Hong Kong: Meanings and Contexts." *Asian Anthropology* 11(1): 107–27.

Pantoja, Luis, Sadiri Joy Tira, and Enoch Wan, eds. 2004. *Scattered: The Filipino Global Presence*. Manila: Lifechange Publishing.

Philippine Statistics Authority. 2020. "Total Number of OFWs Estimated at 2.2 Million." https://psa.gov.ph/statistics/survey/labor-and-employment/survey-overseas-filipinos. Accessed February 10, 2020.

Ruger, Eileen. 2020. "The Nazarene Overseas Filipino Worker: Equipping God's Missionary People in the Church of the Nazarene." PhD diss., Faculty of Intercultural Doctoral Studies, Assemblies of God Theological Seminary, Missouri, USA.

Saint-Blancat, Chantal, and Adriano Cancellieri. 2014. "From Invisibility to Visibility? The Appropriation of Public Space through a Religious Ritual: The Filipino Procession of Santacruzan in Padua, Italy." *Social & Cultural Geography* 15(6): 645–63.

San Juan Jr., E. 2009. "Overseas Filipino Workers: The Making of an Asian-Pacific Diaspora." *The Global South* 3(2): 99–129.

Sapitula, Manuel. 2013. "Overcoming 'Hierarchized Conviviality' in the Manila Metropolis: Religious Pluralism and Urbanization in the Philippines." In *Religious Pluralism, State and Society in Asia*, ed. Chiara Formichi, 138–52. London: Routledge.

Sheringham, Olivia. 2010. "Creating 'Alternative Geographies': Religion, Transnationalism and Everyday Life." *Geography Compass* 4(11): 1678–94. https://doi.org/10.1111/j.1749-8198.2010.00393.x.

Skelchy, Russell. 2020. "The Afterlife of Colonial Radio in Christian Missionary Broadcasting of the Philippines." *South East Asia Research* 28(3): 344–62.

Taylor, Christopher. 2013. "Genocide and the Religious Imaginary in Rwanda." In *The Oxford Handbook of Religion and Violence*, eds. Mark Juergensmeyer, Margo Kitts, and Michael Jerryson, 268–79. Oxford and New York: Oxford University Press.

Tondo, Josefina. 2014. "Sacred Enchantment, Transnational Lives, and Diasporic Identity: Filipina Domestic Workers at St. John Catholic Cathedral in Kuala Lumpur." *Philippine Studies: Historical and Ethnographic Viewpoints* 62(3–4): 445–70.

Ulla, Mark. 2019. "Filipinos as EFL Teachers in Bangkok, Thailand: Implications for Language Education Policy in the ASEAN Region." *RELC Journal*. https://doi.org/10.1177/0033688219879775.

Yap, Valerie. 2015. "The Religiosity of Filipina Domestic Workers in Hong Kong." *Asian Anthropology* 14(1): 91–102.

Christian Missions and the Reconstruction of Identities: The Talaku Karen on the Thailand-Myanmar Borderland

KWANCHEWAN BUADAENG

When the British colonial government took over Burma (known as Myanmar since 1989) in 1885, the classification of ethnic groups was one of several projects. The "Karen" became a generic term for an ethnic group comprised of smaller groups all sharing the Karenic language. At different periods of time, the Karen have been identified differently from one organization to another and the population figure has also varied from one source to another. An earlier survey conducted by the British colonial government in 1931 found 1,367,673 Karen people out of a total of 14,667,146 Burmans, or 9.3 percent of the total population (Enriquez 1933, 81–82). There has been no official survey on ethnic population since Burma's independence in 1948, when many ethnic groups engaged in armed fighting with the Burmese state. According to the Karen National Union (KNU) (1986), the pan-Karen national organization, the Karen include twelve subgroups—Sgaw, Pwo, Pa-Os, Paku, Maw-Nay Pwa, Bwe, White Karen, Padaung (Kayan), Red Karen (Karenni), Keko/Keba, Black Karen, and Striped Karen—with an estimated population of seven million. The Karen thus formed almost 20 percent of the total 35,307,913 population of Burma in 1983 (Department of Population, Ministry of Labour, Immigration and Population 2015). Smith (1999, 30) states that most neutral estimates calculate the Karen population at three to four million.

Smeaton (1887) and Jorgensen (1997) employ the category "Karens" to emphasize these diverse subgroups. The work of Womack (2005) on Karen literature shows that there were at least eleven different systems of writing for the Pwo and Sgaw Karen languages in Burma during the nineteenth and early twentieth centuries. Each system was invented and accepted by a different network along the lines of religion and locality. Religion is thus an important element used in the construction of Karen identity. As described by Ikeda (2012), Karen history, another important element of identity, was written differently by the Christian Karen and the Buddhist Karen. Besides Buddhism and Christianity, Karen people in different locations have developed diverse religious practices with a different sense of belonging and identity (Hayami 1996). Talaku, the religious movement that is the focus of this chapter, is one of them.

The concept of ethnic identity used here, therefore, is not the natural-given essence of shared blood, descending from the same ancestors, or shared culture, but rather a constructed representation that instills in people a sense of belonging. Religious, ethnic, or cultural identities are usually constructed to differentiate between "us" and "them," enforcing a shared imagination which unites the group members. However, ethnic identity is not fixed, as the group boundary may be broken when one or more members have different experiences and no longer share the same imagination. They may create new groups, with new or plural identities depending on the new network or movement they join. In the modern, globalized period, when many people leave their old community permanently or temporarily for education and work, they connect with new networks and include themselves in new communities with new identities.

This chapter will describe the Talaku religious movement which was originally started by the Pwo Karen who were later joined by the Sgaw Karen in their formation of a different religious subgroup of the Karen. This is to illustrate that although their ethnoreligious identity appears to be fixed and sustained, they have gone through a process of rise and fall. For more than a century, their territory has expanded to cover the vast area along the Thailand-Myanmar border at certain periods, while at others it has been reduced following the flight of members to join other groups. The fieldwork conducted in the borderland of the Karen State of Myanmar and the Phobphra and Umphang districts of Tak Province of Thailand over the last two decades, shows that as the Talaku group has been deterritorialized by state and non-state forces, including religious missions, new groups with new identities have emerged. This chapter thus seeks to answer two main questions: why have the Talaku retained their clear ethnoreligious boundary with unique identities for such a long time? And why is it that some Talaku members began to adopt Christianity? This chapter will argue that as young members develop new imaginations and encounter new experiences resulting from their connections with new communities and networks, they develop new or alternative ethnoreligious identities. To support this argument, I will first introduce the Talaku territory and community and how it has been deterritorialized by many forces over a long period of time. The case of Christian missions, which took more than half a century to convert the first group of Talaku, shows that conversion comes when a group loses faith in an old group and accepts the Christian church, which is part of a strong network operating on the borderland and around the world.

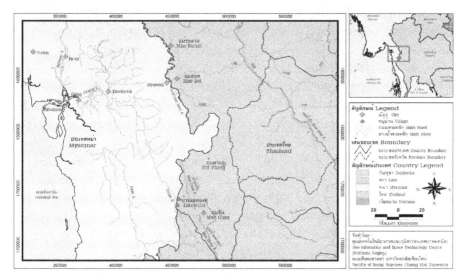

Map 1. Map shows Letawkho/Letongkhu village, the Talaku center at Thailand-Myanmar border (Map by Geo-Infomatics and Space Technology Centre (Northern Region), Faculty of Social Sciences, Chiang Mai University).

The Emergence of Talaku Communities on the Thailand-Myanmar Borderland

Talaku is one of many religious movements of the Karen peoples who reside on the borderland of Thailand and Myanmar.[1] *Talaku* in Sgaw or *Talakhong* in the Pwo Karen dialect comes from the Mon word for "the one who possesses (*tala*) merit/truth (*khong*)." It is said to have been founded in Kyaing, a town in the present Karen State of Myanmar in the 1860s (Hayami 2011). This coincided with the period when Christian and Buddhist missions were competing to convert the Karen, who largely practiced their traditional religions. The Talaku founder is said to have been one of the early Karens ordained as a Buddhist monk. He and some of his friends shared ideas that were different from mainstream Buddhism, and later developed distinctive principles and practices. Talaku members do not identify themselves as Buddhists but as members of the Karens' own religion. They worship Ariya Metteyya, the fifth Buddha who has yet to come, and strictly observe five Buddhist precepts: to refrain from killing, lying, stealing, committing adultery (and other forms of harmful sexual activity), and taking intoxicants (such as alcohol). Those who violate the precepts can be driven out from the village and/or rituals must be conducted to purify the village territory. The Talaku do not raise pigs or chickens and do not consume meat. This observance also makes the Talaku Karen different from other "traditional" Karen who worship ancestral and other types of spirits and conduct rituals involving the sacrifice of pigs and chickens (Hayami 1992; Kwanchewan 2003).

The Talaku group shows similarities with Buddhist organizations. The head of the *ter ro*, the monastery-like place, is called I-Si, a Pali word for "hermit," or Phue i-si, with the addition of the Karen word *phue*, which means "reverend" or "respected," thus reverend hermit or Pujite, another Karen term for a sacred respected person. When a hermit dies, the Talaku select someone to replace him, usually the most senior *ta waw bu*, literally "monasterial boy," the most senior disciple of the late hermit. The Pujite wears a white robe when he assumes the position, and later a yellow robe if he gets the approval to continue in it, often through an auspicious dream. His long hair is wound into a topknot above his forehead. Unlike Buddhist monks who receive food from laypeople who collect alms every morning, the Pujite cultivates the land and cooks his food with the *ta waw bu* within the monastery boundary, which is isolated from the village. The Pujite has two vegetarian meals a day and once a year, at a particular time, he fasts. Every year, the ordination of young boys to become *ta waw bu* is an important mechanism to continue the Talaku organization. *Ta waw bu* spend at least three years in the compound before they can leave. They are trained by the hermit and senior *ta waw bu* to gain knowledge and be skillful in leading Talaku rituals, which require many types of paraphernalia. The hermit and *ta waw bu* observe more precepts than Talaku laypeople, such as no traveling outside the monastery boundary and no intimate relationships with woman.

Fig. 1. The tenth I-si and Talaku leaders at the reception hall inside the monastery compound.

Fig. 2. Monasterial boys (*ta waw bu*) inside the Talaku monastery compound.

At the community level, *bu kho*, the religious leader and his committee whose members are former *ta waw bu*, lead villagers in the organization of Talaku rituals and ceremonies and on religious matters to be dealt with in the Talaku community. He also coordinates with the Pujite on rituals organized within the monasterial compound.

The Talaku, which was formed in the mid-nineteenth century, has a different identity from Buddhist, Christian, traditional, and other Karen groups. As Talaku Karen are subject to many restrictions, such as the prohibition of raising pigs or chickens and not drinking alcohol, they prefer to set up their village in rural and mountainous areas away from others. The story told by Talaku from Letongkhu village, presently in Umphang district on the Thai side of the border, is that they had to flee from attacks by Burmese forces to various places until they came to the present area where they set up a village named Letongkhu, literally, "above the rock." There is no record of the founding date of the village but Stern (1968) estimates that it would have been around the middle of the nineteenth century at a time when many revolts were taking place in Burma. The village is said to be more than a hundred years old as there have been ten hermits from its beginning to the present.

Prior to the 1960s, Talaku villagers expressed their identity through their dress code, eating taboos, and religious practices. At that time, the Thailand-Myanmar borderland was not administrated by any state or non-state agency. It was a sparsely populated area, although long-distance merchants from the north and the south frequently passed by. Powerful local men administered their villages and surrounding territories but did not exert control over a larger area. This does not mean, however, that the Talaku did not change over the century of its existence. For example, in the Karen State of Myanmar, the Talaku monastery once set up by the Talaku founder in the large town of Kyondoe in Myawaddy district, became a Buddhist monastery. However, until 2015 when the author and her team visited this monastery, the Bu Kho, the head of the Talaku lay people, and a few *ta waw bu* were still involved in the organization of Talaku ceremonies, especially Bu U Jong, the annual bonfire ceremony. The Bu Kho revealed that there were three Talaku communities around the monastery containing around three hundred households who considered themselves both Talaku and Buddhist. Other Talaku villages in more remote and mountainous areas have also adjusted their practices in different ways.

On the Thai side of the border, until the 1950s Talaku communities in mountainous areas maintained their relative autonomy over their organization and practices, although they have modified them over time. Letongkhu (also called Tee Maw Klo, the village at Tee Maw stream) has been known as the headquarters of the Talaku with Pujite, the head of the cult. Although there were many Talaku communities which have their own monasteries, Letongkhu was recognized among other communities as the headquarters. Talaku in other communities inside Myanmar, and the Talaku-cum-Buddhist Karen people living as far away as Huay Kha Khaeng National Park in Kanchanaburi Province, Thailand, came at least once a year to worship the Pujite in a big ceremony. At present there are altogether around twenty Talaku villages settled along the Thailand-Myanmar border. Sixteen of these are located on the Myanmar side while four villages, including Letongkhu, are in the area of Mae Chan subdistrict in the Umphang district of Tak Province. The number of Talaku villages and Talaku members has fluctuated, from around seven thousand people in the early 1960s (Stern, 1968) when the Talaku community had not yet been disrupted, to only three thousand in the 1990s after some Talaku had adopted other religions.

Talaku history is based on oral form. In the 1980s, when the Thai government asked Maw A Mee, the late Letongkhu headman, to write a history of the Talaku, he and village leaders concluded that there had been nine Pujite since the time the village was founded. Each Pujite had unique characteristics and sometimes created new practices (The 34th Border Patrol Police Force 1998). It was Phue Tee Maw, the seventh Pujite at Letongkhu, who radically changed the practices as he had a wife and three children which, in principle, was forbidden. In the 1960s, the Talaku community was disrupted when Phue Tee Maw led many Talaku to fight against the Burmese army who had moved near the border. He was the Pujite at the time of the Christian missionary's first visit to Letongkhu in their attempt to convert the Talaku.

Fig. 3. *Pha Cha Long*, the donation of new rice ceremony, organized by Talaku members in Letongkhu, April 2015.

Early Christian Missions among the Talaku

After the first Karen was baptized by the American Baptist Mission in Burma in 1826, there had always been a desire to go to Siamese territory (changed to Thailand in 1939) to convert the Karen there. The Christian missionaries were motivated to evangelize the Karen for two reasons. The first was to spread the "good news" with the intention of liberating poor people from the exploitation of the evil, as expressed by Eubank (2015, xii): "There are still people who are struggling under the power of Satan and waiting for someone to come to demonstrate the love and power of Jesus Christ." Second, their experience in conducting Karen missions in Burma led them to believe that the Karen would convert in large numbers, following their leader. Some missionaries believed that the Karen were waiting for them, convinced that they themselves were the white brother, as in the myth of the "Golden Book of Life," who would bring back the literature, the source of valuable knowledge.

The first missionary visit to the Talaku took place in 1962. According to Hovemyr (1997), the core members of the team belonged to the family of Olivepa,[2] the Karen Christian from Burma who studied law in Bangkok, and two missionaries, Aran Eubank of the United Christian Missionary Society and Paul Dodge from the American Baptist Mission, both working in Thailand. Olivepa contacted Phue Tee Maw, the then-Pujite, through a friend and arranged permission to visit the Letongkhu. The expedition from the church in Sangkhlaburi, a border town in Kanchanaburi Province to the Talaku center at Letongkhu took place at the end of 1962. It took forty days to complete the round trip from central Thailand to Sangkhlaburi in the west and then north to the Talaku center by train, boat, elephant, and on foot, including staying at Letongkhu for two weeks. Along the way to Letongkhu, they met many Talaku who showed a keen interest in the missionaries' preaching. However, on the matter of conversion, they said they would wait for Pujite's decision. After arriving at the Talaku center, and going to see the hermit the next morning, the missionary team was told to remove their shoes before meeting the hermit. Of the first encounter with the Phue Tee Maw, Eubank (2015, 42) wrote:

> He (Phue Tee Maw) was a lean, wiry, stern-faced man who was about forty-five years old ... we introduced ourselves and presented him an axe and a hunting knife, which had been brought from America as personal presents.... Our most important gifts, however, were two gilt-edged leather Bibles, one in Sgaw and the other in the Pwo language. We hoped that he would accept them as the long lost 'Golden Book of Life.' However, after a few meetings with the hermit, in which the team lengthily explained God's revelation in the Bible from creation to the last judgment, Eubank found that 'his [the hermit's] main concern was for the present peace and prosperity of his people.... Although he did not readily commit to belief in Christ, he did say that others would have to choose for themselves, and that the future of his people depended on cooperation with the white missionary brother. The legend of the 'white brother' is definitely true....

However, Phue Tee Maw did not believe that the gilt-edged Bibles were their lost books. According to Eubank (2015, 45), "We felt discouraged when the Pujite told us that the lost book was a magic book that every Karen, whether literate or not, would be able to read at first sight. He could not read our Bibles as he only read the Pwo language written in the Mon alphabet...."

Thus, the first missionary trip ended with no converts, although the team felt that the hermit's acceptance of them as the "white brother" could be a starting point for further negotiation. The missionary team visited the Talaku center again in 1963 and 1964 to see the seventh hermit. Eubank still found that the Pujite's concern was not about religious matters but, rather, economic interests as he was asked to look for a market for minerals found in the area. The result of these trips for the Talaku was that they learned more about Bible stories and their illnesses were treated by medical doctors. The missionary team, on the part, obtained a better understanding of Talaku beliefs and practices. However, as there seemed to be no progress in converting the Talaku, the missionaries did not return to the Talaku center until 1969, a year after Phue Tee Maw was killed. When the missionary team visited Talaku center, they expected that without the presence of the hermit, the Talaku people would decide to convert. But the Talaku villagers were still conducting their rituals while hopefully waiting for the return of the Pujite. After 1970, however, the borderland area was disrupted by the forces of both Thai and Burmese states and also by non-state agencies.

Borderland Transformation and the Deterritorialization of the Talaku Community

Since the 1960s, the borderland has no longer been a mountainous backwater. Many powerful states, quasi-states, and non-state blocs moved into the area, fighting and competing for control of land and resources, and the governing of borderland populations. The Talaku communities were deterritorialized in three ways: their territory was taken to build and operate offices or military bases of these interceptors; Talaku villagers fled their old villages to set up new ones or join existing Talaku villages;[3] and Talaku villagers converted to other religions but continued to reside in the same place together with other Talaku. Deterritorialization took place first from the KNU and Karen National Liberation Army (KNLA), which moved into the area in the 1960s. Then, in the 1970s and early 1980s, parts of the borderland became the operational base of the Communist Party of Thailand (CPT). By the 1990s, the area was fully integrated into the Thai government system and its modern economy.

In 1962, the Burmese General Ne Win staged a coup d'état and inaugurated the policy of the "Burmese Way to Socialism." With the rise of the dictatorship, many ethnic groups started to build up their armies and move to the borderland to set up military bases and governmental strongholds. The KNU and KNLA controlled the borderland in the Karen State of Myanmar opposite Mae Hong Son, Tak, and Kanchana Buri Province of Thailand. Some KNU officials visited Phue Tee Maw and discussed economic and political matters. Phue Tee Maw had once led the Talaku and KNU soldiers fighting the Burmese army, which resulted in fatalities on both sides. This was said to agitate the KNU. Then the Pujite and several of his disciples were taken from their monastery by KNU soldiers to be executed in some remote unknown place. This event was widely known, as some Karen people had seen the Pujite and KNU soldiers walking along the border from the south to the KNU area in the north.

What were the reasons for this execution? Smith (1999, 455) writes that the Pujite was accused of leading KNU soldiers to die. Eubank (2015, 59), however gives a different reason, "He was taken into Burma and executed by the Karen National Union (KNU) Christian soldiers for the murders of the Pujite's wife's first husband and his adopted mother." There is no official statement explaining the reason for his execution by the KNU. For whatever reason, the event shows that in the late 1960s the KNU had assumed control over the borderland, including Talaku territory. As a result of Phue Tee Maw's sudden death in 1968, the Talaku community was in disarray. The missionary team hoped that without a head, the Talaku at Letongkhu would decide to convert to Christianity. But it did not turn out that way, although the team saw that the monastery was run down, only a few *ta waw bu* still lived there, and many villagers had moved elsewhere.

During the 1970s and 1980s, another powerful group that moved into the Talaku territory was the Communist Party of Thailand (CPT). Mong Kuo, a Talaku village, the birthplace of Phue Tee Maw, became a CPT center and military base. Talaku from other villages were sent to study Marxist ideology and acquire the necessary knowledge to become soldiers and nurses. Some Talaku had been with the CPT for many years until its operation stopped in 1982. Some returned to their villages after being with the CPT for a few years. They talked about the new habits adopted while being with the CPT, especially wearing pants instead of a sarong, maintaining short hair, and wearing a hat. Maw A Mee, the late headman of Letongkhu (d. 2008), joined the CPT as a soldier, then after marrying a woman who was trained as a nurse, went back to their village before moving to Letongkhu.

As a result of the expanding operations of the KNU and CPT, the Talaku villages were deterritorialized. In former Talaku villages like Mong Kuo, after the CPT left, the Thai authorities came and set up a permanent camp, a school, and a Buddhist temple. Most villagers changed their identities by becoming Buddhists. Some of Phue Tee Maw's family members maintained their Talaku identity and set up a new cluster, a satellite of Letongkhu. Another group identified themselves as "revolutionary Talaku" by continuing Talaku rituals but with communist rhetoric. The group leader had been a *ta waw bu* before he joined the CPT, so he constructed a new identity from both Talaku and communist ideas and practices. From the 1980s Letongkhu grew in size when other Karen from Myanmar moved in after their lives were disrupted by the fighting between the KNLA and the Burmese army. As Letongkhu is situated on the Thai side of the border and is difficult to access from both the Thai and Burmese states, it provides a good refuge area. Non-Talaku Karen also moved in Letongkhu and later converted to Talaku. A Talaku committee decided to rebuild Letongkhu by inviting a Pujite from a Talaku village in Myanmar to stay at the Letongkhu monastery.

The greatest challenge to the existence of the Talaku at Letongkhu came in the late 1980s when the Thai state extended its operation in the area after the dissolution of the CPT. The Border Patrol Police (BPP) was the first group to set up a station in Letongkhu although access to the village was only possible by an eight-hour walk or by helicopter. In 1989, a BPP high-ranking officer came to visit the BPP station in Letongkhu and found that only two people in Letongkhu, one of them Maw A Mee, could speak some Thai.[4] He then coordinated with the Non-Formal Education Center and the Hilltribe Development and Welfare Center of Tak Province to plan for the "development" of Letongkhu village. A BPP school was finally set up in the village in 1989 after a long process of negotiation. Initially, Talaku villagers rejected the plan to set up a school in the village, saying that it was contradictory to their tradition. After repeated discussions with the BPP, the villagers finally agreed, but with several conditions, such as not bringing pork, chicken, alcohol, or drugs into the village; not interfering with their cultural practices; and not raising pigs, ducks, or chickens. The first BPP teacher agreed to these conditions and gave a ceremonial vow at the hermit's office, but the Talaku people were still worried and hesitant. When an epidemic broke out a few months later, the villagers attributed their illness to the newly constructed school and asked for it to be removed. When a high-ranking officer came to negotiate, the villagers had to agree to let the school operate again (Boonruang Wantha 1991).

However, since the 1990s, things have changed. The new BPP teachers did not keep the promises made by their predecessors. They now eat pork and chicken, drink alcohol, and try to instill modern thinking and behavior in their students. Some villagers still complain about the school and regret the decision they made in the 1980s. In 2012, the school expanded with more students from Letongkhu as well as other villages from both sides of the Thailand-Myanmar border. It has managed to send students to further their studies in secondary schools and colleges in the district town and elsewhere. Students from Letongkhu find it hard to maintain their practices while living in boarding schools with non-Talaku students. For example, they cannot separately cook food without pork or chicken. Boys cannot wear their hair long and make topknots as other boys have short hair. After many years studying in the schools, they have had to give up being Talaku and adopt the practices of other Thai students.

In the meantime, Talaku villagers have become increasingly incorporated into modern and commercial practices. With village funds provided by the government in the late 1990s, some Talaku bought small tractors to replace the cattle formerly used to plough the land. These tractors are also used, at least in the dry season, for transporting commodities from the nearest town via a winding dirt road through Burmese territory. The demand for cash has increased as people must repay village funds they have borrowed to buy more conveniences, including motorcycles and electric appliances. In the early 2010s, the dirt road inside Thai territory from Peng Khleng, the border market town, to Letongkhu was finished but with a rough and muddy surface. Consequently, commuting by car can be undertaken only in the dry season or by motorbike with a skillful rider. The road has since been paved and improved with a hard surface every year until the late 2010s, and a four-wheel drive car can pass even in the rainy season. As the border trade is open, betel nuts, the popular cash crop, are extensively produced and brought out from the village, mainly to be exported to Myanmar. Consumer goods are regularly bought from Peng Khleng to be sold in the many grocery stores established in Letongkhu. Students from Letongkhu who study in many other towns can return home easily. Public officials and Buddhist and Christian missionaries frequently visit Letongkhu. Many television stations show documentary films about the exclusive and unique Letongkhu Karen village, thus attracting more tourists. Young boys and girls aspire to go to cities to work for cash.

Within the disruption caused by many new ideologies and practices being forced upon them by external powers, internal conflict among the Talaku people has increased regarding the best way forward for them. Before 2008, the conflict between Phue Tee Maw's daughter and Maw A Mee's faction was publicly known. Maw A Mee criticized the late Phue Tee Maw for his immorality despite being a Pujite, especially having a wife who bore him three children. Phue Tee Maw's daughter, who lives in Letongkhu, was a strong and outspoken woman who had many relatives living in the village. As a Pujite's daughter, she was highly respected and could guide the political direction in the village. Maw A Mee resigned from being a headman as he was pressured to do so by the Pujite's daughter. But the district office intervened by holding a village meeting in which most villagers voted to have him back. However, in 2008, while walking on a long mountain trail to attend the monthly meeting at the district office, Maw A Mee was shot dead by an unknown assassin. The identity of the murderer(s) and their motivation is still not known. In 2012, the Pujite's daughter and her son-in-law were also killed by unknown forces for unknown reasons.

Networks of Christian Missionaries and the Success in Converting Talaku

The success of Talaku conversion is partly attributed to the relentless effort of the missionaries. Notable among them is Allan Eubank, who joined every mission to Letongkhu since the first one in 1962. The account of his life and missions among the Talaku are recorded in his books (Eubank, 2007, 2015). Eubank has lived in Thailand for over fifty years and is well-known to high-ranking Thai officials. His biography explains his motivation for devoting himself to converting the Talaku. Born into a middle-class Christian family in Texas, USA, in 1929, Eubank writes that after graduating from university, he began to hear God calling him to be a missionary. Later he applied and was accepted by the Christian Church (Disciples of Christ) mission board, which had a plan to start a mission among the Talaku. To prepare for the mission, Eubank was given a report about the Karen, who since the early 1800s had responded en masse to the missionaries because of their legends of the "white brother" and the "golden book."[5] The report explained that the golden book of knowledge had been given to them by Ywa, the Karen creator, but was taken away by the white brother. Eubank learned that the Talaku were a strict religious sect of the Karen, who were also waiting for the return of the white brother and the golden book. After reading the report, Eubank again felt God's call to go to the Talaku. In 1961, he and his wife flew to Thailand to start their mission under the Church of Christ in Thailand.

Eubank and his team have regularly visited Letongkhu since the first mission. But after the trip in 1969 and following the death of Phue Tee Maw, the area was controlled by the Thai Communist Party and missionaries could no longer go there. Only in 1988, when the Thai government had retaken the area, did a missionary team dare to venture to the Talaku center where they met the new hermit. Again, the mission was not successful in converting the Talaku. Thus, the hard work of Eubank alone did not guarantee success of Talaku conversion. The momentum started with the development of the extensive network of local Karen missionaries across the Thailand-Myanmar border with support from the global network of Karen Christians.

How have the Karen missionaries in the borderland been able to gain more converts since the 1990s? By then the KNU and main military bases were seized by the Burmese army, leading to hundreds of thousands of Karen people fleeing across the border to reside in refugee camps and Karen villages on the Thai side of the border. The KNU's Kawthoolei Karen Baptist Churches (KKBC) moved two main Bible schools there.[6] The schools offer a Bachelor of Theological Studies (BTS), which comprises both English and Karen programs. Those graduating in the English program were mainly sent to work with Karen migrants who have constructed their churches after having resettled in third countries, such as the US, Canada, and Australia. Those who finished the Karen program and the BA were sent back to work for the churches and communities and conduct missions in Karen villages on the borderland (Horstmann 2011; Boonsong and Kwanchewan 2017). As the KKBC moved their operations closer to and across the border, their relationship with the Thai Karen Baptist Convention (TKBC) also became closer. In fact, the first Thai Karen was baptized by a Karen missionary from Burma, but their connection was interrupted because of the wars and the unsettled situation. Now that their working area is closer and is even overlapping, the KKBC and TKBC began to work in support of each other. With this link, some churches set up by KKBC missionaries on Thai soil were later included under the TKBC, which is also a part of the Church of Christ in Thailand (CCT), the registered Protestant Christian association.[7] Thus, these churches are recognized and supported in their operation by the CCT. Moreover, Bible schools run by the KKBC have connections with Christian universities in Thailand, the Philippines, India (especially Nagaland), and other countries. The former director who obtained his PhD in theology from the Philippines, had sent his best students for further training in the network universities abroad before they return to teach in Bible schools.

The Global Karen Baptist Fellowship (GKBF) is another network of Karen from Myanmar, Thailand, and Western and non-Western countries worldwide. It was set up in 2007 to support the work of Karen Baptists on the borderland. GKBF leaders consist of migrants to Western countries from half a century ago who are now citizens of those countries and have high socioeconomic status. They had followed the news of the adversity faced by their fellow Baptists, and thus organized the GKBF to support them. The GKBF organizes an annual meeting in Chiang Mai and usually travels to refugee camps and Karen villages on the borderland to give moral and financial support.

When Eubank and other missionaries went back to Letongkhu in 1988, nineteen years after the last trip, both the Christian landscape on the borderland and the village landscape had changed. A school had been set up and Thai government officers had intensified their work with villagers. The missionary team that visited Letongkhu comprised sixteen people, including many local Karen missionaries and a medical team from the Christian hospital in Sangklaburi. They traveled for a day in two four-wheeled vehicles and four-door pickups from Sangklaburi to the village nearest to Letongkhu and then walked for two days to reach the village. The duration of their journey was much shorter than their first trip, which took a month by elephant and on foot. The team met with the new Pujite, who still did not believe that the Bible was the Golden Book of Life in their myth, but many villagers, especially the younger generation, took a keen interest in the message, which gave the missionaries hope of their conversion. Maw A Mee, the then-young headman's words were quoted by Eubank (2015, 65): "We know we are in a hole and cannot get out by ourselves. The younger white brother is reaching down to help us. We cannot jump high enough to reach your hand; but we will before long."

In the years that followed, missionary trips to Letongkhu were more frequent, and included young Karen evangelists who had graduated from Bible schools. These young people related the Gospel via dance, drama, and song from the old Pwo Karen legends, such as the well-known legend of Naw Muh I, which illustrates how Christ died for them. This way of evangelization differs greatly from the first missions conducted by foreign missionaries who had to use translators when making speeches. It corresponds to Hayami's (2018, 279) finding on the "Karen culture of Evangelism," in which she argues that Karen evangelists have successfully converted the Karen and other hill people because they "had successfully spoken things that resonated in the recipients' lives and minds."

In 1990, the missionaries were able to negotiate with the Talaku elders and representatives of three hundred families for a missionary couple to stay and teach Talaku people how to read and to understand and obey God's word. Their response: "We can accept your three proposals, if you will accept ours, as follows: (1) that we retain our five rules of behavior; (2) that we retain our rules of eating and dress; and (3) that we retain our ceremonies of worship" (Eubank 2015, 71) They also demanded that the missionaries join the oath-taking ceremony by drinking together "the water of blessing and curse" to ensure that the missionaries were sincere and honest in their proposal. If those who drank the sacred water did not keep their promise, they would die or their descent would be cursed. The missionaries viewed this practice as something "evil" and were hesitant to accept the conditions. However, Karen evangelists and foreign missionaries who had worked with the Karen for many years convinced the team that this was Karen custom and it was no different from the Christian tradition in which people swore by the words, "I swear to tell the truth, the whole truth, and nothing but the truth, so help me God!" (Eubank 2015, 74). Therefore, the ceremony was organized and the Karen evangelist couple was allowed to live in the Talaku village.

From 1990 to 1993, the Karen evangelists lived in the guesthouse built by Talaku villagers. Within those three years, many Talaku, especially those living near the guesthouse, developed a close relationship with the Karen evangelists. They came to learn Bible passages and listen to preaching in the Karen language. Among those interested in the Bible was Du Pa (pseudonym), Maw A Mee's elder brother. He could read the Bible and always came to discussions with Karen evangelists from Myanmar and elsewhere who came to assist in teaching. Du Pa asked to be baptized many times, but Maw A Mee, his brother and the current headman, always said that the Talaku were not yet ready: if they got baptized, they would have to leave the village. During this time, the Eubank team gave scholarships to several young Talaku women to study to become nurse aides while living with Christians in Chiang Mai. In 1992, Maw A Mee and his friends came to Chiang Mai for medical treatment and stayed at Eubank's house. In 1993, the evangelical couple was asked by the BPP to leave the village after a couple of terrible events: forty-one deaths from measles, mostly children, in April 1992, and five BPP killed by a different Talaku sect in November 1992. Almost every year from 1994, Eubank and other Karen evangelists visited Letongkhu to teach, provide medical services, and celebrate Christmas. The Christian hostel in Peng Khleng, the border town, has increased in size with students from villages on both sides of the border coming to live there while studying in high school.

In early 2008, shortly after Maw A Mee was murdered, four people were baptized. They were all Maw A Mee's close relatives—his elder brother (Du Pa) and wife, and his sister and her husband, who had developed close relationships with the missionaries and wanted to convert earlier but were forbidden by Maw A Mee. According to Eubank (2015, 94), "By February 2014, we have baptized 79 Talaku.... They are rejoicing that Jesus has delivered them from the evil spirits...."

The Talaku who became Christians (from now on Talaku Christians) have gradually formed a new group and developed a new identity. In the early days, as was common with many other highland ethnic communities, once they were converted, they had to move away from the village because the territory was governed by traditional authorities who communicated with certain traditional deities. But in the twenty-first century, it is difficult to find new forest land to set up a new village with new infrastructure and other connecting technologies. At the beginning of conversion in 2008, the Christian group was also asked to move out. In a six-hour meeting, the evangelist who worked with the group argued to be able to continue to live in Letongkhu village, citing a chapter in the Thai constitution stating that a Thai citizen has the freedom to uphold any religion.

They have built their church in Du Pa's upland field; first, a small temporary one, then a larger permanent one. The evangelist who lives permanently in the village is a man of unknown ethnic origin who came from the Myanmar side of the border when he was young. He attended a high school at Peng Khleng and was supported by the Church there to continue his theological training. He then came back to work in Letongkhu. He married Du Pa's daughter and lived and farmed in the village while carrying on the mission.

The Talaku Christians no longer identify themselves as Talaku as they have already left the Talaku group. Some of them no longer follow practices required by the Talaku, such as the wearing of a topknot by the men and avoiding the consumption of pork and chicken meat, but others continue the practices as they feel it does not contradict being a Christian. In the late 2010s, a forestry officer came to the village and accused the Christians of building a church in the reservation forest without permission. In response, the church network on many levels helped to prepare data to show that the Talaku Christians had done nothing wrong, as they have the right to build the church in their own field which is customarily recognized.

Fig. 4. A temporary Christian Church in Letongkhu, 2011.

Conclusion

This chapter has described the process by which the Talaku group has been deterritorialized by many forces: the Karen National Union, the Communist Party of Thailand, the Thai government, and capitalist industries. Whenever these forces operated in Talaku territory, Talaku villagers have either fled the village, which was overtaken by other groups, and set up new villages or joined other Talaku villages. Talaku individuals can change their identities if they (usually men) marry women of other religions. In many former Talaku villages, especially inside the Karen State of Myanmar, Karen villagers identify themselves as Buddhists with Talaku ancestors. They continue to organize and regularly join in Talaku rituals.

The case study of Letongku Talaku village shows that while many other Talaku villages inside Myanmar and Thailand have stopped being Talaku, Letongkhu has long maintained being a Talaku village with clear boundaries and uniform religious and daily life practices among villagers. Although the villages became smaller as some people left during the disruptive period, Letongkhu has continued to be a Talaku village with a Pujite, a Talaku committee, and villagers who all identify as Talaku. The missionary team who first came to Letongkhu in 1962 and continued to come many times until 1969 has not been successful in converting Talaku. After 1990, the headman, his family, and his relatives developed close relationships with the missionary team, some of whom stayed on in the village for three years to teach and help villagers in medical treatments. Others have occasionally joined the events organized by the missionaries outside the village. But conversion took place only in 2008 after the headman was murdered and his close relatives asked to be baptized shortly after.

Letongkhu has long been identified as a unique Talaku village with the Pujite as the head surrounded by the *ta waw bu*, the Pujite's disciples who exclusively reside and work within their sacred territory. Talaku villagers are also widely recognized as observing high morals and complying strictly to Talaku regulations on the organization of sophisticated and colorful ceremonies. But, in reality, after the Thai state established the school in the village and villagers had been integrated into the modern capitalist world, practicing Talaku identity ran into problems. Young people who had left the village for study and work could not follow Talaku regulations, such as those concerning types of food, dressing, etc. When staying outside, they are considered non-Talaku. They can become Talaku again if they return to the village and organize special rituals. People still identify themselves as Talaku although the regulation and practices are adjusted. But once they have different experiences and lose their faith in the Talaku, they convert to other religions and change their ethnoreligious identity.

This chapter has also endeavored to explain why it took forty-six years from the first attempt by missionaries to convert the Talaku in 1962, up to when the first group of Talaku in Letongkhu were baptized in 2008. Conversion pertains to the change of identity from Talaku to Christianity. The decision to leave their old identity and adopt a new one took an unusually long time. People went through a process in which they gradually lost faith in old beliefs or were marginalized from old associations. At the same time, they developed a closer relationship with a new association from which they received more affection and higher hope. In the Letongkhu case, the intensive work by the Karen missionaries among the Talaku who concentrated more on the borderland after the 1990s, created new networks and close association between the missionaries and some of the Talaku, while their association with the old group became less.

To sum up, ethnoreligious identities are not static but can change following a break-up into many groups. In the deterritorialized world, the breaking up of old groups and the creation of new ones and new networks occurs as people can connect to other networks more easily via modern infrastructure including digital technology. Although some groups seem to maintain their identity for a long time through their unique practices, at present individuals in the group often attach themselves to new networks and groups as they reconstruct their imaginations and redesign their religious and mundane practices.

Endnotes: Christian Missions and the Reconstruction of Identities

1. Others are, for example, Leke (Stern 1968; Kwanchewan 2017) and Duway (Hayami 2011), which are not classified as Buddhist or Christian organizations although their beliefs have some elements derived from Buddhism and Christianity.

2. His name is Saw Tha Din. He was once the president of the Karen National Association in Insein, Burma (Hovemyr 1997, 17–18). He was also a member of the four-man Karen Goodwill Mission to the United Kingdom in August 1946 to express to the British government their community's opposition to being included in an independent state dominated by Burmans and their wish was for a Karen autonomous state. He was asked by the American Presbyterian missionary in Bangkok to head the first expedition to the Talaku.

3. Eubank (2015) refers to one village which moved out as the Thai state came to build a school where teachers drank, played games, and did not observe the precepts.

4. They were the first and second official headmen to join the CPT and had thus gained some Thai language ability.

5. The myth of *li thu li che*, literally "golden book silver book," is widely told among Sgaw and Pwo Karen in both Thailand and Myanmar. The myth explains that the Karen, the oldest child and the most loved by the Ywa, the God creater, lost their book of knowledge which was given by the Ywa. The youngest white brother somehow managed to get the book and that is why he gained a lot of knowledge and became rich and powerful, while the Karen remained poor and illiterate.

6. Previously, the Baptist churches of the Karen in Burma belonged to the Karen Baptist Convention. But as they were operating in the borderland under the KNU administered area, in 1983 the KNU Baptist leaders set up the KKBC to independently handle the religious organizations themselves.

7. The Church of Christ in Siam (CCT) was founded in 1934 with the aim of forming a single ecumenical denomination to include all Protestant churches in Thailand, among them Presbyterian churches, the Disciples of Christ, and the American Baptists. With the change of the country's name from Siam to Thailand in 1939, its name was changed to the Church of Christ in Thailand. In 2018, the CCT was active in twenty regions and had around 185,000 members (see USA Board of Foreign Missions 1915 and McGilvary 1912). For those in Burma, see for instance, the missions among the Karen in Mason (1843).

References

Boonruang Wantha. 1991. *Prawat khwam pen ma khong ban Letongkhu lae latthi ruesi* [History of Letongkhu village and hermit cult]. Fieldnote document of the 347th camp of the Border Patrol Police Force, Umphang District, Tak.

Boonsong Thansrithong and Kwanchewan Buadaeng. 2017. "Refugee Camps on the Thailand-Myanmar Border: Potential Places for Expanding Connections among Karen Baptists." *ASR: CMU Journal of Social Sciences and Humanities* 4(2): 89–109.

Department of Population, Ministry of Labour, Immigration and Population. 2015. *The 2014 Myanmar Population and Housing Census. Thematic Report on Population Dynamics*. Census Report, Volume 2.

Enriquez, C. M. 1933 [1883]. *Races of Burma*. 2nd edn. Delhi: Manager of Publications.

Eubank, Allan, L. 2007. *God! If You are Really God ... Ask and Receive*. 5th edn. Chiang Mai: TCF Press.

—————. 2015. *Where God Leads ... Never Give up*. Chiang Mai: Pan Rak Foundation.

Hayami, Yoko. 1992. "Ritual and Religious Transformation among Sgaw Karen of Northern Thailand: Implications on Gender and Ethnic Identity." PhD diss., Brown University.

—————. 1996. "Karen Tradition according to Christ or Buddha: The Implications of Multiple Reinterpretations for a Minority Ethnic Group in Thailand." *Journal of Southeast Asian Studies* 27(2): 320–33.

—————. 2011. "Pagodas and Prophets: Contesting Sacred Space and Power among Buddhist Karen in Karen State." *Journal of Asian Studies* 70(4): 1083–1105.

—————. 2018. "Karen Culture of Evangelism and Early Baptist Mission in Nineteenth Century Burma." *Social Sciences and Missions* 31: 251–83.

Horstmann, Alexander. 2011. "Sacred Networks and Struggles among the Karen Baptist across the Thailand-Burma border." *Moussons* 17(1): 85–104.

Hovemyr, Maria. 1997. *A Bruised Reed Shall He Not Break: A History of the 16th District of the Church of Christ in Thailand*. Chiang Mai: Office of History, Church of Christ in Thailand.

Ikeda, Kazuto. 2012. "Two Versions of Buddhist Karen History of the Late British Colonial Period in Burma: Kayin Chronicle (1929) and Kuyin Great Chronicle (1931)" *Southeast Asian Studies* 1(3): 431–60.

Jorgensen, Anders Baltzer. 1997. "Forward." In *The Karen People of Burma: A Study in Anthropology and Ethnology* by Harry Ignatius Marshall. Bangkok: White Lotus Press.

KNU (Karen National Union). 1986. *KNU Bulletin* no. 2 (November).

Kwanchewan Buadaeng. 2003. *Buddhism, Christianity, and the Ancestors: Religion and Pragmatism in a Skaw Karen Community in North Thailand*. Chiang Mai: Sprint.

————. 2017. "The Karen Leke Religious Movement in the Thailand-Myanmar Borderland: Deterritorialization and Diversification."In *Ethnic and Religious Identities and Integration in Southeast Asia*, eds. Ooi Keat Gin and Volker Grabowsky, 241–79. Chiang Mai: Silkworm Books.

Mason, Francis. 1843. *The Karen Apostle: or Memoir of Ko Thabyu*. Boston: Gould, Kendall and Lincoln.

McGilvary, Daniel. 1912. *A Half Century among the Siamese and in Lao*. New York: Revell.

Smeaton, Donald Mackenzie. 1887. *The Loyal Karens of Burma*. London: Kegan Paul, Trench and Co.

Smith, Martin. 1999. *Burma: Insurgency and the Politics of Ethnicity*. 2nd edn. Bangkok: White Lotus.

Stern, Theodore. 1968. "Ariya and the Golden Book: Millenarian Buddhist Sect among the Karen." *Journal of Asian Studies* 27: 297–328.

The 34th Border Patrol Police Force. 1998. "*I-si kap ban letongkhu*" [Hermit and Letongkhu Village]. BPP case study report.

USA Board of Foreign Missions. 1915. *Historical Sketch of the Missions*. Philadelphia: The Woman's Foreign Missionary Society of the Presbyterian Church.

Womack, William Burgess. 2005. "Literate Networks and the Production of Sgaw and Pwo Karen Writing in Burma, c. 1830–1930." Unpublished PhD diss., School of Oriental and African Studies, University of London.

Buddhist Pilgrimages and Architectural Restoration in the Upper Mekong Basin: Revival of Tai (Transnational) Identities

SIRUI DAO AND VOLKER GRABOWSKY[*]

As a transnational ethnic group, the Tai people[1] have attracted much academic attention. The transborder pilgrimage of Theravada Buddhists in northern Thailand, Sipsòng Panna (Xishuangbanna),[2] and Müang Sing (Muang Sing), which James Taylor (2020) calls "religious nomadism," are examples of the transnational nature of these groups who call themselves Tai.[3] Paul Cohen (2000a, 2000b) discusses the transborder pilgrimages of Khruba Bun Chum in the Upper Mekong region and of the Tai Lü from Sipsòng Panna to Müang Sing during the That Chiang Tüng stupa festival. Wasan Panyagaew (2010, 2018) studies how Tai Lü monks engaged in transborder Buddhist studies, preferably at Tai Lü monasteries (*wat*), in Myanmar and Thailand and the transborder pilgrimages of senior monks, such as Khruba Khüan Kham and Khruba Saeng La. The transborder religious connections of this region can be traced back to the premodern era. According to local chronicles, Theravada Buddhism in Chiang Tung (Kengtung) and Sipsòng Panna was introduced from Chiang Mai (Sāimöng 2002, 122). In a recent study on the relationship between Thai Buddhist pilgrimage and tourism in Myanmar, Neeranooch Malangoo aptly remarks that "the Buddhists' goal of pilgrimage is not a valued ideal in itself, but rather is a means to gain merit" (2020, 20).

The mythical visits of Lord Buddha are recorded in *Tamnan Phra Chao Liap Lok* (The Chronicle about the Buddha's Journeys around the World), a Buddhist chronicle widely spread in Northern Thailand, Chiang Tung and Sipsòng Panna. This chronicle reports Buddha's putative journeys from India to distant places in Southeast Asia where someday his doctrine would find adherents and

---

[*] "Research for this chapter was funded by the EU-supported Horizon 2020 CRISEA project; this is gratefully acknowledged. We are particularly indebted to Roger Casas for his insightful comments and many suggestions for improvements."

would prosper. More local in orientation than many other chronicles, it reflects the worldview of old Lan Na and provides information about the political geography of ancient times, covering the Buddhist world in the Upper Mekong region (Thianchai 2009, 67–70). Moreover, the chronicle provides invaluable information about stupas, reliquaries, and sacred sites as well as legends surrounding the founding of towns and villages all over the Upper Mekong basin, connecting them in a coherent narrative with Lord Buddha as its core. Even after the formation of modern nation-states and their borders, this ancient interconnectedness remains. In 1946, the borders were still porous as we have evidence that four monks from the Burmese and Lao sides of the border came to Müang Phong (Mengpeng), Müang Mang (Mengman), and Müang Yuan (Mengrun) in Sipsòng Panna. At that time, people in Müang Mang and Müang Yuan still crossed the border to make a pilgrimage to Müang Sing (according to an investigation in 1958 launched by the National People's Congress Ethnic Affairs Committee in 1956, "Minzu Wenti Wu Zhong Congshu" Yunnan Sheng Bianji Weiyuan Hui 1983, 94). Transborder ethnoreligious connections also exist among non-Buddhist Tai in the region. For instance, a group of Tai Yai (Shan) Baptist Christians from Chiang Tung and Thai Christians from Thailand (Chiang Mai, Chiang Rai, and Bangkok) were invited to attend the celebration ceremony of the newly completed vihāra in Chiang Rung (Jinghong), Sipsòng Panna, in 2002 (interview with Sadaw, September 12, 2019), even though these Christians nowadays belong to different churches and denominations.

As a contribution to this volume, this chapter aims at studying transborder pilgrimage as a cultural practice to preserve ethnoreligious identity. The focus is on the sizeable Tai Lü communities inhabited by the descendants of refugees and war-captive descendant communities living along the Myanmar-Thai border (see Grabowsky 1999), a group hardly studied by scholars in the field. For the refugee communities living in eastern Myanmar and northern Thailand, the reconstruction of a holy stupa in the Tai Lü homeland of Sipsòng Panna is considered a meritorious deed which not only aims at karmic benefits for the individual donor but also at overcoming traumatic experiences caused by past violence and at rebuilding the donor's emotional connection with his or her homeland. In particular, the descendants of war captives from northern Thailand feel a kind of cultural nostalgia when looking at the contributions to architectural preservation in Chiang Tung and Sipsòng Panna. Apart from interviews with celebrities like well-known monks and artists, our fieldwork also took into consideration the experience of the common people.

This chapter is thus deeply embedded in the overall agenda of this volume, which is concerned with historical and contemporary manifestations of

Map 1. The Upper Mekong basin, designed by Sirui Dao.

Southeast Asian regional identity. Identity, from a transnational perspective, results inevitably from the manifold experiences of people living in the borderlands. The feeling of identity, which is often not perceived in daily routine, is usually enhanced or amplified in the transborder experience. It is through the transnational ethnoreligious connection that the cross-border pilgrimage is fulfilled.

During the early years of communist rule in Vietnam, China, and Laos, Buddhism declined in varying degrees. There was a dramatic reduction in the number of monasteries and of monks and novices in Sipsòng Panna from the 1950s to the 1970s (McCarthy 2009, 76). The 1980s witnessed the revival of Buddhism in Laos and Sipsòng Panna (Stuart-Fox 1999, 169; Kang 2009). The

Buddhist revival in Sipsòng Panna owed a lot to the transborder ethnoreligious connection as well as the remarkable revival of the traditional manuscript culture (Grabowsky 2019). Many monks who later became the core of the Sipsòng Panna Sangha had studied in the Shan State and northern Thailand in the 1990s (Wasan 2010; Kang 2009, 30). Since the 1980s, due to a lack of monks, Tai Lü monks from Myanmar and Laos have been residing in monasteries in Sipsòng Panna (Peters 1990, 349). The assistance from Myanmar and Thailand was crucial to revive Buddhism and restore Buddhist places (Peters 1990, 349; Hasegawa 2000, 128).

Since 1953, the Tai minority of Theravada Buddhists has been incorporated in the nation-state of the People's Republic of China and communication with other Buddhist sects within Chinese territory has been increasingly encouraged. At the same time, while contacts with the Southeast Asian Theravada Buddhist world are not prohibited, they are regulated by the Chinese government and local Buddhist Associations. In 2020, Somdet Luang Chòm Müang, the abbot of Wat Pa Che in Chiang Rung, in his capacity as a standing committee member of the Chinese People's Political Consultative Conference and the vice-president of the Yunnan Provincial Buddhist Association, proposed to the Chinese People's Political Consultative Conference to encourage communication between "Chinese Theravada Buddhism" and Theravada Buddhism in South Asia and Southeast Asia and to enhance the friendship with these countries through Theravada monks (Xishuangbanna Zongfosi 2020).

Transnational pilgrimages and merit-making are parts of the religious practice of Tai people, especially those who live in the borderland. The connections between the borderlands in this region are enhanced by the presence of descendants of war captives and refugees from two different periods. During the late eighteenth to the early nineteenth centuries, a large number of Tai in Chiang Tung, Sipsòng Panna, Müang Yòng (Mongyawng), Müang Sing, and other places were forcibly resettled in Chiang Mai, Lamphun, Nan, and other parts of northern Thailand. Besides Tai Khün from Chiang Tung, Tai Lü from Müang Yòng, Sipsòng Panna, and Müang Sing were the majority of those who were resettled (Grabowsky 1999). In the twentieth century, the political turmoil in Sipsòng Panna and Chiang Tung, the withdrawal of the Kuomintang army into the Shan State, and the Lao civil war (1959–75) turned tens of thousands of people into refugees, fusing into a global diaspora of Tai people. During the rule of the Kuomintang government, some of the Lü people from Sipsòng Panna had already fled to Burma and Indochina for being intolerant of government policies (Yanyong and Ratanaphon 2001, 289). In the mid-twentieth century, Sipsòng Panna lost a large part of its population because of economic and political disturbance. In the early 1950s, after the communist victory of the Chinese civil war, many pro-Kuomintang people, mostly Tai, Lahu, and Yunnanese along the frontier following the Kuomintang army, fled into Burma. By 1953, there were around 500 men and 120 women and children, ethnically Tai and Yunnanese from Sipsòng Panna, in Müang Ma and Müang Yòng. The Tai were mostly from noble families, including Chao Mòm La, the ruler of Müang Hon, who later settled in Mae Sai, Thailand (Central Intelligence Agency, December 1, 1953). In 1958, the policies of China's Great Leap Forward saw monks being forced to disrobe and sent out to work. As a result, Sipsòng Panna lost more than 20,000 people who fled across the border, among whom 4,847 people came from Chiang Rung County (of these 3,541 were hill people from the borderlands, i.e., Akha, Lahu, etc.) (Xishuangbanna Zizhizhou Minzu Zongjiao Shiwu Ju 2006, 21–22). In 1960, more than 3,900 people left Müang Luang district and fled to Myanmar (ibid., 23). In 1969, more than 1,860 from Müang La county fled into Laos, and more than 2,000 in Sipsòng Panna fled China to Myanmar (ibid., 26). Although some of the refugees returned to Sipsòng Panna at the end of the 1980s, many of them chose to remain in Burma, Thailand, and Laos.

Apart from periodic pilgrimages during a stupa festival and the birthday of a senior monk, among other special events, casual pilgrimage is also common. For the Tai people, journeys to the Theravada Buddhist area are usually followed by visits to the local temples and the making of donations. For a long time, when Myanmar had not yet opened Chiang Tung and Müang Yòng for tourists, visitors from Thailand intending to proceed to these places had to accompany monks to attend religious activities. In 1986, Khruba Khüan Kham from Lamphun led a group of monks and lay people from Lamphun, Chiang Mai, Chiang Rai, and other provinces—most of them Tai Lü descendants from Müang Yòng, including Khruba Khüan Kham himself—to donate a Tham script version of the Tipiṭaka to Müang Yòng, which was the first time Thai citizens had ventured into Müang Yòng. The visits to Sipsòng Panna by Tai Lü refugees in the United States usually involve the attending of merit-making Buddhist activities.

Donations for the construction of Buddhist sites are, for the most part, a collective enterprise, conducted by family and village, strengthening the identity of a community. For the diaspora, cross-border donation to sacred Buddhist places in the homeland is an expression of one's emotional attachment and social affiliation to the place of origin. In Müang Sing, almost every village received donations from diasporic villagers (Tai Lü, Tai Nüa) living in the United States (fieldwork, September 15–17, 2018). For Tai migrants, regardless whether they are marriage migrants from the Shan State to Singapore, female marriage migrants retreating to Taiwan with Kuomingtang soldier husbands, or refugees from Sipsòng Panna and Laos driven by the political turmoil in mainland China and the Lao civil war to the United States, participating in Buddhist activities, abroad or at home, like donating to the construction or preservation of a Buddhist site are practices of social networking and community building (Kang 2009; Wu 2015, 117, 132–33).

Transborder support is still found, for example, in the case of Thailand's contributions to the preservation of monasteries in Chiang Tung and Sipsòng Panna, like Wat Yang Khuang of Chiang Tung in the Shan State, Myanmar, and of contributions by descendants of former war captives to the construction of Thai-style architecture at the stupa of Phra That Chòm Yòng in Müang Yòng, and of the donations by more recent refugees to the monasteries of their hometowns in Sipsòng Panna and Müang Sing.

A division of roles exists between males and females in Theravada Buddhist societies. In the Upper Mekong region, traditionally only men are allowed to be ordained as monks. Gender also plays a role in transborder pilgrimage, which can be divided into three categories: pilgrimage of monks, pilgrimage of disrobed monks (*khanan*) and novices, and pilgrimage of other lay people. The former two are only male and their pilgrimages are often related to the Sangha network. In the case of the birthday ceremony of Khruba Saeng La to be discussed below, some *khanan* pilgrims from Sipsòng Panna traveled to Tha Khilek (Tachileik) to attend the ceremony because their study in Thailand in the 1990s had been assisted by Wat Sai Müang (interview, Monk D, August 22–23, 2020). However, in diasporic communities in Taiwan and Singapore, Tai females form the majority, partly because they are part of marriage migration. In Singapore, the Tai female immigrants from Chiang Tung have founded an association and often attend Buddhist ceremonies making donations in the name of the association. However, donations, including those from the diaspora community, are often made by individual households.

The mobility of Buddhist pilgrims often causes tension with the nation-state. This is because of regulatory difficulty, border security, or national cohesion, especially when these activities are not controlled by the government or conflict with governmental policy. Because of the shortage of monks in Sipsòng Panna, the long-standing residency of foreign monks from the Myanmar and Laos side of the border was tolerated and regulated by the Chinese government. However, in 1987, all foreign monks in Sipsòng Panna were expelled from Chinese territory (Kang 2009, 24). However, foreign Tai monks remained in Sipsòng Panna. The policy to register and expel them has tightened in recent years (Casas 2022). Transnational charismatic monks also cause security concerns for government authorities. In 2004, Khruba Bun Chum was forced to leave Myanmar (Amporn 2016, 378). In Laos, the presence of Khruba Bun Chum has also worried some Lao officials. The charismatic monk tradition has also caused friction with Chinese authorities. Chao Bun Saeng Rüang, a disciple of Khruba Bun Chum, is a Tai from Müang La and follows Khruba Bun Chum's practice of a wandering preacher and of long-term isolated meditation in caves. However, he is not recognized by the authorities and the official Buddhist Associations. His sermons in Sipsòng Panna usually attract many pilgrims but worry the authorities.

The Diaspora Community and the Feeling of Belonging

The feeling of belonging for the diaspora community is the awareness of belonging to a displaced ethnic group, connected by religious and spatial dimensions. As mentioned in the previous section, the bustling border town of Tha Khilek in Myanmar has a large diaspora Tai community, especially refugees from Sipsòng Panna (Chaiwan 2012). Many monks exercising transnational influence are based in this area, such as Khruba Bun Chum. This Tai Lü refugee community was formed through ethnic and ancestral home connections and later enhanced by religious practice. Previously, the Tai Lü community conducted Buddhist activities at a Tai Yai (Shan) monastery. Later, partly because of the growth of the Tai Lü population and partly because of some differences in religious customs between the Tai Lü and Tai Yai, a new monastery, Wat Sai Müang, was constructed on the edge of Tha Khilek.[4] Wat Sai Müang is now an important monastery of the town and has significant influence among the Tai Lü refugee villages in Tha Khilek and Mae Sai. Normally, a Tai monastery is named after the village where it is located. However, Ban S, where Wat Sai Müang is situated, is now usually referred to as Ban Sai Müang because of the significance of the monastery. It was also a hub during the Buddhist revival of Sipsòng Panna in the 1980s (Wasan 2010) and contributed to the strengthening of the Tai Lü transnational Sangha connection. Khruba Saeng La was born in 1928 in Müang Hon (Menghun), Sipsòng Panna. He fled from Sipsòng Panna into Myanmar in 1958 when the Great Leap Forward occurred (ibid.). Now he is the abbot of Wat Sai

Müang and has become a spiritual-religious leader in the Tai Lü diaspora communities in Tha Khilek and Mae Sai.

The birthday of a *khruba* (senior monk) is a motive for transborder pilgrimage. On December 21–29, 2018, a grand celebration for Khruba Saeng La's 90th birthday was held at Wat Sai Müang in Tha Khilek, Myanmar. Believers attending the ceremony were a medley of Burmese officers, Tai lay people, and Tai monks from the Upper Mekong region. They included Khruba Bun Chum, Luang Pu Thòng from Chiang Mai, Somdej Atya Tham from Chiang Tung, Khruba Kham Pheng from Denver, lay people from Sipsòng Panna, Luang Namtha, and Bokeo provinces in Laos and Chiang Khòng and Mae Sai in Thailand, most of whom are Tai Lü people, Tai residents from Taiwan, Tai Lü refugees from the United States, Thai and Chinese Thai from Mae Sai, and Thai citizens from Bangkok and other provinces outside Lan Na. The Buddhist Association of Sipsòng Panna and major monasteries of Sipsòng Panna are invited every year to attend the celebration. Monk D, a young male from Müang Hon in Sipsòng Panna, went to Tha Khilek with representatives of the Sangha and the lay community of Sipsòng Panna. The team consisted of more than twenty monks and more than seventy lay people from Chiang Rung, Müang Luang (Menglong), Müang Hai (Menghai), Müang Hon, Müang Chae (Mengzhe), Chiang Lò (Daluo), and Müang Nun (Menglun) (interview, Monk D, February 1, 2019).

The travel of monks via Mongla into Myanmar is comparatively easy,[5] but this time the monks traveled in the company of lay people, which made their crossing more difficult. Thus, the group chose the route through Laos and Thailand to Myanmar that starts at Bò Han (Mohan) and Bò Ten, passes Huai Sai (Houayxay) and Chiang Khòng until reaching Mae Sai, then entering Tha Khilek in Myanmar. Monk D was deeply touched by the ceremony, which made him aware of the belief and cultural cohesion of Tai people in the Upper Mekong region, regardless of their citizenship. Some male believers of Sipsòng Panna attending the ceremony were former monks who had pursued their studies in Thailand during the 1990s with assistance from Wat Sai Müang. Donor K, a middle-aged female, is a Tai Lü from Ban S, Tha Khilek, who now lives in Mae Sai. She often attends the ceremonies held at Wat Sai Müang and goes to the birthday celebration of Khruba Saeng La every year. In 2018, she went to attend the celebration as usual. She said she participated in the celebration because it was considered an auspicious ceremony of her village, and Khruba Saeng La was a monk whom she had respected since she was a child. Moreover, as a villager from Ban S she had the obligation of a host to assist the activities and welcome guests from everywhere. She felt proud to be able to attend the ceremony as a devout Buddhist and was pleased that her community had a good Buddhist leader who followed "good practice," allowing them to encounter only good things. She said that she learned the Thai language at Wat Sai Müang, but Khruba Saeng La requested them to study the Tham script first, as that script was an inseparable part of their culture (interview, Donor K, February 15, 2020). She also expressed her pride in her Tai Lü identity, describing the Tai Lü as a diligent ethnic group (interview, Donor K, January 12, 2020).

The mobility of monks also assists the diaspora community to maintain and develop ethnic consciousness and belonging. In Taiwan, there is a predominantly female community of migrants from the Shan State who have married into Taiwanese society. Buddhism is an important component in the daily life of the Tai diaspora community in the island. The first generation of migrant females from the 1950s, having lived for years in communities without any Buddhist monasteries, still maintain their Buddhist beliefs and some of them have donated money for the construction of monasteries in their hometowns and brought videos of their home villages' Buddhist ceremonies, Buddha images, and other Buddhist items back to Taiwan (Wu 2015, 117, 132–33). Depending on personal preference or resident location, apart from the Burmese monasteries, the Shan State immigrants also join activities with the Thai community, like the Songkran Festival at Songkran New Year, the End of Buddhist Lent (*òk phansa*), and the Kathina Offering (*thòt kathin*), and go to Thai monasteries like the Buddhabaramee Thai Buddhist Temple in Tainan. The Shan State migrants have a Buddhist association, named the Buddhist Light Association Tai Wan. The sign for the association is written in Shan, Tai Khün/ Tai Lü, Burmese, Thai, and English.

Like the Tai people and other ethnic groups in the Upper Mekong region, Khruba Saeng La and Khruba Bun Chum are also respected by the Tai diaspora community in Taiwan. Khruba Saeng La's and Khruba Bun Chum's travels to Taiwan provided opportunities to assemble Shan State migrants distributed throughout Taiwan. In March 2018, Khruba Saeng La and Khruba Kham Pheng of Tha Khilek/Denver visited Kaohsiung. The Shan State migrants went to the Grand Hotel Kaohsiung to donate food to the two Khruba and accompanied them to the Fo Guang Shan Buddha Museum in Kaohsiung. Some of the migrants had never met each other before. Khruba Saeng La was invited to pray at the homes and restaurants of Shan State migrants in Taoyuan, New Taipei City, and other places.

After having traveled to preach in Bhutan and Malaysia, on March 27, 2019, Khruba Bun Chum arrived in Taiwan. Wearing traditional ethnic clothes, migrants from Thailand and the Shan State residing in different cities in Taiwan went to the Kaohsiung International Airport to welcome him. Migrant S was one of the Tai who came to give a warm welcome to Khruba Bun Chum at the airport. She is a Tai Lü from Sipsòng Panna married to a Taiwanese. She said that she was glad to welcome Khruba Bun Chum and pay respect to him because he is a monk held in great esteem by Tai people. She argued that the reason for wearing her Tai ethnic garb was to express their Tai identity through her clothing when attending such activities (interview, Migrant S, January 6, 2020).

Chiang Ngoen Stupa

Theravada Buddhism in Sipsòng Panna was almost destroyed during the political disturbances of the 1950s to 1970s. Buddhist temples were demolished or converted into warehouses or barns for keeping livestock. The reconstruction of temples and stupas began in the early 1980s when religious practice was permitted by the Chinese government (Casas 2010, 4). The Buddhist revival in Sipsòng Panna involved workers from different communities, some of whom were monks and lay people from beyond the borders of China. The latest reconstruction of the stupa Phra That Kesa Luang Chiang Ngoen (referred to as Chiang Ngoen Stupa in this chapter) in Müang Hon reflects the transborder Buddhist practice in Sipsòng Panna. The Chiang Ngoen Stupa is located on a hillock, Khòng Chiang Ngoen, in Müang Hon town. It is the most important stupa in Müang Hon and is considered a sacred site by the Tai Lü of Müang Hon.

Oral and written legends closely relate the stupa to the Buddha, thus consecrating it as a sacred place. According to an inscription on the site, "History of the Phra That Kesa Luang Chiang Ngoen," it is believed that the Buddha had been to Müang Hon, which was known as Müang Chai at that time. The Buddha passed through Müang Chai and then changed the direction of his travels; later this place was named Müang Hon (*hon*: direction). Phraya Chaiya Prasat of Müang Hon offered his son, Chitta Kuman, to the Buddha. When Chitta Kuman turned ten years old, he was ordained as a novice and named Chitta Samanen. By the time Chitta turned seventeen, his father had grown old and finally fell ill. The Buddha commanded Chitta to visit his father. When he greeted (*waisa*) the Buddha before leaving, he was given three strands of hair. However, upon arriving home, he found that his father had already died. After the funeral, Chitta constructed a monument (*chetiya*) with his father's reliquary enshrined. Then he set off to Kuchinarai (Kushinagar) and found that the Buddha had reached Nirvana. He bid farewell to Lord Buddha, went back to Müang Hon, and enshrined two strands of the Buddha's hair in the monument and built a large stupa, naming it the Chiang Ngoen Stupa. When he built the stupa in the Buddhist era (BE) 4, he was a 21-year-old *bhikkhu* (monk or priest). In BE 39, a 42-year-old revered monk, Chitta Phra Khuru Khru Müang (probably Chitta Samanen/Chitta Bhikkhu), put the third strand of hair into the stupa. He passed away in BE 140.

A reliable historical account of the stupa starts from the seventeenth century. In 1677, a local ruler, Phraya Wanna, led the people of Müang Hon to renovate the stupa and build a *vihāra* (prayer hall or ordination hall for novices) nearby. In 1884, a revered high-ranking monk, Atya Thamma Phra Chao Khru, hosted the reconstruction of the 20-*wa* or 40-meter-tall stupa, building also a small stupa and four gates. In 1958, when an earthquake damaged the stupa, a revered high-ranking monk, Phra Chao Khru Maha Phing, together with Thu Luang Saengla (who might nowadays be Khruba Saengla), and Upatchai Nam Kat, hosted the reconstruction and attached the top part. In 1970, during the Cultural Revolution, the stupa was destroyed by fire. From 1983 to 1985 (the 2004 stone inscription records it as 1980), Bhikkhu Kham and Phò Choi Phi hosted the reconstruction of the stupa. The extant stupa was the one constructed between 2000 and 2004.

The latest reconstruction of the Chiang Ngoen Stupa, initiated in 2000, was led by Khruba Saeng La, together with Khruba Luang Chòm (now Somdet Luang Chòm), Khruba Sin Man (Khruba Undi), Bhikkhu Luang Sam of Müang Hon, and Bhikkhu Inkaew. Khruba Luang Chòm is the abbot of the central temple, Wat Pa Che, in Chiang Rung, while Bhikkhu Luang Sam and Bhikkhu Inkaew are native monks. As previously mentioned, Khruba Saeng La is from Müang Hon; he fled from Sipsòng Panna to Burma in 1958 during the Great Leap Forward and later constructed the monastery Wat Sai Müang in Tha Khilek. Khruba Saeng La's involvement in the reconstruction of the Chiang Ngoen Stupa is partly because Müang Hon is his native land and partly because he has a personal connection to the stupa which he helped reconstruct in 1958.

Khruba Undi is the abbot of Wat Tao Kham in Mongla, Myanmar. He followed the tradition of Khruba Siwichai, a charismatic monk from Lamphun in northern Thailand who challenged Thai authorities in the 1920s and 1930s and has rebuilt and reconstructed temples and stupas in many areas of northern

Thailand (Bowie 2017). Starting in the 1980s, he has participated in more construction and renovation projects in Sipsòng Panna than any other monk. Villager A of Müang Hon compared his deeds with the travels of the Buddha (*phra chao liap lok*), touring and reconstructing dilapidated Buddhist places (interview, Villager A, September 22, 2019). Elders of Müang Hon who were interviewed confirmed that both Khruba Undi and Khruba Saeng La are Tai from Müang Hon. Villager D said that because of a shortage of local craftsmen, Khruba Saeng La came to help Müang Hon. He was from Müang Hon and they did not abandon each other (interview, Villager D, September 22, 2019). The elders vividly remember the name of the villages their parents came from, while for younger generations only Khruba Saeng La is considered a Tai from Müang Hon.

Khruba Saeng La and Khruba Undi helped arrange parts of the donations, mostly from Myanmar. Being one of the most influential monks in the Upper Mekong basin, Khruba Saeng La managed to obtain a large number of donations from cities in Myanmar and Thailand, such as Chiang Tung, Tha Khilek, and Mae Sai. The rebuilt stupa was adapted from the 1985 one, similar in overall shape but with differences in the details of the decoration. The body of the 1985 stupa was white, accented with colored painting. The top parts of the main stupa and the affiliated stupas were gilded. The 2004 stupa is completely painted, as Thai gold paint began to be imported into Sipsòng Panna and was popular at that time.[6]

The major donors supporting the reconstruction were mostly Tai Lü refugees in Tha Khilek and Mae Sai. Khruba Saeng La donated 100,000 CNY,[7] CM's household (Ban S, Tha Khilek) 100,000 CNY, PH's household (Tha Khilek) 30,000 CNY, PC's household (Ban S, Tha Khilek) 20,000 CNY, and KY's household (Ban M2, Tha Khilek) 5,000 CNY, a total of 285,000 CNY, together with other donations.

The donors for the eight affiliated stupas surrounding the central stupa were eight families from Myanmar and Thailand, including four families from Ban S (Tha Khilek), one family each from Ban M1 (Mae Sai), Ban H (Chiang Tung), Ban M2 (Tha Khilek), and Ban T (Tha Khilek). Among the four families from Ban S, three were refugees from Müang Hon, Sipsòng Panna, including CM, the former ruler of Müang Hon, and one consisted of a Tai Nüa (husband) and a refugee from Müang Chae in Sipsòng Panna (wife). The family from Ban M1 included two Tai Lü refugees from Müang Hon and a Tai Yuan son-in-law. The family from Ban M2 consisted of refugees and descendants from Müang Hai, Sipsòng Panna. The family from Ban T is Tai Khün. The diaspora members in Tha Khilek had a clear awareness of their local and transborder identity. On the one hand, they considered themselves as villagers of Tha Khilek. On the other, they had a sense of belonging to their original villages or *müang* in Sipsòng Panna. The second generation maintains this feeling as well. The donations for the reconstruction are for the diaspora, considered as a contribution to their homeland (interview, Donor PC's daughter, September 9, 2019).

Construction materials like brick, sand, and cement were donated by local people in Sipsòng Panna. Donations could also be made in the form of labor. Constructing a Buddhist site is considered a merit-making deed. The reasons for donating vary. For the Müang Hon refugees, a donation for the construction of a Buddhist site was a contribution to their homeland. Donor C from Ban H in Chiang Tung said that they heard of the plan for the reconstruction of the Chiang Ngoen Stupa from Khruba Saeng La and were willing to participate. They usually make donations where there are sacred places (interview, Donor C, September 12, 2019). Donating to the Chiang Ngoen stupa, for them, primarily means contributing to Buddhism.

The reconstruction lasted nearly six years. The impetus for the project began in 1998 when people from Ban S collected money and paid a visit to Müang Hon with Khruba Saeng La and found that the stupa was in poor condition after being damaged in an earthquake. Khruba Saeng La decided to reconstruct the stupa. On November 30, 2000, a ceremony was held to apologize for the necessary demolition of the old stupa. On December 13, 2001, the stupa-heart installation (*sai chai that*) ceremony was held. In this ceremony, Buddha images, gemstones, silverwork, and gold items were placed at the bottom and top of the stupa. This process was repeated at the eight affiliated stupas. These items were donated by the residents of Müang Hon, Khruba Undi from Mongla, Khruba Saeng La, and donors from Chiang Tung and Tha Khilek, all of whom had traveled across the border to make donations and attend the ceremony.

From January 31 to February 3, 2004, a grand celebration ceremony (*pòi luang*) was held to mark the completion of the reconstruction. A caravan of around twenty cars transporting monks and lay donors from Chiang Rai, Mae Sai, Tha Khilek, and Chiang Tung set off from the Thai-Myanmar border to Müang Hon via Chiang Tung, Mongla, and Chiang Lò, to attend the ceremony. A *thi* (Burmese loanword, "umbrella"), the golden umbrella to be erected on the top of the Chiang Ngoen Stupa, was carried from Tha Khilek and transported by the first car in the caravan.

The reason for pilgrimage varies. Monks from the city of Chiang Rai were invited by Khruba Saeng La. Monk S is the abbot of Wat SK in Chiang Rai. He was invited by Phra Tham Rachanuwat of Wat PK, the head of the Chiang Rai

Sangha, to attend the ceremony. He felt that the Buddhist religion in Müang Hon was prosperous, and the religious custom was not very different from that of Chiang Rai (interview, Monk S, September 7, 2019). Monk T, who attended the completion ceremony in 2004, now has been disrobed for several years. He vividly remembers the scenes in 2004. He got the opportunity to attend the ceremony because the abbot of Wat Ban L, a village which has many Tai Lü refugees from Sipsòng Panna could not attend. As an abbot in Mae Sai from 1989 to 2014, he was well acquainted with Khruba Saeng La. When he heard the news that it would be a grand ceremony, he was very eager to participate. He rode in an Isuzu Trooper together with Khruba Saeng La. He felt "happy to be able to attend the ceremony at the mercy of Khruba Saeng La, proud to participate in the journey with the Chiang Rai Sangha led by Phra Tham Rachanuwat. He was impressed to witness the Buddhists of Müang Hon and the deeply respected Khruba Saeng La" (interview, Monk T, August 21–22; September 8, 2019). Driver N was formerly a driver for Khruba Saeng La. He was born in Ban R, Chiang Chüang (Jingzhen), a town situated a few kilometers from Müang Hon. He now lives in Ban S, Tha Khilek. He went to Müang Hon to attend the ceremony as the driver for Khruba Saeng La (interview, Donor K, September 17, 2019).

In 2010, six years after the stupa reconstruction, a new temple hall (*vihāra*) was built. The construction of the hall was initiated and led by Khruba Undi. Donations came mostly from Müang Hon, but still included a substantial amount from Mongla and Tha Khilek, making a total of 178,518 CNY, which was much more than the combined local donations by individual households. Some of the Müang Hon-originated donors from Tha Khilek who had already donated for the Chiang Ngoen Stupa also donated for this hall. Some donors in Tha Khilek who were unable to travel to Müang Hon chose to deposit money with a representative.

Buddhist Architecture Preservation

A Buddhist place is not only a field of religious activity but also a symbol of cultural and ethnic identity. For this reason, during the recent cultural revival of Lan Na, the Tai Lü people in northern Thailand replicated stupas from Müang Yòng and Sipsòng Panna in their own communities (Dao 2017, 222). In the Upper Mekong region, partly because of financial stringency and partly because of a lack of awareness of cultural preservation, many Buddhist places of historical and artistic value have disappeared. This phenomenon worried both local and foreign cultural enthusiasts. Since the 1980s, the preservation of many Buddhist sites in Chiang Tung and Sipsòng Panna has been supported by individuals and governmental and non-governmental organizations from Thailand. It usually begins with a tourist pilgrimage to these places, driven by cultural nostalgia. Taking the example of the preservation project of the Wat Ban Y monastery, this section will discuss transborder religious connection as a tool to preserve architectural identity.

Wat Ban Y Project

The reconstruction of Buddhist sites in the 1980s were mostly replicas of the original Sipsòng Panna style. However, since the late 1990s, as many monks and local Tai architects completed their studies in Thailand and returned to Sipsòng Panna, Thai-style Buddhist architecture began gaining in popularity (Kang 2009, 36). The Wat Ban Y Project is an attempt to preserve the local style of Buddhist architecture, which involves cooperation between Thailand and Sipsòng Panna.

Ban Y is a village in Chiang Chüang district. Formerly named Ban Siao, the village was founded in 1450. It is said that once upon a time the villages in Chiang Chüang were struck by lightning and only Ban Siao survived. For this reason, the villagers changed its name to Ban Y ("village of stepping over the sky"). The village temple was built in 1778 but destroyed in 1955. It was rebuilt in 1984.

Later, Donor N, the head of the Art and Culture Office of Chiang Rai Rajabhat University (CRRU), heard the news from Donor B, a student from Ban Y, that the *vihāra* of the monastery of Ban Y would be torn down and reconstructed. Donor N then brought a team from the office to visit the monastery and was dismayed that its historical and art value would disappear if it was replaced by a new style hall (interview, Donor S, January 24, 2020). In 2010, an art exchange activity between Chiang Rai and Sipsòng Panna, organized by CRRU, was held in Sipsòng Panna. As it was held during the Songkran New Year Festival and the Thai artists were interested in local Tai culture, Donor B, the interpreter of the Thai artists, invited them to experience the Songkran custom at her own village, Ban Y.

When the Thai artists visited Ban Y and its temple, Artist S said he was deeply impressed by the local lifestyle, the antiquity of the *vihāra*, and traditional architecture, which did not survive in Chiang Rai. When conversing with village elders after the merit-making ceremony and the welcome-blessing ceremony, they learned that the villagers of Ban Y were planning to tear down the hall[8] and build a new one, as constructing a new *vihāra* would cost less than preserving the old one. Artist S said that during his trip to Sipsòng Panna, he was disappointed to find that many traditional Sipsòng Panna-style Buddhist *vihāra* were replaced by Thai-style *vihāra*. For this reason, these Thai artists were worried about the disappearance of traditional architecture and proposed to assist the reconstruction of Wat Ban Y temple. The villagers of Ban Y were willing to accept help from the Thai artists, as Ban Y is a small village of around sixty to seventy households and local funding for such projects is limited. A reconstruction project was proposed by the Art and Culture Office of Chiang Rai Rajabhat University. Thirty-four artists from Thailand donated their paintings for auction to raise funds for the reconstruction (Samnak Silapa Lae Watthanatham Maha Withayalai Ratchaphat Chiang Rai [n.d.]). Through personal connections, a collector purchased many of the works. To further supplement these fundraising efforts, another charity auction exhibition in Bangkok was arranged to raise money for the project (interview, Artist S, September 8, 2019).[9]

Some of the Thai artists who visited and donated to Wat Ban Y temple are of Tai Lü descent. Artist S is a famous artist from Chiang Rai Province. His Tai Lü ancestor came from Müang Yòng, and after having settled in Lamphun for over a century, his grandparents' generation moved to Chiang Rai Province. His works focus on the Buddhist world and are often inspired by the Buddhist arts of places he visits. When asked why the Thai artists had proposed the preservation project, he replied that there was a period in Thailand when local culture, including architecture, was erased and replaced by central Thai culture. While few pieces of Tai Lü architecture are left in Thailand, Sipsòng Panna has preserved more. Given such considerations, he expressed his hope that Sipsòng Panna should preserve its traditional architectural style, but he found that the architectural conditions in Sipsòng Panna were equally concerning. Under the pressure of the influx of foreign products, local craftsmanship is also endangered according to Artist S. Thus, the Thai artists proposed not only to preserve the original architecture but also to help the local craft by utilizing local building materials (ibid., interview).[10] Timbers were from Müang Ong (Mengweng), tiles from Chiang Nüa (Jingne), earthenware from a Chiang Chüang businessman-owned factory in Müang Luang, and constructors and craftsmen from Müang Ong. Only the gold paint, which the Chiang Rai Rajabhat University chose, was imported from Thailand (interview, Artist K, September 20, 2019). Artist S said that he felt pride that he had contributed to the preservation of traditional Tai Lü-style architecture, which he sees as part of his own cultural heritage (interview, Artist S, September 8, 2019).

The reconstruction committee was headed by the president of CRRU and consisted of the director and six teachers from the Fine Arts Department at CRRU, one teacher from the Faculty of Industrial Technology at CRRU, one Thai artist representative, two Chinese citizens studying at CRRU (one of them the Tai interpreter), the representative of the villagers of Ban Y, and the construction team. Before carrying out the project, the reconstruction committee obtained permission for the reconstruction from the Religious Affairs Bureau of Sipsòng Panna Prefecture. On May 2, 2011, CRRU, villagers of Ban Y, and the reconstruction company signed the contract. On November 24, 2012, the construction celebration ceremony was held. Thai artists, teachers, and personnel of CRRU traveled from Thailand to attend the ceremony (interview, Artist K, September 20, 2019).

Apart from the hall and the house for Buddhist priests, a new Buddha image was built at the southern part of the temple in 2011. The construction of this Buddha image and the temple wall were made possible through a donation by a Tai Lü migrant who had returned from Thailand, who was originally from Ban Y and whose business has been discussed by Wasan Panyagaew (2007).

The reconstruction of Wat Ban Y is praised by some monks and lay people in Sipsòng Panna. However, differing opinions still prevail regarding the reconstruction, not only between elites and local villagers but also between the local villagers of different generations. Roger Casas argues that a Buddhist place becomes the site of confliction between two different notions of modernity: one is the "mainstream Chinese visions of modernity, in which knowledge is depreciated with respect to size and brightness as expressions of wealth," another is to preserve "the past" "very faithfully but in enclosed spaces (such as museums), while the rest of the place and culture is equally transformed and even destroyed by modernization" (pers. com. Casas, March 10, 2022). Since the reconstruction, Wat Ban Y has been considered a model by some local elites, encouraging the Tai people in Sipsòng Panna to preserve the traditional local style of Buddhist architecture. The elders of Wat Ban Y believe that the old *vihāra* is *gudong* (Ch. "antique"; here meaning "treasure") and thus should be preserved (interview, Villager A2, September 23, 2019). Villagers of a younger generation still prefer to build a bigger hall in a new style, but this plan is temporarily shelved for lack of funds. For many local villagers, big and colorfulness implies modernity, while the traditional style is considered "bad technique" (*jishu buhao*) (interview, Villager C, September 23, 2019). Because the Chiang Rai Rajabhat University did not fund the reconstruction of the house for Buddhist monks and novices, which is next to the *vihāra*, the villagers reconstructed it by themselves. Villager E said that right now the house for Buddhist monks and novices is almost as high as the *vihāra*, which is not appropriate (interview, Villager E, September 23, 2019). Another case reveals a general lack of architectural identity preservation awareness among the local people. The *vihāra* of Ban L in Müang Hai County, whose preservation was assisted by Chiang Mai University, later fell into disrepair and was replaced by a new style one (interview, Artist K, September 20, 2019).

Conclusion

The 1980s witnessed the revival of the transborder pilgrimage in the Upper Mekong basin. The absence of native Buddhist monks and the change of national policies at the end of the Cultural Revolution provided monks and lay people outside Chinese territory the opportunity to participate in the reconstruction of Buddhism in Sipsòng Panna. The Sangha network, mentor-disciple relations, kinship, and cultural nostalgia are factors stimulating cross-border pilgrimage. In the peripheral regions of nation-states, cross-border pilgrimage is a strong force to promote the spiritual connection among marginalized people in the borderlands.

Yet, there are still some factors that pose obstacles to integration. Cross-border religious activity is viewed by some nation-states as a potential threat to the stability of frontier regions. Since the 1980s, when religious practice was restored, the Chinese government has stepped up efforts to integrate the Tai minority and Theravada Buddhists into the Chinese nation-state and to promote communication with other sects of Buddhism within the Chinese borders, such as the Han Chinese Mahayana Buddhism and Tibetan Buddhism (Kang 2009, 33). However, contact with the Southeast Asian Theravada Buddhist world is not prohibited. At the national level, Tai Theravada Buddhism in Yunnan has served as a tool to connect geopolitically Southwest China to Mainland Southeast Asia.

Another factor is limited free transborder travel. In recent years, the border control post of Mongla has deeply hindered transborder mobility. In addition, there is no immigration checkpoint along the border between Myanmar and Sipsòng Panna, where passports are invalid and Chinese citizens holding a border resident certificate can only travel a few kilometers from the borderline into Burmese territory. Almost all the informants agreed that residents of Sipsòng Panna cannot make trips southward beyond Mongla, while residents of Chiang Tung and Tha Khilek cannot enter Chinese territory via Mongla, and only the residents of Mongla can proceed to Sipsòng Panna. Except on special occasions, such as a pilgrimage with senior monks like Khruba Saeng La, people from the Shan State and Thailand hardly cross into Mongla.

Our research has demonstrated that the transnational pilgrimages of Tai monks and lay people in the Upper Mekong basin has provided a means of sustaining ethnic and religious identities of the Tai Lü, a group which had been separated as members of four nation-states for quite a long time. Such Buddhist pilgrimages that stimulate other kinds of tourism create a sense of belonging among the Tai people whose long-term impact on the region's integration deserves to be studied in detail.

Endnotes: Buddhist Pilgrimages and Architectural Restoration

1. The Tai people are an ethnolinguistic group extending over a vast territory comprising parts of northeastern India, Kachin State and Shan State in Myanmar, the southwestern parts of Yunnan Province in China, Laos, northern Vietnam, northeastern Cambodia, and Thailand (Keyes 1995, 136). This chapter focuses on a subgroup of the Tai, the Tai Lü, who call themselves simply "Tai" (to distinguish them from non-Tai speaking peoples, and a name equivalent to the Chinese term "Daizu") or "Tai Lü" (relative to the Tai people of other origins), named after the ancient Tai Lü kingdom (Müang Lü). The Tai Lü originally lived in Sipsòng Panna and surrounding areas in the Upper Mekong basin. Because of wars and political upheavals as as well as forced resettlements, especially from the early nineteenth century onward, and the Tai Lü are now displaced to southern regions like northern Laos and northern Thailand, and even as refugees to the United States and Canada. There are roughly 350,000 Tai Lü in Sipsòng Panna, 200,000–300,000 in the eastern part of the Shan State of Myanmar, 150,000 in northern Laos (according to the 2005 census), 400,000 in northern Thailand, and 4,500 in the United States (Liew-Herres, Grabowsky, and Renoo 2012, 8; Kang and Wasan 2014).

2. All toponyms referred to in this chapter are transcribed according to their pronounciation in the respective Tai languages, with official names in brackets.

3. See, for example, Cohen 2000a, 2000b; Davis 2005; Thianchai 2009; Wasan 2010, 2018; Amporn 2016; and Taylor 2020.

4. A similar motive to construct a separate monastery was found in the Tai Lü refugee community in Colorado, US (Kang and Wasan 2014).

5. To distinguish the Müang La in Myanmar and the Müang La in Sipsòng Panna, this article uses Mongla to refer to the former and Müang La to the latter.

6. It might be closer to the previous stupa style. McLeod visited Müang Ma in 1837 and found the stupa there was gilded (Grabowsky and Turton 2003, 363). The French explorer Francis Garnier recounted in 1876 that the Phra That Chom Yòng in Müang Yòng was gilded, and the That Pu Lan and That No in Müang Luang was formerly gilded (Garnier 1872a, 410; Garnier 1872b, 298).

7. According to the Regulation on Religious Affairs of PRC, donations from foreign organizations or individuals are subject to permission from the Religious Affairs Department of the People's Government of County level and above (Zhonghua Renmin Gongheguo Guowuyuan 2017).

8. Most parts of the hall, including the floor, were replaced with new materials. Because of the precious historical and artistic value of the decoration on the original wall, it was preserved. The outer side of the wall is painted with murals depicting scenes from the Jataka stories (tales about previous lives of the Buddha), such as Dasajati Jataka, Vessantara Jataka, Meghvadi Jataka, and Pora Jataka. The inner side of the wall is painted with a gold inlay design (*lai kham*), which is a traditional Buddhist decoration technique in the Upper Mekong basin. Traditionally, *lai kham* employs thin sheets of gold leaf which are hammered onto walls and pillars to form various patterns. It is unclear from what time onwards Sipsòng Panna used gold paint instead. The use of *lai kham* is increasingly rare in Sipsòng Panna due to the disappearance of traditional Tai Lü-style Buddhist architecture. Nowadays in Sipsòng Panna, the Buddhist architecture of modern Lan Na and Central Thai style gains in popularity, and in these buildings *lai kham* is supplanted by gold-painted carved decorations. The reconstruction adopted the *lai kham* patterns of the original forms and of temples from surrounding villages.

9. On June 8–30, 2013, an exhibition titled "Thai Contemporary Art Exhibition," was held at the Museum of Contemporary Art (MOCA), Bangkok.

10. Some of the temples in Sipsòng Panna had been reconstructed with the support of laypeople from Thailand before the reconstruction of Wat Ban Y. For example, the reconstruction of the *vihāra* of Ban L in Müang Hai county in 2004 was done in cooperation with Chiang Mai University, but the tiles were imported from Thailand and the entrance was added with a Lan Na-style pattern (interview, Artist K, September 20, 2019). The unique feature of Wat Ban Y is its emphasis on local crafts.

References

Amporn Jirattikorn. 2016. "Buddhist Holy Man Khruba Bunchum: The Shift in a Millenarian Movement at the Thailand-Myanmar Border." *SOJOURN: Journal of Social Issues in Southeast Asia* 31(2): 377–412.

Bowie, Katherine. 2017. "Khruba Siwichai: The Charismatic Saint and the Northern Sangha." In *Charismatic Monks of Lanna Buddhism*, ed. Paul Cohen, 27–57. Copenhagen: NIAS Press.

Casas, Roger. 2010. "Beyond 'Fantasyland': Religious Revival and Tourist Development in Sipsong Panna." ARNC Workshop "Human Security and Religious Certainty in Southeast Asia," Chiang Mai, Thailand.

————. 2022. "Moving Tai? Cross-Border Mobility and its Discontents on China's Southwest Frontiers." The 14th International Conference of Thai Studies, April 29–May 1, Kyoto, Japan.

Central Intelligence Agency. 1953. "Background on the Chinese Nationalist Problem in Burma." December 1. General CIA Records, National Archives, College Park, CIA-RDP80-00810A003100860001-2.

Chaiwan Saowaree. 2012. "Lue Borderlanders: History, Economy and Locality among the Lue in Mae Sai-Tachileik Border Towns." MA thesis, Chiang Mai University, Chiang Mai.

Cohen, Paul T. 2000a. "A Buddha Kingdom in the Golden Triangle: Buddhist Revivalism and the Charismatic Monk Khruba Bunchum." *Australian Journal of Anthropology* 11(3): 141–54.

————. 2000b. "Lue across Borders: Pilgrimage and the Muang Sing Reliquary in Northern Laos." In *Where China meets Southeast Asia*, eds. Grant Evans et al., 145–61. New York: Palgrave Macmillan.

Dao, Sirui. 2017. "The Cultural Influence of Sipsong Panna on Thailand since the 1980s: The Case of the Lue Literary Work *Kham Khap Lanka Sip Hua*." *Proceedings of the 13th International Conference on Thai Studies: Globalized Thailand? Connectivity, Conflict and Conundrums of Thai Studies*, Chiang Mai, Thailand, July 15–18. Vol. 1: 216–40.

Davis, Sara L. M. 2005. *Song and Silence: Ethnic Revival on China's Southwest Borders*. New York: Columbia University Press.

Garnier, Francis. 1872a. "Voyage d'exploration en Indo-Chine." *Le tour du monde* 23: 353–416.

————. 1872b. "Voyage d'exploration en Indo-Chine." *Le tour du monde* 24: 289–336.

Grabowsky, Volker. 1999. "Forced Resettlement Campaigns in Northern Thailand during the Early Bangkok Period." *Journal of the Siam Society* 87(1): 45–86.

————. 2019. "The Ethno-Religious Identity of the Tai People in Sipsong Panna and Its Resurgence in Recent Manuscripts." In *Engaging Asia: Essays on Laos and Beyond in Honour of Martin Stuart-Fox*, ed. Desley Goldston, 290–322. Copenhagen: NIAS Press.

Grabowsky, Volker, and Andrew Turton, eds. 2003. *The Gold and Silver Road of Trade and Friendship: The McLeod and Richardson Diplomatic Missions to Tai States in 1837*. Chiang Mai: Silkworm Books.

Hasegawa, Kiyoshi. 2000. "Cultural Revival and Ethnicity: The Case of the Tai Lue in the Sipsong Panna, Yunnan Province." In *Dynamics of Ethnic Cultures across National Boundaries in Southwestern China and Mainland Southeast Asia: Relations, Societies, and Languages*, ed. Hayashi Yukio, 121–37. Kyoto: Center for Southeast Asian Studies, Kyoto University.

Kang, Nanshan. 2009. *Theravada Buddhism in Sipsong Panna: Past and Contemporary Trends*. Chiang Mai: Regional Centre for Social Science and Sustainable Development.

Kang, Nanshan and Wasan Panyagaew. 2014. "The Lue in America: Lue-American Community and Their Connectivity to the Sipsong Panna Motherland." The 12th International Conference on Thai Studies "Thailand in the World," April 22–24, Sydney, Australia.

Keyes, Charles F. 1995. "Who Are the Tai? Reflections on the Invention of Identities." In *Ethnic Identity: Creation, Conflict, and Accommodation*. 3rd edn. eds. Lola Romanucci-Ross and George A. De Vos, 136–160. Walnut Creek, CA: Alta Mira Press.

Liew-Herres, Foon Ming, Volker Grabowsky, and Renoo Wichasin, eds. 2012. *Chronicle of Sipsòng Panna: History and Society of a Tai Lü Kingdom, Twelfth to Twentieth Century*. Chiang Mai: Mekong Press.

McCarthy, Susan. 2009. *Communist Multiculturalism: Ethnic Revival in Southwest China*. Seattle: University of Washington Press.

"Minzu Wenti Wu Zhong Congshu" Yunnan Sheng Bianji Weiyuan Hui 《民族问题五种丛书》云南省编辑委员会, ed. 1983. *Xishuangbanna daizu shehui zonghe diaocha (yi)* 西双版纳傣族社会综合调查 (一) [Comprehensive investigation of the Sipsòng Panna Tai society. Vol. 1]. Kunming: Yunnan minzu chubanshe.

Neeranooch Malangpoo. 2020. "Nationalism and Tourism. The Case of Thai Buddhist Pilgrimage in Myanmar." PhD diss., University of Wisconsin-Madison.

Peters, Hinton. 1990. "Buddhism and Ethnicity among the Tai Lue in the Sipsongpanna." *Proceedings of the International Conference on Thai Studies*, Kunming, May 11–13. Vol. 3: 339–52.

Sāimöng Mangrāi, Sao. 2002. *The Pāḍæng Chronicle and the Jengtung State Chronicle Translated*. Center for South and Southeast Asian Studies, University of Michigan.

Samnak Silapa Lae Watthanatham Maha Withayalai Ratchaphat Chiang Rai สำนักศิลปะและวัฒนธรรม มหาวิทยาลัยราชภัฏเชียงราย. [n.d.] *Kan burana wihan thai lü, wat yang fa, sipsòng panna* การบูรณะวิหาร ไทลื้อ วัดย่างฟ้า สิบสองปันนา [Renovation of Tai Lü Hall of Wat Yang Fa Temple, Sipsòng Panna].

Stuart-Fox, Martin. 1999. "Laos: From Buddhist Kingdom to Marxist." *Buddhism and Politics in Twentieth Century Asia*, ed. Ian Harris, 153–72. London: Continuum.

Taylor, James. 2020. "Buddhism, Nomadism, and the Making of New Religio-Political Places: Deleuzian Thought about Borderlands, Movement and Itinerant Theology." *Asia Pacific Journal of Anthropology* 21(2): 103–16.

Thianchai Aksondit. เธียรชาย อักษรดิษฐ์. 2009. *Tamnan phra chao liap lok: kan süksa phünthi thang sangkhom lae watthanatham lan na, phuminam, tamnan, phukhon* ตำนานพระเจ้าเลียบโลก: การศึกษาพื้นที่ ทางสังคมและวัฒนธรรมล้านนา ภูมินาม ตำนาน ผู้คน [Legend of the Buddha's Travel in the World: Study of the Social and Cultural Areas of Lan Na, Names, Legends, People]. Bangkok: Than Panya.

Wasan Panyagaew. 2007. "Re-Emplacing Homeland: Mobility, Locality, a Returned Exile and a Thai Restaurant in Southwest China." *Asia Pacific Journal of Anthropology* 8(2): 117–35.

——————. 2010. "Cross-Border Journeys and Minority Monks: The Making of Buddhist Places in Southwest China." *Asian Ethnicity* 11(1): 43–59.

——————. 2018. "The Two Khruba Lue: Buddhist Place Makers of the Upper Mekong." *Journal of the Siam Society* 106: 279–94.

Wu, Hsiu-Chueh 吴秀雀. 2015. *Chong lajiao de ziwei: Qingjing yimin renqun zhi rentong neihan yu bianqian* 舂辣椒的滋味：清境義民人群之認同內涵與變遷 [The taste of chilli paste: the content and change of identity among veterans in Chingjing]. Taipei: Kaixue Wenhua.

Xishuangbanna Zizhizhou Minzu Zongjiao Shiwu Ju 西双版纳傣族自治州民族宗教事务局, ed. 2006. *Xishuangbanna Daizu Zizhizhou minzu zongjiao zhi* 西双版纳傣族自治州民族宗教志 [Religious and Ethnic Gazetteer of Sipsòng Panna Tai Autonomous Prefecture]. Kunming: Yunnan Minzu Chubanshe.

Xishuangbanna Zongfosi 西双版纳总佛寺. 2020. *Quanguo zhengxie changwei pa songlie long zhuang meng: guanyu jiaqiang yunnan nanchuan shangzuobu fojiao yu zhoubian guojia youhao jiaowang de jianyi* 全国政协常委帕松列龙庄勐：关于加强云南南传上座部佛教与周边国家友好交往的建议 [The Standing Committee Member of the Chinese People's Political Consultative Conference Phra Somdet Luang Chom Müang: Proposal for Promoting the Communication between Theravada Buddhism of Yunnan Province and the Neighbouring countries]. May 23. https://mp.weixin.qq.com/s/HYIA4dxWQJjBaMmP1C8raQ

Yanyong Chiranakhon ยรรยง จิระนคร, and Ratanaporn Sethakul รัตนาพร เศรษฐกูล. 2001. *Prawattisat sipsòng Panna* ประวัติศาสตร์สิบสองปันนา [History of Sipsòng Panna]. Bangkok: Withithat.

Zhonghua Renmin Gongheguo Guowuyuan 中华人民共和国国务院 [State Council of the People's Republic of China]. 2017, "Zongjiao shiwu tiaoli" 宗教事务条例 [Regulation on Religious Affairs]. *Zhonghua renmin gongheguo zhongyang renmin zhengfu*, Zhongguo zhengfu wang, September 7. http://www.gov.cn/zhengce/content/2017-09/07/content_5223282.htm.

Interviews

Artist K, young male, Müang Ong, on-spot interview by Sirui Dao (Chiang Rung, September 20, 2019).

Artist S, middle-aged male, Mae Kham, on-spot interview by Sirui Dao (Mae Kham, September 8, 2019).

Donor C, middle-aged male, Chiang Tung, on-spot interview by Sirui Dao (Chiang Tung, September 12, 2019).

Donor K, middle-aged female, Mae Sai, on-spot interview by Sirui Dao (Mae Sai, February 15, 2020); Interview through instant messaging client (September 17, 2019; January 12, 2020).

Donor PC's daughter, middle-aged female, Tha Khilek, on-spot interview by Sirui Dao (Tha Khilek, September 9, 2019).

Donor S, middle-aged female, Chiang Rai, interview by Sirui Dao through instant messaging client (January 24, 2020).

Migrant S, young female, Tainan, interview by Sirui Dao through instant messaging client (January 6, 2020).

Monk D, young male, Müang Hai, interview by Sirui Dao through instant messaging client (February 1, 2019; August 22–23, 2020).

Monk S, elderly male, Chiang Rai, on-spot interview by Sirui Dao (Chiang Rai, September 7, 2019).

Monk T (now disrobed), middle-aged male, Mae Sai, on-spot interview by Sirui Dao (Mae Sai, September 8, 2019); interview by Sirui Dao through instant messaging client (August 21–22, 2019).

Sadaw, elderly male, Chiang Tung, on-spot interview by Sirui Dao (Chiang Tung, September 12, 2019).

Villager A, middle-aged female, Müang Hon, on-spot interview by Sirui Dao (Müang Hon, September 22, 2019).

Villager A2, elderly female, Chiang Chüang, on-spot interview by Sirui Dao (Chiang Chüang, September 23, 2019).

Villager C, middle-aged female, Chiang Chüang, on-spot interview by Sirui Dao (Chiang Chüang, September 23, 2019).

Villager D, elderly male, Müang Hon, on-spot interview by Sirui Dao (Müang Hon, September 22, 2019).

Villager E, middle-aged female, Chiang Chüang, on-spot interview by Sirui Dao (Chiang Chüang, September 23, 2019).

Death of the Last King: Contemporary Ethnic Identity and Belonging among the Tai Lü of Sipsòng Panna

ROGER CASAS

On October 1, 2017, an elderly man passed away in a hospital in Kunming, the capital of Yunnan Province, in southwest China. The name of this man, Dao Shixun, would not ring a bell among inhabitants of his homeland, Sipsòng Panna (Xishuangbanna in Chinese), a frontier prefecture in the southernmost tip of the same province, much less among those in other parts of China. Despite this, and even though the passing was summarily dealt with in the daily news broadcast from local TV stations (after all, October 1 is National Day in China), this death did not go unnoticed, and funeral services and remembrance ceremonies were arranged in honor of Dao Shixun in Thailand or Taiwan, and even in the United States.

Indeed, Dao Shixun was no ordinary citizen. In his youth, and for a short time, Chao Mom Kham Lü, as he was known in the local language, acted as *chao phaendin*, the highest dignitary and nominal ruler of the Tai Lü of Sipsòng Panna.[1] As a flesh-and-bone symbol of the prosperity of the land, he was then at the top of a ritual and cosmological hierarchy whose origins can be traced back some eight hundred years. Some scholars have referred to his position as that of a "king" (Tanabe 1988; Hsieh 1995).[2]

While deciding whether he was really a "king" or not is probably a moot point, Chao Mom's life[3] is of interest because it runs through many of the political and social upheavals the Tai Lü and many other subaltern collectivities in China underwent throughout the twentieth century—from the turmoil of the Republic and the civil war, through the founding of the People's Republic in 1949, and up to the period of apparent prosperity brought by the "reform and opening up" (Ch. *gaige kaifang*) policy adopted by the state by the end of the 1970s. As an individual, Chao Mom embodied these transformations in a particularly acute and visible manner. After being dethroned and converted into a common citizen of the People's Republic, he went on to work in state academic institutions and to suffer repression during the Cultural Revolution, only to be rehabilitated into a minor political position in the 1980s.

In this chapter, the life of the last *chao phaendin* is used as a vantage point from which to reflect on issues of power in relation to the Tai Lü polity prior to and throughout the twentieth century, as well as to the governance of the so-called "ethnic minorities" (Ch. *shaoshu minzu*) inhabiting the territory of the contemporary Chinese nation-state. While a more in-depth account of his life and circumstances remains to be written, within the limited framework of this chapter Chao Mom Kham Lü will act as a *figure* through which to explore "local, national, and transnational discourses about contemporary social life and its futures" (Barker et al. 2014, 1), in order to obtain "unique insights into ideological formations and their contestations."[4] In particular, the chapter will show how Chao Mom's figure has acted, and continues to act, as a symbol of a traditional, transnational Tai Lü identity that spills over the borders of the Chinese polity, therefore questioning the inward-oriented project of the Communist Party-state of integrating the populations inhabiting its frontier territories into the "Chinese nation."

The *Moeng* and the Last King

Sipsòng Panna, on the southernmost tip of Yunnan Province, is said to be one of the most ethnically and culturally diverse areas in China, with several groups speaking languages ascribed to the Tai-Kadai, Mon-Khmer, and Tibeto-Burman linguistic families. Before the mid-twentieth century, when the region was formally integrated into the administrative structures of the modern Chinese polity, relations between these different groups articulated within the framework of a locally specific entity known as the *moeng*.[5] This Tai term, sometimes translated as "principality" (Hsieh 1995, 306), describes a geopolitical unit comprising both populations living in fertile plains and engaged in wet-rice cultivation (most of them speakers of Tai languages), and peoples speaking other languages, usually living off the scarce and less productive highlands and engaged (even if from a symbolically inferior position) in economically symbiotic relations with the valley dwellers (Condominas 1990, 36–41; Tanabe 2000, 294–95; Turton 2000; Liew–Herres et al. 2012, 13–15). Tai political dominance was traditionally legitimated and naturalized by their possession of Buddhist scriptures and of the male monastic discipline attached to them, the main civilizational markers at the regional level until the contemporary period, according to different authors (Turton 2000, 27; Keyes 2002, 1172–73).

Within the *moeng*, Tai peasants were themselves subject through relations of fealty to a ruling class of landowners collectively known as the *chao*. As all land was considered the property of the *chao phaendin* (see below), free peasants cultivating communal land had to pay corvée to members of the *chao* class, while those working land owned by the *chao* themselves had to pay a fixed rent in paddy to their lords.[6]

Before the emergence of nation-states in the area between the late nineteenth and early twentieth centuries (Keyes 2002, 1174), Sipsòng Panna, alternatively known in the premodern period as Moeng Lü (Liew-Herres et al. 2012, 5–61), was a large principality among several others located in the borderlands shared by the much larger and more powerful Chinese empire and the Burmese and Siamese kingdoms, principalities such as Kengtung (Chiang Tung in the Thai language) in present-day Shan State of Myanmar, or Lan Na in northern Thailand. As these other Tai-dominated polities, *moeng* Sipsòng Panna integrated, in turn, a number of smaller *moeng*, each of them ruled by a male member of the *chao* class, the *chao moeng*.[7] The *chao* ruling over Jinghong[8] was the nominal lord of all other *chao moeng* in Sipsòng Panna and was known as the *chao phaendin* or "lord of the land." Even if, as it is clear from the chronicles, the authority of the *chao phaendin* was regularly and strongly contested by other theoretically lesser *chao* and internecine fighting was chronic in *moeng* Sipsòng Panna, the dynasty managed to stay in power for almost eight centuries.[9]

As the official representative of the emperor in the area, the *chao phaendin* was also the *tuguan* or *tusi* (both Chinese terms can be translated as "indigenous official") of Sipsòng Panna, itself known in Chinese historical records as Cheli.[10] The *tusi* system was set up during the Yuan dynasty (thirteenth to fourteenth century) in order to facilitate control of the peripheral regions of the empire without the need for establishing a formal administration of appointed bureaucrats. Accordingly, the various *tusi* were responsible for maintaining the peace and securing the trade routes in those regions, as well as screening the flow of merchandise and people toward the interior of the empire.[11] Chinese presence in Sipsòng Panna regularly materialized in the form of the military support offered to the *chao phaendin* against neighboring principalities or internal rivals, a support which might have been critical in securing the continuity of the dynasty in Jinghong (Hsieh 1995, 309).

Nevertheless, as Hsieh has also argued, this Chinese military support was not determinant in securing the legitimacy of the Tai regime with regard to the local population, for whom the *chao phaendin* was the highest lord (Hsieh 1995, 303–15).[12] Furthermore, for most of the time after the Tai[13] rulers in this area became vassals of the Yuan Empire, the presence of both imperial bureaucrats, and of Chinese population in general, was very limited.[14] The gradual integration of Sipsòng Panna into the national-level structures of the Chinese polity intensified during the Republican period,[15] a nationwide time of transition between the old, feudal society, and that of the modern nation-state that the People's Republic aspires to become. This process of integration is shown in the different internal administrative reorganizations of Sipsòng Panna implemented by Han Chinese administrators, particularly Ke Shuxun, a military officer-cum-warlord initially appointed by the Nationalist government, and who became the strongman in Sipsòng Panna between the end of the empire in 1911 and his own death in 1927 (Liew-Herres et al. 2012, 67–72; Hsieh 1989, 148–60).

The Last King

When Chao Mom Kham Lü was born in 1928, the authority of the *chao phaendin* and the stability of the *chao* regime as a whole were seriously compromised, as real power lay with Chinese-Guomindang administration personnel and troops. Nevertheless, Chao Mom's education followed the tradition of the court, and he attended a primary school for children of the nobility called Cheli Saen Wi, in Jinghong.[16] As part of his upbringing and in accord with custom in Sipsòng Panna, where temporary monastic ordination was, until very recently, expected of all males of young age (see Casas 2008), in 1939 Chao Mom ordained for three months as a Buddhist novice (Tai *pha*) at a local monastery (Tai *wat*).

Chao Mom Kham Lü's father, Chao Mom Saeng Moeng, was the elder brother of the *chao phaendin* at the time, Chao Mom Suwanna Phakhang. The two children this latter ruler had from his third wife[17] were apparently too young when their father passed away in 1943. Therefore, it was his nephew and adoptive son, Chao Mom Kham Lü, who at the time was studying in a secondary school (Hansen 1999, 92) in Chongqing (then part of Sichuan Province), who ascended the throne. In 1944, he became the 44th *chao phaendin*, although it was not until 1947 that he returned to Sipsòng Panna and was crowned in a formal ceremony. He was nineteen years old.

After "ruling" over the Tai Lü of Sipsòng Panna for little more than a year, in 1948 Chao Mom Kham Lü resumed his studies in Kunming, where he spent the final phase of the civil war fought by the Nationalist and Communist armies. While Chao Mom was away, his father became regent, but due to his connections with the Guomindang officials stationed in Sipsòng Panna in this period, following the Communist takeover he fled into Burma with the retreating Nationalist troops. Many *chao* supported the Nationalists "who had allowed coexistence of the Tai political system and the Chinese administration," while, as we shall see, some other members of the local nobility chose to side with the Communists (Hansen 1999, 92). While Chao Mom Kham Lü's father was back in China by 1954, many others remained abroad, never to return.[18]

Fig. 1. A portrait of the young Chao Mom Kham Lü, published online at the time of his death.

After the victory of the Communist Party in the civil war and the establishment of some sort of border security, in 1950 Sipsòng Panna became officially the Xishuangbanna Dai Autonomous Region, then, in 1953, Prefecture. This latter year, the position of *chao phaendin*, together with that of *xuanwei shi* and the *noe sanam* (Tai) or "council of nobles," were abolished, effectively putting an end to the previous political regime (Liew-Herres et al. 2012, 71).[19]

When Chao Mom Kham Lü, now a common citizen of the People's Republic of China, graduated from his studies in Kunming, he did not return to Jinghong but went on to study linguistics and humanities in Beijing. After completing his education, he acted as advisor in the development of a reformed, simplified script for the Sipsòng Panna *Daizu* in the 1950s, aimed at substituting the old Tham script used traditionally in local temples.[20]

Later, the former *chao phaendin* worked as an assistant researcher at the Yunnan Institute for the Nationalities (*Yunnan Minzu Xueyuan*, today Yunnan Minzu University) in Kunming, where he was also dean of the Institute for Nationalities Languages. As it happened with many other individuals across China during the Maoist period, Chao Mom went through the dramatic shifting in official attitudes toward minority groups and their pre-1950 elites. During the Cultural Revolution he suffered "criticism" (Ch. *pidou*) and was sent, together with other members of the Tai nobility, to a village in Moeng Ban (Jinggu County, in Pu'er Prefecture of Yunnan Province), where he spent several years at the end of that period, engaged in agricultural work.

After the death of Mao Zedong in 1976 and the implementation of the "reform and opening-up" policies in China from the late 1970s onwards, Chao Mom was rehabilitated, and in the mid-1980s he became a member of the Yunnan branch of the Chinese People's Political Consultative Conference (CPPCC). Thirty years after participating in the elaboration of the "new Tai script," he became a proponent of what was ultimately going to be only a temporary return to the use of the old script at the prefectural level.[21]

Although he kept a house in Jinghong, Chao Mom spent most of his time in Kunming with his wife and children in the last decades of his life,[22] returning only occasionally and somehow incognito to Sipsòng Panna. According to one close collaborator of his, Chao Mom was reluctant to attract the attention of the authorities, something unavoidable as scores of locals would inevitably flock to see and pay respects to the last of their *chao phaendin*. In the following section I will explore some of the ideological features of this allegiance, as well as the ways in which the Party-state set out to deal with it after 1950.

Power and Collective Memory

Chao Mom's passing symbolically ended a period in the history of Sipsòng Panna and the Tai Lü determined by the *moeng* context and the rule of the *chao*. As this sociopolitical system and the rituals that sustained it were in place (no doubt undergoing constant transformation) for almost eight centuries, its connection to Tai Lü identity should not require further explanation.[23] Some authors have even argued that allegiance to the *chao phaendin* was the most fundamental marker of such identity, what defined the Tai Lü as Lü vis-à-vis other Tai-speaking groups in the region and living under the authority of other, differently named rulers (Hsieh 1995, 303–8). Leaving aside this somehow limited understanding of Lü identity, the social and political significance of the *chao phaendin* in the framework of pre-1950 Sipsòng Panna is undeniable. I will now elaborate on the nature of this significance, starting with its links to spirit worship.

Spirit worship was a fundamental feature of the political ideology in *moeng* Sipsòng Panna, as reflected in the ethnographic research conducted by Chinese specialists in the 1950s.[24] The realm of the spirits was arranged into a hierarchy mirroring that of the human world. At the lower levels of this hierarchy, Tai Lü peasants worshipped household as well as village spirits; beyond the village every *moeng* in Sipsòng Panna possessed its own tutelary spirit, which was, in turn, the object of propitiating rituals presided by the *chao moeng* of each of these territories.[25]

In this spiritual hierarchy, both village and household spirits were subordinated to the more powerful spirits of the *moeng*. Accordingly, the six or seven spirits of Jinghong, where the *chao phaendin* resided, "were responsible for the entire kingdom" (Tanabe 1988, 15). The most important among them, Phi Moeng Longnan, was regarded as "the ancestor spirit of the king and the founder of the capital" (ibid.).[26] However, in spite of the links of the *chao phaendin* to this particular spirit, and reflecting, according to Tanabe, the lack of centralization in *moeng* Sipsòng Panna, "[t]he king's access to particular guardian spirits in the capital was simply one of the major sources of legitimacy of his authority within the royal territory only, and did not differ from what happened within local *moeng*s [*sic*] of his kingdom" (ibid.). The *chao phaendin* was therefore, at least, the *symbolic* pinnacle of a cosmological system englobing all inhabitants (human and spiritual) of the land, including non-Tai, non-Buddhist groups.[27]

Immediately after the Communist Party gained control of Sipsòng Panna in 1950, the shift in power was accompanied by what can be seen as a series of symbolic recognitions of the old regime.[28] To start with, from 1950 on, Party cadres "used elements of traditional society to habituate the Dai population to the goals and ideas of the new socialist order" (McCarthy 2009, 55). In 1956, the land reform was implemented in a "peaceful, consultative" manner, paying attention to local institutions of power, so that "many preexisting cultural and political structures were left intact and even subsumed into the Party-state structure" (ibid., 53).

This special treatment was not exclusive to Sipsòng Panna. All "autonomous areas" (Ch. *zizhi qu*) in China, that is, regions with significant numbers of minority populations and some minimal degree of autonomy, were exempt of the most heavy-handed measures implemented in other areas of the country to deal with previous land regimes, particularly with the landed classes. This recognition of minority cultures and of local authority on the part of the Communist Party was aimed at differentiating the new approach from the directly assimilationist policies of the Nationalists. At the same time, it can be understood as a strategic policy aiming to facilitate the power transition by gaining the trust of ethnic minorities, which in any case continued to be conventionally represented as backward and in need of guidance from the Han *dage* or "big brother", as in the past (McCarthy 2009, 53; Harrell 1995).

In Sipsòng Panna, the Communist Party used selected elements of so-called "local culture" to make socialism "intelligible and legitimate" to the common folk (McCarthy 2009, 53). More importantly, the Party cooperated with parts of the local elite, members of which were co-opted into the local state apparatus in order to avoid conflict with the Tai population. Consequently, many of the *chao* obtained positions in the new administration.[29] The final goal of these policies was for the Communist Party to succeed the Tai *chao* as the main source of loyalty and allegiance for the local (at least the Tai Lü) population. As McCarthy has pointed out, this strategy was so successful that in the first years of the People's Republic, Tai peasants would identify Communist Party cadres with the previous ruling class, referring to the former as *chao gongchan*, that is, "Communist *chao*" (ibid.).[30]

Special treatment was granted not only to those members of the *chao* class who had cooperated with the Communists, but also to those who had not. In an effort to win back those members of the Tai elite who had fled with the retreating Nationalist troops, the new government guaranteed a safe return and a fresh beginning to those who decided to return to China. One of the individuals to accept this offer was, as mentioned earlier, Chao Mom Kham Lü's father.

Nevertheless, this period of "velvet glove treatment of wayward Dai elites" (McCarthy 2009, 54) and the policy of collaboration with local nobles following the founding of Xishuangbanna Prefecture did not last long. Starting in 1957 with the Great Leap Forward and the Anti-Rightist Campaign, policies became less compromising or outright antagonistic, and during long periods the laws and regulations guaranteeing the recognition of minority "peculiarities" (Ch. *tese*) were ignored, suspended, or simply abolished, allowing in particular for the "criticism" of the feudal order and its representatives, as we saw in the case of Chao Mom Kham Lü and others. Throughout this period of instability, which was to last until the end of the 1970s, new waves of refugees fled Sipsòng Panna for Burma-Myanmar and Laos (McCarthy 2009, 55).

During the Maoist period, the figure of the former *chao phaendin* became particularly problematic. As the former supreme ruler of the Tai Lü, and as the individual at the top of the rituals that assured the prosperity of the land and of its populations, the symbolic power of Chao Mom's position was much greater than that of any other *chao*. Therefore, he had to be dealt with in a special way. First, as many other *chao*, he was co-opted and made part of the new system; unlike Zhao Cunxin, however, he was not given any position of political significance until his old age. In fact, Chao Mom was kept physically away from Sipsòng Panna. This was undoubtedly facilitated by his youth at the time, as well as his lack of familiarity with and strong connections to his native place.

Secondly, the figure of the *chao phaendin* was at the center of a struggle concerning historical narratives. Like what happened with populations all over China, after 1950 a reworking of the so-called "collective memory" (Keyes and Tanabe 2002) of the Tai Lü as a group was set into motion. This implied the selecting, emphasizing, excluding, rearranging, and silencing of different existing accounts of the past. Until that moment, the "official history" of the Tai Lü, recorded in the old chronicles, revolved almost exclusively around events concerning the local ruling dynasty (see Liew-Herres et al. 2012). This narrative was then subject to a radical revision according to a new, allegedly "scientific" perspective, articulated in the Marxist language of modes of production and of exploitation, according to which the *chao*, including the *chao phaendin*, were evil feudal lords who had ruthlessly oppressed and exploited the local peasantry for centuries, a situation from which the Communist Party had "liberated" the *Daizu*, as the rest of *shaoshu minzu* in China.[31] Within this new, expanded framework, the traditional role of the *chao phaendin* was downgraded to that of a mere local ruler whose authority derived exclusively from that of the Chinese emperor.[32]

During the decades following "liberation" (Ch. *jiefang*), and to an important extent until today, elements such as the close political and cultural connections of the previous regime and of the Tai Lü in general to other principalities in the Upper Mekong region, were de-emphasized or expurged from the narrative, while their relationship with the rest of China was portrayed as essential: "Xishuangbanna" was and had always been part of the "Chinese nation" (Ch. *zhonghua minzu*). The creation of the *Daizu* itself, and even the previously discussed reform of the old script used in monasteries, can be seen as part of this process as well.

Furthermore, the post-1950 remaking of the past did not imply only a refashioning of discourses and history textbooks. As Tanabe has pointed out, "[…] in so far as the spirit cults generated the ideological discourse constructing the general bases for the concept of state, they naturally became a vital political issue during the course of the revolution [*sic*]." The suppression of spirit cults, an undeniable part of a tradition anchoring Tai Lü sense of belonging in a certain past, is to be understood in relation to this reworking of local collective memory. While household and village spirit rituals are still held today in Sipsòng Panna, the *moeng*-level spirit cults were not recovered after the Maoist period, due to their overt political character (Tanabe 1988, 16–18).

Return of the King

Whatever the actual ideological fortunes of the *chao* regime in legitimating the traditional social order described above, it is clear that the strategy of the Communist Party has been mostly successful in harnessing the potency of the *chao* rulers. As those individuals who lived in the time before "liberation" gradually disappear, the living memory of the *chao* fades. Apart from their residual prominence as members of the local political and cultural elite,[33] completely integrated into the People's Republic administration anyway, the *chao* have ceased to be a major source of allegiance for the Tai Lü. In the last decades, alternative sources of identification for young Tai Lü as public schooling (where the history of pre-1950 Sipsòng Panna or Tai Lü language and culture are hardly alluded to) and consumerism are substituting for the traditional institutions of cultural reproduction, such as the Buddhist monastery (see Casas 2008). For those Tai Lü born in the last forty years, the *chao phaendin* is fast becoming an irrelevant figure. Many among them have never heard of him, and even those who have may find it hard to picture the centrality of his role in the pre-1950 world.

Nevertheless, it would be premature to declare the end of the *chao* era. Narratives of the past divergent from those promoted by the Party-state continue to circulate among the Lü. The memory of pre-1950 Sipsòng Panna is kept alive with special consistency in certain circles, for instance among members of the Buddhist Sangha,[34] an institution very much connected to the power of the *chao* nobility, as the state-promoted research project of the 1950s emphasized. Furthermore, not only the names and stories, but even some the rituals linked to the *chao* and to their former power, are somehow kept alive today. In relation to this, I will now focus on the significance of two events directly connected to the passing of Chao Mom Kham Lü.

A first public secular funeral for Chao Mom was arranged in Kunming shortly after his death. In August 2018, that is more than ten months after the event, a Buddhist funeral service was held at Wat Pajie,[35] the central temple in Sipsòng Panna.[36] Chao Mom's ashes had been kept at the temple after his cremation, which had taken place in Kunming only a few days after his passing. During the time between both funerals, a display placed on the lower level of the Jinghong temple showed an image of the late *chao phaendin* as a young man, with texts written in Chinese, (old) Tai Lü, and Thai. As Tai Lü celebrate funerals and remembrance rituals during *wassa*, the three-month rainy season of Buddhist lent (usually lasting from July until October), this grander ceremony had to wait until the following year.

Fig. 2. Circumambulation of Wat Pajie during the funeral ceremony, Jinghong, August 2018.

This funeral consisted of a chanting plus water-pouring ritual (Tai *yat nam*) celebrated in the *vihan* (Pali *vihāra*) or prayer hall of Wat Pajie. The resident chapter of monastics as well as other important monks from Sipsòng Panna and beyond were invited to chant at the ceremony. There were speeches by local personalities, some of them members of the former nobility and connected to the prefectural and provincial branches of the Buddhist Association. Apart from the participants from Kunming, several distant relatives of Chao Mom descending from those members of the royal family or the nobility who fled defeat in the civil war or political repression in the twentieth century, and who settled in Thailand decades ago, attended the event. After this part of the ceremony was completed, all participants, joined by groups of dancers and musicians arranged partly through Manting Gongyuan, an entertainment park adjacent to the monastery, circumambulated the urn with Chao Mom's ashes three times around the *vihan*. The ashes were taken to a white stupa built for the occasion on temple grounds, where they were laid to rest, with more chanting by the monks and a final pouring of water. The whole ceremony was presided by the head of the Sipsòng Panna Buddhist Association and of the local monastic community, Somdet Longjom Wannasiri (see Casas 2008).

The ritual just described can be seen as a formal activity of remembrance, celebrated according not only to regional and globally sanctioned standards of "proper" Buddhism, but to the official representation of religion that has become commonplace all across China since the "reform and opening-up" period.[37] Interestingly, an even more significant event concerning the memory of Chao Mom Kham Lü had taken place only a few weeks after his death. This was the ritual by which the former *chao phaendin* was made into a *chao moeng*, a lord spirit protector of the *moeng*. As explained earlier, the relation between the *chao* and the land, mediated by the cults of tutelary territorial spirits, is a fundamental feature not only of traditional political ideology in Sipsòng Panna but also among other cultures across Southeast Asia. Accordingly, the symbolic significance of the *chao* is maintained after their death.

This third (second in chronological order) ceremony started in Wat Pajie as well. This time, the central object of the ritual were not the ashes of the *chao phaendin* but a set of personal items embodying the spirit or soul of the ruler, an immaterial entity known in different Tai languages as *khwan*. In contrast to the funeral held in August 2018, no monks participated in this ritual, as activities involving spirits or *phi* are seen as external and in tension to Buddhism.[38] The master of ceremonies was a ritual specialist mediating with the world of the spirits, known among the Tai Lü by the general term *pò mò*.[39] Reflecting the already mentioned hierarchy in the spirit world, the *pò mò* specifically dedicated to the service of the *chao phaendin* ranks highest among all of Sipsòng Panna.

Once this preliminary ritual in Wat Pajie was complete, the objects making up Chao Mom's *khwan* were taken to Moeng Ham, a densely populated valley area around 40 kilometers to the southeast of Jinghong City, by a group of around a dozen people. The members of the group carried different offerings, a *phasat* or commemorative stupa, and portraits of the deceased ruler. In the past, the trip was made on foot while the *khwan* of the *chao phaendin* was carried on a horse. On this occasion, the first such ceremony since the 1940s, a paper horse was instead used, and the whole party traveled between Jinghong and Moeng Ham sitting comfortably in minivans.

Fig. 3. The group leaving Wat Pajie for Moeng Ham with the *khwan* of Chao Mom Kham Lue, the paper horse, and the *phasat* bearing a portrait of the deceased, October 2017.

Apart from one of Chao Mom's sons, the members of this group came from a single village in Moeng Ham, Ban Dap-Ban Tao.[40] According to tradition, only villagers from this particular community are allowed to publicly mourn the deceased *chao phaendin*; only after these villagers have finished their mourning can members of the ruler's family take their turn. As it was, these same villagers who were historically in charge of arranging the cremation of the *chao phaendin*'s corpse, a group from Ban Dap-Ban Tao traveled to Kunming in October 2017 in order to be present at Chao Mom's cremation.

The destination of the party traveling from Jinghong was the village of Ban Suon Kham,[41] another village in Moeng Ham intimately connected to the royal dynasty, where a large group of locals, including dancers and musicians, awaited their arrival. Once the two groups came together, the procession continued on foot from the village to a bounded area in a nearby forest, known in Tai Lü as *dong kham ten kham*.

In another ceremony, the *khwan* of Chao Mom Kham Lü was ceremonially deposited in a small, roofed building within this area. Inside this structure, *ho ma* in Tai, dwell the souls of some of the former *chao phaendin*—in total, the *khwan* of twenty-two out of the forty-four recorded rulers. Here they are worshipped every year as a way of securing the fertility of the land and their inhabitants. In the ritual, which takes place on the third day of the waxing moon of the third month in the Tai Lü calendar (usually in December), twenty-two male villagers of Ban Dap-Ban Tao prepare food for each of the twenty-two *chao moeng*. The ceremony includes offerings and prayers at a nearby altar, again, led by the *pò mò*.

From this day on, the spirit of Chao Mom Kham Lü joined those of his ancestors, and together with them he will be worshipped and fed as a *chao moeng*, a tutelary spirit of *moeng* Sipsòng Panna.

Conclusion

After centuries of practically autonomous existence at the interstices of the Chinese and Burmese empires, in the 1950s the regime of the Sipsòng Panna *chao* came to an end. Since then, the new power in the region, the Party-state of the People's Republic of China, strived to replace the *chao* as the main source of political allegiance for the local Tai Lü population. This involved, first, the eradication of the ideology that sustained the power of this local ruling class, achieved through the suppression of territorial spirit cults; second, the co-option of some of the *chao* into the new administration; and finally, a shift in the historical narrative, from one centered on the *chao* as symbols of Tai Lü identity to one fashioned in terms of the exploitation of the common people at the hands of the landed class, and their "liberation" by the Communist Party. Chao Mom Kham Lü was to be treated according to this new framework. After having been stripped of his previous position, he was made into a common citizen and "invited" to collaborate with the new regime. Chao Mom, the last *chao phaendin*, passed away on National Day 2017, far away from Sipsòng Panna and in a radically different world from the one he was born into.[42]

While the strategy of the Party-state has mostly succeeded in erasing the memory of *chao* rule and in integrating the Tai Lü into the "Chinese nation," the history of the *chao* might not be over. After all, hegemony is never complete. Ethnic difference persists in China despite (and partly thanks to) the problematic state-promoted recognition of ethnic identities. Mingled in inextricable and paradoxical ways with their being part of a *shaoshu minzu* or "ethnic minority" that reaches beyond the limits of Sipsòng Panna but remains within the limits of China's "imagined community,"[43] the Tai Lü stubbornly adhere to the markers of a transnational, pre-1950 identity, such as their language, Buddhist rituals, and spirit cults—even the pejorative stereotypes against non-Tai. The rituals concerning household and village spirits are still respected, and in spite of the social contradictions Tanabe identified in relation to the *moeng* spirit cults, which concealed the exploitation of the Tai peasantry on the part of the *chao*, and of the decades-long "ideological work" implemented by the Party-state, at least some Tai Lü in Sipsòng Panna continue to revere the *chao* as part of their sense of belonging to a certain place and a certain community. As long as rituals, such as the feeding and celebration of the deceased *chao moeng* continue, the power of the *chao phaendin*, even if latent, will go on.

Endnotes: Death of the Last King

1. The ethnonym "Tai Lü" (sometimes spelled "Lue") designates the Tai-speaking populations in Sipsòng Panna, numerically and politically dominant in the region before 1950. Since then, these populations have been included, together with other Tai-speaking groups living mainly in Yunnan Province but historically unrelated to the Lü, in the Dai *minzu* or *Daizu*, one of the 55 *shaoshu minzu* or "ethnic minorities" in the state-produced ethnic classification system of the People's Republic. The populations of Sipsòng Panna also include smaller communities of other Tai-speaking groups, such as Tai Ya and Tai Neua.

2. Liew-Herres et al. refer to the *chao phaendin* as "local ruler." See for example 2012, 38.

3. In this chapter I will often refer to Chao Mom Kham Lü simply as "Chao Mom". As this is an honorary title carried by other (male) members of the royal family of Sipsòng Panna, when referring to other individuals of that family using the same title their complete name will be specified.

4. Barker et al. (2014, 2–3) define a figure as "someone whom others recognize as standing out and who encourages reflexive contemplation about the world in which the figure lives."

5. A cognate of the term *muang* or *müang*.

6. On the pre-1950 socioeconomic system in Sipsòng Panna, see especially Tanabe 1988, 6–8 and Liew-Herres et al. 2012, 18–33; also McCarthy 2009, 55. Chinese researchers identified the regime of Sipsòng Panna at the time of "liberation" as "feudal manorialism" (Ch.: *fengjian lingzhu zhuyi*); see McCarthy 2009, 53. Tanabe, based on Chinese sources, describes these relations as exploitative, as "a considerable burden of corvée fell on those households which received an allotment [of land]" (1988, 7). McCarthy, however, downplays the significance of social inequality and of the burden placed upon peasants (2009, 55, 58).

7. According to a local informant, up to 26 different, lesser *moeng* were part of *moeng* Sipsòng Panna in the past. See also Liew-Herres et al. 2012, 28–31.

8. Chiang Rung in Thai, the current administrative capital of Xishuangbanna Prefecture.

9. Liew-Herres et al. (2012, 5–72) is by far the best English-language resource covering the pre-twentieth century political and social history of Sipsòng Panna. Whether and to which extent Sipsòng Panna was "a centralized state" is also subject to debate, at least among scholars outside of China. See Hsieh 1995, 303.

10. More specifically, the formal designation of the local ruler within the empire's administration was *xuanwei shi* (an abbreviation of the full title) or "pacification commissioner." On the name "Cheli," see Liew-Herres et al. 2012, 5. Sipsòng Panna became a "pacification commission" or *xuanwei si* under the Ming dynasty, at the end of the fourteenth century (Liew-Herres et al. 2012, 38–39).

11. A vivid example of this task is provided by the journal of British envoy Captain McLeod, who visited Sipsòng Panna in the late 1830s and left a detailed account of court life and politics at the time. See Grabowsky and Turton (2003). On the *tusi* system, see Liew-Herres et al. 2012, 31–36.

12. See also Liew-Herres et al.: "In the eyes of the imperial court of China the chieftains were just 'aboriginal officials;' in the eyes of the tribal [*sic*] peoples they were, in the case of the Tai, the *cao* [*chao*] *fa* (lord of heaven)" (2012, 36).

13. I am indulging here in an anachronism, as it is impossible to know how these peoples, the forerunners of the present-day Tai Lü, called themselves. On the risks of applying current ethnic categories to the distant past, a common practice in Chinese historiography until today, see Churchman (2016, 13).

14. But see Giersch (2006) on the vibrant cultural and social diversity of the frontier under imperial rule. According to Liew-Herres et al. (2012, 67–69), the first direct intervention of Chinese officials in internal affairs of the Jinghong court was in 1729, concerning the collection of taxes on tea production. It was only during the last years of the empire and its immediate aftermath that the Chinese presence in Sipsòng Panna became significant, following a clash between local *chao* in whose outcome Chinese troops, as was traditionally the case, would play a key role.

15. The dominant force in mainland China during most of this period was the *Guomindang* or *Kuomintang*, the Nationalist Party founded by Sun Yat-sen and Song Yaoren immediately after the overthrow of the empire in 1911.

16. According to Hansen (1999, 93), the first Chinese schools were established in Sipsòng Panna by the Nationalist government in 1911. These institutions, like their predecessors, the Confucian schools set up during the empire, were mostly attended by members of the *chao* class, in general the only ones among the Tai population who became fluent in Chinese language and writing (see also Liew-Herres et al. 2012, 36).

17. Chao Mom In Moeng and Chao Mom Mahacai (Liew-Herres et al. 2012, 71).

18. "By 1950, when Sipsòng Panna was declared 'liberated', many Tai had fled to Thailand and Burma, where some took refuge with leading Chinese Nationalists" (Hansen 1999, 92–93). After staying in the Shan State for a time, many of these high-standing refugees would move to Thailand, where they and their descendants have resided until today.

19. According to historian Gao Lishi, who sets that final point in 1956, the year of agrarian reform and therefore the end of feudal property of the land, the dynasty had reigned for a total of 786 years. See Liew-Herres et al. 2012, 307 fn 342.

20. The person responsible for the project of creating and reforming minority scripts at the national level was Fu Maoji. Hsieh himself "asked Dao [Shixun] why he agreed to reform the Dai writing [sic]. He said, 'Because Fu was my former teacher. Also we were carrying out the order from the central government'" (Hsieh 1989, 244). On the cultural politics behind the use of the "old" and the "new" Tai scripts (in Chinese, lai daiwen and xin daiwen), see Casas 2022.

21. "[I]n 1987, after the new writing system had been in use for 32 years, the People's Congress of Xishuangbanna passed a resolution to decide [sic] to resume the old style of Dai character. Zheng Peng, one of the vice-chairmen of the Xishuangbanna Branch of the CPPCC, told me that, 'Dao Shixun argued in favour of resuming use of the old style. It is only because he was Chao Phaendin, that people follow what he asks.'" Pointing to the significance of this decision, Hsieh remarks that "to reuse the old Dai character [sic], in my interpretation, symbolizes a resurgence of traditional Dai identity" (Hsieh 1989, 44–45). See also Casas 2022.

22. Chao Mom had four children, two sons and two daughters.

23. The moeng maintains its relevance at least in terms of local toponymy, as Chinese authorities kept the term when translating place-names in Sipsòng Panna into Chinese through the use of the Chinese character meng. In connection with this, most Tai Lü in Sipsòng Panna still identify in terms of the moeng they belong to.

24. On this research and the state project of "ethnic identification" (Ch.: minzu shibie), see Mullaney 2011. The results of the work conducted in Sipsòng Panna were later published in series, such as the early 1980s multivolume A Research on the Social History of the Dai People: Sipsong Panna (Daizu shehui lishi diaocha: Xishuangbanna).

25. Scholars concerned with the practices and cosmologies related to the tutelary spirits of the land in moeng domains have stressed the fundamental role played by the ruling chao as intermediaries between land spirits and peasant populations (Tanabe 1988, 2000; Trankell 1999). The relation between tutelary spirits and those associated to the spirits of the land, embodied by the lak moeng or "pillar of the moeng," is quite complex. Sometimes they are conflated, sometimes not. For instance, in Sipsòng Panna some places possess a lak moeng, which is the object of regular cults, but worship other tutelary cults related to the moeng or the village separately. See Tanabe (2000).

26. On ancestor cults in Southeast Asia and among Tai-speaking peoples, see Tannenbaum and Kammerer (2003).

27. In the past, those rituals concerning the tutelary spirits of the land across Tai domains in mainland Southeast Asia often involved the participation of representatives of the so-called "autochthonous" populations (usually populations speaking Mon-Khmer languages). Different specialists see this as a recognition of such peoples as previous rulers of the land by the Tai (Condominas 1990; Tanabe 2000; Trankell 1999).

28. As acknowledgement of the previous dominance of the Tai Lü, the Xishuangbanna Autonomous Prefecture was explicitly linked to this group (the Daizu), at the expense of the Hani, Lahu, Bulang, and all other groups in the area (Hansen 1999, 93).

29. According to McCarthy, "[w]hole sections of the Dai aristocracy were absorbed into the local Party-state apparatus" (2009, 53). See also Hansen (1999, 93).

30. The foremost example of this policy of collaboration with the local chao is that of Zhao Cunxin or Chao Tsengha, a member of the Tai government in Jinghong, who showed his support for the Communists long before the end of the civil war and became the first head of the Xishuangbanna Autonomous Prefecture, a position he would hold for forty years (McCarthy 2009, 53–54; Hansen 1999, 92). Nevertheless, even Zhao Cunxin could not escape "criticism" at the height of Maoist political paroxysm, and during the Cultural Revolution he too was sent to a village along with other former members of the Tai nobility.

31. Of course, the Communist Party "liberated" not only the non-Han ethnic minorities of China from oppression but also the Han "uneducated masses" of the country (see Harrell 1995, 26–27).

32. This has not prevented Chinese media reporting Chao Mom's death from referring to him as *daiwang*, or "king of the Tai." The new context and the fact that it was almost seventy years after his stepping down of the position, allowed for this linguistic liberty (from the perspective of the Party-state). Sipsòng Panna was indeed a territory under the suzerainty of the Chinese empire, but this should be qualified and understood within the framework of the *tusi* system. Besides, conceptions of suzerainty were different then, as proven by the fact that the rulers in Jinghong (as those of other *moeng* in the area) paid allegiance to several sovereigns simultaneously. The "Chinese Nation" is a contemporary notion that emerged in the final period of the empire, and therefore applying it to the past is an anachronism.

33. Members and descendants of the ruling class can be recognized by the surnames "Dao" and "Zhao" in their Chinese names. Tai Lü commoners carry no surname.

34. "Sangha" is the Pali and Sanskrit term commonly used to refer to the community of monastics living in temples and sustained by the laity in Buddhist societies, although sometimes it is used in a broader sense which includes the laity.

35. Sometimes spelled "Pajay" or "Pache."

36. As the most important monastery in the region and the seat of the Sipsòng Panna Buddhist Association, Wat Pajie has symbolized the local recovery of Buddhist practice after the re-establishment of the policies regulating religious activities at all administrative levels in the late 1970s (see Casas 2008).

37. The activities held at Wat Pajie, the same as any others belonging in the official category of "religion" (Ch. *zongjiao*) held in the region, fall under the jurisdiction of the local Bureau for Ethnic and Religious Affairs, which has to approve applications submitted through the respective religious associations, in this case through the Sipsòng Panna Buddhist Association (Ch. *Xishuangbanna fojiao xiehui*).

38. This dichotomy is always problematic as village monks often participate in apotropaic rituals targeting accidents, illnesses, etc. involving *phi*. Spirit worship is known among the Tai Lü (and other Tai groups) as *ling phi*. The term *ling* means "feeding" or "nurturing." On the issue of the abundance of non-Buddhist elements in the daily practice of Buddhist specialists in Thailand, see the seminal work by Terwiel ([1975] 2012).

39. *Po* means "father" in Tai Lü, while the word *mo* designates a specialist in ritual or medical practices (the two might be hard to differentiate), as in the Tai Lue term for "doctor," *mo ya* (*ya* is the word for "medicine"). Female spirit specialists are therefore known as *mae* ("mother") *mo*.

40. As this village (Tai *ban*) resulted from the merging of two previously separated settlements, it retains a double name.

41. In Tai Lü language, Suon Kham means "golden gardens," referring to an appropriately paradise-like residence for the *chao* in their afterlife.

42. Some Tai Lü pointed out to me the fact that even when the actual passing may have taken place on the previous day, the authorities conveniently placed Chao Mom's death on October 1, anniversary of the founding of the People's Republic and its National Day.

43. A notion first coined by Benedict Anderson in his seminal work *Imagined Communities* (1983).

References

Anderson, Benedict. 1983. *Imagined Communities: Reflections on the Origin and Spread of Nationalism*. London and New York: Verso.

Barker, Joshua, Erik Harms, and Johan Lindquist. 2014. "Introduction." In *Figures of Southeast Asian Modernity*, eds. Joshua Barker, Erik Harms, and Johan Lindquist, 1–17. Honolulu: University of Hawai'i Press.

Casas, Roger. 2008. "Theravada Buddhism in Contemporary Xishuangbanna." In *Challenging the Limits: Indigenous Peoples of the Mekong Region*, eds. Prasit Leepreecha, Don McCaskill, and Kwanchewan Buadaeng, 289–305. Chiang Mai: Mekong Press.

————. 2022. "Intangible Enclosures and Virtual Scripts: The Cultural Politics of the Tham Script in Sipsòng Panna." In *Manuscript Cultures and Epigraphy in the Tai World*, ed. Volker Grabowsky, 383–406. Chiang Mai: Silkworm Books.

Churchman, Catherine. 2016. *The People between the Rivers: The Rise and Fall of a Bronze Drum Culture, 200–750 CE*. Lanham, MD: Rowman & Littlefield.

Condominas, George. 1990. *From Lawa to Mon, from Saa' to Thai: Historical and Anthropological Aspects of Southeast Asian Social Spaces*. Canberra: Australian National University.

Giersch, Charles Patterson. 2006. *Asian Borderlands: The Transformation of Qing China's Yunnan Frontier.* Cambridge, MA: Harvard University Press.

Grabowsky, Volker, and Andrew Turton, eds. 2003. *The Gold and Silver Road of Trade and Friendship: The McLeod and Richardson Diplomatic Missions to Tai States in 1837.* Chiang Mai: Silkworm Books.

Hansen, Mette Halskov. 1999. *Lessons in Being Chinese: Minority Education and Ethnic Identity in Southwest China.* Seattle: University of Washington Press.

Harrell, Stevan. 1995. "Introduction: Civilizing Projects and the Reaction to Them." In *Cultural Encounters on China's Ethnic Frontiers,* ed. Stevan Harrell, 3–36. Seattle: University of Washington Press.

Hsieh Shih-Chung. 1989. "Ethnic-Political Adaptation and Ethnic Change of the Sipsòng Panna Dai: An Ethnohistorical Analysis." PhD diss., University of Washington, Seattle.

—————. 1995. "On the Dynamics of Dai/Tai Lü Ethnicity: An Ethnohistorical Analysis." In *Cultural Encounters on China's Ethnic Frontiers,* ed. Stevan Harrell, 301–28. Seattle: University of Washington Press.

Keyes, Charles F., and Shigeharu Tanabe, eds. 2002. "Introduction." In *Cultural Crisis and Social Memory: Modernity and Identity in Thailand and Laos,* eds. Charles F. Keyes and Shigeharu Tanabe, 1–39. London: Routledge.

Liew-Herres, Foon Ming, Volker Grabowsky, and Renoo Wichasin, eds. 2012. *Chronicle of Sipsòng Panna: History and Society of a Tai Lü Kingdom, Twelfth to Twentieth Century.* Chiang Mai: Mekong Press.

McCarthy, Susan. 2009. *Communist Multiculturalism: Ethnic Revival in Southwest China.* Seattle: University of Washington Press.

Mullaney, Thomas. 2011. *Coming to Terms with the Nation: Ethnic Classification in Modern China.* Berkeley: University of California Press.

Tanabe, Shigeharu. 1988. "Spirits and Ideological Discourse: The Tai Lü Guardian Cults in Yunnan." *SOJOURN: Journal of Social Issues in Southeast Asia* 3(1): 1–25.

—————. 2000. "Autochthony and the Inthakhin Cult of Chiang Mai." In *Civility and Savagery: Social Identity in Tai States,* ed. Andrew Turton, 294–318. Richmond: Curzon Press.

Tannenbaum, Nicola, and Cornelia Ann Kammerer, eds. 2003. *Founders' Cults in Southeast Asia: Ancestors, Polity, and Identity.* Yale Southeast Asia Studies 52. New Haven: Yale University Press.

Terwiel, Barend Jan. [1975] 2012. *Monks and Magic: Revisiting a Classic Study of Religious Ceremonies in Thailand.* Copenhagen: NIAS Press.

Trankell, Ing-Britt. 1999. "Royal Relics: Ritual and Social Memory in Luang Prabang." In *Laos: Culture and Society,* ed. Grant Evans, 191–213. Chiang Mai: Silkworm Books.

Turton, Andrew. 2000. "Introduction." In *Civility and Savagery: Social Identity in Tai States,* ed. Andrew Turton, 2–30. Richmond: Curzon Press.

VIOLENCE

Anticriminality and Democracy in Southeast Asia

ERRON C. MEDINA AND BIANCA YSABELLE FRANCO

When former president Rodrigo Duterte won via a landslide in the 2016 elections, he launched a bloody war on drugs with a promise that drug suspects and other criminals would be executed. His successor, Ferdinand "Bongbong" Marcos, Jr., who garnered more than 31 million votes in the 2022 elections, has also mentioned that he will continue the campaign and has remained mum about human rights violations during Duterte's term (Patag 2021). It is also important to note that Marcos Jr. is the son and namesake of the late dictator whose twenty-year rule in the country was marked by massive corruption and human rights violations, which have been well-documented. Marcos Jr. has refused to apologize or even acknowledge the atrocities committed during Marcos Sr.'s martial law (CNN Philippines 2021b). Further, Marcos Jr.'s running mate and now vice-president, Sara Duterte, is the former president's daughter who was urged to run by her father's supporters in order to continue the Duterte legacy.

Rodrigo Duterte's legacy campaign, the war on drugs, has claimed 6,235 lives as of February 28, 2022, according to the Philippine Drug Enforcement Agency (PDEA 2022). However, human rights groups estimate that there are around 30,000 casualties, including executions by unidentified perpetrators linked to the police (Lalu, 2021; Robertson, 2020). These killings have been classified as extrajudicial killings (EJKs), which are defined as slayings perpetrated or encouraged by government officials without due process. EJKs also include executions by groups, which are encouraged by the government (Sommer and Asal, 2019). Observers of Southeast Asian politics claim that so-called draconian measures against criminality are not unique to the Philippines but might be a pattern across Southeast Asia (Lasco 2016; Sombatpoonsiri and Arugay 2016). Thailand's former prime minister Thaksin Shinawatra implemented a war on drugs in 2003 similar to Duterte's, resulting in 2,500 casualties. Thaksin, like the former Philippine president, also enjoyed sustained popularity throughout his leadership. Indonesian President Jokowi Widodo is reportedly following in Duterte's footsteps by enforcing a shoot-to-kill directive against illegal drug personalities (Reuters 2017b). In Cambodia, the drug users are illegally arrested and detained (Human Rights Watch 2010; Global Commission on Drug Policy 2017). While despotic detention began a decade ago, Cambodian prime minister Hun Sen declared a crackdown on illegal drugs in 2017 that prompted thousands of arrests (Reuters 2017a).

Capital punishment is also standard across Southeast Asia. The Philippines was the first Asian country to abolish the death penalty in 1987. It was then reimposed in 1993 by Fidel Ramos and abolished again in 2006 by Gloria Macapagal-Arroyo. The reinstatement of capital punishment in the Philippines was a central issue during Duterte's term. The former president is a staunch advocate of the death penalty and even publicly urged legislators to favor it in his fourth State of the Nation Address (Ranada 2019). In Vietnam, deaths through capital punishment have been reported since 2013 (Killalea 2017). Between 2013 and 2016, it has been reported that 429 people have been executed in Vietnam (ibid.). In 2018, Thailand executed a death row inmate for the first time since 2009 (Amnesty International 2018).

Meanwhile, Indonesia has consistently been in the headlines for administering the death penalty, particularly against foreign nationals (Anya 2019). In 2016 Mary Jane Veloso, a Filipino domestic worker, got caught up in the war on drugs when she was sentenced to death in Indonesia for allegedly smuggling drugs into the country (Holmes 2016). Veloso insists she was duped by her recruiters who wanted to use her as a drug mule (Rappler 2015). She has since been spared the death penalty upon public outcry both in the Philippines and Indonesia but has been detained for more than twelve years. Veloso's case is still ongoing, and her recruiters are currently being prosecuted by the Philippine government (Rappler 2022).

These punitive policies have resulted in the arbitrary loss of lives and prolonged suffering for the underprivileged sectors of the population. Such harsh measures are seemingly begging for a response from human rights advocates and opposition personalities, yet any reaction is bound to provoke retaliation from disciplinary governments. In 2017 Senator Leila de Lima was arrested for trumped-up drug charges, including extorting money from New Bilibid Prison inmates to fund her senatorial campaign (Buan 2017). De Lima is a known critic of the Duterte administration who led the Senate investigation on Duterte's war on drugs. While in detention, De Lima sought reelection in the 2022 elections but failed to garner a seat in the senate. In 2022 her supporters are urging her release after key witnesses have retracted their statements against her (Al Jazeera 2022). Since De Lima's arrest, other personalities, and even government offices, have been subjected to political attacks. For example, the Commission on Human Rights, an independent constitutional body, has been critical of the violations of the Philippine National Police in implementing the campaign against illegal drugs (Gavilan 2017). In 2018, the House of Representatives, where Duterte's political party has a "supermajority," threatened to give the Commission a budget of only P 1,000 (US$20). Perhaps more infamously, the Duterte government has been trying to take down independent media. The crackdown against critical media includes the online outlet Rappler. Rappler is known for its critical reports against the Duterte administration, particularly regarding the government's "troll army" and the extrajudicial killings in the war on drugs since 2017. Rappler's CEO and Nobel Prize laureate Maria Ressa has been repeatedly arrested for trumped-up charges, including cyber libel and alleged tax offenses (Gunia 2019; Stevenson 2019). Further, right before Duterte's term ended in 2022, the Philippine Securities and Exchange Commission ordered Rappler's shutdown, revoking its license to operate because of alleged foreign ownership (Wang and Regan 2022). On May 5, 2020, while the country was battling the COVID-19 pandemic, ABS-CBN, the Philippines' largest media network, was shut down for the first time since 1972 when then-dictator Ferdinand Marcos declared martial law. In 2017 President Duterte accused the network of "swindling" and multiple times threatened to block the renewal of their legislative franchise (ABS-CBN News 2020). Nowadays, with Marcos Jr. as president and Duterte's daughter Sara as vice, the crackdown against critical media is expected to continue. During their campaign, the Marcos-Duterte tandem did not attend any of the public debates scheduled by media outlets and the Commission on Elections. They also granted very few interviews and denied access to media personalities critical of them (Demegillo 2022).

Thaksin Shinawatra's war on drugs received criticism from across the globe. The *New York Times* reported that he imposed a "war on media" with severe censorship of media practitioners (Cumming-Bruce 2005). Thailand's war on drugs was also the subject of a Human Rights Watch report (2004). The report divulged details of extrajudicial killings and the so-called "blacklisting" of drug suspects (eerily similar to Duterte's drug "watchlist"). The report also described the government's delaying tactics concerning the investigation on the human rights violations. In contrast, Hun Sen's crackdown on illegal drugs has not received the same amount of scrutiny, unlike Duterte's and Thaksin's. In Cambodia, drug war is enforced with unjustified mass arrests, with detainees cramped in overcrowded and inhumane cells (Salvá 2017). The crackdown was reportedly implemented right after Hun Sen and Duterte's meeting in 2017. Amnesty International reported that the Cambodian government dissolved the Cambodia National Rescue Party, an opposition party that promoted strengthening human rights and Cambodian democracy. Subsequently, the party's leader, Kem Sokha, was arrested on bogus charges.

This chapter will analyze how anticriminality policies are shared among Southeast Asian nations. Why are draconian measures common across Southeast Asia as an approach to criminality? We emphasize that there is a pattern of punitive measures across Southeast Asia, and this includes the responses of human rights advocates and opposition parties. While this does not set the Philippines apart, it will be our case study and our point of comparison with other countries. The following questions will frame the chapter: (1) How are punitive anticriminality policies shared across Southeast Asia? and (2) What social and institutional factors make this anticriminality rhetoric comparable across Southeast Asian "democracies"? The following sections will elaborate on the relationship of anti-criminality campaigns and their challenges to developing democracies in the region.

Democracy in Southeast Asia

The gravity of punitive measures in addressing criminality and order in Southeast Asian states lies primarily in how democracy is instituted and practiced in the region. Despite differences in cultural heritage and forms of government, democracies in Southeast Asia demonstrate a lot of convergence in their regime structures, ranging from "electoral authoritarianism" to "low-quality democracy" (Case 2009, 91). Two important factors explain these political arrangements. First, there are traditional cultural outlooks rooted in ethnic and social stratification that hold firm ground. These traditional outlooks, which reduce prospects for participation and contestation, contribute to "authoritarian contours" in Southeast Asian politics (ibid., 95). Second, the "persistence" of this authoritarian inclination is very much affected by leadership factors and patronage. These are made possible by state institutions that are molded according to the leader's capriciousness (ibid., 98). Indeed, prospects for democracy, while not completely absent, as shown by civil society mobilizations, are still endangered because of the failure of government institutions to check abuse of power and provide material progress. Moreover, the elites and the military still command these regime structures, which enjoy reserved powers despite democratic constitutions. Thus, these systems directly set the path for authoritarian measures in the economic sphere and in domestic peace, order, and crime reduction.

Given these characteristics, Southeast Asian democracies are far from consolidation. These "developing" democracies struggle not only with producing economic growth but also delivering political goods. Securing order and peace for the public is one of the crucial dimensions of this political performance (Diamond 1999, 89). Criminality is one of the top concerns in developing democracies. It may endanger support for democracy, especially in poorer and developing countries (ibid.). This happens for three reasons. First, weak state capacity may magnify the strength of the issue of criminality and criminal groups. State capacity is said to be weak when police corruption is widespread and dispensing justice is too slow. Doubt about the deepening of democracy spreads because of perceived heightened criminality. The slowness or failure to deliver public goods, such as security, tends to be the weak spot of unconsolidated democracies. Second, pervasive and violent crimes can threaten economic activities by undermining trust and discouraging smooth transactions. In this case, even the appearance of rising criminality can portray a country as unwelcoming of direct investments. This then affects a democracy's capacity to raise revenues and fund social services. Finally, criminality, if not controlled, can damage not only public security but respect for the law, undermining the credibility of the state as protector and source of order. State agents, with their desire to manage criminality, may rely on extrajudicial means of hunting suspects, which most often take the form of vigilante killings.

In the above view, fighting criminality seems to be at odds with strengthening democratic institutions and human rights. The issue is not new. In the late 1990s, Singapore, Malaysia, and Indonesia were known voices of democracy with "Asian values," a position that rejects the aggressive promotion in the region of the human rights and freedom of the West (Mauzy 1997). These societies also emphasize the value of "consensus and cooperation rather than confrontation and conditionality" in promoting human rights in the region (ibid., 221). The notion of shared essential Asian values is far from reality given the cultural diversity in the region. However, there are some significant cultural values that manifest themselves in many Asian societies, including moderation, duties and responsibilities, emphasis on community and family orientation, respect for authority, and "a belief in punishment as a deterrent to and retribution for crimes" (ibid., 216; Fukuyama 1995). Since Southeast Asian states generally prefer to achieve growth through strong and controlling governments, the antigovernment protests in the name of democratic mobilization in the United States was worrisome (Mauzy 1997). This has been a hotly debated topic. With the alarming cases of punitive punishments in addressing criminality, this seeming conflict in values is certain to resurface in justifying such measures in Southeast Asia (Huntington 1993).

These key demands—peace and order and crime reduction—from Southeast Asian democracies seem to be at odds with liberal goals limiting political power and protecting individual human rights. Since addressing these issues is undeniably important, it is easy to understand why anticriminality constitutes political discourses for order, stability, and discipline in the region.

Anticriminality in Southeast Asia

In 2018, the former Indonesian police chief Tito Karnavian awarded the "Bintang Bhayangkara Utama" (Medal of Honor) to former Philippine national police chief Ronald "Bato" Dela Rosa for giving them "inspiration" in the fight against illegal drugs in Indonesia (Cahiles 2018). The award was presented in a solemn ceremony in Jakarta. It was the first time a non-Indonesian citizen had received the medal. The Human Rights Watch criticized the event, but it points to something important. Even in its bloody and violent form, addressing illegal drugs and criminality is a shared vision, at least between Indonesia and the Philippines. Many observers state that the Indonesian government might be imitating the Duterte-style drug war to boost its existing antidrug and anticriminality campaigns (Bevins 2017; Kine 2017). The forty-nine drug-related police shootings in Indonesia in early 2017 compared to twenty-four killings from 2015 to 2016 is a testament to this (McRae 2017). The sustained support for Duterte's war on drugs (Viray 2018) and the praise given to it by then-US president Donald Trump may have raised the popularity and acceptability of the campaign. The war on drugs remained Duterte's top social agenda throughout his term. In 2019 Dela Rosa, the former chief of police was elected senator for a six-year term with a platform that reinstates the death penalty (Senate of the Philippines 2020) and sustains the war on drugs (Talabong 2019).

Despite the violence and strong "genocidal" character of Duterte's drug war in the Philippines (Simangan 2018), the death penalty remains the ultimate anticrime policy in Southeast Asia. While not all Southeast Asian states implement capital punishment, it still takes lives in Indonesia, Singapore, and Malaysia, especially for drug-related crimes (International Federation for Human Rights 2016). Moreover, eight of the ten ASEAN member countries continue to impose the death penalty even though some have ratified the

International Covenant on Civil and Political Rights (ibid.). This is an apparent contradiction to their international obligations.

While the Covenant has reserved the death penalty for "most serious crimes," the implementation of capital punishment in Southeast Asia confronts issues that are too important to be overlooked. First, the vague definitions of "terrorism" influence human rights principles that protect people from death row. Second, secrecy or lack of transparency among governments blurs hope for accountability in prosecuting suspects. Third, trial rights and due process are at stake given accusations that executions, specifically in Indonesia, are based on admissions made under torture (ibid., 4). Finally, the growing number of crimes punishable by the death penalty is alarming. Currently, Indonesia imposes the death penalty for crimes such as "murder, terrorism-related offenses, gang-robbery, drug trafficking, drug possession, treason, and spying" (ibid., 8). Laos also maintains the same policies for similar offenses by claiming that death sentences "deter" the most severe crimes. Singapore takes a similar position on offenses related to illegal drugs. During the 32nd session of the United Nations Human Rights Council held between June and July 2016, Singapore claimed that "capital punishment is a legitimate exercise of state power" (ibid., 13). Such glaring scenarios show that the punitiveness of anticrime policies is still evident in the region. Why are these policies punitive? What accounts for this "shared and persistent" state aggressiveness in addressing crime? This section deals more seriously with the "punitive" character of anticriminality measures in Southeast Asia.

The illegal status of certain drugs and its connection with criminality, violence, and disorder needs to be examined (Roberts and Chen 2013). In this situation, a government is essential because of its capacity to sanction or criminalize specific behaviors. Unraveling the punitive character of antidrug campaigns and overall anticrime policies means looking at the policies and laws implemented by the state. Sociological analysis has contributed much to this topic. Drug policies work as "social and political construction based on factors like moral panics, misinformation, political and religious ideologies, or professional and organizational interests" rather than medically oriented policies (Stevens 2011; Roberts and Chen 2013). This discourse comes from the "association of drug use with … marginal and dangerous members of society," which significantly affects the way illegal drugs are criminalized. For example, in the Americas, African Americans and foreign migrants are known for illegal vices and petty crimes that mark their drug use as an extension of criminal behavior. But over time, as economic and social change take place, illegal drugs become more prevalent in other marginalized groups including the urban working class as they face harsh working conditions to survive in the cities (Lyttleton 2004; Lasco 2014). Thus, even in Southeast Asia, drug policy serves as a "basis of an inflexible morality politics" (Roberts and Chen 2013, 109). The question of morality then becomes a strong policy initiative on order and strong authority that endangers democratic opposition based on human rights and liberal values.

Given this context, it is not impossible to argue that countries such as the Philippines, Indonesia, and Cambodia resort to political and military measures which have been a common approach of Southeast Asian states to security and crime problems. The region faces a myriad of security challenges, such as terrorist networks, drug and human trafficking, and environmental issues. The expectation in the early 2000s was that ASEAN members would focus their security efforts on military capabilities and links with extraregional powers (Ward and Hackett 2003). But recent events show that strengthening the police and military also enhances these states' punitive capacity to enforce domestic policies.

Another factor contributing to this grim scenario are the illicit activities entangled with the character of some Southeast Asian countries considered "dirty money states" (Baker and Milne 2015). In this account, shadow economies are encouraged by Southeast Asian states to use "dirty money" for political benefits. In their study of six Southeast Asian countries' taxation practices, expenditure patterns, and legal-administrative capacity (all measures of fiscal power), they found that these states are fiscally weak. Moreover, there are other sources of revenue absent from these official data—illicit sources of wealth. Some examples are illicit revenue from Indonesia's timber, Vietnam's furniture, and the Philippines' gold. Southeast Asian nations also comprise six of the fifteen top exporters of illicit capital. Illegal trades in the region are worth billions of US dollars. Baker and Milne (2015) argue that this is because corruption and unlawfulness are historically embedded in Southeast Asia state formation. It also explains the prominence of strongman figures in the region. Criminal figures are planted in government agencies, and opposition figures are framed as the actual lawbreakers. In the same vein, it can be argued that it is not necessarily beneficial for states to eradicate illicit economies. The more practical approach is to utilize the threat of these illegal activities for political gain. Generally, these states do not sincerely oppose their respective illicit economies but rather cultivate them through "political accommodation, economic management, and institution building" (ibid., 156).

Anticriminality as a Political Discourse

In general, moral crusades against drugs and criminality have been effective platforms for political leaders in authoritarian and low-quality democratic regimes to establish legitimacy (Roberts and Chen 2013, 113). However, developing countries, characterized by weak law enforcement and susceptibility of police to corruption, may find it challenging to push for genuine and humane drug control policies. As these developing states grapple with the increasing complexity of social life and citizen demands, insecure leaders need to gain a strong foothold to establish control and continuing relevance. For example, a "populism of fear" enables politicians to draw on fear of criminals to garner votes (Chevigny 2003). Using fear of criminals as a campaign strategy politicizes criminality, which entails trimming procedural rights of suspects, criminals, and prisoners. The lack of state capacity and weak bureaucracy also leads to unreliable service delivery and administration. These weakened state functions thus become the source of dissatisfaction and discontent, especially in developing democracies. Such problems contribute to more disillusionment in the capability of democratic states to generate public goods like peace, security, economic development, and order.

Recent political events in Southeast Asia appear to exhibit the phenomenon of "voting against disorder" whereby political leaders run for office in the name *not* of law and order but for order *over* law (Pepinsky 2017, 120). The success of "order-first political strategies" in Southeast Asia can be traced to the belief that political order and economic development can only be achieved by annihilating all "disorderly elements" within the countries' respective territories (ibid., 121). This narrative revolves around the "anxiety and hope" of the public for change (Curato 2016). This position has a class dimension. Supporters of Duterte and other similar candidates in the region have come from the elites and the middle class. These classes invest a great deal in their campaigns and have a lot to lose from the social problems caused by disorderly elements (Teehankee and Thompson 2016). As the hunt for targeted groups allegedly causing "disorder" continues, politicians' aggressive policy approaches for security and order often lead to more punitive measures that may endanger human rights and democratic norms. These corrective measures are exacerbated through appeals to national security and nationalism, as can be seen in Indonesia (Aspinall 2015) and the rising challenge of populists in the region (Kenny 2019). To clarify this point, it is important to define what punitiveness means and the situations in the region where punitive policies are employed.

Punitive means "being tough on crime" (Enns 2014, 858). Recently, punitiveness has been an important overtone of social campaigns led by populists in addressing order. In societies with vulnerable democratic safeguards, anticriminality easily achieves popular support as people desire someone who will bring stability, even at the expense of procedural rights. Punitiveness also pertains to the tendency and willingness of elected officials to adopt harsher measures in punishing criminals and hunting down suspects. It also refers to the penalization of various activities that do not usually constitute a criminal act. What is alarming about increased punitiveness is that it criminalizes activities associated with the poor. In the Philippines, even though vagrancy was decriminalized in 2012, the new anti-*tambay* (idling or loitering) directive of former president Duterte in 2018 targeted the poor for simply being in public places for no obvious reason. The directive was justified as a crime-prevention mechanism that limited potential troublemakers (*Philippine Star* 2018). During the quarantine lockdown implemented in early 2020 because of the Covid-19 pandemic, the same directive was implemented to arrest violators of quarantine protocols. This seemed to be an overreach given that some studies had already provided a nuanced account on idling in the Philippines (Batan 2012). Other activities, such as legitimate protests, were also subject to police action.

More recently, Jolovan Wham, an activist in Singapore, was arrested for "holding up a smiley face sign in public" in violation of the law on "illegal public assembly" even though he was alone at the time (BBC News 2020). The absurdity of such an arrest gains media attention and questions the likelihood of democratic change in Singapore. In Indonesia, new nationalist sentiments fuel harsher death penalties for drug offenders. This is because brutal punishments are framed as an opportunity for Indonesian leaders to strengthen national dignity and identity, one that is not pressured by international norms and criticism from human rights groups (Aspinall 2015, 79). This increased punitiveness blurs the line between criminal acts and legitimate political protests or otherwise innocuous activities. To be punitive means to require more retribution than restoration for the offender or suspect. Punitiveness can also be a shared attitude across the population. It refers to how citizens rank criminality as their most important concern. This public sympathy was favorable for Duterte as he was able to catapult criminality and drugs to the top of Filipino concerns during the 2016 campaigns. Heightened attention toward criminality, however, depends on several attitudinal factors, including opinions regarding the rights of criminals and the kind (and degree) of punishment for them; support for capital punishment; support for more significant funding for crime and the criminal justice system, and confidence and trust in the criminal justice system (Enns 2014, 861).

It is concerning to witness how people see disorder and criminality as a significant cause of economic or political instability rather than the other way around. When criminality and legitimate protests are wrongly framed as synonymous because they are both associated with conflict, people are more willing to listen to candidates who appeal for moral crusades that criminalize "disorderly behavior," even if this is vaguely defined. More importantly, the low quality of social services that breeds poverty and conflict in the lower ranks of society contributes to this worsening condition. More surprising is how these punitive approaches come to be shared by Southeast Asian states irrespective of their differences in national income, language, and culture. Some lessons from other contexts seem to fall on deaf ears. Given the prohibitionist and punitive character of antidrug campaigns in Latin and North America, many unintended consequences occur. These include a rise in criminality since old drugs are just being replaced by new drugs; the prioritization of law enforcement rather than public health in budget resources; the shift of illegal drugs supply from one country to another; and the increased stigma surrounding drug use (Roberts and Chen 2013, 119). These effects can be mirrored in the Southeast Asian experience.

Putting a Face on Punitiveness: The Case of Duterte's War on Drugs

In the Philippines, the consequences of Duterte's punitive approach to crime have been widely documented by local and international media and human rights organizations. We were able to document some of these consequences. From 2017 to 2018, as part of a research grant awarded by the Australian National University and the Department of Foreign Affairs and Trade of Australia, we examined community responses to Duterte's bloody war on drugs that involve religious congregations (Cornelio and Medina 2019), urban poor hotspots, and detainees of drug-related cases. We observed an urban poor community in Metro Manila that had witnessed a spate of killings and sought to understand how the war created and disrupted formal and informal networks. We studied the various sectors that were affected by the war, namely the families left behind by the victims, local church leaders, arrested persons, and the police.

The most significant cost of this so-called war on drugs has been the loss of lives. Duterte launched his brutal campaign against illegal drugs in 2016, promising that drug suspects and other criminals would be killed. Since then, human rights advocates and media outlets estimate that as many as 30,000 people have been killed (Lalu 2021; Roberston 2020). Many of those slain were men from low-income communities working as garbage collectors, tricycle drivers, and construction workers (Atun et al. 2019). They were the apparent victims of the drug war. The other victims were the survivors who bear the brunt of the victims' deaths. These include widows, mothers, and children who struggle to survive while grieving the sudden and sometimes inexplicable deaths of their loved ones. Survivors also include those arrested for drug crimes who suffer at the hands of police officers who were ordered to show no mercy toward drug offenders.

We spoke to detainees in a city jail, most of whom denied the crimes they are accused of (i.e. selling crystal meth) but admit they were occasional drug users. Nevertheless, Simon's story is striking because of the torture he suffered at the hands of police officers. A 42-year-old carpenter, he was on his way home from work on a rainy day when police officers abducted him. For days he was tortured with electrical shocks and kept in a secluded room in the police station, with his family unaware of his whereabouts. The following is Simon's recount of the incident: "I was on my way home from work on a rainy day. I hurriedly got off the bus, running to the tricycle terminal when an SUV stopped in front of me and the passengers pointed a gun at me. They were in plain clothes so I did not think they were police officers. They proceeded to try to cuff me but I resisted. I hit one of them with my equipment bag, injuring him. The others retaliated and they beat me up on the sidewalk. When they were done, they loaded me onto their SUV."

Simon figured out they were the police when he was taken to the police station. He was being accused of theft. When the victims did not point to him as the perpetrator, the arresting officers continued to interrogate him. In Simon's words, "The police were furious with me because I wounded one of them. They tortured me for two days, electrocuting me and putting a plastic bag over my head to suffocate me. They wanted to kill me." Simon is serving jail time for possession of illegal drugs. His torturers finally set him free when his distraught wife caused a scene at the police station.

Women who lost their kin to the drug war may not have experienced the physical trauma that Simon did, but their experiences were just as horrifying. Clarita was sixty years old when she got home to the small compound she shares with her son to find him dead with his three other friends after a police raid. This is how Clarita tearfully recalled the events that day: "When I got home from church with one of my grandchildren, there were crowds of people in our neighborhood. There were ten police motorcycles outside our house. My youngest child shouted, 'Kuya is dead!' I wet my pants upon hearing those words. In my head I said, 'What do I do now? Who is going to look after my grandchildren? Who will look after us?' I went inside the house despite restraints to look for him since he was not one of the three corpses lined up outside. I went inside his bedroom to see him lying on the ground with one bullet hole on his head and another on his chest. I held him and said, 'Why would anyone do this to you?' He should have just been arrested if he did anything wrong. The police said I couldn't touch the body, but I ignored them. His body was still warm. I told my son, 'Why did this happen to you?'" Clarita said the police were looking for crystal meth. Her son's house was turned upside down, but no evidence of drug dealing was found. With the help of a local Catholic parish, Clarita, and the three other victims' families, filed charges against the police officers who killed their loved ones.

Unlike Clarita's case, many families did not get the opportunity to fight back against the perpetrators. We spoke to more than twenty women whose close male kin had been killed in either legitimate police operations, like Clarita's son, or by masked shooters. Whether they were killed for fighting back or shot by vigilantes, the suffering left behind was just the same. The Human Rights Watch produced a report in 2017 linking the police to the vigilante-style killings in the Philippines (Human Rights Watch 2017). For instance, Carla's longtime partner and father of her five children went to the market one morning and never returned. She searched for him at police community precincts and relatives' homes, to no avail. When she visited Camp Karingal as a last resort, she found his motorcycle in the parking lot. Officers told Carla at Camp Karingal that her husband had involved in a shootout with the police after a failed robbery. She was instructed to claim his body at a funeral home, where she found him almost unrecognizable. His body showed signs of torture—so damaged that only his tattoos could prove his identity. In her own words, this is how Carla found her partner: "The police told me he was involved in a robbery and when they were hunted down, it ended in a shootout with my partner and his supposed accomplice dead. My question is, where would he get a gun? And when we saw his body at the funeral parlor, I could barely identify him. His face was shattered. I only recognized him because he has my name and the names of our children tattooed on his body."

In Socorro's case, both her son and daughter-in-law were on the receiving end of impunity. Socorro is a woman in her eighties whose son was on the drug watch list of their *barangay* (village). He fled the *barangay* to keep his family safe, but the police jailed his pregnant wife instead. As a result, she had to give birth in jail. Socorro's son went home one morning for his daughter's birthday. The following day, police officers raided his house and shot him while he knelt on the ground begging for his life. The incident was identified as a case of *nanlaban* (the term used to identify suspects who were killed for fighting back). Socorro was on her way home from the convenience store when she was warned by her neighbors that "Duterte's squad" was at their doorstep. Socorro hurried home to find several men barging into their home. She was prevented from entering. This is how she remembers the moment her son was gunned down: "The person who killed my son was masked and wearing black. Through the windowsill of our home, I begged him, 'Sir, please don't kill my son! What did he do wrong?' He said, 'We won't kill your son as long as he doesn't fight back.' My son did not fight back but they still killed him!"

These stories are only a few of perhaps tens of thousands of lives suffering the consequences of the Philippine drug war. These would not have been possible without policies that encourage the violence and a leader that pardons the perpetrators. This approach to crime is rendered futile when compared to the piles of corpses that it has produced.

We also interviewed police officers implementing the war on drugs in communities considered "hotspots" for illegal drugs. Police officers associate crime with drug use. This exacerbates the stigma surrounding drug use and ignores the underlying causes, such as poverty and unemployment (Lasco 2014). For example, a police station commander described drug users as those with the guts to rape a woman. "Most of those charged for crimes are associated with illegal drugs. Those who rape and steal are drug users because they need drugs to lose their inhibitions," he argued. This statement echoes former president Duterte, who advocated for the lethal injection for crimes specified in the anti-illegal drugs law (Limpot 2020). On the other hand, retired police general Guillermo Eleazar, who was chief of police during Duterte's term, believes that people living in poverty use drugs because "when they take shabu, they feel they are important" (Gutierrez and Franco 2020, 234).

Concerning Carla's suspicious story of a gun found in her partner's possession and a report by the UN Human Rights Office, the police said that guns were easily accessed by those involved in illegal drugs (United Nations High Commissioner for Human Rights 2020). The same station commander mentioned above argued that "firearms worth 5,000–6,000 [are] very available in the black market," which drug peddlers may purchase from their earnings. The station commander insisted that "the PNP will not kill someone who did not fight back." However, it is important to point out that in several instances, members of the police have been charged for illegally using force. In 2018 three police officers were convicted of murdering Kian delos Santos, a seventeen-year-old boy. The police officers insisted that delos Santos had fought back, but security camera footage showed them dragging the boy to the spot where he was killed (Lalu 2018). In 2020 a viral video showed a police officer killing a mother and son point-blank because of a neighborhood squabble (CNN Philippines 2021a).

The Duterte administration espoused violence and harsh punishments for other issues too. In 2018 the president made a verbal directive that led to the arrest of around 3,000 loiterers (local term *tambay*) (Talabong 2018). This baseless mass arrest resulted in the death of a detainee in an overcrowded detention cell, which was probed by the Commission on Human Rights (Mateo 2018). And as mentioned above, in the context of the COVID-19 pandemic, the president also ordered police to gun down quarantine violators in an effort to curb the spread of the disease (Tomacruz 2020).

Explanation

The examples above demonstrate that Southeast Asian leaders share punitiveness in terms of their various anticrime policies. The Philippine war on drugs under Duterte exhibited this brutality, in which killings of drug-related persons became normalized and murder was transformed into an "enterprise" (Coronel 2016). Outside the Philippines, the same punitive measures and toughness on crime continue in Southeast Asian countries. This toughness on crime is usually carried out in the name of order and moral unity, a way to save societies from deterioration or destruction caused by alleged enemies like drugs, criminals, and even the foreign media. Sometimes this aggressiveness also points toward legitimate political groups who show opposition to the incumbent administration.

While a clear source for this alleged destruction is never fully identified, many people in such societies approve of the punitive style of their leaders. Singapore's intolerance of public protest, the Philippines' war on drugs and its antivagrancy directive and antiterror law, Cambodia and Indonesia's death penalty for illegal drug cases, Brunei's stoning punishment for members of the LGBT community (Magra 2019), are just some glaring state policies that endanger not only democratic potentials but also the diversity of identities in the region. These policies impede further development of civil liberties and freedoms. By punishing and criminalizing behaviors, these states prefer to address public issues through punitive and sometimes militaristic methods. While these policies are supported by the people, they also endanger their future capacity to hold their leaders accountable. Criminalizing behaviors also compromises peaceful conflicts that can contribute to the development of other policy agendas and alternatives. How are these punitive policies shared? We argue that constructed Asian identities and values play a significant part as cultural and political justifications to deviate from liberal and humanitarian standards in addressing crime and social concerns. This argument also resembles a broader "de-Westernization" pattern in which Southeast Asian countries critically oppose Western liberal orientation in the name of order, collectivism, and national identity. The weakness of liberal opposition groups (or lack thereof) within these countries also exacerbates the already predominant position of a punitive approach to criminality.

One way of understanding how punitiveness is shared is by looking at how Southeast Asian states "reference" each other when choosing policy initiatives. Here, we would like to borrow the concept of "inter-Asian referencing." It is a concept from media and cultural studies that pertains to the academic practice of refining and developing social science theories and concepts using the Asian context and cultures. This is not a complete rejection of Western contributions to theory-building and research practice but a way of avoiding the one-way application of such ideas in different geographical and cultural environments. Inter-Asian referencing acknowledges that while Western experiences and theories are helpful in knowledge production, "theory always requires a subtle spatio-temporal translation" in interpreting and explaining events in other social contexts (Iwabuchi 2014, 45). Thus, inter-Asian referencing is an effort "to advance innovative knowledge production through reciprocal learning from other Asian experiences" (ibid., 47). However, it is important to remember that inter-Asian referencing is not limited to purely academic interest. It also pertains to "people's mundane practice of encountering Asian neighbors and making reference to other Asian modernities" or contexts. Seeing and experiencing trans-local and region-bound practices may help produce regional identities and familiarity with each other. These practices constitute "identities, consciousness, and mentalities within [a] cultural geography" (Cho 2011, 393). Adopting this concept from cultural studies can be helpful. Nonetheless, we acknowledge the limits of the application of this concept in a sociopolitical context. Instead, we use it as a framing device in understanding how a punitive approach has become a shared phenomenon in Southeast Asian societies today.

In the Philippines, it is common to hear about the late Singaporean prime minister Lee Kuan Yew's iron-fist approach as a strategy for reforming the Philippines' political and economic predicaments. In fact, it is President Ferdinand "Bongbong" Marcos Jr., the namesake of the late dictator, who idealizes the Singaporean leader in his political campaigns or interviews, even though Lee Kuan Yew distanced himself from the older Marcos (de Jesus 2015).

This referencing to Yew has been a practical political discourse in campaigning for a stricter and more rigorous approach to governance, one that emphasizes strong governmental control over social affairs. This discourse also resonates with Overseas Filipino Workers located in neighboring countries. As these overseas workers witness effective governance without the liberal dimension of democratic politics in other countries, it becomes tempting to support such a governance style rather than the democratic practice prevailing in one's own country. This discourse also leads to unwarranted statements such as the cause of social ills in the Philippines is the result of too much democracy brought about by the February 1986 People Power Revolution, also known as the EDSA Revolution. Such a claim devalues the democratic movement that ousted the dictatorship in favor of a less democratic but controlled society.

The drug war in the Philippines also reflects a similar referencing phenomenon in Indonesia as President Jokowi Widodo appears to be adopting a Duterte-style war on drugs in his country. In 2017 local media in Indonesia quoted Widodo instructing police to shoot drug traffickers as Indonesia faces a "a narcotics emergency" (Hutton 2017), a familiar phrase of the former Philippine president. Furthermore, the number of deaths in Indonesia's antidrug campaign has increased since Jokowi announced a similar anticrime drive in the early years of Duterte's presidency. The referencing was also evident when the Indonesian police gave a police award to Ronald Dela Rosa, Duterte's former police chief. In this way, Duterte and Widodo share a similar strategy in addressing criminality and drugs. Rather than approaching illegal drugs as a public health issue, they prefer to increase police power and the criminalization of drug users and offenders. It would be interesting to know why these leaders deliberately choose police and military-centered strategies rather than other methods. Moreover, Indonesia shows no inclination to repeal its death penalty for capital punishment; the Philippine Congress is also deciding whether to revive the death penalty for heinous crimes. These agendas are raising many human rights concerns given the weakness of rule of law and corruption in these countries. More broadly, the violence and gravity of Duterte's war on drugs seems to have become the basis and point of comparison of antidrug campaigns in other Southeast Asian societies.

The gravity of police-led action against criminality is not the only measure of punitiveness. A more dangerous attack on democracy is the subtle and even outright criminalization of legitimate political activities. Some forms of political opposition and protest are gradually being criminalized in Southeast Asia. This toughness on political defiance attempts to silent critical opposition and other voices challenging the current regimes. In Singapore, the arrest of Jolovan

Wham is testimony to this political intolerance. The heightened tension between government forces and pro-democracy activists in Bangkok also displays Thailand's strong punitive stance. This show of force suppresses peaceful protests, including the banning and penalizing of "selfie photos" captured during pro-democracy movements, as it is believed that these social media posts can incite others to go against the Thai state (Phoonphongphiphat 2020). Violators of selfie rules can be apprehended and may face up to two years in prison.

What factors help cultivate a shared punitiveness in anticrime campaigns in Southeast Asia? The low quality of democracy and welfare provisions prevailing in the region is a significant factor. The lack of accountability of leaders and endemic corruption and "disorder" give impulse to the need for strong leadership. However, strong leadership without liberal democratic safeguards still needs to have legitimacy. One way these governments legitimize their rule is through performance. Thus, anticriminality is a perfect area to showcase performance through police and military action. One explanation looks at anticriminality campaigns as concerns of countries with weak welfare (Chevigny 2003). In such countries, cultivating fear among citizens is an important electoral tool to maintain political support and relevance. The ASEAN principles of noninterference and national sovereignty may also contribute to the sharing of similar punitive campaigns (ASEAN 2017). Since ASEAN as an organization cannot enforce liberal democratic norms at the regional level, states and their governments may not be called out if they commit bold human rights violations. The regional integration envisaged by ASEAN is thus far from being realized. Another factor is the increasing appeal of autocratic models, especially those of China and Russia, in weak democracies (Diamond 2019). The absence of a strong liberal democratic atmosphere in the region makes Southeast Asian societies vulnerable to autocratic influences. These authoritarian models will not pay attention to political suppression and worsening human rights violations. Without a critical check on human rights violations, prevailing undemocratic practices will only get worse.

Conclusion

The punitive approach in anticriminality campaigns in Southeast Asia is shared through heavy police and military involvement. The harsh approach toward crime not only involves severe punishment for activities related to drugs and other petty violations, but also includes many different activities and behavior that are penalizable and punishable through laws or local ordinances. This punitive strategy is boosted through an electoral narrative. To win votes and gain support, Southeast Asian leaders capitalize on building an internal enemy to strengthen their political base. When critical issues such as economic development, worsening inequality, poverty alleviation, or territorial integrity are difficult to address, it is easier for some leaders to use strong force in maintaining control to exhibit regime performance. More alarming in this situation is that political activities such as the exercise of protest are being criminalized by the state. Hence, some behaviors—criminal or political—are being watched by the state so that anyone who shows opposition can face exaction of penalties or immediate imprisonment.

Some social and institutional factors also allow anticriminality rhetoric to be comparable across the region. The perceived "conflict of values" in appreciating and protecting human rights is still being used by these punishing regimes to justify their tough stance against crime. The priority of discipline and order as a precondition for economic growth still resonates with the public. This discourse makes anticrime campaigns popular while still being dangerous and menacing for democratic change and good governance. What makes this issue important for the region, moreover, is how leaders show sympathy and admiration for punitiveness by referencing each other as justification or inspiration for toughness on crime and society at large. The weakness of liberal norms in the region and the increasing presence of autocratic alternatives might soon play a significant role in discrediting human rights and democratic accountability in the region. This demands critical reflection on the part of pro-democracy movements regarding their strategies and other sympathizers for reforms.

Finally, the gravity and seriousness of these anticriminality campaigns should not be reduced to mere numbers and journalistic reporting. The loss of lives is the price that is paid for a punitive approach to crime—an emerging phenomenon in key Southeast Asian countries such as the Philippines, Indonesia, and Thailand. Lives are lost while the survivors bear the brunt. Vulnerable populations across the region suffer the consequences of governments imposing harsh policies against criminality. But a punitive approach to crime is a necessary evil to attain political ambitions. A "strong" government is not an effective one in the case of Southeast Asia, at least not in terms of delivering proper services to its citizens. It is only effective in establishing fear and panic. Further, the regional neglect of human rights is a neglect of democracy because when voices are silenced, when protesters are arrested, and when innocent people are jailed, democracy erodes. Economies will not truly grow if the growth only benefits a few at the top. Thus, as long as punitiveness continues across the region, so will the decline of democracy and the quality of lives of the people.

References

ABS-CBN News. 2020. "TIMELINE: ABS-CBN Franchise Renewal." February 23. https://news.abs-cbn.com/news/02/23/20/timeline-abs-cbn-franchise-renewal.

Al Jazeera. 2022. "Leila de Lima release urged after witnesses retract testimony." May 4. https://www.aljazeera.com/news/2022/5/4/leila-de-lima-release-urged-after-witnesses-retract-testimony.

Amnesty International. 2018. "Thailand: Country's First Execution since 2009 a Deplorable Move." Amnesty.Org. June 19. https://www.amnesty.org/en/latest/news/2018/06/thailand-countrys-first-execution-since-2009-a-deplorable-move/.

Anya, Agnes. 2019. "15 Foreigners among 48 Handed Death Penalty in Indonesia Last Year: Amnesty." *Jakarta Post*, April 11. https://www.thejakartapost.com/seasia/2019/04/11/15-foreigners-among-48-handed-death-penalty-last-year-amnesty.html.

ASEAN. 2017. *The ASEAN Charter*. Jakarta: ASEAN Secretariat.

Aspinall, Edward. 2015. "The New Nationalism in Indonesia." *Asia & the Pacific Policy Studies* 3(1): 72–82.

Atun, Jenna Mae, Ronald Mendoza, Clarissa David, Radxeanel Peviluar Cossid, and Cheryll Ruth Soriano. 2019. "The Philippines' Antidrug Campaign: Spatial and Temporal Patterns of Killings Linked to Drugs." *International Journal of Drug Policy* 73: 100–111.

Baker, Jacqui, and Sarah Milne. 2015. "Dirty Money States: Illicit Economies and the State in Southeast Asia." *Critical Asian Studies* 47(2): 151–76.

Batan, Clarence. 2012. "A Conceptual Exploration of the Istambay Phenomenon in the Philippines." *Philippine Sociological Review* 60 (Special Issue): 101–30.

BBC News. 2020. "Singapore: Jolovan Wham Charged for Holding up a Smiley Face Sign." News. BBC News. November 27. https://www.bbc.com/news/world-asia-55068007.

Bevins, Vincent. 2017. "Indonesia Might Be Copying the Vigilante Violence of Duterte's Drug War." *The Washington Post*, August 4. https://www.washingtonpost.com/news/worldviews/wp/2017/08/04/indonesia-might-be-copying-the-vigilante-violence-of-dutertes-drug-war/.

Buan, Lim. 2017. "Senator Leila de Lima arrested." *Rappler*, February 24. https://www.rappler.com/nation/161278-leila-de-lima-surrender-drug-charges/.

Cahiles, Gerg. 2018. "Indonesian Police Chief: Bato Inspires Us." CNN Philippines. February 14. https://cnnphilippines.com/news/2018/02/14/PNP-Chief-Ronald-Bato-dela-Rosa-Indonesia-award.html.

Case, William. 2009. "The Evolution of Democratic Politics." In *Contemporary Southeast Asia*, edited by Mark Beeson, 2nd edn., 91–110. New York: Palgrave Macmillan.

Chevigny, Paul. 2003. "The Populism of Fear: Politics of Crime in the Americas." *Punishment & Society* 5(1): 77–96.

Cho Younghan. 2011. "Desperately Seeking East Asia amidst the Popularity of South Korean Pop Culture in Asia." *Cultural Studies* 25(3): 383–404.

CNN Philippines. 2021a. "Tarlac Courts Convicts Cop Nuezca for Murder of Mother and Son." August 26. https://www.cnnphilippines.com/news/2021/8/26/Jonel-Nuezca-Gregorio-murder-guilty-police.html?fbclid=IwAR3f65rg1257mVSLgRFL87XXrMatn1cdffdIxgnCu_ZLVkrJn2OuAn4A_ZU.

————. 2021b. "Bongbong Marcos not sorry for father's reign: 'I can only apologize for what I've done.'" October 7. https://www.cnnphilippines.com/news/2021/10/7/Marcos-not-sorry-father-dictator-martial-law-crimes-.html.

Cornelio, Jayeel, and Erron Medina. 2019. "Christianity and Duterte's War on Drugs in the Philippines." *Politics, Religion, & Ideology* 20(2): 151–69.

Coronel, Sheila. 2016. "Murder as Enterprise: Police Profiteering in Duterte's War on Drugs." In *A Duterte Reader: Critical Essays on Rodrigo Duterte's Early Presidency*, ed. Nicole Curato, 167–98. Quezon City, Philippines: Ateneo de Manila University Press.

Cumming-Bruce, Nick. 2005. "Thaksin Accused of 'dirty War' on Media." *New York Times*, June 25. https://www.nytimes.com/2005/06/25/world/asia/thaksin-accused-of-dirty-war-onmedia.html.

Curato, Nicole. 2016. "Politics of Anxiety, Politics of Hope: Penal Populism and Duterte's Rise to Power." *Journal of Current Southeast Asian Affairs* 35(3): 91–109.

De Jesus, Edilberto. 2015. "The Luck of Bongbong Marcos." *Philippine Daily Inquirer*. October 17. https://opinion.inquirer.net/89472/the-luck-of-bongbong-marcos.

Demegillo, Angelica. 2022. "Group hits Marcos-Duterte's no-show at debates: Crucial for public to know platforms." March 19. https://www.cnnphilippines.com/news/2022/3/19/ph-debate-union-bbm-duterte-debate-refusal.html.

Diamond, Larry. 1999. *Developing Democracy toward Consolidation*. Maryland: The Johns Hopkins University Press.

——————. 2019. *Ill Winds: Saving Democracy from Russian Rage, Chinese Ambition, and American Complacency*. New York: Penguin Press.

Enns, Peter. 2014. "The Public's Increasing Punitiveness and Its Influence on Mass Incarceration in the United States." *American Journal of Political Science* 58(4): 857–72.

Fukuyama, Francis. 1995. "Confucianism and Democracy." *Journal of Democracy* 6(2): 20–33. https://doi.org/10.1353/jod.1995.0029.

Gavilan, Jodesz. 2017. "CHR's Gascon Reiterates Concern over 'sense of Impunity' in PH." Rappler. November 24. https://www.rappler.com/nation/commission-on-human-rights-chito-gascon-concern-impunity-philippines-drug-war-killings.

Global Commission on Drug Policy. 2017. "ASEAN: Drugs Might Harm Individuals, but Current Policies Undermine Social Cohesion." November 9, 2017. https://www.globalcommissionondrugs.org/asean-drugs-might-harm-individuals-but-current-policies-undermine-social-cohesion.

Gunia, Amy. 2019. "Philippines Journalist Maria Ressa Arrested Again." *Time*, March 29. https://time.com/5561018/philippines-maria-ressa-arrested-fraud/.

Gutierrez, Filomin C., and Bianca Ysabelle Franco. 2020. "Violence and Police Accountability: Interview with a Police District Director on the Philippine Drug Problem." In *Crime and Punishment in the Philippines: Beyond Politics and Spectacle*, ed. Filomin C. Gutierrez, 233–53. Quezon City: Philippine Social Science Council.

Holmes, Oliver. 2016. "Tragic Story of Death-Row Maid Caught up in Asia's War on Drugs." *Guardian*. September 16. https://www.theguardian.com/world/2016/sep/17/philippines-president-heroin-deterte-mary-jane-veloso-death-row.

Human Rights Watch. 2004. "Not Enough Graves: The War on Drugs, HIV/AIDS, and Violations of Human Rights." Vol. 16 No. 8. https://www.hrw.org/reports/2004/thailand0704/thailand0704.pdf.

——————. 2010. "'Skin on the Table': The Illegal Arrest, Arbitrary Detention and Torture of People Who Use Drugs in Cambodia." January 25. https://www.hrw.org/report/2010/01/25/skin-cable/illegal-arrest-arbitrary-detention-and-torture-people-who-use-drugs.

——————. 2017. "'License to Kill': Philippine Police Killings in Duterte's 'War on Drugs.'" https://www.hrw.org/report/2017/03/02/license-kill/philippine-police-killings-dutertes-war-drugs.

Huntington, Samuel. 1993. "The Clash of Civilizations?" *Foreign Affairs* 72(3): 22–49.

Hutton, Jeffrey. 2017. "Is Widodo Following Duterte's Playbook in War on Drugs?" *South China Morning Post*. August 12. https://www.scmp.com/week-asia/geopolitics/article/2106293/widodo-following-dutertes-playbook-war-drugs.

International Federation for Human Rights. 2016. *Going Backwards: The Death Penalty in Southeast Asia*. No. 682a. Paris: International Federation for Human Rights.

Iwabuchi, Koichi. 2014. "De-Westernisation, Inter-Asian Referencing and Beyond." *European Journal of Cultural Studies* 17(1): 44–57.

Kenny, Paul. 2019. *Populism in Southeast Asia*. Cambridge: Cambridge University Press.

Killalea, Debra. 2017. "Vietnam, China Hiding Deadly Secret on Execution Figures, Amnesty International Reveal." News.Com.Au. April 11. https://www.news.com.au/travel/travel-updates/incidents/vietnam-china-hiding-deadly-secret-on-execution-figures-amnesty-international-reveal/news-story/d0c7df7f07a0f1d91b47ac890ece4e15.

Kine, Phelim. 2017. "Duterte's 'Drug War' Migrates to Indonesia." New Mandala, August 23. https://www.newmandala.org/DUTERTES-DRUG-WAR-MIGRATES-INDONESIA/.

Lalu, Gabriel Pabico. 2018. "3 Policemen Guilty of Killing Kian Delos Santos—Court." November 29. https://newsinfo.inquirer.net/1058265/3-policemen-guilty-of-killing-kian-delos-santos-court.

Lalu, Gabriel Pabico. 2021. "52 out of 30,000 deaths? Rights group disputes gov't claims of DOJ drug war probe." November 20. https://newsinfo.inquirer.net/1517512/52-out-of-30000-deaths-petitioner-in-icc-case-disputes-doj-probe-of-drug-war.

Lasco, Gideon. 2014. "Pampagilas: Metamphetamine in the Everyday Economic Lives of Underclass Male Youths in a Philippine Port." *International Journal of Drug Policy* 25(4): 783–88.

Lasco, Gideon. 2016. "Southeast Asia's War on Drugs Doesn't Work—Here's What Does." The Conversation, December 21. https://theconversation.com/southeast-asias-war-on-drugs-doesnt-work-heres-what-does-69652.

Limpot, Kristel. 2020. "Duterte Calls for Revival of Death Penalty by Lethal Injection for Drug-Related Crimes." July 27. https://www.cnnphilippines.com/news/2020/7/27/Duterte-death-penalty-revival-fifth-SONA.html.

Lyttleton, Chris. 2004. "Relative Pleasures: Drugs, Development and Modern Dependencies in Asia's Golden Triangle." *Development and Change* 35(5): 909–35.

Magra, Iliana. 2019. "Brunei Stoning Punishment for Gay Sex and Adultery Takes Effect despite International Outcry." *New York Times*, April 3. https://www.nytimes.com/2019/04/03/world/asia/brunei-stoning-gay-sex.html.

Mateo, Janvic. 2018. "CHR Probes Death of 'Tambay' in Jail." *Philstar*, June 22. https://www.philstar.com/headlines/2018/06/22/1826915/chr-probes-death-tambay-jail.

Mauzy, Diane K. 1997. "The Human Rights and 'Asian Values' Debate in Southeast Asia: Trying to Clarify the Issues." *The Pacific Review* 10(2): 210–36.

McRae, Dave. 2017. "Is Indonesia Embarking on a Philippine-Style War on Drugs?" Indonesia at Melbourne. August 8. https://indonesiaatmelbourne.unimelb.edu.au/is-indonesia-embarking-on-a-philippines-style-war-on-drugs/.

Patag, Kristine Joy. 2021. "Marcos to pursue Duterte's 'war on drugs' with same vigor, but different approach." *Philstar*, October 7. https://www.philstar.com/headlines/2021/10/07/2132430/marcos-pursue-dutertes-war-drugs-same-vigor-different-approach.

Pepinsky, Thomas. 2017. "Southeast Asia: Voting against Disorder." *Journal of Democracy* 28 (2): 120–31.

Philippine Drug Enforcement Agency (PDEA). 2022. "#RealNumbersPH (As of February 28, 2022)." https://pdea.gov.ph/index.php?option=com_content&view=edit&id=279.

Philippine Star. 2018. "20 Things You Need to Know about the 'anti-Tambay' Drive." June 29. https://www.philstar.com/headlines/2018/06/29/1829055/20-things-you-need-know-about-anti-tambay-drive.

Phoonphongphiphat, Apornrath. 2020. "Thailand's Young Protesters Keep up Pace despite 'Selfie Rules.'" *Nikkei Asia*. October 19. https://asia.nikkei.com/Politics/Turbulent-Thailand/Thailand-s-young-protesters-keep-up-pace-despite-selfie-rules.

Ranada, Pia. 2019. "Duterte Pushes for Return of Death Penalty for Drug Crimes, Plunder." Rappler, July 22. https://www.rappler.com/nation/duterte-pushes-return-death-penalty-drug-crimes-plunder-sona-2019.

Rappler.com. 2015. "The story of Mary Jane Veloso, in her own words." April 24. https://www.rappler.com/nation/91026-mary-jane-veloso-narrative/.

————. 2022. "SC decision on Mary Jane Veloso's deposition good news, says lawyer." June 22. https://www.rappler.com/nation/lawyer-says-supreme-court-decision-mary-jane-veloso-deposition-good-news/

Reuters. 2017a. "Cambodia Promises Harsher Drug Crackdown as Arrests Soar." February 8. https://www.reuters.com/article/uk-cambodia-drugs/cambodia-promises-harsher-drug-crackdown-as-arrests-soar-idUKKBN15N18Z.

————. 2017b. "Indonesian President Orders Officers to Shoot Drug Traffickers." July 22. https://www.reuters.com/article/us-indonesia-drugs/indonesian-president-orders-officers-to-shoot-drug-traffickers-idUSKBN1A708P.

Roberts, Bryan, and Yu Chen. 2013. "Drugs, Violence, and the State." *Annual Review of Sociology* 39: 105–25.

Robertson, Phil. 2020. "Another Spike in Philippines' 'Drug War' Deaths: Latest Data Shows Police Killings Rising amid Covid-19 Pandemic." Human Rights Watch. https://www.hrw.org/news/2020/09/28/another-spike-philippines-drug-war-deaths.

Salvá, Ana. 2017. "Why Are Abuse Claims in Cambodia's War on Drugs Being Ignored?" *South China Morning Post*, May 17. https://www.scmp.com/week-asia/politics/article/2094693/why-are-abuse-claims-cambodias-war-drugs-being-ignored.

Senate of the Philippines. 2020. "Bato Bats for Reimposition of Death Penalty." July 29. http://legacy.senate.gov.ph/photo_release/2020/0729_06.asp.

Simangan, Dahlia. 2018. "Is the Philippine 'War on Drugs' an Act of Genocide?" *Journal of Genocide Research* 20(1): 68–89.

Sombatpoonsiri, Janjira, and Aries Arugay. 2016. "Duterte's War on Drugs: Bitter Lessons from Thailand's Failed Campaign." The Conversation, September 29. https://theconversation.com/dutertes-war-on-drugs-bitter-lessons-from-thailands-failed-campaign-66096.

Sommer, Udi, and Victor Asal. 2019. "Examining Extrajudicial Killings: Discriminant Analyses of Human Rights' Violations." *Dynamics of Asymmetric Conflict* 12(3): 185–207.

Stevens, Alex. 2011. "Sociological Approaches to the Study of Drug Use and Drug Policy." *International Journal of Drug Policy* 22(6): 399–403.

Stevenson, Alexander. 2019. "Maria Ressa, Journalist Critical of Duterte, Is Arrested Again in Philippines." *New York Times*, March 28. https://www.nytimes.com/2019/03/28/business/media/maria-ressa-arrested-philippines-rappler.html.

Talabong, Rambo. 2018. "Filipinos Feel Safer but Trust Police Less in Metro Manila in 2017." Rappler, February 5. https://www.rappler.com/nation/195303-filipinos-feel-safer-trust-police-less-metro-manila-2017-pnp-napolcom.

——————. 2019. "In 2019 Campaign, Dela Rosa Wins with His Heart and Duterte." Rappler, May 10. https://www.rappler.com/newsbreak/in-depth/ronald-dela-rosa-wins-with-his-heart-and-duterte-campaign-2019.

Teehankee, Julio, and Mark Thompson. 2016. "The Neo-Authoritarian Threat in the Philippines." New Mandala, April 29. https://www.newmandala.org/the-neo-authoritarian-threat-in-the-philippines.

Tomacruz, Sofia. 2020. "'Shoot Them Dead': Duterte Orders Troops to Kill Quarantine Violators." Rappler, April 1. https://www.rappler.com/nation/duterte-orders-troops-shoot-kill-coronavirus-quarantine-violators.

Tostevin, Matthew, and Neil Jerome Morales. 2019. "War on Numbers: Philippines Targets Drug Killing Data." Reuters, July 18. https://www.reuters.com/article/us-philippines-drugs-idUSKCN1UD1CJ.

United Nations High Commissioner for Human Rights. 2020. "Situation of Human Rights in the Philippines: Report of the United Nations High Commissioner for Human Rights." UNHCHR. https://www.ohchr.org/Documents/Countries/PH/Philippines-HRC44-AEV.pdf.

Viray, Patricia Lourdes. 2018. "Drug War, Fighting Criminality Duterte's Top Achievement—Pulse Asia." *Philstar*, July 23. https://www.philstar.com/headlines/2018/07/23/1836071/drug-war-fighting-criminality-dutertes-top-achievement-pulse-asia.

Wang, Philip, and Helen Regan. 2022. "Philippines orders news site Rappler to shut down, founder Maria Ressa says." June 29. https://edition.cnn.com/2022/06/28/media/rappler-shut-down-philippines-ressa-intl-hnk/index.html.

Ward, Adam, and James Hackett. 2003. "Security Cooperation in Southeast Asia." *Strategic Comments* 9(8): 1–2.

Papuan Youth Identity:
Violence, Oppression, and Marginalization in the Context of ASEAN Integration

VIDHYANDIKA DJATI PERKASA

This chapter focuses on the construction of Papuan youth identity as the result or impact of the contestation of violence, oppression, and marginalization. The western half of the island of New Guinea is located in the eastern part of Indonesia and comprises two provinces—West Papua (Papua Barat) and Papua. It is a conflict-stricken area characterized by human rights violations and economic backwardness.[1] Geographically, the smaller West Papua Province is shaped by the coastal plain, while the larger Papua Province encompasses the mountainous areas. Physically distinct from most Indonesians who are of Malayan Mongoloid origin, Papuans belong to the ethnogeographic group of Pacific Islanders known as Melanesians.

My research is about how conflict and the narrative of violence, oppression, and marginalization have played a significant role in the construction of Papuan identity. As such, the dominant narrative that emerges is that national identity or Indonesian nationalism is undermined or challenged by an exclusive form of local identity known as Papuan nationalism, especially among Papuan youth. A referendum on Papuan independence has become their goal, a struggle that has been a source of prolonged conflict in the provinces. As such, it has become an Indonesian domestic issue, one that can have an impact on ASEAN stability and integration. Instability in a particular ASEAN country can bring about negative consequences for the surrounding countries, especially when the region is struggling to maintain its relevance and cohesiveness through its so-called "ASEAN identity."

Maintaining a distinct Papuan identity, whether that pertains to physical characteristics or the rejection of Indonesian nationalism is part of the way Papuan people "contest" the violence, oppression, and marginalization which they have experienced for generations. This contestation can be viewed as the Papuan "agency" to fight against "structural" misconduct.

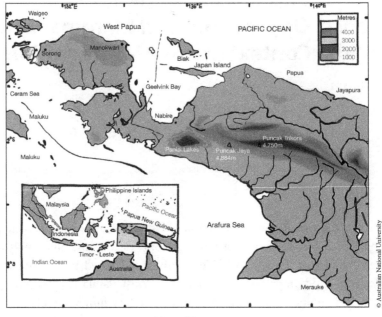

Map of Papua.

I begin this chapter with a discussion of Papua's multidimensional complexity and the conceptualization of violence. This will be followed by an analysis of how violence influences the construction of Papuan identity and the attitudes of Papuan youth toward a particular type of Papuan nationalism. Exploring the points of view of Papuan youth is extremely important since they are part of the generation that will determine the future of Papua. They can be regarded as the progressive element with respect to the referendum for Papua independence. Most demonstrations objecting to the government's mishandling of Papua are also led by youths, who use social media to campaign for independence. At the macro level, the younger generation, known also as millennials, will play an important role because they will be in the "driving seat" and will determine ASEAN's future. According to Indonesia's 2020 population census, 25.9 percent of the country's total population comprise millennials (born 1981–96). This is the second largest generation after the Z generation (born 1997–2012), which constitutes 27.94 percent of the population of Indonesia.

Finally, based on empirical investigation, I will discuss the components of identity construction among Papuan youth. This study draws on Focus Group Discussions (FGDs) and in-depth interviews with Papuan youths in Jakarta, Salatiga, Yogyakarta, and Jayapura. These youths are university students or activists in various organizations. In my interactions with them, I focused on understanding the Papuan youth's experience in violence and how they construct their identity.

Understanding Papua's Complexity

The concept of Papua has been controversial since its integration with Indonesia following the withdrawal of the Dutch administration from the Netherlands New Guinea through the New York Agreement of October 1, 1962, and the implementation of Indonesian administration in 1963. This was followed in 1969 by the Act of Free Choice when 1,026 Papuan leaders were handpicked and "intimidated" to vote unanimously in favor of Indonesian control. The "integration" or "annexation" narratives have been much disputed. Most Papuans, who have accused integration of being an illegal act, demand a "review" of the Act of Free Choice. Experts say this controversial process was contrary to the "one man one vote" principle in a democratic system.

To complicate the issue, Indonesia's New Order regime opted to continue an earlier Dutch colonial government initiative, the Indonesian Transmigration Program (*transmigrasi*), whereby more than two million landless people were moved from the densely populated inner islands of Java, Bali, and Lombok to the less populous islands of Sumatra, Kalimantan, Sulawesi, and Irian Jaya (now named Papua). This had the unanticipated effect of promoting socioeconomic and cultural inequality vis-à-vis the indigenous Papuans, known as Orang Asli Papua, or OAP. The immigrants under the transmigration program became settlers in the region and gradually took control of the local economy and bureaucratic positions. However, this has not been accompanied by affirmative action to protect and empower the OAP, resulting in alienation and marginalization towards OAP in their homeland, which has generated paranoia across generations.

In addition, Papua has become the target of massive exploitation by predatory business actors who rely on military protection and interests. A constant flow of bribes to the military has ensured inhumane treatment of Papuans and has weakened local participation in development. This situation has inevitably created an undeniable record of human rights abuses. Sadly, the violators have never been brought to trial and enjoy a high level of impunity.

These unresolved grievances have led to the emergence of "Free Papua" separatist movements, such as Organisasi Papua Merdeka (OPM) or the Papua Independence Organization, also known as Kelompok Kriminal Bersenjata

(KKB) or the Armed Criminal Group, who fought for independence from Indonesia. In April 2021 the government declared Papua KKB a terrorist organization since the organization has carried out brutal and massive killings and violence. Security forces are quick to take decisive action against the KKB. The international community, as well as countries in the Pacific Islands, have strongly expressed their support of Papuans who wish to voice their political, economic, social, and cultural rights within the trajectory of independence (Wangge and Djali, 2016).

In an effort to improve the situation in Papua, in 2001 Indonesia's parliament ratified the Special Autonomy Law (2001–2021), purportedly aimed at boosting development with a special autonomy fund but regarded by Papuans as a "political contract" negotiated against the demand for independence. It is known that from 2002 to 2020, 138,65 trillion rupiahs were distributed to Papua and West Papua provinces. However, the law led to considerable disruption as the locals claimed that it failed to increase social welfare among indigenous Papuans. Rumor has it that the policy has only been profitable for local elites and migrants.

Moreover, local Papuans complained about increasing conflict and human rights abuses during the Special Autonomy era. Aggressive attacks were made by the KKB in Nduga and Intan Jaya as abuses began to escalate. The tension was real. Special Autonomy was a disaster due to rampant corruption by Papuan elites, exacerbated by a lack of managerial capacity to administer the funds. Bad governance is a widespread phenomenon in Papua. It concerns cultural factors, lack of capacity and managerial skills, and weak law enforcement (Perkasa, 2011).

After the transfer of funds ended in 2021, the government extended the Special Autonomy fund for a further twenty years. The fund, also known as Special Autonomy Part 2, will now operate until 2041, despite its wide rejection by the public, especially by church leaders, students, and civil society organizations. The rejection was not only an indication that the law was ineffectual, but various important articles within it, such as the establishment of the Commission for Truth and Reconciliation and the right to form a local political party, have never been implemented. However, some segments of society openly supported the continuation of the law, and this has increased polarization within Papuan society.

Special Autonomy Part 2 focuses on increasing the funds while regulating the area expansion in the province (*pemekaran*). There has always been suspicion among Papuans that *pemekaran* is intended to "divide and weaken" indigenous people along ethnic and territorial lines and to intensify security measures. There is insufficient proof that *pemekaran* successfully increased the welfare of

Papuans. As such, political observers criticized the government for perceiving the complexity of Papua only in economic terms, neglecting other fundamental issues such as human rights, equality, and justice.

With the Special Autonomy Part 2 coming into effect and with the KKB declared a terrorist organization, welfare, order, and stability have not improved for Papuans. Instead, conflict has escalated. In early March 2022, separatist KKB killed eight technicians who were fixing a telecommunications tower in Puncak district. Only one worker survived (Reuters, March 4, 2022). Among the eight victims was Beby Tabuni, the son of a tribal chief in Ilaga, Puncak Regency, Papua. Separatist KKB also injured a contract worker in Intan Jaya in early March 2022. Given the frequency of such incidents, there is an urgent need to review both the security apparatus strategies and the developmental approach in Papua.

Racism, embedded in the daily lives of the Papuan population, has also become an alarming and unresolved problem. After protests erupted because of the use of racist and hate speech against Papuan students in Surabaya, East Java, in August 2019, domestic and international sources were quick to respond. The racist abuse involved allegations that the security apparatus and its local organization mocked Papuan students with derogative words such as "monkeys" and "pigs" before they were arrested and questioned for desecrating the national flag, as will be explained further.

Following the emergence of the "Black Lives Matter" campaign across the world, the hashtag #PapuanLivesMatter trended in Indonesia, reflecting the growing awareness among Indonesians of state oppression and racism against Papuans. There is also a power struggle to distinguish Papuans from the majority of Indonesians in terms of identity. Physical characteristics matter here.

The indigenous population of Papua is dark-skinned and belongs to the Australo-Melanesian group, whereas Indonesians have Malay ancestry (Maulia 2020). Thus, there is also a trend towards shifting from "dual nationalism" (being Papuan and being Indonesian) to "single-state" nationalism, which is "Papuan nationalism," which I will explain in a later section of this chapter. Unresolved racism has become extra ammunition for Papuans to fight for independence.

Conceptualizing Violence in Papua

Three words best describe the atrocities and harsh conditions that Papuans have had to contend with for generations: violence, oppression, and marginalization. Oppression and marginalization can also be categorized as forms of violence.

Violence is a complex phenomenon, not only because of its different categories but also because of its multiple causes (Moser and Shrader 1999). Since it is so complex, there are no clear definitions for it. It is understood differently by different people and in different contexts.[2]

While there is no standard definition of violence, it is important to have a clear understanding of what it is and the context in which it occurs. In 2002, in a report on world violence and health, the World Health Organization (WHO) defined violence as "The intentional use of physical force or power threatened or actual against oneself, another person or against a group or community, that either results in or has a high likelihood of resulting in injury, death, psychological harm, maldevelopment or deprivation."

WHO's definition encapsulates the extent to which violence pertains to threats committed by a community, which I will address as collective violence. It refers to the instrumental use of violence by people who identify themselves as members of a group—whether this group is transitory or has a more permanent identity—against another group or set of individuals, to achieve political, economic, or social objectives. This can manifest itself in several forms, including genocide, repression, terrorism, and organized crime (ibid.)

However, it is crucial to acknowledge the characteristics of states that employ collective violence. This context is arguably important in the shaping of violence in Papua. Geoffrey Robinson (cited in Grabowsky et al. 2020) points out that most states in Southeast Asia have conditioned mass violence as perpetrator, facilitator, or even role model. This includes the mass killing of certain segments of its own citizens based on their ethnicity, class, and political or religious affiliation. Many scholars believe that this situation can be equated with "massacre." In addition, state authorities have also promoted violence in collaboration with non-state actors by deploying their own security forces to commit outrageous and unlawful violence, thus participating in the spread of violence as a political strategy (ibid., 22). In the case of conflict in Papua, civilians are normally implicated in this violence and become the victims of security forces (military), non-state actors, and KKB misconduct.

In this section, I will propose that the argument of Grabowsky et al. can also be interpreted as vertical violence. Bobby Anderson (2015) states that there is both vertical and horizontal violence in Papua. Vertical violence is defined as political violence due to its separatist agenda, whereas horizontal violence comprises domestic, identity or clan violence, witchcraft, resource-related violence, and crime violence (ibid.). In the following I intend to focus only on vertical or political violence.

Many domestic and international actors have highlighted the widespread nature of violence in Papua. A 2018 report by Amnesty International Indonesia, "Don't Bother, Just Let Him Die: Killing with Impunity in Papua," stated that there are two categories of unlawful killings—one which relates to political activities and the other unrelated to political activities. The report also stated that from 2010 to 2018 there were 69 cases of unlawful killings involving 95 victims. Of these, 28 cases with 39 victims were related to political activities and 41 cases with 56 victims unrelated to political activities. These numbers could just be the tip of the iceberg.

How does the state settle these cases or show its accountability in unlawful killings? Amnesty International Indonesia observed that in 2018 only two cases were still ongoing investigations; 26 cases had been investigated but the results were not made public; and 25 cases were not investigated. Of the 26 cases investigated, these were dealt with either via internal police discipline, or through a traditional settlement mechanism or remedy, or through military tribunal. These settlement numbers are considered well below the total cases that occurred.

In the case of Papua, military occupation since 1962 is seen as an era in which the OAP were considered by Indonesian armed forces as the enemy.[3] Elmslie and Webb-Gannon (2013) argue that explicit and implicit government policy has been consistently directed towards countering and eliminating Papuan attempts to create an independent state for their nation or to enjoy political freedom on a par with other Indonesians.

Contextualizing the misery of indigenous Papuans in their experience of violence, Selpius Bobii (cited in Elmslie and Webb-Gannon 2013) states:[4]

> Military operations during this time have included bombings, shootings, kidnapping, murder, forced disappearances, detention and imprisonment, torture, rape, theft of domestic livestock, destruction of crops/vegetable gardens (which are people's source of survival), burning of homes to the ground, burning of churches, killing by poisoning of food and water and others. There have been killings carried out in sadistic ways such as victims whilst still alive, having their body parts chopped off with a short machete/chopping knife or axe; or victims being sliced up with razors or knives, then the open flesh being filled with chili water; males and females being forced to have sex before their torturers then the male genitals being cut off and their wife forced to eat them, following which they are both killed; being killed by being suspended (strung-up) until dead; being thrown alive into deep chasms

where there is no way out; being placed tied alive into a sack then thrown into the sea or a lake or river; being buried in the earth alive; iron bars being heated in a fire then inserted into the anus, the mouth or into the female internally through the genitals.

Bobii's testimony, a combination of first-hand experience and storytelling, demonstrates the sadistic acts of violence used against indigenous Papuans. He uses the term "annihilation" to describe the acts of violence experienced.[5]

These atrocities are generally categorized as "slow motion genocide" (Elmslie and Webb-Gannon 2013), the condition whereby most Papuans did not only die because of intentional killings but also "unjust" government policies. A study by Dutch scholars in Papua on infant mortality rates in 2012 describes structural discrimination against indigenous Papuans, who have an infant mortality rate of 18.4 percent compared to 3.6 percent for the non-indigenous population in Papua (Elmslie and Webb-Gannon 2013).

Kjell Anderson (2015) uses demographic indicators to illustrate depopulation in Papua. She argues that in 1971 indigenous Papuans represented 96.9 percent of the total population whereas in 2020 it would likely represent only 29 per cent. Selpius Bobii (cited in Elmslie and Webb-Gannon 2013) argues that the decline of indigenous Papuans is a result of the impact of the Family Planning Program, which allows each Indonesian family to only have two children, exacerbated by the massive transmigration program.

Infectious diseases such as TB, tapeworm infections, typhoid, cholera, hepatitis, venereal diseases, HIV/AIDS, and others transmitted from unmedicated new settlers to the Papuan people have played a role in accelerating the death rate. Prior to the arrival of new settlers, these diseases were unknown to the ancestors of indigenous Papuans. These types of infections/diseases spread quickly due to inadequate health services and infrastructure in Papuan villages.

Selpius Bobii and Kjell Anderson's views on the "mistreatment" of indigenous Papuans mirrors observations made by RW, a student from a public university in Jayapura, Papua. RW complained that the Indonesian government had "destroyed" Papua through various policies involving family planning, HIV, and intensifying migration, causing the Papuan to become "extinct" (*punah*) (interview, Jayapura, May 10, 2019). KSM, a student from a private university in Yogyakarta agreed that this was part of a plan to depopulate indigenous Papuans (interview, Yogyakarta, January 7, 2021).

Extinction and depopulation contribute to Papuans' loss of identity. In addition, there is great concern about massive transmigration to the island, according to FRN, a student from a mountainous district who at the time of this research was studying at a public university in Jayapura. Transmigration would bring in more non-Papuans with a religion "distinct" from most Papuans who are predominantly Protestant and Catholic. Transmigration in a way is part of a plan to Islamize indigenous Papuans (interview, Jayapura, May 9, 2019). This will contribute to the extinction of indigenous Papuans.

As can be seen from the above, Papua has become a land of violence. Apart from direct violence, which is observable and evidence-based, rumors and stories of political violence are widespread in Papua. Rumors are a more subjective phenomenon of violence as they are vulnerable to appropriation or manipulation by the state. Rumors tend to exacerbate instead of ameliorating the problems of political violence (Kirsch 2002). Through rumors, people explicitly experience the threat of violence to express their concerns. Any parties, whether the state, military/police, OPM/KKB, or civilians can be the perpetrators of such rumors aimed at creating fear and hatred, and even to justify certain actions.

Stuart Kirsch provides a few examples of rumors and narratives of political violence in Papua. For example, there is concern about the spread of HIV/AIDS which is believed to have contributed towards the "extinction" of indigenous Papuans. The rumors claimed that state agencies had sent prostitutes infected with HIV to deliberately infect the local people of Papua. Papua has the highest proportion of Indonesians with HIV/AIDS despite its small population compared to other islands in Indonesia. There are endless rumors accusing the Indonesia government, the military, the fishing industry, and the Freeport mine of being primary vectors for the introduction and spread of sexually transmitted diseases, including HIV/AIDS.

Rumors can be interpreted in several ways. On the one hand, if perceived from the perspective of the state, the Indonesian government/military/police, it shows the power domination of the "oppressor" over the "oppressed," the latter in this case the indigenous Papuans. The HIV/AIDS phenomenon signals the penetration of political violence into the most private and intimate areas of life, which causes fear (Kirsch 2002). The security apparatus would then be justified in acting oppressively towards infected indigenous Papuans because they are considered a danger to society. Conversely, seen from the perspective of indigenous Papuans, rumors can generate hatred towards the state/military/police, especially when they highlight the alleged intention to spread the disease to annihilate indigenous Papuans. The indigenous people would also be justified in committing violence towards those responsible for orchestrating the spread of HIV/AIDS.

In the early 1970s, another rumor spread that the Indonesian government was sponsoring a program of biological warfare against indigenous Papuans. It allegedly sent pigs into the province as a gift to military forces that were posted there to exert control over the disputed Paniai Lakes district after the Act of Free Choice in 1969. President Suharto at that time sent the "gift" from Bali, the home province of some soldiers in the armies involved in solving the dispute. Observers believe that the pigs were not meant to compensate military action but rather to weaken the opposition, that is, indigenous Papuans who opposed the Act of Free Choice. Rumors had it that the pigs were deliberately infected with cysticercosis, a parasite that infects brain, muscle, or other tissue and is a major cause of seizures in young adults.

The infected pigs were seen as a counterinsurgency tactic to decimate and demoralize the enemy (David Hyndman, cited in Kirsch 2002). In time, there was no proof whatsoever that the pigs were indeed infected and caused sickness or death among indigenous Papuans. However, this rumor followed "the trail" of motivation and impact from the previous example of HIV/AIDS. It demonstrated power domination, fear, hatred, and acts intended to annihilate indigenous Papuans. Using pigs, which are considered "sacred" animals by Papuans and are used for traditional rituals and ceremonies and also determine social status, was an affront to local beliefs.

Rumors and the narrative of political violence have exacerbated conventional violence. Kirsch (2002) argues that rumors can provide for a historical reading of power and its abuses, a symbol of inequality and exploitation, and a classic weapon against the weak. Finally, rumors and the narrative of political violence culturally sustain collective memory and influence indigenous Papuan identity. Eventually, being Melanesian is a crucial political assertion and aspect of identity politics for Papuans, whose attitudes toward Indonesians have been shaped by the racialized discourse that discriminates against them (ibid.).

Contextualizing Violence and Papuan Youth Identity Construction

Experience of violence strongly influences how Papuan youth identify themselves, as stated by Selpius Bobii (cited in Elmslie and Webb-Gannon 2013) and Elizabeth Brundige (cited in Bobby Anderson 2015). Indigenous Papuans are frequently tortured, raped, mutilated, and killed in their own land. Their properties and livelihoods are destroyed or stolen. They face discriminative treatment just because they are physically distinct from other Indonesians.

Moreover, Papuans as an "ethnic" group are gradually declining in numbers or in the process of becoming "extinct" while the number of non-Papuans originating from various ethnic groups is increasing and they are living in better conditions on Papuan soil. Indeed, the stigma of "being different" from other Indonesians has influenced indigenous Papuan's confidence and self-esteem, a subject discussed in the next section. Papuans feel they are becoming "alienated" in their own land. They question why they are living in poorer conditions compared to other ethnic groups even though all are part of Indonesia as a nation-state. They question what it means to be Indonesian. These are the factors which emotionally or psychologically influence identity construction, especially with reference to Papuan youth. The communal feeling among all OAP of being oppressed acts as a component of identity construction. As Manuel Castells stresses, conceptually it is identity that is the source of people's meaning and experience: "We know of no people without names, no language or cultures in which some manner of distinctions between self and others, we and they, are not made.... Self-knowledge is always a construction no matter how much it feels like a discovery—is never altogether separable from claims to be known in specific ways by others" (2010, 6).

As social actors, Papuans undergo the process of identity construction based on a related set of cultural attributes that are given priority over other sources of meaning. Cultural attributes may refer to a nation (Indonesia), race, clan, sub-clan, ethnicity, language, religion, cultural artifacts, even territorial origin. There is always a plurality of identities. As such, this plurality is a source of stress and contradiction in terms of self-representation and social action (ibid.). For Amartya Sen (2007), however, identity is multifaceted and there is no reason to allow any dimension of identity to predominate over all others.

Despite the debate over whether the plurality of identities should be contested or harmonized, it has been argued earlier that all identities are a product of historical evolution (Fearon and Laitin 2000). The real issue is how, from what, by whom, and for what. There are many sources available for constructing [Papuan] identity: history, geography, biology, productive and reproductive institutions, collective memory, personal fantasies, power apparatuses, and religious revelations.

Social construction of identity always takes place in a context marked by power relationships. Castells (2010, 8) proposes a distinction between three forms of identity building. The first is "Legitimizing Identity," which is introduced by the dominant institution of society—in this case, the state—to extend and rationalize their domination vis-à-vis social actors. This is about domination and authority and draws on theories of nationalism. In the

Papuan context, being Indonesian should, in theory, be a legitimizing identity, especially as it is supported by state-building policies such as the Pancasila or Five Principles, which highlight the importance of maintaining unity as a nation, complemented by principles of justice and humanity. There is also the state motto of Bhinneka Tunggal Ika ("Unity in Diversity"), which focuses on maintaining cohesiveness amidst cultural and ethnic diversity. Diversity is seen as a strength. There is also the national red and white flag and the Indonesian national anthem Indonesia Raya ("Great Indonesia"). Separate versions of the Indonesian identification card, Kartu Tanda Penduduk (Residential Identity Card) exist for Indonesian citizens and non-Indonesian residents. The question is, should Papuans be subservient to "Legitimizing Identity" after all the mistreatment they have experienced?

Castell's second origin of identity building is "Resistance Identity," or an identity generated by those actors who are in positions or live under conditions that are devalued and stigmatized by forces of dominion. These only engender resistance. In other words, "Resistance Identity" is about identity politics. I have noted above how Papuans experience violence and stigmatization and are treated as inferior human beings by state actors or even by non-Papuans. As a result, Papuans reject being Indonesian as defined by the state.

Castell's third form of identity building, "Project Identity," is when social actors or, in this case, Papuans, based on whatever cultural materials are available to them, build a new identity that redefines their position in society and by doing so transforms the overall social structure. This is where Papuan nationalism becomes relevant.

Papuan nationalism involves strengthening their distinction vis-à-vis non-Papuans, whether that be physical (dark skin and curly hair) or not; proudly highlighting their origin as part of the Melanesian race; having a symbolic flag (*bintang kejora* or "morning star"); communicating in the local dialect and language; and possessing other cultural attributes and artifacts specific to them. The notion of changing the overall social structure means that Papuans are challenging the dominant narrative of being Indonesian with the goal of fighting for separation from the nation state. Thus, Papuan nationalism is seen as an essential element of an independent Papuan state.

Redefining identity can also be a strategy to contest racism or, in a broader context, violence, oppression, and marginalization. Yuyun Surya (2016) argues that Papuans are consolidating their identity by raising their distinctive ethnic consciousness. They are emphasizing their affiliation to the Melanesian race to redefine their ethnic identity and to contest the negative stereotype previously attached to them in order to empower themselves. Marginalization, oppression, and economic exploitation, along with being recognized by their black skin and curly hair, have made Papuans "the Blacks of Indonesia." Papuan ethnic consciousness is facilitated by the Facebook platform which allows them to choose and post messages to support their preferred online identity.

Through social media, Papuans are showing determination in the power struggle by constructing identity according to their values and interests. There is no notion of their "giving in" regarding experiencing racism, violence, and oppression. Identity in this case is not only about who they are but also who they ought to be (Daniel Miller cited in Surya 2019, 95). Social media allows people to show rather than tell; it is the expression of hoped for possible self (Surya 2019, 95). Black skin and curly hair are attributed to Papuans; these become markers of an "ideal Papuan." Black skin and curly hair are a symbol of political unity rather than a distinct physical characteristic. In line with this argument, Dale Gietzelts (in Surya 2019, 100) states: "This identification with blacks has political motivations in that it is used to arouse sympathy for and indeed empathy with, the Papuan cause among black minorities elsewhere who may be sensitive to charges of lingering colonialism. Thus, the black skin and curly hair are not only markers of Papuan ethnic identity but also symbols of resistance" to oppression, marginalization, discrimination, and economic exploitation.

To understand why Papua nationalism becomes a significant part of "project identity" can be explained through the "uncertainty-identity" theory (Hardie-Bick 2016, 1036). Because of violence, racism, and oppression, Papuan identity tends to be one of uncertainty concerning attitudes, values, beliefs, and feelings that are uncomfortable. Papuans will do their best to manage, avoid, or significantly reduce these uncertainties. Michael Hogg (cited in Hardie-Bick 2016, 1037) argues that the experience of having stronger social identity reduces uncertainty by enhancing self-esteem and provides a framework for understanding how one should think and behave: "We are particularly motivated to reduce uncertainty if, in a particular context, we feel uncertain about things that reflect on or are relevant to self, or if we are uncertain about self per se; about our identity, who we are, how we relate to others, and how we are socially located. Ultimately, people like to know who they are and how to behave and what to think, and who others are and how they might behave and what they might think" (ibid.).

Experience prolongs violence, racism, oppression, and marginalization from generation to generation, that to some degree can result in an "identity crisis." To escape from this identity crisis or uncertainty some people express their identity by joining armed groups, for example, the separatist KKB (Kelompok Kriminal Bersenjata or Armed Criminal Group). Joining this group provides members with protection, inspires loyalty and a strong sense of identity that promotes a sense of "them" and "us," and justifies the use of violence and hatred (Papachristos et al., cited in Hardie-Bick 2016, 1041). As discussed earlier, some Papuans affirm their identity by using social media as a form of power struggle. Others find expression through the use of group identification to strengthen Papua nationalism and fight for independence in a more "peaceful" way, such as through demonstrations, petitions, and public discussion.

Papuan Youth and Nationalism

Papuan identity construction as the result of contesting violence, oppression, and marginalization is a dynamic and progressive process. This is where the role of Papuan youth becomes significant. As mentioned above, identity is constructed from history, geography, collective memories, and personal imaginations. Since violence, oppression, and marginalization have been omnipresent in Papua, these experiences are transmitted from generation to generation, partly through storytelling and partly through personal encounters. Papuan youth are now in the "driving seat" of absorbing collective memories which have the power to determine the future and fate of Papua through their actions.

People's experiences from a particular generation are connected to and intertwined with conflict and violence. Previously I discussed how Papuans are being mistreated and feel discriminated and marginalized, eventually becoming the embryo of Papuan nationalism which contests the Indonesia nationalism dating from the colonial era and shared by various generations of indigenous Papuan.

According to Chauvel (2009), the emergence of a Papuan identity with reference to and in opposition to Indonesian nationalism has its roots in the structures of the Dutch colonial administration in Papua. During the colonial era until the 1960s, the Dutch employed Indonesians (non-Papuans) who held key positions in the provincial government. This positioning continued in the New Order administration under President Suharto. The indigenous Papuans felt the sense of rivalry with Indonesians. Due to this state of affairs, the first generations of Papuan have been debating what it meant to be Papuan and whether they wanted to establish a Papuan state.

This hierarchical structure based on ethnicity or race is dynamic in its nature. The colonial government of the Dutch Indies had somehow contributed to the emergence of a perpetuating racism by exercising the politics of *divide*

Fig. 1. A glimpse of economic injustice and inequality, especially between the indigenous Papuans (OAP) and migrant communities. Here, young Papuan (millennials) are employed as becak (pedicab) drivers, while the surrounding stores are owned by migrant communities.

at impera.[6] In the Papuan case, accordingly, there is always the fear that the "oppressed" group, the indigenous Papuans, will rebel and fight for its rights. Thus, racism is activated as a tool to maintain a culture of subordination and sustain the hegemonic culture of the oppressor. As a result—and this will be discussed further—racism tends to create a sense of low self-esteem, low confidence among Papuans due to their cultural differences, and assumed inferiority. With racism, potentially it could "weaken" the Papuan struggle to achieve equality and justice.

In the New Order era, the situation became even more complex when religion was incorporated into the construction of a Papuan identity. Christianity is seen as a core element of Papuan identity. Churches are regarded as "liberating institutions" and as "bearers" of new hope for a society shackled by the cold ideology of development that the New Order Government taught (Chauvel 2009). Papuan identity and nationalism are further strengthened by demographic changes resulting from the transmigration policy, as mentioned earlier. Javanese, Chinese, Bugis, Buton, and Makassar are influential ethnic groups that dominate the Papuan economy. There is widespread fear that the Indonesian government has the intention of Islamizing Papua through this transmigration policy, as suggested by one Papuan student. In this case, Papuan identification evolves from both religious and ethnic factors.

In the current situation, Papuan expressions of identity vis-à-vis other groups, particularly Indonesians, are made in the dichotomy of "we" Papuans against "you" Indonesians (ibid.). Papuan identity entails a form of nationalism based on ethnicity and race. Chauvel argues that Papuans distinguish their own from Indonesian values by emphasizing and linking together their Christianity, Melanesian cultural values, and respect for human rights.

Even though there is a slight improvement in the economic indicators in Papua under President Joko Widodo, problems in Papua are far from over. Demands for independence flourish due to the lack of political will by the government to solve human right abuses, both past and present. First, second, and even current generations have experienced traumatic human rights violations that have not yet been resolved. Apart from human rights issues, "indigenous Papuan rebels" also question Papua's integration into Indonesia. They regard this act as illegitimate.

The war for independence has shifted from armed struggle to a more political cyber diplomacy and "soft" strategy involving youth and millennials. One event which showed the active role of youth occurred in Bali when thirty students of the Papua Student Alliance (AMP) held a rally on August 2, 2017 to demand Papuan independence. The students denounced the Papua Act of Free Choice of 1969 as undemocratic; rather, it was full of terror, intimidation, and manipulation (Erviani, *The Jakarta Post*, August 2, 2017).

A research project conducted by the Indonesian Institute of Sciences (LIPI) has highlighted the role of youth in the Papuan struggle (Elisabeth et al. 2017). These young people received their education mostly at universities in Java and Sulawesi. Compared to the older generations, young people use technological tools such as instant messaging and other communication technologies online to better organize and disseminate their actions and ideas, as discussed earlier. According to Napoli (2014), social media are not only used as a means for the political struggle but are also intra- and intergenerational communicative practices among various generational cohorts. This seems clearly the case in the Papua context.

The young generation is full of people who have never been involved in Indonesian politics in the era before the 1998 reforms and thereafter. It is interesting to note that the idea of independence, or even the call for a referendum, is transmitted from one generation to the next through collective experiences and shared memories of physical abuse, oppression, and marginalization.

In the LIPI report (Elisabeth et al. 2017, 18), the younger generation of Papuans confronts the older generations' political traditions by accusing them of not having developed a coherent ideology and continuous tradition of liberation struggle. The younger generation accuses the older generations of pursuing diverse self-interests. Appealing to the Papuan diaspora abroad to "campaign" the horrific occurrences in Papua, some activists are trying to mobilize support from international actors, which makes the Papuan struggle a transnational issue.

The older generations are also accused of being too much inclined towards "elitist-feudal" attitudes and patronage. As the result of such perceived deficiencies within the older generations, members of the younger generation began to transform their resistance movement through building a more solid organizational structure with democratic and participatory principles. "Knowledge" plays an important role for the youth to carry on their struggle. They apply the Marxist perspective to understand the context of their struggle which they see as the impact of colonialism, imperialism and militarism. The youth are taught to find common ground in terms of analysis, strategy, and methods of struggle and to build mutual trust and intensive communication among the leaders of the youth movement (Elisabeth et al. 2017, 21).

As mentioned earlier, Papuan youth also focus on political diplomacy and the right of self-determination through referendum. Their approach differs fundamentally from that of the older generations, which favor armed struggle in remote forest areas to attain independence. In addition, this Papuan youth movement also stresses the important role of women in the struggle. Women are encouraged to build progressive women's organizations to address the oppression and exploitation of women in the economic and political spheres as part of the national liberation of Papua.

It is also interesting to investigate how identity and nationalism are ingrained within the context of the Papuan youth struggle. Papuan youth regard nationalism to be inseparable from the interests of national and international capital. The LIPI scholars further argue: "Economic and political dimensions of oppression towards Papuan people have supported the emergence of a more consolidated nationalist feeling and forged an embryo of collective identity among members of youth resistance group. Nationalism of 'oppressed nation' is different with a strong ethno-nationalism and/or primordialism. Occupation over Papua is part of Indonesia's domination and international interest towards economic capital. The definition of independence has been broadened not only as a nation but also freedom from all structural and systematic oppression" (Elisabeth et al. 2017, 22).

From the above argument, the idea of nationalism as a core objective among Papuan youth has been broadened in the sense that it is not only directed against the Indonesian occupation but also against all other actors who colonize and destroy Papua. It is not a narrow form of nationalism which is primordial and ethnocentric, considering the fact that there are hundreds of subethnic groups in Papua, but it is seen as an integrative nationalism for all people who live in Papua, especially the indigenous Papuans, but including the migrant populations in Papua who adhere to various religions.

Components of Papuan Youth Identity Construction: Empirical Observation

I was intrigued to ask my interlocutors what "Indonesia" means to them. LEJ, a student at a private university in Yogyakarta, firmly stated that Papua is not Indonesia. She highlighted the racial differences. Papuans are Melanesians, characterized by dark skin and curly hair, while the rest of Indonesians originated from the Malayan Mongoloid race, characterized by fairer skin and straight dark hair. The other reason why she argued that Papua is not Indonesia is related to the failure of Indonesia's nationalism "project" initiated by Indonesia's first president Sukarno (interview, Yogyakarta, January 7, 2021).

According to LEJ, there is no such thing as "Indonesian nationalism" since some regions are experiencing insurgencies with a strong political identity agenda, such as in Aceh, Kalimantan, and Maluku. In addition, the other reason Papua is not seen as part of Indonesia relates to historical events. When other islands were fighting the Dutch prior to Indonesia's independence in 1945, Papua was not part of that struggle. Hence, Papua followed a different historical path (ibid., interview). This non-availability of a collective past is one factor accounting for the centrality of the "recent past" in Papuan identity construction, which is link with violence (Goumenos 2006).

Another interlocutor, YANG, "imagines" Indonesia as a country colonizing Papua (interview, Yogyakarta, January 7, 2021). This millennial has learnt history from her parents and ancestors through storytelling. She stresses that in 1961 Papua achieved its independence from the Dutch. However, due to the economic and political interest of Sukarno and his allies, Papua was annexed to Indonesia. This statement from YANG leads us again to the history of "integration" where the Act of Free choice in 1969 was believed to be full of fraud and manipulation. Consequently, the process of "integration" was considered invalid and illegal. During that process, there have been many military operations that claimed hundreds of Papuan lives.[7] Thus, for YANG there is no such thing as loving or expressing loyalty to Indonesia, a place where she "temporarily" lives.

Other interviews with Papuan youth always touched upon the history of integration or, in their own words, "annexation" which needs to be reviewed to get it straight (*meluruskan*). POS and RON, both students coming from Jayapura, argue that there is a need to "reconcile" the history of "integration" (interview, Jayapura, May 11, 2019). But again, this reconciliation is seen only as a means to fight for a referendum. In this case, Papuans manipulate "integration" into Indonesia a discursive element that influences identity construction.

Before discussing other components of Papuan identity construction, it is interesting to observe the differences in "life orientation" between Papuans living in the coastal area (*pantai*) and those living in mountainous areas (*pegunungan*). One of the challenges in this study was avoiding generalizations based on various opinions. The so-called Papuans of Melanesian race are not a cohesive entity. The mountainous Papuans tend to have a stronger standpoint in favor of fighting for independence compared with the coastal Papuans.

An informant from the mountainous area argues that once the coastal Papuans received jobs or material benefits from the government, they would soften their aspiration for independence and would support integration with the Indonesian nation-state. RW explained that once "engaging in the system," coastal Papuans will be less outspoken (interview, Jayapura, May 11, 2019; interview with FRN, May 11, 2019). This is also an accusation toward the older generation. Consequently, mountainous Papuans accuse coastal Papuans as traitors. Coastal Papuans are also seen as "closer" to the migrant population and as supporting "mixed marriages" which the mountain Papuans object to (interview with RON, May 10, 2019). RW explained, for exemple, that in a marriage ceremony, coastal Papuans will raise the red and white Indonesian flag (interview, Jayapura, May 10, 2019). Coastal Papuans stereotype the mountain Papuan as "dead-brain," headstone, stupid, backward, and having a more vicious character.

Racism and discrimination have been a continuous and unresolved issue among Papuans. These have intensified again recently. One event occurred in Surabaya, East Java, before the Indonesian independence celebration on August 17, 2019 mentioned earlier. Security personnel and local mass organizations hurled racist slurs at Papuan students who were accused of refusing to celebrate Indonesia's 74th Independence Day. The racist abuse involved the students being called "monkeys" and "pigs" before they were arrested and questioned for allegedly desecrating a national flag.

Such events have incited anger and antiracist protests amongst the people in Papua and West Papua. There also have been mass riots which involve the destruction of public facilities in some cities, such as in Manokwari, Sorong and Jayapura. Demands for a referendum were raised. In response, the government decided to block Internet access to prevent a wider spread of hoaxes. Thirty-four students suspected of being provocateurs were arrested, while thousands of Papuan students who study outside Papua felt threatened and decided to return to their hometowns.

The government's response in addressing this issue has been deemed to be slow and unfair. Papuans' demand for the racist perpetrators to be put on trial also has not been met. Another violent riot broke out in Jayapura and Wamena on September 23, 2019. In Jayapura, the violent protests took place after the police and Cendrawasih University's rector decided not to allow Papuan students to carry out their plan to open a center in the university's compound to accommodate students from outside Papua who had just returned to their hometown. The students were taken by the military forces (TNI) and the police to Expo Waena, where a riot took place. Four people reportedly died, including one TNI member.

Meanwhile, in Wamena, riots accompanied by the destruction of public facilities, began suddenly after rumors spread about an allegedly racist incident involving a high school teacher and a student. At least sixteen people were reportedly killed during the clash. According to the government, the attack was intended to attract the attention of state officials who were attending the United Nations General Assembly at that time.[8] On the other hand, the conflict in Wamena is moving toward a horizontal conflict between the Papuan indigenous population and the migrants from outside the region. The root causes of this clash are social inequality and injustice. Meanwhile, the government attempted to restore order in Papua and West Papua by sending additional TNI troops. Thousands of migrants returned to their hometown for safety.

For Papuan students studying in a few universities in Java, racism is a daily experience. For example, YANG complained she was humiliated by her own lecturer in class when discussing gender issues. She also thinks she does not fit in the socially constructed beauty standards accepted by many Indonesian women, that is, being fair-skinned and slim, having a sharp nose and long straight hair (interview, Yogyakarta, January 7, 2021). She was considered not beautiful. That was a traumatic experience for YANG. She also has difficulties in finding a boarding house in Yogyakarta because she is Papuan. The public has stigmatized Papuans as criminals, alcoholics, and troublemakers.

The government has also perpetuated "differences" both regarding physical appearance and character (Papuans are considered as being uncivilized and backward). Political violence is reproduced in and through representations of culture and difference (Kirsch 2002). One FGD participant became furious when another Indonesian fellow thought that she originated from Africa (FGD, Papuan millennials, Jakarta, January 25, 2019). This is a sign that Papuans are not well "introduced" to the rest of the Indonesian society. One informant also observed that his Indonesian fellow visualized Papua as "traditionalist" and backward. Papuan youth feel that there is always an attempt to "force" Papuans to be Indonesians but there has never been any effort to make Indonesians understand Papuans.

According to YANG, racism is socially constructed with strong economic and political motivations. It is a means to create a sense of inferiority and lack of self-confidence among Papuans so they will not rebel when outside forces are exploiting the natural resources in their home province. YANG and her friends have experienced the impact of racism. She felt afraid to interact with non-Papuans and to take opportunities that were offered to her. She is afraid of being teased and humiliated. Therefore, she has chosen to avoid interaction with non-Papuans.

Like YANG, LEJ faced similar experiences with racism when she was attending high school in Semarang, Central Java. Her classmates mocked her with the word *kobong*, which means "burn down," because of her dark skin. During her undergraduate studies in Yogyakarta, she had difficulties to meet her lecturer to arrange her grades and felt this was motivated by racism. In a WhatsApp group composed of peers in the university, all members communicate in Javanese which LEJ does not understand. In her view, this was also a form of racism. Like YANG, at first LEJ also experienced a sense of inferiority due to racism. She was reluctant to express her Papuan identity. She lacked self-confidence and was afraid to express an opinion in public.

Learning from such unpleasant experiences, both YANG and LEJ view racism as a blessing in disguise. They started to study theories of racism and had the courage to join public discussions, writing opinions on social media and organizing campaigns to fight racism. It became a turning point for them to "fight against racism." LEJ asserts: "I will not fight racism frontally and with force. I will fight my way. I am also a human being like the others. I want to prove that I am capable. I came with a different physical appearance and political struggle with the others, but I can interact with all of you. I am challenged to build emotional connection with people different from me so you can understand that I have suffered by the experiences of racism. I want to unite different thoughts."

Despite facing racism, both YANG and LEJ have not denied their Papuan identity. They continue to listen to traditional songs, speak their local languages, maintain a distinct physical appearance (hair, skin), and use a traditional bag (*noken*). For both YANG and LEJ, the #BlackLivesMatters movement, which inspired the establishment of #PapuanLivesMatter, encouraged them to fight against racism.

Besides the racist practice implicating Papuan students enrolled at universities outside of Papua, racism is also experienced by indigenous Papuans in their homeland. At Cendrawasih University in Jayapura, a student explains that Papuans and non-Papuans do not mingle with each other. Non-Papuans tend to discriminate against local Papuans. It is difficult for indigenous Papuans to find jobs. There is mutual distrust. However, the phenomenon is more complex because it also involves stereotypes about the mentality or character of Papuans, for example, being lazy, having no entrepreneurial skills, getting habitually drunk, not planning for the future, and committing criminal activities. These stereotypes are not merely stigma made by others but internalized by the Papuans themselves.

Another component of identity construction is obviously related to violence. RW has experienced seeing her brother being chased by the military and having to hide in the attic during the Cendrawasih University bloody incident in 2006. She heard gunshots and witnessed the brutality of the military toward the students (interview, Jayapura, May 10, 2019). Another youth, EV, witnessed his grandfather being beaten by soldiers in the early 2000s (interview, Jayapura, May 11, 2019). POS witnessed the military forcefully confiscating his family's pigs and other belongings in the district of Hitigima (interview, Jayapura, May 11, 2019). YANG has learnt from her parents of the brutality of the military during the "integration" of Papua into Indonesia. People who refused to join Indonesia were killed. Her grandfather was a member of the OPM and was killed in front of her father.

YANG and LEJ also witnessed the brutality of the police when one of their close friends was beaten until his head bled during a demonstration in Yogyakarta. He was finally jailed without trial (interview, Yogyakarta, January 7, 2019). KSM, a student in Yogyakarta, witnessed a friend being caught by people from a local organization and seeing his friend's neck being stepped on. He was finally jailed for six months without trial. Military and police brutality followed by their impunity have caused *memoria passionis* or the memory of suffering among youth. These experiences have caused anger and a thirst for revenge.

Finally, the last component of identity construction from the youth perspective is resentment toward the migrant population. Harsh words from Papuan youths are directed at migrants, who are considered "poison" for the Papuans because they dominate the economy. Migrants undervalue the capacity of Papuans (interview with POS, Jayapura, May 11, 2019). Migrants are accused of stealing Papuan resources and exacerbating Papuan marginalization.

My interlocturs also believe that migrants are better treated compared to indigenous Papuans. They are given houses and accommodation by the government, which they believe never controls the influx of migrants. There is fear of extremism brought in by the migrant population (interview with FRN, Jayapura, May 9, 2019). There are also complaints that the local legislative and bureaucracy are now filled with an increasing number of migrant people. It is easy to say that the government has failed to protect the rights of the indigenous Papuans, and that resentment toward the migrants is partly due to the Papuans' envy and their sense of not being able to compete with the migrants. There is also suspicion by indigenous Papuans that migrants have participated intentionally in a program to reside in Papua as a pro-Indonesian support base in a region of dubious loyalty (interview with FRN, Jayapura, May 9, 2019).

In general, the complexity of Papuan identity has brought detrimental effects toward identity construction among Papuan youth. The majority opt for independence and call for a referendum to separate from the nation-

Fig. 2. The market scene also shows economic inequality. The OAP sell their goods in the streets while the migrants have their own stores.

state of Indonesia due to various and complex "unresolved" components of identity that have been discussed above. Given better education and access to the Internet, Papuan youths are regarded as a "progressive" element fighting for independence. The Papuans from the mountains are also aware that independence will entail bleak consequences of a "horizontal conflict," with Papua eventually becoming a "failed" province.

However, this does not discourage Papuan youth from demanding independence from the nation-state of Indonesia. In this case, as argued by Goumenos (2006), "Papuan nationalism had a political-territorial character (just as like the Indonesian nationalism and other anti-colonial nationalist movements). It was based on the common aim of independence or 'freedom' (*merdeka*) on behalf of the indigenous residents of an artificially created unit."

Goumenos further states that "Papuan nationalism does not seek to construct an a-historical national continuity, but primarily focuses on the recent past (and the collective present), namely on developments that relate to the decolonization of the region and its integration into the Indonesian state. The core argument is that the Papuan past does not build on the activation and dissemination of myths of common descent but is rather understood and represented through collective popular memories, which refer to these developments."

In connection with the above statement and as mentioned earlier, collective memories of violence and torture have been passed down from generation to generation through storytelling and even have become their own life experience. Papua is about *memoria passionis* or the memory of suffering and unjust treatment, a common set of grievances and memories which draw from the recent past, from the often traumatic experiences of Papuans under Indonesian rule (ibid.).

Papuan youths reject "being Indonesian" as part of their identity. They have no sense of loyalty to Indonesia. They refuse to "fight" for Indonesia when the country is in "danger." Indonesia is considered only a territory where Papua happens to be located. Indonesia is only what is written in their identification card. When asked "What is your identity?" the answer is "I am Papuan" and "I am proud to be Papuan" because Papuans are physically different from the rest of Indonesian people. They have dark skin and curly hair. This is part of the resistance identity discussed earlier.

As far as identity construction is concerned, Papuan national identity has been characterized as a negative identity, that is, in opposition to an anti-Indonesian identity. "Papuanness" appears to encompass two definitional criteria: it is "firmly based on the racial difference between Indonesians and Papuans," and it builds on a distinct interpretation of Papua's integration into

Indonesia (Goumenos 2006) along with other factors that has been previously discussed. Hence, the keywords of Papuan nationalism also include political repression, de-Papuanization of the regional bureaucracy, land alienation, and unequal development.

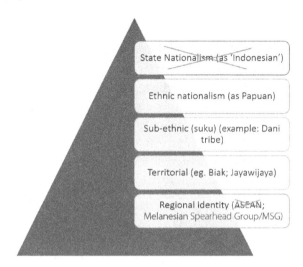

Fig. 3. Layers of Papuan identity.

Figure 3 shows various layers of identity that Papuans could identify themselves with. From conducting several FGDs and in-depth interviews, it is clear they rejected the state-nationalism-cum-Indonesian identity (FGD with Papuan millennials, Jakarta, January 25, 2019). Dual nationalism (Indonesian and Papuan) does not exist. There is only Papuan nationalism based on subethnic, territorial, and regional identities which the Papuans acknowledge. Interestingly, as far as regionalism is concerned, Papuans opt for MSG (Melanesian Spearhead Group) identity. The MSG is one of three subregional groupings in the Pacific Island region. It comprises the Melanesian countries of the southwest Pacific which support Papua independence.

When ASEAN is brought into the equation, it becomes evident that Papuans do not have any faith in ASEAN to solve their problems. They also reject ASEAN membership since ASEAN investment would steal their resources and not bring economic and other benefits for them. Papuans have become resentful of "external and foreign" interests. As for the international actors, Papuans rely on the United Nations to act as mediator. From both the FGD and in-depth interviews, this study also finds that Papuan youth have minimal understanding of ASEAN. News about ASEAN does not interest them, let alone enhance their confidence in ASEAN to solve the complex Papua problem, as stated earlier.

Without a clear understanding of and interest in ASEAN, there is no point speaking about ASEAN identity.

Conclusion

This study has shown that the situation in Papua involves a multicomplex and multidimensional configuration which has been left unresolved for many years. This could become a "time bomb," which might even destabilize the province and influence domestic stability in Indonesia. The Indonesian government has been accused of having failed in managing the situation in Papua.

At the external level, unrest and instability in Papua can also jeopardize ASEAN integration. It has the potential to disrupt the prospects of economic activities from ASEAN countries in Papua or their cooperation with Indonesia in general. However, if the internationalization of Papua is intensified by involving bigger powers such as the US, China, Australia, and the European Union, it can potentially change the geopolitical landscape of this multilateral cooperation. Would ASEAN member states still feel a commitment to be "faithful" to maintain its noninterference principle in the Papuan case, or would ASEAN submit under pressure from those superpower countries to delve into the issue?

Another alarming image of a "fragile Papua" is linked to refugees. There have been cases of Papuans seeking refuge in Australia, which has resulted in tensions between Indonesia and Australia. Papuans could also potentially seek refuge in ASEAN member states. This would become a very sensitive regional issue, just like the case of the Rohingya in Myanmar.

As far as identity issues are concerned, in the discourse and literature review on Papua, it was once believed that the concept of dual nationalism of Papuans (Nationalisme Ganda Orang Papua) was feasible, meaning that Papuans could identify as being Papuans and as being Indonesians at the same time. However, this idea of a dual nationalism has vanished and has been replaced by a single nationalism—Papuan nationalism. There is no such option as an Indonesian nationalism or identity in the eyes of Papuans. Papuan youth feel obliged to carry on the mission inherited from their predecessors to fight for the independence of Papua via referendum.

Social media and the Internet are now the technological tools used to realize this goal. The components of Papuan nationalism stem from complex historical issues, such as "integration," violence, oppression, marginalization, racism, and resentment toward the migrant population. In other words, Papuan nationalism is the result of contested forms of violence, including the appropriation of land and resources, forced relocation of indigenous communities, racial and ethnic discrimination, civil rights violations, human rights abuses, physical assault and torture, sexual violence, and extrajudicial killings (Kirsch 2002, 53).

So far, the government has only recognized the Papua problem as being rooted in economic underdevelopment. Therefore, it focuses on pouring billions of rupiah into the province through the Special Autonomy Law. This is, in fact, the wrong way of trying to overcome the complexity of the issues at stake, especially those relating to the violation of human rights, military/police impunity, economic marginalization, and racism, which are all crucial issues in Papua.

Too many "invisible hands and interests" have been delving in Papua for decades. This may hamper any government or administration to have the courage or commitment to solve the problems in Papua because any effort to touch the "untouchable" may bring detrimental consequences on the current political leadership. Despite these challenges, a breakthrough is needed to deal with the complexity in Papua. If not, it can be imagined that further "forces" will erode stability not only in Papua but also in Indonesia and this would bring about detrimental effects on ASEAN integration.

Endnotes: Papuan Youth Identity

1. In this chapter I use the word Papua to describe the context in both provinces of West Papua and Papua, even though in some cases there are distinct characteristics which I will highlight. In July 2022, the province of Papua was split into four smaller provinces called South Papua, Central Papua, Highland Papua, and Papua (the latter extending along the northern coast).

2. Saferspaces.org.za/understand/entry/what-is-violence. Accessed January 27, 2020.

3. It is difficult to obtain an exact number of victims. However, between 1963 and 1998 the violence of the security forces in the region resulted directly or indirectly in the death of an estimated 100,000 Papuans (Neles Tebay, cited in Goumenos, 2006).

4. Selpius Bobii at that time was the general chairperson of The United Front of the Struggle of the People of Papua and a political detainee in Abepura Prison in Jayapura, Papua. He wrote his article on March 25, 2013, while in prison.

5. Other reports describe various acts of violence in Papua, for example, a 2013 article by Markus Haluk, Papuan human rights activist, titled "Mati atau Hidup: Hilangnya Harapan Hidup dan Hak Asasi Manusia di Papua" [Dead or Alive: The Loss of Life and Human Rights in Papua], and "We Will Lose Everything: A Report on a Human Rights fact-Finding Mission to West Papua" conducted by the Catholic Justice and Peace Commission of the Archdiocese of Brisbane in 2016.

6. *Divide at impera* aims to gain and maintain power by breaking up larger concentrations of power.

7. One example is when an Indonesian campaign was launched in the early 1970s (Operasi Koteka) that forced the highland Papuan tribes to abandon their traditional appearance and get accustomed to textile clothing. This was not only a military operation but also an effort to suppress Papuan cultural identity and expression.

8. "Kerusuhan di Papua: Tentara dan Polisi Diminta Tidak Terpancing." *Kompas*, September 24, 2019. https://kompas.id/baca/nusantara/2019/09/24/tentara-dan-polisi-diminta-tidak-terpancing.

References

Amnesty International Indonesia. 2018. "Don't Bother, Just Let Him Die: Killing with Impunity in Papua." Jakarta: Amnesty International Indonesia.

Anderson, Bobby. 2015. "Papua's Insecurity: State Failure in the Indonesian Periphery." *Policy Studies* 73. Honolulu: East West Center.

Anderson, Kjell. 2015. "Colonialism and Cold Genocide: The Case of West Papua." *Genocide Studies and Prevention: An International Journal* 9(2): 9–25.

Castells, Manuel. 2010. *The Power of Identity*. Oxford, UK: Wiley-Blackwell.

Catholic Justice and Peace Commission of the Archdiocese of Brisbane. 2016. "We Will Lose Everything: A Report on a Human Rights Fact-finding Mission to West Papua." May 1. https://cjpcbrisbane.files. wordpress.com/2016/05/we-will-lose-everything-may-2016.pdf.

Chauvel, Richard. 2009. "Papuan Nationalism: Christianity and Ethnicity." In *The Politics of the Periphery in Indonesia: Social and Geographical Perspectives*, eds. Minako Sakai, Glenn Banks, and J. H. Walker. Singapore: NUS Press.

Elisabeth, Adriana, Aisah Putri Budiarti, Amorisa Wiratri, Cahyo Pamungkas, Wilson. 2017. *Executive Summary: Updating Papua Road Map: Peace Process, Youth Politics and Papuan Diaspora*. Jakarta: Indonesian Institute of Sciences (LIPI).

Elisabeth, Adriana et al. 2019. "Menuju Papua Yang Stabil dan Sejahtera." *Policy Brief.* Jakarta: Indonesian Institute of Sciences (LIPI).

Elmslie, Jim, and Camellia Webb-Gannon. 2013. "A Slow-Motion Genocide: Indonesia Rule in West Papua." *Griffith Journal of Law and Human Dignity* 1(2): 142–66.

Erviani, Ni Komang. 2017. "Students Rally for West Papuan Independence in Bali," *The Jakarta Post*, August 2.

Fearon, James D., and David D. Laitin. 2000. "Violence and the Social Construction of Ethnic Identity." *International Organization* 54(4): 845–77.

Goumenos, Thomas, 2006. "The Activation of the Recent Past: National Identity Formation and Conflict in West Papua." Paper presented at the ASEAN 16th Annual Conference, "Nations and Their Past, Representing the Past, Building the Future." London, UK, 28–30 March.

Grabowsky, Volker, Jayeel Cornelio, and Medelina Hendytio. 2020. "Shaping Alternative Identities in Southeast Asia: Youth, Violence and Transnationalism. State of the Art and Theoretical Framework, Working Paper WP 4." CRISEA Working Paper Series No. 4.

Haluk, Markus. 2013. *Mati atau Hidup: Hilangnya Harapan Hidup dan Hak Asasi Manusia di Papua* [Dead or Alive: The Loss of Life and Human Rights in Papua]. Jayapura: Deiyai.

Hardie-Bick, James. 2016. "Escaping the Self: Identity, Group Identification and Violence." *Onati Social Legal Studies* 6(4): 1032–52.

International Coalition for Papua and the West Papua-Netzwerk. 2017. *Human Rights in West Papua 2017. Fifth Report 2015–2016*. Wuppertal, Germany: International Coalition for Papua (ICP).

Kirsch, Stuart. 2002. "Rumour and Other Narratives of Political Violence in West Papua." *Critique of Anthropology* 22(1): 53–79.

———. 2010. "Ethnographic Representation and the Politics of Violence in West Papua." *Critique of Anthropology* 30(1): 3–22.

Maulia, Erwida. 2020. "George Floyd Protests Inspire Campaigns against Racism across Asia," *Nikkei Asia*, June 9. https://asia.nikkei.com/Spotlight/Society/George-Floyd-protests-inspire-campaigns-against-racism-across-Asia. Last accessed on 20 August 2022.

Moser, Caroline, and Elizabeth Shrader. 1999. *A Conceptual Framework for Violence Reduction*. Urban Peace Program Series. Latin America and Caribbean Region. Sustainable Development Working Paper No. 2. Washington, DC: The World Bank.

Munro, Jenny. 2019. "Indigenous Masculinities and the 'Refined Politics' of Alcohol and Radicalization in West Papua." *The Contemporary Pacific* 31(1): 36–63.

Napoli, Antonella. 2014. "Social Media Use and Generational Identity: Issues and Consequences on Peer to Peer and Cross-generational Relationships—An Empirical Study." *Participations: Journal of Audience and Reception Studies* 11(2): 182–206.

Perkasa, Vidhyandika D. 2011. "Memotret Stagnasi dan Krisis Berkepanjangan di Papua." *Jurnal Analisis CSIS* 40(1): 87–99.

Reuters. 2022. "Separatists in Indonesia's Papua Kill 8 Workers at Telecom Tower." March 4. https://www.reuters.com/world/asia-pacific/separatists-indonesias-papua-kill-8-workers-telecom-tower-2022-03-04/. Last accessed on 20 August 2022.

Robinson, Geoffrey. 2010. "Mass Violence in Southeast Asia." In *Political Violence in South and Southeast Asia: Critical Perspectives*, eds. Itty Abraham et al., 69–90. Tokyo: United Nations University Press.

SaferSpaces. 2021. "What is Violence?" https://www.saferspaces.org.za/understand/entry/what-is-violence.

Sen, Amartya. 2007. *Identity and Violence: The Illusion of Destiny*. New York: W.W. Norton and Company.

Surya, Yuyun W. I. 2016. "The Blacks of Indonesia": The Articulation of Papuan Ethnic Identity on Social Media." *Media and Jornalismo* 16(29): 93–110. Coimbra University Press.

Wangge, Hipolitus, and Gafur Djali. 2016. "Indonesia Must Confront Its Papua Problem: Jakarta Should Tackle the Issue Head On." *The Diplomat*. https://thediplomat.com/2016/03/indonesia-must-confront-its-papua-problem/.

World Health Organization (WHO). 2002. *World Report on Violence and Health*. Geneva: World Health Organization.

Violence and Belonging: Conflict, War, and Insecurity in Arakan, 1942–1952

JACQUES P. LEIDER

The decade from 1942 to 1952 was a period of abrupt political and social change in Burma's province of Arakan (Rakhine since 1982).[1] Power and political agency shifted and were redistributed in a context of warfare, transition from colonization to independence, and struggles for autonomy. Devastation, bloodshed, and rampant poverty were features of this troubled period where regionally dominant Buddhist and Muslim populations went through a process of increased self-awareness and a reshaping of ethnohistorical identification. The present chapter, a contribution to this volume on identity formation in Southeast Asia, looks at the interaction of multiple forms of violence with the consolidation of belonging.[2] Violence and belonging were underpinned by the politics of community formation which persisted and hardened during the following decades, engendering new intercommunal strife.

The significance of investing in research on Burma's pre-1962 period of early independence calls for a word of explanation. While anthropological research on the borderlands, often generated by development studies, has been flourishing, the history of Myanmar's territorial periphery is still poorly understood (Sadan 2018). The neglect is linked to the unequal development of ethnohistorical studies on and in Myanmar due to recent political conditions and habits of state-centric framing of political history. Knowledge-production on ethnically denominated states remains mostly organized within constitutional, legal, developmental, and transnational approaches highlighting issues of state-minority discontent.

This chapter aims to fill a gap in our current knowledge on the conflict etiology in late colonial and early postcolonial Arakan. It demonstrates a hierarchy of interacting levels of violence, including communal riots, civil violence involving political groups, warfare, and coercive as well as oppressive state policies. It is organized in three parts.

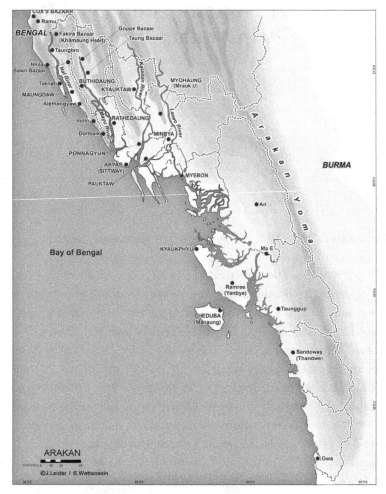

Arakan 1942–48.

The first part presents the thematic, methodological, and conceptual framework. The second part describes three arenas of conflict: the Buddhist-Muslim riots and ethnic cleansing during Britain's war with Japan (1942–44), the anticolonial struggle of the Rakhine and the Nationalist-Communist revolt led by U Seinda (1942–49), and, finally, the early phase of the insurgency of the Mujahids and the struggle for an autonomous Muslim state (1946–52). The rather better-known regional theater of war between Japan and the Allied Forces is not part of the investigation but forms the background, contextualizing the situation of the people within the region. These empirical data do not aggregate as a comprehensive narrative of the period but prioritize those elements which sustain the chapter's main argument. This is discussed in part three, where I contend that the experience of war and ongoing violence and insecurity after the war hastened a process of self-identification and belonging because they entrenched a hostile set-up between competing parties—Buddhists, Muslim communities, and the state—that was grounded in conflicting territorial stakes, rival elite interests, and an emotional regime of lingering fear and resentment. The most recent cycle of violence, which followed the outbreak of communal riots in Rakhine State in 2012, culminated in the mass exodus of several hundred thousand Muslim Rohingyas in 2017 and led to accusations of genocide. It generated an avalanche of humanitarian and human rights reports sidelining the complexity of the historical background. The present chapter aims at filling a gap by detailing some of the historical roots of contemporary developments. It also throws light on domestic actors and their profile some eight decades ago. On the one hand, there were the majority Arakanese (or Rakhine) Buddhists who acted politically in line with regional differentiations and traditional interests. On the other hand, there were the Muslims who were a historically stratified community with roots in Bengal and who were differentiated by the level of their social integration in the majority society. In 1942, 80 percent of the Muslims descended from the successive waves of colonial migrants who had settled in North Arakan since the 1850s, known as Chittagonians. The political endeavor of the Chittagonian elite to reidentify and merge with the older local Muslim identities was at the heart of the dynamics which propelled the Rohingya movement in the 1950s.

Exploring a Distressing Decade and the Impact of Violence

The multiple stories of Arakan from 1942 to 1952 have largely remained untold. The colonial order collapsed with the Japanese invasion, uncertainty took over and endured, while threats and coercion did not fade away when the tide of war ebbed. Radically new opportunities emerged for the people of Burma with the prospect of liberation from foreign rule. The birth of two nation-states, Pakistan (1947) and the Union of Burma (1948), meant a "tectonic shift" for people in Arakan as it neatly divided an area of fluid transitions across the Naf River into a borderland of ethnicized domestic conflict.[3]

Violence, as is often signified in introductions to the subject, is loathed by mankind. Yet, when it is in the right cause, namely when it is perceived as justified in the name of principles, can obtain collective approval.[4] During the ten years under examination, violence in Arakan became normalized and spread as a mode of political action, an "action resource" available in various forms and accessible to nearly everyone (Baberowski 2015, 17). What violence does to the bodies and can do to the hearts and minds of people has been extensively studied. Jörg Baberowski has invoked this transformative power of violence: "One enters a space of violence and experiences that nothing is like it was.... Violence changes everything and someone who has been exposed to violence will be a different person. The experience of violence is like a trip into a new world where other rules are valid and other people live" (ibid., my translation).

The present chapter argues that the traumatic experience of violence and turmoil strengthened existing and emerging *patterns of political and ethnic self-identification* among Buddhists and Muslims of Arakan and contributed to the rise of competing subnationalisms in the 1950s. It puts forward this argument by a description of connected arenas of violent action and the presentation of the dynamics of violence. New forms of organizational mobilization conditioned by the outbreak of war were prolonged by latent insecurity after World War II. Arms and ammunition were easily available. When independence loomed, "centrifugal ideologization" by ethnocentrism, nationalism or/and communism soon took apart what the anticolonial struggle had, to a certain extent, temporarily united (Malešević 2010, 8–15). However, the national or universal claim of ideological garb alone cannot account for the links between violence and belonging. By drawing on two analytical frames—territory and emotion—two important elements in the formation of political communities, I contend that the local dynamics of violence led to an increased sense of belonging among the people living in Arakan. Belonging marks both a claim of ownership, such as the possession of the land, and an expression of emotional attachment. It can be evoked with reference to textual and material evidence and is grounded in ideational claims of historical and cultural embedding. By choosing "belonging," an admittedly soft expression when investigating the roots of violence-prone nationalism, this chapter heeds Frederick Cooper's call for "more differentiated analytical language" when dealing with identity, this "hopelessly ambiguous" and "all-purpose" term (2005, 62, 76). By doing so, I also try to go beyond the terminology swirling around ethnic identities, such as "Rakhine" or "Rohingya," reified in the contemporary activist jargon in an ahistorical use. "Belonging" appears also as a sufficiently broad term to hew as close as possible to what the fuzziness of the archive reveals or hides.

In the section on conflict arenas, I deal with three distinct "micro-theaters" of violence. The first one includes both the Rakhine Buddhist attacks driving Muslims out of Central Arakan in early 1942 and the ethnic cleansing of Buddhists by Muslims in North Arakan. In the second one, which concerns

Central and South Arakan from 1945 to 1948, I describe the simmering conflict and outbreaks of confrontation between the British administrators and Rakhine nationalists. The third one features the early phase of a Muslim insurrection which roiled North Arakan for over a decade and began when Burma's independence loomed and British oversight waned.

Ethnic Cleansing and Territorial Division

Starting on March 28, 1942, as sources seem to agree, Rakhine Buddhist villagers violently attacked their Muslim neighbors, set their houses on fire, destroyed their mosques, seized their cattle, and forced them to leave their villages in Minbya and Myebon townships in Central Arakan (Murray 1942; Merrells 1943). Many died and thousands fled North to Muslim-majority areas and into Bengal. What circumstances released this wave of communal violence which spilled over into surrounding townships (Pauktaw, Myohaung, Kyauktaw) during the next months? Making firm statements is hampered by a lack of primary accounts and the hegemony of ethnoracial interpretations hovering over the reconstruction of events (Leider 2017).

Violence also broke out in April 1942 in the townships of Maungdaw and Buthidaung in North Arakan, where Muslims dominated. But here the violence was directed against members of the Rakhine Buddhist minority who fled south and took a more organized character in May after several thousand Rakhine had already been evacuated by British troops from Maungdaw town. Buddhists remaining in the countryside were ejected by the local Muslim leaders who took possession of the land abandoned by the evacuees and divided up administrative control over the township: "In the area nearest the Indian border, the Maungdaw Township down to near Foul Point and the Buthidaung Township to about 20 miles south of Buthidaung, the Maghs [Rakhine] were killed or driven out (except for small groups in Maungdaw and Buthidaung towns, which had always been predominantly Magh); all Buddhist buildings, pagodas and monasteries, were razed or burnt, all Magh villages burnt and all Magh property (mainly cattle) seized" (Murray 1942; Merrells 1943; Mole 2001, 169).[5]

Writing nearly thirty years later, Moshe Yegar combined the two outbreaks of violence: "[T]he refugees reaching Maungdaw incensed the local Muslim majority with their stories, and the latter began to mete out similar punishment upon the Buddhist minority in their midst. These acts of mutual murder soon caused the Buddhist population in northern Arakan to flee, even as the Muslims had fled from the south" (Yegar 1972, 95).

Nonetheless, the rationalization of anti-Buddhist violence as a retaliatory campaign, however arguable, cannot be traced to contemporary observers. Peter Murray, commissioned with the Military Administration of North Arakan in 1943, wrote that "the area of mixed population was the scene of repeated large-scale massacres in which many thousands of people perished or died subsequently of starvation and exposure" (Murray 1949). Bertie Pearn noted that "in April 1942, Akyab district was the scene of civil war, in which unknown numbers were slaughtered and many perished of starvation and exposure in attempting to find refuge elsewhere" (Pearn 1952).[6] While some correlation between the brutal events is undeniable, communal tensions surely existed *previously* in *both* areas. Still, how can we make sense of the outbreak of atrocities without following colonial explanations of tribalism or treating actors just in ethnoreligious terms? I look at Randall Collins' theory of violence as particularly apt to provide a point of departure for an alternative enquiry. He characterizes violence as a "situational process ... shaped by an emotional field of tension and fear" and invites us to reflect on situational dynamics at the micro-level (Collins, 2008, 19). This approach allows us to look at situational processes which were simultaneously determined by the same macro-circumstances: the socioeconomic conditions of the colonial regime and the outbreak of war.

After aerial attacks in December 1941, Burma was invaded by Japan in January 1942. The rapid progress of Japan's military forces led to the evacuation of Rangoon on March 7, the retreat of the British army, the mass flight of the Indian urban population (estimated at over 400,000 of the more than one million Indians in Burma) and the collapse of the colonial administration (see Tinker 1975, 1–15; Leider 2017, 207–8). These events affected Arakan, a region geographically isolated from Burma's central Irrawaddy valley, with immediate effect. Following the bombing of Akyab, the provincial capital on March 23–27, the British Commissioner Abigail left on March 30, leaving the administration to local officers. The progress of the Japanese was supported by an initially small troop of nationalist Burmese who had undergone military training, the Burma Independence Army (BIA). Many Burmese and Rakhine alike wished for freedom from colonial rule.

Burmese nationalism was strongly anti-Indian, and many Indians in Burma were terrified. They were despised as economic rivals and tools of imperial control. They were not only central actors in the colonial economy and urban society but also occupied many administrative and judicial positions. However, in comparison with central Burma, the situation in rural Arakan was different. Between 1860 and the 1930s, Muslim cultivators from Chittagong district in East Bengal had settled in great numbers in North Arakan. At first reluctantly, but increasingly attracted by favorable conditions to transform wastelands into ricefields, they moved into the northern Mayu valley. As settlers moved further south, they entered Buddhist majority areas and mixed with ancient, yet smaller Muslim communities. This settlement migration was not systematically recorded by the colonial administration at the time it took place. Rather, annual reports mentioned the more visible seasonal migration of Chittagonians which sustained the yearly cycle of harvesting. Only in the 1921 and 1931 census reports did the colonial administration start to differentiate the two main resident Muslim groups by ethnohistorical criteria—Chittagonians and Arakanese Mahomedans (for a detailed analysis, see Leider 2020).

While seasonal migration was uncontroversial, the rapid growth of Chittagonian settlements created social tensions which impacted the situational dynamics in March 1942. The tensions were passed over in official documents before the war but explicitly mentioned afterwards. Noting that "it is not surprising that the Arakanese should feel that they were being driven out of their own homeland," Pearn talks about "unavoidable" communal tensions which appeared to him like an innate quality of communal relations. He writes: "The tension found its expression in 1938" during the anti-Muslim rioting and "the collapse of authority in 1942 ... gave an opportunity for this friction to express itself once more" (Pearn 1952). An impression of unmanageable tribalism is also conveyed by Murray's description of the Arakanese as the "hereditary enemies" of the North Arakan Muslims (Murray [1980]).

Myanmar historians have commonly blamed colonial rule for ethnic divisions and mistrust. So does Rakhine historian Than Than Oo, who links mistrust and the *outbreak* of violence to a mix of panic and uncertainty, with rumors about hordes of Indians fleeing from Burma, real and imagined threats linked to the move of armed troops, and a rush on both sides of the divide to obtain arms (Than Than Oo 1992, 46–48).

A pattern of antagonistic confrontation was undoubtedly in place and, to follow Collins' theory, a sudden break in the solidarity of latent fear and tensions among the numerically dominant Buddhist community was very likely, allowing a splinter group to take the initiative, unleash a herd-like behavior, and do real harm (Collins, 2008, 8). The initial event, it seems, was the killing of the village headman of Rakchaung and his younger brothers in Minbya township (Aye Chan 2005; Yu Yu Aung 1999, 38).[7] This was a township with a Buddhist majority of at least 85 percent, but its population increase since the 1920s and the marked increase of the Chittagonian minority could have led to competition for agricultural land and explain rising frictions. Other elements, such as information circulating about earlier anti-Indian riots and gendered factors such as the temporary presence of mostly young male seasonal labor, may have had an impact.

Virulent anti-Muslim violence in 1942 took place in the townships of Minbya, Myebon, Pauktaw, Myohaung, and Kyauktaw. Except for the township of Kyauktaw where Muslims formed one-third of the total population since at least the late nineteenth century, Muslims formed an average of just 14 percent in the four other townships in the 1930s and probably numbered around 60,000 in 1942.[8] Communal violence was highly contagious and easily reignited in the shadow of the war between British and Japanese troops from late 1942 to 1943.

In an internal note of November 10, 1942, Raibeart MacDougall, the Counsellor of the Governor of Burma in exile, noticed "expulsion of minorities in both cases now an accomplished fact." The main impact of the explosive violence was the large-scale exodus from local populations rather than the number of killed, effectively dividing the territory into an exclusive northern Muslim zone mostly under British military control, and a southern Buddhist majority zone under the Japanese.[9] Colonel Phelips, the military administrator of North Arakan, maintained that "massacres of Muslims by Buddhists [had been] exaggerated" [MacDougall 1942]. But anti-Muslim aggressions seem to have continued in Kyauktaw township until at least June 1942 (Merrells 1943). Many Muslims risked death from starvation, such as "30,000 … refugees" who failed to cross into Maungdaw township in mid-June 1942 when the Japanese in Buthidaung blocked the road toward Bengal [MacDougall 1942]. Venerable Pinyathiha, a community leader, allegedly intervened in favor of a "conflict-free" departure of Chittagonian villagers. British authorities later put him on the list of people connected to the forceful expulsion of Muslims (Duckett 2019, 163).

In the north, the systematic expulsion of an estimated 40,000 Buddhists was organized by Peace Committees whose leaders confiscated and redistributed the agricultural lands of the evicted in order to generate tax income.[10] The British condoned these frauds. It was seemingly the price paid for enlisting local Muslims for V-Force, a special troop formed to collect intelligence along the frontline.[11] During the war against Japan, the British saw the Rakhine Buddhists as traitors and praised the loyalty of the Muslims. During the Allied Forces' First Arakan Campaign (December 1942–May 1943), "most of the villages on the West bank of the Mayu River [Rathedaung township] were burnt and destroyed" by Chittagonian V Force members and the population went into hiding in the jungle. Once the British had to leave, Buddhist Rakhine took their revenge against the Muslims remaining in Central Arakan: "The Indians in the Kaladan have had a bad time and another lot of them around the mouth of the Pi Chaung were slaughtered.... They estimate that out of 40–50,000 about 5–8,000 are now left. Their cattle have been stolen and they have had to pay ransom" (Burnside 1944). The consequences of the mutual ethnic cleansing were buried by the sequence of immediate events of the war between the Allied Forces and the Japanese. But competing Buddhist and Muslim narratives of grief and victimhood formed a layer of constructed memories emerging in later decades. Their propagandistic use, alleging for example an attempted extermination, seems misguided, because violence was less nihilistic—about killing—than opportunistic—about reterritorializing economic and political interests, as I will argue below.

Social and Political Contestation in Central Arakan, 1945–48

The three-year period from Arakan's reconquest by the Allied Forces in January 1945 to Burma's independence on January 4, 1948, was a restless contest between Buddhist leftist actors and the British administration reestablished in Central and South Arakan. The Burmese community, the paramilitary, and party leaders eagerly wished for Burma's independence but were divided over how to achieve it. Communist practices and ideas enjoying increasing popularity provoked ideological militancy and division.

U Pinyathiha, a leader who had joined the anti-Japanese struggle early on, rallied the unity call of General Aung San and the Anti-Fascist People's Freedom League (AFPEL) for ethnic cooperation launched at the Panglong Meeting in February 1947. Aung San had built his anti-fascist alliance into the dominant political force and successfully pushed for negotiating independence, thus paving the political transition toward Burma's freedom (Tinker 1986, 473–74). But he was unable to convince Arakan's entire political class. A nationalist minority among tradition-minded urban and leftist rural Rakhine fancied Arakan's independence, although the region suffered from dismal destitution and widespread insecurity. A faction led by U Seinda, another respected monastic leader within the anti-Japanese front, combined a call for independence arms in hand with radical political dissent. The monk's efforts to unseat the British authorities in Arakan together with the outlawed Red Flag Communists met ruthless British repression. I highlight U Seinda's revolt because it was significant for the political community formation in Rakhine, turning its population against colonial rule as much as the prospect of a centrist Burmese state ruling over Arakan.[12]

In the war against the Japanese, after the failure of the First Arakan Campaign, British troops regained control over North Arakan only in January 1944. Their next attempt to take foot further south started in late 1944, after beating back the Japanese at Kohima in what is today Nagaland (Northeast India). The attack against Akyab was launched on November 8 and the invasion made good progress in December 1944 and January 1945, thanks to the cooperation with Rakhine rebels trained in India by British special forces called Operation Billet of Force 136 (Duckett 2019, 151–64). Parachuted with wireless telegraphs into Japanese-held territory to guide aerial attacks, they helped in building a communications network from July 1944. Yet, these men were often former members of the village-based Arakanese Defence Force, which had been recognized by the Japanese as a paramilitary formation called Rakhine Youth Home Guard.[13] The British might, therefore, doubt their loyalty and, indeed, the Rakhine mix of opportunism and calculation to navigate shifting interests made the Civil Affairs Service (Burma), widely known as CAS(B), suspicious. Things were complicated by the very different approach of the *army*. CAS(B) administrators were former members of the Indian Civil Service (ICS), Burma Civil Service (BCS), or the police, keen to arrest suspects known for anti-British activities. Their view ran across the hands-on approach of Force 136 officers, who pushed for temporarily arming the anti-fascist resistance which it saw as an asset against the Japanese in Burma. After the end of the war, when Governor Dorman-Smith returned from exile in October 1945 to restore civil government, a wave of arrests of Rakhine rebels antagonized the population.

U Seinda, blacklisted as anti-British, went into hiding when CAS(B) administrators clamped down on underground leaders in February 1945. His role became more significant when other leaders, among them U Pinyathiha, U Kra Hla Aung, and U Kyaw Mya, were lured to Calcutta under the pretense of political discussions (Kyaw Mya 1946, 14–15) and prevented from returning to Arakan for two months. Another monk, U Narada, was thrown into prison until December 1945 without clear reasons, while the search for hidden weapons often led to excessive repression (Than Than Oo 1992, 93–97). U Kyaw Mya, then General Secretary of the AFPFL in Arakan, writes that the village of Kra In Daung, U Seinda's place of residence, was encircled in May 1945, and although no weapons were found 84 men between the ages of 18 and 70 were herded like cattle to the police station in Myebon where they were kept under duress and barely fed for seventeen days (Kyaw Mya 1946, 93–97). The leaders who returned from Calcutta in late April 1945 immediately tried to calm the explosive situation and negotiated the liberation of the imprisoned rebels. U Seinda, on the other hand, sent a delegation to Aung San in Rangoon, arguing that the rebels had to stay underground with their arms to face the British if needed. The monk himself stayed in hiding because CAS(B) refused to soften its strict position on his case.

Developments in Arakan took place in conjunction with Aung San's struggle for the creation of a Burmese army and his party's representation at the government level. In 1946, steps were taken to integrate members of the Patriotic Burmese Forces (the renamed Burma National Army raised under Japanese rule) into the newly founded Burma Army (December 1945). But as all the men, including anti-Japanese rebels in Arakan, could not be recruited, a paramilitary formation was created, the People's Volunteer Organization (PVO, often referred to as PYT, the Pyithu Yebaw Tat) to prevent them from losing their military skills and to have them assist in the suppression of crime. The PYT units were also supposed to stand by the AFPFL buttressing law and order policies.[14] While many did, others were instrumentalized by local political entrepreneurs or joined the illegal Communist Party of Burma. In September 1946, Aung San joined the Governor's Executive Council. With the negotiation of the Attlee-Aung San agreement in January 1947, independence came in close sight, but still, in Arakan, hardcore opponents mistrusting the British called for *immediate* independence.

U Seinda's ideological credentials are uncertain. In a leftist revolutionary tradition, he definitely saw armed struggle as the only road to freedom from colonial rule, putting him in opposition to those influential Rakhine who supported the AFPFL and national unity. Therefore, he brought the Arakan People's Freedom League he had founded in December 1945 in close alliance with the Red Flag communists under Thakin Soe. In sum, from 1945 U Seinda was a controversial albeit popular figure, commanding a "large armed following" and described as "a thorn in the Arakanese administration flesh."[15]

When the administration proved unable to suppress banditry or respond to the risk of people starving because markets were not provided with goods, U Seinda exhorted farmers to refuse tax payment and to defer land rents and the repayment of loans. Setting up a parallel administration, including courts in Myebon and other townships, demonstrated the government's effective loss of authority. U Seinda's Arakan Youth League was accused of paramilitary activities and judged illegal. When strikes destabilized the whole country in September 1946, it was accused of attacking police stations.[16] In reaction to U Seinda's threats, Arakan's civil authorities called for a clearance operation which lasted from October 19 to November 5. Thirty villages were raided by the army in an area covering 3000 square kilometers; eleven were burnt to the ground. Arms and ammunition were seized, but only 34 rebels were arrested, including the monk himself. The Under-Secretary of State for India and Burma, Arthur Henderson, judged the operations "pretty drastic treatment and on the face of it very difficult to justify" and called for explanations (Tinker 1983, 38–39. But Governor Hubert Rance opined that "the military operations were justified" and the "burning of villages ... legal" (Tinker 1986, 44–45). For the Rakhine, the excessive repression was outrageous, and the entire Rakhine political class advocated for the liberation of U Seinda. Those who mistrusted the AFPFL felt confirmed in their earlier suspicion because the clearance operations took place barely a month after Aung San had entered the Governor's Executive Council. Aung Zan Wai, the Rakhine AFPFL member of the Council, took U Seinda's defense, arguing that he was not "anti-social" but "forced into his anti-government position by indiscriminate arrests and by issue of warrants for arrest of guerillas of Force 136 and leaders arising out of misunderstanding between V Force and U Sein Da who had supported guerillas and co-operated with OSS unit of US forces" (ibid.).

Rance's personal view was that "U Sein Da's rising was part of an over-all scheme organized by AFPFL cum Communists against the Government."[17] These explanations only partially caught the complexity of the rebellion. On December 17, 1946, an amnesty set the monk free with the hope that he would cooperate "in the maintenance of peace and tranquility."[18] In 1947, however, the situation further deteriorated. Entire village tracts were shut off in isolation, communications were disrupted for lack of water transport, and Akyab, the regional capital, lay in ruins until its reconstruction in the early 1950s. With ubiquitous poverty, the threat of famine was endemic and made state welfare not just a matter of urgency but also legitimacy. Relief measures in September 1947, when 30,000 Rakhine were facing starvation, were caught up in lengthy negotiations about deliveries with authorities in Yangon.

Clearly U Seinda's *resistance violence* to perceived injustice and the state's law-sanctioned regime of *punishment* were locked in opposing logics of legitimacy. At a crucial conference in Myebon in early April 1947, U Seinda broke away from the AFPFL under the influence of a communist faction which rejected the Aung San-Attlee agreement—the agreed roadmap towards independence. When he incited another no-tax campaign, he was rearrested and imprisoned at Tharrawaddy.[19] Efforts by his supporters to set him free failed.[20] His closest ally, Bonpauk Tha Gyaw, a famous communist rebel in his own right and only loosely connected to Burma's communists, carried on nevertheless. Mass demonstrations were organized with revolutionary slogans, tax tickets were burnt, police outposts went up in flames, money was collected or extorted to support the rebellion, military trucks were ambushed, village headmen threatened to stop cooperation with the authorities, and parallel courts were set up once again. In South Arakan, where the Red Guard communists dominated thanks to their presence in the delta region, public administration was brought entirely to a standstill. The lawlessness in the countryside was reinforced by strikes of village headmen and occasionally of police officer unions, too. The conclusion that the administration was rapidly becoming not just "powerless but also functionless" led the authorities to call for another military intervention.[21] Battalions of the Chin Rifles and later the Burma Rifles, altogether 2,000 men, were sent to Arakan. The effect was limited. Larger groups of what the authorities termed "dacoits" were broken up into smaller groups. But the revolt was in no way extinguished and communist organizations affiliated with U Seinda kept a grip on the countryside until the late 1950s.

Crime was a serious problem. Statistics in 1946 and 1947 show that banditry was rampant in Arakan's three districts. The Commissioner's monthly reports restate, monotonously, that numbers did not represent the "true state of affairs" because many cases went unreported.[22] Rebels and criminal gangs recruiting from the same pool of unemployed males were at odds with each other but sometimes indistinguishable. Acts of coercion were facilitated by the easy availability of arms and ammunition. To drive the Japanese out of Arakan, the British military had distributed arms to the Rakhine rebels, commonly known as *pyaukkya*. Guns of various sorts not returned to the authorities after the war were estimated at between 3,000 and 10,000 (Than Than Oo 1992, 93). Villages formed self-defense groups aggressively opposing the gangs but could themselves become the target of police reprisals.

The tensions and collective fear in the majority Buddhist areas of Arakan led to forms of violence which were different from those described in the preceding section. Both the state's security forces and the rebels were structurally weak, and one may wonder why, after years of exhausting struggle, the violent chain was not broken. Collins suggests an interesting approach when he draws attention to the "audience before whom the fight is performed" becoming the "focus of emotional attention" (2008, 19). Arguably, the local administration had to prove itself to the central authorities by fulfilling its duty as a law-and-order agency as much as the leftist Rakhine organizations had to demonstrate their newly gained relevance to the rural population by their violent agitation.

Mention must be made of two types of often-violent coercion exerted by the rebels to strengthen their authority. Village headmen were targeted by the rebels as spies or as tools of the state to enforce tax payment. Venting their anger, they went on strike, retreated to Akyab town, or went into hiding. Furthermore, young men were recruited by force to bolster rebel troops. This appears as a fuzzier form of coercion, but the enormous sympathy which U Seinda enjoyed in his home region suggests that such measures to enforce internal cohesion strengthened collective bonds rather than antagonizing the population. But our understanding of the period cannot stop at a superficial perception of U Seinda as a monastic warlord. U Seinda rose from a context of anticolonial militancy of the 1930s, and the fruits to be derived from a change of power after 1945 were not just threatened by the hegemony and the interventions of the central state. Guns were widely available, bandits roamed the countryside, and insecurity was rife, therefore creating the circumstances for perpetuating internal rivalries as well. To be sure, fighting violence with more violent means was not a recipe to increase his political capital. But U Seinda failed less because of his radicalism than his parochialism, unable to expand his struggle beyond the limits of a few townships.

Insurrection for a Muslim State in North Arakan, 1946–52

The anonymous mass of North Arakan's Muslim population, uniformly referred to as Chittagonians, entered political history with their role as auxiliaries loyally supporting the British return to Burma in late 1942–44. Their leaders distributed territory, taxed the land for income, stabilized control by swiftly ejecting the Buddhist minority, and met the needs of the military administration when prompted. After the war, they were determined to turn their political capital into state recognition and provisions for an autonomous Muslim zone. Betting on British support, they wanted North Arakan, with its Muslim majority, to be classified as a Frontier Area separated from the rest of Arakan. Yet, British wartime sympathies did not help and the civil administration turned down the request as there was no historical precedent.[23] Facing a rapidly changing situation with the imminent independence of India, Pakistan, and Burma, the imagination of North Arakan's political entrepreneurs was pulled into opposing directions: becoming part of a Muslim state under the inspiration of India's Muslim League, or investing into relations with the AFPFL, Burma's emerging powerhouse under Aung San.[24] The fast-track option of joining Pakistan was off the table when Pakistan's Jinnah refused to call into question the India-Burma border and raise territorial claims.[25] The long-term option of lobbying for an exclusive Muslim zone was ultimately successful with the creation of the Mayu Frontier Administration in 1961 by Prime Minister U Nu. The intervening years, however, were a period of political contestation, with the rebellion of the Muslim Mujahids under their leader Jafar Kawal leading to military campaigns, brutal repression, and increased communal resentment.[26]

Unlike Central and South Arakan, North Arakan had been rather stable between 1945 and 1948.[27] The region had suffered less material war damage. Some Muslim entrepreneurs prospered during and after the war and rice harvests were sufficient despite flooding. Land taxes were paid at a stunning rate of 100 percent. These favorable conditions attracted "substantial further immigration from Chittagong."[28] Smuggling of rice and cattle to East Pakistan was rife and enriched the local elite. Displeasure arose only after Pakistan's independence in mid-1947, when a regular Burmese administration and the creation of posts along a poorly checked border threatened vested interests.

An autonomous Muslim state was not a novel idea in early 1948, as it had found a charismatic voice in Jafar Kawal, the founder of a Muslim Freedom Party in North Maungdaw in 1946 and the leader of the Mujahid Party, as the rebels called themselves. His call for *jihad* and the articulation of grievances about land that had not been returned to the Muslims and arrogant Burmese officials humiliating the local population helped to mobilize troops under the Mujahid banner from April 1948 (Yu Yu Aung 1999, 83–94). Like elsewhere, the vagaries of an uncertain future and a lingering sense of injustice sustained tensions. The early Mujahids built on an extended network of sympathizing low-level Pakistani officers in the transborder area which supported the idea of a Muslim-controlled state of North Arakan.[29] The question if this state would still be part of Burma is nowhere clearly addressed. The Mujahids were likely raised among those who had gained military experience during the war.[30] They were estimated at 2,000 in August and 3,000 in December 1948 by Pakistani observers, but sources in Burma quoted their numbers merely in the hundreds.[31] The Mujahids did not need to shed blood to get control over the Muslim villages because the state's effective administrative infrastructure was limited to the towns. For a living, the Mujahids perceived taxes and depended on donations, extortions, and income from smuggling.

From September to December 1948, Burmese troops led attacks in the area north of Maungdaw, Bawli Bazaar, and Taungbro, where the Mujahids held a fortified position on Maung Hnama Mountain.[32] From 1949 onwards, communal violence intensified with looting and killing. The brutal interventions of the Burma Territorial Forces (*sitwundan*), a paramilitary unit of local Rakhine recruits raised to supplement regular troops, deepened the perception of a hostile state. So did air bombings and the scorching of villages during clearance operations (Yegar 1972, 98). Army offensives remained inconclusive as the troops returned to Burma at the end of the dry season or found themselves locked up in defensive positions.[33]

While this situation might have generated greater Muslim solidarity, factionalism soon took over. Mujahid activities in the Buthidaung area were run by Kassim, a warlord, who pushed against the northern leaders Abdul Hussein and Abdul Rashid after Jafar Kawal was killed in 1950 (see Yegar 2002, 83–94).[34] Kassim's men famously hoisted Pakistan's flag, wore green uniforms, and branded the slogan "Pakistan Zindabad." Mujahids moved at ease across the border with the collusion of local Pakistani officers, and maintained headquarters in East Pakistan despite the fact that their activities received no official encouragement from the government in Karachi.[35] The Burmese operations in late 1948 and 1949 led to a mass flight of several thousand people to East Pakistan, many finding refuge with relatives, others being hosted in camps.[36] Reports by diplomats, journalists, and military personnel present a state-centered perspective of the Mujahid rebellion with rebels, soldiers, and the governments as main actors. They say very little about the communal antagonism which thrived, with acts of looting and killing when one of the contending parties saw itself in a position of marginal superiority. In late 1949, a Central Arakanese Muslim Refugee Organization, which had been formed across the border, accused the "unruly forces of North Arakan" of disobeying their government and castigated an "extremist Arakanese Leadership" planning "to wipe out the Rawangyas (Arakan Muslims)."[37] The military balance changed only after 1952 when the Burmese army improved its grip on the security situation throughout Burma.

While it is difficult to disentangle political factions before 1960, what united Muslim rebels and Muslim parliamentarians was a set of core objectives. One was the recognition of a Muslim ethnicity, increasingly associated with the name "Rwangya/Rawangya" or "Roewhengya," precursors of "Rohingya."[38] The other objectives were Muslim autonomy to manage their religious, social, educational, and cultural affairs, the introduction of Islamic law, and the use of Urdu as the sole medium of instruction in schools.

To be sure, not every protester was a militant bending toward Pakistan. Still, culture and the colonial migrant past of many projected a uniform impression of North Arakan Muslims. The Jamiat ul-Ulama (Council of Religious Scholars) in Maungdaw, claiming to speak "on behalf of the people of North Arakan," had pleaded with the British for the "frontier state" status in 1947 while, a year later, it appealed to Prime Minister U Nu for the creation of an autonomous Muslim area.[39] Both politically and socially, the population and its leaders were engulfed in a process of rapid and contradictory change animated by opportunities, ideologies, and collective moods. While the Jamiat was domestically perceived as the civil face of the separatists, it suffered internal divisions that are reflected in paths chosen by its members. Abdul Ghafar from Buthidaung, an elected member of the Constituent Assembly (1947), maintained that Muslims in Arakan were an indigenous population rather than a recent migrant community. He became one the leading lights of the Rohingya movement in the 1950s fighting for the recognition of an indigenous Muslim ethnicity. On the other hand, Omra Meah, who had led the expulsion of the Buddhist population in 1942 as chief of the Maungdaw Central Peace Committee, became one of the underground Mujahid leaders.[40] Political versatility is salient in the life of the region's best-known politician, Sultan Ahmed. He became the Parliamentary private secretary of U Aung Zan Wai, the Minister of Minorities, a Rakhine Buddhist, but was also described in a secret report from East Pakistan as a Mujahid leader (Niblett 1948).

Like the rebellions further south, the organized violence of the early Mujahid insurrection remained territorially limited. Despite brief contacts between Kassim, the Muslim warlord, and U Seinda, the rebellious monk, cooperation between Buddhist leftists and Muslim rebels did not materialize. Until 1951 Mujahid attacks against Burmese infantry and naval craft dominated the timeline of events in North Arakan. The Burmese army led annual military campaigns deploying land, sea, and air forces, but gained ground only after 1951. Meanwhile, the organized robbery of Kassim's Mujahids hurt Muslim civil society (Yu Yu Aung 1999, 88; Yegar 1972, 96).

Territory, Emotion, and the Perpetuation of Conflict

Territoriality matters and it does so in various ways. Territorial stakes were at the center of the three conflict arenas. As a frame to review events of the 1942–52 decade, territory has a strong explanatory potential. From 1942 to 1945 Arakan was frontline in the confrontation between Japanese and British forces and a theater of military confrontation. After the British reoccupation in early 1945, the region turned into a troubled margin at Burma's western periphery. Even after independence on January 4, 1948, it remained out of government control due to local rebellions. The situation worsened and Arakan found itself further divided, first by the impact of nationwide rebellions against the central state and, second, by the communal conflict between a dominant Muslim population of migrant origins in the north not welcoming the Buddhists who had become a minority. While "Arakan" was validated as a geographically, administratively, and historically meaningful spatial entity, and has remained so until today, the unity of the territory had imploded. With independence, Arakan was free of the British and Japanese but perceived by Buddhist Rakhine as territorially diminished due to the loss of North Arakan to the Chittagonian migrants. Before the British (1826), older acculturated Muslim communities who had lived along the rivers and the coast for centuries had never demographically dominated a *single* area.

The leadership of the North Arakan Muslims, not an entirely homogenous community due to the stratified pattern of migrant settlements mixed with older communities, did not want to lose the territory that Muslims farmed as landowners. The Buddhist areas were torn between opposing forces, those keeping Arakan within the Union, be it in cooperation with the AFPFL Union government or the Burmese communists' nationwide struggle, and a parochial drive to rebuild Arakan with the strength of its own people and a yet-to-be defined project of independence or autonomy entertained both by local leftists and conservative urbanites.

Territoriality, however, is more than a physical expression.[41] Territorial brokenness was not commensurate with the way that territories and their nexus with the resident population were imagined both culturally and politically. The kingdom of Arakan was twice the size of the eponymous colonial division, including parts of southeast Bengal, and since its decline in the late seventeenth century its history had been a story of territorial diminishing. Arakan imagined by Buddhist Rakhine was both significant as a site of historical belonging and ambiguous in its geographical and cultural configuration, alluring yet with borders undefined. Was Arakan the land that the Rakhine could possibly control because they formed a majority? Was it a land to be reconquered? Or was it a wider cultural space where people who identified as Rakhine lived? Remember that pockets of Rakhine people lived far away in Tripura and Bengal's Cox' Bazaar, Sunderbunds, and the Chittagong Hill Tracts. They had migrated there in the late eighteenth century due to the political anarchy in their homeland and after the Burmese conquest in 1784. A similar disparity existed regarding centers of political mobilization. There was an unequivocal Buddhist focus on the former royal capital of Mrauk U (colonial Myohaung), which had seen a restoration of several of its ancient temples since the 1920s. But the headquarters of U Seinda was not the venerated Myohaung but the rural outback of Minbya. Nor did Rakhine nationalists gain access to or even voice their claims from Akyab (Sittway), the commercial and administrative center, evenly populated by Buddhists and Muslims. South Arakan, as shown above, was drawn politically toward Lower Burma.

In North Arakan similar incongruence existed. Its Muslim masses developed into a community of purpose, united by the minimal goal of cultural autonomy but divided on the means of gaining political autonomy. History became an important reference point, but the territory where North Arakan Muslims lived was different from the territory conjured in the political imagination of the emerging Rohingya movement. Like the Rakhine Buddhists, Muslim historical references pointed to the memory of the old royal capital and the ruins of a single mosque associated with an early presence of Muslims. It is important to be aware of the discontinuities of imagined communities of the past and the way they mapped their identities on the territory to understand the later confrontational discussions about historical legitimacy between Rohingya and Rakhine elites in the 1990s. It is because territory was divided, contested, redistributed, and reimagined that territoriality was driving longing and belonging.

Emotion matters, too. It is a political factor and not an accoutrement (Jasper 2006). Fear and collective tension have been named as conditions in the outbreak of violence. The enthusiasm among Buddhist and Muslim leaders is a transversal theme pervading rival causes. Shame may have prevented much talk about the mutual ethnic cleansing in 1942, but traumatic experiences surely impacted identifications (see Leider 2017). The territorial differentials were inescapably linked to emotional regimes of frustration. Frustration, resulting from the gap between expectation and full-blown anger, was also the dominant mood in the years following the violent decade. Differences and their perception were strengthened as political, territorial, and cultural aspirations of communal and state leaders clashed. The Rakhine in the center fought for an autonomous, ethnically denominated state; southern Rakhine was reluctant about such a project and in North Arakan, the emerging Rohingya movement, dreading Rakhine oversight, lobbied for an autonomous Muslim area at all costs and ethnic state recognition.

Seeds of discord having jumped during the violent decade came to fruition when a semblance of order settled in the 1950s. It was poisonous resentment, bitterness, pain, regret, and nostalgia that were driving the increasing bonding of Rakhine on the one hand and North Arakan Muslims on the other. The emotional call for North Arakan Muslims to self-identify as Rohingyas mobilized the younger generation long before the movement became ideologized. The melting of intraethnic differences among Rakhine from various regions happened during the shared experience of resistance to the Japanese and the British. Yet, if solidarity did not entirely survive the ideological conflicts after 1946, ethnic belonging became more deeply entrenched.

Conclusion

The politics of the decade 1942–52 were extremely confusing as the description of the three conflict arenas has shown. Individual and communal belongings newly emerged or were reshaped by a myriad of pressures, challenges, and shifting loyalties. With kinds and causes of violence often lacking clear-cut lines of conflict, we must step back and refrain from adjudicating blame and reduce complexity to a simple frame of victims and perpetrators. The overlapping waves of ethnic cleansing in 1942 had likely resulted from years of frustration and competing elite ambitions which were ignored by the colonial state. In Central Arakan, Rakhine who had fought for freedom from any subjugation, though divided by factions, soon grew desperate after 1945 when they sensed the risk of losing their triumph to a hostile yet overstretched government. Similarly, the Mujahids saw themselves as rightful in laying claims for autonomy in a land where migrant Muslims had settled for decades, and their struggle would then deepen existing communal divisions. In all these conflict arenas, the fateful mix of violence and a sense of righteousness promoted by leading elites invariably strengthened communal links and grounded collective cohesion in emotional response and territorial claims.

Investigating Rakhine Buddhist or Rohingya Muslim nationalism and their ethnic armed organizations since the 1960s and today needs, therefore, an understanding of the violent decade. Increasing ethnic solidarity and emotion-driven mobilization outpaced the conflictual binary of pro-British Muslim versus anticolonial Rakhine of the war period. Still, the nexus of ethnicity, territorial belonging, and nationalist struggle did not lead to social homogeneity. In the twenty-first century, social and political differences persist between North and South Rakhine (as elections show) and between Muslims who alternately identify as Rakhine Muslims or Rohingyas.

Writing about contemporary Rakhine State, one is "condemned" to provide explanations for a long track record of armed rebellions, mass flights, communal riots, poverty and state dereliction, oppression, and the disenfranchisement of the Rohingyas. Global appeals behind the 2012 and 2017 mass violence in Rakhine State have grounded Rakhine's ethnopolitical issues in Myanmar's hyper-ethnicized politics, Islamophobia, and alleged systematic state-engineered persecution of the Muslim minority. They have favored an interpretation of the past seen in retrospect as a tragedy rather than a demonstration of their political strength, and a predication of their victimization under the military regime. This is admittedly wrong. This study shows the power and agency of multiple elite actors before the military coup of 1962, and their consequential political choices. By looking at the events through the prisms of territoriality and emotion, a more humane understanding of the process of newly forming patterns of belonging and embedded conflicts becomes possible.

Endnotes: Violence and Belonging

1. The vernacular term *rakhuiṅ*, transcribed as Rakhine or Rakhaing, can be traced in epigraphic witnesses since the early modern period. It is related to Pali forms such as Rakkha or Rakkhaṅga, referring to the lord of successive city-states which flourished in the Kaladan and Lemro valleys as well as its Buddhist population. Mrauk U, the capital of a kingdom which lasted from 1430 to 1784, was generally denoted as "city of Arakan" on early Western maps. Arakan, a term which has appeared in a vast array of spellings in various Western languages since the late fifteenth century, has remained a widely used name of the coastal region in English, even after its official renaming as "Rakhine State" in 1982.

2. Research for this chapter was enabled by funding of the EU-supported Horizon 2020 CRISEA project and is gratefully acknowledged. Collaborators and friends working within the multinational project in Myanmar, Thailand, and the UK have contributed to the progress of my thinking and understanding of topics discussed here. I am particularly indebted to Andrew Hardy's insightful comments for revising and improving the final version. My thanks finally go to the editors for their questions and careful observations.

3. The Naf River forms the border between Bangladesh and Myanmar.

4. As Collins notes, "... 'good' violence—which is not seen as violence at all ... is not subject to analysis since it is part of normal social order" (2008, 2).

5. Mole writes that in 1943 "the entire population of this area was now Muslim" (2001, 191). According to Hayden, "Acts made to remove an ethnic or religious community from a specific territory, especially one of strategic importance," are now commonly referred to as ethnic cleansing (2008, 504).

6. Pearn was researcher at the Foreign Office and former history lecturer at Rangoon University.

7. Than Than Oo also mentions confrontations of Rajput troops with Buddhists villagers in Myebon, and attacks by Indian Muslims against Rakhine at Sittway in March 1942 (1992, 48).

8. Muslims in these five townships numbered about 50,000 at the census of 1931 (see Bennison 1933).

9. Pockets of the Muslim population remained in the south. Merrells notes that "This division, however, was not absolute; numbers of Chittagonians, chiefly those of families settled in the Akyab District for a fairly long time, remained in Buddhist areas and were not further molested" (Merrells 1943). An Australian weekly, The Age, quoted Omra Meah, the Muslim chief in Maungdaw stating that 1,000 Muslims had been killed by the Buddhists (July 24, 1942). This is a low figure compared with the 100,000 routinely cited by Rohingya propaganda today (https://www.thestateless.com/2016/09/the-muslim-massacre-of-arakan-in-1942. Accessed November 28, 2020.

10. This is an admittedly low estimate derived from the data of the 1931 census. It presumes a population of 270,000 in Buthidaung and Maungdaw, with Buddhists forming 34 percent of the total (93,000). For descriptions of the Peace Committees, see Merrells (1943) and Murray 1942).

11. Merrells, an officer with the Military Administration, writes: "We allowed the various Peace Committees to continue their schemes of realizing rents in kind from occupants of land left vacant by refugee Arakanese cultivators" (Merrells 1943).

12. An interpretation of U Seinda's revolt either as an expression of anti-colonialism, Rakhine nationalism, or communist insurrection is not a central concern of the present study.

13. Like the Chittagonian Muslims of V Force, the duty of Force 136 men was to collect intelligence along the front. Under Japanese rule, a training course for guerrilla warfare had been organized and a school for officer cadets was set up in Laung Gadu near Paletwa in 1943. See Than Than Oo (1992, 63–64); also Thompson and Adloff (1955, 152).

14. See, for example, intelligence report, no. 1036 from May 1946: "The ex-guerrilla Association of Akyab has been converted into a PYT with Kra Hla Aung as Deputy District Leader. He has offered his assistance in the suppression of crime to the District Superintendent of Police" (British Library, IOR M/4/2537).

15. Intelligence report, August 1946. British Library, IOR M/4/2537.

16. British Library, IOR M/4/2635.

17. Thakin Soe's Red Flag Communists was not an illegal organization before January 1947.

18. Monthly report June 1947. British Library, IOR, M/4/2503.

19. Monthly report April 1947. National Archives, FO643-74.

20. "U Hla Tun Pru's letter to Secretary of State for Burma presenting a memorandum on U Seinda," June 30, 1947. British Library, IOR, M/4/2503.

21. Monthly report April 1947. National Atchives, FO643-74.

22. British Library, IOR M/4/2503; M/4/2635; M/4/2655; NA, FO643/74.

23. "Submission by Jamiat ul-Ulama North Arakan to Arthur Bottomley, the under-secretary of state for Dominion Affairs, 24 February 1947," with comments by E. N. Larmour. http://www.networkmyanmar. org/ESW/Files/1947-Jamiat.pdf; Yu Yu Aung (1999, 81–87).

24. A section of the Muslim League in Maungdaw became affiliated with the Muslim League of India on May 5, 1946. Contacts were probably first established in the wake of the preparations for the Constitutional Assembly whose elections took place on April 9–10, 1947.

25. Aung San met Md Ali Jinnah during a stop in Karachi on January 7, 1947, on his way to London for negotiating the path to Burma's independence. See also Bayly and Harper (2008, 253, 293).

26. The 1950s saw also the rise of the Rohingya movement. See Leider (2018, DOI: 10.1093/acrefore/9780190277727.013.115).

27. Bengal, stricken by famine and communal riots after the war, was described as "a subcontinental version of Hell" by Bayly and Harper (2008, 243–51).

28. See Peter Murray's comment "there has been substantial further immigration from Chittagong." National Archives, FO371/69489; Thompson and Adloff mention "postwar illegal immigration of Chittagonians … on a vast scale" (1955, 154). Yegar notes "The mujahideen interest in the illegal immigrants from East Pakistan was as workers who would cultivate abandoned land and grow rice on it" (2002, 45); in a message of 8 February 1947 to the Governor of Bengal, Burma's Governor Rance mentioned "63,000 illegal entries to Buthidaung and Maungdaw." National Archives, FO643/61/4.

29. The name Mujahid implies a religious motivation but the recurrent expression Mujahid party points to their political character.

30. National Archives, FO371/69489 6; National Archives, DO142/453.

31. Major L. H. Niblett's report (1948) mentions "3000 volunteers." National Archives, DO142/453. Britain's Ambassador Bowker informed the Foreign Office that "there are perhaps 500 Muslims under arms" in his dispatch of 12 February 1949. National Archives, FO371/75660. Yu Yu Aung (1999, 44) indicates "2700" based on Myanmar army archives.

32. Yu Yu Aung provides a somewhat disparate overview of military actions (1999, 83–94).

33. A report of the British Services Mission talks about "marauding expeditions," 15 July 1949. National Archives, FO371/75661.

34. On Kassim's fame as a "national hero" in Pakistan, see Yegar (1972, 101).

35. Details are provided in a 1949 report by Major L. H. Niblett. National Archives, DO142/453.

36. British Embassy, Rangoon to UK High Commissioner, Karachi, 28 February 1949. National Archives, FO371/75660.

37. Central Arakanese Muslim Refugee Organisation, "Resolution No. 5 of Meeting No. 12/49." National Archives, DO142/453.

38. There was no standard written form of the name in English until approximately 1963. Since the mid-1960s, the use of "Rohingya" in the names of eponymous armed groups has established the spelling globally in the twenty-first century. The use of various spellings between 1947 and 1963 reflects the existence of different Muslim groups claiming the term, mainly, as sources would suggest, the descendants of the precolonial Muslims on the one hand, and the descendants of the colonial migrant communities on the other.

39. "Address Presented by Jamiat Ul Ulema North Arakan on Behalf of the People of North Arakan to the Hon'ble Prime Minister of the Union of Burma … on the 25th October 1948." GUB, Foreign Office. http://www.networkmyanmar.org/ESW/Files/J-U-25-October-1948.pdf.

40. On Omra Meah as a leader of the Peace Committees and later as a member of the Jamiat ul-Ulema, see Merrells (1943, 57); Niblett (1949); Murray (1942); and "Address Presented by Jamiat Ul Ulema" (fn 39).

41. For reasons of space, the Burmese state-centric perspective cannot be treated in detail. Creating a sense of belonging to the Union by improving the commonwealth of the people in Arakan did not emerge as a state priority. More "care" meant essentially more law and order. Arakan was an administrative unit with a majority of Buddhist people culturally akin to the Burmese. The security forces played an important role after independence, the army's main goal being the control of the border and a law-abiding obedient population.

References

"Address Presented by Jamiat Ul Ulema North Arakan on Behalf of the People of North Arakan to the Hon'ble Prime Minister of the Union of Burma ... on the 25th October 1948." GUB, Foreign Office. http://www.networkmyanmar.org/ESW/Files/J-U-25-October-1948.pdf.

"Submission by Jamiat ul-Ulama North Arakan to Arthur Bottomley, the under-secretary of state for Dominion Affairs, 24 February 1947." [Comments by E. N. Larmour]. http://www.networkmyanmar.org/ESW/Files/1947-Jamiat.pdf.

Aye Chan. 2005. "The Development of a Muslim Enclave in Arakan (Rakhine) State of Burma (Myanmar)." *SOAS Bulletin of Burma Research* 3: 396–420.

Baberowski, Jörg. 2015. *Räume der Gewalt*. Frankfurt am Main: Fischer.

Bayly, Christopher, and Tim Harper. 2008, *Forgotten Wars: The End of Britain's Asian Empire*. London: Penguin Books.

Bennison, J. J. 1933. *Census of India 1931* vol. XI, *Burma* Part II. Rangoon: Office of the Superintendent.

Burnside, Major P. "Major P. Burnside, 81st WAP Division, to Brigadier R. S. Wilkie, 14th Army, 2 March 1944." National Archives, WO203/309.

Collins, Randall. 2008. *Violence: A Micro-sociological Theory*. Princeton: Princeton University Press.

Cooper, Frederick. 2005. *Colonialism in Question Theory, Knowledge, History*. Berkeley: University of California Press.

Duckett, Richard. 2019. *The Special Operations Executive in Burma. Jungle Warfare and Intelligence Gathering in World War II*. London: Bloomsbury.

Hayden, Robert M. 2008. "Mass Killings and Images of Genocide in Bosnia, 1941–5 and 1992–5." In *The Historiography of Genocide*, ed. Dan Stone, 487–516. New York: Palgrave Macmillan.

British Library. IOR M/4/2503; M/4/2635; M/4/2655.

Jasper, James M. 2006. "Motivation and Emotion." In *The Oxford Handbook of Contextual Political Analysis*, eds. Robert E. Goodin and Charles Tilly, 157–71. Oxford: Oxford University Press.

Kyaw Mya. 1946. *Rakhine under the British: Grievances of the Rebels and the Problems of Rakhine (Britishy lak auk ra khuiṅ praṅ Ra khuiṅ praṅ i prassanā nhaṅ. pyauk krāḥ tui. i nac nā khyak)*. Yangon: Printing Press on Churchill Road.

Leider, Jacques P. 2017. "Conflict and Mass Violence in Arakan (Rakhine State): The 1942 Events and Political Identity Formation." In *Citizenship in Myanmar: Ways of Being in and from Burma*, eds. Ashley South and Marie Lall, 193–221. Singapore: ISEAS/Chiang Mai: CMU.

—————. 2018. "Rohingya: The History of a Muslim Identity in Myanmar." In *Oxford Research Encyclopedia of Asian History*, ed. David Ludden. New York: Oxford University Press. DOI: 10.1093/acrefore/9780190277727.013.115.

—————. 2020. "The Chittagonians in Colonial Arakan: Seasonal and Settlement Migrations." In *Colonial Wrongs and Access to International Law*, eds. Morten Bergsmo et al., 177–227. Brussels: Torkel Opsahl Academic EPublisher.

[MacDougall, Raibeart]. 1942. "Note [to the Governor of Burma], 10 November 1942." British Library, IOR R/8/9.

Malešević, Siniša. 2010. *The Sociology of War and Violence*. Cambridge: Cambridge University Press.

Merrells, George L. 1943. "Notes on Events and Administrative Arrangement in North Arakan during the Period August 1942 to May 1943." British Library, Mss Eur F 180/38.

Mole, Robert. 2001. *The Temple Bells are Calling: A Personal Record of the Last Years of British Rule in Burma*. Bishop Auckland: Pentland Books.

Murray, Peter. 1942. "North Arakan 1942." [1980]. British Library, Mss Eur E 390.

—————. 1949. "Peter Murray, Foreign Office, to Robert Fowler, Commonwealth Relations Office, 26 January 1949." National Archives, FO371/75660.

—————. [1980]. North Arakan 1942, detailing the collapse of British Administration in the area, with a brief historical introduction and a short account of subsequent events. British Library. India Office Collections, Mss Eur E 390.

National Archives. FO371/69489 (Burma 1948: Situation in Arakan); FO371/75661 (Political and Military Situation in Burma 1949); Arakan643/74 (Monthly Reports of Commissioners of Division: Arakan Division 1947); DO142/453 (Burma: Arakan 1948).

Niblett, Major L. H. 1948. "Enclosure to Ref. 144 dated the 16th December 1948 from the Deputy High Commissioner, Dacca." National Archives, DO142/453.

[Niblett, Major L. H.]. 1949. "Copy of report dated Rangamati, 7th February 1949 by the Deputy Commissioner, Chittagong Hill Tracts." National Archives, DO142/453.

Pearn, Reginald B. 1952. "The Mujahid Revolt in Arakan." 31 December 1952. National Archives, FO371/101002.

Sadan, Mandy. 2018. "Contested Meanings of Postcolonialism and Independence in Burma." In *The Postcolonial Moment in South and Southeast Asia*, eds. Gyan Prakash et al., 49–65. London/New York: Bloomsbury.

Than Than Oo. 1992. "The Part of the Rakhine in the History of the Struggle for Myanmar's Independence (1936–48)" [Mran mā. lvat lap reḥ kruiḥ pamḥ mhu sa muiṅḥ tvaṅ ra khuiṅ tuiṅḥ raṅḥ sāḥ tui. i akhanḥ kaṇṭa 1936-48]. MA thesis, Yangon University.

Tinker, Hugh. 1975. "A Forgotten Long March: The Indian Exodus from Burma, 1942." *Journal of Southeast Asia Studies* 6(1): 1–15.

————. 1986. "Burma's Struggle for Independence: The Transfer of Power Thesis Re-Examined." *Modern Asian Studies* 20(3): 461–81.

————. 1983. *Burma—The Struggle for Independence, 1944–48. Documents from Official and Private Sources*. Vol. 2. *From General Strike to Independence 31 August 1946-4 January 1948*. London: HMSO.

The Age (Melbourne). 1942. "Civil War in Burma—Moslems fight enemy adherents." July 24.

Thompson, Virginia, and Richard Adloff. 1955. *Minority Problems in Southeast Asia*. Stanford: Stanford University Press.

Yegar, Moshe. 1972. *The Muslims in Burma*. Wiesbaden: Harassowitz.

————. 2002. *Between Integration and Secession: The Muslim Communities of the Southern Philippines, Southern Thailand, and Western Burma/Myanmar*. Lanham/Oxford: Lexington Books.

Yu Yu Aung. 1999. "History of the Mujahid, Red Flag and White Flag Rebellions in Rakhine Province after Independence 1948-58 (Lvat lap reḥ ra prīḥ khet rakhuiṅ desa mūgyāhac alaṁ nyī alaṁ phrū chū pū soṅḥ kyanḥ mhu samuiṅḥ 1948-58)." MA thesis, History Department, Yangon University.

Democratic Kampuchea's Revolutionary Terror in the 1970s: The Role of Cambodian Youth in Mass Violence

VOLKER GRABOWSKY[*]

Although the top Khmer Rouge leaders like Pol Pot (1925–98), Nuon Chea (1926–2019), Ieng Sary (1925–2013), and Khieu Samphan (1931–), to name but a few, were in their forties or early fifties when in power,[1] the middle and lower ranks of the Khmer Rouge movement, colloquially called Angkar ("Organization"), both civilian and military, were rather young people, in their twenties, and many even much younger. The violence these young people experienced either as perpetrators or as victims shaped their social, political, and generational identities.

This chapter seeks to analyze how the leadership of the Communist Party of Kampuchea (CPK) or Pak Kommiunit Kampuchea led by Pol Pot exploited the idealism of Cambodian youth for their political ends. Furthermore, it studies the mechanisms of recruitment of young cadres into the military and political apparatus of the CPK, especially the Communist Youth League of Kampuchea (Yuvakak). Special attention is given to the relationship between young people from rural areas and their peers who came from resettled urban families and were in numerous cases stigmatized as class enemies. The role of education as a means of mobilizing Cambodian youth for the revolution and committing acts of violence will be given special attention. Finally, a demographic survey discusses the human costs of war and revolution during Cambodia's bloody decade of the 1970s.

---

* The research for this chapter was funded by the Horizon 2020 project "Competing Regional Integration in Southeast Asia" (CRISEA). I am grateful to Pong Pheakdey Boramy and Prum Savuth for their help in transcribing handwritten Khmer language documents for me and their excellent explanations of Khmer terms. I would also like to express my deep gratitude to Youk Chhang, Ros Sampeou, and Morm Sophat from the Documentation Center of Cambodia for providing me with precious primary source material. I am in particular indebted to Jacques Leider and Andrew Hardy for their insightful comments for improving the final version.

The deportation of the urban population to the countryside after April 17, 1975, the constant movement of mobile youth brigades to difficult construction sites, and the reshuffle of military personnel and civilian cadres in the wake of political purges raise questions related to migration. Moreover, these purges were mainly motivated by an overarching concern of Pol Pot's Party Centre with security issues—the fear that foreign forces, notably the former ally Vietnam, might try to subvert the CPK through internal agents and destroy the nation's independence. Finally, gender is a pervasive theme since the Cambodian revolution had a great impact on the relationship between men and women both within the core family and in society at large. The prominent role of women in the Khmer Rouge administration at different levels, and even in the military, should not be overlooked. In his study of Khmer Rouge policy on women, Zal Karkaria (2003, 28) provides evidence for the empowerment of women among the rank and file of the Khmer Rouge earned through their work at the front.[2]

Sources

The project is largely based on written material which the Khmer Rouge produced themselves during the five-year civil war and the four years they were in power. This material is considerably larger than what we might expect from a regime known for relying almost exclusively on oral communication due to its ostensibly anti-intellectual and anti-technological orientation. The documentary material from the Khmer Rouge period has gradually been unearthed after the Vietnamese invasion and made accessible to scholars since the late 1990s thanks to the admirable efforts of the Documentation Center of Cambodia (DC-Cam) and its director Youk Chhang. This independent Cambodia research institute, which has a fine reputation as an international leader for memory and justice, has built an impressive collection of tens of thousands of documents not only from the Khmer Rouge period but also from the two war periods 1970–75 and 1979–91. Some of these documents were used as evidence in the Khmer Rouge tribunal, officially called the Extraordinary Chambers in the Courts of Cambodia (ECCC).[3]

During its proceedings over more than a decade—the final judgement in Case 002/02 was held in November 2018—the Khmer Rouge tribunal produced an enormous amount of additional material, such as the transcripts of accounts of witnesses as well as of Cambodian and international experts, translations into English and French of the minutes of meetings of the Standing Committee of the Central Committee of the CPK, telegrams documenting the chain of command within the party and state, and also Khmer Rouge magazines and school textbooks. For my study of violence, in particular youth violence, in Democratic Kampuchea, the following materials were identified as core sources.

The first category of primary sources comprises the issues of two CPK magazines published approximately on a monthly basis. The magazines *Tung Padevoat* and *Revolutionary Male and Female Youth* (*Yuvachun nueng Yuavaneary Padevoat*) started publication prior to 1975, but during the national liberation war period only a small number of handwritten and stenciled copies were made for distribution. From May 1975 until the end of 1978, both magazines were printed at printing house facilities known under the code names K-25 and K-26. These facilities were placed under the authority of the Ministry of Propaganda and Information led by Hu Nim until his purge in April 1977, and thereafter by defense minister Son Sen's wife Yun Yat. Both magazines were distributed only to party members, though not each of the roughly 20,000 full or candidate party members got his or her own copy.[4] Copies were delivered to ministries, military units, and offices as well as units of the Revolutionary Youth Organization at the levels of zone, sector (region), district, and subdistrict. Moreover, they were expected to be shared amongst several members of a unit.[5]

We do not know who penned the exclusively anonymous articles in the two magazines. But in one court statement Nuon Chea admitted that the articles in *Revolutionary Flag* were written by members of the CPK Standing Committee, principally by himself and Pol Pot.[6] Later he withdrew this statement, denying that he authored any articles published in *Revolutionary Flag* and claiming that Pol Pot had "his own personal assistants who were fully in charge of writing the articles."[7] While *Revolutionary Flag* was used for political training sessions of party members, *Revolutionary Male and Female Youth* was targeted at the Youth League known under its acronym Yuvakak.[8] It is believed that at least some articles of that magazine were authored by propaganda minister Yun Yat herself. The two magazines contain similar materials: speeches of CPK leaders, articles on the history of the Party, the alleged achievements of the regime, the general political line of the Party, and future economic plans. A special feature of *Revolutionary Male and Female Youth*, however, were the regular columns dealing with revolutionary short stories and poetry to instill a spirit of "revolutionary vigilance" and patriotism among young people. It is interesting to note that the youth magazine attached some importance to gender issues, stressing the role of women in the production process and national defense. A total of twenty-four issues of the *Revolutionary Flag* magazine and twenty-eight issues of *Revolutionary Male and Female Youth* were accepted by the Chamber as authentic. Less than one-third of these issues have so far been translated into English.

Fig. 1. Cover of the April 1978 issue of the magazine *Thung Padevoat* (*Revolutionary Flag*).

The second category of documents comprise notebooks of youth cadres containing handwritten notes about their participation in political study sessions, interpretations of the statute of the Revolutionary Youth Organization of Democratic Kampuchea, and experiences in regularly held "lifestyle sessions" (*Prachum chivapheap*) in which participants of work units had to engage in criticism and self-criticism in order to eliminate any vestiges of individualistic thinking and lifestyle. Immediately after such lifestyle meetings, discussion meetings would be organized to jointly read and discuss the CPK and Yuvalak magazines.[9] These notebooks, stored in the DC-Cam Archives, contain interesting and informative insights into how the ideological indoctrination was perceived by young cadres in the light of the radical social and economic transformations of the time. Of particular interest are notebooks taken by the mostly young staff of Cambodia's state security prison S–21 or Tuol Sleng. Very few scholars have so far systematically studied such notebooks, with Path Kosal and Angeliki Kanavou (2015 and 2017) being rare exceptions.

The third group of source material is related to education. It includes school textbooks, particularly for classes on geography and society, but also political slogans, poems, songs, and dance performances as forms of "popular education." In a predominantly oral society, which Democratic Kampuchea undoubtedly was, "music emerged as a dominant mode of artistic expression by which a correct political consciousness could be fashioned" (Tyner 2019, 95). It was by radio broadcasting that songs were preferably transmitted. This had the greatest impact on people living in agricultural cooperatives or working at construction sites, like the mobile youth brigades. Khmer Rouge songs combine traditional and popular peasant music with revolutionary lyrics and serve as narratives of revolution and nation-building. A lot of these songs have been collected by the Documentation Center of Cambodia whose archives also contain a collection of oral testimonies, including interviews with former Khmer Rouge performing artists and those who witnessed such performances.

Full translations or at least summaries of selected documents from all three categories of material presented above were regularly published in the English edition of the magazine, *Searching for the Truth* (Khmer edition *Svaeng rok karpit*, with 223 issues from 2000 to 2018) by the Documentation Center of Cambodia between 2000 and 2015.

Theoretical Framework

In the next section I will consider the factors which contribute to mass violence and facilitate a sense of belonging among groups having experienced such violence, either as perpetrators or as victims. First, I briefly reflect on the concept of *Gewalträume* (Spaces of Violence). Thereafter, I will discuss how the "youth bulge" theory can be applied to the Cambodian case.

Spaces of Violence

Mass killings, including the extermination of entire peoples, as well as mass deportations and forced resettlements, are by no means unique to the modern era. However, it is evident that the modern "biopolitical state" (Foucault 1980) possessed the ability to maximize human resources with projects to eliminate enemies on a large scale, putting the biological existence of a population at stake. A strong biopolitical state, the modern Leviathan, claims the exclusive right to use physical violence, including the right to kill. In his seminal essay *Räume der Gewalt* [Spaces of Violence], the German historian Jörg Baberowski, a specialist on Russian and Soviet history, argues that even in the most civilized and technologically advanced societies normal human beings—people who could certainly not be described as abnormal sadists—were able to get involved in mass killings if encouraged by the highest authorities, as in war times, while they would be the most peaceful citizens in times of peace, knowing and fearing that the same acts of violence would be strongly sanctioned by the state (Baberowski 2015). To a certain extent, all forms of modern states, from the most authoritarian dictatorships to liberal democracies, need to discipline their subjects to internalize the state's monopoly of biopower. In societies where a culture of obedience is prevalent, mass violence might be instigated by state authorities more easily.[10]

Besides obedience, other characteristics of a culture or society enhance the potential for group violence (Staub 1989). Hierarchy and honor have been identified by Hinton (1998, 117), along with Cambodian cultural models of obedience, as decisive factors facilitating mass violence. However, sociopolitical transformations alone do not necessarily trigger such large-scale violence against civilians, as the revolutions in Vietnam and Laos demonstrate. They must be accompanied by a violent ideology which dehumanizes a real or perceived "enemy," external or internal. This was precisely what happened in Democratic Kampuchea where the Khmer Rouge divided the population into two antagonistic classes, the "old people" (*pracheachun chah*) or "base people" (*pracheachun multhan*), those rural people who had been living in the revolutionary zones prior to the "liberation of Phnom Penh," on the one side, and the "new people" (*pracheachun thmey*), the people of the capital and a few other urban enclaves of the Lon Nol regime. Dissidents within the Communist movement were dehumanized as "enemies of the people." This explains why the perpetrators of violence, the executioners of the Cambodian state security as well as the perpetrators of the Indonesian mass killings of 1965–66 and Thai soldiers shooting at radical students in the compound of Thammasat University in October 1976, felt no guilt about their deeds.[11]

Cambodia's Youth Bulge

A major factor that has facilitated mass violence in Southeast Asia is the participation of youth. The rank and file of the Khmer Rouge were recruited in large numbers from among the poor peasant youth, and these indoctrinated and generally fanatical youthful cadres were the most feared by almost everyone during the regime's reign of terror (Dith Pran, 1997). Many of the most notorious killings in Indonesia during the witch-hunt of Communists were committed by members of Muslim youth organizations. Many other examples from Southeast Asia and elsewhere can be cited to underline the impact of youth. There exists a wide range of literature demonstrating the impact of a "youth bulge," characterized by a very high percentage of youth especially in the age group 15–24 years. Such a "youth bulge" increases the probability of armed conflicts and mass violence in a society.

The term "youth bulge" was first introduced in the academic discourse by the American political scientists Jack Goldstone in 1991 and Gary Fuller in 1995 and later popularized by the German sociologist and genocide specialist Gunnar Heinsohn in 2003. Heinsohn argues that an excess of young adult males in the population, notably in cases where the cohort of those aged 15–29 is higher than 25 percent of the total, leads to social unrest, internal and external armed conflicts, and terrorism. This is especially the case if the "third and fourth sons," who do not find economic opportunities and prestigious positions in their own societies, rationalize their desire to compete for such opportunities and positions by turning to religion or political ideologies. Marxist-Leninist movements in Third World countries during the 1960s and 1970s, or radical Islam in present times, are examples of such ideological justifications. Heinsohn's provocative thesis appears highly plausible in the light of the Cambodian experience. Cambodia's "youth bulge" had increased from 24.3 percent in 1962[12] to 26.4 percent in 1970,[13] with many thousands of high school students unable to find employment in the state bureaucracy of Prince Sihanouk's autocratic regime and thus were receptive for radical political mobilization in the late 1960s and early 1970s.

The younger age cohorts (below 15 years) increased from 33.4 percent in 1962 to 43.9 percent in 1970, laying the ground for a further increase of the youth bulge in the early 1970s. The young average age was certainly one of the major demographic characteristics at the beginning of the Cambodian tragedy.[14] Although the birth rates declined during the Khmer Rouge regime, as is reflected by the significantly smaller age group 20–24 in Cambodia's age pyramid of 1998, the country experienced a baby boom until the early 1990s, ensuring a youth bulge until recently (31.5 percent in 2008), which has been declining only during the last decade (27.4 percent in 2019). Recently, Heinsohn modified his youth bulge theory by introducing a so-called "war index" (Kriegsindex) which measures the ratio between young men aged 15–19 who are going to join the "struggle ahead of them" (Lebenskampf) in competition to adult men aged 55–59 who are going to leave their positions in the near future. With a war index above 2.5 (2,500 young men are going to replace 1,000 elderly men), a range of reactions can be anticipated: flight and migrations, prostitution, forced labor, gang killings, terror, coup d'états, revolution, civil war, and genocide. Whereas Cambodia had a war index of 5.0 in 1970, the highest in Asia at that time, this index has modestly declined to 3.72 in 2018. This is still high and surpassed in Southeast Asia only by Timor-Leste (4.55), but by 2030 the Cambodian war index will have further declined to 2.50 giving hope to a less violent future (Heinsohn 2019, 18, 30, 34).

State and Society in Democratic Kampuchea: Historical Background

The Cambodian revolution of the 1970s has widely been acknowledged as perhaps the most violent revolution in the twentieth century, if not in world history. When a 150,000-strong Vietnamese army invaded Cambodia on Christmas Eve 1978 and only two weeks later removed the Khmer Rouge regime of Democratic Kampuchea from power in Phnom Penh, up to two million Cambodians had lost their lives. This bloody decade started in March 1970 with a pro-Western coup d'état against the neutralist regime of Prince Sihanouk, provoking a ferocious civil war between Marshal Lon Nol's Khmer Republic and the pro-Communist forces of the Front Uni National du Kampuchea (FUNK).

The collapse of the Khmer Republic on April 17, 1975 began with the complete evacuation of the Cambodian capital and several provincial towns and enclaves along the border to Thailand. An estimated two and a half million, perhaps up to three million people were forced to embark on a march to their new living quarters in the countryside. In contrast to their Vietnamese and Lao comrades, the Cambodian communists discarded the possibility of a long-term transformation phase toward a classless egalitarian society with no poor, no rich, and no exploitation. Inspired by the Chinese "Great Leap Forward," the new regime of Democratic Kampuchea (Kampuchea Pracheathippadey) turned the country into a huge construction site by initiating hundreds of ambitious irrigation projects, including the construction of huge dams, like the "1 January dam" in Kampong Thom Province in central Cambodia, with the aim of substantially increasing rice production. "There has never been a modern regime that placed more emphasis and resources towards developing irrigation," writes Jeffrey Himel, a water resource engineer, in his study of Cambodia's irrigation system.[15] "If we have water, we have rice. If we have rice, we can have everything: steel, factories, energy, and tractors" (quoted after Ponchaud 1979, 716–17; cf. Martin 1981). Such was a well-known slogan at the time visualized by the national coat of arms of Democratic Kampuchea. This shows a chessboard system of dikes and canals symbolizing modern agriculture, and in the background a factory as an icon of industry and modernity. Khmer Rouge publications deplored the almost non-existent heavy and light industry, the poor technological foundation of the country, and the dependence on foreign countries for raw materials.[16] Thus, the total mobilization of the country's workforce based on manual labor was carried out to ensure the massive build-up of an agricultural infrastructure that aimed at a rapid increase of the areas under wet-rice cultivation. The ambitious Four-Year Plan to Build Socialism in all Fields, 1977–1980 promulgated in July–August 1976 envisaged unrealistic, even utopian, goals for annual yields of up to three to six tons per hectare (Chandler et al. 1988, 53–79 (tables 1–28)).

Although hundreds of thousands of tons of paddy, along with other agricultural products, were exported to China, Hongkong, and Madagascar in 1977 and 1978, there was hunger and inadequate medical care in wide parts of the country. However, in this respect there were considerable regional variations to which Michael Vickery pointed as early as November 1980.[17] Although official Khmer Rouge documents divided the population in compliance with orthodox Marxist-Leninist analysis into social classes, social reality was determined by a classification dividing the 7.5 million inhabitants between the rural people who had been living under Khmer Rouge control before April 1975, on the one hand, and those predominantly urban people in the newly "liberated," but in fact conquered zones, on the other. In a sense, these "new people" (*pracheachun thmey*) or "17 April people" (*pracheachun dap-prampi mesa*), making up nearly three million people[18] or almost two-fifths of the whole population, were treated like "war captives" who deserved to be deported and resettled to augment the manpower of the victorious side, echoing a long-established feature of traditional warfare in Southeast Asia.[19] This resettlement strategy was already implemented by the Khmer Rouge before April 1975, for example, after the seizure of the ancient Cambodian capital of Oudong situated some 40 kilometers north of Phnom Penh: "We liberated Oudong in 1974. We pulled out all the people. When they (the Lon Nol forces) took it back, they had no forces."[20]

According to all accounts, deaths as a result of inadequate food rations, overwork in the ricefields, and lack of access to medicine were significantly higher among the "new people" than among the "old people" (*pracheachun chah*), also called "base people" (*pracheachun multhan*). They were privileged because only members of this rural core could become full members (*penh sith*) of the agricultural cooperatives, which could comprise up to 1,000 families or

5,000 individuals by March 1978,[21] and be recruited as Khmer Rouge cadres. Khmer Rouge documents acknowledge that by mid-1976 less than half of the country's cooperatives were under full control of the Party. It was planned to expand the CPK village cooperative branches from 40 percent to 50 percent until the end of 1976, as "[w]hen a cooperative does not have a Party branch directly leading correctly, that cooperative is not strong ... in fulfilling its obligations in every aspect."[22] According to a party directive of spring 1977, an ideal "advanced cooperative" of 1,000 families needed to have at least thirty party members and fifty core organization members.[23] This meant that it was targeted to increase the total non-military membership to roughly 0.6 percent of the population or up to 50,000 persons. Fragmented data from the Northwest Zone indicate that in June 1977 roughly 4 percent of the zone's military forces but only 0.3 percent of the population living in the cooperatives were party members.[24] An extrapolation of these figures to the whole country might indicate a total CPK membership of at least 20,000–25,000 in mid-1977, that is, before the internal purges had been in full swing.

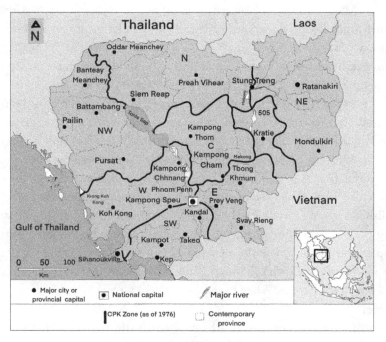

Map 1. Former provincial boundaries and CPK zone level administrative boundaries, ca. 1976.

Since autumn 1976, segments of the "old people" had been suffering due to a series of internal purges within the CPK. Several hundred thousand

Cambodians perished in the more than 150 prisons which were established all over the country at the levels of zone (*phumipheak*), region/sector (*tambon*), and district (*srok*). The most notorious secret prison was that of the State Security (Khmer Santebal) established on the grounds of a former high school in Phnom Penh's Tuol Sleng district. An estimated 12,000–14,000 prisoners, two-thirds of them Khmer Rouge cadres and family members, were executed in the infamous killing fields of Choeng Ek, situated 15 kilometers south of Phnom Penh, after having been forced to write confessions of their involvement in antigovernment plots, being agents or spies of the American CIA, the Soviet KGB, or the Vietnamese (Chandler 2000, 36). Because of the hasty retreat of the Khmer Rouge in early January 1979, the Vietnamese forces captured and saved thousands of Santebal documents, allowing a better understanding of the functioning of Democratic Kampuchea's terror machine as well as the dynamics of inner-party disputes and power struggles.

Fig. 2. Political slogans in the assembly hall of the Communist Party of Kampuchea, Phnom Penh, July 1978.

Recruitment of Youth for the Revolutionary War

In his long speech of September 27, 1977, in which he revealed the very existence of the Communist Party of Kampuchea (CPK), and in the Black Paper (*Livre noir*) of September 1978 disclosing the background of the conflict with Vietnam, Pol Pot praised the loyalty of the hill people in northeastern Cambodia, the so-called Khmer Loei, the backbone of the Party's armed struggle in the final years of Sihanouk's Sangkum regime. He described them as "completely illiterate people who did not have even the slightest idea of cities, automobiles and Parliament [but who] dared to fight under the guidance of the Party" (cited in Quinn 1989, 236). Although young boys from these national minorities made careers in the Revolutionary Army and the CPK, some of them, like I Chien, the later governor of Pailin, even became the bodyguards of Pol Pot and other top Khmer Rouge leaders. But the vast majority of young people recruited for the revolutionary movement were ethnic Khmer. In the early 1970s, thousands of young Khmer from poor peasant backgrounds in remote villages were recruited into the Khmer Rouge army, which rapidly expanded from 15,000 soldiers in early 1971 to over 40,000 only two years later. In late 1974, the movement comprised up to 200,000 fighters, including local militias. As Prince Sihanouk observed, some of these young people were still children at the age of twelve or younger when they started their military careers. Removed from their home villages and separated from their families, these young soldiers (*yothea*) grew up with their peers in the Khmer Rouge indoctrination camps, considering it as the greatest honor that the CPK praised them as "the dictatorial instrument of the Party" (*Oppakar Phdachkar Robas Pak*).

Absolute dedication for the revolutionary cause and loyalty to Angkar—a generic term literally meaning "organization" and designating the CPK and all its auxiliary organizations—was propagandized in numerous short stories, such as those collected in the anthology *Khèm, die junge Kämpferin und andere Erzählungen des kambodschanischen Widerstands* [Khèm, the young female combatant and other stories of the Cambodian resistance].[25] Among the many stories published in the *Revolutionary Youth* magazine, the story of Comrade Phin who had joined the revolution as early as 1966, is striking. When captured in 1968, young Phin, who had been serving as a messenger for the Party's East Zone leadership, vehemently repudiated his own mother when the latter was led by the police to his prison cell to identify him as her son. Finally, the police had to release Phin who reunited with his old mother several years later when visiting his native village as a Khmer Rouge combatant not long after the liberation of Phnom Penh.[26] Other short stories from the final phase of the war against "American imperialism and the Lon Nol traitorous clique" glorify the "patriotic anger" (*kamhueng chiat*) and "class anger" (*kamhueng vanna*) of Cambodian youth, such as in the story of Comrade (*mit*) Say, born as the son of poor peasants in Kampong Speu in the Southwest Zone, who joined the revolution after the March 18, 1970 coup d'état and participated in the final offensive against Phnom Penh in early 1975. Say's firm determination to sacrifice himself on the battlefield makes him a model for the revolutionary youth cadres.

His last words before dying were allegedly: "Our beloved motherland is close to be liberated. I have already fulfilled my task. Dear comrades-in-arm, do not worry about me. March forward and attack! March forward! Phnom Penh will indeed be liberated!"[27]

The corrupt and abusive behavior of officials of the Khmer Republic and the relentless bombings by the US persuaded poor peasant families to give at least one of their sons or daughters to the Communist resistance to serve the revolution. The brutality of the Lon Nol army and the devastations caused by the bombing were memorialized in songs like the following one, which was taught to children after the war:

> Baribo village sheds it tears
> The enemy dropped bombs and staged a coup.
> The screams of a combatant; friend, where are you?
> The hated enemy killed my friend.
> When you died away, friend, you were still naked,
> Chest and stomach asunder, liver and spleen gone,
> You floated them away like a river's current. (…)
> When you died away, friend, you reminded me
> that the hated enemy had swallowed Cambodia

> (quoted from Kiernan 1996, 422).

The vast majority of the young fighters were male, but the Khmer Rouge were particularly proud of their women's battalions. Gender equality featured prominently in the Communist propaganda to win over support from rural female youth. Some of the heroes portrayed in short stories as revolutionary models were young women, such as Comrade Sao from Kampong Speu, who joined the revolution in early 1971 at the age of seventeen and was fighting in a women's battalion at the front northwest of Phnom Penh.[28] The revolutionary ideal of a Cambodian youth is most vividly described in the fictional story "The Red Heart of Dam Pheng," presumably written by a senior Khmer Rouge leader and published in a 1973 edition of *Revolutionary Youth*. Dam Pheng was the son of a poor peasant family from Prey Veng Province in eastern Cambodia. Having become an orphan when he was still very young, he was adopted by a monk who taught him literature and mathematics in a village pagoda. Later, the intelligent and diligent young boy was sent by the monks to pursue his studies in the capital Phnom Penh. There Dam Pheng joined the youth organization of the illegal Communist Party and became a role model in carrying out educational propaganda in youth circles against the "US imperialists." When arrested by the enemy in 1968, he withstood all kinds of torture and refused to confess, expressing "his pure and deep sentiment to the revolutionary organization, the people, and the poor who he respected, served and loved more than his life." Dam Pheng died in his cell sacrificing his life for the revolutionary cause by "taking an absolute stance of struggle."[29]

Short stories regularly published in *Revolutionary Male and Female Youth* highlight the atrocities of the Lon Nol regime, recalling brutal methods of physical torture and atrocities, such as the taking out of livers and gall bladders of murdered revolutionary fighters, thus mirroring acts of revenge committed by the Khmer Rouge after their victory.[30] The "revolutionary story" about Comrade Ret, who sacrificed his young life in the battlefield of the Cardamon mountains in southwestern Cambodia, ends with the appeal to consider the sacrifices during the war of national liberation as an obligation to safeguard with "revolutionary vigilance" the interests of the workers and peasants in the postliberation phase of socialist revolution and the building of socialism.[31]

The Communist Youth League of Kampuchea (Yuvakak)

How did the Khmer Rouge organize those they considered the future of their socialist revolution? In 1960 it formed the Democratic Kampuchea Youth League (acronym Yuvakap). Serving as the "right hand of the Party," it was renamed the Communist Youth League of Kampuchea, also known by its acronym Yuvakak, in January 1971.[32] According to its statutes, the Yuvakak is defined as "the right hand" (*day sdam*) and a "core strength" (*kamlang chumchuay*) of the CPK consisting of a "class element" and a "pioneer element." While the first element refers to the tasks to educate and struggle "among all circles of the youth workers, youth laborers, youth farmers, and youth students," the pioneer element pertains to the implementation of the political guidelines of the CPK in the economy, social affairs, defense, transportation, and other fields. Membership was restricted to "all progressive youths of Cambodian nationality from the ages of 17 to 30, who agree to abide by the statutes, secret plans and fundamental political guidelines" of the Yuvakak (Membership, Article 1).[33]

Admission into membership required a pledge of allegiance in front of the party flag by swearing loyalty to Angkar, the Yuvakak, and the working class and to serve the revolutionary struggle to the utmost of one's own life (Article 6). The statute of the CPK, in return, referred to the Yuvakak as a pillar (*bangkoul*) and core organization of the Party "in implementing the Party's political line, ideological principles and stances, and organizational lines among the popular masses, the workers-peasants [alliance] and the Revolutionary Army of Kampuchea" (chapter V, article 26).[34]

Strong emphasis was laid to "maintain all kinds of secrecy" (*trouv ksa kar samngoat khrop baep yang toang os*) (Article 7).[35] An obsessive concern with secrecy was indeed an overarching feature of the leadership of Democratic Kampuchea.[36] This explains why we lack reliable data about membership of both the CPK and its Youth League. The military statistics of June 1977 from the Northwest Zone mentioned above indicate that around 6 percent of the military and 0.5 percent of the people living in the cooperatives were members of the party's "core organizations," that is, mainly Yuvakak members.[37] Thus, a tentative extrapolation to the whole country would indicate a total membership of 30,000–40,000. This pool of young and highly indoctrinated cadres was the reservoir from which new CPK members were recruited and losses from continuous purges within the party were to be compensated.

The Role of Youth in the Socialist Revolution

The privileged role assigned to young people, especially from the disadvantaged strata of the population, is glorified by Pol Pot in his famous speech of September 27, 1977, in which he disclosed the existence of the CPK to the outside world: "Youth is a period of life in which there are very rapid changes. It is a time when consciousness is most receptive to revolution and when we are in a full possession of our strengths. This, then, is a general directive of our Party. It is the youth of today who will take up the revolutionary tasks of tomorrow" (Pol Pot 1977, 48–49). Pol Pot's words were echoed by Luong Ung, who was sent to a children's camp during the Khmer Rouge period. She recalls the incessant lectures of the communist cadres on the preeminent role of children in the revolution: "Your number one duty is to Angkar.... You are the children of the Angkar! In you lies our future. The Angkar knows you are pure in heart, uncorrupted by evil influences, still able to learn the ways of the Angkar! ... That is why the Angkar gives you so much power. You are our saviours" (Ung 2000, 129–130, 132, quoted from Hinton 2005, 131).

Though Khmer Rouge publications consistently stressed the necessity to instill the "new revolutionary worldview" into Cambodian youth regarding cultural habits, much emphasis was placed on knowledge and know-how of increasing production. Citing the ancient Khmer saying "Only a hot flame can forge steel to be good and hard," the October 1975 issue of *Revolutionary Youth* called for youth to fully participate in the production process of the cooperatives without fearing any hardship "in order to temper and re-fashion themselves to be as hard as steel in order to carry on making socialist revolution and communist revolution until they seize a complete and permanent great victory."[38] These overarching goals are reflected in a number of short stories and poems, such as in the following one:[39]

The Cambodian homeland is liberated
Now leaping forward fast
Just one year out of the war
A grieving landscape is turning into a cheerful one.
Plains, mountains, islands and sea
Cities, countryside, and all other places
Were converted by male and female youths.
Become pleasurable places.
Gaze at dikes and water channels
Crisscrossing endlessly, making new scenes….
For male and female youths who believe
In the Communist Party of Kampuchea….
Young farmers are strong
Remain at the work sites without the need for families
Cultivating the fields giving their best
To achieve three tons per hectare.

In his exploration of the social meaning of songs written and performed during the Khmer Rouge regime, John Marston concludes that most revolutionary songs celebrated agricultural work (2002, 119). This is confirmed by a closer look at collections of Khmer Rouge songs from two extant song books.[40] Many of these songs appeal to the revolutionary youth to consider their manual labor in irrigation projects as a kind of military campaign aiming at the transformation of nature. However, although traditional forms of education were eradicated by closing schools and universities, ransacking libraries and burning "reactionary" books, and killing teachers of the old regime, the widespread notion that *any* kind of education ceased to exist in Democratic Kampuchea's "stone-age communism" is wrong. George Chigas and Dmitri Mosyakov have argued this point persuasively by referring to the circulation of written party documents among young peasant cadres who were expected to complete their handwritten biographies and answer questions from special questionnaires.[41] While the old "feudalist-bourgeois" educational institutions were dismantled, the Cambodian communists introduced a qualitatively different system of education, which put the main emphasis on communal and more participatory forms of learning that took place outside the classrooms and emphasized the crucial importance of manual labor to transform *human* nature along with a transformation of the *physical* landscape (Tyner 2019, 107). This revolutionary pedagogy is reflected in textbooks printed during the Democratic Kampuchea period to teach Khmer language at primary schools. Lesson 53 of a Khmer Language textbook (from 1976) used for children of Class One describes an idealized everyday school life: in the morning learning Khmer language and mathematics, at noon performing physical work by helping the adults in all kinds of agricultural activities while singing revolutionary songs.[42] The more elaborate Khmer language Class Two textbook (from 1977) arranged its 42 lessons thematically from the "happy life" of children in the cooperatives to agricultural production, various kinds of industry to the "patriotic sacrifices" of the Revolutionary Army of Kampuchea.[43]

This kind of education was directed at the children of the poor and lower-middle peasants, many of them illiterate, rather than the children of the "new people" who on their part would have considered Angkar's educational approach as an almost total lack of teaching. The four American journalists from the Maoist newspaper *The Call* who visited Cambodia in April 1978, were proudly shown an electronic trade school in Phnom Penh where peasant boys and girls 10–14 years old, had to devote almost half of their six-month schooling to learning reading and writing as well as to "political instruction" before starting with the learning of specialized electronics skills. The US journalists introduced their report with the words: "What could a battle-hardened guerilla fighter and a 14-year-old electronics student have in common? Everything, if the student happens to be Kampuchean."[44] It appears evident that the rationale behind Democratic Kampuchea's new education system was to create a sense of belonging to a peasant-worker collectivity, any kind of individualistic behavior and thinking being eradicated. Violence played a crucial role to forge this collective identity among the peasant youth.

Youth and Violence

Accounts of survivors of Cambodia's "Killing Fields" persistently report that adults were most afraid of the *chhlop*, the local militia that was responsible for the internal security in a village or commune. As most adult *chhlop* were transferred to the Revolutionary Army of Kampuchea after April 1975, the Khmer Rouge recruited young people of poor peasant background, very often teenagers, to fulfill the task. In fact, these young *chhlop* were feared as spies who tended to misuse their power. Absolute loyalty to Angkar and pride at forming the future elite of a communist utopia was instilled into these *chhlop* as well as into children in general through various methods. Young children were often compared to "a piece of white paper that will change its color according to the paint." The Party had to assure that the color with which this "piece of white paper" would be painted was red.[45] Very young soldiers, among them many girls, were trained to mercilessly execute "enemies" as the final judgement of Pol Pot and Ieng Sary rendered by the Heng Samrin regime's People's Revolutionary Tribunal expressed: "Pol Pot and Ieng Sary sought to use children under fifteen years of age as spies in the 'people's communes' and to enlist them in army units or mobile shock brigades. They considered children at that age to be pure, and loyal to them." Thus, even young children were considered suitable for key positions in the administration, "because the children will grow up in the movement."[46]

Fig. 3. Youth mobile group marching to a working site, July 1978.

Sentimental attachments to parents, the wider family, or even the village were perceived as obstacles to ensuring absolute loyalty for the revolution. That even supporters of the revolution hesitated to see their children recruited in mobile teams and enduring hardships was bluntly criticized in lifestyle meetings as "a wrong standpoint on childrearing."[47] Slogans like "Young ones, you are the sons and daughters of the Angkar. Report everything to us who are your parents," and "If you wish to know how things happen, ask adults: if you wish to see them in a clear light, ask children," reveals how the Khmer Rouge manipulated children, encouraging them to denounce and spy on adults (Locard 2004, 142). In some, probably rare, cases "Khmer Rouge youths were ordered to kill their teachers or even their own parents," as recalled by the Cambodian journalist Dith Pran who coined the term "killing fields" (Quinn 1989, 239). In any case, even very young children (*komar*) were taught to address adults in the cooperatives—other than their own parents—in kinship terms, calling them either "aunties and uncles" (*ming-mia*), "grandparents" (*yiay-ta*) or even "parents" (*puk-mae*), instilling a sense of belonging to a large people's community transcending loyalties to one's family.

The children's ideological training was very intensive. This is reflected not only in the extant notebooks of Khmer Rouge youth cadres but also in the memoirs of participants from the ranks of the "new people" recalling how the Khmer Rouge cadre unceasingly lectured about the youth's pivotal role in the revolution and the gratitude they owed to Angkar, that is, to the Communist Party.[48] Path Kosal and Angeliki Kanavou (2015, 323) demonstrate in their analysis of notebooks left by military personnel that "lifestyle meetings" (*prachum chivapheap*)—a euphemism for public sessions of criticism and self-criticism—during the last eighteen months of the Khmer Rouge regime went beyond the core themes of politics, consciousness, and work tasks but degenerated into witch-hunt sessions going hand in hand with the escalation of the border war with Vietnam and the fear of Vietnamese spies within the Democratic Kampuchean administration and army.

The Cambodian communists considered violence an inherent feature of their revolutionary struggle. A Geography Class Two textbook (1977) gives the following revealing definition of violence (*hingsa*): "The resort to attacks to annihilate the people at large or a political group against an adversary to whom there is a life-and-death contradiction."[49] As for the impact of violence on identity during the period of Democratic Kampuchea, the American anthropologist Alexander Hinton identifies hierarchy and honor as characteristic features in Cambodian society which, along with Cambodian cultural models of obedience, facilitated murderous acts (see Hinton 2005). Dissidents within the communist movement were dehumanized as dangerous "microbes" and members of "secret networks" (*khsae somngat*) and deserved to be "smashed into pieces."[50] The atrocities committed by the Lon Nol army against Khmer Rouge fighters and civilians, as well as the devastations caused by the American terror bombing, were continuously picked up by Khmer Rouge propaganda[51] and memorized in revolutionary songs, including the National Anthem of Democratic Kampuchea.[52] This explains why the perpetrators of violence in Democratic Kampuchea hardly felt any guilt about their deeds, and it also explains how violence created a sense of belonging or group identity among the Khmer Rouge hardcore supporters, enabling them a "second life" after January 1979 for another twenty years, now no longer under the banner of communism but of nationalism.

Though organized Buddhism, such as the Sangha, represented a serious threat to the regime of Democratic Kampuchea, the Cambodian communists nevertheless resorted to Buddhist notions to transmit their collectivist ideology to the rural masses as suggested by Hinton (2005, 126ff). Phrases like "Angkar has [the many] eyes of a pineapple" (*Angkar mean phnaek mnoah*) portray the CPK and its organizations as an enlightened, omnipotent being comparable to a Bodhisattva (Locard 2004, 112).[53] Path Kosal and Angeliki Kanavou agree that some Buddhist beliefs, in particular the concept of renunciation of personal belongings, desire, greed, and the lure of material kinds, inspired the zeal of the Cambodian communists to purify the society and facilitate total social control. They surmise that "the notion of internal purification from all desires and sins in life," which Ponchaud (1989, 175) defined as one of Buddhism's supreme virtues, shows that the Khmer Rouge obsession with confessions had "deep roots in the ontology of Theravada Buddhism, i.e. the concepts of self-renunciation and self-examination."[54] Whether this was a deliberate political strategy—several Khmer Rouge leaders, including Pol Pot, had spent parts of their youth in monkhood—or, rather, an unconscious process, needs further examination. In any case, the allusions to Buddhist worldview and cosmology are mirrored in several Khmer Rouge songs, such as the one titled "The revolutionary Angkar is the soul of every Kampuchean citizen" where it is stated: "The revolutionary Angkar had goodness, which is as heavy as Mount Meru, and more valuable than our lives. We are committed to following its good virtue."[55]

The Human Cost of War and Revolution

The mass violence of the late 1970s enforces the question about the human costs: "How many people lost their lives as a result of the murderous Khmer Rouge revolution?" One might well rebuke such "body counting" as impious in view of the human tragedy inflicted on countless Cambodians. However, figures of the victims of the Khmer Rouge have been used for political ends since the Vietnamese invasion and even before. The Vietnamese-installed government of the People's Republic of Kampuchea headed by Khmer Rouge dissident Heng Samrin claimed more than 3.3 million deaths of the "Pol Pot-

Ieng Sary clique" and just over 4 million survivors when sentencing Pol Pot and Ieng Sary to death in absenstia for genocide in August 1979. This estimate was based on a nationwide effort at collecting evidence of crimes committed by the previous regime, including statements of surviving individuals and groups called "petitions," which involved a significant amount of multiple counting.[56] The Khmer Rouge themselves denied any mass killings of that magnitude, denouncing such allegations as mere Vietnamese propaganda. In a memorandum issued in the second half of the 1980s, they argued that during the "three-year period of 1976–1978, the population increased by 640,000" and that due to a census taken by the Democratic Kampuchea regime in mid-1978 "Kampuchea had 8.4 million inhabitants." The unrepentant Khmer Rouge leadership conceded only "more than 20,000" deaths from illness and food shortage, 10,000 deaths from executions (carried out by "Vietnamese agents") and "over 3,000 people" considered to be "minor offenders or innocent civilians" killed in the effort to counter "the subversive activities of Vietnam's agents."[57] It is evident that the Khmer Rouge's own estimate of under 40,000 victims as a result of their murderous policies is simply ridiculous and contradicts their own population figures of spring 1976—total population 7,330,000 people— used for designing the Party's Four-Year Plan (1977–1980).[58] The Cambodian communists' disrespect for life stands in contrast to their pro-natalist policies promulgated in 1978 to double the country's population to 15–20 million inhabitants within less than two decades.[59]

The first figures released by the Heng Samrin regime at the end of 1980 indicated a population of roughly 6.6 million people, not including those Cambodians who fled to Thailand and third countries since January 1979 or lived in areas under resistance control.[60] These figures lasted until 1998 when a nationwide census was taken in Cambodia. The 1998 census revealed a total Cambodian population of 11.44 million, which further increased to 13.4 million in 2008 when a new census was taken. According to the preliminary results of the latest census of 2019, Cambodia's population reached 15.3 million in spring 2019 (see National Institute of Statistics, Ministry of Planning 2002, 2009, and 2019).

Any serious demographic study of the Cambodian tragedy of the 1970s faces the problem that no census had been taken in the twenty-six years between 1962 and 1998. All censuses before 1962 were based on colonial tax registers or rather incomplete provincial censuses undercounting the population, notably in remote areas.[61] The census of 1962 was the first to meet the international standards of the time. The census counted a total of 5,728,771 inhabitants, with females outnumbering males by only 3,000.[62] There is no agreement about the population development during the following eight years. Thus, we do not know for certain the size of Cambodia's population in March 1970 when the civil war and the Cambodian tragedy started. Depending on different scenarios about the likely increase of life expectancy and reduction in mortality as well as decline of fertility for the post-1962 years, the population of Cambodia in early 1970 would have been between 6.9 and 7.4 million. UN demographer George Siampos (1970) considers a figure of 7.14 million as most likely, whereas Jacques Migozzi (1973) prefers the higher number of 7.36 million, taking into account a possible undercounting of 1–2 percent for the 1962 census.[63]

Furthermore, there is no agreement about the human losses during the war between 1970 and 1975. The Khmer Rouge announced in 1975/76 that "almost 800,000" people were killed during that period either on the battlefield or due to the severe American bombing campaign. Almost a quarter of a million people had become either invalids (40,000) or were otherwise seriously wounded.[64] A demographic study of the CIA from January 1980 titled *Kampuchea: A Demographic Catastrophe* refers to "US Government sources" putting the "assumed number of war-related deaths ... unofficially at 600,000 to 700,000" but considers this figure "debatable" (Central Intelligence Agency 1980, 8). Kiernan (1996, 458) estimates the number of deaths caused by US bombing only at 150,000, but he does not provide any figures about other war casualties, especially fighters killed on the battlefield. Bannister and Johnson (1993, 66) assume about "275,000 excess deaths during 1970–1974, caused by civil war, bombing, and growing food shortages." Given the fact that the total payload of the B-52 bombers was dropped mainly on the densely populated area around Phnom Penh and between the capital and the Vietnamese border was over half a million tons, I consider the estimate of Polish demographer Marek Sliwinski (1995) that 310,000 Cambodians died during the civil war as a rather realistic estimate but assume 200,000 and 400,000 as the possible range for total war casualties. Depending on which population figure is accepted for March 1970, the April 1975 population would range between 7.4 and 8.1 million. As about 350,000 people, mostly ethnic Vietnamese, had left Cambodia during the war, I accept a maximum of 7.9 million and a minimum of 7.0 million as the starting population for the Democratic Kampuchea period, with 7.5 million as the most likely figure.

Table 1. Estimated number of excess deaths, 1970–1980

Age	1980 expected population (Normal mortality)			1980 observed population (Backward projection)			Estimated number of excess deaths		
	Male	Female	Total	Male	Female	Total	Male	Female	Total
0–4	642,710	611,156	1,253,866	496,086	522,108	1,018,194	146,624	89,048	235,672
5–9	617,044	583,624	1,200,668	421,971	448,923	870,894	195,073	134,701	329,774
10–14	584,174	552,081	1,136,255	445,725	472,789	918,514	138,449	79,292	217,741
15–19	509,769	485,061	994,830	390,297	418,850	809,147	119,472	66,211	185,683
20–24	411,417	403,226	814,643	277,494	356,144	633,638	133,923	47,082	181,005
25–29	345,910	350,139	696,049	206,483	291,081	497,564	139,427	59,058	198,485
30–34	303,797	264,341	568,138	177,448	228,785	406,233	126,349	35,556	161,905
35–39	260,493	203,110	463,603	146,241	183,679	329,920	114,252	19,431	133,683
40–44	163,754	183,874	347,628	126,381	156,531	282,912	37,373	27,343	64,716
45–49	154,861	164,263	319,124	112,766	137,633	250,399	42,095	26,630	68,725
50–54	132,516	137,297	269,813	98,781	117,714	216,495	33,735	19,583	53,318
55–59	103,668	109,396	213,064	82,817	96,049	178,866	20,851	13,347	34,198
60–64	80,040	86,049	166,089	71,150	79,628	150,778	8,890	6,421	15,311
65–69	61,741	67,372	129,113	49,695	58,384	108,079	12,046	8,988	21,034
70–74	40,818	45,397	86,215	31,041	36,425	67,466	9,777	8,972	18,749
75+	44,266	52,888	97,154	28,627	35,442	64,069	15,639	17,446	33,085
Total	4,456,978	4,299,274	8,756,252	3,163,003	3,640,165	6,803,168	1,293,975	659,109	1,953,084

Source: Ricardo. F. Neupert and Virak Prum. 2005. "Cambodia: Reconstructing the Demographic Stab of the Past and Forecasting the Demographic Scar of the Future." *European Journal of Population* 21: 217–46.

Limits of space and time do not permit a detailed critique of alternative serious studies about the population development during the three years and nine months the Pol Pot regime stayed in power. These estimates vary between 740,000 (Vickery 1984) and 1.87 million (Sliwinski 1995). The methodologically most convincing analysis by Neupert and Prum (2005) of the age cohorts as derived from the 1998 census data substantiates Vickery's well-argued assumption of a dramatic decline of the natural birth rates from more than 40 per thousand to 30 per thousand due to the precarious living conditions during the Democratic Kampuchea regime (Vickery 1984, 185–87; see also Vickery 1988).[65] Moreover, their backward projection suggests a population of 6.8 million in 1980. This figure is compared to the expected population that remained in the country "with reduced fertility, but on the assumption that it was subject to normal mortality levels and trends" (Neupert and Prum 2005, 234). The 1980 population obtained by this hypothetical projection is calculated at 8.75 million. Thus, Neupert and Prum arrive at the conclusion that the total number of "excess deaths" for the *whole* period from early 1970 until early 1980 was 1.95 million. They conclude that "[d]isaggregated by sex, the number of male deaths during the tragic decade was 1.3 million and that of female deaths 0.7 million (not including normal deaths)." Of these excess deaths Neupert and Prum (ibid., 237) attribute 1.4 million to the Pol Pot regime, leaving more than half a million victims of the 1970–75 civil war and the famine haunting Cambodia in the second half of 1979 and early 1980.[66]

Using a different methodological approach, Judith Banister and Paige Johnson (1993, 90) calculated 1.3 million "excess deaths" for the 1970s of which 1.05 million occurred during the Khmer Rouge period.[67] We may thus conclude that most probably between one and one million and a half, that is, one-seventh to one-fifth of the April 1975 population, died as a result of the policies devised by the CPK leadership. At least one-third of these deaths, but likely many more, were victims of killings, including purges within the party and state apparatus. Given the short period of time during which this mass violence occurred, the Cambodian revolution was indeed probably the most violent revolution in modern history.

Children and youth suffered enormously. The table above shows that the excess mortality among children below the age of 15 (born between 1966 and 1980) was 783,181. Youth aged 15–29 (born between 1951 and 1965) suffered excess deaths of 565,173. Both groups combined (1,348,354) made up almost 70 percent of the total excess deaths. Most deaths among the children—as was the case for most elderly people—were not due to combat casualties or political executions but caused by hunger and disease, mostly during the Khmer Rouge regime, as young children and the elderly are the most vulnerable segments of the population with regards to health conditions. On the other hand, most excess deaths among youth as well as of the age cohort 30–59 were presumably violent deaths.

Conclusion

The communist movement in Cambodia was dominated by young people with low- and middle-ranking cadres in their twenties entrusted with positions of political responsibility during the short-lived regime of Democratic Kampuchea. Cambodian society as a whole had a youth bulge until the late 1980s and was thus particularly prone to youth violence, which was nurtured by the radical Maoist-inspired version of Cambodian communism. The mobilization of young cadres was carried out through the selection of children in their early teens from poor peasant backgrounds and their integration into a close-knit community where they could grow up as dedicated young revolutionaries totally loyal to Angkar, as the ruling Communist Party of Kampuchea (CPK) was generally called. The Communist Youth League of Kampuchea (Yuvakak) was the most important recruitment basis for the CPK, whose very existence had been kept secret for two and a half years after the Khmer Rouge victory of April 17, 1975. Intensive ideological indoctrination in public sessions of criticism and self-criticism, euphemistically called "lifestyle meetings," was crucial for ensuring a sense of belonging, a group identity, among these youthful followers of the revolution by replacing traditional family bonds with loyalty to Angkar.

As Kosal and Kanavou have observed, a "cult of confession took over the entire society" and the Khmer Rouge regime effectively brainwashed segments of the society (2017, 90), including its youth, some of whom stayed with the movement after the Vietnamese invasion as they were also motivated by a strong sense of nationalism. Though numerous young Cambodians, along with their families, became victims of the communist reign of terror, it needs to be explained why even after the fall of the Pol Pot regime a sufficiently large number of Cambodians, albeit a minority, continued to support the movement, now no longer for achieving an ideal communist society but for defending the nation against a foreign invader. Moreover, the perceived existential threats by outside enemies, first the United States (CIA), later the Vietnamese and their Soviet backers (KGB), justified the witch-hunt against supporters or "agents" within the Khmer Rouge ranks since late 1977. It is my hypothesis that the paranoia of the Party Center under Pol Pot and Nuon Chea was not completely based on pure fabrications but fueled by real opposition actively encouraged by the decision of the Vietnamese Communist Party's Politburo in February 1978 to support a "regime change" in Phnom Penh to solve the escalating border war with Democratic Kampuchea (Chanda 1986, 216). Though the Vietnamese invasion of early 1979 ended the Khmer Rouge terror regime, it contributed to a further round of mass violence in Cambodia lasting at least another decade.

The mass violence of the 1970s is by no means a phenomenon of the past. It has long-term repercussions such as post-traumatic stress disorder (PTSD) not only among the people who experienced war and revolutionary terror but also among their children (van Schaack and Reicherter 2016). Disrespect of life and arbitrary killings, including those politically motivated, are still a social reality and a concern for human rights activists. The legacy of a decade of arbitrary arrests, mass killings, and actions classified as "genocide," either in a legal or a political and sociological sense left its mark on Cambodian society until today.

Endnotes: Revolutionary Terror in the 1970s

1. For short biographies of Khmer Rouge leaders and high-ranking cadres, see Corfield and Summers 2003, and Kane 2011.

2. Karkaria interviewed a woman who despite her sufferings during the Pol Pot regime stated: "We had equal rights. Women even asked for that. We all struggled and carried guns with strength. Women may be stronger than men. Men were leaders, women were also leaders" (Karkaria 2003, 28).

3. The ECCC became fully operational in June 2007 and has so far convicted and sentenced three former high-ranking Khmer Rouge leaders for crimes against humanity, namely, Kaing Guek Eav (alias Duch), the former security chief and director of Tuol Sleng (Case 001), Nuon Chea, the former deputy secretary of the Communist Party of Kampuchea (CPK) (Case 002/01), and Khieu Samphan, the former head of the state presidium of Democratic Kampuchea (Case 002/02).

4. Witness Kim Vun, who worked for the Ministry of Propaganda and Information under Hu Nim was unable to give a precise estimate of the number of copies printed but stressed that "stacks of magazines" were packed for delivery. See Case 002/02 Judgement. 16 November 2018, Case File/Dossier No. 002/19-09-2007/ECCC/TC (Archive No. E465), §474, 259.

5. See Case 002/01 Judgement. 7 August 2014, Case File/Dossier No. 002/19-09-2007/ECCC/TC (Archive No. E313), §263, 143.

6. This statement is dated 15 December 2011 (ECCC, E1/23.1), 73–74.

7. Case 002/02 Judgement. 16 November 2018, Case File/Dossier No. 002/19-09-2007/ECCC/TC (Archive No. E465), §474, p. 260. See also Statement on 9 July 2013 (ECCC, E1/220.1, 20).

8. In 1960 the Communist Party of Kampuchea decided to establish a youth organization called the Democratic Kampuchea Youth League (abbreviated Yuvakap) with the purpose of instigating Cambodian youth to become involved in the struggle against the Sihanouk regime and US interference. In January 1971, at the beginning of the civil war, the league was renamed Kampuchean Communist Youth League (Yuvakak). See "Kampuchean Communist Youth League: The Right Hand of the Party." *Revolutionary Youth*, Issue 5, May 1977. Reproduced in *Searching for the Truth*, No. 20, August 2001, 5.

9. See *Revolutionary Flag*. Issue 2–3, February–March 1976. DC-CAM, Archive No. E3/166, 18.

10. Stanley Milgram (1974) notes that people obeying orders do not lose their moral sense but this moral sense shifts to a consideration of what his or her superior expects. Thus "a soldier does not ask whether it is good or bad to bomb a hamlet; he does not experience shame or guilt in the destruction of a village: rather he feels pride or shame depending on how well he has performed the mission assigned to him" (quoted in Hirsch 1995, 125).

11. During the political polarization of the 1970s, a right-wing political monk named Kittivudho Bhikkhu even justified the killing of Communist insurgents for the sake of the Thai nation's survival. See Jackson 1989. As for the 6 October 1976 massacre at Thammasat University and how this outburst of violence shaped collective memories, see Thongchai Winichakul 2020. In his book *Die Farbe Rot* [Colour Red], Gerd Koenen reports an insightful event from the Soviet purges of the mid 1930s. The wife of the imprisoned organizing head of the Communist International, Ossip Pjatnitzki, one of the main defendants of the fourth show trial, noted down on the day when Bucharin and other defendants were executed: "Today at four o'clock these monsters were anhilated [*sic*]. With their anhilation [*sic*], however, my hatred does not get lower" (Koenen 2017, 919).

12. According to the 1962 census, 1,391,500 of the 5,728,800 inhabitants were in the age group 15–29 years, while another 1,914,000 were below 15 years old. See Migozzi 1973, 237.

13. According to a moderate population projection proposed by the American demographer George Siampos, 1,883,400 persons out of a total of 7,143,000 were in the age group 15–29 years. See also the discussion of these data in Migozzi 1973, 267.

14. As Migozzi (1973, 215) puts it aptly: "L'extrême jeunesse de la population est sans conteste l'une des caractéristiques majeures de la situation démographique actuelle du Cambodge."

15. Quoted from Thomas Fuller, "Cambodia revives Pol Pot's deadly canals," *The New York Times*, December 4, 2008.

16. See "Determine to Build Socialism in a Great Leap Forward Following the Line of the Party by Depending on Agriculture as the Foundation." *Revolutionary Flag*, Issue 8, August 1976. Reproduced in *Searching for the Truth*, Special English Edition, 4th quarter 2015, 10.

17. See Michael Vickery, "Kampuchean Demography: Cooking the Books," unpublished paper, November 10, 1980. Later he enlarged this paper to the monograph Cambodia 1975–1982 (1984) which became one of the main reference works on Cambodia in the 1980s and 1990s.

18. The February–March 1976 issue of *Revolutionary Flag* boldly admits that "nearly 3,000,000 people had to exit the various cities empty-handed, without food supplies, without any means and tools at all to increase production. This was a very heavy burden for the party and for our revolutionary state authorities in the base areas that had to feed and supply everything to nearly 3,000,000 people." See ECCC, Archive No. E3/166, 19.

19. It was a well-established pattern of premodern warfare in Southeast Asia that the victorious armies sought to deport and resettle large parts of the conquered population to augment the manpower in their own core areas, leaving waste large tracts of the conquered territories. The control over people, not over land, was considered the key to political supremacy. See, for example, Grabowsky 1999, 45–86.

20. *Revolutionary Flag*, Special Issue, December 1976–January 1977. See ECCC, Archive No. E3/25, 31. The same issue of the publication rationalizes the strategy of forced relocations of conquered populations as follows: "The line of taking away the people from the enemy was very correct. This never happened in the world. When the enemy has the people, the enemy has an army and an economy. When the enemy has no people, the enemy has no military and no economic strength. Our reasoning is correct. Thus our line is very correct. We fight to capture the people at every location."

21. According to the publication *Kampuchea Democratique en Mars* 1978, 3, 50% of the cooperatives comprised 700–1,000 families, 30% 400–600 families, and 20% 100–300 families, each family with an average of 5–6 members.

22. *Revolutionary Flag*. Issue 7, July 1976, 30. ECCC, Archive No. 3/4.

23. *Revolutionary Flag*. Special Issue, April 1977, 15. ECCC, Archive No. 3/742.

24. "Activity of Pol Pot military in the year 1977, military statistics in all sections in the Northwest Zone" (in Khmer). DC-CAM, Archive No. D01608. According to the statistics compiled by the zone's military leadership, 519 out of 12,990 soldiers were CPK members but only 45 out of 13,539 people living in three supporting cooperatives. According to Vietnamese figures, the CPK had only 14,000 members when they "liberated" Phnom Penh. See Carney 1989, 84.

25. Botschaft des Demokratischen Kampuchea (Embassy of Democratic Kampuchea), 1976a. Khèm, the young heroine of this anthology, joined the liberation struggle in early 1972 and participated in the fighting along National Route No. 6 (running from Phnom Penh via Kompong Thom to Siem Reap). Heavily wounded and losing one of her legs, Khèm nevertheless participates in a mobile production unit in the Southwest Zone admired by the local people as a model revolutionary.

26. *Revolutionary Youth*, Issue 10, October 1975, 16–23. ECCC, Archive No. E3/729.

27. "The life of comrade Say remains eternally in the consciousness of our nation" (in Khmer). In *Virakam robas prachiachun nueng kongtoap pativoat kampuchea* [The heroism of the people and the Revolutionary Army of Kampuchea], Vol. 3, February 1975, 15.

28. "I attack the enemy constantly until they are completely destroyed and anhilated from the territory of Kampuchea" (in Khmer). In *Virakam robas prachiachun nueng kongtoap pativoat kampuchea* [The heroism of the people and the Revolutionary Army of Kampuchea], Vol. 2, March 1974, 33–48.

29. "The Red Heart of Dam Pheng" (written by a possible Khmer Rouge senior leader). *Revolutionary Youth*, 1973. Reproduced in *Searching for the Truth*, Special English Edition, 3rd quarter 2016, 51–56.

30. As is highlighted in the short story "The struggling life in the great storm of the revolution" on the life of a fifteen-year-old boy from a poor peasant family in the southwestern province of Takeo who had joined the revolution in his earliest childhood. See *Revolutionary Flag*. Issue 11, November 1976. DC-CAM, Archive No. E3/139, 15.

31. "The sacrifice of our combattant [*sic*]." *Revolutionary Male and Female Youth*. Issue 3, March 1976, 15–21. ECCC, Archive No. E3/751.

32. See "Kampuchean Communist Youth League: The Right Hand of the Party." *Revolutionary Youth*, Issue 5, May 1977. Reproduced in *Searching for the Truth*, No. 20, August 2001, 5.

33. See "Under the bright leadership of the Communist Party of Kampuchea, our Democratic Kampuchea Youth League worked actively on propaganda and education by taking the political line, policy, and various decisions by the Party to disseminate among the crowd of the Kampuchean male-female youths and [the] general population." *Revolutionary Male and Female Youth*. Special Issue August–September 1974, 6. ECCC, Archive No. E3/146.

34. "Statute of the Communist Party of Kampuchea", ECCC, document E3/130, 25. For the Khmer original, see "*Lakkhantika Pak Kommunit Kampuchea*". DC-CAM, Archive No. D00674.

35. See "Temporary Statutes of the Communist Youth League of Kampuchea of the Communist Party of Kampuchea." Reproduced in *Searching for the Truth*, No. 13, January 2001, 12. As for the Khmer original, see *Lakkhantika Samphoan Yuvakak* 1972 [Statute of Yuvakak League, 1972]. DC-CAM, Archive No. D06792.

36. This obsession with secrecy was explained in much detail by Nuon Chea, the deputy secretary-general of the Standing Committee of the CPK, to a delegation of the pro-Chinese Danish Communist Party in late July 1978. In this conversation, Nuon Chea defined secrecy as a fundamental principle of the revolutionary struggle of the Cambodian communists. He stressed: "Only through secrecy can we be masters of the situation and win victory over the enemy who cannot find out who is who." See Nuon Chea 1987, 27.

37. "Activity of Pol Pot military in the year 1977, military statistics in all sections in the Northwest Zone" (in Khmer). DC-CAM, Archive No. D01608. According to the statistics compiled by the zone's military leadership, 831 of 12,990 soldiers were CPK members but only 68 of 13,539 people living in three supporting cooperatives.

38. "Kampuchean Youth Must Forge and Re-Fashion Themselves in the Movement to Strengthen and Expand Production Cooperatives." *Revolutionary Youth*, Issue 10, October 1975. Archive No. E3/729, 8.

39. "Male and Female Revolutionary Youths Determine to Fight, Defend, and Rebuild the Country in Great Leaps." *Revolutionary Youth*, Issue 12, December 1976. Reproduced in *Searching for the Truth*, No. 23, November 2001, 50.

40. See Marston 2002, Appendix 122–25; see also *"Chumriang Padevoat"* [Revolutionary Songs]. Stenciled booklets. DC-CAM, Archive Nos. D21452 and D21501.

41. Chigas and Mosyakov cite the example of a notebook that was obtained in 1979 in the former headquarters of the Democratic Kampuchean Department of Information and Propaganda. This notebook dated 1978 belonged to a 19-year-old Khmer Rouge cadre named Ly Sok Khy who was born on May 14, 1959 in region 25 (Kandal Province, Southwest Zone) and had entered the revolution in April 1975. It is obvious that even peasant cadres were expected to learn at least basic writing and reading skills. They conclude: "To rise in the state and party hierarchy, one needed to know how to read and write … the Khmer Rouge were not, in principle, afraid of the ability of common people to read and write. It was, therefore, what and how one read, rather than the ability to read and write, that made certain kinds of people suspect. As with every other aspect of daily life, the Party Center wanted to be in complete control of how, when and what people, wrote, read, and thought." See George Chigas and Dmitri Mosyakov, Literacy and Education under the Khmer Rouge. https://gsp.yale.edu/literacy-and-education-under-khmer-rouge. Last accessed January 31, 2020.

42. *Siavphouv rian aksòr thnak ti muay* (in Khmer). Language textbook, Class 1. Phnom Penh, 1976. DC-CAM. Archive No. D21486.

43. *Siavphouv aksòr thnak ti pi* (in Khmer). Language textbook, Class 2. Phnom Penh, 1977. DC-CAM, Archive No. D21478.

44. "Youth are a vital force in Kampuchea." *Kampuchea Today: An Eyewitness Report from Cambodia.* 1978. Chicago, Ill.: Call Pamphlets, 30–34.

45. "Bringing up the Children of the Khmer Rouge Revolution." Excerpted from KR notebook 008. Reproduced in *Searching for the Truth*, No. 34, October 2002, 8. The excerpt continues as follows: "In short, children are influenced by our guidance. If we have brought them up well from a young age, they will be good people. In contrast, they will be arrogant if they have been spoiled."

46. Quoted from Chen 2015, 12. In her paper Chen basically analyzes the live stories of children under the Khmer Rouge compiled by Dith Pran in 1997.

47. "Bringing up the Children of the Khmer Rouge Revolution," 11.

48. Hinton (2005, 131) quotes an informant recalling the following lecture: "You are the children of the Angkar! In you lies our future. The Angkar knows you are pure in your heart, uncorrupted by evil influences, still able to learn the ways of the Angkar! That is why the Angkar loves you above all else. That is why the Angkar gives you so much power. You are our saviors."

49. *Phumisat Kampuchea Pracheathipadey phnaek nayobay* [Political Geography of Democratic Kampuchea]. Phnom Penh 1977, 69. DC-CAM, Archive No. D00475.

50. See Weitz (2003, 155) who comments on Pol Pol's remark from December 1976: "[S]ometimes there is not active opposition; there is only silence" by stating: "[Pol Pot] meant that the party had constantly to seek out its opponents, even when only silence reigned. It meant, too, that the prosecution of actions did not suffice. The party had also to investigate the thoughts of people to see what the silence signified, a kind of theological investigation of consciousness" (ibid., 156).

51. See, for example, the childhood memoirs of Comrade Khorn, which describe in detail such atrocities, including the cutting out of the liver and gall bladder of captured Khmer Rouge soldiers by Lon Nol forces. See *Revolutionary Male and Female Youth*. Issue 11, November 1975, 15–22. DC-CAM, Archive No. E3/570.

DEMOCRATIC KAMPUCHEA'S REVOLUTIONARY TERROR IN THE 1970S

52. See Botschaft des Demokratischen Kampuchea, '*Khèm, die junge Kämpferin*' und andere *Erzählungen des kambodschanischen Widerstands*. Berlin (Ost), 1976a, 71.

53. Intriguingly, Roeland A. Burgler (1990) has chosen "The Eyes of the Pineapple" as the main title of his book.

54. Kosal and Kanavou (2015, 312) who even further speculate that "a complete extinction of all sexual desires, one of the goals of Buddhist asceticism, sat comfortably with the anti-sexual-desire precept of KR indoctrination."

55. "Khmer Rouge Song: The Revolutionary Angkar is the Soul of every Kampuchean Citizen." Reproduced in *Searching for the Truth*, No. 3, March 2000, 49.

56. For a critical discussion of the statistics released by the "Research Committee into the Crimes of [the] Pol Pot Regime" set up by the Salvation Front Reanakse, see Tabeau 2009, 9–11.

57. See Democratic Kampuchea. n.d. "Census of the Population under Democratic Kampuchea from 1975 to 1978," 5–6. In defiance of allegations of having committed genocidal actions against its own population, the Khmer Rouge memorandum states: "To be fair, the number of people who died in Kampuchea from 1975 to 1978 is less than people who die by car accidents in some countries where each year 30,000 people or more die from road accidents," 12.

58. See Democratic Kampuchea, 1976, in Chandler et al. 1988, 53. This figure must be taken with great caution as most population figures for individual zone or special regions are rounded. Khmer Rouge publications from 1978 used to give the figure of "eight million Kampuchean people." See, for example, *Revolutionary Flag*. Issue 8, August 1978, 16, 23. ECCC, Archive No. E3/747.

59. See, for example, two slogans related to improving the living conditions of the people announced at the third anniversary of the liberation of Phnom Penh. Slogan 1: "Hold aloft the banner to implement the plan to achieve a maximum increase of population to 15–20 million people within 10–20 years"; Slogan 2: "Hold aloft the banner to implement the plan to achieve a maximum increase of population within one year, within three years, within five years, within ten years, within twenty years." In *Notebook No. 76: Peak Slaok 17 Mesa 1978* (Slogans for the [celebrations] of 17 April 1978). DC-CAM, Archive No. D21571.

60. See National Institute of Statistics, Ministry of Planning 2009, 21. Ewa Tabeau (2009, 6) comments: "Unlike the 1980s studies, the recent projections of the 1980 population proved that the overall number of about 6.590 million observed by end-1980 was not at all that unlikely and impossible as some authors thought in early post Khmer Rouge years."

61. According to French colonial statistics, the population of Cambodia was estimated at 2,403 million in 1921 and 3,406 million in 1936. In 1950, the colonial authorities counted 4,046 million inhabitants. These figures, if considered reliable, would indicate an annual increase of population of 1.6 percent during the period 1921–1936 and of 2.3 percent during the period 1936–1950. See Zadrozny 1955, 96.

62. There were 2,862,939 males against 2,865,882 females, which corresponds to a ratio of 999 males per 1,000 females. See Migozzi 1973 and Siampos 1970.

63. Siampos (1970, 346–47) accepts a reduction in mortality based on an increased life expectancy at birth of about two and a half years for the period 1965–1970 and a decline of fertility for each quinquennial period after 1960 by 5 percent of the sex-age adjusted birth rate.

64. See Botschaft des Demokratischen Kampuchea, 1976b, 61.

65. Comparing the expected population with an alternative projection for which normal fertility is assumed, Neupert and Prum infer the deficit of birth: 207,000 births for the period 1970–1975 and 495,000 births for 1970–1980. They emphasize that "these deficits are caused not only by a fertility decline but also by deaths and emigration of women in reproductive ages" (2005, 235).

66. Due to the chaos following the Vietnamese invasion and heavy fighting between Vietnamese troops and loyalists of the toppled Pol Pot regime during the first half of 1979, a famine broke out in the second half of the year. Though an international relief program averted the death of millions of Cambodians, the death toll resulting from starvation is estimated at up to 200,000 people, many of them in Khmer Rouge controlled areas close to the border to Thailand. See Ea Meng-Try 1981.

67. Etcheson (2005, 118) refutes the conclusion drawn by Banister and Johnson and prefers the higher figure of 2.2 million as excess mortality during the Khmer Rouge regime given by demographer Patrick Heuveline (1998, 2001, and 2015). In fact, Heuveline's numercial modelings (2015, 214) provide space for a much larger span ranging from 1.2 to 2.25 million excess deaths. Besides, several of the 47 variable parameters used for his modelings are highly questionable. Thus, he grossly minimizes the number of deaths caused by the civil war 1970–75 (parameter 15) and the famine of later 1979 and early 1980 (parameter 41), distorting the outcome of his calculation.

401

References

Baberowski, Jörg. 2015. *Räume der Gewalt [Spaces of Violence]*. Frankfurt am Main: S. Fischer.

Banister, Judith, and E. Paige Johnson. 1993. "After the Nightmare: The Population of Cambodia." In *Genocide and Democracy in Cambodia: The Khmer Rouge, The United Nations and the International Community*, ed. Ben Kiernan, 65–139, New Haven, CT: Yale University Southeast Asia Studies, Monograph Series 41.

Botschaft des Demokratischen Kampuchea (Embassy of Democratic Kampuchea). 1976a. *Khèm, die junge Kämpferin und andere Erzählungen des kambodschanischen Widerstands* [Khèm, the Young Female Fighter and Other Stories of the Cambodian Resistance]. Berlin (Ost).

——————. 1976b. *Ein Jahr Demokratisches Kampuchea* [One Year Democratic Kampuchea]. Berlin (Ost).

Burgler, Roeland A. 1990. *The Eyes of the Pineapple: Revolutionary Intellectuals and Terror in Democratic Kampuchea*. Saarbrücken and Fort Lauterdale: Breitenbach Publishers.

Carney, Timothy. 1989. "The Organization of Power." In *Cambodia 1975-1978: Rendezvous with Death*, ed. Karl D. Jackson, 79–107. Princeton, NJ: Princeton University Press.

Central Intelligence Agency (CIA). 1980. *Kampuchea: A Demographic Catastrophe*. Washington, DC.

Chanda, Nayan. 1986. *Brother Enemy: The War after the War*. San Diego: Harcourt Brace Jovanovich.

Chandler, David P. 2000. *Voices from S–21: Terror and History in Pol Pot's Secret Prison*. Chiang Mai: Silkworm Books.

Chandler, David et al. eds. 1988. *Pol Pot Plans the Future: Confidential Leadership Documents from Democratic Kampuchea, 1976-1977*. New Haven, CT: Yale University of Southeast Asian Studies, Monograph Series 33.

Chen Yanzhou. 2015. "Lambs in the Slaughter House: Children and the Savage Utopia of Khmer Rouge." Unpublished paper. https://www.academia.edu/ 15319923/Children_and_the_Savage_Utopia_of_Khmer_Rouge.

Chigas, George, and Dmitri Mosyakov. n.d. *Literacy and Education under the Khmer Rouge*. Cambodian Genocide Program, Yale University. https://gsp.yale.edu/literacy-and-education-under-khmer-rouge.

Corfield, Justin, and Laura Summers. 2003. *Historical Dictionary of Cambodia*. Lanham, MD: Scarecrow Press.

Democratic Kampuchea. n.d. "Census of the Population under Democratic Kampuchea from 1975 to 1978." Unpublished document (12 pp.).

——————. 1976. "The Party's Four-Year Plan to Build Socialism in All Fields, 1977–1980" (Party Center, July–August 1976, 111 pp.). In *Pol Pot Plans the Future: Confidential Leadership Documents from Democratic Kampuchea, 1976-1977*, eds. Chandler et al. 1988, 36–119. New Haven, CT: Yale University of Southeast Asian Studies (Monograph Series 33).

——————. 1978. *Kampuchea Democratique en Mars 1978*. Phnom Penh.

Dith Pran. compiler. 1997. *Children of Cambodia's Killing Fields: Memoirs by Survivors*. New Haven, CT: Yale University Press.

Ea Meng-Try. 1981. "Kampuchea: A Country Adrift." *Population and Development Review* 7(2): 209–28.

Etcheson, Craig. 2005. *After the Killing Fields: Lessons from the Cambodian Genocide*. Lubbock, TX: Texas Tech University Press.

Foucault, Michel. 1980. *The History of Sexuality, Vol. 1: An Introduction*. New York: Vintage.

Fuller, Gary. 1995. "The Demographic Backdrop to Ethnic Conflict: A Geographic Overview." In *The Challenge of Ethnic Conflict to National and International Order in the 1990s*, ed. Edward Gerwin, 151–54. Washington: Central Intelligence Agency (RTT 95-10039, October).

Goldstone, Jack A. 1991. *Revolution and Rebellion in the Early Modern World*. Berkeley: University of California Press.

Grabowsky, Volker. 1999. "Forced Resettlement Campaigns in Northern Thailand during the Early Bangkok Period." *Journal of the Siam Society* 87(1/2): 45–86.

Heinsohn, Gunnar. 2019 [2003]. *Söhne und Weltmacht: Terror im Aufstieg und Fall der Nationen* [Sons and World Power: Terror in the Rise and Fall of Nations]. 2nd edn. Zürich: Orell füssli.

Heuveline, Patrick. 1998. "Between One and Three Million: Towards the Demographic Reconstruction of a Decade of Cambodian History (1970-79)." *Population Studies* 52: 49–65.

Heuveline, Patrick. 2001. "Approaches to Measuring Genocide: Excess Mortality during the Khmer Rouge Period." In *Ethnopolitical Warfare: Causes, Consequences and Possible Solutions*, eds. Daniel Chirot and Martin E. P. Seligman, 93–108. Washington, DC: American Psychological Association.

——————. 2015. "The Boundaries of Genocide: Quantifying the Uncertainty of the Death Toll during the Pol Pot Regime in Cambodia (1975–79)." *Population Studies* 69 (2): 201–18.

Hinton, Alexander Laban. 1998. "Why Did You Kill? The Cambodian Genocide and the Dark Side of Face and Honour." *Journal of Asian Studies* 57(1): 93–122.

——————. 2005. *Why Did They Kill? Cambodia in the Shadow of Genocide*. Berkeley, CA: University of California Press.

Hirsch, Herbert. 1995. *Genocide and the Politics of Memory: Studying Death to Preserve Life*. Chapel Hill, NC: University of North Carolina Press.

Jackson, Peter A. 1989. *Buddhism, Legitimation, and Conflict: The Political Functions of Urban Thai Buddhism*. Singapore: Institute of Southeast Asian Studies.

Kampuchea Today: An Eyewitness Report from Cambodia. 1978. Chicago, Ill: Call Pamphlets.

Kane, Solomon. 2011. *Dictionnaire des Khmers rouges: Édition révisée et augmentée*. Paris: Les Indes savantes.

Karkaria, Zal. 2003. "Khmer Rouge Policy on Women." MA thesis, Concordia University, Montreal. Excerpt reproduced in *Searching for the Truth*, Special English Edition, Fourth Quarter, 17–32. Phnom Penh: Documentation Center of Cambodia.

Kiernan, Ben. 1996. *The Pol Pot Regime: Race, Power, and Genocide in Cambodia under the Khmer Rouge, 1975–79*. New Haven, CT: Yale University Press.

——————. 2003. "The Demography of Genocide in Southeast Asia: The Death Tolls in Cambodia, 1975–79, and East Timor, 1975–80." *Critical Asian Studies* 35(4): 585–97.

Koenen, Gerd. 2017. *Die Farbe Rot: Ursprünge und Geschichte des Kommunismus* [The Colour Red: Origins and History of Communism]. München: C.H. Beck.

Kosal, Path and Angeliki Kanavou. 2015. "Converts, Not Ideologues? The Khmer Rouge Practice of Thought Reform in Cambodia, 1975–1978." *Journal of Political Ideologies* 20(3): 304–32.

——————. 2017. "The Lingering Effects of Thought Reform: The Khmer Rouge S-21 Prison Personnel." *Journal of Asian Studies* 76(1): 87–105.

Locard, Henri. 2004. *Pol Pot's Little Red Book: The Sayings of Angkar*. Chiang Mai: Silkworm Books. Original French edition *Le 'Petit Livre Rouge' de Pol Pot ou Les Paroles de l'Angkar*. Paris: L'Harmattan, 1996.

Marston, John. 2002. "Khmer Rouge Songs." *Crossroads* 16(1): 100–27.

Martin, Marie Alexandrine. 1981. "La riziculture et la maîtrise de l'eau dans le Kampuchea démocratique." *Études rurales* 81(1): 7–44.

Migozzi, Jacques. 1973. *Cambodge: Faits et problèmes de population*. Paris: Éditions du Centre national de la recherche scientifique.

Milgram, Stanley. 1974. *Obedience to Authority: An Experimental View*. New York: Harper & Row.

National Institute of Statistics, Ministry of Planning (NIS-MP). 2002. *General Population Census of Cambodia 1998: Final Results (2nd Edition)*. Phnom Penh.

——————. 2009. *General Population Census of Cambodia 2008: National Report on Final Census Results*. Phnom Penh.

——————. 2019. *General Population Census of the Kingdom of Cambodia: Provisional Population Totals*. Phnom Penh.

Neupert, Ricardo F., and Virak Prum. 2005. "Cambodia: Reconstructing the Demographic Stab of the Past and Forecasting the Demographic Scar of the Future." *European Journal of Population* 21(2/3): 217–46.

Nuon Chea. 1987. "Statement of the Communist Party of Kampuchea to the Communist Workers' Party of Denmark, July 1978." *Journal of Communist Studies* 3(1): 19–36.

Pol Pot. 1977. *Long Live the 17th Anniversary of the Communist Party of Kampuchea*, September 29. Phnom Penh: Ministry of Foreign Affairs, Democratic Kampuchea.

Ponchaud, François. 1979. "Kampuchea: une économie révolutionnaire." *Mondes en développement* 28: 716–31.

——————. 1989. "Social Change in the Vortex of Revolutions." In *Cambodia 1975–1978: Rendezvous with Death*, ed. Karl D. Jackson, 151–77. Princeton, NJ: Princeton University Press.

Quinn, Kenneth. 1989. "Explaining the Terror." In *Cambodia 1975–1978: Rendezvous with Death*, ed. Karl D. Jackson, 215–40. Princeton, NJ: Princeton University Press.

Siampos, George. 1970. "The Population of Cambodia 1945–1980." *Milbank Fund Quarterly* 48(3): 317–60.

Sliwinski, Marek. 1995. *Le génocide Khmer Rouge: une analyse démographique*. Paris: L'Harmattan.

Staub, Ervin. 1989. *The Roots of Evil: The Origins of Genocide and Other Group Violence*. Cambridge: Cambridge University Press.

Tabeau, Ewa. 2009. *Khmer Rouge Victims in Cambodia, April 1975–January 1979: A Critical Assessment of Major Estimates*. Demographic Expert Report for the Extraordinary Chambers in the Court of Cambodia, September 29. https://www.eccc.gov.kh/sites/default/files/documents/courtdoc/D140_1_1_Public_ Redacted_EN.PDF. Last accessed January 19, 2020).

Thongchai Winichakul. 2020. *Moments of Silence: The Unforgetting of the October 6, 1976 Massacre in Bangkok*. Honolulu, HI: University of Hawaii Press.

Tyner, James A. 2019. *The Nature of Revolution: Art and Politics under the Khmer Rouge*. Athens, OH: University of Georgia Press.

Ung Luong. 2000. *First They Killed My Father: A Daughter of Cambodia Remembers*. New York: Harper Collins.

Van Schaack, Beth, and Daryn Reicherter, eds. 2016. *Cambodia's Hidden Scars: Trauma Psychology and the Extraordinary Chambers in the Courts of Cambodia*. Documentation Series No. 22. Phnom Penh: Documentation Center of Cambodia.

Vickery, Michael. 1980. "Kampuchean Demography: Cooking the Books." Unpublished paper, November 10.

——————. 1984. *Cambodia, 1975–1982*. Boston, MA: South End Press.

——————. 1988. "Correspondence." *Bulletin of Concerned Asian Scholars* 20(1): 70–73.

Weitz, Eric D. 2003. *A Century of Genocide: Utopias of Race and Nation*. Princeton, NJ: Princeton University Press.

Zadrozny, Mitchell G. ed. 1955. *Area Handbook on Cambodia*. Human Relations Area Files. Chicago: University of Chicago.

Archival Sources

Extraordinary Chambers in the Courts of Cambodia (ECCC)

Case 002/01 Judgement. 7 August 2014, Case File/Dossier No. 002/19-09-2007/ECCC/TC (Archive No. E313).

Case 002/02 Judgement. 16 November 2018, Case File/Dossier No. 002/19-09-2007-ECCC/TC (Archive No. E465).

Nuon Chea's Closing Brief in Case 002/02. 28 September 2017 (Archive No. E457/6/3/1).

Nuon Chea's Request for Reconsideration of the Supreme Court Chamber's Decision not to Summons Heng Samrin and Robert Lemkin and to Admit Evidence Produced by Robert Lemkin on Appeal. 4 February 2016. Case No. 002/19-09-2007-ECCC/SC (Archive No. F2/10).

Nuon Chea's Sixth Request to Consider and Obtain Additional Evidence in Connection with the Appeal Against the Trial Judgement in Case 002/01. 11 September 2015. Case No. 002/19-09-2007-ECCC/SC (Archive No. F2/8).

Revolutionary Flag. Issue 8, August 1975. Archive No. E3/5.

Revolutionary Flag. Issue 10, October 1975. Archive No. E3/729.

Revolutionary Flag. Issue 2–3, February–March 1976. Archive No. E3/166.

Revolutionary Flag. Issue 7, July 1976. Archive No. E3/4.

Revolutionary Flag. Issue 11, November 1976. Archive No. E3/139.

Revolutionary Flag. Special Issue, December 1976–January 1977. Archive No. E3/25.

Revolutionary Flag. Special Issue, April 1977. Archive No. E3/742.

Revolutionary Flag. Issue 8, August 1978. Archive No. E3/747.

Revolutionary Male and Female Youth. Special Issue August–September 1974. Archive No. E3/146.

Revolutionary Male and Female Youth. Issue 11, November 1975. Archive No. E3/750.

Revolutionary Male and Female Youth. Issue 3, March 1976. Archive No. E3/751.

Revolutionary Youth. Issue 10, October 1975. Archive No. E3/729.

Revolutionary Youth. Issue 12, December 1976. Archive No. E3/729.

Transcript of Trial Proceedings Public. 15 December 2011. Trial Day 11, Case File No. 002/19-09-2007-ECCC/TC (Archive No. E2/23.1).

DEMOCRATIC KAMPUCHEA'S REVOLUTIONARY TERROR IN THE 1970S

Transcript of Trial Proceedings Public. 9 July 2013. Trial Day 207, Case File No. 002/19-09-2007-ECCC/ TC (Archive No. E2/220.1).

Documentation Center of Cambodia (DC-CAM)

"Bringing up the Children of the Khmer Rouge Revolution." KR Notebook 008. Reproduced in *Searching for the Truth*, No. 34, October 2002, 8–12.

Chumriang Padevoat [Revolutionary Songs]. Stenciled booklet, ca. 1975. Archive No. D21452.

Chumriang Padevoat [Revolutionary Songs]. KR Notebook 006. Archive No. D21501.

Democratic Kampuchea. 1977. *Phumisat Kampuchea Pracheathipatey* [Geography of Democratic Kampuchea], Class 2. Archive No. D21494.

"Determine to Build Socialism in a Great Leap Forward Following the Line of the Party by Depending on Agriculture as the Foundation." *Revolutionary Flag*, Issue 8, August 1976. Reproduced in *Searching for the Truth*. Special English Edition, 4th quarter 2015, 9–13.

"Kampuchean Communist Youth League: The Right Hand of the Party." *Revolutionary Youth Magazine*, Issue 5, May 1977. Reproduced in *Searching for the Truth*, No. 20, August 2001, 5–6.

Karkaria, Zal. 2003. "Khmer Rouge Policy on Women." *Searching for the Truth*, Special English Edition, 4th quarter, 17–32.

"Khmer Rouge Song: The Revolutionary Angkar is the Soul of every Kampuchean Citizen." Reproduced in *Searching for the Truth*, No. 3, March 2000, 49.

Lakkhantika Pak Kommunit Kampuchea [Statute of the Communist Party of Kampuchea]. Archive No. D00674.

Lakkhantika Samphoan Yuvakak 1972 [Statute of Yuvakak League, 1972]. Archive No. D06792.

"Male and Female Revolutionary Youths Determine to Fight, Defend, and Rebuild the Country in Great Leaps." *Revolutionary Youth*, Issue 12, December 1976. Reproduced in *Searching for the Truth*, No. 23, November 2001, 50.

"News for Revolutionary Male and Female Youth." *Revolutionary Flag*, Issue 10, September 1975. Archive No. D21389). Reproduced in *Searching for the Truth*, Special English Edition, 2nd quarter 2016, 7–12.

Notebook No. 76: *Peak Slaok 17 Mesa 1978* [Slogans for the (celebrations) of 17 April 1978]. Archive No. D21571.

Phumisat Kampuchea Pracheathipadey phnaek nayobay [Political Geography of Democratic Kampuchea]. 1977. Phnom Penh, 69. Archive No. D00475.

"Revolutionary Male and Female Youth Must Strive to Destroy the Standpoint of 'Sufficient', and Temper Ourselves in Order to Fiercely Fight the Enemy, Nature, Defend and Committedly Build Our Country." *Revolutionary Flag*, Issue 10, October 1978. Reproduced in *Searching for the Truth*, Special English Edition, 3rd quarter 2015, 7–12.

Siavphouv rian aksòr thnak ti muay (in Khmer) [language textbook, Class 1], Phnom Penh, 1976. Archive No. D21486.

Siavphouv aksòr thnak ti pi (in Khmer) [language textbook, Class 2), Phnom Penh, 1977. Archive No. D21478.

"Statute of the Communist Party of Kampuchea on Party Membership and Party Branches" (in Khmer). Archive No. D21502.

"Temporary Statutes of the Communist Youth League of Kampuchea of the Communist Party of Kampuchea." *Searching for the Truth*, No. 13, January 2001, 10–14.

"The Communist Youth League of Kampuchea is the Right Hand of the Party." *Male and Female Revolutionary Youth*, Special Issue, August–September 1974. Archive No. D21380. Reproduced in *Searching for the Truth*, Special English Edition, 3rd quarter, 2016, 5–9.

"The Red Heart of Dam Pheng" (by a possible Khmer Rouge senior leader). *Revolutionary Youth*, 1973. Reproduced in *Searching for the Truth*, Special English Edition, 3rd quarter 2016, 51–56.

Mass Violence, Ethnic Conflict, and the Expanding State in the Vietnamese Highlands: The Sơn Hà Revolt as Event and Memory

ĐÀO THẾ ĐỨC AND ANDREW HARDY[*]

The house was narrow, most of the space between its brick walls filled by a bed covered by a mat. In the afternoon of March 20, 2010, four visitors stepped out of a car outside the house, but inside there was only room for two. Đào Thế Đức settled on the mat beside its owner Đinh Giới, Andrew Hardy perched on a stool by the bed, and the two other men—an official of the culture department and a young policeman—sat by the open door as they listened to the old man's stories.

Đinh Giới was a veteran of Vietnam's wars. Napalm had scarred his ankles and bombs had impaired his hearing, but he spoke with a strong calm voice in good Vietnamese, perfected after 1954 during a long stay in northern Vietnam where he met his wife. His mother tongue is Hrê, the minority language spoken in his home village of Ta Meng in the hill country of Quảng Ngãi. This is where he was born in 1915, he said, to a poor family that became poorer when his father was killed on the riverbank in a battle between village landlords. He told us how he had joined the communist party in 1945, enlisted in the resistance army and served as the commune's first party secretary, and how they had set up the village militia, youth organization, women's association, and a tax system. He talked for two hours, giving a rare insider's account of the early years of Vietnam's revolution in the highlands. In the doorway, the policeman occasionally wrote something in a tiny notebook.

In 1948 the army posted Đinh Giới to another district. At this point in the conversation, unprompted by any question, he related the circumstances of his return home. "When I got back—I'd been away for a year and a half—I had just got home and the same night a revolt broke out, a revolt where they were killing

---

* The research for this chapter was funded by the Horizon 2020 project CRISEA "Competing Regional Integrations in Southeast Asia" (https://crisea.hypotheses.org/) and received logistical and administrative support from the EFEO's center in Hanoi and from VASS.

Kinh people and burning their houses in chaos everywhere. Our minority people were doing that, killing people, so I had to run, out to the road, and down the road to the district town...."[1]

At this point the culture department official stepped into the narrow space of Đinh Giới's room. "Stop, there's no need for you to talk about that. Just talk about culture, and if you do talk about that, then you must take responsibility for what you say—I won't talk about that, because I don't know what sort of work these men are doing—if you talk about that subject in particular, politics, you don't have our permission." This intervention was surprising for its delivery in a loud voice and an angry, aggressive tone. A short exchange of words followed, and then Đinh Giới's visitors thanked him, got back in their car and left.

$$* * * *$$

The present chapter presents the results of research into the event of mass violence that Đinh Giới witnessed in January 1950. The research had three aims. First, to understand the historical context and causes of the violence that took place in Sơn Hà district (Quảng Ngãi Province, central Vietnam). Second, to produce an account of what happened. Third, to explore the impact of the memory of the event. This chapter summarizes the first strand and makes a preliminary analysis of the second and third strands. It is a case study of how violence in a community's past may shape that community's identity in the present, affecting the terms of its members' integration at national and regional levels.

The culture department official's behavior during the interview with Đinh Giới sheds light on the third strand. In our experience of working in Vietnam, his intervention was unusually aggressive and cannot be explained with reference to routine state surveillance of ethnographic research. It reflected, rather, the high level of stress and fear this man suffered as he listened to Đinh Giới speak about the past in the presence of the police. The intervention revealed the tense local politics that inhabit the memory of the historical violence it was intended to conceal.

We collected data using ethnographic, historical, and cartographical methodologies. After receiving the local authorities' permission to do interviews on this subject, we made several field visits to Quảng Ngãi in 2017-20, especially to the commune where the massacre started, Sơn Linh. We consulted the archives of the French army in Paris and the Democratic Republic of Vietnam (DRV) in Hanoi.[2] As for the cartographical component, Map 1 uses archival sources to indicate the territorial extent of the violence, while Map 2 records the event as it took place at Sơn Linh, described to us by survivors.[3]

The chapter's three sections develop our argument that the violence resulted from the DRV state's expansion in the late 1940s. The first section on the history of Sơn Hà recalls how, in the nineteenth century, the Vietnamese imperial state had excluded this highland area from the empire's territory through the construction of a wall and how, at the turn of the twentieth century, the French colonial rulers allowed nonstate institutions of political control to persist there. This section argues that Vietnam's postcolonial state, as it established its rule after the 1945 revolution, placed the indigenous elites that ran those institutions under increasing pressure.

The second section on the massacre as event uses ethnographic data to make narrative and cartographical reconstructions of the massacre's first day. The data confirm the role of indigenous highlander elites as organizers of the killing, which was carried out by male civilian members of the subaltern populations they ruled. The violence was an act of resistance by nonstate elites against the encroachment of a modern state. As Đinh Giới said, it was a revolt. It was an attempt by traditional Hrê leaders to assert an ancient autonomous political identity as the French "colonialists" faded from the territorial picture and the Vietnamese "communists" moved in at the head of a new state, their state, a Vietnamese state.

The third section on the massacre as memory observes differences in the way the event was understood in the periods before and after the Vietnam War ended in 1975. A postwar taboo on the subject means that younger generations understand little of its political origin, while commemorative rituals ensure that the mass death and its ethnic dimension are not forgotten. In this section we argue that the simplifications of memory have led the Sơn Hà revolt to be exclusively understood as an incident of ethnic conflict.

Background to the Revolt: Sovereignties Collide in the Highlands of Quảng Ngãi

The historical context to the event involved two long-term sociopolitical processes. The first was the Vietnamese empire's southward expansion into the territory of the kingdom of Champa. In Quảng Ngãi, this occurred in the sixteenth to seventeenth centuries and involved the in-migration of Kinh people (ethnic Vietnamese) who settled on land inhabited by ancestors of a people known today as Hrê, and in 1950 as Chàm, Hre, or Rhe.[4] This colonial encounter gave rise to two territories each with its own ethnic community—a coastal plain inhabited by the incoming Kinh and a hinterland inhabited by the indigenous Hrê (Hardy and Nguyễn Tiến Đông 2019). With its source on the plateaus to the west, a river crossed both territories, known as the Hrê River in the hill country of Sơn Hà and the Trà Khúc on the plain.

The second process was the formation of the border apparatus known as the Long Wall of Quảng Ngãi. This consisted of an ancient road defended by a network of eighteenth-century forts, reinforced in 1819 by a hundred-mile-long wall, hedge, and ditch. An initiative of the Vietnamese empire, the wall was designed to separate the two communities and was negotiated and built by both. The Hrê sought to block Vietnamese imperial expansion onto the fertile paddy land of their valleys, while the Vietnamese hoped to stop Hrê raids on Kinh villages. It embodied a territorial settlement under which Kinh people would remain to the east, Hrê to the west. Trade between them took place in the vicinity of the wall (Hardy 2015).

With the advent of French rule, the army that manned the Long Wall was disbanded and military posts were established inside Hrê territory. The first was built in 1898 at Làng Rí (Sơn Giang commune (see Map 1). These forts aside, the French presence in the hills was minimal. Within the federal model that underpinned their rule over the highlands of Indochina, they made strategic use of preexisting nonstate political arrangements involving indigenous elites.

These arrangements were based on networks of village heads. Each Hrê village had a head, who regularly met neighboring village heads at ceremonies and feasts. The networks thus formed were dominated by a few "influential chiefs," as they were described by contemporaries. They had no army or police, but these networks gave them a considerable capacity for military mobilization. Village heads easily raised 50–100 men to fight field boundary disputes, while influential chiefs assembled forces of many hundreds. With spears, knives, and crossbows ready to hand, fighters could be mobilized at short notice for internecine warfare and cross-border raiding.[5]

The highlands of Quảng Ngãi were ruled by these chiefs, whose sovereignty was reinforced in the nineteenth century by the wall that excluded the Vietnamese empire. In the twentieth century, the French federated them into the colonial state hierarchy, appointing them as canton heads (*chánh tổng*), requiring them to raise corvee labor but no tax. They posted French officers with Kinh troops to punish internecine fighting and border raiding and to protect a minor mandarin. Within this framework, Hrê networks of rule changed little from precolonial times.

The dismantling of the Long Wall reduced Hrê raiding on lowland villages. It also meant Kinh people could circulate freely in Hrê country where upstream-downstream trading was lucrative. They built shops and homes along the banks of the river west of the wall, sojourning and settling with their families. Living on the outskirts of Hrê villages, many were traders, while others fished the river, farmed fields on its banks, or provided boat services. This proximity nurtured friendly relations between many members of the two communities, though intermarriage was rare. By 1950 about 3,000 Kinh lived alongside the 23,000 Hrê inhabitants of western Quảng Ngãi.[6]

In Sơn Hà, colonial rule was thus deeply dependent on the Hrê chiefs. This was an archetypal protectorate, a federal regime of indirect rule with limited ambitions, defined as "hegemonic" (by Ferguson and Whitehead 1992, 7, after Luttwak 1976) and characterized by the "establishment of military superiority and indirect control through local authorities." Then came the 1945 revolution, a national revolution when the DRV authorities announced they would claim all of Vietnam as national territory, including upland areas the precolonial empire had never occupied. The expanding ambitions of this postcolonial state produced a shift in the model of sovereignty. The DRV aimed at full territorial control, involving direct rule over the whole population and its integration into national political structures. With this shift, the revolution inaugurated the Hrê districts' first transformative experience of state rule. It involved state-building and national revolution on Vietnamese terms, it paid no attention to the long-abolished Long Wall, and it was accompanied by new Kinh in-migration, this time of soldiers, officials, factory workers, and farmers. This program implied a challenge to the political primacy of the indigenous elites.

Immediate Causes: The Expanding DRV State

In the early days of the revolution, DRV officials courted the Hrê chiefs, encouraging them to join the government and party committees that replaced the colonial cantons and to stand in the 1946 elections. At first the chiefs went along with this. In the late 1940s, however, relations began to strain. During these early years of the Indochina War, the revolutionaries retained control of Quảng Ngãi and several neighboring provinces of Interzone V, which formed a "liberated zone" that extended for hundreds of miles along the coast. But the French were not far away, maintaining a military presence on the edge of Hrê country, at Kom Plong (see Map 1), and elsewhere in the Central Highlands. As they established their rule in Sơn Hà, DRV officials sought to modernize Hrê customs and transform their economic, social, and political relations. These policies threatened the chiefs' interests.

The revolt's leaders mentioned this threat in a letter they sent to the French in February 1950: "Until 1946 there were no serious difficulties with the Vietnamese. After 1946 the [Viet Minh] asked the Montagnards to share their wealth, which the latter refused until the end of 1949."[7] French reports similarly noted that "The V.M. authorities thought they should apply communist principles to the highlander regions.... Too preoccupied with gaining the masses for their cause, the V.M. thought they could ignore the authority and ancestral ascendancy of the "Chiefs." The latter were not fooled by communist propaganda and rose up to defend their inheritance."[8]

DRV analysts concurred. Regional leaders realized that the violence had been provoked by cadres who "transferred the full framework of popular democratic revolution in the plains to the circumstances [of the highlands], using orders to implement policy."[9] In November 1950, President Ho Chi Minh sent two telegrams to Sơn Hà—one to the highlanders, the other to officials—rebuking officials for using dictatorial methods to raise excessive contributions of land, cattle, and capital.[10] A few months later, Ho Chi Minh expressed deep concern to regional leader Võ Chí Công, who explained how officials' imperious implementation of revolutionary ideals had "impinged on the interests of a few members of the elite or canton heads" (Võ Chí Công 2001, 135–36).

Hrê, Kinh, and French records thus support our hypothesis that the violence stemmed from the postcolonial state's threat to the chiefs' power. In the revolution's early days, the communist leadership understood that it should not confront two enemies at once. Prioritizing national independence over class struggle, it focused first on defeating the French (the anti-imperialist agenda), deferring the fight against traditional elites (the antifeudal agenda) to a later date (Marr 2013, 3, 9, 463). In Sơn Hà, however, it appears that DRV officials, made complacent by the French absence from Quảng Ngãi and by a misunderstanding of Hrê politics, failed to defer the "antifeudal" agenda. On the contrary, in the late 1940s they implemented policies aimed at reducing the Hrê chiefs' power.

The consequence was an act of resistance the French described as a *révolte* (Bodard 1950); its name in Vietnamese, *phiến loạn*, has a similar meaning.[11] The revolt took place at a pivotal moment in the DRV's prosecution of the war. As aid started to arrive from China in 1950, the DRV adopted a new strategy of "war communism," massively expanding the reach of the state through mobilization of people and resources at the expense of traditional elites. With the turn to war communism in 1950, the antifeudal agenda was no longer deferred, but it was pursued gradually, incrementally, in a "slow burning coup d'Etat," in Goscha's words, that led to the land reform policy launched in 1953 (Goscha 2022, 11). As Ho Chi Minh's reaction shows, the communist authorities fully understood the revolt's political significance. It was a rejection of DRV rule.

The Revolt as Event: Chronicle of a Killing

Our ethnographic research into the revolt as event had two aims. We wanted to produce an account of the violence, and we wanted to use ethnographic sources to test the hypothesis we had developed to explain it, outlined in the paragraphs above. No ethnographic research had previously been done and few accounts have been published.[12] Our findings allowed us to chronicle the event. They confirm that it was organized by indigenous chiefs who raised a fighting force among the civilian population under their control, and that it was indeed a revolt against the DRV. But they also reveal that this act of political violence did not specifically target the administrative and military personnel of the Vietnamese state. It was an indiscriminate massacre of the district's entire civilian Kinh population.

The following account is drawn from interviews with Kinh and Hrê inhabitants of Sơn Hà. It adopts two perspectives. The first is spatial. The hour-by-hour reconstruction presented below is the basis for a map of the violence in Sơn Linh commune (Map 2). The second is sociological. Social analysis of the Kinh and Hrê communities help identify which groups were involved in the violence and in what ways.

The Massacre

The violence started on January 25, 1950, which in the lunar calendar was the 8th day of the 12th month of the Kỷ Sửu year. Kinh people in Quảng Ngãi set aside this season for visiting the ancestors' graves (*chạp mả*), a lineage ritual usually led by men. This meant that on the day of the attack many male members of Hrê River's Kinh communities were away in their home villages on the Quảng Ngãi plain. The violence was planned in advance, including its timing during this festive period.

One of the larger Kinh villages on the river was Gò Da (Sơn Linh commune, see Map 1). From here, soon after dawn, a group of women hawkers set out on their morning rounds. When they entered the Hrê village of Vi Sinh (point 1 on Map 2), villagers attacked them and killed one woman. Not long after, the men of Vi Sinh came out, armed with throwing spears and stabbing spears, some with crossbows.

They went first to a collective farm at Ba Rinh field (point 2). Here they seized rice and buffaloes and torched buildings. The twenty migrant workers there fled. By 8 a.m. Kinh people throughout the area were shouting "There's a revolt (*phiến loạn*)! They're killing Kinh people." Commune officials sent a soldier downstream to inform the district authorities and told people to go to Gò Da school, a large building with several classrooms and a big yard, where they hoped to defend them. Over the morning, the Kinh population assembled, 600–800 people.

The state authorities had thirty militiamen. But ten were Hrê and they were with the attackers. In the late morning, the remaining twenty Kinh soldiers formed a line in the village street outside the house of local party leader Đặng Ngọc Liên (point 3). They had four guns but no bullets. Hrê men arrived from their villages in groups of thirty or forty to form an army several thousand strong, and around noon the militia slowly moved back. At 1 p.m. they reached the shop of a trader, Chiêm (point 4). The attackers seized cloth, liquor, and other goods, then set the house alight. They took a hundred cattle from his neighbour Toàn and torched his house too. Soon all the houses were ablaze, the bamboo cracking as it burned. Đặng Ngọc Liên was away. When people heard loud explosions from his house, they realized it had contained a supply of bullets. It was at this point that the attackers started firing arrows.

By 2 p.m. they reached the school (point 5). The militia commander took up a loudhailer but his attempts to parley—"What's the problem? Don't kill people, we'll give you buffaloes"—were greeted with stones and arrows. The militia threw grenades—they had three boxes of locally manufactured grenades, 25 to a box—but they failed to explode. The attack intensified and the commune chairman gave the order to retreat. Calmly, without speaking, they walked down the village street towards the river. The attackers advanced apace, hollering, shouting *xung phong* (attack) in Vietnamese and *vik Kloi* (stab the Kinh) in Hrê.

They forded the stream and by 3 p.m. reached the cemetery in Làng Ghè village (point 6). A hundred or so women, children, and elderly hid in the bushes here, while the others followed the militia down to the river, running now, some struck by arrows and spears. They planned to head downstream to Xà Nay (Sơn Nham commune), to the well-guarded mint where money and stamps were printed. But at 4 p.m. they were cut off by another Hrê army advancing upstream. Some swam to safety, but most died here, hundreds of people stabbed to death on the bank of the river (point 7).

The killing stopped at nightfall. The killers went home for their evening meal, taking the stolen livestock and leaving guards to watch the road. Plunder and killing continued the following day, and the massacre spread up and down the

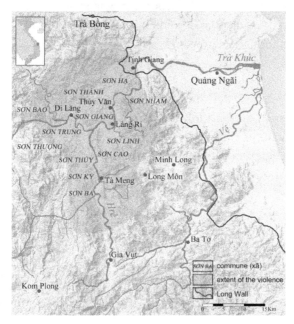

Map 1. The Sơn Hà Revolt (Sơn Hà district, Quảng Ngãi province). Drawn by Federico Barocco from a 1950 French army map (Service Historique de la Défense 10H1281).

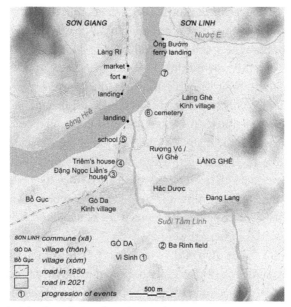

Map 2. The Sơn Hà Revolt in Sơn Linh commune, January 25, 1950. Drawn by Federico Barocco from ethnographic data gathered in Sơn Linh (2017–21).

valley. The bodies remained on the ground or floated down the river. When the DRV army arrived ten days later, soldiers and relatives buried the dead where they lay, many in unmarked graves.[13]

Survivors

The above account depicts the killers and the people they killed, but other groups were present at Sơn Linh that day. Some people survived the attack. Kinh survivors gave us the account summarized above, and this is clear from its perspective. Understandably, none of the Hrê we met gave us an eyewitness narrative from the perpetrators' point of view. Our main informant—Lâm Quyển, aged twelve at the time—was a survivor. He saved himself by hiding in a bush in the cemetery where he saw his parents and sisters killed by men he knew. Survivors like him were numerous, he said, a third of the Kinh community. But the other two-thirds perished, and with killings going on upstream, downstream, and on the far bank, escape was not easy.

After night fell on January 25, Lâm Quyển left his bush and moved to a nearby Hrê village where he hid in a garden. Eating bananas and vegetables, he changed hiding place nightly, keeping to the Hrê village, as the killers continued killing and stealing but did so in the Kinh village. He had learned this trick, he said, in military training at school. His ordeal ended nine days later when DRV troops arrived. The cover of darkness also helped Yên, aged sixteen. He spent the day on a boulder in the river, then at nightfall floated downstream to Thủy Văn, coming ashore in the small hours to hide in a ditch until troops arrived.

Those who escaped by swimming were men. Women and children mostly followed the militia to the riverbank. But some fled in other directions and got away. Among them was Nguyệt, aged thirty. She and five other young women lived for days in a forest hut, then walked the trails to the safety of the next valley, beating sticks to frighten the tigers.[14] Others stayed in the bushes at the cemetery. This was the choice of Thu, aged thirteen, where her family hid in a thicket of thorny rattan. After dark they crept out and cooked rice in the embers of their smouldering house. Next morning, the perpetrators stabbed through the rattan, killing her parents, wounding her. Thu survived, as the blood from her wounds helped her play dead for the next nine days.[15]

Eleven-year-old Tuấn also hid in a thicket. The cemetery, where both communities buried their dead, was taboo, he told us, so they fired arrows in but few dared enter. On the second day, some Hrê passed on their way to plunder. One was Mr. Dui, a customer of Tuấn's mother. His sister called out and Dui took them to a hut in the forest where his wife and children were, hiding them there until they heard the soldiers' loudhailers ten days later.[16]

A similar thicket failed to protect Minh, aged nineteen. They used a dog to find him, pulled him out and started stabbing. But their leader was a friend of Minh's father. He recognized Minh, took him to the hills 10 kilometers away in Sơn Cao commune, and placed him in the safekeeping of his family hiding there. When the soldiers arrived, he handed him over.[17]

Hrê Non-combatants

The survivors' stories reveal the presence of a further group—Hrê non-combatants hiding in the hills. A proportion of the Hrê population was not involved in the massacre but took cover in the forest to avoid the violence and the reprisals they expected would follow. Many of them, but not all, were women and children.

These stories record Hrê efforts to rescue and hide Kinh people. As noted above, close relationships had been formed, particularly through trade. One man recalled how his father was saved by a Hrê friend who said, "Go, quickly, or I have to kill you." But rescuing people was not easy. The evidence suggests that the rescuer either had high social status or had to act discreetly. These points—that some Hrê did not join in the killing and some Hrê helped people escape, and that both acts depended on the actor's social position and relations—highlight the social limits to the mobilization capacity possessed by the massacre's organizers.

On January 25, the four or five Kinh families at Làng Môn village (Sơn Cao commune) heard news of the violence downstream at Sơn Linh. In the early afternoon they fled to the hills, heading for the neighboring district of Minh Long. Among them was Hiền, aged ten. After she lost her parents in the melee, she spent three hungry days and nights wandering in the wild. Then they ran into some Hrê men on the trail. The men killed the others in her group, but one of them knew Hiền's father. He took her home, gave her Hrê clothes, and set her to fetching water and babysitting, working as the family's slave. Then a fortnight later, fearing reprisals, he released her.[18]

Interviews revealed several instances of high-status rescuers. Eight-year-old Lợi was sheltered by a village head at Gò Da, who knew his parents. Other villagers saw this, but no one touched the boy.[19] A young adult from Làng Ghè fled upstream to Đồng Sạ village (Sơn Cao commune), where he hid in the house of one of his customers, a wealthy woman and head of the village. At Vi Ghè, too, the village head took in a Kinh neighbor. This man must have been surprised. He owed his life to Trưởng Đời, the main leader of the massacre in Sơn Linh.[20]

417

Other rescues were kept secret. One involved the family of Đặng Ngọc Liền. He was away but his pregnant wife and her mother were at home. When they heard hollering and saw their Hrê neighbors leaving, they asked to go with them. The Hrê women hid them in their hut in the forest, where days later the child was born.[21]

On the night of January 25, four Kinh men approached the house of Đinh Đô in the hills above Ta Meng village (Sơn Kỳ commune). They were traders and Đinh Đô was an old friend and customer. Đô's son told us how the men told Đô about the killings and asked for refuge with their families, waiting outside. Đô fed the thirty refugees, hid them in the forest, and led them out of the valley to safety. Đô's brother Gô rescued twenty others in the same way. Using a pejorative term for Kinh people, a party of perpetrators came asking, "Are there any Kloi here? If so, we'll kill them." The brothers replied, "There are none."[22]

Perpetrators

Among the Hrê who left for the forest was Đinh Mai, a teenager at the time. "We fled to the mountain," he recalled, adding that many Hrê fled there. "Many families ran away, there was no one left at home." He recalled a Kinh neighbor who stayed with them, "a boy, the same age as me, we used to tend the cattle together … he was alone, his parents had already died." For ten days they shared the same difficult conditions—banana leaves to keep off the rain, nothing against the cold and mosquitoes. Then they heard the soldiers calling and went back to the village.[23]

The existence of Hrê non-combatants like Đinh Mai raises the question: who were the perpetrators? If we believe the author of a French report, all the Hrê were involved: "The young men massacred, the women and children plundered, the old people burned and posted up slogans."[24] There is ethnographic evidence for a gender division of labor as several eyewitnesses saw women plundering on day two. But interviews do not bear out the impression conveyed here that the entire Hrê population took part. They show that all the children, most of the women, and many men moved away from the massacre site before it started.

Regarding Hrê men, we may distinguish between non-combatants, fighters, and leaders. This was not, however, a simple military-civilian distinction. Besides a few who had served in the DRV army, none were soldiers. The fighting force that gathered on 25 January was raised among Hrê civilians using ancient methods of military mobilization that relied on the village heads' networks and power. Many were pressed to join. Besides the war cry "plunder—kill—burn," a second slogan, "pillage and kill those who don't follow us," was directed at ordinary Hrê men.[25] The threat was enforced, but only unevenly. At Sơn Linh we heard of one Hrê man killed for not joining. But in the commotion it was possible to get out of the way and some Hrê men did so.

One was Đinh Đeo, a teenager of fighting age. When he heard the hollering, he fled to the hills with his sick mother: "If I hadn't left, they would have killed me," he told us. He heard people going through the streets of his village shouting threats, but no one was checking the houses to see if people complied. He told us that many Hrê fled to the forest. He did not hear of any Hrê men killed, he said. People who did not flee had to join the killing.[26] This was the choice faced by Đinh Đao, son of the revolt's leader in Làng Ghè. He was a party member, so DRV officials sent him to parley, but he joined the killing instead.[27] Another party member at Sơn Linh made a different call. Đinh Nít refused to join the killing and escaped death himself only because he was related to a leader of the revolt (Ban Chấp hành Đảng bộ huyện Sơn Hà 1993, 71–72).

Not all the perpetrators were coerced. According to Đinh Mây, a Hrê intelligence officer with the DRV at the time, many were low-status men motivated by the opportunity for material gain. The revolt's followers were paupers or slaves, he explained. Rich people owned valuables like buffalos and gongs. The poor had no property, but they worked for the rich, so did not go short. The only poor who went hungry were lazy people, who cared little about making a living, ate from meal to meal, and preferred jaunts to work. Few rich people joined the revolt because they worried about their valuables, which they moved into safety. Only the poor wanted to go, for the plunder. If you paid them, they would go.[28]

There was also an ideological dimension to the revolt, as its slogans show. A French report listed several, one with a political target, "down with the V.M. invaders," another with an ethnic and territorial focus, "the mountain for the minorities, the delta for the Kinh."[29] A similar refrain, "the highlands for the highlanders," appears in a DRV report, alongside a rallying cry that merged Viet Minh and Kinh into a single category: "Kill the V.M. cadres and inhabitants of the delta."[30] Before the attack, ethnic targeting was used to get men to swear oaths at a buffalo sacrifice, like this slogan urging men to attack villages near the Long Wall: "Anyone who does not go down to the wall and kill Kinh is not a man."[31] During the massacre, the war cry was ethnic: "Stab the Kinh." The authors of these slogans fused the ancient ethnic divide embodied in the Long Wall with the contemporary political objective of ousting the DRV.

These data suggest that the perpetrators were Hrê men either coerced by their leaders or driven by opportunities for material gain and ideologies of ethnic division. In the absence of evidence from the perpetrators, it is impossible to gauge each factor's motivating power. But in all three cases, the issue of authority was central.

The Revolt's Leaders

A DRV ethnography commissioned after the revolt stressed the importance of authority in Hrê society. Using the class terminology of contemporary Vietnamese communism, it described the economic inequalities and social hierarchies of Hrê society. The "aspirations" of members of the farmworker classes—a subaltern group "bought off by the rich, obedient to the strongest"— contrasted with the conservative outlook of the landowning classes, who preferred the status quo. These groups were, in turn, subject to the authority of two elite classes, aristocrats (*quí tộc*) and village heads (*cà rá*).[32]

Archival and ethnographic sources identify the revolt's leaders as belonging to these two elites. The first consisted of the former canton heads, the "aristocrats," characterized by several informants as big men figures, men who "spoke and the people listened." They are the chiefs named in the 1950 Ethnography as responsible for the violence: "Enh, Diêu, Di, Lải, whose loss of power and economic interests motivated them to embroil a number of ordinary people in revolt."[33] Đinh Mây was one of several informants who named the revolt's leaders as Chánh Đí (former head of the canton that covered modern Sơn Cao, Sơn Linh, Sơn Giang communes), Chánh Ênh (Sơn Trung, Sơn Thượng, Sơn Bao), Chánh Lãi (Sơn Nham, Sơn Hạ, Sơn Thành), and Chánh Lộc (Sơn Thủy, Sơn Kỳ, Sơn Ba).[34] As Map 1 shows, these men's territory covered most of Sơn Hà, and that indeed is what they claimed in a request for arms sent to the French after the revolt—to represent the population of the whole district.[35]

A French report gives an insight into the status, character, and motivation of one such man. The *résident* in Kon Tum described Chánh Lãi as the "instigator and soul of the revolt against the Viêt-Minh in January 1950; former canton chief of Son Ha [=Sơn Hạ] (on the Tra-Khuc River) ... Authoritarian and oversensitive, Dinh Loi [*sic*] is the true political head of Hrê country. He maintains a solid hatred of the V.M.—which he regrettably tends to confuse with Vietnamese in general—which seized all his possessions (600 head of cattle, old jars, jewels, a thousand acres of paddy fields)."[36]

In 1945 men like Chánh Lãi lost their posts as canton chief, though some found new roles in the DRV. None, however, lost their ability to mobilize men through networks of relatives, clients, and dependents. Thus, when Đinh Mây noted that most rich people and village heads did not join the revolt, this reflected a general truth, that wealth made people risk averse, to which there were exceptions. Some, like the chiefs listed above, were prepared to risk their property if something more important was at stake—their political and economic power, threatened by the expanding DRV state.

The chiefs exercised their authority through the second elite group, the village heads (*lý trưởng* in Vietnamese, *kara plây* in Hrê, lit. village elder), whose status was similarly threatened by the new regime. One was Đinh Đời, known as Trưởng Đời from his status as head of the Hrê village Vi Ghè at Làng Ghè. Among the wealthiest men on the river, he was richer even than canton chief Chánh Đí. He owned paddy fields, buffaloes, jars, and a hundred slaves. Yet fear of losing power prevailed over concern for property, and thus he led the revolt at Sơn Linh. After it was over, when he moved his family into hiding in the forest, Đời did indeed lose his property—livestock, jars, pots, gongs—smashed and stolen by soldiers.[37]

In 1949 the threat to the interests of both elite groups came to a head when the DRV announced a policy to abolish slavery. In Hrê society, slaves were debt defaulters obliged to work in perpetuity for their creditor. Abolition threatened elites politically, as slavery underpinned the Hrê system of justice run by village heads who fined offenders and enslaved defaulters. It threatened elites economically, as landowners not only faced the loss of a workforce but also of ownership of their fields. Abolition was associated with land reform. For Lâm Quyền, this policy triggered the violence because "liberating the slaves meant that land would be shared out to the landless, something the rich did not like." His view that "this was a lesson for the party and a lesson for the revolution, as it was the party's fault, the revolution's fault, and not the fault of the people," voiced by a survivor of the revolt and former commune leader, was echoed by other retired officials we interviewed.[38] It was the culmination of a process of reappraisal that started immediately after the revolt. At a meeting in March 1950, DRV officials recognized abolition as a factor and asked, "Was this policy right?"[39]

Village heads were thus networked with canton chiefs in hierarchical relations of political, social, and economic dependence. Both groups faced an existential threat emanating from the DRV state. It was the village heads – like Trưởng Đời, Vok Lâm and Vok Gào at Làng Ghè or Vok Cho Cha, Vok Lung, Vok E and Hương Ná at Gò Da – who sacrificed the buffalos that fed the perpetrators the night before the massacre. Many of them led groups of 30–40 armed men down to the school at Gò Da. It was one of them who saw a Kinh doctor he knew in the crowd and ordered him spared, saving his life. Not all these men later followed the canton chiefs to join the French in Kon Tum, but many played leadership roles on the day of the revolt.

In the aftermath of the revolt, DRV officials understood the importance of authority and the role of the village heads. Party analysis of the "character of the revolt" recognized that many people were involved in the killing—"more than half the population in some places"—but found that coercion, plunder, and "unconscious imitation" were factors in their participation. The key decisions were made by a very small number of people, they concluded—"the chiefs and their sidekicks." In the months after the revolt, this understanding orientated DRV policy, which sought to undermine the chiefs' power by appealing to ordinary Hrê people to return home without fear of punishment.[40]

During the revolt, moreover, it was impossible to mobilize the Hrê without the village heads' active involvement. A party of perpetrators went downstream to Sơn Nham where the village head, an army officer named Đinh Mô, remained loyal to the DRV and urged his villagers to do the same. Despite rumors that the DRV had killed Hrê soldiers, the village did not join the revolt. Former canton chief Chánh Nhá similarly prevented the violence spreading into the district's westernmost communes (now Sơn Tây district).[41] Few Hrê inhabitants of the neighboring districts of Ba Tơ and Minh Long were involved. They too were beyond the reach of the Sơn Hà canton chiefs' networks of influence (see Map 1 for the revolt's geographical limits).[42]

* * * *

Ethnographic research yields sociological insights into both the communities involved in the events of January 25, 1950. For the Kinh, the stand-off at the Gò Da school was the moment it became clear that no response would work. Attempts to parley failed, the guns had no bullets, the grenades were duds. The authorities' last act was an orderly retreat, which was quickly overwhelmed. After the collapse of the DRV state at Sơn Linh, the social and economic complexity of the Kinh community of trading, farming, and fishing folk, of civilians, officials, and ill-armed militiamen, was reduced to a simple binary—those who died, including many women and children, and those able to escape.[43]

Within the Hrê community there was greater sociological complexity to the event. Women and children hid in the forest while some women joined in the plunder. The men who took up arms in January 1950 were poorer members of the community, civilians pressed and led by their village heads, who themselves obeyed the former canton chiefs. A few had been DRV soldiers and officials. Some men and some villages avoided getting involved, some saved the lives of people they knew. Yet the Sơn Hà Revolt demonstrated the immense strength of the canton chiefs' mobilization capacity. They arranged for village heads on both banks of the river for over 30 kilometers of its length to induce thousands of civilian men to murder an entire community of civilian women, children, and men, who, the day before, had been their friends, neighbors, and partners in trade.

The Revolt as Memory: The Changing Meaning of the Violence

Killing on this scale deeply marked the community that suffered it. We examine the revolt's aftermath at two levels. The first is the level of politics. As we have seen, the revolt was a rejection by Hrê elites of the DRV state's expansion of power at their expense. Their action drew the inhabitants of Sơn Hà into Vietnam's mid-twentieth-century wars for the first time. We call this the "political aftermath." It is about developments in the political conflict of which the revolt was an expression. The second level focuses specifically on the consequences of mass death. The massacre was not forgotten, but the way it came to be remembered bore little relation to the political situation that caused it. We call this the "aftermath of memory." It is about how the meaning of the violence changed over time. We briefly summarize the political aftermath in the following section, before turning to a fuller analysis of the aftermath of memory.

The Political Aftermath: Ethnic Politics Reframed

For the DRV, the revolt was a disaster. One report recorded losses of "more than 500 killed, 700 houses burned, 200 cows and buffaloes lost, and money losses valued at 20 million to 30 million piastres."[44] Another regretted the death of "over 1,000 people," including "many Kinh officials in all communes."[45] Ethnographic research suggests that these estimates are too low. The figure of 2,000 casualties (80 percent of the Kinh population) cited in a French report seems more accurate. The French also reported the death of 400 Hrê officials of the DRV, which is unlikely, as Hrê were killed only if they refused to join the revolt. Quantities of rice and salt were destroyed, as well as a weapons factory and the regional mint, several warehouses, and all the Kinh people's houses.[46] In military terms, the western districts of Quảng Ngãi, a province previously under full DRV control, became a contested zone. The DRV recognized the revolt as a "failure of national significance."[47]

In the weeks after the revolt, its leaders turned to the French. The French army had no prior knowledge of the revolt and moved quickly to capitalize on the new support for its own political reasons. The canton chiefs and some of their men moved to the French posts at Kom Plong and Kon Tum, above the cliff that separates the valleys of Quảng Ngãi from the plateaus to the west controlled by the French. Through 1950 and 1951, Sơn Hà became an actively contested frontier area where French troops and Hrê guerrilla bands launched attacks, hoping to capture the Hrê River valley, break into Quảng Ngãi, open a route to the sea, and cut the DRV-held area of Interzone V in two. It took the DRV two years to regain control in Sơn Hà, which it exercised now with great caution. By 1952 it was clear that the revolt had failed to expel the revolutionaries and the French had proved unable to turn the windfall into strategic advantage.

Most of the canton chiefs never returned to Sơn Hà. But return was an option, and many subaltern participants did go home. One man from a poor family told how he served for two years in a highlander unit of the French army in Kon Tum before returning to his village in Sơn Linh, where we met him in 2020.[48] Also still living in Sơn Linh was a former village head at Làng Ghè, a son of Trưởng Đời, the revolt's leader in Sơn Linh, but he was too frail for interview. For canton chiefs, return presented greater risks. Only one attempted it. Not long after the revolt, Chánh Đí went home to Thủy Văn (Sơn Giang commune). Cautiously pursuing a no-vengeance policy, the DRV left him alone. But early in 1954, with the valley firmly under their control, officials ordered his arrest. He was tried and executed, not for organizing the revolt but for conspiracy with the French after his return. The trial was a public event designed to send a clear message. In the words of a DRV report, it "mobilized the people to hate the enemy and its spies, rise up and smash the power of the enemy's evil lackeys, at the same time as highlighting the government's ethnic policy." The trial publicly marked the traditional chiefs' demise as a political force.[49]

The revolt had two further political consequences. It obliged inhabitants of Sơn Hà to take sides in Vietnam's wars, as the chiefs' fight was subsumed in the broader geopolitical conflict. From 1950, Hrê people had to navigate the presence near their villages of pro- and anti-communist forces. In 1954, while the country's partition obliged DRV partisans to withdraw from Quảng Ngãi and other provinces south of the 17th Parallel, many remained in hiding and the DRV maintained a parallel administration. Some Hrê who had joined the French after the revolt transferred their allegiance to Ngô Đình Diệm's Republic of Vietnam (RVN). But after 1954 few veterans of the revolt were politically active in Sơn Hà and none served the cause of the indigenous elites. The lines of fracture had shifted. Competing for the population's loyalty now were RVN forces in the towns and DRV insurgents in the hills, who depended heavily on Hrê support. Here, as elsewhere, the communist victory of 1975 was the culmination of a long process of contested expansion by the DRV state.

The war thus reframed ethnic politics in Sơn Hà. The highlanders no longer chose between the DRV and the Hrê chiefs, as they had in January 1950. Instead, they chose between the DRV and the RVN. [50] But the fact of the mass death remained. This fact was the revolt's longest-lasting political consequence. At a May 1950 meeting in Quảng Ngãi, its "disastrous results" were underlined by a DRV official: "It is a political defeat for us, giving rise to doubt and distrust among the population and hatred between highlanders and Vietnamese."[51] This assessment made in the immediate aftermath of the killing raises a question about its long-term impact: how were ethnic relations affected by the memory of the event?

The Aftermath of Memory: Official Amnesia, Popular Remembrance

Our main informant, Lâm Quyền, had a remarkable recall for the violence he witnessed in January 1950. Other villagers defer to him for this knowledge, saying "If you want to know about that event, talk to Quyền." In this section, we contrast his narrative (presented above, p. 413–416) with the knowledge possessed by younger people, people who did not see what happened.

To research this, we interviewed community members involved with the production and consumption of memory. They include province, district, and commune officials, many of them retired; history teachers at local schools; participants at Kinh rituals commemorating victims' deaths; and Kinh and Hrê villagers living near the massacre site. Our findings led us to distinguish between two contexts of memory. The first was official, focusing on government offices and schools. The second was social, focusing on the Kinh community. Our investigation of Hrê memories is in its early stages and not discussed here.

The Official Context

Among officials, we found that memory of the event changed over time. During the period from 1950 to 1975, leaders of the insurgency in Sơn Hà regularly attended meetings where the revolt was discussed. The revolt was a salutary reminder, DRV cadres told them, of the importance of good community relations, especially with minorities. When Lâm Quyền spoke of "a lesson for the party and a lesson for the revolution," he was articulating a sense of political caution developed at those meetings. As one retired official described the lesson, the violence happened because "we were not close to the people, not near the people, and didn't understand the minorities."[52]

When the Vietnam War ended in 1975, leaders of the DRV's parallel provincial administration left their highland refuges and moved to the city. Physical distance from wartime minority hosts, exacerbated by poor mountain roads and postwar economic hardships, led to growing political distance between the provincial government and the highlanders. The distance grew under the impact of threats to the state emanating from ethnic minorities in the Central Highlands—the 1980s FULRO insurgency, the 1990s growth of Protestantism, and the Dega riots of 2001 and 2004. In this context, officials ceased to talk about the revolt. There was no formal ban, but a taboo took root and older cadres who remembered the lesson it embodied did not pass it on to younger colleagues. The state no longer depended for its existence on the highlanders; political caution lost its sense of urgency and its practice of discussion. As the revolt passed into history, the official fear that memory of a past killing might cause new ethnic divisions wrapped itself in silence. It was that fear that created the conditions in the post-war period for the development of a memory impasse (Thongchai 2020, 17–19).

During this period, several books voiced an official memory of the event. The party histories of the district and province offer accounts of the revolt that openly acknowledge the revolutionary leaders' mistakes and the political motivation of the revolt's organizers (Ban Chấp hành Đảng bộ huyện Sơn Hà 1993, 65–101; 2015, 59–72; Ban Chấp hành Đảng bộ tỉnh Quảng Ngãi 1999, 95–103; 2019, 217–18, 236–42). The accounts are remarkably detailed and accurate. They err only in their claim that the French were involved. [53] French archives show that, on the contrary, French officers were surprised by this "spontaneous revolt," claimed no credit for it, and moved quickly afterwards to turn the DRV setback to their advantage. [54]

Produced for sale in shops, these books are given to senior party members, are consulted by teachers, can be read at the city public library, and were recently made available online. [55] They present the revolt as containing lessons for party leaders, including "lack of attention to the masses" and "insufficient democracy" (Ban Chấp hành Đảng bộ tỉnh Quảng Ngãi 1999, 96). They are not exercises in political whitewashing. Their length, moral seriousness, historical accuracy, and didactic presentation indicate that learning from past mistakes to improve present governance was among their authors' ideals.

Yet, the books also facilitate the freezing of official memory. One retired official we knew was reluctant to speak about the revolt. He was also unwilling to feign ignorance. He resolved the dilemma by taking down his copy of the provincial history and reading out extracts to answer our questions. The approved narrative relieved him of the need to use his own words.

In official contexts in Sơn Hà's district town Di Lăng, the impasse is especially strong. During our 2009–12 fieldwork on Hrê history and culture, we were formally instructed not to ask about the revolt. After the ban was lifted in 2017, questions posed in official contexts were met with embarrassment or evasion, even when we were not accompanied by a security official. Officials we know confirmed that the revolt rarely comes up in conversation. History teachers we met said the curriculum has only one local history class per term, so there is no time to mention the revolt. Junior officials or teachers risk reprimand if they discuss it with outsiders. For local elites, the subject is taboo.

Attempts to memorialize other events fell afoul of the taboo. In 1997–98, a project to erect an inscription to mark the 1946 creation of the first party cell in the district was quashed. The proposed site was Gò Da, where the revolt started. Senior provincial leader Phạm Thanh Biền recalled: "We could not do that. It would provoke the minorities, because to erect that would be to consider ourselves in the right, to consider ourselves as the norm, and place the responsibility for the crime on them.... If you erected that, you would have trouble. At Sơn Hà, we were damaged through our own fault, the damage was our own doing, it wasn't as though they spontaneously started killing people.... We can't erect that, it's dangerous."[56] Here, too, we see how the political prudence learned in the aftermath of the revolt took on a new form—silence and fear.

In this context, there has been no question of memorializing the massacre. Elsewhere in the province, the 1968 killing of Kinh civilians by American forces at Mỹ Lại village (Sơn Tịnh district) is remembered at an on-site museum, the Sơn Mỹ Memorial. State-sponsored ceremonies, inscriptions, and statues commemorate the killing of Kinh civilians by American forces at Khánh Giang-Trường Lệ (Nghĩa Hành district) in 1969 and by South Korean forces at Diên Niên-Phước Bình (Sơn Tịnh district) in 1966 and Giếng Thí market (Đức Phổ district) in 1965. But in Sơn Hà, the ethnic communities of the perpetrators and the victims still live side by side. Fear of renewed conflict between them has prevented the state from making any gesture of remembrance to those killed in January 1950. The state achieved power over the living in Sơn Hà, but fear of ethnic conflict has rendered it powerless as a commemorative force for the dead.

The Social Context

In his study of late twentieth-century Vietnamese death and ritual, Malarney (2002, 180, 188) explained the inadequacy of state provisions for the remembrance of war dead in northern Vietnam. State rituals cannot bring the soul (*hồn*) to its proper place, which is why families continue to observe traditional forms of commemoration (Malarney 2001, 61; 2002, 180, 188). Kwon's books (2006, 2008) on the aftermath of mass death in the central region further explore the distinction between state and social contexts of remembrance. They underline, in particular, the difficulty of political positioning the state faces in cases of mass death of civilians and their consequent absence from the national memory (Kwon 2006, 24). These observations apply acutely in Sơn Hà, where the state neither honors nor recognizes those who died in the revolt, while the large number of people who died means their killing is not forgotten. Prudent state positioning has produced official amnesia, yet the fact of mass death ensures that social memory persists.

We identified three contexts where Kinh inhabitants of Sơn Hà transmit this memory—family rituals, community rituals, and conversations outside ritual contexts.

For families, the main ritual event is the death anniversary (*giỗ*). In cases of mass death, many death anniversaries fall on the same day. In Sơn Linh this is the 8th day of the 12th lunar month, the date of the massacre, while across the river in Sơn Giang it is the 7th day, the eve of that date. Households hold rituals at the family altar in their house, followed by a meal to which they invite friends and neighbors. Many Kinh people here are descendants of massacre victims and survivors, giving the date an important place in the community's social calendar.

The occasion encourages talk about the massacre. Younger family members ask why so many died on the same day. The older men speak freely about it at table, more freely than normal. Conversations focus on the people and their experience of the event—the identities of victims, the relationships between them, stories of people running, rescued, killed. The massacre's political meaning rarely comes up. If it does, it can be settled conveniently with reference to the French. "They did that because they were put up to it by the French," as two people commented separately to us on the day of the *giỗ* we attended in January 2020.[57]

At these rituals, the venerated dead are "ancestors," named members of the extended family. Here, families make no distinction between ancestors who died good deaths, peacefully at home (*chết nhà*), and those who died unnatural "grievous deaths," "deaths in the street" (*chết oan, chết đường* (see Malarney 2002, 179–80; Kwon 2006, 12–16). The dead venerated on this day in Sơn Hà all died in violent circumstances. Many of their bodies were never recovered nor identified, and many ancestors' graves contain no body or only part of one. The important thing is that the ancestor is kin and is known by name.

For the community, the main ritual event is the Thanh Minh festival in the 3rd lunar month. In northern Vietnam, Thanh Minh is when people visit family graves (*tảo mộ*; see Phan Kế Bính 2006, 46). In Quảng Ngãi and Bình Định, however, lineages hold these rituals in the 12th month (*chạp mả*), and the Thanh Minh festival serves instead for the worship of wandering ghosts (*cô hồn*, or *cô bác*; see Kwon 2006, 12, 90), done elsewhere on the 15th day of the

7th month. The Thanh Minh festival is thus of particular importance to the Kinh inhabitants of Sơn Hà, as this is when they venerate the anonymous dead, the dead for whom ceremonies are not held by their descendants. On this day, men clean the graves, both those of their ancestors and those of unknown people, while women prepare food. The rituals are held in community locations—at small public shrines (*đàn*, there are three in Sơn Linh) or a goddess temple (there is one, named *đình bà*, at Thuỷ Văn in Sơn Giang)—and followed by a community meal. The ritual specialist we met in Sơn Giang said the petition read out at the ceremony indicated the violent nature of the deaths: "They died because they were stabbed by highlanders" (*chết vì mọi đâm*).

Some years ago, the date of the Thanh Minh festival at Sơn Linh and Sơn Giang was fixed on the 10th day of the 3rd lunar month. In 2007 the state created a new public holiday on this day—the Hùng Kings Festival, popularly known as the ancestors' death anniversary (*giỗ tổ*)—in a gesture intended to nurture national sentiment, to remind all Vietnamese of their shared ancestral kings. For Thanh Minh, this choice of date is convenient as the schools are closed and children can join in the celebrations. But when people adopt a national(ist) holiday to memorialize a local conflict between two ethnic groups, they overturn the ethnic solidarity of the national myth. Their use of the state holiday also serves to legitimize the ceremony, as for some years after 1975 such rituals were banned as "superstition."

In these ritual contexts, Kinh people in Sơn Hà deal with the two ways evoked by Kwon (2008, 27) by which ghosts come into being. Ghosts are either "unknown dead existing near home" or known "dead missing from home burial." The unknown dead are venerated in community rituals held at shrines or temples, while the known but missing dead join the ancestors on the family altar. This is a simplification, as the unknown dead also benefit from rituals closer to home, corresponding to the dual gestures described by Kwon (2006, 90) whereby ancestors are worshipped in the house and ghosts outside. In Sơn Linh, one such ritual takes place after the ceremony that closes the family's year (*tất niên*), held before the 23rd day of the 12th lunar month, when people place food offerings on their doorstep for those who died unnatural deaths.

The difficulty of locating tragic deaths in this dual ritual framework emerges from Kwon's study (2006, 93–94). He shows how the ambiguity of death in a civilian massacre—a bad death that happened at home—complicates the practice of domestic remembrance by forcing people to ask, "Which direction do we turn, the ancestral side or the ghost side?" Our research suggests a slightly different conclusion. We found that Kinh inhabitants of Sơn Hà have resolved this dilemma by making pragmatic use of the dual framework, by shifting between ritual contexts located in house and street, in family and community, "between the house of genealogical memory and the outer terrain of anonymous death" (Kwon 2006, 94), between the death anniversary at home and the Thanh Minh festival at the shrine. During the seventy years since the massacre, they settled the matter using appropriate rituals and, if necessary, empty graves (*mộ giố*, literally graves of wind). Further research will be necessary to determine whether this process involved innovatory ceremonies, as Malarney (2002, 180) observed in the north.

There are, finally, several non-ritual contexts where knowledge of the event is transmitted. Our interviews showed that within the family one such context is the bedroom, where several younger informants reported long late-night conversations with a grandmother or aunt. Another context for such conversations was the marketplace and local shops and hairdressers, where the public space created its own intimacy. One Kinh migrant from outside the region told us that it was here that she learned about the massacre—from traders in the market.[58] Most of the traders are women, and in all these contexts we observed a gendered dimension. Women seemed more comfortable to engage in informal talk in intimate places about the event and less concerned outside official contexts by the taboo in play there. Men talked about the massacre on the ritual occasions assigned for such talk. In non-ritual contexts, women played a key role in the transmission of memory.

Conclusion

Our findings raise a question about the revolt as event. In what sense was this mass violence an incident of ethnic conflict? To answer it, we may examine the resources that created the conditions for the violence. The first resource was military—Hrê men possessed and regularly used spears, knives, and crossbows. The second resource was economic—people were motivated to kill by opportunities for material gain, in the form of the meat of buffaloes sacrificed the night before, and the plunder of Kinh homes afterwards.

The third resource was political—the availability of an authority with capacity to mobilize armed forces. Ethnographic and archival evidence show that the revolt was led by a small number of chiefs who continued to exercise power over subaltern Hrê populations in the years after 1945. In Sơn Hà, the revolution inaugurated not only a new state but also a new type of state possessing vastly increased ambitions for rule. Its policies on slavery, land reform, and other issues, coupled with the overbearing attitude of its officers, threatened the autonomy of traditional elites. They reacted by mobilizing their men to violence.

As Katz noted in his study of the Ta-pa-ni Incident in Taiwan, rebellions were commonly led by local elites who "simply opposed any state that attempted to encroach on their interests." For Katz, a central issue was "how these elites reacted to state attempts to restrict or usurp their control over local communities" (Katz 2005, 55, 239). The tripartite relation between the expanding state, traditional elites, and subaltern highlanders observed in colonial India by Arnold (1982, 140), was further complicated in Sơn Hà by the presence in the hills of a community of migrants from the plains.

This brings us to the question of why this political violence did not target the agents of the encroaching state but struck the men, women, and children of the migrant community? Why did it take the form of civilian mass violence? The distinction between political violence, mass violence, and ethnic conflict, and the way they merged in January 1950, is a key problem here. The issue hinges on the fourth type of resource mobilized in Sơn Hà, which was ideological.

Some of the revolt's slogans, such as "the mountain for the minorities, the delta for the Kinh," invoked history associated with the Long Wall of Quảng Ngãi. In the nineteenth century, this border had embodied a law barring Hrê from the delta and Kinh from the hills. The regime was abandoned in 1898, thanks to the federal nature of the French colonial empire, and Kinh migrants started settling in the hills. But after 1945, as the Hrê chiefs became aware that the DRV was establishing direct rule in their territory, the ideology of ethnic divide associated with the Long Wall took on renewed political relevance. In the same way, the presence of Kinh settlers took on new political meaning. Associated with the intrusive state, they were now seen as its agents. In 1950 the Hrê chiefs resuscitated the discourse of the Long Wall to legitimate their retaliation against the DRV. They deployed it as an "othering" device to offer their subalterns an ethnic justification for killing that was rooted in history, territory, and customary law. This context helps us interpret the French portrait of Chánh Lãi, described (above) as maintaining "a solid hatred of the V.M.—which he regrettably tends to confuse with Vietnamese in general." The device conflated Kinh settlers and the DRV state, with its imperial predecessors, into a single enemy.

Fueled by ideologies of territoriality, xenophobia, and hills-plains divide (see Arnold 1982, 141–42), this ethnic othering dehumanized the victims and distracted from the fundamental reason for the violence—the maintenance of the chiefs' power. It turned a political revolt into a civilian massacre, and a handful of chiefs' refusal to relinquish control over their subalterns into an incident of conflict between two ethnic groups. Many perpetrators made exceptions for individual friends, but nonetheless targeted the Kinh as a group.

* * * *

These insights help us understand the revolt as memory. As noted above, the Kinh memory of the massacre developed in two contexts—official and social—where different understandings of its political and ethnic dimensions took shape.

The DRV leadership immediately understood the revolt's political significance, as Ho Chi Minh's telegrams show. Thereafter, learning lessons from the debacle underpinned DRV policy in Sơn Hà, taking two forms. During the war, officials applied the lesson as part of their political education, while after the war the policy of discussion gave way to a prudent practice of silence. Today, an officially sanctioned memory may be read in the party histories but is rarely articulated elsewhere.

In the social context, memory of the revolt followed a different path. On the day of the massacre, few Kinh or Hrê inhabitants of Sơn Hà understood the politics of the violence. In its aftermath, they were not privy to official discussions about lessons to be learnt and their understanding did not increase in the postwar years. If the political dimension came up, the violence was seen in the context of the Indochina War, as incited by the French.

As a result, the event's political meaning is now more or less unknown in both contexts. The dead, however, are not forgotten and the violence of their death is not forgotten. On two days every year, family and community rituals place their memory at the forefront of people's minds. This has affected the way the massacre is thought about. Its perpetrators' intention was political (targeting the DRV), but their method was ethnic (targeting the Kinh). The political intention has slipped from memory, leaving only the knowledge of mass death, experienced and remembered as ethnic conflict.

Today, Hrê relations with Kinh people are no better or worse than those of other minorities in Vietnam, where ethnic relations are peaceful. And despite the fears the massacre engendered, we believe that a repeat is unlikely. This is partly thanks to the DRV's lesson-learning in the revolt's aftermath, when diplomatic engagement with the Hrê population was favored over the pursuit of vengeance. It also reflects the contemporary state's possession of overwhelming military superiority. But mainly, we believe, it is because the political conditions for the mass violence that existed in 1950 no longer exist. As Phạm Thanh Biền noted, this killing did not happen spontaneously. It was organized by a group of powerholders who acted according to a political logic—the Hrê chiefs weaponized the ethnic divide to defend their interests. In the decades after 1950, the Vietnamese state established its rule in Sơn Hà, while the chiefs left. The chiefs have gone, and with them the political logic for violence has also gone.

The Sơn Hà Revolt was the final act of resistance of a nonstate indigenous elite against the encroachment of a modernizing state. In its outcome, the revolt was a defeat for that elite as it was for the DRV. Through the memory of mass death and its legacy of fear, today's inhabitants of the district, Kinh and Hrê, still suffer the traumatic effects of the chiefs' last stand.

Endnotes: Mass Violence, Ethnic Conflict, and the Expanding State

1. Interview with Đinh Giơi (b. 1920), Sơn Kỳ commune, March 2010.

2. In Paris, we read documents kept at the Service Historique de la Défense (SHD), Vincennes. In Hanoi, we read documents kept at Trung tâm Lưu trữ Quốc gia III, Cục Văn thư Lưu trữ nhà nước (VNA3—National Archives Centre III, State Records and Archives Department) and Cục Lưu trữ Văn phòng Trung ương Đảng (APCC—Archives Department of the Office of the Party Central Committee).

3. We are deeply grateful to survivors of the violence and many others in Sơn Linh, Sơn Giang, and other communes of Sơn Hà district, who agreed to share their memories. We have changed the names of people we interviewed (here, Hrê given names are preceded by Đinh, the only Hrê surname in Sơn Hà; Kinh given names appear without surnames); the names of others involved in historical events are not changed. Special thanks to the families at Gò Da village who warmly welcomed us to their death anniversary celebrations in January 2020, and to Luyện Thị Thu Thủy and Phan Thị Kim Tâm for their help with our research on this occasion. We thank the authorities in Sơn Hà district and Sơn Linh and Sơn Giang communes. Thanks too to Phạm Thanh Biền (1922-2022, secretary of Sơn Hà district party committee from 1950 and of Quảng Ngãi province party committee in 1959–62 and 1965–71) and to Lâm Quyền (1938-2022, former secretary of Sơn Linh commune party committee). We thank Patrick Desbois, Patrice Bensimon, and their colleagues at Yahad-In Unum in Paris, who shared their methodological insights into collecting data on mass violence: "The important question to ask is 'where?'" This greatly improved the quality of our findings. Thanks to Elisabeth Lacroix and Nguyễn Hồng Minh for their logistical help, Christopher Goscha for his perceptive comments on an early draft, and Jayeel Cornelio, Andrew Gibbs, Volker Grabowsky, Jacques Leider, Penny Kane, and Rachel Leow for their many suggestions for improvements. Finally, thanks as ever to Nguyễn Tiến Đông and to Federico Barocco for his maps.

4. Hrê people speak an Austroasiatic (north Bahnaric) language. DRV documents used the ethnonym Chàm. See, for example, an ethnography (hereafter referred to as the 1950 Ethnography) commissioned by the DRV in 1950: "Bảng tổng kết tình tục thượng du tỉnh Quảng Ngãi" [Summary of the customs in the highlands of Quảng Ngãi province], Uỷ ban Kháng chiến Hành chính tỉnh Quảng Ngãi, undated study commissioned by Ministry of Interior on 26/8/1950 (VNA3, Uỷ ban Kháng chiến Hành chính Miền Nam Trung Bộ (hereafter UBKCHCMNTB) 252). The ethnonym Rhe (borrowed from French) appears in a 1953 Party report: "Tổng kết âm mưu phát triển 'goums' của địch, hoạt động phá 'goums' của ta" [Summary of the enemy's plot to develop 'goums' and our action to destroy the 'goums'], (APCC, hồ sơ 'Báo cáo về phong trào đấu tranh ở Liên khu năm 1953, "phòng Liên khu ủy V (1949-1975)," phòng số 01, mục lục số 01, đơn vị bảo quản 180). The terms Rhé, Rhe, and Hre appear in the French sources cited here.

5. This and the following two paragraphs are written from ethnographic data we gathered in Sơn Hà in 2009–12 and 2017–20. Historical accounts attest to the power of "influential chiefs," as they were known to Nguyễn Tấn (1871), Haguet (1905), and Trinquet (1908), or "aristocrats," as the 1950 Ethnography (VNA3 UBKCHCMNTB 252) called them.

6. "La situation de Song-Ha (Rapport prononcé à la réunion de la Haute Région de Quang Ngai du 24 au 25.5.50)," translated captured DRV report (SHD 10H643).

7. "Déclaration de Dinh Loi ex-Chef de canton de Son Ha (pho chu tich chez les rebelles) et de Dinh Dieu ex-garde de I. Classe de la G.I. en retraite (chu tich de son village), Kon Tum 16/2/1950" (SHD 10H1281).

8. "Bulletin de renseignements no. 0.213/C Enseignement militaire Lien Khu V Province de Quang Ngai, Hue," 7/3/1950 (SHD 10H1281).

9. "Một năm hoàn thành chuẩn bị chuyển mạnh sang tổng phản công và nhiệm vụ sắp đến của Liên khu V (báo cáo chung tại Hội nghị Liên khu ủy mở rộng từ 29-12-1950 đến 2-1-1951)" [One year's preparations for counterattack and coming tasks for Interzone V (general report at the [expanded Interzone Party Committee Conference held from 29-12-1950 to 2-1-1950], signed Can [Nguyễn Duy Trinh], bí thư Liên khu ủy, Liên khu V, 29/12/1950 (APCC, hồ sơ 'Hội nghị Liên khu ủy V từ ngày 29-12-1950 đến ngày 2-1-1951, tháng 10, tháng 12-1951: "Báo cáo, nghị quyết về công tác tổng phản công," phòng 'Liên khu ủy V (1949-1975)," phòng số 01, mục lục số 01, ĐVBQ 34).

10. "Điện gửi đồng bào Sơn Hà" [Telegram to compatriots in Sơn Hà], "Điện gửi các cán bộ chính quyền và đoàn thể miền Nam Trung" [Telegram to the South Central region's officials and organization]. The original telegrams are archived in the file "Hai bức điện của Hồ Chủ Tịch gửi cán bộ chính quyền các đoàn thể Miền Nam Trung Bộ và đồng bào huyện Sơn Hà tỉnh Quảng Ngãi năm 1950 (14.11.1950)" [Two telegrams from Ho Chi Minh to the government officials and organizations of the South Central Region and compatriots in Sơn Hà district, Quảng Ngãi Province in 1950 (14 November 1950)] (VNA3 Phủ thủ tướng (hereafter PTT) 271). The telegram to officials is now classified, but texts of both are published in Ho Chi Minh (2000, 117–118) and Ban Chấp hành Đảng bộ huyện Sơn Hà (1993, 80–82).

11. See Đào Duy Anh's dictionary (1996, 119): "Phiến loạn – 片亂 "Xui giục làm loạn (provoquer une révolte)."

12. See Bodard (1950); Ban Chấp hành Đảng bộ huyên Sơn Hà (1993, 65–101); Ban Chấp hành Đảng bộ huyện Sơn Hà (2015, 59–72).

13. We owe this account to Lâm Quyền, Sơn Linh commune, Sơn Hà, April 2017, April 2018. Many details are corroborated by Yên (b. 1934), Tuấn (b. 1939), and other survivors of the massacre at Sơn Linh.

14. Interview with Nguyệt (b. 1920), Sơn Linh commune, April 2017.

15. Interview with Thu (b. 1937), Sơn Linh commune, April 2017.

16. Interview with Tuấn, April 2017.

17. Interview with Minh (b. 1931), Sơn Thủy commune, Sơn Hà, April 2017.

18. Interview with Hiền (b. 1940), Sơn Thủy commune, April 2017.

19. Interview with Lợi (b. 1942), Sơn Thủy commune, April 2017.

20. Interview with Lâm Quyền, April 2017.

21. In April 2017, several informants told us this remarkable story.

22. Interview with Đinh Mai (b. 1930s), Sơn Linh commune, Sơn Hà, June 2019.

23. Interview with Đinh Đỏ's son (b. 1930), Sơn Kỳ commune, Sơn Hà, April 2017.

24. "Les jeunes massacraient, les femmes et les enfants pillaient, les viellards incendiaient et affichaient des slogans comme: -A bas les envahisseurs V.M., - La montagne pour les minorités, le delta pour les 'Kinh." "Bulletin de renseignements no. 0.213/C Enseignement militaire Lien Khu V Province de Quang Ngai, Hue 7/3/1950" (SHD 10H1281).

25. Interview with Đinh Mây (b. 1921), Di Lăng town, Sơn Hà, January 2020: cướp của! giết người! đốt nhà! and không theo, đốt nhà đốt của, according to his translation of the Hrê words.

26. Interview with Đinh Đeo (b. ca. 1930), Sơn Linh commune, April 2018.

27. Interview with Lâm Quyền, April 2017.

28. Interviews with Đinh Mây, April 2017, April 2018, June 2019, January 2020.

29. "Bulletin de renseignements no. 0.213/C Enseignement militaire Lien Khu V Province de Quang Ngai, Hue 7/3/1950" (SHD 10H1281).

30. These slogans appear in a translated captured DRV report, "Bulletin de renseignements," signed Lacroix, 1/3/1950 (SHD 10H3729).

31. Interview with Lan, Tịnh Giang commune, Sơn Tịnh, April 2018. This was the oath of Hrê men at Đèo Gió, Sơn Hạ commune, sworn at a buffalo sacrifice ceremony before raiding Tịnh Giang during the revolt.

32. 1950 Ethnography (VNA 3 UBKCHCMNTB 252).

33. Ibid.

34. Interviews with Đinh Mây, April 2017, April 2018, June 2019, January 2020. Đinh Điêu had not been a canton leader but a soldier with the colonial guard (garde indigène).

35. The request's ten signatories included Dinh En, Dinh Di and Dinh Luc. "Population Montagnarde (Moï), dépendant le Poste de Gi Lang, région de Son Ha, province de Quang Ngai" to "Chef de Poste de Kon Plong," 13/2/1950 (SHD 10H3729).

36. "Note sur l'Action Hre," 20/3/1951, résident de France à Kontum, G. Riner (SHD 10H3729).

37. This and the next two paragraphs are written from data provided by Lâm Quyền, April 2017, April 2018, June 2019.

38. Interview with Lâm Quyền, April 2017.

39. "Ban chap hanh tinh Dang bo Quang Ngai, Dai bieu hoi nghi tinh tu 14 thang 3-1950 den 20-3-1950, Bao cao ve chinh quyen" [Quang Ngai Party Executive Committee, Delegates to the provincial congress 14-20/3/1950, Report on administration] (VNA3 PTT 183).

40. "Báo cáo đặc biệt miền tây Quảng Ngãi số 6U-TT" [Special report on western Quảng Ngãi no. 6U-TT], 20/12/1950 (APCC, hồ sơ 'Báo cáo tổng kết các mặt công tác: chỉ đạo quân sự, chính trị, kinh tế, đoàn thể từ năm 1949-1950, tình hình thượng du của tỉnh Quảng Ngãi," phông "Liên khu ủy V (1949-1975)," phông số 01, mục lục số 01, ĐVBQ 775).

41. On Đinh Mô and Chánh Nhá, see Ban Chấp hành Đảng bộ huyện Sơn Hà (1993, 72). The rumors nearly succeeded in mobilizing the villagers, according to Đinh Cao (b. 1935), Sơn Nham commune, Sơn Hà, interviewed September 2011.

42. There was violence in the communes of Long Sơn, Long Môn (Minh Long), Ba Ngạc, Ba Vì (Ba Tơ), and Tịnh Giang (Sơn Tịnh), but not elsewhere in these districts. Ethnographic data show that some of the attacks (e.g. in Tịnh Giang) were made by people from Sơn Hà. See Ban Chấp hành Đảng bộ huyện Sơn Hà (2015, 59).

43. The high proportion of women and children among the dead came up in many interviews and is mentioned in an Interzone V Party Committee report, which estimated that "500 Kinh people in Sơn Hà, mostly women and children, were killed." "Báo cáo đặc biệt miền tây Quảng Ngãi số 6U-TT," 20/12/1950 (APCC, hồ sơ "Báo cáo tổng kết các mặt công tác: chỉ đạo quân sự, chính trị, kinh tế, đoàn thể từ năm 1949-1950, tình hình thượng du của tỉnh Quảng Ngãi," phông "Liên khu ủy V (1949–1975)," phông số 01, mục lục số 01, ĐVBQ 775).

44. "La situation de Song-Ha (Rapport prononcé à la réunion de la Haute Région de Quang Ngai du 24 au 25.5.50)," translated captured DRV report (SHD 10H643).

45. "Báo cáo liên khu 5 (làm ngày 23/5 [1950]) (Theo các công văn nhận được từ 10/5 đến 22/5)" [Interzone 5 report (made on 23/5 [1950]) (from official correspondence received from 10/5 to 22/5] (VNA3 PTT 269).

46. "Bulletin de renseignements no. 0.213/C Enseignement militaire Lien Khu V Province de Quang Ngai, Hue 7/3/1950" (SHD 10H1281). "Báo cáo liên khu 5 (làm ngày 23/5 [1950]) (Theo các công văn nhận được từ 10/5 đến 22/5)" (VNA3 PTT 269).

47. "Tom tat hoi nghi cua lien khu uy mo rong cuoi 1950" [Expanded Interzone conference summary late 1950], undated report for the Liên Khu 5 Party Committee conference held in December–January 1950 (VNA3 UBKCHC MNTB 68).

48. Interview with Đinh Điem (b. 1933), Sơn Linh, January 2020.

49. We learned about Chánh Đí's arrest and crowded trial proceedings from the arresting officer, Đinh Mây, interviewed April 2017. A DRV report notes: "viec xet xu bon Dinh Dy, te diep cu da lam, I cach day du, phat dong duoc nhan dan cam thu giac va te diep, dung day dap tan uy cua bon tay sai gian ac cua dich va dong thoi lam sang to duoc chanh sach dan toc cua chinh phu" [holding a proper trial for Dinh Dy and the former spies mobilized the people to hate the enemy and the spies, shattered the power of the enemies' cruel lackeys, and clarified the government's ethnic policy]: "Bao cao tinh hinh hoat dong tup hap trong thuong ban nien 1954" [Operations situation report, first half of 1954] signed Quach Tao of Interzone 5 People's Court, 24/6/1054 (VNA3 UBKCHC MNTB 439). The court records remain classified: "Hồ sơ v/v. xử lý Đinh Đý, Đinh Trồi, Đinh Rà can tội làm tay sai cho giặc Pháp, hành động phương hại đến nên độc lập của nước VNDCCH do Tòa An ND Đặc biệt miền Tây Quảng Ngãi và TAND LKV xử năm 1954 (05.12.1954 [sic]-19.04.1954)" [File on the trial of Đinh Đý, Đinh Trồi, Đinh Rà, convicted of working as French agents and of actions harmful to the DRV's independence by the Western Quảng Ngãi Special People's Court and the Interzone 5 People's Court in 1954 (05.12.1954 [sic]-1904.1954)] (VNA3 UBKCHC MNTB 444).

50. This process of shifting allegiances started in the revolt's immediate aftermath, as a DRV report suggests: "the revolt's troops have already dispersed and no longer have the nature of a revolt force, those who fled have become soldiers of the puppet regime, while the others are gradually surrendering." "Thuong vu LKU5 dien Trung uong" [Telgram from Interzone 5 Standing Committee to Central Committee] 3/12/1950 (VNA3 PTT 269).

51. "La situation de Song-Ha (Rapport prononcé à la réunion de la Haute Région de Quang Ngai du 24 au 25.5.50)," translated captured DRV report (SHD 10H643).

52. Interview with a former provincial official, Quảng Ngãi city, April 2018.

53. "On 25-01-1950, French colonialists and reactionaries joined forces with discontented Hrê village heads," according to Ban Chấp hành Đảng bộ tỉnh Quảng Ngãi (2019, 237). See also Ban Chấp hành Đảng bộ huyện Sơn Hà (2015, 71–72); Ban Chấp hành Đảng bộ tỉnh Quảng Ngãi (1999, 95).

54. "For "révolte spontanée" and "Le mouvement de révolte aurait été amorcé par les Hrê," see "Extrait d'un rapport de Mr Belot (du 12.2.1950)" attached to "Révolte des populations de la region de SON HA," Lt-col Morvan au Général commandant la Zone Sud et Plateaux, 18/2/1950 (SHD 10H1281).

55. In 2020 they were made available for download from the library's website www.thuvienquangngai.vn.

56. Interview with Phạm Thanh Biến (b. 1922), Quảng Ngãi city, June 2019. On the party cell's creation in 1946, see Ban Chấp hành Đảng bộ huyện Sơn Hà (2015, 49).

57. Interviews with Mr. Hải (b. 1959) and Mrs. Vi (b. 1940s), Sơn Linh commune, January 2020.

58. Interview with Sen (b. 1949), Sơn Linh commune, June 2019.

References

Arnold, David. 1982. "Rebellious Hillmen: The Gudem-Rampa Risings 1839–1924." In *Subaltern Studies I*, ed. Ranajit Guha, 88–142. Oxford: Oxford University Press.

Ban Chấp hành Đảng bộ huyện Sơn Hà. 1993. *Lịch sử Đảng bộ huyện Sơn Hà (1930–1990)* [History of the Party in Sơn Hà District (1930–1990)]. Quảng Ngãi: Xí nghiệp in Quảng Ngãi.

———. 2015, *Lịch sử Đảng bộ huyện Sơn Hà (1930–2010)* [History of the Party in Sơn Hà District (1930–2010)]. Quảng Ngãi.

Ban Chấp hành Đảng bộ tỉnh Quảng Ngãi. 1999. *Lịch sử Đảng bộ Tỉnh Quảng Ngãi (1945–1975)* [History of the Party in Quảng Ngãi Province (1945–1975)]. Hanoi: Nxb Chính trị Quốc gia.

———. 2019, *Lịch sử Đảng bộ tỉnh Quảng Ngãi (1930–1975)* [History of the Party in Quảng Ngãi Province (1930–1975)]. Hanoi: Nxb Chính trị Quốc gia Sự thật.

Bodard, Lucien. 1950. "La révolte des Rhés." *Sud-Est Asiatique* 17: 26–33

Đào Duy Anh. 1996, *Từ điển Hán Việt* [Hán Việt dictionary], rev. edn. Hanoi: Nxb Khoa học Xã hội.

Ferguson, R. Brian, and Neil L. Whitehead. 1992. "The Violent Edge of Empire." In *War in the Tribal Zone: Expanding States and Indigenous Warfare*, eds. R. Brian Ferguson and Neil L. Whitehead, 1–30. Santa Fe, New Mexico: School of American Research Press.

Goscha, Christopher E. 2022. *The Road to Dien Bien Phu: A History of the First War for Vietnam*. Princeton: Princeton University Press.

Haguet, H. 1905. "Notice ethnique sur les Mois de la région de Quảng Ngãi." *Revue Indochinoise* 1419–26.

Hardy, Andrew. 2015. "La muraille de Quảng Ngãi et l'expansion territoriale du Vietnam: projet pluridisciplinaire de recherche historique." *Comptes-rendus des séances de l'Académie des Inscriptions et belles-lettres* III: 1117–134.

Hardy, Andrew, and Nguyễn Tiến Đông. 2019. "The Peoples of Champa: Evidence for a New Hypothesis from the Landscape History of Quảng Ngãi." In *Champa: Territories and Networks of a Southeast Asian Kingdom*, eds. Arlo Griffiths, Andrew Hardy, and Geoff Wade, 121–44. Paris, EFEO.

Ho Chi Minh. 2000. *Hồ Chí Minh toàn tập 6 1950–1952* [Ho Chi Minh Collected Works 6 1950–1952], 2nd edn. Hanoi: Nxb Chính trị Quốc gia.

Katz, Paul R. 2005, *When Valleys Turned Blood Red: The Ta-pa-ni Incident in Colonial Taiwan*. Honolulu: University of Hawai'i Press.

Kwon, Heonik. 2006, *After the Massacre: Commemoration and Consolation in Ha My and My Lai*, Berkeley: University of California Press.

———. 2008, *Ghosts of War in Vietnam*. Cambridge: Cambridge University Press.

Luttwak, Edward N. 1976. *The Grand Strategy of the Roman Empire: From the First Century AD to the Third*. Baltimore and London: Johns Hopkins University Press.

Malarney, Shaun Kingsley. 2001. "'The Fatherland Remembers Your Sacrifice': Commemorating War Dead in North Vietnam." In *The Country of Memory: Remaking the Past in Late Socialist Vietnam*, ed. Hue-Tam Ho Tai, 46–76. Berkeley, University of California Press.

———. 2002. *Culture, Ritual and Revolution in Vietnam*. London and New York: RoutledgeCurzon.

Marr, David G. 2013. *Vietnam: State, War and Revolution (1945–1946)*. Berkeley: University of California Press.

Nguyễn Đức Cung. 1998. *Lịch sử vùng cao qua Vũ man tạp lục thư* [History of the Highlands through the Chronicles of the Barbarian Districts]. Philadelphia: Nhật-Lệ. (This includes the original in characters of Nguyễn Tấn's 'Phủ Man Tạp lục' with a Vietnamese translation.)

Nguyễn Tấn. 1871. "Phủ Man Tạp Lục" [Chronicles of the Barbarian Districts]; see Nguyễn Đức Cung (1998).

Phan Kế Bính. 2006. *Việt Nam Phong tục*. Hanoi: Nxb Văn học.

Thongchai Winichakul. 2020. *Moments of Silence: The Unforgetting of the October 6, 1976 Massacre in Bangkok*. Honolulu: University of Hawaii Press.

Trinquet, Charles-Marie. 1908. "Le poste administratif de Lang Ri (Quảng Ngãi)." *Revue Indochinoise* 347–82.

Võ Chí Công. 2001, *Trên những chặng đường cách mạng (hồi ký)* [On the Roads of the Revolution (A Memoir)], Hanoi: Nxb Chính trị Quốc gia.

Youth, Violence, and Identities of Insecurity in Timor-Leste

JANINA PAWELZ

From ASEAN to Timorese Identity

Timor-Leste, formerly known as East Timor, occupies the eastern half of the island of Timor, the western half being Indonesian West Timor; Timor is the largest of the Lesser Sunda Islands. Home to 1.3 million inhabitants, Timor-Leste is a multicultural and multilingual state that has undergone tremendous progress in terms of democratization and development in the past decades. The state went from twenty-four years of Indonesian occupation (1975–99) to a referendum in 1999 seeking independence from Indonesia, followed by a period of United Nations administration before officially gaining independence in 2002. Despite its small population, Timor-Leste is home to a huge array of collectives and identity groups, ranging from veteran associations and civil society organizations to youth groups, disaffected groups, ritual arts groups, and martial arts groups. While most of the groups are peaceful, three martial arts groups have frequently been associated with violence and were declared illegal by the government in 2013.

In terms of conflicts of identity, martial arts groups play a major role up until the present day in Timor-Leste. They provide social identities to their members based on lifelong commitment and loyalty. They also influence the dynamics of conflicting priorities and individual needs that overlap with party politics, the security sector, and national identity. In addition to its local social identities, Timor-Leste seeks to gain regional identity as a Southeast Asian country by joining the Association of Southeast Asian Nations (ASEAN). Established in 1967 as a loose intergovernmental organization, at the 11th ASEAN Summit held in Kuala Lumpur in December 2005, leaders signed the ASEAN Charter and adopted an official motto for the organization—"One Vision, One Identity, One Community"—with the purpose of forming a truly collective identity and community. According to the ASEAN vision, dubbed "ASEAN Vision 2020," charted in 1997, Southeast Asia planned to share a collective regional identity by the year 2020.

Because Southeast Asia is extremely diverse in regard to history, religion, language, and culture, it is central to identify the "we" feeling in the process of identity construction. However, Southeast Asia is a "unity-in-diversity" region (Jönsson 2010, 41) and a "patchwork of networks, life-worlds, trading systems" (Noor 2017, 1) rather than a region with shared similarities. ASEAN leaders recognize this patchwork, arguing that "[o]ur rich diversity has provided the strength and inspiration to us to help one another foster a strong sense of community" (ASEAN 2012, 1). Acknowledging that differences are not in conflict with successful commonality is prevalent throughout Southeast Asia, as exemplified by Indonesia's national motto *Bhinneka Tunggal Ika* (Unity in Diversity). The solution to bridging the gap between diversity and a common identity is termed "the ASEAN Way." As Grabowsky, Cornelio, and Hendytio (2019, 2) argue, "the peoples of Southeast Asia have not yet developed a common identity," while ASEAN as a regional organization "shapes collective imaginings about the future of the region." Is there a conflict of identity, after all, and if so, on which level? The multitiered layers of identities and how they affect one another, if at all, remains at question.

This chapter uses the case of Timor-Leste, an aspiring contender to join ASEAN, to illustrate the various kinds of collective identities in a multiethnic, multilinguistic, and multicultural society which can be a challenge in the quest for a common regional identity. Data for the project were derived from interviews with members of violent groups, NGO workers, politicians, youth, and religious representatives. In addition, I used secondary data from scholarly articles and books, reports published by international organizations and official government documents, reports by local NGOs, news articles, roundtable discussions featured by television station RTTLEP, and videos posted by private individuals on Faceclip.net and YouTube. The interviews were conducted in 2014 in Timor-Leste in Tetum, the official language of Timor-Leste, and English; in this chapter I indicate when I have translated interview excerpts from Tetum to English. The more recent interviews were conducted via Facebook messenger and WhatsApp in 2019.

In the following section I outline major findings of my research. First, as a contribution to this volume on identities and regional integration, I found that the opinion of Timorese on joining ASEAN is multifaceted and shaped by both hopes and fears about the future. This raises the question whether the construction of an ASEAN identity is an elite-driven project. Second, in terms of identity and violence, the occurrence of violence among martial arts groups is persistent, and the featuring of street fights on social media is worrisome. Identification with martial arts groups is shaped by emotions—pride, self-esteem, a sense of belonging—and social gains such as loyalty and brotherhood, patronage and protection. Third, regarding identity and security, I found that the group identity of martial arts groups is very strong and harbors potential friction with national identity, political identity, and police identity.

Violence, Identity, and Social Media

The issue of identity is a central theme in various disciplines, among them sociology, political science, psychology, criminology, and peace and conflict studies. Identity—understood as social identity based on (perceived) group membership that conveys the feeling of belonging, unity, and cohesion—plays an important role in conceptualizing youth violence, radicalization, and the functioning of social media.

Several scholars have highlighted the importance of peer groups and the connection between violence and identity-making practices of violent groups (Esser and Dominikowski 1997; Littman and Paluck 2015; Trotha 1974; McEvoy-Levy 2010; Hazen and Rodgers 2014). Identity construction involves creating a distinction between "us" and "them." Identities are not static but are created through modes of differentiation between in-group and out-groups. Campbell (1998) highlights the importance of understanding "who we are" and "who we are not" in identity-building processes. Peer groups have an important social function for identity creation. Peer groups, including violent groups and armed groups, become more than a substitute for families: they may become the most important social network, one that offers protection, orientation, identity, and self-confidence (Esser and Dominikowski 1997). In the case of Timor-Leste's martial arts groups, these can provide young people with a sense of structure, trust, mutual help and support, solidarity and security. Beyond that, joining a peer group can be a means of attaining social status and enhance self-confidence through the demonstration of power and the feeling of control over other youths. Members of peer groups get the chance to achieve moral, historical, and political significance by participating in political group actions (McEvoy-Levy 2010).

Violent groups commonly use brute force to generate "power, status and a sense of belonging" among members (Littman and Paluck 2015, 90). Furthermore, acts of violence may raise someone's self-esteem, especially in cultures where certain traits like strength, toughness, aggression, and assertiveness are considered prestigious (Trotha 1974). Esser and Dominikowski (1997) explain that the use of violence is a potentially well-arranged and target-oriented act of high significance, which functions as a way of forming identity and in-group orientation. Violence directed at people outside of a group can increase individuals' identification with the unit (Littman and Paluck 2015). Violence and the threat it contains play a remarkable role in the group as it increases solidarity, uniting them against enemy collectives (Decker 1996; Esser and Dominikowski 1997). These dynamics have an essential impact on the members' emotional attachment and commitment to one another.

In the digital age, social media plays a fundamental role in the processes of identity creation of groups. Social media platforms such as Facebook, YouTube, and Twitter are essential components of everyday life for today's youth. This trend also applies to young people actively engaged in violence and crime. Scholars have found that delinquent youth groups, such as gangs, use the Internet predominantly for expressive actions to increase their reputation, spread fear, and advocate their pride (Storrod and Densley 2017). Pawelz and Elvers (2018) also found that street gangs use music and social media to glorify their lifestyle, to display power, and send threats to generate motivational support for criminal activities and to bond socially and mourn collectively. In a similar vein, Pyrooz et al. (2013, 23) have argued that "gangs exploit the Internet to further their collective identity." Social media thus offers an opportunistic structure of expression, recruitment, and the exchange of threats.

Regional Identity: Timor-Leste as the Final Missing Member of the ASEAN Family

The *Jakarta Post* has stated that "Timor Leste is the final missing piece" of ASEAN (Jianheng Yu 2018). In July 2005, Timor-Leste became a member of the ASEAN Regional Forum. Two years later, it signed the ASEAN Treaty on Amity and Cooperation. A year further on, in 2011, Timor-Leste submitted a request to join ASEAN. The admission has still not been decided at the time of writing, but in the following section I outline the key points of discussion.

Timor-Leste actively presents itself as part of the ASEAN family. After officially gaining independence in 2002, Timorese politicians began to assert the state's identity as a Southeast Asian nation (Sahin 2014, 10). Former president and Nobel Peace Prize laureate José Ramos-Horta was an early advocate of ASEAN membership. ASEAN was viewed as an opportunity to boost foreign investment, tourism, and trade. The Timor-Leste Strategic Development Plan 2011–2030 makes clear reference to ASEAN: "Timor-Leste's aspiration to join ASEAN is based on our geographical location, the wishes of our leaders and people, and our cultural affinity with our Asian neighbours" (Government of Timor-Leste 2011, 172).

After several years of applying for membership, the question remains as to why Timor-Leste has not yet been accepted into the organization. Seixas, Mendes, and Lobner (2019) find that there is a consensus in international online media of a "narrative of readiness" for Timor-Leste to join ASEAN. This narrative is based on the progress Timor-Leste has made along the lines of admission requirements of nation-building, human development, democracy, and economy. However, ASEAN has long engaged in constructing a certain image of Timor, ranging from labeling it a "communist threat" (1974–98) to a "failing state" (1999–2011) to a "not-quite-ready partner" (2012–present) (Ortuoste 2019, 303). It is believed that some ASEAN members, for example, Singapore and Laos, were against Timor-Leste joining the team because "the tiny nation is an outspoken advocate of democracy and human rights" (Talesco 2016). Democratic activism can, indeed, be viewed as "disturbing and uncomfortable by some members" (Hägerdal and Berlie 2018, 102). During my interview with former president Ramos-Horta, he claimed that Timor-Leste's high democratic standards are "not really an issue" with regard to joining ASEAN, but that countries like Singapore worry that Timor-Leste might lack infrastructure and human resources (interview, March 9, 2019).

It also remains to be seen whether ASEAN membership bears as many positive advantages as Timor-Leste expects. Douglas Kammen (2013, 4) points out that probably the biggest change is at the diplomatic level when certain diplomats have to attend meetings and conferences. He further points out that ASEAN membership would benefit "members of East Timor's elite" and not the average citizen. Alternately, as a member of ASEAN, Timor-Leste could become "the voice of the poor, the dispossessed, and a voice opposed to exploitation and elitism" (ibid.). Ramos-Horta, an outspoken supporter of joining ASEAN, believes that becoming a member of ASEAN is widely supported by the Timorese population: "Urban youth, students, community leaders, civil society are all very aware and supportive of TL joining ASEAN" (interview, March 9, 2019). In contrast, a young Timorese student explained: "I only have one identity which is Timorese nationality. ASEAN is great! But our nation Timor-Leste is not ready yet to take part because we need to develop first our cultural and social sector, agriculture and security. Because we are still fractured in some parts" (interview, February 21, 2019, author's translation.)

ASEAN promotes itself as the sixth largest economy in the world with the third largest population. The difference that Timor-Leste could bring to the table in terms of trade and population is thus comparatively tiny. A representative of a Timorese human rights NGO explained in an interview that ASEAN membership is "the next time bomb" as it will "open the gates for well-educated foreigners who come and take over the businesses." He outlined his fears for the future. When Timor joins ASEAN, "Timorese will be second-class people in their own country" as they might not be able to compete for jobs with highly educated and skilled foreigners (interview, Dili, October 9, 2014). "We are not ready yet in terms of the labor issue. Then when we join (ASEAN), the gate will be opened, then there will be more workers—well equipped, well educated, they will come like a tsunami! And we will not be able to compete" (ibid.). In contrast, a young martial arts (PSHT) leader sees the positive side of joining ASEAN: "In my opinion it is important because [it] could free the people from difficulties and poverty. Joining ASEAN would be good because our nation is so young, and we'd be so proud as Timorese if we could join. It's important to give opportunities to our people" (interview, 14 April 2019, author's translation).

Local Identity: Martial Arts Groups, Violence, and Loyalty

The largest and best-known martial arts groups in Timor-Leste are Persaudaraan Setia Hati Terate (PSHT), Ikatan Kera Sakti (IKS), and Kmanek Oan Rai Klaran (KORK). Of Timor-Leste's population of 1.3 million population, 35,000 are members of PSHT, the largest and most influential martial arts group in Timor-Leste (interview with secretary-general PSHT, Dili, October 16, 2014). Reportedly, Kera Sakti has 18,000 members and KORK 12,000 (interview with PSHT top leader, Dili, December 8, 2014). Although the bulk of members consist of young men, high-ranking leaders are often well-educated, with university degrees and hold high positions in government (ibid.). The geographic range is nationwide, but there are stronghold districts and neighborhoods in Dili, the capital of Timor-Leste, which has become "the main battleground" for martial arts groups (TLAVA 2009b, 1).

The violence perpetrated by martial arts groups includes street fights, stone throwing, attacks with machetes and knives, and arson (interview with NGO representative, Dili, 7 October 2014). Most confrontations are fought with deadly weapons such as wooden spears, machetes, swords, rocks, and *rama ambons*—crude darts made from electrical cable or old nails, which are fired into the air with slingshots made from rubber bands. The tips of the darts are sometimes dipped in battery acid or poison (TLAVA 2009b, 6).

There are few opportunities for banned martial arts groups to redirect their energies into other channels, such as competitive sports, causing young members to choose "informal and often violent ways" (Fundasaun Mahein 2018, 1). Despite the government ban in 2013 of three martial arts groups, violent incidents continue, as "young people will naturally gravitate towards MAGs, which offer an outlet for their aggression" (ibid.). A UNDP study revealed that conflicts of identity have conquered the digital sphere. Social media use in Timor-Leste is dominated by Facebook (95 percent) and almost 70 percent of all Facebook users in Timor-Leste are below the age of twenty-four (UNDP 2018, 89).

Facebook and video platforms such as YouTube and Faceclip.net, are particularly popular sites for uploading videos of violent fights. Almost daily, low-quality videos recorded on smart phones capture violent fights between martial arts members. Most commonly these videos feature duels between individual members of PSHT on one side and IKS on the other, with two young male protagonists fighting one another using their *pencak silat* skills, watched by dozens of cheering people. Frequently, these one-on-one fights escalate into group fights involving dozens of youths. In addition to showing fights, some videos show rivals burning martial arts equipment, a clear provocation (Komik Timor Leste 2019c), or even burning down houses (Komik Timor Leste 2019a; 2019b). Some videos show dozens of predominantly young men engaging in violent street fights, throwing stones, breaking furniture, and destroying property, accompanied by the sound of loud cheering at every stone thrown. The videos capture the atmosphere of aggressiveness among male youth burning for a fight and show why local families feel unsafe in their communities when such fights break out.

In Timor-Leste, the concepts of identity and loyalty play a major role in the dynamics of violence. Explaining this link between violence and identity, Henri Myrttinen (2008, 7) argues that martial arts groups can be seen as "identity creation vehicles for youth, especially men, caught in between tradition and modernity, as vehicles for attaining economic, social, and political power for their leaders." Martial arts groups offer "a sense of belonging and purpose" as "social associations for young people" (Fundasaun Mahein 2018, 1). In the case of Timor-Leste, "gangs and MAGs offer these youths companionship, status and protection, free cigarettes and alcohol and often a source of livelihood" (TLAVA 2009a, 2).

Central to their martial arts philosophy is the concept of *persaudaraan*, an Indonesian term meaning "brotherhood" or *maun-alin* (in Tetum, siblings), thus including brothers and sisters regardless of gender. *Persaudaraan* describes the loyalty between members and refers to a concept of mutual help based on lifelong commitment and loyalty (Pawelz 2019) in which members claim they "can't be separated until death" (interview with PSHT leader, Ermera district, November 1, 2014). Full members of martial arts swear an oath of loyalty, known as *juramentu*. A martial arts member explained to me that "we have something that we call *juramentu* which is a concept that you can't exit ... until death." He explained that the oath of loyalty is like an "inseparable bond, like brothers and sisters," which means that members "look out for each other" (interview with PSHT top leader, Dili, December 8, 2014, author's translation).

The solidarity among members based on *juramentu* means that "they will always stick together" (interview with journalist, Dili, 5 December 2014). This is often regarded as the root of violent conflicts as members may get involved in confrontation on behalf of their friends "without questioning" (interview with NGO worker, Baucau district, 21 October 2014). Group members support and fight for one another in case of an attack, which might involve a confrontation on behalf of their friends without questioning the circumstances (Pawelz 2019). An NGO activist explained this rationale as follows: "If one of the members of my group got attacked, then I have to defend. If one [is] sick, then everybody is sick. But this might actually lead to something negative: Okay, my brother got attacked; for what reason I don't care, but I will join them to do a contra act [revenge]" (interview with NGO activist, Dili, 8 October 2014). Therefore, the concept of brotherhood is the basis of lifelong commitment and group loyalty which can lead to violent conflict. Beyond that, I found that violent martial arts group identity generates potential friction with national identity, political identity, and police identity, which I outline in the following section.

Martial Arts Groups versus National Identity

Timor-Leste's martial arts groups have complex histories dating back to the Indonesian occupation of 1975–99, which was marked by violence and brutality and conflict-related deaths. Some of the members of martial arts groups were partly involved in the liberation struggle and are thus politically and personally affiliated, creating a complex nationwide network of alliances. Some groups actively supported the independence movement by changing their names and participating politically in the clandestine front. PSHT and Kera Sakti are originally from Indonesia but were brought to Timor by Indonesian soldiers in the early 1980s during the war of independence. KORK, from the district Ainaro, is proud to be of Timorese origin. While martial arts groups of Indonesian origin are regarded as traitors, today they claim to have always supported the independence movement.

However, the Indonesian origin of some groups and continuing links with Indonesia remain a source of conflict today. For example, the geographic origin and spiritual "mecca" of PSHT and Kera Sakti is Madiun in Jawa, Indonesia. But Timorese citizens who aspire to become members of PSHT have always traveled to Madiun to take their exams and buy their uniforms and belts (Suara Timor Lorosae 2014; interviews with members of Kera Sakti, Dili, October 25, 2014). However, after the three martial arts groups were banned by the government they went underground and started to operate secretly. Their symbols of identity went from being uniforms to T-shirts and necklaces. Public gatherings and training were held in secret. During an interview, an NGO activist explained: "So the government thinks 'ok, let's ban it.' So since then, banned. But now they are still hiding. The training is in a hidden way and sometimes they cross the border to have their ceremonial exams in Indonesia and Indonesia accepts it! For the sake of the future time bomb, they accept it!" (interview, Dili, October 9, 2014). However, numerous members have been caught at the border to Indonesia with their bags full of martial arts equipment according to the Diariu Timor Post. In the same vein, a NGO worker of Dili reported, "You know the police just captured somewhere close to 300 [martial arts members] now trying to cross the border to Indonesia to go become a full member of PSHT, a ceremony that only takes place in Indonesia but not in Timor-Leste, where they have to take oath under the Indonesia flag, so the whole ... you know, it is quite bizarre. I think it is more because of that ... you being a Timorese citizen you have to go to Indonesia to take an oath under an Indonesian flag!" (interview with NGO worker, Dili, November 31, 2014).

The connection of martial arts groups to former occupier Indonesia has long been a thorn in the side of the Timorese authorities. On a local television program in 2018, a representative of the Secretariat of State for Youth and Sports (SSYS) stated that martial arts groups are "Indonesian culture," and members should identify with Timorese customs. While good relations with Indonesia are fine, he worries about an identity conflict and Indonesian infiltration via martial arts groups (RTTLEP 2018). A major-general from the Timorese armed forces (F-FDTL) stated on television in February 2019 that they need to find the root of the problem of violent confrontations. He maintained that "martial arts exist in Timor since the Indonesian invasion until today" and added that they will cooperate with Indonesia to make sure that Timorese won't go to Indonesia secretly to do their activities (RTTLEP 2019a).

In contrast, a young leader from PSHT believes that martial arts identity is not in conflict with national identity. He explained that members go to Indonesia to take exams because the big leaders (*ema boot*) are from Indonesia, but they do not pledge allegiance to the Indonesian flag: "Their values are our values because the big leaders from Indonesia give the graduation to us. But SH terate [PSHT] doesn't swear to the flag *merah putih* [Indonesian flag]. They don't. We are born in Timor, we pledge allegiance to Timor. We swear to this country, to improve this country" (interview, Dili, November 10, 2014, author's translation). In a similar vein, a PSHT leader said, "I am Timorese, of Timorese origin" (interview, April 14, 2019, author's translation). A young female KORK member emphasized this stand: "I only have one identity which is Timorese nationality" (interview, February 21, 2019, author's translation).

Martial Arts Groups versus Political Parties

Another source of potential friction regarding identity is between martial arts groups and political parties. Many martial arts groups exhibit a political stance and are often affiliated with a particular party or are used as electoral muscle by that party. Yet, martial arts groups deny any political affiliation as their members are allowed to become politically involved only as individual citizens of the nation, not as a collective of martial arts. Although links between martial arts groups and politicians or political parties are often denied, they remain fluid, informal, and connected by personal alliances. The power that martial arts groups have is based on their high membership numbers, combined with a hierarchical organizational structure and blind loyalty to superiors. This makes them a major source of quick political mobilization (Pawelz 2019). Supporting a political party during election campaigning raises hopes of receiving a favor, a job, or even a political position in return, as an interviewee explained: "Some of the groups began to think: "Ah, maybe it's better to be with a political party, if they win [the elections] the groups have better opportunities. So some groups tried that ... they supported a party because they wanted a [political] position, they wanted money, they wanted a better position for their groups" (interview with PSHT contender, Dili, October 4, 2014, author's translation). An NGO activist said that "It is indeed effective to be in a dangerous martial arts group and then be incorporated into the government. It is easier when you have a big group in the back. If you are not a member it is more difficult" (interview with NGO activist, Dili, 5 December 2014). These electoral muscle mechanisms are processes of political patronage that reward members or leaders of martial arts groups with positions or financial gain. Although the leaders of the martial arts groups profit from it, the bulk of members don't profit, as a resident from the district Baucau pointed out: "The martial arts leader and political party leader, they are friends, have a good relation or … we don't know exactly. Maybe when the elections are coming up, the politicians say 'ok, you come, you organize our campaign, and then you make the security for us.' It's a secret relation. It's an opportunity for the martial arts leader, but not for the members, the members don't understand" (interview with youth worker, Baucau, October 22, 2014).

In 2013, the International Crisis Group (ICG) warned that this electoral muscle strategy may lead to future deadly conflict: "The patronage system of rewarding violent spoilers with contracts … threatens to promote a dangerous dynamic seen in other fragile post-conflict situations, in which violence is perceived to offer rewards—or at least to be without downside—raising further prospects for recurrence" (ICG 2013, 7). The Timor-Leste Armed Violence Assessment blames politicians for using the groups in an irresponsible way with unintended consequences, such as fostering the power of attraction: "The irresponsible use of gangs by political parties as personal security and agents provocateurs has entrenched the power of these groups and made them more attractive to impoverished youths as a source of income" (TLAVA 2009b, 2).

The electoral muscle mechanism is a reciprocal game of give and take with blurred lines as to who is manipulating who. On the one hand, interviewees explained that violence-prone groups are co-opted or paid off due to their violent potential; on the other hand, politicians "use them as the force or as the right hand to support their political interest" (interview with youth worker, Baucau, October 22, 2014). There are examples of connections between politicians and martial art groups, with KHUNTO (Kmanek Haburas Unidade Nasional Timor Oan) being a well-known one. In the 2012 parliamentary elections, KHUNTO, a new party, participated for the first time and only missed the 3 percent threshold by 150 votes (Pawelz and Myrttinen 2012, 6). The surprisingly high support for KHUNTO can be explained by its affiliation with the group KORK (Pawelz 2015). In an interview with the leaders of the party during the 2012 campaign period, they did not divulge their relationship to KORK to me as an election observer. Yet, the relationship is an open secret and "in this case the state doesn't have any clue how this could have happened" (interview with NGO activist, Dili, October 8, 2014). In the 2017 parliamentary elections, KHUNTO gained 6.4 percent of the vote and five seats. KHUNTO, FRETILIN (Frente Revolucionária de Timor-Leste Independente), and PD (Partido Democrático) were about to form a government coalition, but KHUNTO withdrew at the very last minute. Instead, KHUNTO joined the opposition alliance comprising AMP (Alliance for Change and Progress), CNRT (Congresso Nacional de Reconstrução Timorense), and PLP (Partidu Libertasaun Popular) under the leadership of Xanana Gusmão and presented themselves as an alternative to the government.

The minority government of FRETILIN and PD could neither enforce its government program nor a state budget. President Francisco Guterres therefore dissolved the national parliament in January 2018 and called for early elections on May 12, 2018. The 2018 special elections ended in victory for a pre-electoral formed coalition. AMP formed by CNRT and two smaller parties, PLP and KHUNTO, won an absolute majority of 49.6 percent (309.663 votes), 34 of 65 seats. This meant that Xanana Gusmao's party CNRT had allied with a martial arts-backed party to regain power. As a result, talks on lifting the ban on the three martial arts groups began.

According to my interviewees, lifting the ban on martial arts groups was not only an election promise made by AMP but also by FRETILIN. It was a strategically smart decision to put the reactivation of these groups back on the table, as this is a popular issue which thousands of citizens—and voters—support. Ramos-Horta stated that "the original decision [to ban the groups] made no sense" and after reactivating the groups "they can go either way, become gangs, organized crime or force of good" (interview, March 9, 2019). In a television roundtable discussion with representatives of banned martial arts groups in December 2018, a representative of the Secretary of State for Youth and Sports (SSYS) emphasized that martial arts as a sport has not been forbidden by the state, but only the three groups who practice it. Guest speakers discussed the possibility of lifting the ban on the three groups. The SSYS representative opined that engagement in sports and participation in competitions like the ASEAN Games would contribute to the state (RTTLEP 2018). Martial arts representatives used the opportunity during the roundtable to remind group members what is most important "to contribute to stability, peace and development of the nation." On February 18, 2019, politicians also met to discuss the issue of martial arts. The major-general urged that justice institutions need to cooperate with the police and army in capturing and convicting criminals. Likewise, representatives of the SSYS stated that they needed to find the root of martial arts problems: "Is it a political problem? Or martial arts? Or individual? Or is the problem related to laws and tribunals?" (RTTLEP 2019b, author's translation).

Martial Arts Groups versus the Police

Timor-Leste's martial arts groups are strongly entangled with the political arena and security forces (Scambary 2006, 1–4). Not only have they traditionally been both official and unofficial protection providers for communities, but many members have also joined the police or the army (interview with former high-ranking politician, Dili, 26 September 2014). The large number of martial arts group members in the police force has led to various problems, such as informing fellow martial arts members about scheduled raids and taking sides during street fights, leading to arbitrary arrests, hence providing no solution to community problems. The overlapping identities have caused conflict as police officers inform their fellow martial arts members about planned raids, or only arrest members of a martial arts group different from their own when two groups get into a violent fight (interview with an NGO activist, Dili, October 9, 2014). "In some cases, people who are about to be attacked call the police, but the police are not coming. So they have to defend themselves and sometimes they become victims and they are angry at each other and start to chop them [with a machete] or throw [things]" (interview with secretary-general of PSHT, Dili, October 16, 2014, author's translation).

The overlap between the police force and martial arts groups has caused bias which has led to police ineffectiveness and inefficiency. An NGO worker believes that although martial arts groups infiltrate the police, they remain loyal to their martial arts groups: "Martial arts members are inside the police. They are not well [loyal] to the police institution but they are well [loyal] to the martial arts group. The martial arts also destroyed the institutions" (interview with NGO activist, Dili, 9 October 2014.)

This conflict of identities has been of great concern to the Ministry of Defense and Security. In January 2014, then prime minister Xanana Gusmão ordered members of the police (PNTL) to quit their martial arts groups, which resulted in 993 members, including 654 from PSHT, 243 from KORK, and 96 from Kera Sakti, declaring their loyalty to the police force and officially surrendering their martial arts uniforms (*Jornal Nacional Diário* 2014). These numbers are evidence of a massive infiltration of martial arts members into the police. "I call this the rule of MAG not the rule of the law! The PNTL guys don't obey loyal to the constitution, the PNTL, but they are loyal to their big boss inside the MAG groups, [they] influence them. That's why when they are doing their [police] interventions, then they are not neutral" (interview with NGO activist, Dili, 9 October 2014.) It is also of concern to the Timorese authorities. During the 2018 television roundtable, the SSYS representative stressed that there would be "zero tolerance" for PNTL (police force) or FDTL (army) members who seek to participate in martial arts, "no discussion, he will be suspended from duty" (RTTLEP 2018, author's translation). His statement is an example of a conflict of identities which might lead to insecurity and fear.

Discussion and Outlook

The case of Timor-Leste shows that identity, which is understood to be social identity based on group membership, conveys a feeling of belonging, unity, and cohesion, has several levels. On an abstract level, rational aspects predominate, while on an individual level emotional and social aspects prevail. Interviews show that Timorese citizens and civil society organizations view the issue of Timor-Leste joining ASEAN through the lens of costs and benefits. Political leaders of ASEAN and Timor-Leste also highlight the benefits of becoming part of a large regional association. In contrast, the Timorese I interviewed feared an increasingly competitive job market and becoming second-class citizens in their own country. They hoped that by becoming a member of ASEAN, problems related to poverty in Timor-Leste would be solved by providing jobs and opportunities. In conclusion, Timorese opinion on joining ASEAN is multifaceted and shaped by both hope and fear of the future. For Timorese civil society, and youths in particular, the issues of quality education, access to the job market, and opportunities for economic participation are crucial, and the idea of joining ASEAN thus triggers hopes and fears. These hopes and fears are not directly linked to a lack of ASEAN identity, a concept that appears to be propagated by political leaders and scholars.

The focus shifts away from the question of whether regional integration can be successful despite a lack of common identity to the question of whether joining ASEAN comes with benefits or disadvantages for the people of member states.

On a more individual level, identity appears to be more linked to the dynamics of conflict and violence. The above analysis of the role of martial arts groups has shown that they are social identity groups and a source of pride and self-esteem. Membership includes aspects of guidance, patronage and protection, belonging and purpose. Martial arts groups also play a major role as a vehicle for youth identity and belonging. These groups exhibit strong ties of loyalty, concepts of brotherhood and unity, and mutual assistance. The violence featured on social media reinforces aspects of rivalry, thus fostering an in-group orientation. The concept of brotherhood is the basis of lifelong commitment and group loyalty which can lead to an escalation of violent conflict because group members tend to defend one another unconditionally.

More specifically, I found an overlap of social identity groups which can lead to a conflict of interest. First, the Achilles' heel of identity conflicts among martial arts groups in Timor-Leste is the Indonesian origin of PSHT and Kera Sakti. While members of martial arts groups do not see their identity as conflicting with national identity and loyalty to the state, non-members highlight the hypothetical threat, fueled by the historical legacy of Indonesian occupation, that Indonesia could secretly infiltrate Timorese society. Second, martial arts groups play an important role in the politics of Timor-Leste as electoral muscle. Politicians take a keen interest in these organizations because they have thousands of members who are eligible to vote. The hierarchical structure of command, loyalty to the group, and obedience to leaders make it easy to influence voting behavior, which can be readily used for generating political support. Thus, martial arts groups, despite being officially politically neutral, become an electoral muscle in a system of patronage that mostly benefits leaders. Third, there is an overlap between the police force and martial arts groups. Martial arts groups have traditionally been protection providers for communities and many members have joined the police or the army. The police are not perceived as corrupt, but rather an integral part of martial arts groups. The overlap impairs the police's impartiality, and to this end, the effectiveness of law enforcement.

Joining ASEAN will bring challenges and opportunities alike. In terms of martial arts groups and ASEAN membership, there can be positive synergies if the illegalized groups were to be legalized. The sport practiced by martial arts groups offers the potential to engage in athletic competitions on a national and even international level. Besides being an outlet for recreational activity and an outlet for energy, participation in international competitions can contribute to the consolidation of an identity both as a Timorese and as a Southeast Asian country. A positive connotation of Timorese martial arts can raise international visibility and stimulate tourism and, to this end, contribute to employment opportunities.

References

ASEAN. 2012. "ASEAN Vision 2020." ASEAN One Vision One Identity One Community. https://asean.org/?static_post-asean-vision-2020.

Campbell, David. 1998. *Writing Security: United States Foreign Policy and the Politics of Identity.* Minneapolis, MN: University of Minnesota Press.

Decker, Scott H. 1996. "Collective and Normative Features of Gang Violence." *Justice Quarterly* 13(2): 243–64.

Diariu Timor Post. 2020. "Ekipa Konjuntu Kaptura PSHT Timoroan Nain 37 Fila Hosi Indonézia." September 9. https://diariutimorpost.com/2020/09/09/ekipa-konjuntu-kaptura-psht-timoroan-nain-37-fila-hosi-indonezia/.

Esser, Johannes, and Thomas Dominikowski. 1997. *Die Lust an der Gewalttätigkeit bei Jugendlichen: Krisenprofile, Ursachen, Handlungsorientierungen für die Jugendarbeit.* Frankfurt am Main: ISS.

Fundasaun Mahein. 2018. "The Government Must Address the Root Causes of Youth Violence." December 13. http://www.fundasaunmahein.org/2018/12/13/the-government-must-addressthe-root-causes-of-youth-violence/.

Government of Timor-Leste. 2011. "Timor-Leste Strategic Development Plan 2011–2030." https://www.laohamutuk.org/econ/SDP/2011/Timor-Leste-Strategic-Plan-2011-20301.pdf.

Grabowsky, Volker, Jayeel Cornelio, and Medelina Hendytio. 2019. "Shaping Alternative Identities in Southeast Asia: Youth, Violence, and Transnationalism." Working Paper WP4. Competing Regional Integrations in Southeast Asia (CRISEA). http://crisea.eu/publications/working-paper/.

Hägerdal, Hans, and Jean A. Berlie. 2018. "Timor-Leste and ASEAN." In *East Timor's Independence, Indonesia and ASEAN*, ed. Jean A. Berlie, 91–112. Cham: Palgrave Macmillan. https://www.palgrave.com/de/book/9783319626291.

Hazen, Jennifer M, and Dennis Rodgers. 2014. *Global Gangs: Street Violence across the World.* Minneapolis, MN: University of Minnesota Press.

International Crisis Group (IGG). 2013. "Timor-Leste: Stability at What Cost?" Asia Report 246. International Crisis Group.

Jianheng Yu, Truston. 2018. "2019: The Year of Timor Leste in ASEAN?" *Jakarta Post*, December 13. https://www.thejakartapost.com/academia/2018/12/13/2019-the-year-of-timor-leste-in-asean.html.

Jönsson, Kristina. 2010. "Unity-in-Diversity? Regional Identity-building in Southeast Asia." *Journal of Current Southeast Asian Affairs* 29(2): 41–72.

Jornal Nacional Diário. 2014. "Membrus PNTL 993 Entrega Atributu Artemarsiais." January 16. http://www.jndiario.com/2014/01/16/membrus-pntl-993-entrega-atributu-artemarsiais/. Accessed June 30, 2016.

Kammen, Douglas. 2013. "Timor-Leste and ASEAN." Paper presented at the Timor-Leste National Political Consensus: One Vision and Commitment Towards ASEAN Membership, Dili, Timor-Leste, April 23.

Komik Timor Leste. 2019a. "PSHT vs IKS |Baucau Timor Leste| Sejumlah Motor Dan Rumah Dibakar - YouTube." January 31. https://www.youtube.com/watch?v=LzaofJ5f3Qo&has_verified=1.

—————. 2019b. "PSHT vs IKS Kera Sakti Timor Leste." Faceclips.Net. February 6. https://www.faceclips.net/video/mxJnrjHS-KE/psht-vs-iks-k.html.

—————. 2019c. "Mantan PSHT Bakar Atribut PSHT." Faceclips.Net. February 7. https://www.faceclips.net/video/DkRugDs_WIk/mantan-psht-b.html.

Littman, Rebecca, and Elizabeth Levy Paluck. 2015. "The Cycle of Violence: Understanding Individual Participation in Collective Violence." *Political Psychology* 36: 79–99.

McEvoy-Levy, Siobhán. 2010. "Die Rolle von Peer-Gruppen. Mehr als ein Ersatz für Familie und staatliche Institutionen?" In *Jugendliche in gewaltsamen Lebenswelten: Wege aus den Kreisläufen der Gewalt*, eds. Sabine Kurtenbach, Rüdiger Blumör, and Sebastian Huhn. Stiftung Entwicklung und Frieden. Baden-Baden: Nomos.

Myrttinen, Henri. 2008. "Timor-Leste: A Kaleidoscope of Conflicts." *Watch Indonesia!* April 1. http://www.watchindonesia.org/1222/timor-leste-kaleidoscope-of-conflicts?lang=en. Accessed June 30, 2016.

Noor, Farish A. 2017. "ASEAN Identity, Now and Into the Future: The Interaction across Borders in Southeast Asia." August 2. Heinrich Boell Foundation. https://www.boell.de/en/2017/08/02/asean-identity-now-and-future-interaction-across-borders-southeast-asia.

Ortuoste, Maria. 2019. "Timor-Leste and ASEAN: From Enmity to Amity, Exclusion to Semi-Inclusion." In *Routledge Handbook of Contemporary Timor-Leste*, eds. Andrew McWilliam and Michael Leach, 303–13. London: Routledge. https://www.routledge.com/Routledge-Handbook-of-Contemporary-Timor-Leste-1st-Edition/McWilliam-Leach/p/book/9781138654563.

Pawelz, Janina. 2015. "Security, Violence, and Outlawed Martial Arts Groups in Timor-Leste." *Asian Journal of Peacebuilding* 3(1): 121–36.

—————. 2019. "Well-Known and Little Understood: Martial Arts Groups in Timor-Leste." In *Routledge Handbook of Contemporary Timor-Leste*, eds. Andrew McWilliam and Michael Leach, 197–209. London: Routledge.

Pawelz, Janina, and Paul Elvers. 2018. "The Digital Hood of Urban Violence: Exploring Functionalities of Social Media and Music Among Gangs." *Journal of Contemporary Criminal Justice* 34(4): 442–59.

Pawelz, Janina, and Henri Myrttinen. 2012. "Wahlen in Timor-Leste: Feuerprobe für Sicherheit und Konsolidierung" 7. GIGA Focus Asien. GIGA German Institute of Global and Area Studies.

Pyrooz, David C., Scott H. Decker, and Richard K. Moule. 2013. "Criminal and Routine Activities in Online Settings: Gangs, Offenders, and the Internet." *Justice Quarterly* 32(3): 471–99.

RTTLEP. 2018. "Sala Redasaun—Arte Marsiais." Faceclips.Net. https://www.faceclips.net/video/NWgGe09Awy8/sala-redasaun.html. Accessed March 1, 2019.

—————. 2019a. "Estadu Presiza Buka Tuir Fukun Husi Problema Arte Marsiais." Faceclips.Net. https://www.faceclips.net/video/ehfOMTj1NSs/estadu-presiz.html. Accessed February 17.

—————. 2019b. "Governu No KRAM Diskuti Problema Artes Marsiais." Faceclips.Net. https://www.faceclips.net/video/lZB2PNk_uCU/governu-no-kr.html. Accessed February 18.

Sahin, Selver B. 2014. "Timor-Leste's Foreign Policy: Securing State Identity in the Post-Independence Period." *Journal of Current Southeast Asian Affairs* 33(2): 3–25.

Scambary, James. 2006. "A Survey of Gangs and Youth Groups in Dili, Timor-Leste." Australian Agency for International Development (AusAID). http://www.etan.org/etanpdf/2006/Report_Youth_Gangs_in_Dili.pdf.

Seixas, Paulo Castro, Nuno Canas Mendes, and Nadine Lobner. 2019. "The 'Readiness' of Timor-Leste: Narratives about the Admission Procedure to ASEAN." *Journal of Current Southeast Asian Affairs* 38(2): 149–71.

Storrod, Michelle L., and James A. Densley. 2017. "'Going Viral' and 'Going Country': The Expressive and Instrumental Activities of Street Gangs on Social Media." *Journal of Youth Studies* 20(6): 677–96.

Suara Timor Lorosae. 2014. "PNTL Kaptura PSHT 122 Hasai Sabuk Iha Indonesia." November 24. https://stlnews.co/notisias-online/pntl-kaptura-psht-122-hasai-sabuk-iha-indonesia/ Accessed November 24, 2020.

Talesco, Cristian. 2016. "How East Timor's Democracy Is Making It an Outcast." *Foreign Policy* (blog). May 10. https://foreignpolicy.com/2016/05/10/how-east-timors-democracy-is-making-it-an-outcast-asean-southeast-asia/. Accessed November 24, 2020.

Timor-Leste Armed Violence Assessment (TLAVA). 2009a. "Groups, Gangs, and Armed Violence in Timor-Leste." 2. Issue Brief. Small Arms Survey. http://www.timor-lesteviolence.org/pdfs/Timor-Leste-Violence-IB2-ENGLISH.pdf. Accessed June 10, 2016.

—————. 2009b. "Groups, Gangs, and Armed Violence in Timor-Leste." http://www.timor-leste-violence.org/pdfs/Timor-Leste-Violence-IB2-ENGLISH.pdf. Accessed June 10, 2016.

Trotha, Trutz von. 1974. *Jugendliche Bandendelinquenz: Über Vergesellschaftungsbedingungen von Jugendlichen in den Elendsvierteln der Grossstädte*. Soziologische Gegenwartsfragen, n. F, Nr. 39. Stuttgart: F. Enke.

United Nations Development Programme (UNDP), ed. 2018. *Planning the Opportunities for a Youthful Population*. Timor-Leste National Human Development Report, 4.2018. New York: UNDP.

Contributors

FILOMENO V. AGUILAR JR. is professor in the Department of History, School of Social Sciences, Ateneo de Manila University. He received his Ph.D. from Cornell University, and has taught previously at the National University of Singapore and James Cook University. From 2003 to 2021, he was chief editor of *Philippine Studies: Historical and Ethnographic Viewpoints*. He is the author of *Migration Revolution: Philippine Nationhood and Class Relations in a Globalized Age* (2014) and *Maalwang Buhay: Family, Overseas Migration, and Cultures of Relatedness in Barangay Paraiso* (2009).

ROGER CASAS obtained a Ph.D. in anthropology from the Australian National University with a thesis on Buddhist monasticism and masculinity among the Tai Lü of Sipsòng Panna, a region where he has lived and conducted extensive research since 2004. At present he is visiting researcher at the Faculty of Social Science, Chiang Mai University, and conducting research for the Austria-Japan joint project, Religion, Economy and Gender in the Upper Mekong Region: Anthropological and Historical Perspectives, of which he is one of two principal investigators.

JAYEEL CORNELIO is associate professor of development studies and associate dean for research and creative work at Ateneo de Manila University. He is also an associate editor of the journal *Social Sciences & Missions* and a regular contributor to *Rappler*. He is the author of *Being Catholic in the Contemporary Philippines: Young People Reinterpreting Religion* (2016) and lead editor of the *Routledge International Handbook of Religion in Global Society* (2021). With Volker Grabowsky, he led the Work Package on Identity for the Competing Regional Identities in Southeast Asia (CRISEA), a project funded by the EU's Horizon 2020 Framework Programme.

DAO THE DUC has a Ph.D. in anthropology from the University of Washington. He is a researcher at the ICS and deputy chief editor of its journal, *Van hoa Dan gian* (Folk Culture). His research focuses on the Long Wall of Quảng Ngãi, social institutions, religious practices, cultural heritage, and ethnic relations. He has participated in projects such as SEATIDE (2013–16), The Role of Culture in Sustainable Development of Central Highlands (ICS 2013), and Local Cultural Institutions: Case Studies Project (UNESCO 2014).

SIRUI DAO is a Ph.D. student at the University of Hamburg. He obtained his M.A. in comparative literature with a thesis titled "On the Reception of the Sipsong Panna Lue Literary Work *Kham Khap Lanka Sip Hua* in Thailand," which was revised as a conference paper for the 13th International Conference on Thai Studies, Chiang Mai, 2017. His doctoral dissertation, "Travels and Investigations in the Yunnan-Burma Borderlands, 1837–1911," focuses on the historical encounters between Westerners and the natives of Chiang Tung, Sipsòng Panna, and Chiang Khaeng.

ALAN DARMAWAN is a postdoctoral researcher at SOAS, University of London. He is currently working on Malay manuscripts in the Palace Library of the former Palembang sultanate in a project, Mapping Sumatra's Manuscript Cultures, funded by a Leverhulme Research Leadership Award. He obtained his Ph.D. in Malay and Indonesian Studies at University of Hamburg, Germany, where he wrote a dissertation on Mak Yong theater performance and cultural revitalization in the Riau Islands, Indonesia. His research interests include the revival, reinvention, and heritagization of the writing and performing traditions in insular Southeast Asia.

BIANCA YSABELLE FRANCO recently graduated with a M.A. in sociology from the University of the Philippines Diliman. She was formerly a research associate at the Development Studies Program of the Ateneo de Manila University where she worked on projects about human rights, deliberative democracy, and conflict studies. Her written work has been published on the academic blogs New Mandala (Australian National University) and Broad Agenda (University of Canberra), and on the news websites Globe Post (United States) and Rappler (Philippines).

VOLKER GRABOWSKY is professor of Thai Studies at the Asia-Africa Institute, University of Hamburg. He is (co-)author of several books on the history and culture of Tai ethnic groups, including the translations and analyses of Tai Lü chronicles, such as *Chronicles of Chiang Khaeng* (2008) and *Chronicles of Sipsòng Panna* (2012). Affiliated with the Centre for the Studies of Manuscript Cultures (CSMC) in Hamburg, he has directed various projects pertaining to the manuscript cultures of the Tai peoples in the Upper Mekong valley. Among his most recent publications are the edited volumes *Manuscript Cultures and Epigraphy in the Tai World* (2022), and *Ethnic and Religious Identities* and *Integration in Southeast Asia*, co-edited with Ooi Keat Gin (2017).

ANDREW HARDY is professor of Vietnamese history at the Ecole Française d'Extrême-Orient (French Institute of Asian Studies). He coordinated the Horizon-2020 project, Competing Regional Integrations in Southeast Asia (CRISEA). His research focuses on Vietnamese migration and ethnic relations in Southeast Asia, including an interdisciplinary study of the Long Wall of Quang Ngai, a 127-km border built in 1819. In 2020, with Eric Guerassimoff, Nguyen Phuong Ngoc, and Emmanuel Poisson, he published *Les migrations impériales au Vietnam, Travail et colonisations dans l'Asie-Pacifique français, XIXᵉ XXe siècles.*

MEDELINA K. HENDYTIO is the deputy executive director of the Centre for Strategic and International Studies (CSIS) in Jakarta, where she has also been a senior researcher in the Department of Politics and International Relations since 1985. Her research areas cover administrative development, bureaucratic reform, education, and gender studies. She also teaches at Diponegoro University and is a trainer on policy advocacy and gender issues. She received her M.A. in development administration from the Australian National University, and her Ph.D. from the University of Indonesia in 2008. Her doctoral research concerned the recruitment process of the government civil servant with particular attention to utilizing scenario planning for implementing a reform agenda.

CONTRIBUTORS

KWANCHEWAN BUADAENG is associate professor in the Department of Sociology-Anthropology, Faculty of Social Sciences, Chiang Mai University. Her latest works include "A Karen Charismatic Monk and Connectivity across the Thai-Myanmar Borderland," in *Charismatic Monk of Lanna Buddhism*, ed. Paul T. Cohen (2017), and "The Karen Leke Religious Movement in the Thailand-Myanmar Borderland: Deterritorialization and Diversification," in *Ethnic and Religious Identities and Integration in Southeast Asia*, eds. Ooi Keat Gin and Volker Grabowsky (2017).

JACQUES LEIDER is a historian of Arakan (Rakhine State) and early modern Myanmar. He has led the research centers of the Ecole Française d'Extrême-Orient (French Institute of Asian Studies) in Yangon, Chiang Mai, and Bangkok. A trained teacher with extensive professional experience, he had stints in diplomacy and consulting with UN organizations on contemporary conflict issues. From 2017 to 2021 he was the scientific coordinator of Competing Regional Integrations in Southeast Asia (CRISEA), a project funded by the European Union's Horizon 2020 Framework Programme. His latest publication is *The Arakan Army, Rakhine State, and the Promise of Arakan's Independence* (2022).

ERRON C. MEDINA teaches in the Development Studies Program of the Ateneo de Manila University. He is finishing graduate studies in political science (comparative politics) at the Department of Political Science, University of the Philippines Diliman. He co-wrote with Jayeel Cornelio "Christianity and Duterte's War on Drugs in the Philippines," *Politics, Religion, & Ideology* (2019), and "Neoliberal Christianity and the Rise of the New Prosperity Gospel in the Philippines," *Pneuma* (2021). His research interests include populism, democratization, regime legitimacy, politics of religion, politics of development, and social theory.

JANINA PAWELZ is a researcher at the Institute for Peace Research and Security Policy at the University of Hamburg (IFSH) and associate researcher at the German Institute of Global and Area Studies (GIGA). She conducts research on political, collective and urban violence, security and radicalization. Currently she leads a research consortium on conspiracy theories and right-wing extremism in Germany. Her work has been published in several journals, including *Terrorism and Political Violence; Conflict, Security and Development;* and *Peacebuilding.*

PRASIT LEEPREECHA is a faculty member in the Department of Social Science and Development, Faculty of Social Sciences, Chiang Mai University. He earned his Ph.D. in social anthropology from the University of Washington, Seattle, in 2001. His research interests range from ethnicity, indigeneity, tourism, and religious beliefs, to development. His recent publications include *Becoming Indigenous Peoples in Thailand* (2019), *Heroes of the Plain of Jars: Hmong Monuments and Social Memory in Laos and America* (2020), and *Transnational Hmong Protestant Evangelism in Mainland Southeast Asia* (2021).

NATASHA PAIRAUDEAU is a research associate with the Centre of South Asian Studies at the University of Cambridge. Her research interests include migration, interethnic relations, and the dynamics of citizenship, race and status in colonial systems. Her book *Mobile Citizens: French Indians in Indochina, 1858–1954* (2016), addresses the making of French citizenship among French Indian migrants to Indochina. Her study of Shan migration in the Thai-Indochinese borderlands complements a larger project concerning the exile and intrigues of Burmese Prince Myngoon.

VIDHYANDIKA DJATI PERKASA is a senior researcher in the Department of Politics and Social Change, Centre for Strategic and International Studies (CSIS), Jakarta. His research focuses on issues of conflict, human trafficking, poverty, ethnic relations, social policy, and local governance, with particular reference to Papua. His recent publications are "Colliding Disasters: Conflict and Tsunami in the Context of Human Security in Aceh, Indonesia," in Carolina Hernandez et al. *Human Security and Cross-Border Cooperation in East Asia* (2019) and, with Amelinda Bonita Leonard, "Strategizing Religious Oppression: Christianity and Indonesia's Democratic Resilience," in Brendan Howe, ed., *Consolidating Democracy: Resilience and Challenges in Indonesia and South Korea* (forthcoming).

JAN VAN DER PUTTEN is professor of Malay and Indonesian Literature in the Department of Southeast Asia, Asia-Africa Institute, at the University of Hamburg. He teaches and publishes on insular Southeast Asian texts. He is affiliated with the Centre for the Study of Manuscript Cultures (CSMC) in Hamburg where he leads research projects and is one of the primary investigators of the Digital Repositories of Endangered and Affected Manuscripts in Southeast Asia (DREAMSEA) Programme, supported by the Arcadia Foundation in the UK.

OLIVER TAPPE is senior researcher at the Institute of Anthropology, University of Heidelberg. His current research project, funded by the German Research Foundation, addresses historical and anthropological questions of tin mining in Laos. His research interests include the historical anthropology of Laos, with a focus on labour relations, migration and mobility, and sociocultural change. His recent publications include a special issue of the journal *Social Anthropology* (2021), co-edited with Rosalie Stolz, and the volume *Extracting Development: Contested Resource Frontiers in Southeast Asia* (2022), co-edited with Simon Rowedder.

DANNY WONG TZE KEN is dean of the Faculty of Arts and Social Sciences, Universiti Malaya, where he is also professor of history in the Department of History where he teaches the history of Southeast Asia and the history of China. His research interests include the Chinese in Malaysia, China's relations with Southeast Asia, and the history of Sabah. Among his recent publications are *Wang Gungwu and Malaysia* (ed., 2021), *One Crowded Moment of Glory* (2021), and *Lead & Grow: 115 Years of the Chinese Chamber of Commerce & Industry of Selangor and Kuala Lumpur* (2021).

Index

A

Abigail (British commissioner of Arakan) 352
Aboriginal Advancement Leagues of Victoria 130
Aboriginal Land Rights Act 130
Act of Free (1969) 319, 326, 332–34
Agriculture 95, 112, 381, 443
   Rice Cultivation 109
   Rice Production 380
   Wet-Rice Cultivation 82, 272, 381
Akha 251
Akyab 352, 356, 358, 360, 364, 368n
Alam Melayu (Malay cultural space) 155, 158
Alienation 4, 163, 327
Alliance of Indigenous Peoples of the Archipelago
   (AMAN) 141
Alliance Party (Malaya) 68
Allied Forces (in World War II) 348, 354–55
American Baptist Mission 231
Amnesty International 294, 296
Amnesty International Indonesia 323
Anderson, Bobby 322, 326
Anderson, Kjell 324
Angkar 94, 97, 373–84, 386–87, 390–92, 397
   and see Communist Party of Kampuchea
Angklung 49
Annam 111
Anti-*tambay* directive (of Duterte) 302
Anticrime Campaign 24, 310–11
Anticrime Policy 298–99, 307
Anticriminality 293, 296, 298–99, 301–02, 310–11
Appadurai, Arjun 152, 170, 175, 168
Arakan 347, 349–50, 351–57, 359–66 *and see*
   Rakhine State
   Arakan (Autonomous Muslim State) 348, 361
   Arakan Muslims 353, 362, 364–65
   Arakanese Defence Force 356
Ariya Metteyya 227
ASEAN 1–2, 6–13, 19, 22–23, 25, 33–52, 126,
   131–33, 135, 145–47, 181–82, 298, 300, 310,
   317, 341–43, 439–40, 442–44, 450, 452–53
   ASEAN Agenda 36
   ASEAN Charter 8, 34, 439
   ASEAN Civil Society Conference 131–32
   ASEAN Community 34, 134, 138, 145, 147, 182

ASEAN (*continue*)
   ASEAN Community Vision 2025 34
   ASEAN Cooperation 43, 46–47
   ASEAN Economic Community (AEC) 43, 47,
     132, 133, 181
   ASEAN Foundation 50
   ASEAN Identity 7, 34–38, 48–52, 133, 317,
     342, 440, 452
   ASEAN Integration 8, 33–35, 37, 45, 47, 50,
     52, 132, 181, 199, 317, 342–43
   ASEAN Intergovernmental Commission on
     Human Rights (AICHR) 132
   ASEAN People's Forum 10, 131–32
   ASEAN Political-Security Community (APSC)
     132
   ASEAN Secretariat 50, 145
   ASEAN Socio-Cultural Community (ASCC)
     33, 132–33
   ASEAN Vision 2020 34, 440
   ASEAN Way 49, 440
   ASEAN Youth Programs 44, 52
Asia Indigenous Peoples Pact (AIPP) 130,
   132–35, 138–44
Asian Values debate 297
Assemblies of God (Philippines) 213
Attapeu 109
Atya Thamma Phra Chao Khru 257
Aung Zan Wai 358, 363
Australian Aborigines' League (AAL) 130
Australian National University 303, 318, 457–58
Authoritarian Regimes 11, 22, 38, 296–97, 301,
   310, 378, 420
Aw Boon Haw 62–64
Aw Boon Par 62

B

Bachelor of Theological Studies (BTS) 238
Bahasa Melayu (Malay language) 154
Baihua *see* Mandarin
Baird, Ian 147
Ban Bonaeng 116
Ban Dap-Ban Tao 283–84
Ban Muangkhai 114, 117
Ban Sai Müang 253

INDEX

Ban Siao 261
Ban Suon Kham 283
Bangsawan 167–68
Bao An 56
Barangay 305, 457
Basel Church 57, 63
Battambang Province 86, 88, 94–95, 97
Bhikkhu (Buddhist monk) 257
  Inkaew 257
  Kham 257
  Luang Sam of Müang Hon 257
Bhinneka Tunggal Ika (Unity in Diversity) 328, 440
Bible 85, 214, 216, 232, 237–40
Bintan 153–54, 158, 161, 164–66, 169–71, 173–74
  Darul Masyhur 160, 171, 174
  Kingdom of Bentan 171
  Bhayangkara Utama (Medal of Honor) 298
  Kejora (Morning star) 328
Black Lives Matter 321
Black Paper (Livre Noir) 383
Black, Stewart 79–81, 84, 87–88
Blanadet, Roger 91–92
Bò Han (Mohan) 254
Bo Laphok 84
Bo Luo 56
Bo Phloy 97
Bo Rai 97
Bò Ten 254
Bobii, Selpius 323–24, 326
Bodhisattva 392
Bodineo 84
Bonaeng 111, 116
Bonpauk Tha Gyaw 358
Borders (national) 4–5, 46, 75, 88, 96, 127, 155, 157, 162, 174, 225–27, 229–30, 233–35, 237, 248, 259, 380, 394, 401n
Border Patrol Police (BPP) 230, 235
Borneo 59–60, 62, 151, 162
Boyakar 84
Boyan 152
Briggs Plan 65–66
Brundige, Elizabeth 326
Brunei 19, 151
Buddhabaramee Thai Buddhist Temple (in Tainan) 255
Buddhism 226–27, 249–50, 255–56, 259, 264, 282, 392, 459
  Theravada 82, 247, 250, 257, 264, 392
  Han Chinese Mahayana 264
  Tibetan 264
  Buddhist Lent (òk phansa) 255, 281
  Buddhist Light Association Tai Wan 255

Buddhism (continue)
  monks 17, 25, 98, 210, 228, 247–56, 258–69, 261, 263–65, 281–82, 268n, 385
  Pilgrimages 247, 265
  Sangha 17, 280
Bugis 152, 170, 331
Bukidnon Province 213, 217
Bumiputera Community 68
Bunda Tanah Melayu 152, 161, 168, 175, 176
Burma Independence Army 352
Burmese 3, 15, 20, 23, 75, 76, 78, 80–85, 89–92, 99, 101n, 137, 225, 229–30, 233–34, 236–37, 248, 254–55, 259, 264, 273, 284, 352, 355–56, 357, 361, 362–64, 369
  Military 15, 20, 229–30, 234, 237, 254, 357, 361–63
  Ethnicity 80–81
Buthidaung 351, 354, 362–63, 368

C

Cambodia 1, 17–20, 23, 75, 77, 83, 88, 90–92, 94–96, 98–99, 101, 132, 134–35, 141, 144, 147, 151, 207, 212, 266, 294–96, 300, 307, 373–74, 377, 380, 383, 385–86, 389, 393–398, 400–401
  Communism 378, 380, 388, 391–93, 396 400
  Nation–State 15, 91, 378
  Cambodian Tragedy 379, 393–94
  Cambodian Youth 24–25, 373, 384–85, 387, 398
Cambodia National Rescue Party 296
Camp Karingal 305
Cantonese (Guangfu) 56, 58–59, 65, 67
Capital Punishment 294, 298–99, 302, 309
Cardamom Mountains 75, 78, 87, 97, 100
Carling, Joan 140
Carlisle, Tom 79, 82, 88, 89
Casas, Roger 24, 247, 253, 256, 263, 271, 274, 280, 282, 287–88
Castells, Manuel 327
Catholic Church 111, 206, 209
Cayuga Nation 128
Center for Malay Studies at the University of Riau 161
Chanthaburi 75, 76, 80, 82, 85, 101
Chao Bun Saeng Rüang 253
Chao Fa 24, 101, 286
Chao Moeng 273, 277, 282, 284, 285
Chao Mom Kham Lü 271–72, 274–75, 279, 281–84
Chao Mòm La 251
Chao Phaendin 271–77, 279–87
Chayang Association (Dapu) 56
Chiang Chüang (Jingzhen) 260–62

462

INDEX

Chiang Kai Shek 60
Chiang Khòng 254
Chiang Lò (Daluo) 254
Chiang Mai 11, 137–40, 142, 144–45, 238, 240, 247–48, 250–51, 254, 264, 266
Chiang Ngoen Stupa 256–58, 260
Chiang Nüa (Jingne) 262
Chiang Rai 139, 143, 248, 251, 259–63
Chiang Rai Rajabhat University 261–63
Chiang Rai Sangha 260
Chiang Rung 248, 250, 254, 257 and see Jinghong
Chiang Rung County 251
Chiang Tung, see Kengtung 247–48, 250–52, 254, 258–59, 261, 264, 273
Chin Human Rights Organization (CHRO) 137, 144
China 7, 45, 56, 59–64, 70–72, 105, 107–08, 118, 141, 145, 152, 155, 170, 184–85, 222, 249–52, 256, 264, 266, 271–72, 275–76, 278–79, 282, 284, 286–87, 310, 342, 381, 412
China Relief Fund 62
Chinese Cemeteries or Zhonghua Yishan 57
Chinese Chamber of Commerce 57–59, 62
Chinese Community 55–56, 59, 65, 67–69
Chinese Identity 22, 55, 59, 61–62, 67, 69, 72
Chinese People's Political Consultative Conference 250, 276
Chinese Polity 24, 272, 274
Chitta Kuman 256
Chitta Samanen 256–57
Chittagonians 349, 353, 360
Choeng Ek, see Killing Fields 383
Christian Conference of Asia (CCA) 139
Christian Missions 217, 225–26, 231, 244
Christians 3, 65, 206–7, 210, 214–17, 220, 222n, 237, 240–41, 248
  Filipino 206, 216–17
  Hakka 65
  Karen 237, 241
Christianity 207–09, 211, 214–16, 219–20, 222n, 236, 234, 242, 244n, 266n, 332
Chronicles (Buddhist) 247
Chung Hwa 58
Church of Christ in Thailand (CCT) 238, 244
Civil Affairs Service (Burma) CAS(B) 256–57
Cohen, Paul 247, 266
Cola Tribe, see Kola 97, 100
Colin Grafton 93–94, 101
Collective Memory 20, 21, 25, 276, 279–80, 326–27
Commission for Truth and Reconciliation 320
Commission on Filipinos Overseas (CFO) 184, 189–90
Communism 66–67, 350, 388, 392, 396, 412, 420

Communist Party of Kampuchea (CPK) 24, 94, 373, 383, 388, 397, 398n, 399n
  Standing Committee 374, 375, 400
Communist Party of Thailand (CPT) 233–35, 237, 241, 244
Communist Party of Burma 357
Communist Party of China 272, 275, 277–80, 284, 287n
Communist Party of Indonesia 18
Communist Party of Vietnam 407
Communist Youth League of Kampuchea (Yuvakak) 373, 375, 386–87, 397, 398n, 399n
Compagnie Fermière des Étains d'Extrême-Orient 110
Contemplacion Flor, 182
Cordillera Peoples Alliance (CPA) 141–42
Criminality 293, 296, 297–99, 301–03, 308–09, 311
Cultural Revival 260
Cultural Revolution 12, 257, 264, 272, 276, 287

D

Dabo Gong (Tai Pak Kung) 57
Dai 277–78, 286 and see Tai
Daik Bonda Tanah Melayu 161
Dao Shixun 271, 287
De La Pena, Guillermo 130
De-Westernization 308
Deetes, Tuanjai 139
Dela Rosa, Ronald 298, 309
Democratic Kampuchea 18, 375–78, 280–81, 386–87, 389, 391–402
  Four-year Plan 381, 393
Demography 10, 14, 39, 108, 111, 185, 324, 331, 364, 373, 379, 393–94
Department of Foreign Affairs and Trade of Australia 303
Depopulation 324
Deportation 374
Dialect groups 55–59, 66, 72
Dialog Selatan 157, 176
Dialog Utara 157, 176
Diaspora 12, 151, 185, 219, 250–55, 258–59, 333
Dinar 153, 172–73, 177
Documentation Center of Cambodia (DC–Cam) 373–74, 377
Dodge, Paul 231
Dong Kham Ten Kham 283
Dunia Melayu Dunia Islam (DMDI, Malay World Islamic World) 158, 176
Duterte, Rodrigo 293–95, 298, 301–03, 306–07, 309
Duterte, Sara 293

INDEX

E

Economy 1, 23, 47, 75, 82, 91, 100, 107, 112, 133, 158, 172, 183, 185, 189, 194, 233, 319, 331, 339, 352, 386, 399n, 443–44
  mining economy 75, 91
Eleazar, Guillermo 306
Erviani 332
Ethnic cleansing 348, 350–51, 355, 365–66
Ethnicity 1, 5, 11, 16–17, 55, 83, 100, 134, 199, 322, 327, 330, 332, 362–63, 366
Ethno-nationalism 127
Ethno-religious boundaries 226
Ethno-religious identities 226, 242–43, 248
Ethnoscape 155, 159
Eubank, Aran 231–33, 237–40
Extinction 324–25, 327, 401
Extraordinary Chambers in the Courts of Cambodia (ECCC) 374, 401

F

Facebook 329, 440, 442, 445
Federal Council of the Advancement of Aborigines 130
Federation of Nanyang Hakka Associations 58, 62–63
Federation of National Writers Association of Malaysia (Gabungan Persatuan Penulis Nasional/GAPENA) 157–58, 161
Festivals
  Cultural festivals 157, 159–60, 163, 167
  Festival Mak Yong Mantang 167
  Festival of Penyengat Island (Festival Pulau Penyengat) 164
  Festival Sungai Carang 163–64, 175
  Festival Sungai Enam 166
  International Literary Festival of Mount Bintan (Festival Sastra Internasional Gunung Bintan/FSIGB) 165–66
  Malay Civilization Festival (Festival Tamadun Melayu) 165
  Songkran New Year Festival 261
  Stupa Festival 251
  That Chiang Tüng Stupa Festival 247
Filipino/Filipina 189, 196, 198, 208, 218
  Filipino Catholic Church 208
  Filipino migrants 182, 190, 192, 194, 196, 199, 201, 202, 209, 215, 217
  Filipino missionaries 23, 205–06, 209, 211, 214, 220–21
  Filipino nationalism 187, 191, 198–99
  Filipino professionals 181–82, 189–92, 199, 201
  Modes of being in Singapore 189–99
Filleau de Saint Hilaire, Gilbert 82

Fo Guang Shan Buddha Museum 255
Four-Year Plan of Democratic Kampuchea (1976–1980) 381, 393 *and see* Democratic Kampuchea
Franco-Siamese Treaty (1907) 88
Free Prior and Informed Consent (FPIC) 133
Friendship Forum of Indonesian Archipelago Palaces (Forum Silaturahmi Keraton Se–Nusantara 171
Fujian Community 57
Fujian Province 59
Furnivall, John 199

G

Generations 2–4, 22–23, 35–36, 38–42, 46, 50, 51, 67, 85, 99, 107–08, 118, 137, 166, 258, 263, 317, 319, 321, 330, 332–33, 409
  Baby Boomers 5, 35, 38–43, 45–48
  Generation X 5, 35, 38–43, 45, 47
  Generation Y or Millennials 5, 35–48, 50–52, 318, 331–32, 337, 341
  Generation Z 5, 38–39, 41–42, 45, 47, 318
Genocide 17, 129, 322, 324, 349, 379–80, 393, 397
  Rwandan Genocide 211
  See Cambodian Tragedy
Gewalträume 377
Ghafar, Abdul 363
Global Karen Baptist Fellowship (GKBF) 238
Global Sufi Movement 168
Globalization 1, 112, 126, 128, 130, 132, 138, 145, 152, 193
Grabowsky, Volker 24, 35, 434n, 440
Grand River Land 128
Grandmother Yat *see* Yeay Yat, 97, 100
Great Leap Forward 254, 257, 278, 380, 398
Guangdong 56–57, 73
Gunn, Geoffrey 112
Gunung Bintan, also Mount Bintan 166
Guomindang 274, 286

H

Hainanese (Hainan) 59
Hakka (Kejia) 59
  Hakka Affiliated Association (Keshu Gonghui) 56
  Hakka Associations 56–58, 62–64, 69, 71
  Hakka Christians 57
  Hakka Community 56–57, 64, 73
  Hakka Dialect 55, 58, 63, 67, 69, 71–72,
  Hakka Dialect Identity 55–56, 71–72
  Hakka Identity 58–60, 62–64, 66–67, 69, 71–73
  Hakka Organizations 56, 58, 62–64
  Hakka Studies 58, 63, 70, 72–73
  Hakka–ness 58, 60, 61, 63–64, 69, 72

INDEX

Henghua (Xinhua) 59
Hill Area and Community Development
  Foundation 139
Hilltribe Development and Welfare Center of Tak
  Province 235
HIV/AIDS 324–26
Hlawnching, Famark 137, 144
Hmong Association for Development 144
Hogg, Michael 329
Hokkien (Fujian) 56, 58–59, 65, 67
Homeland 12, 15, 24, 151–53, 155, 160, 163–64,
  167, 191, 248, 252, 259, 271, 319, 338, 353,
  364, 388
Hong Kong 57, 64, 69, 73, 85, 205, 209, 218
Houayxay see Huai Sai, 254
Housing Development Board (HDB) 183,
  195–96, 201
Hu Shih 61
Hu Wenfu 58
Huai Sai (Houayxay) 254
Huizhou Association 56
Huizhou Prefecture 56–57
Human Rights 11, 45, 140, 147, 332
  Abuses 11, 319–20, 343
  Violations 3, 10, 45, 51, 133, 293, 295, 310,
    317, 332
Human Rights Watch 294–95, 298, 305
Hun Sen 97, 294–96
Huzrin Hood 171–74, 178
Hymne Tanah Melayu 162–63
Hyndman, David 326

I

Identity Construction 2, 25, 318, 326–27, 330,
  334–35, 338–40, 440–41
Ieng Sary 96–98, 373, 390, 393
Ieng Thirith 96–98
Ieng Vuth 98
Ikhsan, Mohammad Fajar 34
Indians 68, 81, 130, 185, 352–53, 355
Indigenism 125, 127–28, 131, 134, 137–38,
  141–42, 145–47
  transnational 125, 131–32, 138–39, 141, 145, 147
Indigenism movement 131, 138–39, 147
Indigenous people 11, 130, 133, 135–38, 140,
  146, 320, 325
Indigenous Peoples' Foundation for Education
  and Environment (IPF) 140
Indigenous women 136, 140–41
Indonesia 3–5, 9, 17–23, 38, 46–47, 49, 51, 56,
  141, 151–52, 154–55, 157, 162, 169–71,
  173–76, 212–13, 294, 297–302, 309, 311,
  317–21, 323, 325, 327–28, 330, 332, 334–35,
  338, 340–43, 379, 439, 446–48, 453

Indonesia (continue)
  Indonesia Raya 328
  Indonesia–Malaysia–Thailand Growth Triangle
    (IMT–GT) 157
  Indonesia–Malaysia–Singapore Growth
    Triangle (IMS–GT) 157
  Indonesian Institute of Sciences (LIPI)
    332–33
  Indonesian Mosque Council (Dewan Masjid
    Indonesia) 171
Inter–Asian Referencing 308
Inter–Mountain Peoples' Education and Culture
  in Thailand (IMPECT) 137, 139
International Alliance of Indigenous and Tribal
  People in the Tropical Forests (IAITPTF)
  140
International Christian Assembly 212–13, 219
International Covenant on Civil and Political
  Rights 129, 134, 299
International Covenant on Economic, Social and
  Cultural Rights 129, 134
International Indian Treaty Council 129
International Indigenism 134
International Work Group for Indigenous Affairs
  (IWGIA) 133–34, 139–40, 146
Irrigation 380, 388
Ismail Hussein 157

J

Jafar Kawal (Mujahids) 361–62
Japan 139, 141, 348, 352, 353
  Japanese invasion in World War II 55, 62,
    64–65, 72, 349, 352, 354–57, 359, 354–365,
    368n
Jambi 155, 158, 162, 176
Jamiat ul–Ulama 362, 369
Jaringan Orang Asal Se Malaysia (JOAS) 141
Jawa 152, 447
Jesselton (present–day Kota Kinabalu) 63
Jesus is Lord (JIL) Church 213, 215, 217–18
Jia Yin Zhou Prefecture 56
Jiaying Zhou Association 56
Jinghong, see Chiang Rung 248, 273–77, 281–83,
  286–88
Joget Dangkong 167, 176
Johor 63, 154, 157, 161, 164–65, 171, 176,
Jokowi Widodo 294, 309, 332

K

Kampong Speu 384–85
Kampong Thom Province 380
Kaoshiung Normal University 70

INDEX

Karen 20, 23, 79, 225–34, 236–44
  Identity 225
  Languages 225
  Literature 225
  Migrants 210, 238
  Missionaries 237–38, 243
  Karen National Liberation Army (KNLA)
    233–34
  Karen National Union (KNU) 225, 233–34,
    237, 241, 244
  Karen Network for Culture and Environment
    144
  Karen State 226–27, 230, 233, 242
Karnavian, Tito 298
Kassim (Mujahids) 362–63
Kathina Offering (thòt kathin) 255
Kawthoolei Karen Baptist Churches (KKBC)
  237–38, 244
Ke Shuxun 274
Kengtung see Chiang Tung, 247, 273
Kepri 153, 155, 159–64, 166–69, 174–176
Khammouane Province 105, 106
Khanan 252
Khieu Samphan 96–97, 373, 398
Khmer 16, 18, 75–78, 80–82, 86, 88, 91–93, 95,
  99, 272, 287, 373, 377, 384, 387, 389, 399–400
  Khmer Issarak 91
  Khmer Krom 16, 92
  Khmer Republic 380, 385
  Khmer Rouge 17, 20, 24–25, 77, 94–100,
    373–75, 377– 89, 391– 94, 396–401
  Khmer Santebal 383
Khòng Chiang Ngoen 256
Khruba Bun Chum 247, 253–56
Khruba Kham Pheng 254–55
Khruba Khüan Kham 247, 251
Khruba Luang Chòm (now Somdet Luang Chòm)
  257
Khruba Saeng La 247, 252–55, 257–60, 265
Khruba Sin Man (Khruba Undi) 257–60
Khruba Siwichai 257
Khruba Undi 257–60
Khwan 282–83
Kiernan, Benedict 18, 93–96
Killing Fields (of Cambodia) 383, 389, 391
Kingdom of Jesus Christ 221
Kingship 153, 167, 168
Kirsch, Stuart 325–26, 337, 343
KKB (Kelompok Kriminal Bersenjata or Armed
  Criminal Group) 320–22, 325, 329
Kola, also as Koula /Gula 75–80, 82–83, 85–96,
  98–101
  Kola autonomy 86, 91, 99
  Kola identity 75, 77–78, 85, 95

Kota Kinabalu 58, 63, 70–71
Kuala Lumpur 58, 68, 70, 158, 172, 205, 208,
  218, 439
Kuchinarai (Kushinagar) 257
Kui Culture 144
Kuomingtang Soldier 252
Kuomintang 60, 251,
Kuomintang Army 250–51
Kuomintang National Government 61
Kwangsi (Guangxi) 59
Kyauktaw 351, 354

L

Lahiri–Dutt, Kuntala 117
Lahu 251, 287n
Lajarca Jr, Mario 196
Lamphun 250–51, 257, 262
Lan Na 248, 254, 260, 266, 273
Laolung (Longchuan) 56
Laos 4, 11–12, 15–16, 18, 23, 105, 107–115, 118,
  120, 132, 141, 207, 212, 214–25, 249–55,
  266, 279, 299, 378, 443
  Lao (People) 15–16, 19, 23, 71, 81, 84, 88,
    105–118, 248, 253
  Lao Civil War 250, 252
  Lao nation–state 15, 110
  Lao peasants 108–110
Lasimbang, Jennie 140
Leach, Edmund 81
League of Nations 128
Lee Hsien Loong 187
Lee Kuan Yew 308
Legitimizing Identity 327–28
Letongkhu 227, 229–32, 234–43
Letongkhu Monastery 235
Levi General Deskaheh 128
Liaodong 60
Liberating Institutions 331
Lingga Island 161
Lon Nol 378, 381, 384–86, 391
Longue Durée 107
Low–Quality Democracy 296
Luang Namtha 254
Luang Prabang 109
Luang Pu Thòng 254
Luingam Luithui 139
Lukuo Qiao (Marco Polo Bridge) 62
Luo Xianglin 58, 63, 70, 72

M

Macapagal–Arroyo, Gloria 294
Mae Sai 251, 253–54, 258–60
Magh 351
Mak Yong 166–68, 176

466

INDEX

Malangoo, Neeranooch 247
Malaysia 1, 9, 18–19, 22, 38, 49, 51, 55–61,
 66–67, 70–72, 135, 140–41, 151, 154–59,
 162, 169–70, 172–73, 176, 183, 201, 207,
 256, 297–98
 Malay Cultural Space 155, 158, 164
 Malay Identity 151–56, 158–59, 162, 164, 168,
  171, 174–77
 Malay Peninsula 56, 63, 66–67, 109, 151–52,
  154, 157, 160,165, 167, 173, 176
 Malay Royal Traditions 154
 Malay Sultanate of Patani 16
 Malay World Conference 158, 176
Malayan Communist Party (MCP) 65, 72
Malayan Indian Congress (MIC) 68
Maluku Islands 3, 49
Manchu 60
Manchuria 62
Mandarin 58, 61, 67, 69, 72
Mantang Island 166–67
Manuel, George 129
Marcos, Ferdinand 293, 295, 308
Marginalization 24, 66, 131, 138, 156, 317, 319,
 321, 328–30, 332, 339, 342–43
Marston, John 388, 400
Martínez–Cobo, José R. 146
Marxism–Leninism 379, 381
Mass violence 14, 17, 20–21, 24, 322, 366, 373,
 377–79, 392, 396–97, 407–08, 430–432, 434
 and see violence
Massacres 3–4, 21, 330, 352, 354, 368n, 309n,
 408–9, 413–14, 423, 425, 427–32, 435n
Maulia, Erwida 321
Maung Keng 86–90
Maung Say 88–90
Maungdaw 351, 354, 361–63, 368
Maw A Mee 230, 234–36, 239–40
May Fourth Movement 58, 60
Mazu 57
Me Khin Me 95–96, 98
Medan 156–57, 162–63
Meizhou (Meixian) 56
Mekong River 111, 113, 214
Melaka 154–55, 158, 160–62, 169–70
Melanesians 317, 334
Merlan, Francesca 130
Metro Manila 303
Migration 3, 6, 12, 23, 33, 36, 56, 63–64, 67, 81,
 107, 111–13, 115, 118, 151, 156, 160–62,
 166, 181–85, 187–95, 197–199, 201n, 202n,
 205–8, 220, 252, 264, 319, 324, 353, 361,
 374, 380, 401n, 409, 411
 skilled labour migration 181–99
 transmigration 156, 319, 324–25, 331–32

Migration (*continue*)
 transnational 2, 13, 118, 199
 Vietnamese 107, 111–12, 458
Min Yuen 65
Min Zhou 189
Minbya 351, 353–54, 364
Miner–Peasant Identity 117
Ministry of Planning and Investment 114
Minzu 272, 279, 284, 286n, 287n
Mise En Valeur 108, 118
Mission Fields 218
Missions Étrangères 111, 120
Moeng 272–73, 276–77, 280, 282, 285–87
 Moeng Ham 282–83
 Moeng Lü 24, 273
Mogok 91
Mohamad, Mahathir 156, 172
Mohan *see* Bò Han, 254
Mongla 254, 257, 259–60, 264–66
Mongyawng *see* Müang Yòng, 250
Moro 211
Motherland of The Malays 152, 159, 161, 163
Mount Ledang 162
Mount Meru 392
Mount Zion 210
Mountain View College 217
Müang 82, 286n
Müang Chae (Mengzhe) 254, 258
Müang Chai 256
Müang Hai (Menghai) 254, 258, 264, 266
Müang Hon (Menghun) 251, 253–54, 256–260
Müang La 251, 253, 266
Müang Luang 251, 254, 262, 266
Müang Ma 251, 266
Müang Mang (Mengman) 248
Müang Nun (Menglun) 254
Müang Ong (Mengweng) 262
Müang Phong (Mengpeng) 248
Müang Sing (Muang Sing) 247–48, 250, 252
Müang Yòng (Mongyawng) 250–52, 260, 262,
 266
Müang Yuan (Mengrun) 248
Muang Chong Soo 88–89
Mujahids 348, 361–63, 366
Munshi, Abdullah 154
Murabitun 153, 172–74, 177
Mutual Recognition Agreements (MRAs)
 181–82, 210
Myanmar 1, 3, 11, 15, 17–18, 24, 63–64, 137,
 141, 144, 225–27, 229–30, 233–38, 240–42,
 244, 247–48, 250–54, 257–59, 264, 266, 273,
 279, 342, 347, 353, 368
Myanmar Morning News Sin Chew Daily 64
Myanmar-Thailand border 24

467

INDEX

Myebon 351, 354, 356–58, 368
Myohaung 351, 354, 364

N

Naf River 349, 368
Nai Phasi 86, 88, 101
Nakhon Phanom 113
Nam Phathaen 105–110, 112, 114, 117–18
Nanjing 61
Nanjing Government 59, 61
Nanlaban 306
Napoli, Antonella 332
Nash, June 117
National Central University 70
National Chiao Tung University 70, 73
National Indian Brotherhood of Canada 129
National Operations Council 68
Native Union in Western Australia 130
Navong 78, 87
Ne Win 233
Negeri Sembilan 56
Netherlands 319
Network of Indigenous Peoples in Thailand
(NIPT) 137, 142–43
New Bilibid Prison 294
New Economic Policy (NEP) 55, 68, 72
New Order regime 319
New People 378, 381, 389, 391
New Vision Policy 68
Ngee Ann City Civic Plaza 187
Nghe Tinh Region 112
Niezen, Ronald 127–29, 146
Nirvana 257
Norodom Sihanouk 93, 101, 380, 384
North Borneo 59–60
Nuon Chea 96, 97, 373, 375, 397–90, 400

O

OAP (Orang Asli Papua or Indigenous Papuans)
319, 323, 327, 331, 339
OFW (Overseas Filipino Workers) 206
Old People (Pracheachun Chah) 378, 381, 382
Omra Meah (Mujahids) 363, 368–69
OPM (Organisasi Papua Merdeka or Papua
Independence Organization) 319, 325, 338
Oppression 21, 24, 287, 317, 321, 328–30,
332–33, 342, 366
Ortiga, Yasmin 183, 185–86
Osborne, Milton 6, 8, 93, 101
Oudong 381
Overseas Chinese Diaspora 185
Overseas Filipino Workers 205, 219, 309

P

Pacific Islanders 317
Paclarin, Jelen 131
Pagarruyung 158
Pailin 23, 75–101, 384
  Population 77–79, 86, 92
Pailin Peacock Dance 100–101
Pakistan 349, 360–63, 369
Pakse 111
Palembang 153, 155, 158, 162, 166, 170, 177
Palembang Prince Sri Tri Buana (also known as
Sang Nila Utama) 170
Pancasila (Five Principles) 328
Pantuns 161
Panyagaew, Wasan 247, 263
Papua 3, 317, 318–25, 330–34. 336–40, 342–44
  Ethnic consciousness 329
  Identity 317–18, 326–27, 329–32, 334–35,
  337–39, 341
  Nationalism 3, 317–18, 321, 328, 330, 340–42
  #PapuanLivesMatter 321, 338
  Youth identity 24, 317, 326, 334
  Violence 322–23
Papuans 3, 317, 319–21, 323–342, 344
Pauktaw 351, 354
Patriotic Burmese Forces (renamed Burma
National Army) 357
Pavie, Auguste 75
Peace Committees 354, 368–69
Pei Feng 58
Peiping (Beijing) 60
Pemekaran 320
Penang Chinese Girls School and Sin Min 58
Pendet Dance 49
Penyengat 164, 171
Penyengat Island 164, 171
People Power Revolution 309
Perak civil wars of the 1860s–1870s 56
Perkasa, Vidhyandika D. 24, 317, 320
Phi Moeng Longnan 277
Philippines 1, 5, 18, 20, 38, 43–46, 131–32,
  135, 139–41, 147, 173, 182, 184, 190–92,
  194–201, 205–07, 209, 211–13, 216–18,
  220–22, 238, 293–96, 298, 300, 302–03, 305,
  307–09, 311
  Philippine Congress 309
  Philippine Drug Enforcement Agency PDEA
  293
  Philippine Nationalism 187, 191, 196
  Philippine National Identity 198–99
  Philippine National Police 295, 298
  Philippine Securities and Exchange
  Commission 295
Phillip, Captain Arthur 129

Phnom Penh 11, 20, 77, 90–91, 94, 96, 378, 380–81, 383–85, 389, 394, 397, 399–401
Phò Choi Phi 257
Phra Chao Khru Maha Phing 257
Phra Tham Rachanuwat 259–60
Phra Tham Rachanuwat of Wat PK 259
Phra That Chòm Yòng 252, 266
Phra That Kesa Luang Chiang Ngoen 256
Phraya Chaiya Prasat of Müang Hon 256
Phraya Wanna 257
Phue Tee Maw 230–34, 236–37
Pilgrimage 247–48, 252, 259, 261
Casual 251
Periodic 251
Transborder 24, 247–48, 252, 254, 264
Transnational 250, 265
Pilipino Independence Day Council (PIDC) 187
Pinyathiha (Buddhist monk) 354
Pol Pot 18, 96, 373, 375, 383–84, 387, 390, 392–93, 395–401
Political Violence 322, 325–26, 337, 413, 431 and see violence
Populism 301
Poverty 4, 9, 33, 43, 45–46, 68, 93, 113, 133, 136, 218, 303, 306, 311, 347, 358, 366, 444, 452
Prasert Trakarnsupakorn 139, 140
President Jokowi Widodo 294, 309, 332
President Soekarno 66, 334
President Suharto 154, 169, 326, 330
Prophet Muhammad 172–73
Proton Saga 49
Pujite 228–33, 235–36, 239, 242
Pungyi Kyoung 82
Pwo 225–27, 232, 239, 244 and see Karen

Q
Queen Wan Seri Beni 170

R
Racism 129, 187, 196, 321, 328–31, 335–38, 342–43
Radio Veritas 206
Rahman, Abdul 68, 170, 177
Raja Ali Haji 164
Raja Malik Hafrizal 164
Rajaratnam, S. 36
Rakhine State 11, 15, 349, 366, 368 and see Arakan
Ramos, Fidel 194
Rappler 294–95
Raquez, Alfred 105, 109
Rasa Sayange 49
Rattanakrachangsri, Kittisak 140
Red Flag Communists 355, 357

Referendum 317–18, 332–33, 335–36, 339, 342, 439
Religious Affairs Bureau of Sipsòng Panna Prefecture 263, 288n
Religious imaginary 205–06, 209–212, 214, 219–22
Resistance identity 328, 340
Ressa, Maria 295
Revival of Buddhism 250
Revolutionary Flag 375–76, 398–401
Revolutionary Youth Organisation 375–76
Riau Islands 152–53, 159, 161–62, 167, 170, 174–76
Riau–Lingga 160
Ribao, Yangon 64
Richard Chauvel 330–32
Robinson, Geoffrey 17–18, 21, 322
Rohingya 15, 42, 45, 342, 349–50, 362–63, 365–66, 368–69
Rohingya Movement 11, 349, 363, 365, 369
Royalty 167–68, 170
Rwanda 211

S
Sabah 19, 57, 59, 63, 67, 70–71, 140
Sacralization 206, 211, 214, 220
Saenmi, Sakda 137–38, 143
Sakai 134
Samlaut Uprising 94
Samnak Silapa Lae Watthanatham Maha Withayalai Ratchaphat Chiang Rai 262
Sandakan 57
Sangha, see Buddhism
Sandakan Chinese Chamber of Commerce 58
Sani, Arsul 169
Santacruzan 208, 222
Santos, Kian delos 306
Sapphires and Rubies Limited 87
Sarawak 19, 57, 59–60, 63, 66
Sarawak Clandestine Organisation (SCO) 66
Savannakhet Province 108, 111–12
Sawbaw 87, 101
Searching for the Truth 377, 398–401
Security 1, 6, 8, 12, 14, 18, 25, 34, 36, 39, 65–67, 113–14, 116, 133, 147, 252–53, 275, 297, 300–01, 306, 320–322, 325, 344n
Insecurity 25, 113–14, 185, 189, 349–50, 355, 360
Sejarah Melayu 154
Selangor 56–57, 59, 66
Selangor Chinese Chamber of Commerce 59
Sen, Amartya 327
Sepon or Savannakhet Province 108
Seri Aman 66

INDEX

Serumpun 48
Seventh-Day Adventist Church 217
Sgaw 225–27, 232, 244
Shadow Economies 300
Shaikh Vadillo 173
Shan State 87, 250, 252, 255–56, 265–66, 273, 287
   Migrants 255
Shaohua Zhan 189
Shenyang (Mukden) 62
Shimray, Gam 140
Shun Ren 58
Siak 158, 170
Siam 16, 76, 79, 84, 86–87, 92, 101n, 107, 244n
   and see Thailand
Siam Exploring Company Limited 87–88
Siamese (ethnic group) 16, 75–76, 80–82, 85, 87–90, 99, 101, 109, 118, 231, 273
   Administration 75, 77, 79–80, 86–88
   Kingdom 16, 273
Sin Bin Ribao 64
Singapore 22–23, 43, 56, 63, 70, 126, 151–54, 157, 162, 169–71, 176–77, 181–202, 205, 207, 218–19, 251, 297–99, 302, 309, 443
   2011 General Elections 186–89
   Anti-immigrant Resentment 185–89
   Drive for Foreign Talent 183–84, 193
   Filipino migrants 182–200, 201n, 202n
   Multiculturalism 186, 199–200, 201n
   Naturalization 188, 193–96, 198, 201n
   Population 183–84, 188
   Racism 185, 187
Singapore, Johor, and Riau (SiJoRi–growth triangle) 157, 171
Sinsiam Ribao 64
Sipsòng Panna (Xishuangbanna) 12, 24, 247–54, 256–66, 271–82, 284–88
Sipsòng Panna Buddhist Association 282, 288
Sipsòng Panna Sangha 250
Social Media 40–41, 50–51, 186–87, 310, 318, 329–30, 332, 337, 342, 441–442, 445, 452
Société des Étains de l'Indochine 110
Société des Étains du Cammon 110
Société des Étains et Wolframs du Tonkin 110
Société des Études et Éxplorations des Mines de l'Indochine (SEEMI) 110–11
Somdej Atya Tham 254
Somdet Longjom Wannasiri 282
Somdet Luang Chòm Müang 250
Southeast Asian Community 199
Soviet Union 118
Special Autonomy 320–21, 343
Spirit Worship 277, 288
Sreymo, Ban 98

Structural Discrimination 324
Stupas 24, 82, 247–48, 251–52, 256–60, 266 n. 6, 282–83
Suffering 207, 218, 294, 305–06, 338, 340, 382
Sulalatu 'l-Salatin 154, 162, 170
Sultan 153, 165, 167–69, 171, 173–75, 177
Sultan Abdul Rahman 170, 177
Sultan Ahmed 363
Sultan Mahmud 165, 167, 176,
Sultanate 154, 171, 177
Sultanate of Bintan Darul Masyhur 160, 171, 174, 176
Sultanate/Riau–Lingga Sultanate 169–70
Sumatra 151–53, 155–60, 162, 167, 176
Surya, Yuyun 328–29
Syaikh Abdalqadir as-Sufi 172
Syaikh Umar Ibrahim Vadillo 172–74

T

Tachileik *see* Tha Khilek, 252
Tai (people) 75, 81–82, 101, 247–48, 250–56, 258, 260–66, 271–88
Tai Khün 250, 255, 258
Tai Lü 12, 24, 247–48, 250–56, 258, 260, 262–63, 265–66, 271–72, 274, 276–88
Tai Müang 82
Tai peasantry 285
Tai Yai (Shan) 248, 253
Taiping Rebellion 60
Taiwan 70–72, 141, 207, 210, 212–13, 215, 252, 254–56, 271, 431
Taiwan Normal University 70
Talaku 8, 23, 225–37, 239–44
   Talaku Communities 227, 230, 233
   Talaku Karen 23, 225, 228–29, 234
   Talaku Religious Movement 226
Tamnan Phra Chao Liap Lok 247
Tan Gong (Tham Kung) 57
Tanah Melayu 157, 159–60, 162–63
Tanjungpinang 159, 163–66, 170, 176
Tappe, Oliver 23, 105, 108, 112–13, 115, 117, 120
Tawi–Tawi 217
Taylor, James 247
Tengku Mohammad Shawal Ibni Tengku Abdul 169
Tengku Ryo Riezqan 162
Tentera Nasional Kalimantan Utara (North Kalimantan National Army) 66
Teochiu (Chaozhou) 56, 58–59
Tha Khilek (Tachileik) 252–55, 257–60, 264
Thai Karen Baptist Convention (TKBC) 238

470

INDEX

Thailand 1, 3, 15–19, 23–24, 43, 56, 75, 95–96, 101, 105, 107–08, 112–14, 126, 134–37, 139–44, 151, 157, 176, 205–07, 209–17, 219–20, 225–27, 229–33, 237, 241–42, 244, 247–48, 250–52, 254, 256–58, 260–63, 265–66, 271, 273, 282, 287–88, 294, 311, 368, 380, 393, 401 *and see* Siam
  Conflict in Southern Thailand 15–16, 20
  Conflict with Cambodia 19, 75, 96
  Conflict with Laos 19
  Thailand–Myanmar Borderland 8, 210, 225, 227, 229, 238
Thakhaek 107, 111–13
Thaksin Shinawatra 3, 293, 295
Tham script 251, 255, 276
Thammasat University 3, 378, 398
That Chiang Tüng 247
Theology 219, 221, 238
Theravada Buddhism 82, 247, 250–52 , 256, 264, 392 *and see* Buddhism
Tiger Balm 62
Timor-Leste 1, 17, 19–20, 25, 141, 162, 380, 439–50, 452–53
Tin Mining 105, 107–12, 114, 116–17
Tipiṭaka 251
Tonkin 110–11
Trade 6, 13, 23, 33, 44, 76, 82, 88, 92, 96–97, 101n, 111, 133, 170, 172, 174, 236, 273, 300, 410–12, 414, 417–18, 423, 430, 443–44
Transborder ethnoreligious connections 248
Transmigration 156, 319, 324–25, 331–32
Transnational activities 6, 155, 157
Transnational entanglements 159–60
Transnational indigenism 125, 131–32, 138–39, 141, 145, 147
Transnational influence 253
Transnational Malayness 159
Transnational Sangha 253
Transnationalism 2, 3, 5–6, 10–12, 22, 123, 126–27, 151, 155, 157, 160, 168, 209, 220
Trauma 1–3, 5, 21, 24, 156, 248, 304, 332, 336, 340, 350, 365, 397, 433
Trat Province 97
Treaty ASEAN Treaty on Amity and Cooperation 442
Treaty Bowring Treaty (1855) 79
Treaties
  Franco–Siamese Treaty (1907) 88
  London Treaty (1824) 155
Tribal Peoples 130, 134, 140
Trump, Donald 298
Tshing Tsin Secondary School 58
Tshung Tsin 58, 64, 70
Tshung Tsin Association 64, 70

Tsunami (Indian Ocean, 2004) 198
Tuguan 273
Tung Padevoat, *see* Revolutionary Flag 375
Tunku Abdul Rahman 68
Tunku Abdul Rahman University 70
Tusi 273, 286, 288

U

U Kra Hla Aung 356
U Kyaw Mya 356
U Seinda 348, 355–50, 363–64
Uncertainty Identity Theory 329
United Christian Missionary Society 231
United Malays National Organisation (UMNO) 68
United Nations (UN) 97, 129, 134, 140, 142, 145–46, 229, 306, 336, 341, 439
United Nations Declaration on the Rights of Indigenous Peoples (UNDRIP) 134–35, 137, 146
United Nations Human Rights Council 299
Universal Declaration of Human Rights 129
University of Malaya Malaysian Chinese Research Centre 70
Upatchai Nam Kat 257

V

V Force 354, 358, 368
Van Klinken, Gerry 169
Veloso, Mary Jane 294
Versailles Accord (1919) 60
Vertovec, Steven 6, 127, 151
Vientiane 111
Viet Minh 91, 412, 419–20
Vietnam 1, 4, 16, 18, 20, 91, 101, 105, 107–08, 111–13, 118, 132, 141, 151, 249, 266, 294, 374, 378, 383, 391, 407–09, 411, 424–25, 427–28, 432, 434
Vihan *see* Vihāra, 281–82
Vihāra *see* Vihan, 248, 257, 260–64, 266, 281
Violence 1–3, 14–18, 20–25, 94, 100, 129, 221, 248, 298–99, 306–7, 309, 317–26, 328–30, 334, 337–40, 342–43, 344n, 347, 349–55, 358–61, 363, 365–66, 368n, 373, 375, 377–79, 389, 391–92, 396–97, 398n, 408–09, 412–13, 417, 420–23, 425, 430–33, 434n, 436n, 439, 441–42, 444–46, 449, 452
  Intercommunal 2, 347
  Mass violence 17, 20–21, 24, 322, 366, 377–79, 392, 306–97, 408, 430–32, 434n
  Political 322, 325–26, 337, 413, 431
  Youth 375, 396, 441

471

INDEX

W

War on Drugs 293–95, 298, 303, 306–07, 309
Warawut Silapa–Archa 135
Warington Smyth, Herbert 76, 78–84, 86–87, 101
Wat Ban Y 261–63, 266
Wat Khaong Kang 95, 98
Wat Pa Che (Wat Pajie) 250, 257, 281–83, 288
Wat Pa Hy 98
Wat Phnom Yat 95
Wat Sai Müang 252–55, 257
Wat Tao Kham 257
Wat Yang Khuang 252
Wee, Kellynn 193
West Coast Hakka Association 57
Wham, Jolovan 302, 310
Winichakul, Thongchai 3, 17, 21, 125–26, 131,
393, 426
World Bank 43, 108, 142
World Council of Indigenous Peoples (WCIP)
129
World Hakka Conference 69–70, 72
World Health Organization (WHO) 322
World Islamic Mint 172–73
World Islamic Trading Organization 172
Wuhua (Zhangle) 56

X

Xaysomboun Province 108
Xishuangbanna Dai Autonomous Region 275
Xishuangbanna Zizhizhou Minzu Zongjiao
Shiwu Ju 251
Xishuangbanna 247, 250–51, 271, 275, 278–79,
286–88 *and see* Sipsòng Panna

Y

Y Chhien 98
Yat–Sen, Sun 60–61
Yeay Yat *see* Grandmother Yat, 97
Yeoh, Brenda 193
Younger Bear Clan 128
Youth 2–5, 21, 25, 44, 47, 52, 141, 145, 171, 175,
194, 332–39, 356, 379, 388–89, 396, 439–43,
445, 449, 452
Cambodian Youth 24–25, 373–74, 376, 378,
384–87, 391, 396–98
Papuan Youth 24, 317–19, 321, 327, 330,
333–35, 337, 339–42
Timor–Leste Youth 439, 440, 442–43, 445
Violence 375, 396, 441
Youth Bulge 21, 377–79, 396
Yuan Shih Khai 60
Yunnan 81, 101, 264, 266, 271–72, 276, 286
Yunnan Institute for the Nationalities 276
Yunnan Minzu University 276

Yunnan Provincial Buddhist Association 250
Yunnanese 251
Yuvakak *see* Communist Youth League of
Kampuchea
Yusuf, Yusmar 161

Z

Zamboanga 217
Zeng Cheng Association 56
Zhong Yuan 63
Zhonghua Yishan or Chinese Cemeteries 57
Zijin 56

Printed in the USA
CPSIA information can be obtained
at www.ICGtesting.com
LVHW090807260823
756101LV00004B/12